A COMPLETE LITERARY GUIDE TO THE BIBLE

A COMPLETE LITERARY GUIDE TO THE BIBLE

EDITED BY
LELAND RYKEN
AND
TREMPER LONGMAN III

ZondervanPublishingHouse
Academic andProfessionalBooks
Grand Rapids, Michigan
A Division of HarperCollins*Publishers*

A Complete Literary Guide to the Bible

Requests for information should be addressed to:
Zondervan Publishing House
Academic and Professional Books
Grand Rapids, Michigan 49530

Library of Congress Cataloging-in-Publication Data

A complete literary guide to the Bible / edited by Leland Ryken and Tremper Longman III.
p. c.
Includes bibliographical references and indexes.
ISBN 0-310-51830-X
1. Bible as literature. 2. Bible—Criticism, interpretation, etc. I. Ryken, Leland. II. Longman, Tremper.
BS535.C56 1993 93-4326
220.6'6—dc20 CIP

Cover design: Gary Gnidovic
© 1993 Marbled Art by Peggy Skycraft
Interior design: James E. Ruark
Copy editor: Gerard Terpstra

Printed in the United States of America

93 94 95 96 97 98 / DH / 10 9 8 7 6 5 4 3 2 1

Contents

Acknowledgments

The following Scripture versions are cited in the chapters indicated:

KJV The King James or Authorized Version is used in chapters 8, 15, 23, 29, 35.

Authors use their own translations in chapters 7 and 16.

Preface

Since the late 1970s, the literary approach to biblical interpretation has swept through the field of biblical studies and has claimed a lasting place in the methodological arsenal of scholars whose main focus is the Bible. Not only monographs but also commentaries and even introductions to the Bible advertise themselves as a "literary approach." And while biblical scholars have been discovering literary methods of analysis, literary scholars have rediscovered the Bible as a book to teach and study.

But not all that claims to be literary is genuinely literary. Or perhaps it is fairer to say that not all that goes by the label of "literary approach" actually leads to an appreciation and analysis of the Bible from a literary point of view.

For one thing, much that is presented as literary is really literary theory that makes no pretense to move toward interpretation. In these cases the literary approach to the Bible partakes of developments in recent literary theory. The question that dominates this approach is meaning: Do literary texts carry meaning, and if so, where is that meaning located—with the author, the text, or the reader? These are obviously important questions, but often the "literary approach" to the Bible fails to move beyond them to literary analysis.

A second weakness of much "literary" commentary on the Bible is that it fails to achieve true integration between biblical studies and literary criticism, doing little more than providing a new name for old approaches. There can be no doubt that biblical scholars increasingly embrace a literary approach to the Bible at a theoretic level, a stance that they often articulate with impeccable clarity in the opening chapters of their commentaries. But when these same scholars begin their actual analysis, they show a marked tendency to revert to the conventional categories and concerns that their discipline has bequeathed to them.

A third failure of many approaches that claim to be literary is their lack of definition regarding what constitutes a literary approach. The classic case is a popular volume entitled *The Literary Guide to the Bible,* edited by Robert Alter and Frank Kermode (published by Harvard University Press in 1987). Although the title announces a definitive and thoroughgoing literary approach to the Bible, the volume offers no discernible or systematic literary method. The book is a journey through the miscellaneous, with summary and paraphrase of content predominating over analysis of biblical texts. The book is a collection of isolated comments about the books of the Bible. The editors' claim that their view of criticism is "pluralist" turned out to mean that whatever a contributor produced was labeled literary, even if, for example, it was a historical survey of commentary on a given book of the Bible.

Our reaction to *The Literary Guide to the Bible* led us to embark on the present project. Our leading aim has been to insure consistency in method and scope. Overriding all other concerns was the desire to integrate literary and biblical studies more carefully than has been done to date. Biblical scholars are often amateurs at literary analysis, while literary scholars run roughshod over issues that have plagued biblical scholars for years.

Here, too, as editors we learned a lesson from the Alter/Kermode volume. Although the editors of that book were literary scholars, most of the contributors were biblical scholars. As editors of the present volume, we represent the two disciplines, and we solicited essays equally from literary and biblical scholars. All essays, moreover, were critiqued by readers from both disciplines.

All of this was done in the interest of achieving genuine integration. The exercise revealed different expectations and skills in the two fields, even though both sets of scholars share important preoccupations and assumptions that we will articulate in the introductory chapter that follows.

As editors we wish to express our gratitude to our contributors. We asked them to contribute because we had confidence in their abilities, and our only surprise was the extent to which they exceeded our expectations. They endured a strong editorial hand designed to bring individual chapters into a coherent whole, and they did so with a grace and humility not always found in the scholarly community.

Our book is divided into four parts. The opening five essays are introductory. The first was written jointly by the two editors and lays the foundation for what follows. Of special interest in this essay is the middle section that highlights some of the differences, even tensions, that arise between literary scholars who analyze the Bible and biblical scholars who use a literary method. Esteemed author and novelist Frederick Buechner then adds a writer's perspective on what it means to view the Bible as a literary book. Yet another overview traces the history of literary approaches to the Bible, beginning with the Bible itself and ending with the current scene. Since the two overarching genres of the Bible are narrative and poetry, two additional chapters describe these dominant modes.

The middle two sections of the book provide literary commentary on the individual parts of the Old and New Testaments. Each section begins with an introductory essay that delineates the literary features of the Old and New Testaments as a whole. Constraints of space prevented our assigning a chapter to every book in the Old and New Testaments. For instance, we combined Exodus through Deuteronomy into a single chapter on the basis of common subject matter, themes, narrative thread, and literary milieu. Similarly, Old Testament prophecy is covered by a chapter that treats prophecy as a genre and by individual chapters devoted to representative specimens that show the range of the genre—Isaiah, Daniel, Amos, and Jonah. The New Testament epistles are treated together.

Contributors were free to emphasize different aspects of their assigned book and to develop original points, provided they did justice to the common issues of genre, unity, and style. In keeping with the literary premise that the subject of literature is human experience, we asked our contributors to say something about the recognizable or universal human experience in their texts.

Literary approaches to the Bible are characterized partly by what they do *not* take up, and this is true of our book as well. We asked contributors to avoid issues of the historicity of events, theories of authorship, and background material.

The concluding section of the book extends the scope beyond commentary *on* the Bible to other areas with which the Bible intersects. An opening chapter surveys how literature has served as a source and influence for imaginative literature. Follow-up essays by Chaim Potok and Gene Warren Doty give us instructive glimpses into how a novelist and poet experience the Bible and are influenced by it. And since the literary approach to the Bible has huge implications for preaching, a concluding essay by homiletician Sidney Greidanus explores what difference it makes in the pulpit to believe that the Bible is a very literary book.

We envision our book as a reference book as well as a commentary. We accordingly asked our contributors to make sure that their "Works Cited" pages include the secondary sources that they considered of primary importance to anyone wishing to pursue a literary study of their assigned genre or biblical book.

In quoting the Bible, contributors chose the English translations that they preferred. Biblical scholars inclined toward their own translations or the New International Version. Literary critics gravitated most naturally to the King James Version and the Revised Standard Version.

LELAND RYKEN

TREMPER LONGMAN III

PART 1

CHAPTER 1

Introduction

Leland Ryken and Tremper Longman III
Wheaton College
Westminster Theological Seminary

At a time when scholars and publishers are eager to claim that their approach to the Bible is literary, it has become a common practice to accept all claims as valid. As editors of this volume we have not taken this easy way out. To accept every piece of commentary as literary that claims to be such undermines the credibility of the very concept of a literary approach to the Bible. The purpose of this chapter is to define what we mean by a literary approach to the Bible, to identify differing emphases among literary critics and biblical scholars, and to provide an overview of some leading literary traits of the Bible.

The Literary Study of the Bible

Biblical scholars have been using the terms *literature* and *literary criticism* for at least half a century, but until recently they did not define these terms in the same way that literary scholars in the humanities did. Two decades ago Amos Wilder rightly recorded his "astonishment that the term 'literary criticism' should have such different connotations for biblical scholars as for students of literature generally," noting specifically the preoccupation of biblical scholars with authorship, sources, dating, and purpose as opposed to "those appreciative and interpretive questions which are the goal of criticism everywhere else" (*Rhetoric* xxii).

Literary critics themselves have presented a splintered scene in recent years, and it is of course impossible to reduce the field to a single approach. Yet as one looks at the deep structure that underlies the amorphous thing called literary criticism in the last half century, it is apparent that the influence of traditional literary criticism remains a subtext for the new approaches that have succeeded each other with accelerating frequency. If we ask what most characterizes traditional literary criticism, the answer is that a concern with genre does, provided that we acknowledge that literature itself constitutes a genre with identifying traits (Fowler 1–19).

To forestall potential resistance, we need to say at once that the Bible is a mixed book that contains three dominant types of material and therefore invites multiple approaches. The three main interests of biblical writers are the theological, the historical, and the literary. The focus of this book is on only one of these, which is not, however, offered as a complete approach. To say that a literary approach is limited in what it can do with a biblical text is to say nothing that cannot be said of any other approach.

It is a truism that each scholarly generation creates its own critical vocabulary, yet certain principles have remained constant under the changing styles of criticism. One is that the subject of literature is human experience, concretely presented. The Classical tradition spoke of literature as an imitation of reality, whereas the Romantic tradition championed the idea that literature is an image of human experience. What both traditions have in common is an assumption that literature does not consist primarily of abstractly stated ideas but of truthfulness to human experience and life.

When a writer comments that his book will "consider how the Bible, as literature, uses images in a great variety of ways" (Fischer 39), we do not need to inquire into the author's scholarly discipline before we know that the approach is literary. The authentic literary note is similarly sounded by the statement that the stories of the Bible "tell of mankind's experience at its most moving and most memorable in words that go beyond mere chronicle: words that strike the heart and light up the vision" (Roche xvi). Or, to take another specimen, a literary commentary on the gospel of Luke comments regarding the story of Jesus on the road to Emmaus that "a story is a story is a story. It cannot be boiled down to a meaning. Here the power is in suggestion rather than outright doctrine" (Drury 217). Contrariwise, a piece of scholarship that primarily discusses the ideas or historicity of a biblical text removes itself from what we mean by literary criticism.

Literature enacts rather than states, shows rather than tells. Instead of giving abstract propositions about virtue or vice, for example, literature presents stories of good or evil characters in action. The commandment "you shall not murder" is propositional and direct, while the story of Cain and Abel embodies the same truth in the distinctly literary form of narrative—a narrative, we should note, that does not even use the word *murder*. When we read a literary text, we do not feel primarily that we have been given new information but rather that we have undergone an experience.

Several corollaries follow from the incarnational nature of literature. One is that literature conveys its meanings by a certain indirectness and therefore calls for interpretation. Novelist Flannery O'Connor claimed that the storyteller speaks "*with* character and action, not *about* character and action" (76). About what, then, does the storyteller tell us by means of character and action? About life, human experience, reality, truth. Inherent in O'Connor's formula is the idea that the indirection of literature places a burden of interpretation on a reader. Literary texts do not come right out and state their themes. They embody them.

This means, in addition, that literary texts are irreducible to propositional statements and single meanings. The whole story or the whole poem is the meaning. A propositional statement of theme can never be a substitute or even the appointed goal of experiencing a literary text. At most it is a lens through which we see the incarnated experiences—something that brings the experiences embodied in the text into focus.

The chapters that follow will have a lot to say about the form in which the Bible comes to us and the relation of that form to ideology, but they will say relatively little about ideas per se. They will have more to say about the human experiences presented in the Bible than about theological ideas. A noted theologian has said that "we are far more image-making and image-using creatures than we usually think ourselves to be and . . . are guided and formed by images in our minds," adding that the human race "grasps and shapes reality . . . with the aid of great images, metaphors, and analogies" (Niebuhr 151–52, 161). The essays in this volume share this literary bias and believe that the Bible confirms it.

With a literary text, form is meaning. This implies that we cannot grasp the truth of story or poem, for example, without first interacting with the story qualities or poetic images. We cannot understand the religious and human themes of the story of Abraham's offering of Isaac without first reliving the progress of this test story and analyzing the characterization of Abraham and God in the story. The sheep-shepherd metaphor that pervades

Psalm 23 itself embodies the truth of the poem. The literary critic's preoccupation with the forms of biblical literature is more than an aesthetic delight in craftsmanship, though it is not less than that. It is also part of a concern to understand the truth of the text at a deeper level than a propositional summary extracted from the text.

A second identifying trait of literature is its self-conscious artistry. Literature is more saturated with technique and pattern than ordinary writing is. The proportion of commentary devoted to matters of how something is expressed is proportionately higher with a literary text than with an expository text. Literature calls attention to its own technique in a way that ordinary discourse does not. We can legitimately speak of literary writers' exploiting and even flaunting their verbal and artistic resources. Whereas ordinary discourse is most effective when it is most transparent, pointing efficiently and unambiguously to a body of information, literary writing continually asks us to interact with the "how" of the utterance.

Given the range of contemporary literary approaches, the interest that contributors to this volume show in literary form does not mean just one thing. To some it means an aesthetic interest in artistic form—the delight in something carefully crafted and intricately patterned. To others it is part of a rhetorical interest in how discourse is structured to achieve its effects. Structuralist analysis maintains a strong appeal to biblical scholars who associate certain verbal structures such as repetition and chiasm with the distinctiveness of the Bible. Narratology has its own preoccupation with technique, pattern, and conventions. Robert Alter's theory of type scenes that carry expectations for both author and reader has elicited the loyalty of many biblical scholars. Underlying the range of current critical approaches, however, is a shared conviction that literature is the result of conscious composition, careful patterning, and an awareness of literary conventions prevalent at the time of writing and subsequently.

A particular manifestation of this preoccupation with literary form and technique is the prominence of genre in literary discussions of the Bible. The contributors to this volume give us variations on the theme that genre is a "norm or expectation to guide the reader in his encounter with the text" (Culler 136). Literary approaches to the Bible agree that an awareness of genre tells us what to look for in a text and how to organize our experience of it. Beyond this descriptive function is a shared assumption that genre also influences how we interpret a biblical text. Northrop Frye sounds the keynote when he says that the "right" interpretation is the one "that conforms to the intentionality of the book itself and to the conventions it assumes and requires" (*Great Code* 80). Although this statement uses the term that has been such a preoccupation with biblical scholars for half a century—

intentionality—we should note that Frye locates intentionality in the text and its conventions, not in the author. This bias is evident in current literary approaches to the Bible (which is not to say that it has obliterated the concern with authorial intention among biblical scholars).

A related feature of literary approaches to the Bible is a focus on the text in its present form and an acceptance of the text as a unified whole. Literary critics have never needed conversion to this viewpoint; it has been their presupposition from time immemorial. Richard Moulton, the early champion of modern literary study of the Bible, said a century ago that "no principle of literary study is more important than that of grasping clearly a literary work as a single whole" (1718).

For biblical scholars to accept this principle has required a shift from the preoccupations of a century or more of scholarship, in which the main activity consisted of conducting excavations into the stages of composition and redaction behind a text and arranging biblical texts into a patchwork of fragments. Before the recent paradigm shift occurred, biblical scholars generally accepted Klaus Koch's claim that "the literary critic . . . approaches the text with, so to say, a dissecting knife in his hand. . . . Literary criticism is the analysis of biblical books from the standpoint of lack of continuity, duplications, inconsistencies and different linguistic usage, with the object of discovering what the individual writers and redactors contributed to a text, and also its time and place of origin" (69–70).

In such a critical climate, Northrop Frye's oft-quoted verdict was nothing less than a throwing down of the gauntlet: "a purely literary criticism would see the Bible, not as the scrapbook of corruptions, glosses, redactions, insertions, conflations, misplacings, and misunderstandings revealed by the analytic critic, but as a typological unity" (*Anatomy* 315). Today Frye's claim for unity is axiomatic for anyone claiming to take a literary approach to the Bible. The essays in this book assume the unity of biblical books and are uninterested in how the text came to its present form.

Any approach to the Bible can be formulated as a process of questioning the text. It is easy to summarize a literary approach to the Bible in terms of the questions that it asks of a biblical text. They include the following: What human experiences have been embodied in this text? To what genre(s) does this text belong, and how does an awareness of the relevant generic conventions guide our encounter with the text? What are the unifying patterns and structure of the text? What artistry does the text exhibit? What devices of disclosure has the author encoded in the text to guide our interpretation of its religious and other meanings?

Literary Critics and the Bible

Within the broad areas of agreement noted above, literary critics and biblical scholars continue to pursue their mutual interests with differing emphases and occasional uneasiness about what the other group does with the Bible. We might note in passing that a decade or two ago the previous sentence would have read "rival group" rather than "other group." In this section and the following one, we discuss what we as representatives of our respective disciplines find distinctive to our literary interest in the Bible and what we find either surprising or potentially troubling when we see members of the other discipline pursue literary analysis of the Bible.

A preliminary point to note is that both groups of scholars become novices when they take their first excursions into the other discipline's territory. Judged by the expertise of biblical scholars, literary critics of the Bible show obvious shortcomings when they discuss the Bible, especially in such areas as historical context, linguistic nuances of texts in their original languages, and theological sophistication.

Biblical scholars, for all their professed enthusiasm for literary methods, sometimes seem amateurish to literary critics in their use of literary terms and their application of literary methods of analysis. They sometimes seem unable to differentiate good from bad literary methodology, and although they make a good case for a literary approach in the introductory chapters to their commentaries, they quickly lapse into conventional preoccupations when they actually conduct their exploration of a biblical book. The integration between theory and practice sometimes seems deficient. In the present book we attempted to guard against the potential deficiencies of both literary and biblical scholars by having members of the two disciplines critique each other's chapters.

In the view of literary critics, biblical scholars continue to run the risk of isolating the Bible in an ancient world, sealed off both from the current literary interests of ordinary readers of the Bible and the experience of people today. Several strands make up this tendency.

A historical orientation continues to evidence itself among biblical scholars who share the new interest in the literary nature of the Bible. It has been an axiom from the time of Aristotle that history deals with the particular and literature with the universal. History tells us what happened; literature tells us what happens. The Bible invites both approaches, but biblical scholars do not find it natural to discuss the universal experiences portrayed in a biblical text. They are generally content to discuss the events and characters in the Bible as data of the ancient world, and not to worry about modern applications. To literary critics, biblical literature is a mirror in which we see ourselves. Biblical scholars might not dispute this, but it does not excite their enthusiasm.

In a landmark essay earlier in this century, Krister Stendahl proposed that interpretation of the Bible must be governed by two questions—"what it meant" and "what it means." By training and temperament, biblical scholars have gravitated toward the first of these and literary critics toward the second, a divergence that quickly surfaced as we collected the essays for this book.

The divergence between "then" and "now" is also evident in the handling of genre. Both groups of scholars believe that biblical texts will yield their meanings most fully if approached in terms of their genres. But the genres that the two groups apply to the Bible only partly overlap. Literary critics apply the generic considerations with which they are familiar in their study of English, American, and comparative literature. Biblical scholars show a hesitance to use generic terms that came on the scene after the Bible's date of composition; James Kugel, for example, claims that we should not use the word *poetry* for the Bible because biblical writers did not use it.

To literary critics, this skittishness about using the best critical terms available today is as self-defeating and arbitrary as it would be to discuss the history of the Bible using only the historical methods and terminology available in the ancient world, or to discuss the grammar of the Bible using only ancient grammatical terms, or to discuss biblical poetry without using such terms as *parallelism* and *lyric* and *imagery* because biblical poets did not use them. Literary critics generally apply a pragmatic test: if a given generic term or critical method helps us to see what is present in a biblical text, it would be perverse not to use it.

For biblical scholars, genres cannot be divorced from their origin in a specific moment in literary history. Literary critics are more inclined to regard generic traits as universal tendencies of literature itself. Northrop Frye thus theorized that "if . . . genre has a historical origin, why does the genre of drama emerge from medieval religion in a way so strikingly similar to the way it emerged from Greek religion centuries before? This is a problem of structure rather than origin, and suggests that there may be archetypes of genres as well as of images" ("Archetypes" 12). By such reasoning, biblical scholars' preoccupation with the historical rootedness of genres is an unnecessary confinement.

A related dichotomy is evident in the parallel literature to which the two groups of scholars compare biblical texts. Both agree that one of the criteria by which we judge whether a text in the Bible is literary is whether and how it resembles extrabiblical texts that we commonly classify as literature. But biblical scholars tend to compare the Bible to ancient texts.

Literary critics, by contrast, compare biblical stories and poems to familiar works of literature taught in literature courses in high school and college. By their taste, biblical scholars run the risk of making the Bible seem remote in the very process of applying literary methods of analysis.

The question of accessibility is important to literary critics. Biblical scholars have generally warmed to Robert Alter's claim that modern readers "have lost most of the keys to the conventions out of which [biblical narrative] was shaped" (47). Most literary critics are skeptical of the claim. A story is a story. A metaphor is a metaphor. We do not need special methods of analysis simply because a text is ancient. Of course every body of literature and every literary era exhibit distinctive traits. For the most part, observant reading will reveal what is in a text. Like literature generally, biblical literature displays a mixture of the familiar and the unique, and expositors of the Bible can choose to accentuate either quality. Literary critics have generally seen their task as taking the Bible out of the specialist's study and returning it to what one of them called the common reader (Chase).

Although both groups of scholars believe in the usefulness of genre studies, a difference emerges even here. Biblical scholars have been preoccupied with genre as a basis for classification and have often given the impression that mere classification is the goal of genre studies. They have also sometimes multiplied the classifications almost without limit (e.g., Westermann on the Psalms). Again the practical bent of literary critics is evident: they are interested in the ways in which an awareness of genre yields interpretive insight into a text. To cite a specific example, biblical scholars have been preoccupied with identifying the source or model for the New Testament Gospels, while literary critics have simply proceeded to look at the properties of the text before them.

Although biblical scholars rightly find literary critics to be frequently naïve in their theological judgments, their own theological orientation also carries a price tag. Biblical scholars are often content with formulations that strike literary critics as reductionist. Whereas literary critics are likely to see the manysidedness of real life in a biblical text, biblical scholars often reduce biblical texts to a unifying idea.

They do this with individual books of the Bible, for example. A common strategy is to find a prominent repeated pattern and then read individual parts of a book as illustrations of this theme. A common reading of the book of Judges, for example, is to read it as a cyclic pattern of Israel's apostasy, servitude, supplication, and deliverance. We can contrast this approach with a literary critic's comment that what the judges "have in common . . . is their rich diversity. The book of Judges delights in surprises, in diversity of character and situation, in reversals of expectations" (Gros

Louis 160). These are two very different versions of the book of Judges. We do not have to choose between them. But by comparison with the literary critic's version, the biblical scholar's emphasis on a repeated pattern runs the risk of being reductionist.

Or consider the following two versions of the story of Ruth: (1) "When the narrative 'trimming' is stripped away, the story of Ruth takes its place as simply one more bit of *Heilsgeschichte*" (Hals 19); (2) "I hold up a picture of the author of Ruth as an artist in full command of a complex and subtle art, which art is exhibited in almost every word of the story" (Rauber 176). Both of these viewpoints can be supported, but literary critics would again register their dissatisfaction with the impulse of the first formulation to reduce the rich complexity of the story to a single theme or purpose.

A final stricture that literary critics might make is that biblical scholars have been overly impressed by the changing fashions in contemporary criticism. They have tended to forget that behind the changing fashions is bedrock traditional literary criticism, which has never gone out of date to the extent that biblical scholars have inferred. Dazzled and perplexed by the splintered voices of "cutting edge" literary criticism, biblical scholars have not known exactly how to conduct literary criticism of the Bible. They have been more comfortable in writing surveys of literary approaches to the Bible than in conducting actual literary analyses of biblical texts. Literary critic John Sider has written that "what biblical scholars need to hear most from literary critics is that old-fashioned critical concepts of plot, character, setting, point of view and diction may be more useful than more glamorous and sophisticated theories" (19–20).

It would be wrong to amplify the foregoing analysis of differing emphases between literary critics and biblical scholars into a rivalry or conflict. Two decades ago such a characterization was accurate (Ryken, "Fallacies"). Today the two groups share the most essential assumptions about what it means to approach the Bible as literature. The differing biases within this body of shared procedures are viewed today as complementary rather than contradictory.

Biblical Scholars and the Bible

This section evaluates the literary approach to the Bible from the perspective of a biblical scholar. It considers the work of literary scholars as they ply their trade on the Bible, and the work of biblical scholars as they apply a literary method to the Bible. While the overall assessment of both is positive, points of tension remain between the literary approach and traditional biblical scholarship. For biblical scholars, literary analysis of the Bible still carries the aura of "the new kid on the block." In assessing the potential of literary analysis, we can speak of both its perils and its promise.

Some of the perils can be traced to the fragmented nature of contemporary literary theory. Most biblical scholars are not formally trained in the study of literature. The best method of self-training is through reading. Biblical scholars naturally want to read the most up-to-date literary theory. It does not take long to discover that the field of literary theory consists of radically different schools of thought. Left to their own designs, biblical scholars often simply accept the most current approach. In a day when scholarship is increasingly faddish, moreover, publishers seem interested in promoting the latest fashion in literary theory—until the next controversial perspective appears. In effect, many biblical scholars opt for fashionable contemporary forms of literary criticism without an awareness of traditional forms of literary criticism.

The more recent literary approaches, structuralism and deconstruction in particular, focus on theory and minimize the practice of literary analysis. Although biblical scholars are not trained in literary theory, many have studied philosophy in college or seminary and are captivated by philosophical studies of meaning. Important as these "literary" issues are, they sidetrack and even throw into question the possibility of illuminating the meaning of a biblical text.

The point is this: literary theory itself has been a frequent diversion from literary criticism of biblical texts. It has diverted commentators on the Bible away from the explication of texts toward philosophical discussion of the possibility of meaning.

This body of literary theory carries with it a related pitfall. Contemporary literary approaches have generated their own "in-language," with a result that they have difficulty in communicating with other members of the guild of biblical scholarship, to say nothing of clergy and laypeople who look to scholars for help in the elucidation of biblical texts. *Actant, signifié, narratology, interpretant, différance,* and *aporia* are only a few among the many esoteric terms of the field. Biblical scholars would do best to follow the advice of John Reichert when he urges the development of "a view of reading and criticism that cuts through the plethora of competing critical languages to recover and redignify the simple procedures of reading, understanding, and assessing literature" (x). But many biblical scholars have been powerless to resist the allure of esoteric literary theory.

An additional danger of a literary approach to biblical interpretation is the possible imposition of modern Western categories on the biblical text in a way that distorts the Bible. Literary scholars generally do not worry about this, but biblical scholars do. In their view, the possibility is very real that foreign concepts and categories will be applied to the Bible in ways that lead to misinterpretation.

The Old Testament, for example, is a collection of writings radically distanced from modern readers by a gap of time and culture. There is no reason to think that the conventions for writing poetry and prose were the same in ancient Near Eastern times as they are in the modern Western world. As Robert Alter has stated (13):

> Every culture, even every era in a particular culture, develops distinctive and sometimes intricate codes for telling its stories, involving everything from narrative point of view, procedures of description and characterization, the management of dialogue, to the ordering of time and the organization of plot.

This is not the place for a detailed analysis of how valid this theory is. The point is rather that the view summarized by Alter is a deeply ingrained tenet among biblical scholars and any rapprochement will require literary critics to acknowledge the depth of feeling that biblical scholars have on this point.

Biblical scholars are certain that the discontinuities of literary convention have often led to false characterization of the literary devices of the Bible. One example was the early attempt to discover meter in Hebrew poetry, especially by comparison with Latin forms. Both Josephus and Jerome (Kugel 152) described meter, which itself may be foreign to biblical poetry (Longman, "Critique"), in such terms as iambic pentameter. Another example of the distorting effect of modern categories is demonstrated by the use of Yugoslavian epic ballads to argue for the originally oral nature of biblical poetry (Cross 112–44).

Of course the application of wrong categories is not limited to, nor inherent in, the practice of applying modern and Western categories to the Bible. But biblical scholars want to see biblical literature placed in the context of ancient Near Eastern literature before it is studied in the context of modern literature and with the help of modern literary terms and categories. The Song of Songs and its imagery need first to be read in the light of Mesopotamian and Egyptian love poetry. Once we acknowledge the foreignness of the Old Testament, we can profitably recognize its similarities to familiar literature. The Song of Songs, for example, resembles not only ancient Near Eastern love poems but also Renaissance love poetry.

The final pitfall of a literary approach is the most significant: a literary approach to the Bible often entails a denial of the historical function of the biblical text. Indeed, the move away from the question of history is often the great seduction offered by the literary approach. Biblical criticism since the Enlightenment has majored on the historical dimension of the origin and composition of biblical texts, as well as the question of the connection between the contents of the Bible and real history. Source criticism of the Pentateuch is an example of the former, while the question of the reconstruction of the history of premonarchical history of Israel illustrates the latter.

The lure of the literary approach is in part a desire to "move beyond" such historical concerns, many of which have already exhausted discussion or reached an impasse. Furthermore, many biblical scholars have been frustrated by the obstacles that a historical approach to the text often places before a theological appreciation of the message of the Bible. The literary approach and the closely related canonical approach (Childs; see Barton 83–103 for the analogy with New Criticism) are avenues into a postcritical perspective on the Bible and theology. We should note that because literary approaches often express disinterest in the issues of historical reference, some evangelical scholars rightly or wrongly see literary approaches as a means to enter the broad arena of biblical scholarship.

Although not all literary theory denies the historical function of a text, the belief that literary texts have no external interests is an old one. According to Renaissance poet Sir Philip Sidney, the poet "nothing affirms." Frank Lentricchia's masterful book *After the New Criticism* follows the history of literary theory for the last forty years, using the theme of the denial of any external reference for literature. In this view, literature represents, not an insight into the world, but rather language play.

In short, the rupture between the literary and referential is an axiom of much modern literary theory. As one might expect, recognition of the literary characteristics of the Bible has led scholars to equate the Bible and literature, with the corollary that the Bible as a literary text does not refer outside of itself and especially makes no reference to history. This position leads, on the part of some, to a complete or substantial denial of a historical approach to the text—a denial that most often takes the form of disallowing or denigrating traditional historical-critical methods. Source and form criticism are special objects of attack. The following quotations are typical specimens of the prevailing rejection of historical reference in the name of literary criticism:

> Above all, we must keep in mind that narrative is a form of representation. Abraham in Genesis is not a real person any more than the painting of an apple is real fruit. (Berlin 12)

> Once the unity of the story is experienced, one is able to participate in the world of the story. Although the author of the Gospel of Mark certainly used sources rooted in the historical events surrounding the life of Jesus, the final text is a literary creation with an autonomous integrity, just as Leonardo's portrait of the Mona Lisa exists independently as a vision of life apart from any resemblance or nonresemblance to the person who posed for it or as a play of Shakespeare has integrity apart from reference to the historical characters depicted there. Thus Mark's narrative contains a closed and self-sufficient world with its own integrity. . . . When viewed as a literary achievement the statements in Mark's narrative, rather than being a representation of historical events, refer to the people, places, and events in the story. (Rhoads and Michie 3–4)

> As long as readers require the gospel to be a window to the ministry of Jesus before they will see truth in it, accepting the gospel will mean believing that the story it tells corresponds exactly to what actually happened during Jesus' ministry. When the gospel is viewed as a mirror, though of course not a mirror in which we see only ourselves, this meaning can be found on this side of it, that is between text and reader, in the experience of reading the text, and belief in the gospel can mean openness to the ways it calls readers to interact with it, with life, and with their own world. . . . The real issue is whether "his story" can be true if it is not history. (Culpepper 236–37)

For these authors, the truth of "his story" is independent of any historical information.

Similar evaluation may be seen in the hermeneutics of Hans Frei, who pinpoints the major error in both traditional critical and conservative exegesis as the loss of understanding that biblical narrative is historylike and not true history with an ostensive or external reference. In addition, we may cite Alter's often brilliant analysis of Old Testament narrative coupled with the assumption that the nature of the narrative is "historicized fiction" or "fictional history."

The result of this approach is a turning away from historical investigation of the text as impossible or irrelevant. The traditional methods of historical criticism are abandoned or radically modified or given secondary consideration. Concern to discover the original *Sitz im Leben* or to discuss the traditional history of the text languishes among this new breed of scholar. Traditional critical scholars have rightly objected, so that we find articles like Leander Keck's "Will the Historical-Critical Method Survive?" While evangelicals might in some respects be glad to see the end of historical criticism as practiced by "higher critics," they along with historical critics have a high stake in the question of history.

Recent signs are encouraging to those who believe that a literary approach to the text does not exclude its historical claims. Meir Sternberg has made a passionate case that the Bible is multifunctional, delineating the literary, historical, and ideological interests of the texts. It is possible to follow Sternberg's lead and see the latter category as a "theological" function, serving at the same time didactic and doxological functions (Longman, *Literary Approaches* 68–70). V. Philips Long's recent study of the Saul narrative is a model of combining literary and historical methods. Some of the early claims of the literary approach, such as Robertson's statement that "nothing depends on the truth or falsity of [the Bible's] historical claims" (548), now seem quite naïve.

There can be no denial of the dangers that the literary approach presents to biblical interpretation. But these dangers are not inevitable or even inherent in a literary approach. The positive values of that approach, to which we now turn, are testimony to its significance.

The literary approach to the Bible has restored a wholeness to biblical interpretation. Biblical scholarship in the twentieth century has been consumed with interest in composition and origins, with the historical paradigm paramount. The literary approach has reminded the guild that the Bible is literature, indeed great literature. This is new to modern scholarship, but as Prickett has shown so well, it is not new to the long tradition of biblical scholarship (1–3). The rupture between literary studies and biblical studies took place in the early nineteenth century. The modern literary approach has challenged biblical scholars to transcend the barriers to which the division into disciplines had driven them and has brought with it a breath of fresh air.

The renewed interest in the literary approach to biblical texts has also helped biblical scholars of all stripes to recover a healthy interest in whole texts. Before the ascendancy of a literary approach, liberal biblical scholars focused on the sources behind the present text. Conservative scholars, with their belief in the verbal inspiration of the Bible, concentrated on words, not on whole texts or even paragraphs. Under the influence of literary criticism, scholars who write critical commentaries, while not completely abandoning source theories, now analyze a biblical book as a whole. Conservative scholars now rarely adopt a word-by-word approach in their commentaries and instead opt for a holistic reading of a passage or book of the Bible.

Beyond affording a renewed recognition of the whole text, the literary approach assists the scholar in understanding the conventions of biblical storytelling and poetry. For biblical scholars, the most effective literary approaches, and the ones having the most widespread influence, are those that take as their task the uncovering and description of the conventions of writing during the biblical period, supplemented by what we know about the study of literature more generally.

After all, a literary text is an act of communication from a writer to a reader. The text is the message. For it to communicate, the sender and receiver have to speak the same language. Through the use of conventional forms, the writer sends signals to the readers to tell them how they are to take the message. We all know the generic signals in English (e.g., "once upon a time," "a novel by"). The literary approach to the Bible uses modern tools and categories (genre, plot, character, setting) in the light of the ancient literary context to throw light on our reading of the ancient biblical texts.

Even the philosophical question of the location of the meaning in a text has elicited a debate that has led to a better-nuanced understanding of the relationship between the author, the text, and the reader. We now appreciate, for instance, the role of the reader in the interpretive process. Readers are not blank slates who dispassionately or objectively read texts that are "out there." We come to a text, especially a text like the Bible, as readers with different agendas, as well as different educational and cultural backgrounds. These inevitably shape our reading. Helped by literary analysis, we may become increasingly *aware* of our readerly preunderstanding, but we can never completely divest ourselves of it.

In the final analysis, the goal of interpretation is to ascertain the author's intention (a hypothetical construct to be sure, as Strickland shows). But the author's intention can be reached only through the text, which prohibits arbitrariness and total relativity in interpretation. To focus on the biblical text in this way is synonymous with literary criticism of the Bible.

There will continue to be bad literary readings of the Bible and abuses of the literary approach, but as we survey the work of the past four or five years from our perspective as biblical scholars, we find that readings of the Bible based on a literary approach to the Bible are increasingly balanced and insightful. It seems likely that literary analysis will become a natural component of biblical interpretation for many years to come.

Distinguishing Literary Features of the Biblical Literature

Before we are likely to regard the Bible as literature, it must strike us as resembling familiar literature. The Bible is initially so distinctive as a book that most modern readers need some coaching before they think of it as literature. With coaching, we might add, perception happens at a faster than normal rate.

The resemblance of the Bible to ordinary books is not hard to see. Its overriding genre is that of the anthology of diverse writings produced by dozens of writers over many centuries. The Bible shares with other literary anthologies a reliance on genres, archetypes, and literary conventions (such as verse form for poetry and a beginning-middle-end construction for stories). The subject of biblical literature is human experience concretely presented, and like the entries in *The Norton Anthology of Poetry,* biblical texts display conscious artistry. All of this is familiar and will be apparent in the chapters that follow. What needs elaboration here at the outset is some of the distinctive features of biblical literature.

The literary feature of the Bible that is perhaps most noticeable is the heterogeneous nature of the material. Judged by classical standards of unity, the Bible is an untidy patchwork of diverse material. Nonliterary material like genealogies, historical notes, commands, and travel itineraries is mingled with literary material. Poetry appears right in the middle of expository and narrative prose. As we read the stories of the Bible, we seem always to be interrupted by extraneous documentary or didactic material. Narrative and discourse jostle for supremacy in the Gospels. Nearly every book in the Bible exhibits a mixed-genre format in a degree unparalleled in other literature.

Further distinctiveness stems from the presence of unfamiliar genres. Most of the Bible falls into conventional genres such as hero story, epic, tragedy, comedy, satire, lyric poetry, proverb, epistle, and such like. But other genres have no very precise parallels in English and American literature (even though they have influenced that literature). One thinks at once of prophecy, apocalypse, and Gospel, each with numerous subgenres that are equally unknown in ordinary literature.

The Bible combines three main impulses and types of writing in a way that makes it unique. They are the theological, the historical, and the literary. We are accustomed to finding these in separate books, but in the Bible they merge together. The Bible thus requires multiple approaches to a degree that an ordinary anthology of literature does not.

The patchwork or collage effect of the Bible is heightened by the biblical writers' preference for the brief unit. T. R. Henn correctly notes that "we have a literature concerned with an immense *range* of events, but the units . . . are relatively small" (30). Poetry in the Bible, for example, means lyric and prophetic poems, not epics. Biblical narrative lacks the kind of unity we find in the novel or even the short story, consisting instead of collections of relatively self-contained episodes. Wisdom literature takes the form of collections of proverbs.

The brevity of the units is accentuated in the narrative parts by the unembellished narrative style in which the stories of the Bible are usually told. The classic source on the subject is Erich Auerbach's essay in which he compares storytelling technique in Homer and Genesis. Whereas Homer elaborates the details of his story, biblical storytellers give only the essentials and leave much unstated. In biblical narrative, writes Auerbach, we find

> the externalization of only so much of the phenomena as is necessary for the purpose of the narrative, all else left in obscurity; the decisive points of the narrative alone are emphasized, what lies between is nonexistent; thoughts and feeling remain unexpressed, are only suggested by the silence and the fragmentary speeches; the whole, permeated with the most unrelieved suspense and directed toward a single goal . . . , remains mysterious and "fraught with background." (11–12)

The effect of this unembellished storytelling technique is that the stories of the Bible "require subtle investigation and interpretation" (15).

Clarity and mystery thus mingle in biblical literature. In the formula of one scholar, the authors of the Bible tell us the truth, but rarely the whole truth (Sternberg 230–63). What they tell us is reliable, but they leave much unsaid. Biblical storytellers narrate but do not explain what happens. With so little interpretive help forthcoming from biblical authors, the possibility for variability of interpretation repeatedly asserts itself in literary treatments of the Bible, which are not cordial to the "single meaning" approach of some biblical scholarship.

But the Bible seems to have a built-in safeguard against misinterpretation that goes beyond what we find in literature generally. Meir Sternberg calls it "foolproof composition." By this he means that while the Bible is hard to interpret correctly or definitely, it is nearly impossible to misread totally:

> By foolproof composition I mean that the Bible is difficult to read, easy to underread and overread and even misread, but virtually impossible to . . . counterread. . . . The essentials are made transparent to all comers: the story line, the world order, the value system. The old and new controversies among exegetes, spreading to every possible topic, must not blind us (as it usually does them) to the measure of agreement in this regard. (50–51)

The spare, unembellished narrative style of biblical narrative has large ramifications for characterization. One is that (in the words of Mark Van Doren) "these stories of the Bible . . . have no psychology in them, no discussion of motivation" (66). Someone else notes that "the great figures move in somewhat remote fashion, their characters illuminated as it were from the side by flashes of magnanimity, pity, anger; heroism, deceit, covetousness; suffering and the frequent cry of despair" (Henn 31). The result is a technique of "miniature vignettes, dramas of individuals" (Henn 31). This biblical technique is in obvious contrast to the modern novel, which tends to give us full-fledged portraits of characters, with detailed psychological portrayal of motivation and complexity.

We should not overstate the case for the simplicity of the Bible's style. Some stories of the Bible (e.g., the book of Esther and the hero stories in Daniel 1–6) are narrated with copia of language, replete with synonyms, epithets, and repetition. Far more important and usually overlooked is that the Bible *does* contain the high style—in its poetry. Even the verse form of parallelism is a form of embellishment in which we are led to consider every idea or feeling at least twice and often repeatedly. Biblical poetry tends toward an "oratorical high style" (Whallon 125), as evidenced by its epithets and synonyms and periphrastic impulse to take more words than necessary to express a thought. The distinctiveness from Greek literature that Auerbach found in biblical narrative is not present in biblical poetry, where the tendency is away from the unique individuality of biblical narrative and toward a universality similar to what we find in Greek literature (Whallon). If we compare the psalms that have headnotes linking them to specific events (e.g., Pss. 3, 18), we find that the poem makes no specific reference to the event but instead universalizes the experience.

The dramatic impulse permeates the Bible. Everywhere we turn we find an abundance of quoted speeches, snatches of dialogue, and stationing of characters in a setting. To read the Bible is to become an implied listener of the spoken voice. Of the four means by which a story can be told—direct narrative, dramatic narrative, description, and commentary—dramatic narrative dominates in the stories of the Bible (Licht 24–50), where direct quotation of speeches is a staple. The book of Job is a narrative drama, and many stories in the Bible are dramas in miniature, ready for staging.

Realism is also a feature of biblical literature. Compared to other ancient literature, the Bible is distinctive in its choice of common experience as its subject. Amos Wilder writes that the kind of nonaristocratic subject matter that in classical Greek and Roman literature had "been proper only to the low style of comedy and satire was . . . dealt with in terms of the sublime and the eternal" in the Bible (*Theology* 69). Erich Auerbach comments regarding the Bible that "the sublime influence of God here reaches so deeply into the everyday that the two realms of the sublime and the everyday are not only actually unseparated but basically inseparable" (22–23). The experience of the biblical writers, claims Auerbach, "engenders a new elevated style, which does not scorn everyday life and which is ready to absorb the sensorily realistic, even the ugly, the undignified, the physically base" (72).

The result of this realism is an astonishing sense of reality. Jewish novelist Chaim Potok has said it well:

> The people of the Hebrew Bible . . . were my early heroes, all of them mortals with smoldering passions, jealousies, many of them experiencing moments of grandeur as well as pitiful lowliness and defeat. . . . Above all, there was always for me a sense of the real when I read about those people—a feeling that the Bible did not conceal from me the truth about the less pleasant side of man. (75)

The focus of biblical literature is on elemental human experience. John Livingston Lowes notes that the vocabulary of the Bible is filled with "the primal stuff of our common humanity—of its universal emotional, sensory experiences" (31). Howard Mumford Jones writes:

> The themes of the Bible are simple and primary. Life is reduced to a few basic activities—fighting, farming, a strong sexual urge, and intermittent worship. . . . This elemental quality in the themes of the Bible is at once ground and occasion of a life and outlook quite as primary as and often more primitive than that in Homer or the Greek tragic poets. We confront basic virtues and primitive vices. . . . The world these persons inhabit is stripped and elemental—sea, desert, the stars, the wind, storm, sun, clouds and moon, seedtime and harvest, prosperity and adversity, famine and plenty. . . . Occupation has this elementary quality also. (52–53)

T. R. Henn similarly observes that the situations in biblical literature are based on "simplified dichotomy; rain and drought, evil against good, the idols against the One God, the little cities and their heroes against the enemy" (31).

Stylistic features of the Bible also distinguish it. Patterns of repetition are numerous and intricate (see, e.g., Muilenburg; Licht 51–95; Alter 88–113; Kugel). A major theme in recent biblical scholarship (e.g., Welch) is the prevalence of chiastic structure or ring composition, in which the second half of a passage repeats motifs of the first half in reverse order. The Hebrew preference for concrete language is well known, even though visual descriptions in the Bible are minimal (Baker). Irony is pervasive (Good; Duke). The Bible is also an affective book that conveys much of its meaning by getting the reader to feel certain ways toward the subject matter that is presented. The style of the Bible combines simplicity and majesty; in the words of Northrop Frye, "The simplicity of the Bible is the simplicity of majesty" (*Great Code* 211).

A combination of conciseness and syntactic tightness gives the Bible an aphoristic quality that is evident throughout. English poet Francis Thompson, writing about books that had influenced him, commented regarding the Bible that "beyond even its poetry, I was impressed by it as a treasury of *gnomic* wisdom. . . . This, of course, has long been recognised, and Biblical sentences have passed into the proverbial wisdom of our country" (543).

If we turn from form to content, what strikes us about the Bible is that it is a predominantly religious book, a fact that a literary approach will reveal rather than obscure. The Bible is pervaded by a consciousness of God. It constantly interprets human experience from a religious perspective. The implied (and sometimes stated) purpose of biblical writers is solidly didactic—revealing God to people, instructing them about how to order their lives, and asserting a religious system of values and morality. This is why C. S. Lewis has claimed that the Bible is

> through and through, a sacred book. Most of its component parts were written, and all of them were brought together, for a purely religious purpose. . . . It is . . . not only a sacred book but a book so remorselessly and continuously sacred that it does not invite, it excludes or repels, the merely aesthetic approach. (32–33)

Reading the Bible has a strong element of encounter to it. The Bible does not merely invite a response—it requires it. "The Bible's claim to truth," writes Auerbach, "is not only far more urgent than Homer's, it is tyrannical—it excludes all other claims. The world of the Scripture stories is not satisfied with claiming to be a historically true reality—it insists that it is the only real world" (14–15).

Part of the didacticism of biblical literature is its premise of the primacy of the inner and spiritual. Significant action consists of a person's response to external reality and does not reside in external reality itself. According to the Bible, people's problems do not stem primarily from outward events or the hostility of the environment. External events, whether large or small, provide *the occasion for* significant moral action, whether good or bad. In such a view, everything that happens to a person is important, since it represents an opportunity to choose God or repudiate him.

At the level of both form and content, the Bible is a multilayered book in which readers can find what their experience of life and literature enables them to see. The Bible has a surface simplicity that children can understand and relish. It is also a book in which scholars find sophistication of technique and subtlety of content. Scholars have shown the immense complexity that lies below the surface, but there is no requirement that we read the Bible at this level in order to understand and enjoy it. The Bible is the most flexible of all books.

The Literary Unity of the Bible

The range and diversity of the Bible are truly impressive. Written by a variety of writers over a span of many centuries, the Bible is an anthology, as the very name *Bible* (*biblia,* "books") suggests. Every aspect of life is covered in this comprehensive book. Because the Bible is both comprehensive and varied, it preserves the complexities and polarities of human experience to an unusual degree. The paradoxes of life are held in tension in what can be called the most balanced book ever written.

But if we stress only the variety of the Bible, we distort the kind of book it is. The Bible is also an amazingly unified book. The most obvious element of literary unity is narrative unity. The Bible tells a story with a beginning (the creation of the world), a middle (fallen human history), and an end (the consummation of history with the eternal defeat of evil and the triumph of good). The very arrangement of the Bible, beginning with Genesis and ending with Revelation, shows a literary shapeliness.

Corresponding to the narrative shape of the Bible is the fact that its arrangement is loosely chronological. If we link the phases of biblical history with the literary forms that we particularly associate with them, the resulting outline is this:

1. The beginning of human history: Creation, Fall, and covenant (story of origins)
2. Exodus (law)
3. Israelite monarchy (wisdom literature and psalms)
4. Exile and return (prophecy)
5. The life of Christ (Gospel)
6. The beginnings of the Christian church (Acts and the Epistles)
7. Consummation of history (Apocalypse)

The skeleton of the entire sequence is historical narrative.

The overall story of the Bible has a unifying plot conflict consisting of the great spiritual and moral battle between good and evil. A host of details makes up this conflict: God and Satan, God and his rebellious creatures, good and evil people, inner human impulses toward obedience to God and disobedience to God. Almost every story, poem, and proverb in the Bible contributes to this ongoing plot conflict between good and evil. Every act and mental attitude shows God's creatures engaged in some movement, whether slight or momentous, toward God or away from him.

The protagonist in the Bible's overarching story is God. He is the central character, the one whose presence unifies the story of universal history with its constantly changing cast of human characters. Roland Frye comments:

> The characterization of God may indeed be said to be the central literary concern of the Bible, and it is pursued from beginning to end, for the principal character, or actor, or protagonist of the Bible is God. Not even the most seemingly insignificant action in the Bible can be understood apart from the emerging characterization of the deity. With this great protagonist and his designs, all other characters and events interact, as history becomes the great arena for God's characteristic and characterizing actions.

This story of God is the story of universal history, viewed in terms of God's providence, salvation, and judgment.

In addition to its narrative unity, the Bible exhibits a unity of reference. In a vast interlocking system of allusions and echoes, writers keep referring to a common core of events, images, and doctrines. This network of foreshadowings, fulfillments, and reinterpretations includes, but is not limited to, the relationship between the Old Testament and the New Testament. The Bible is the example par excellence of intertextual literature. It constitutes a unity of cross-reference that no other anthology even comes close to approximating.

Literary unity also stems from the archetypes in the Bible (Ryken, *Bible as Literature* 187–93). Archetypes are master images that recur throughout literature and life. They fall into three categories: plot motifs (e.g., quest, initiation, rescue), character types (e.g., hero, villain, tempter), and images (e.g., light, darkness, mountaintop). Archetypes fall into a dialectical pattern of opposites—ideal and unideal, wish fulfillment and anxiety, longings and fears. Together they consist of a single composite story on which we can plot every piece of literature that we encounter. This "monomyth" is a circle having four phases that can be given the literary labels of romance, tragedy, antiromance, and comedy. The individual parts of the Bible continually reenact the up-and-down movement of this scheme.

Finally, the literature of the Bible is unified by recurrent subjects or preoccupations. In brief, they are the character and acts of God, the nature of people, the divine-human relationship, the nature of virtue and vice, and the mystery of human evil and suffering. The twin themes of what God does and what people do accounts for much of what we read in the Bible. In regard to human action, the Bible follows the same twofold pattern that literature as a whole does—the *via negativa* that presents examples of vice to avoid and the presentation of positive or heroic examples to emulate.

The Bible is an encyclopedic work that meets Northrop Frye's description of epic as "the story of all things" (*Return of Eden* 3–31). But it is not a formless or confusing book. It possesses a literary unity that encompasses a narrative shapeliness; a network of allusions, echoes, and archetypes; and thematic unity.

WORKS CITED

Alter, Robert. *The Art of Biblical Narrative.* New York: Basic Books, 1981.
Auerbach, Erich. *Mimesis: The Representation of Reality in Western Literature.* Trans. Willard Trask. Princeton: Princeton UP, 1953.
Baker, Dom Aelred. "Visual Imagination and the Bible." *Downside Review* 84 (1966): 349–60.
Barton, John. *Reading the Old Testament.* Philadelphia: Westminster, 1984.
Berlin, Adele. *Poetics and Interpretation of Biblical Narrative.* Sheffield: Almond, 1983.
Chase, Mary Ellen. *The Bible and the Common Reader.* New York: Macmillan, 1944.
Childs, Brevard S. *Introduction to the Old Testament as Scripture.* Philadelphia: Fortress, 1979.
Cross, Frank M. *Canaanite Myth and Hebrew Epic.* Cambridge, Mass.: Harvard UP, 1973.
Culler, Jonathan. *Structuralist Poetics.* Ithaca: Cornell UP, 1975.
Culpepper, R. Alan. *The Anatomy of the Fourth Gospel.* Philadelphia: Fortress, 1983.
Drury, John. *Luke.* New York: Macmillan, 1973.
Duke, Paul D. *Irony in the Fourth Gospel.* Atlanta: John Knox, 1985.
Fischer, James A. *How to Read the Bible.* Englewood Cliffs, N.J.: Prentice-Hall, 1981.
Fowler, Alastair. *Kinds of Literature: An Introduction to the Theory of Genres.* Cambridge, Mass.: Harvard UP, 1982.
Frei, Hans. *The Eclipse of Biblical Narrative.* New Haven: Yale UP, 1974.
Frye, Northrop. *Anatomy of Criticism.* Princeton: Princeton UP, 1957.
———. "The Archetypes of Literature." *Fables of Identity: Studies in Poetic Mythology.* New York: Harcourt, 1963. 7–20.
———. *The Great Code: The Bible and Literature.* New York: Harcourt, 1982.
———. *The Return of Eden.* Toronto: University of Toronto Press, 1965.
Frye, Roland. "Introduction." *The Bible: Selections from the King James Version for Study as Literature.* Boston: Houghton Mifflin, 1965. ix–xxxix.
Good, Edwin M. *Irony in the Old Testament.* Philadelphia: Westminster, 1965.
Gros Louis, Kenneth R. R. "The Book of Judges." *Literary Interpretations of Biblical Narratives.* Ed. K. Gros Louis et al. 2 vols. Nashville: Abingdon, 1974. 141–62.
Hals, Ronald. *The Theology of the Book of Ruth.* Philadelphia: Fortress, 1969.

Henn, T. R. *The Bible as Literature.* New York: Oxford UP, 1970.
Jones, Howard Mumford. "The Bible from a Literary Point of View." *Five Essays on the Bible.* New York: American Council of Learned Societies, 1960.
Keck, Leander. "Will the Historical-Critical Method Survive?" *Orientation by Disorientation.* Ed. R. A. Spencer. Pittsburgh: Pickwick, 1980. 115–27.
Koch, Klaus. *The Growth of the Biblical Tradition: The Form-Critical Method.* New York: Scribner, 1969.
Kugel, James L. *The Idea of Biblical Poetry: Parallelism and Its History.* New Haven: Yale UP, 1981.
Lentricchia, Frank. *After the New Criticism.* London: Methuen, 1980.
Lewis, C. S. *The Literary Impact of the Authorized Version.* Philadelphia: Fortress, 1963.
Licht, Jacob. *Storytelling in the Bible.* Jerusalem: Magnes, 1978.
Long, V. Philips. *The Reign and Rejection of King Saul: A Case for Literary and Theological Coherence.* Chico, Calif.: Scholars, 1989.
Longman, Tremper, III. "A Critique of Two Recent Metrical Systems." *Biblica* 63 (1982): 230–54.
———. *Literary Approaches to the Bible.* Grand Rapids: Zondervan, 1987.
Moulton, Richard. *The Modern Reader's Bible.* New York: Macmillan, 1895.
Muilenburg, James. "A Study in Hebrew Rhetoric: Repetition and Style." *Vetus Testamentum Supplements* 1 (1953): 97–111.
Niebuhr, H. Richard. *The Responsible Self.* New York: Harper & Row, 1963.
O'Connor, Flannery. *Mystery and Manners.* Ed. Sally and Robert Fitzgerald. New York: Farrar, Straus, and Giroux, 1957.
Potok, Chaim. "Heroes for an Ordinary World." *The Great Ideas Today.* Ed. Robert M. Hutchins and Mortimer J. Adler. Chicago: Encyclopaedia Britannica, 1957. 71–76.
Prickett, Stephen. *Words and the Word: Language, Poetics, and Biblical Interpretation.* Cambridge: Cambridge UP, 1986.
Rauber, D. F. "The Book of Ruth." *Literary Interpretations of Biblical Narratives.* Ed. Kenneth R. R. Gros Louis et al. Nashville: Abingdon, 1974. 163–76.
Reichert, John. *Making Sense of Literature.* Chicago: University of Chicago Press, 1977.
Rhoads, David, and Donald Michie. *Mark as Story: An Introduction to the Narrative of a Gospel.* Philadelphia: Fortress, 1982.
Robertson, David. "Literature, the Bible as." *The Interpreter's Dictionary of the Bible Supplementary Volume.* Nashville: Abingdon, 1976. 548.
Roche, Paul. "Introduction." *The Bible's Greatest Stories.* New York: Mentor, 1990.
Ryken, Leland. *How to Read the Bible as Literature.* Grand Rapids: Zondervan, 1984.
———. "Literary Criticism of the Bible: Some Fallacies." *Literary Interpretations of Biblical Narratives.* Ed. Kenneth R. R. Gros Louis et al. Nashville: Abingdon, 1974. 24–40.
Sider, John W. "Nurturing Our Nurse: Literary Scholars and Biblical Exegesis." *Christianity and Literature* 32, no. 1 (1982): 15–20.
Stendahl, Krister. "Biblical Theology, Contemporary." *The Interpreter's Dictionary of the Bible.* Ed. George A. Buttrick. Nashville: Abingdon, 1962. 1:418–32.
Sternberg, Meir. *The Poetics of Biblical Narrative: Ideological Literature and the Drama of Reading.* Bloomington: Indiana UP, 1985.
Strickland, Geoffrey. *Structuralism or Criticism? Thoughts on How We Read.* Cambridge: Cambridge UP, 1981.

Thompson, Francis. *Literary Criticisms.* Ed. Terence L. Connolly. New York: Dutton, 1948.

Van Doren, Mark, and Maurice Samuel. *In the Beginning, Love: Dialogues on the Bible.* Ed. Edith Samuel. New York: 1973.

Welch, J. W., ed. *Chiasmus in Antiquity: Structures, Analyses, Exegesis.* Hildesheim: Gerstenberg, 1981.

Westermann, Claus. *Praise and Lament in the Psalms.* Trans. Keith R. Crim and Richard N. Soulen. Atlanta: John Knox, 1981.

Whallon, William. "Old Testament Poetry and Homeric Epic." *Comparative Literature* 18 (1966): 113–31.

Wilder, Amos. *Early Christian Rhetoric: The Language of the Gospel.* Cambridge, Mass.: Harvard UP, 1971.

———. *Theology and Modern Literature.* Cambridge, Mass.: Harvard UP, 1958.

CHAPTER 2

The Bible as Literature

Frederick Buechner
Novelist

As an occasional writer of novels, I have always thought that the most appealing aspect of the form is that it allows you to do anything you can get away with. I think of *Moby Dick* with its endless excursions into the minutiae of whaledom, or *Ulysses, Tristram Shandy, The Countesse of Pembroke's Arcadia* with their endless excursions into everything else. Or I think of the later novels of Henry James—*The Golden Bowl,* for instance—where the star of the show is not the story it tells or the characters it tells about but the sheer madness of the style, or of Anthony Trollope's *The Warden,* which has virtually no style at all but like a clear window pane allows you to watch the dance of old Septimus Harding's delicate conscience leading him without the sound of anyone's voice in your ears except his own. The Bible is not a novel, needless to say, but like a novel there is almost nothing it does not attempt and by and large not much that it fails to get away with. In that sense it is not only The Good Book but also a book which, except for a few notorious *longueurs,* is a remarkably good one. You might better say that it is not really a book at all but a library of some sixty-six of them written over the course of centuries by Heaven only knows whom, or for how many divergent purposes, or from how many variegated points of view, yet in some sense it manages to be one book even so. Something holds it together. When we think of it, we think of it somehow as a whole.

A novelist, for example, might well envy the way the opening chapters of Genesis set the stage for everything that is to follow and foreshadow all the great biblical themes. Creation is one of them. "In the beginning God *created,*" the opening words proclaim, and from there right on to the book of Revelation creation is proclaimed again and again. More almost than anything else he does, as the Bible depicts him, God makes things. He makes the world in all its splendor, and the psalms never stop stammering out their wonder at it—"Praise him, sun and moon, praise him all you shining stars! Praise him, you highest heavens, and all you waters above the heavens! Let them praise the name of the LORD! For he commanded and they were created" (Ps. 148:3–5).

When God presents his credentials to Job in what is perhaps the greatest of all his arias, it is the creation that he himself points to—the springs of the sea and the storehouses of the snow are his, he says; the young lions crouch in their dens, the ostrich waves her proud wings, Behemoth makes the deep boil like a pot, because with his fathomless ingenuity he made them that way. Men and women he made too, of course, and perhaps because he loved them most, perhaps to make it up to them for all the trouble he saw in store for them because they were so bad at loving him back, he made them a little like himself. Even after their fall and the terrible sentence pronounced upon them, he "made for Adam and for his wife garments of skins, and clothed them," Genesis says (3:21), and in a way the entire remainder of the Bible is about how history itself is the record of the Creator's endless efforts to restore his creation to himself, to clothe it again in the glory for which he created it in the first place.

He also made a people, Israel, to be a blessing to all peoples. He raised up prophets to bring them to heel when they strayed. Somewhat reluctantly he anointed kings to rule over them. When his people abandoned him to follow wantonly after other gods, he made a people within a people out of the faithful few who were left—"brought forth a shoot out of the stump of Jesse"—and when those few fell away also, he came down finally to making one single Person, a second Adam, who was like no other because "in him all the fullness of God was pleased to dwell" as Saint Paul tried to explain the mystery of it to the Colossians (Col. 1:19). Finally, having funneled down to that single Person, the whole vast creative process starts funneling out again through the twelve disciples to, little by little, a new people altogether—a new Israel, the church—which, ragged and inadequate as it must always be in its humanness, in its holiness is yet another garment that the Creator has fashioned for the sheltering of the creation that for better or worse, as

Genesis suggests, he can never stop loving because he made it, and it is his. Being what it is, the human race will go on failing till the end of time, but even at the end of time God is there again, as John finally tells it. "Behold, I make all things new!" he calls forth (Rev. 21:5), and while the words are still on his lips, the new Jerusalem he has created comes down out of heaven like a bride.

Creation is perhaps the greatest of the themes adumbrated in the opening chapters of this extraordinary book of books, but of course all the other great themes are implicit in those chapters too. The old covenant of law grows out of God's telling Adam and Eve that all Eden is theirs if only they will not eat of that one fatal tree; and the whole tragic history of Israel, not to mention of the rest of us, stems from their eating it anyway; and out of those garments of skins as emblematic of the love that will not let them go grows the new covenant of grace where nothing is asked of them except that they allow themselves to be clothed. As Saint Paul understood it, in the face of Adam, who went wrong, are already faintly visible the features of Jesus, who went right, was right, lived and died to make all things finally right and whole. "Happy families are all alike; every unhappy family is unhappy in its own way," is how Tolstoy wonderfully and unforgettably sets the stage for all eight hundred pages or more of the *Anna Karenina* to come. The opening pages of Genesis do much the same for the whole great library that it unlocks.

Genesis sets the stage for the drama, and then of course there is the cast of characters. Who can count their number? Who can describe their variety?—patriarchs and judges, kings and courtesans, peasants and priests; in short, men and women of every possible sort, heroes and scoundrels and some, like ourselves, who from time to time manage to be something of both. The central character, of course—the one who dominates everything and around whom all the others revolve—is God himself. The Bible is God's book. It is as unimaginable without him as *Moby Dick* would be without the great white whale, yet like the great white whale, God is scarcely to be seen. He appears briefly walking in Eden in the cool of the day, but there is no description of him there, nor is there one anywhere else in all those thousand pages and more that come later. Such is his holiness that to look upon him is death, and the commandment to make no graven image of him or of anything else in the heaven above or the earth beneath that might be supposed to be like him is basic to the faith of Israel. When Moses is allowed to take refuge in the cleft of a rock so that he may see his glory passing by, God tells him, "You shall see my back; but my face shall not be seen" (Ex. 33:23), and when Moses comes down from talking with God on Mount Sinai, his own face shines with such an unearthly light that the people are afraid to come near him until he puts on a veil (Ex. 34:29). God is not to be seen in this book that is his except as he is reflected in the faces and lives of people who have encountered him, and the whole New Testament grows out of the experience of those who, like Saint Paul, encountered "the glory of God in the face of Christ" (2 Cor. 4:6).

God is not to be seen in space because in space he is not seeable any more than in *La Comédie Humaine* Balzac is seeable. But he can be *heard.* God's words can be heard because words move forward not through space but through time, and although time cannot be inhabited by eternity, it can be impinged upon by eternity the way the horizontal can be impinged upon by the vertical. God is known in the Bible as he speaks—speaks to and through the prophets and patriarchs, the priests and poets, speaks through the mighty acts he works both in the history of Israel and in the small histories of men and women whose ears and lives are in some measure attuned to him, or sometimes even if they are not. The Bible is the Word of God—the word about God and God's word about himself—and it is also the endless words of God, the unanticipatable and elusive self-disclosures of God to countless numbers of people through the medium of what in Hebrew is called *dābār,* which means both *word* and *deed*—the word that is also a deed because it makes things happen, and the deed that is also a word because through it is revealed meaning.

How remote, inaccessible, and amorphous all this makes God sound, yet as the Bible depicts him, he is anything but that. God is now wrathful, now loving. He is jealous. He laughs. He cries out like a woman in labor. He is Abraham's friend. He destroys cities. He speaks in the still, small voice that Elijah heard and answers Moses in thunder. He makes himself known to thousands through the cataclysms of history and hides himself from thousands of others, hides himself—inexplicably, horrifyingly—even from Christ in his dying. It is God himself who says what he ultimately is, the only one who can do it. "I the LORD your God am holy," he says to Moses (Lev. 19:2), which is another way of saying, "I am who I am." Mystery, power, righteousness, love even—all the words that we use to describe him are in the end as crude as the behavior the Bible ascribes to him. He is none of them. He is all of them. He is who he is experienced to be by Eve, by Rachel, by Ahab, by Hannah, by Bathsheba, by Judas. He is who he is experienced to be by each one of us. He is holy. He is God.

As to the Eves and Hannahs, the Judases and Ahabs themselves—the rest of the cast—we wish we could know what they looked liked, but for the most part the Bible is interested much less in seeing than in hearing and tells us as little about these matters as it does in the case of God. We are told that David was a handsome redhead with beautiful eyes. We are told that Joseph had a coat that was the envy of his brothers, that the bride in Solomon's song had breasts like two fawns, twins of a gazelle, that feed among the lilies. We are told that when Jesus fell asleep in the stern of the boat, he had a pillow under his head, and that Paul was weak in his bodily presence and his speech of no account. But how much we would give to see more—especially when it comes to the leading characters, the ones who not only loomed large in their time but have continued to do so ever since. Abraham and Sarah, for instance. Just one glimpse of their ancient, sand-blasted faces when the angel told them they were to have a child at last would be as precious almost as to them the child was. Or the way Moses looked as he stood on Mount Pisgah letting his gaze wander from the lands of Dan and Naphtali in the north to the Negeb and the Jordan valley in the south knowing that he would not live to set foot on any of it. Or Solomon in all his glory, or Mary when the angel came upon her with his troubling word. We are allowed to see that pillow under Jesus' head where he lay sleeping in the stern as the storm came up, but his head we never see. We know nothing of how he sounded when he talked, how he looked when he was asleep or awake, the slope of his shoulders when he was tired. Yet we know much without seeing, of course. We know him as we know all of them, as we know God, through their *dābᵉrîm*—through the words they speak, which are also their deeds.

The Bible is full of their marvelous words. Isaac, hoodwinked into thinking that it is Esau who is kneeling before him instead of Jacob dressed up in Esau's clothes, sniffs the air as he blesses him and says, "See, the smell of my son is as the smell of the field that the LORD has blessed" (Gen. 27:27), and suddenly the blind old man is there before us in chiaroscuro as rich and moving as even Rembrandt could have managed it. "O my son Absalom, my son, my son Absalom! Would I had died instead of you, O Absalom, my son, my son!" (2 Sam. 18:33)—we see, without seeing, all that is most kingly about David as well as all that is most human about him in those words he speaks when he learns that the son who betrayed him has fallen in battle; and we see Elijah's face in an ecstasy of derision as with scalding words he taunts the rival prophets whose frenzied efforts have all failed to persuade Baal to touch off the sacrificial pyre. "Cry aloud, for he is a god," Elijah says, his voice shrill with mockery. "Either he is musing, or he has gone aside, or he is on a journey, or perhaps he is asleep and must be awakened" (1 Kings 18:27). A camera could capture the scene no better.

There are also dialogues which not only evoke the character of the speakers but bring them alive before our eyes. Guiltily and in disguise King Saul goes at night to ask the witch of Endor to summon from the dead old Samuel, who in life had been his friend, his conscience, his most implacable enemy.

> "Divine for me by a spirit, and bring up for me whomever I shall name to you."
> The woman said to him, "Surely you know what Saul has done, how he has cut off the mediums and the wizards from the land. Why then are you laying a snare for my life to bring about my death?"
> But Saul swore to her by the LORD, "As the LORD lives, no punishment shall come upon you for this thing."
> Then the woman said, "Whom shall I bring up for you?"
> He said, "Bring up Samuel for me."
> When the woman saw Samuel, she cried out with a loud voice, and the woman said to Saul, "Why have you deceived me? You are Saul."
> The king said to her, "Have no fear. What do you see?"
> And the woman said to Saul, "I see a god coming up out of the earth."
> He said to her, "What is his appearance?"
> And she said, "An old man is coming up; and he is wrapped in a robe."
> And Saul knew that it was Samuel, and he bowed with his face to the ground, and did obeisance. (1 Sam. 28:8–14)

Or take the words that Pilate and Jesus speak to each other when they come face to face for the first time.

> "Are you the King of the Jews?"
> "Do you say this of your own accord, or did others say it to you about me?"
> "Am I a Jew? Your own nation and the chief priests have handed you over to me; what have you done?"
> "My kingship is not of this world; if my kingship were of this world, my servants would fight that I might not be handed over to the Jews; but my kingship is not from the world."
> "So you are a king?"
> "You say that I am a king. For this I was born, and for this I have come into the world, to bear witness to the truth. Everyone who is of the truth hears my voice."
> "What is truth?" (John 18:33–38)

It was by speaking his creative word into the primordial darkness that God on the first day brought forth light, and it is by speaking and listening to each other that out of our separate mysteries is brought forth the truth of who we are.

They speak, this huge gathering of people who crowd the pages of the

Bible. They listen. They emerge, if we in turn listen to them, not as allegorical embodiments of Goodness and Badness but as flesh-and-blood men and women who no less ambiguously than the rest of us are good one day, bad the next, and occasionally both at once. Of all people in the world, Noah is the one who found favor with God, but Noah is also the one who quaffs so deeply of the fruit of his own vines that he passes out cold. No less a one than Father Abraham himself—the exemplar of faith, God's friend—willingly abandons the wife of his bosom to Pharaoh's harem rather than risk his neck trying to save her. Jacob is a schemer and a crook, but he is also the one whom God visits with holy dreams and chooses over his apparently blameless twin Esau to be Israel, the father of the twelve tribes and bearer of the promise. In religious art, the disciples of Jesus appear wearing haloes, but in the gospel story they are largely indistinguishable from everybody else—vying with each other for first place, continually missing the point, and, when the going gets rough, interested in nothing so much as saving their own skins down to the last man. Even Jesus himself comes through as far more complex and human than generations of piety have portrayed him. His fellow townspeople at Nazareth are so offended by him that they all but throw him headlong off a cliff. He speaks sharply if not downright cruelly to his mother. When the full horror of what lies ahead comes through to him at Gethsemane, he sweats blood and pleads with God to let him off. As Mark tells it, the last words he ever spoke were not a ringing affirmation of faith but a cry of dereliction and despair.

Whatever else they may be, they are real human beings, in other words, and it is not the world of the Sunday school tract that they move through but a Dostoyevskian world of darkness and light commingled, where suffering is sometimes redemptive and sometimes turns the heart to stone. It is a world where, although God is sometimes to be known through his life-giving presence, there are other times when he is known only by his appalling absence. The Bible is a compilation of stories of what happened to these human beings in such a world, and the stories are not only as different from one another as the people they are about but are told in almost as many different ways. Side by side in the opening pages of Genesis, for instance, there are two stories of the creation, one of them as stately and rhythmic as plainsong, the other as homely and human as the way you might tell it to your grandchildren. The groups of stories about Jacob and his son Joseph, told in as unpretentious a style as the second creation story, are nonetheless complex, full of psychological motivation and rich with detail; and in the case of Jacob in particular, no character in fiction is more multifaceted, fascinating, or believable.

In a different style altogether is, say, the story of Nebuchadnezzar's golden idol as it appears in the book of Daniel.

> King Nebuchadnezzar made an image of gold, whose height was sixty cubits and its breadth six cubits. He set it up on the plain of Dura, in the province of Babylon. Then King Nebuchadnezzar sent to assemble the satraps, the prefects, and the governors, the counselors, the treasurers, the justices, the magistrates, and all the officials of the provinces to come to the dedication of the image which King Nebuchadnezzar had set up. Then the satraps, the prefects, and the governors, the counselors, the treasurers, the justices, the magistrates, and all the officials of the provinces, were assembled for the dedication of the image that King Nebuchadnezzar had set up; and they stood before the image that Nebuchadnezzar had set up. And the herald proclaimed aloud, "You are commanded, O peoples, nations, and languages, that when you hear the sound of the horn, pipe, lyre, trigon, harp, bagpipe, and every kind of music, you are to fall down and worship the golden image that King Nebuchadnezzar has set up; and whoever does not fall down and worship shall immediately be cast into a burning fiery furnace." Therefore, as soon as all the peoples heard the sound of the horn, pipe, lyre, trigon, harp, bagpipe, and every kind of music, all the peoples, nations, and languages fell down and worshiped the golden image which King Nebuchadnezzar had set up. (Dan. 3:1–7)

Here all is sophisticated artistry—the wondrously satiric effect of those sonorous, deadpan repetitions of musical instruments and officials, which continue to occur through the story, for example, and the way each time the words "the image which King Nebuchadnezzar set up" appear, they manage to convey again not only that all the setting up in the world will fail to prevent the golden image from someday tumbling down but that even on a Babylonian scale all human glory in general is a vain and transitory thing. Not even the book of Ecclesiastes conveys it better. The author of the book of Job takes an ancient folktale and with a different kind of artistry entirely uses it as the frame for his fathomless poem, which comes closer to classic drama than any other work that Israel produced. The mission of Israel is to preach God's mercy to all nations, and to dramatize that point the author of the book of Jonah tells a story which seems to me the one example of sheer wit in the Bible—the recalcitrant prophet preaching salvation to the heathen while grumbling all the way, and God at the end pretending to mistake Jonah's anger at the sun for scorching him as pity for the shriveled vine that no longer gives him shade.

In the realm of historical as distinct from fictional narrative, the apparently eye-witness account in 2 Samuel 9–20 and 1 Kings 1–2 of the intrigues of David's court is as psychologically convincing, thorough, and full of life as any history the ancient world produced. One thinks also of the unforgettable portrait it provides of the ruthless, emotional, vulnerable character of David himself, who could order Uriah's murder without batting an eye yet give sanctuary to the crippled son of his dead friend Jonathan, and of the particularly vivid account of the last years of his reign when Bathsheba was nagging him about the succession and not even having the beautiful young Abishag for a bedmate was able to drive the chill of approaching death out of his old bones.

There could hardly be a greater miscellany of stories, characters, styles than are contained in this massive volume. There could hardly be a greater divergence among the ways God is portrayed—vindictive and bellicose, loving and merciful—or the ways human beings are portrayed either and the ways God is shown as wanting them to be related to him and to each other. Yet for all of that, the whole great drama somehow holds together.

Genesis is part of what does it—the prologue in which the stage is set and all the major themes first introduced. And the major themes themselves are part—creation, covenant, law, grace, weaving in and out through all the histories and stories, all the poems, psalms, prophecies. And the leading characters are part—God in his holiness pervading every page, and such heroes of the faith as the epistle to the Hebrews lists—Abraham and Sarah, Moses and Rahab, David and Samuel and the prophets—who both appear in their places and then keep on reappearing in the long memory of their people. And for Christians, of course, Jesus holds it together because it is both his Bible and the Bible about him.

Finally, I think it is possible to say that in spite of all its extraordinary variety, the Bible is held together by having a single plot. It is one that can be simply stated: God creates the world; the world gets lost; God seeks to restore the world to the glory for which he created it. That means that the Bible is a book about you and me, whom he also made and lost and continually seeks, so you might say that what holds it together more than anything else is us. You might also say, of course, that of all the books that humanity has produced, it is the one which more than any other holds us together.

CHAPTER 3

The Bible as Literature: A Brief History

LELAND RYKEN
Wheaton College

The Literary Awareness of Biblical Writers

The current literary study of the Bible reflects a paradigm shift for both biblical and literary scholars. Among biblical scholars, literary approaches have increasingly replaced traditional ways of dealing with the Bible. For literary critics the revolution has not been methodological but canonical: the Bible is now part of the canon of works that literary scholars teach in their courses and about which they publish critical essays and books.

There is a very real danger that the current fashionableness of the Bible-as-literature movement will engender the misconception that literary critics and biblical scholars have discovered something new. An inquiry into the history of literary approaches to the Bible can serve as a corrective to this and other fallacies.

The idea that the Bible is literature is as old as the Bible itself, as we know from both explicit and implicit evidence. One biblical writer provides a brief anatomy of how he composed his work, and it turns out to be a thoroughly literary conception of the writer's task. The passage occurs near the end of the Old Testament book of Ecclesiastes:

> Besides being wise, the Preacher also taught the people knowledge, weighing and studying and arranging proverbs with great care. The Preacher sought to find pleasing words, and uprightly he wrote words of truth. (12:9–10)

Several things are important here. One is the picture of the writer as self-conscious composer, carefully choosing from among available options as he selects and arranges his material "with great care." A second keynote is the preoccupation with artistry and beauty of expression, as suggested by the phrase "pleasing words," or "words of delight." We also catch a glimpse of the writer as stylist—as someone interested in form as well as content. Yet another literary aspect of this writer's theory of writing is his awareness that he is writing in a definite literary genre, in this case the collection of proverbs.

A second piece of explicit evidence that the writers of the Bible were literary craftsmen is the frequency with which they refer to their writings with technical precision as belonging to various literary genres, such as chronicle, saying, song, complaint, parable, gospel, apocalypse, epistle, and prophecy. These labels signal a more sophisticated awareness of genres than the general reader of the Bible today is likely to realize. For example, in two New Testament epistles we find the list "psalms, hymns and spiritual songs" (Eph. 5:19; Col. 3:16). Our inclination is to attach no particular significance to this nomenclature, but in their original context these terms are likely to have referred to distinct types of religious music.

The implicit evidence of literary awareness among biblical writers is even more compelling. One proof is that their writings display conventional literary qualities. Biblical narrative, for example, displays such time-honored principles of storytelling as beginning-middle-end construction, dramatic irony, foreshadowing, and climax. Biblical poets knew that praise psalms have three main parts, that lament psalms have five ingredients, and that poetry consists of the skillful use of figurative language.

The literary sophistication of biblical writers is evident simply in the excellence with which they exploited the resources of literary art, but the case is strengthened if we place their writings in their ancient context. When we do so, we find that they wrote in apparent awareness of the literature being produced in surrounding nations. The Ten Commandments (Ex. 20) and the book of Deuteronomy, for example, bear all the marks of the suzerainty treaty of ancient Hittite kings. Psalm 29 imitates (and ultimately parodies) the motifs of Canaanite poems written about the exploits of Baal. The Song of Songs contains poems that resemble Egyptian love poetry. The book of Acts has affinities with travelogues from Greek literature. And on and on.

The Bible itself advertises its literary nature in both direct and indirect ways. Throughout history, interpreters have been able to approach the Bible as literature precisely because the authors of the Bible did so before them.

Athens and Jerusalem: The Unresolved Question of the Early Church

The question of how literary the Bible is became a point of debate among the church fathers. Steeped in classical rhetoric and literature as well as the Bible, these men struggled to know how to relate the Bible to the rules and practice of classical writing. Their general tendency was to set up an opposition between the Bible and classical literature and to celebrate the superiority of Christianity to paganism by arguing that the simplicity of the Bible triumphed over the ornateness of classical art (Lind 3–7). In general, the Middle Ages was at odds with modern conceptions of the Bible as literature (Lewis 5–8).

But there were notable exceptions, and indeed the whole discussion was filled with unresolved contradictions. When the early church compared the Bible to classical literature, it did not agree on what it saw. Origen represents the majority opinion when he asserts regarding the writers of the New Testament that "it was not any power of speaking, or any orderly arrangement of their message, according to the arts of Grecian dialectics or rhetoric, which was in them the effective cause of converting their hearers" (424).

But even the argument for the superiority of the Bible over classical literature often made implicit claims for the literary nature of the Bible. Consider, for example, Jerome's famous question, "How can Horace go with the Psalter, Virgil with the gospels, Cicero with the apostle?" (*Letters* XXII, 29). Jerome here pairs classical and biblical versions of the same literary genre (lyric, epic or narrative, and rhetoric/epistle/essay, respectively). He thereby enacts what became a standard practice of viewing the Bible as a body of sacred literature parallel to classical literature.

Equally prominent was an early tradition that regarded biblical poetry as written in meters similar to those found in Greek and Roman poetry (Kugel 140–70). The view is as old as Josephus and was articulated most systematically by Jerome, who tried valiantly (and by modern standards futilely) to apply such classical meters as hexameter and pentameter, dactyl, and spondee. The significance of the attempt is that familiar (classical) literature was the touchstone by which to test whether the Bible was literary.

We should not fault the Fathers for this, because any discussion of the Bible as literature must be based on what we know literature to be.

The towering figure in the early church's attempt to define the literary nature of the Bible is Augustine, in whom we find the same tension that the era itself displayed when it tried to relate the Bible to classical literature. In his *Confessions* Augustine recalls that when he first examined the holy Scriptures they "seemed to me unworthy to be compared to the stateliness of Tully; for my swelling pride shrunk from their lowliness" (III, 5).

But this was not Augustine's final word on the issue. For his final word we must turn to his treatise *On Christian Doctrine* (IV, 6–7), the most important early statement about the Bible as literature. Trained as a rhetorician, Augustine approached the literary dimension of the Bible through the specific avenue of rhetoric or style. Four key principles emerge from his discussion.

One is that the Bible does, indeed, display the literary traits of classical writing. To prove this point, Augustine conducts extended explications of passages from the epistles of Paul and the prophecy of Amos to show that the authors of the Bible followed "the laws of eloquence" laid down by classical rhetoric. The eloquence of Scripture, Augustine claims, "is of the same kind as that I do understand" as a classical rhetorician.

A second literary strand in Augustine's approach to the Bible is the value that he places on eloquence or beauty of expression. He is at pains to show that the writers of the Bible were not only wise but also eloquent. "It seems to me," he writes, "not only that nothing can be wiser" than what we find in the Bible, "but also that nothing can be more eloquent." According to Augustine, "all those powers and beauties of eloquence" that enthusiasts of classical literature treasure "are to be found in the sacred writings which God in His goodness has provided."

Third, Augustine implies agreement with a cornerstone of modern literary theory that views literary form and meaning as inseparable. For all his appreciation of stylistic beauty, Augustine also sees a function to such expression. Having asserted that "nothing can be more eloquent" than the Bible, he immediately adds that "all who truly understand what these writers say, perceive at the same time that it could not have been properly said in any other way." The literary eloquence of biblical writers is "an inseparable attendant" of their wisdom, following it "without being called for."

Fourth, along with this exuberance over the excellence of biblical rhetoric we find in Augustine an uneasiness about claiming that the Bible is literary in the same ways that ordinary literature is. He claims, for example, that "it is not the qualities which these writers have in common with the heathen orators and poets that give me such unspeakable delight in their eloquence; I am more struck with admiration at . . . an eloquence peculiarly their own." The traits of eloquence of the biblical writers, moreover, "seem not so much to be sought out by the speaker as spontaneously to suggest themselves." Again, the eloquence of the Bible was not "composed by man's art and care, but it flowed forth in wisdom and eloquence from the Divine mind; wisdom not aiming at eloquence, yet eloquence not shrinking from wisdom."

It would hardly be an overstatement to say that the subsequent history of the Bible as literature is a series of footnotes to Augustine. The key ingredients are all here—an assumption that to approach the Bible as literature means relating it to known literature, delight in the form and beauty of the Bible, sensitivity to the interplay between form and religious meaning in the Bible, and a cautionary awareness that conventional literary criteria, though relevant, do not fit in all the ordinary ways.

The Renaissance and Reformation Synthesis

The sixteenth and seventeenth centuries represented a remarkable flowering of literary appreciation for the Bible. Whereas Augustine had voiced a minority opinion, it became the majority opinion of the Renaissance that the Bible is in many ways a work of literature. While Augustine's approach to the subject was a strictly limited one—by way of eloquence and rhetorical style—the approach of the Renaissance and Reformation was a manysided inquiry into both the content of the Bible and its genres and style. The literary approach, moreover, represented the combined insight of both exegetes like Luther and Calvin and also the leading literary figures of the day.

On the literary scene, much of the impetus for seeing the Bible as literature came from the attempt to provide a Christian defense of imaginative literature (Baroway). Sir Philip Sidney's *Apology for Poetry* may be taken as the definitive example. Faced with the charge that imaginative literature is immoral and a waste of time, Sidney repeatedly appeals to the literary nature of the Bible in defending literature from the attacks. His references to the literary nature of the Bible extend to both form and content.

Three key insights shape Sidney's concept of the Bible as literature. One is that the subject matter of much of the Bible is concrete human experience—"a figuring forth" of reality and "a speaking picture." Second, when Sidney thinks of the Bible as literature he thinks naturally in terms of familiar literary genres, such as "poem," "songs," and "parables." Third, Sidney locates the literary nature of the Bible partly in its use of figurative or poetic style—a style that possesses an ability to move the reader and to delight by its "unspeakable and everlasting beauty."

Sidney's three themes—the experiential concreteness of the Bible, the presence of literary genres, and the prevalence of a distinctly poetic style—are the keynotes of both imaginative writers and biblical interpreters throughout the era of the Renaissance and Reformation. In the wake of Barbara Lewalski's epoch-making book *Protestant Poetics and the Seventeenth-Century Religious Lyric,* it is now a commonplace among literary scholars that Reformation exegetes and Renaissance poets shared a body of literary assumptions about the Bible. On the exegetical side, Lewalski shows the extent to which "an extensive and widely accessible body of literary theory . . . can be extrapolated from such sixteenth- and seventeenth-century materials as biblical commentaries, rhetorical handbooks, poetic paraphrases of scripture, emblem books, manuals on meditation and preaching" (5). The ideas making up this matrix of assumptions were biblical genre theory, the poetic texture of Scripture, and the biblical symbolic mode.

The practice of poetry was strongly influenced by this exegetical tradition. Lewalski shows at length how the Bible afforded the Protestant poet "a literary model [to] imitate in such literary matters as genre, language, and symbolism" (6–7). Chiefly by their practice, but also in their incidental comments in their prose writing, these poets reinforced the Renaissance and Reformation habit of viewing the Bible as literary in nature and effect.

Milton is a typical example. His poetry is rooted in the Bible at every turn—at the levels of genre, imagery, allusion, plot, and character. In a prose passage where he talks *about* the Bible, moreover, Milton shows the characteristic views of his day by speaking of various parts of the Bible as belonging to such genres as pastoral drama, tragedy, odes, hymns, and songs (669). In the same passage, he makes the claim, also commonplace, that biblical songs are incomparable "over all the kinds of lyric poesy," not in "their divine argument alone, but in the very critical art of composition." Here is the Renaissance synthesis—between poet and biblical interpreter, between biblical form and content, between Christian faith in the Bible as a sacred book and literary appreciation of it as an aesthetic accomplishment.

The Romantic Secularizing of the Bible

That synthesis was lost during the next great era of literary interest in the Bible, the Romantic movement of the nineteenth century. I have labeled the Romantic interest in the Bible "secular" because it represented a literary interest in the Bible devoid of the Christian faith in it that had characterized earlier eras. It was, in fact, largely a poet's movement.

The single most influential figure in the movement was Robert Lowth, whose inaugural lectures when he became Professor of Poetry at Oxford University became a landmark work, not only in the history of the Bible as literature but also as an influence on the Romantic literary tradition. Lowth's book *Lectures on the Sacred Poetry of the Hebrews* was printed in Latin in 1753 and in English in 1787. An outline of the book's three-part organization itself tells us a lot about Lowth's approach: Hebrew meter gets one chapter, poetic style fourteen, and poetic genres seventeen.

Five characteristics make Lowth's book noteworthy in the history of the Bible as literature. The most famous is his discussion of the parallelism of biblical poetry. Generally credited with having discovered the rules of biblical parallelism, Lowth identifies three main types of parallelism in biblical poetry (synonymous, antithetical, and synthetic), a formulation that gave modern understanding of biblical parallelism "its definitive form" (Kugel 287). In view of this, anyone reading Lowth's book will be genuinely surprised to see how small a part of the book (a single lecture) is devoted to the subject of parallelism. Lowth's main interests lay elsewhere.

Second, Lowth is singlemindedly devoted to an analysis of the poetic *form* of the Bible. In modern terms, he is an arch formalist. His focus is on the style and genres of biblical poetry. Poetic imagery and figurative language receive seven lectures. Lowth is interested in the Bible as poetry, not as a source of religious truth. He himself insists that his work is "purely critical: and consequently theological disquisitions will be avoided" (4). In the words of one of his own contemporaries, Lowth spoke "not as a churchman . . . but as a poet speaking about poetry" (Johann Michaelis, qtd. in Hepworth 39).

An important corollary is that Lowth thus avoids the preoccupation with sources that has been such an obstacle to literary criticism of the Bible in our own century. To the extent to which he attributes a source to the forms of biblical poetry, that source is either nature or God.

Third, Lowth maintains a balance between the literary uniqueness of biblical poetry and its affinities with classical literature. Part of Lowth's implied agenda is to restore the Bible to a literary stature in no way inferior to that of classical literature. He laments that "the writings of Homer, of Pindar, and of Horace, should engross our attention and monopolize our praise, while those of Moses, of David and Isaiah pass totally unregarded" (26). At the outset Lowth promises to compare "Hebrew poems . . . with those of Greece and Rome" (3), and he makes good on his promise on page after page.

But more prominent is Lowth's inclination to identify the distinctively Hebraic qualities of biblical poetry. Phrases like "peculiar to the poetry of the

Hebrews" (74) and "peculiarities which serve to distinguish the poetical diction of the Hebrews" (127) abound, along with assertions that this or that feature occurs "much more frequently" (122) in Hebrew poetry than in other poetry. Biblical poetry emerges in Lowth's treatment as distinctively Hebraic, characterized by simplicity, affectiveness, rootedness in Oriental culture and topography, prophetic vision, and a distinctive prosody (parallelism).

Fourth, Lowth approaches biblical poetry with the best literary theory and methods that his own day afforded. He decisively disavows that a modern critic should be limited by the literary classifications of the ancient Hebrews (146). He thus talks about biblical poetry as he would have talked about any other body of poetry. It has become a commonplace of recent scholarship that Lowth gave major impetus to the Romantic view of the Bible, a view that at the same time represented how the Romantic era viewed poetry itself. The keynotes are clearly evident in Lowth's lectures: Orientalism, passion, primitivism, lyricism (Lowth even denies that the book of Job has a plot), sublimity, and poetry.

Finally, Lowth's greatest strength is the confidence with which he defines the object of his study. He knows what makes a text poetic (his opening lecture is entitled "Of Poetry"). Lowth knows where to find such poetry in the Bible (in fact, a main thrust of his lectures is to define the canon of biblical poetry). He knows what to discuss when a text is literary and goes about that task systematically.

Judged by its influence, Lowth's book is a landmark in the history of the Bible as literature, but its underlying principles are what make it relevant today. Except for the description of parallelism, Lowth's specific insights and critical terms today seem quaint and long since superseded. But the deep structure of his approach remains a model and a corrective—the focus on form as the differentia of literature, the awareness that biblical literature is a blend of the familiar and the unique, the application of the best contemporary critical tools to the Bible, and a confidence that it is possible to define what is literary about the Bible.

Lowth's stature is currently high. His book is hailed by historians of ideas as "the book that was to transform biblical studies in England and Germany alike" (Prickett 105) and the book that "changed the way we read the Bible" (Kugel 286). It is more accurate to say that Lowth's views on the poetry of the Bible helped to chart the course for English Romantic poets, who valued the Bible in three main ways.

To begin, the Romantics treasured the primitive simplicity of the Bible. Whereas the early churchmen had seen the simplicity of the Bible as evidence that it was nonliterary, Romantics like Coleridge and Wordsworth made this primitivism the very mark of its literary excellence. C. S. Lewis speaks of how with the Romantic movement "the primitive simplicity of a world in which kings could be shepherds, the abrupt and mysterious manner of the prophets, the violent passions of bronze-age fighting men, the background of tents and flocks and desert and mountain, the village homeliness of our Lord's parables and metaphors, now first . . . became a positive literary asset" (27; cf. also Roston).

Second, the Romantics were enamored of sublimity as a literary quality. The poetry of the Bible, especially that of the prophets, became both inspiration and model, partly via the influence of Lowth (Morris 159–70), who had devoted four lectures to the subject.

Third, the Romantic imagination was essentially mythic and visionary. As Western society became increasingly secular, poets strove to put spiritual reality back into life. Hungry for mythology, they came to look upon the Bible as containing (in the words of English poet William Blake) "the Great Code of Art" (*The Laocoon*). The Bible, popularly viewed as a visionary and Oriental book, exerted a strong and steady influence on Romantic poetry as a mythological book (Shaffer). Instead of viewing the Bible as a single book inspired ultimately by God, Romantic poets regarded it as they regarded other imaginative literature. When Blake asserted that "Jesus and his Apostles and Disciples were all Artists," the statement carried a different meaning than it would have for a Renaissance poet or exegete.

The truth that the Romantic poets saw in the Bible was the same truth that they found in other works of imaginative literature—truthfulness to human experience, especially human feelings. The Bible was a supreme work of literature, not a source of religious belief. This secular valuing of the Bible has persisted right to the current time and is, in fact, the dominant twentieth-century tradition, a fact that has produced its own reaction among evangelical Christians, who value the Bible chiefly for its religious content.

The Bible and Literary Criticism, 1900–1975

Two scholarly traditions converged in the twentieth century to produce the current interest in the Bible as literature: the teaching of the Bible in college literature courses and the work of liberal biblical scholarship.

Among literary scholars, interest in the Bible during the first three quarters of the twentieth century can be pictured as an underground stream that finally came to the surface around 1960. For half a century the tradition was kept alive by Bible-as-literature courses taught at a handful of secular universities and a smattering of books and anthologies that this teaching produced.

At the start of it all was the work of Richard G. Moulton. In 1895 he published two landmark volumes. One was a literary analysis of the Bible entitled *The Literary Study of the Bible* (it is still in print today). It is mainly a genre approach to the Bible, and its strength is its ability to impose literary categories on the Bible. This book provided inspiration and direction to generations of literary critics of the Bible. It did so for at least two reasons: it established the possibility that the Bible possesses many of the same literary traits that literature in general does, and it opened the way for one to admire the Bible for its literary beauty. The other Moulton book was *The Modern Reader's Bible* (which went through at least eighteen printings during the first two-thirds of the century). It arranged the books of the Bible to fit Moulton's generic categories. Three hundred fifty pages of notes at the back of the book reinforced the general effect of the book, which was to introduce readers to a whole new way of looking at the Bible.

Anthologies in the same vein played a crucial role in keeping the tradition alive in English departments. Specimen titles and prefaces confirm their link with university courses: *The English Bible, Being a Book of Selections from the King James Version* (ed. Wilbur O. Sypherd, 1923); *The Bible Designed to be Read as Living Literature* (ed. Ernest S. Bates, 1936); *The Bible for Students of Literature and Art* (ed. G. B. Harrison, 1964); and *The Bible: Selections from the King James Version for Study as Literature* (ed. Roland M. Frye, 1965).

In addition to the anthologies, there were occasional critical books whose methods now strike us as old-fashioned but that were genuinely literary in their intuitions (for examples, see the books by Dinsmore, Gardiner, Innes, Reid, Sands). Symptomatic of the continuing interest in the Bible by literary scholars, the approach of these books was largely generic and stylistic.

The landmark piece of literary criticism appeared at mid-century from an expert in comparative literature. Erich Auerbach's classic comparison of storytelling technique in Homer's *Odyssey* and the book of Genesis is to this day a model of what literary analysis of the Bible should look like. Ostensibly Auerbach's essay is a stylistic study that contrasts the embellished, fully delineated style of Greek narrative to the spare, unembellished style of Hebrew narrative. But Auerbach actually covers much more territory than this, including characterization, the dynamics of narrative, and ultimately worldview. Auerbach had no immediate influence on biblical scholars, but literary critics at once resonated with what he had done.

By 1960 the underground stream had surfaced. The main spokesperson was Northrop Frye. In *Anatomy of Criticism,* the most influential work of literary theory in our century, the Bible emerged as the chief organizing framework for Western literature—a definitive source of literary archetypes and by implication a book that was itself literary. Equally important was Frye's contention that "the Bible forms the lowest stratum in the teaching of literature. It should be taught so early and so thoroughly that it sinks straight to the bottom of the mind, where everything that comes along later can settle on it" (*Educated Imagination* 110). Eventually this vision produced a multivolume literature curriculum intended especially for use in Canada.

The decade of the seventies saw a plethora of high school and college courses in the Bible, usually taught in the English Department. Courses in the Bible as literature became one of the ten most popular high school English electives. Anthologies multiplied. Scholarly articles on the Bible began to appear in literary journals. The topic of the Bible as literature became a nearly constant topic at regional meetings of the Conference on Christianity and Literature. The Indiana University Summer Institute on Teaching the Bible in Secondary English, accompanied by half a dozen books (especially the two edited by Kenneth Gros Louis), became one of the visible "institutions" for the movement over the span of a decade.

The second tributary that fed the present literary interest in the Bible is the tradition of liberal biblical scholarship. This tradition is much less coherent than biblical scholars commonly claim. Of the customary approaches taken by biblical scholars (literary criticism, redaction criticism, source criticism, form criticism), only form criticism bears much resemblance to the approach of literary critics in the humanities. In 1971 Amos Wilder recorded his "astonishment that the term 'literary criticism' should have such different connotations for biblical scholars as for students of literature generally" (xxii).

The astonishment was well founded. Consider the following standard definition of literary criticism by a biblical scholar: "Literary criticism is the analysis of biblical books from the standpoint of lack of continuity, duplications, inconsistencies and different linguistic usage, with the object of discovering what the individual writers and redactors contributed to a text, and also its time and place of origin" (Koch 70). This is virtually the opposite of what literary criticism has traditionally meant to literary scholars.

When Northrop Frye made the claim that "a genuine higher criticism of the Bible" would see the Bible, "not as the scrapbook of corruptions, glosses, redactions, insertions, conflations, misplacings, and misunderstandings revealed by the analytic critic, but as the typological unity which all these things were originally intended to help construct" (*Anatomy* 315), he was implicitly challenging the entire tradition of mainstream biblical scholarship during the first half of the century. Biblical scholars produced genuine literary criticism of the Bible only when they began to turn their backs on the entrenched practices of their own discipline.

This is not to say that the tradition of liberal biblical scholarship was devoid of genuine literary analysis. But the forrays into the literary field were unsystematic and often coincidental to the critics' main interests. (The quickest access to these scattered examples of literary criticism by biblical scholars is by way of the excerpts collected in companion volumes of literary criticism on the two Testaments edited by Preminger/Greenstein and Ryken.) While literary critics can look back to the pronouncements of Northrop Frye as codifying the new movement in their discipline, biblical scholars cite the importance of James Muilenburg's 1968 call (published in 1969) to move beyond form criticism to what he called rhetorical criticism and is now known as literary criticism. If we are looking for a visible "institution" of biblical scholars' literary interest in the Bible, we can look to Sheffield, England, publishing site of *Journal for the Study of the Old Testament* and the Almond Press series of book-length literary studies of the Bible.

It is futile to try to ascertain who deserves "credit" for the current convergence of literary interest in the Bible by both biblical and literary scholars. My own assessment is that the paradigm shift occurred very informally. Biblical scholars and literary critics started talking together in the hallway and began teaching courses together. Biblical scholars intuitively sensed that traditional methods in their discipline were somewhat exhausted, and they spontaneously started to apply to the Bible what they had learned in their college literature courses. The prefaces to their books often tell this informal history.

One thing that has inhibited the flowering of literary approaches to the Bible to this day is biblical scholars' distrust of the work of literary critics. Biblical scholars want things stated in the terminology of their own discipline and by members of that discipline. Their bibliographies and footnotes show how little they have read (or how unimpressed they are by) the published work of literary critics. Robert Alter is virtually the only scholar to enjoy the full support of both biblical scholars and the literary establishment.

After 1975: The New Pluralism

To say that the literary approach to the Bible has become fashionable during the past two decades is an understatement. While Northrop Frye's vision of the Bible's becoming "the basis of literary training" (*Educated Imagination* 111) was never fully realized, in a modified sense it was. The

Bible is now part of the canon that literary scholars teach in their literature courses and about which they publish books and articles. Publishers of biblical scholarship, meanwhile, are eager to claim a literary approach in their book titles and advertising blurbs. Several presses (including Indiana University, Almond, and Westminster/John Knox) have established series on a literary approach to the Bible.

As I turn to a survey of recent trends, several questions constitute my analytic grid. What do literary critics mean by "literary criticism of the Bible"? What parts of the Bible interest them most? What do critics do with the texts that they choose for analysis?

The first question yields a clear answer: there is at present no common understanding as to what it means to approach the Bible as literature. Any authors or publishers can hang out their shingle without challenge. Book reviews have played a leading role in the recent Bible-as-literature movement, and reviewers have overwhelmingly left unchallenged the claims that writers and publishers have made to represent a literary approach.

For traditional literary critics, a literary approach continues to imply a focus on the biblical text—on plot, setting, and characterization in a story, for example, or an exploration of pattern, imagery, and figurative language in a poem. But a "literary" approach can as well consist of an analysis of the ideas in a text, or in matters beyond the text such as cultural context or a history of commentary on a text. Equally popular are interdisciplinary approaches that do not resemble any traditional methods of literary criticism. At the very moment that books and articles are claiming to be literary in their approach, the scholarly world lacks standards by which to assess the claims, a situation nowhere more apparent than in book reviews.

The question of what parts of the Bible literary critics find most attractive also yields a decisive answer. Literary critics currently gravitate to the narrative parts of the Bible. In fact, the literary approach to the Bible is now almost synonymous with an interest in the stories of the Bible, to the comparative neglect of other genres. This is in contrast to earlier centuries of literary interest in the Bible, where poetry was assumed to be the chief thing that made the Bible literary.

On what do literary critics today focus in the biblical text? They are especially interested in the problematical. The stories of the Bible, writes a leading critic, "problematic in their ancient versions, have become less problematic, smoother, but also less interesting, in their modern cultural uses" (Bal, *Lethal Love* 5). Returning biblical texts to their problematic status as ancient and "primitive" texts is currently high on the agenda of literary critics of the Bible. A review praises a commentary on the book of Ruth (the first volume in a new "Literary Currents in Biblical Interpretation" series) for its walking "the line with apparent ease between celebrating indeterminacy on the one hand and reading for ideological subversion on the other" (Beal 77).

In such a process, critics tend to write in an awareness of a dominant tradition of interpretation that has prevailed under the long reign of biblical scholars and the pious reading public. The idea of producing "alternate readings" or "counter readings" of what is usually called the "dominant reading" is currently fashionable. Thus one feminist critic sees her task in terms of "breaking open the too-monolithic readings projected on the Hebrew love stories" (Bal, *Lethal Love* 132). Harold Bloom aspires to nothing less than "a reversal of twenty-five hundred years of institutionalized misreading" (16), a feat that requires "a reading that is partly outside every normative tradition whatsoever" (15). In short, a literary approach to the Bible among upper-echelon critics is today virtually synonymous with original or unconventional readings of biblical texts.

Part of the quest for originality is the focus on aspects of the Bible that have traditionally been slighted. Freudian influence in the form of finding sexual overtones wherever possible is proportionately stronger in literary criticism of the Bible than in criticism of other literature. The current critical climate is one in which we can expect to find Jael as a wily woman who had sexual intercourse with Sisera in the process of subduing him (Brenner 118–19), Ruth as a seductress of Boaz (Brenner 106–8), the sheaves of grain in the same story viewed as phallic symbols (Fewell/Gunn 126), and Judges described as a book "full of virgins" (Bal, *Death and Dissymmetry* 69). There is a similar preoccupation with violence, as suggested by book titles (*Texts of Terror; Lethal Love*) and chapter/section headings ("Violence and the Sacred," "Slaughter and Shattering," "The Scandal of the Speaking Body," "Virginity Scattered"). Both sex and violence are prominent concerns in feminist criticism, which has placed a new focus on issues of gender and power.

In keeping with trends in literary criticism generally, claims of ambiguity and indeterminacy of meaning are common. Frank Kermode's book on the gospel of Mark is concerned with "the radiant obscurity of narratives" (47) in the gospel, and Kermode's avowed purpose is to explore the "different ways in which narratives acquire opacity" (75). In a similar vein, Gabriel Josipovici writes that the readers of the Bible who "want certainty" are bound to "misread the Bible because they ask too much of it" (17). Whereas "in works of art in the West there is usually a place at which interpretation stops and the truth appears, the Hebrew Bible does not seem to work like that. . . . When we think we have found at last a place from which to interpret we find that it too is subject to conflicting interpretations" (82).

One result of this trend to find indeterminacy has been a distinct antididacticism, in the form of either a denial that the Bible teaches definite religious truth or an assumption that the "how" of biblical writing is everything, the "what" inconsequential. Meir Sternberg, for example, claims that biblical narrative "breaks every law" that governs didactic storytelling (37–38). The next-to-last sentence in Mieke Bal's literary study of biblical love stories is that "the point of literary analysis is that there is no truth, and that this contention can be reasonably argued" (*Lethal Love* 132). Harold Bloom claims that the time has come to "rid ourselves of the arbitrary presupposition that [the biblical writer's] prime motive for writing was piety" (35).

Current literary criticism of the Bible is also governed by the assumption of complexity. Critics assume that biblical texts are enormously intricate and that critical discussions of them should likewise be complex and prolix. Here is a typical statement of the presuppositions with which a leading literary critic approaches a biblical text:

> It is an extremely sophisticated piece of literature. Embedded in a complex and, in its very complexity, problematic narrative structure, it is also an extremely sophisticated narrative unit. As an example as well of an extremely complex confusion of gender relations, it makes a case for a problematic of representation as related to gender. (Bal, *Lethal Love* 36)

The key terms here appear repeatedly in current discussions of the Bible: sophisticated, complex, problematic, confusion. Equally typical of the current scene is the claim that the story of Ruth "is a complex narrative, even if on the surface it may appear to some readers to be simple" (Fewell/Gunn 17).

Another feature of the current landscape is a loss of classical aesthetic tastes and rhetorical conventions. Traditional literary criticism accepted as axiomatic such aesthetic principles as unity, coherence, and whole-part relationships in a text. But Harold Fisch believes that "the mistake" of much commentary on the Bible "is to look for coherence, unity, . . . [and] an artistic shape having a beginning, a middle, and an end" (38–39), while someone else calls the rhetorical convention of three-part construction "alien to biblical culture" (Bal, *Death and Dissymmetry* 15).

Current approaches eschew holistic and unified readings of texts. Microscopic analysis of details in a text is preferred, so that we can find (for example) a nineteen-page discussion of the nameless man in the field who directs Joseph to his brothers at Dothan (Josipovici 176–294) and a fifteen-page discussion of whether Uriah knows about his wife's adultery when David coaxes him to spend a night with Bathsheba (Sternberg 199–213).

Interest in literary theory is also prominent. Much of the influential recent literary criticism of the Bible has been interested in something other than the biblical text. "This book is about interpretation, an interpretation of interpretation," writes Frank Kermode in his influential *Genesis of Secrecy* (2). Another critic ends her analysis of the story of David and Bathsheba with the comment, "The real issue of the discussion was not the text but the critics" (Bal, *Lethal Love* 36).

The attempt to formulate a "poetics" of biblical literature is now popular (witness such book titles as *Poetry with a Purpose: Biblical Poetics and Interpretation* and *The Poetics of Biblical Narrative*). So is the application of current literary theories to the Bible (e.g., *The Book and the Text: The Bible and Literary Theory,* ed. Regina Schwartz). Increasingly absent is the practice of explicating biblical texts—close readings of biblical texts as literary wholes, allowing the texts to set the agenda of topics to be covered and including a sequential reading of the text at some point.

Many of the trends currently on the scene can be viewed under the format of the desacralizing of the Bible and/or reading it outside the context of a community of religious faith. Through the centuries, the Bible has been of interest mainly to religious readers. Most current literary criticism of the Bible presupposes an audience whose interest in the Bible is academic rather than religious. The dominant metaphor for the literary critic of the Bible is not the travel guide who accompanies readers as they revisit familiar sites enriched with literary analysis, but rather the liberator who unlocks the prison house of conventional (religious) interpretations of the Bible. Harold Bloom prefers the homier metaphor of the critic as varnish remover, "scrubbing away the varnish that keeps us from seeing . . . the original work" (47). Whereas literary criticism of the Bible earlier in this century aimed to illuminate the Bible for what Mary Ellen Chase called "the common reader," recent criticism—armed with specialized vocabulary, microscopic analyses, a theory of indeterminacy of meaning, and unorthodox readings—has returned the Bible to specialists.

The trends that I have traced are the ones with visibility in the world of scholarship. They do not tell the whole story. Traditional literary criticism continues to be applied to the Bible, especially in the classroom but also in published criticism. Much of it is performed by biblical scholars who have only recently caught the vision for a literary approach and who therefore apply simplified critical schemes to biblical texts. Traditional literary criticism is not devoid of theory, but it consists of what M. H. Abrams calls old theory as opposed to new theory. With a little simplifying, we can say that the mainstay of old theory was a formalist or New Critical focus on the text itself, including its genre, artistry, and embodiment of human experience. There was also an interest in master images or archetypes.

The essays in the current volume lean decidedly toward old theory, but not because the authors are unfamiliar with the current critical landscape. Contributors would generally agree with the claim of John Sider that "what biblical scholars need to hear most from literary critics is that old-fashioned critical concepts of plot, character, setting, point of view and diction may be more useful than more glamorous and sophisticated theories" (19–20).

That description accurately describes the agenda of interests of the most notable current practitioner of literary criticism of the Bible, Robert Alter. Alter has delineated his literary theory at length in his book *The Pleasures of Reading in an Ideological Age,* and his theoretic undergirdings have virtually nothing in common with the trends I have surveyed above. Rather, Alter espouses the ideas that "the language of literature is distinct from the use of language elsewhere in its resources and in its possibilities of expression," that "literature is not just a self-referential closed circuit but is connected in meaningful and revelatory ways with the world of experience outside the text," that the focus of literary analysis should not be on something beyond the text but rather on the "formal resources of literary expression, susceptible to analysis and to critical definition," and that "there is a crucial difference between interpretive pluralism . . . and interpretive anarchy" (19). The essays in this book assume the same premises.

Learning From History

The history of the idea of the Bible as literature is useful in several ways. It allows us to assess the implied claims for originality in current literary approaches to the Bible. To view the Bible as literature is not new. Nor is there reason for complacency in the midst of the current vogue of interest in literary approaches to the Bible. In many ways the contemporary scene represents a decline from the promise that the literary study of the Bible offered two decades ago.

The history that I have sketched suggests the obstacles that perennially stand in the way of viewing the Bible as literature. The Bible has been viewed as literature only when interpreters have been willing to analyze it in relation to familiar (classical) literature and through the use of ordinary tools of literary analysis. Conversely, literary approaches to the Bible have waned when the Bible has been viewed as being unique and completely unlike other books. Of course literary interpreters have belabored the point that the Bible is not *totally* similar to other literature. But it is possible to talk about the literary distinctiveness of the Bible only if the Bible is first seen as meeting ordinary definitions of literature.

The history of the Bible as literature highlights another prerequisite as well: the Bible's literary status emerges only when we talk about its form and technique. This does not mean that literary criticism is indifferent to the religious and broadly human meanings embodied in the Bible. But the interpreters I have surveyed were able to view the Bible as literature only as they looked at *how* biblical texts communicate. Having interacted with the "how" of biblical writing, they were able to talk about *what* it said. Contrariwise, eras or traditions that were content to talk only about the ideas of the Bible did not come to see the Bible as a literary work.

There is, finally, a corrective value that emerges from the history that I have sketched. For example, contemporary literary approaches to the Bible are generally hostile to evangelical convictions about the Bible, but the larger history of the movement shows that literary criticism of the Bible can be fully compatible with an evangelical viewpoint. Again, current literary criticism of the Bible offers no consensus on what it means that the Bible is literary, but earlier eras were decisive about what they regarded as the literary genius of the Bible (even though they varied on their definitions of literature).

The history of the movement also gives us a perspective from which to assess the current landscape. Specialized contemporary literary approaches to the Bible pose discernible obstacles to biblical scholars and ordinary readers, including the tendency toward contradictions among the approaches themselves, obscurantism, elimination of authorial intention, and denial of referential quality to the Bible (Longman 47–58). But traditional literary criticism shows that it is possible to conduct literary analysis of the Bible without participating in these trends. Earlier eras can also stand as a ballast against an excessive attention to narrative, the escape from the text, the assumption that the Bible says nothing definite, the disinterest in such classical aesthetic norms as unity and coherence, and the inability to respond to the simple, obvious appeal of biblical literature instead of being preoccupied with the complex and problematical.

WORKS CITED

Abrams, M. H. "How to Do Things With Texts." *Partisan Review* 46 (1979): 566–88.

Alter, Robert. *The Pleasures of Reading in an Ideological Age.* New York: Simon & Schuster, 1989.

Auerbach, Erich. *Mimesis: The Representation of Reality in Western Literature.* Trans. Willard R. Trask. Princeton: Princeton UP, 1953.

Augustine. *Confessions* and *On Christian Doctrine. Great Books of the Western World.* Ed. Robert M. Hutchins. Chicago: Encyclopaedia Britannica, 1952. Vol. 18.

Bal, Mieke. *Death and Dissymmetry: The Politics of Coherence in the Book of Judges.* Chicago: University of Chicago Press, 1988.

———. *Lethal Love: Feminist Literary Readings of Biblical Love Stories.* Bloomington: Indiana UP, 1987.

Baroway, Israel. "The Bible as Poetry in the English Renaissance: An Introduction." *Journal of English and Germanic Philology* 32 (1933): 447–80.

Beal, Timothy K. Review of *Compromising Redemption: Relating Characters in the Book of Ruth,* by Danna Fewell and David Gunn. *Christianity and Literature* 40, no. 1 (1990): 75–77.

Blake, William. *The Laocoon. Blake's Poetry and Designs.* Ed. Mary L. Johnson and John Grant. New York: Norton, 1979. 425–27.

Bloom, Harold. *The Book of J.* New York: Grove Weidenfeld, 1990.

Brenner, Athalya. *The Israelite Woman: Social Role and Literary Type in Biblical Narrative.* Sheffield: JSOT Press, 1985.

Chase, Mary Ellen. *The Bible and the Common Reader.* New York: Macmillan, 1952.

Dinsmore, Charles A. *The English Bible as Literature.* Boston: Houghton Mifflin, 1931.

Fewell, Danna, and David Gunn. *Compromising Redemption: Relating Characters in the Book of Ruth.* Louisville: Westminster/John Knox, 1990.

Fisch, Harold. *Poetry With a Purpose: Biblical Poetics and Interpretation.* Bloomington: Indiana UP, 1988.

Frye, Northrop. *Anatomy of Criticism.* Princeton: Princeton UP, 1957.

———. *The Educated Imagination.* Bloomington: Indiana UP, 1964.

Gardiner, John H. *The Bible as English Literature.* New York: Scribner, 1906.

Gros Louis, Kenneth R. R. et al., eds. *Literary Interpretations of Biblical Narratives.* 2 vols. Nashville: Abingdon, 1974.

Hepworth, Brian. *Robert Lowth.* Boston: Twayne, 1978.

Innes, Kathleen. *The Bible as Literature.* London: Jonathan Cape, 1930.

Josipovici, Gabriel. *The Book of God: A Response to the Bible.* New Haven: Yale UP, 1988.

Kermode, Frank. *The Genesis of Secrecy: On the Interpretation of Narrative.* Oxford: Oxford UP, 1979.

Koch, Klaus. *The Growth of the Biblical Tradition: The Form-Critical Method.* New York: Scribner, 1969.

Kugel, James L. *The Idea of Biblical Poetry: Parallelism and Its History.* New Haven: Yale UP, 1981.

Lewalski, Barbara K. *Protestant Poetics and the Seventeenth-Century Religious Lyric.* Princeton: Princeton UP, 1979.

Lewis, C. S. *The Literary Impact of the Authorized Version.* Philadelphia: Fortress, 1963.

Lind, Nils Wilhelm. *Chiasmus in the New Testament.* Chapel Hill: University of North Carolina Press, 1942.

Longman, Tremper, III. *Literary Approaches to Biblical Interpretation.* Grand Rapids: Zondervan, 1987.

Lowth, Robert. *Lectures on the Sacred Poetry of the Hebrews.* Ed. Calvin E. Stowe. Boston: Crocker & Brewster, 1829.

Milton, John. *The Reason of Church Government. John Milton: Complete Poems and Major Prose.* Ed. Merritt Y. Hughes. New York: Odyssey, 1957. 640–89.

Morris, David B. *The Religious Sublime: Christian Poetry and Critical Tradition in 18th-Century England.* Lexington: University of Kentucky Press, 1972.

Moulton, Richard G. *Literary Study of the Bible.* Boston: Heath, 1895.

———. *The Modern Reader's Bible.* New York: Macmillan, 1895.

Muilenberg, James. "Form Criticism and Beyond." *Journal of Biblical Literature* 88 (1969): 1–18.
Origen. *Against Celsus. The Ante-Nicene Fathers.* Ed. Alexander Roberts. Buffalo: Christian Literature Company, 1885. Vol. 4.
Preminger, Alex, and Edward L. Greenstein, ed. *The Hebrew Bible in Literary Criticism.* New York: Ungar, 1986.
Prickett, Stephen. *Words and the Word: Language, Poetics and Biblical Interpretation.* Cambridge: Cambridge UP, 1986.
Reid, Mary Esson, ed. *The Bible Read as Literature.* Cleveland: Howard Allen, 1959.
Roston, Murray. *Prophet and Poet: The Bible and the Growth of Romanticism.* Evanston: Northwestern UP, 1965.
Ryken, Leland, ed. *The New Testament in Literary Criticism.* New York: Ungar, 1984.
Sands, P. C. *Literary Genius of the New Testament.* Oxford: Oxford UP, 1932.
Schwartz, Regina. *The Book and the Text: The Bible and Literary Theory.* Cambridge: Basil Blackwell, 1990.
Shaffer, E. S. *"Kubla Khan" and The Fall of Jerusalem: The Mythological School in Biblical Criticism and Secular Literature, 1770–1880.* Cambridge: Cambridge UP, 1975.
Sider, John W. "Nurturing Our Nurse: Literary Scholars and Biblical Exegesis." *Christianity and Literature* 32, no. 1 (1982): 15–20.
Sidney, Sir Philip. *An Apology for Poetry. Criticism: The Major Statements.* Ed. Charles Kaplan. New York: St. Martin's, 1975. 109–47.
Sternberg, Meir. *The Poetics of Biblical Narrative: Ideological Literature and the Drama of Reading.* Bloomington: Indiana UP, 1985.
Trible, Phyllis. *Texts of Terror: Literary-Feminist Readings of Biblical Narratives.* Philadelphia: Fortress, 1984.
Wilder, Amos N. *Early Christian Rhetoric: The Language of the Gospel.* Cambridge, Mass.: Harvard UP, 1971.

CHAPTER 4

Biblical Narrative

Tremper Longman III
Westminster Theological Seminary

Prose and poetry are the two basic modes of literary communication. What constitutes the one over against the other differs in various cultures and time periods, and it is always difficult to make a hard and fast distinction between them. In general terms, though, prose is much like the language of normal conversation, and thus poetry is often considered a language characterized by a higher degree of literary artifice.

Literature has a variety of functions. It informs readers, arouses their emotions, stimulates their imaginations, and appeals to their will. Prose is often the discourse of choice for those written acts of communication whose predominant aim is to inform. This statement does not intend to preclude the informative function of poetic discourse, but it does take into account the accentuated artifice of poetic language.

It is not surprising, therefore, to discover that most of the Bible is prose, since its authors intend to communicate a message. What is striking to most readers of the Bible is the occurrence of large portions of poetic material (see next chapter).

Much of the Bible is written in a prose format and, more specifically, narrative. Narrative may be distinguished from other prose forms like the essay or the report by its storylike nature. Quite simply, narrative prose tells a story. That is, its events are related to one another by an explicit or implicit cause-and-effect structure. It is the purpose of this chapter to explore the nature of biblical narrative.

The Literary Quality of Biblical Narrative

The literary nature of biblical poetry has been unquestioned for centuries. The same is not true for the narrative portions of the Bible.

The church has focused our attention on the Bible's theological message, and scientific theology has concerned itself with the question of sources and historical referentiality. Both tend to denigrate its literary function (Prickett). However, because of recent studies by biblical and literary scholars an interest in the storylike character of biblical narrative has resurfaced.

When allowed to stand as unified compositions, the stories of the Old and New Testaments work powerfully on the imagination, vividly evoking a world long since past. Some of the more memorable include the episodic account of Abraham, Sarah, and Isaac, the novellalike Joseph story, the dramatic crossing of the Red Sea, the tragedy of Samson and Delilah, the epic episode of David and Goliath. The list could continue. Not only are these stories literary masterpieces themselves, but they have exerted an incredible influence on the form and content of all subsequent Western literature (Frye). Until very recent times, authors and poets, whether sympathetic or hostile to the Judeo-Christian tradition, wrote from a deep knowledge of Scripture and assumed the same from their readers.

Robert Alter ("A Response" 113) has reminded us that each culture tells stories differently:

> Every culture, even every era in a particular culture, develops distinctive and sometimes intricate codes for telling its stories, involving everything from narrative point of view, procedures of description and characterization, the management of dialogue, to the ordering of time and the organization of plot.

This conviction encourages us to look closely at biblical narrative rather than simply assuming that it is like narrative from our own culture. We will see that there are traits that distinguish modern narrative from ancient biblical narrative. We can, however, group Old and New Testament narrative together. The two narrative traditions are very similar, perhaps because most of the New Testament, though written in Greek, was authored by people steeped in the Old Testament and its culture.

As mentioned, the Bible contains a number of memorable narratives. These stories display an impressive variety of theme and character. But the Bible as a whole constitutes a single narrative. The main characters and the setting are introduced in the first two chapters of Genesis. They are God and the human race as they interact in the latter's earthly home. Suspense is introduced into the story by the Fall, narrated in Genesis 3. The sin of Adam and Eve has led to alienation from God. The bulk of the Bible narrates what God does about this problem and how people react to God's actions. The whole story comes to denouement in the last two chapters with the vision of the New Jerusalem and the restoration of relationship between God and his people.

The Dynamics of Narrative

All stories have four elements, though the way in which these elements are presented in a story may and do differ from culture to culture and even within the same culture. These four are plot, characters, setting, and narrator/point of view. These are closely interrelated with one another, but for purpose of description I will give each a separate discussion.

PLOT

The plot of a literary narrative is the succession of events, usually motivated by conflict, which generates suspense and leads to a conclusion. Abrams calls it a "structure of actions" (137) and points out that plot analysis is not a simple recitation of the episodes that make up a story, but happens "only when we say how this is related to that" (137). In other words, the reader must decide how each part contributes to the whole. This narrative trait of plot is so pervasive that readers will automatically attribute causation between narrative episodes even if they are not explicit in the text itself.

Thus, while one is analyzing narrative in the Bible, it is illuminating to describe the plot. One way of proceeding is to identify the central plot conflict of a book and then see how the different episodes of the story fit into the progression toward the resolution of the conflict.

I will illustrate this by a brief look at the book of Jonah. The central conflict of the book of Jonah becomes obvious in the first three verses. God gives Jonah a command to preach in the city of Nineveh, and Jonah refuses by hopping on a boat that is sailing in the opposite direction. Jonah's reluctance, motivated by an intense hatred of Assyria that is rooted in his ethnocentrism, is contrasted to God's concern for his creatures in that city.

There are four major scenes in the book that constitute the plot and correspond roughly to the four chapters of Jonah as they are divided in the English Bible (the Hebrew differs). These are Jonah's flight from God in a boat, God's rescue of Jonah by means of a great fish, Jonah's preaching in Nineveh, and Jonah's final conflict with God after God spares Nineveh. As we will see, the four episodes are easily distinguished by means of their different settings.

The first episode heightens the conflict between God and Jonah and thus heightens the tension that the reader feels. Jonah is trying to get as far away from Nineveh as he possibly can. In so doing, he is attempting to flee from God as well, something that he soon finds impossible to do. God's long arm reaches out and causes the sailors to reluctantly throw Jonah overboard.

The second episode illustrates how impotent Jonah is as he stands against God and his purposes. God rescues Jonah from certain death by causing a large fish to swallow him. This fish provides Jonah with safe, if admittedly uncomfortable, haven until God delivers him onto the shore. Though undignified, his arrival on the shore points him toward Nineveh, and there he resignedly goes.

The third episode shows Jonah doing God's will. The brevity of Jonah's sermon as reported in the book highlights his reluctance: "Forty more days and Nineveh will be overturned." In spite of the fact that he provides no door of hope to the Ninevites, they repent and are spared. Jonah's reaction to Nineveh's deliverance shows that the conflict with God is not resolved. Jonah fusses and fumes over God's deliverance of Nineveh, presumably because God shows compassion to a people who have oppressed and tormented Israel. But God has the last word. The book closes with God's question to Jonah: "Should I not be concerned about that great city?" Although we never hear Jonah's response, the question is rhetorical, and thus the reader is left with the obvious conclusion that God's way of compassion and mercy is the right one, while Jonah is satirized as a narrow-minded Israelite (see below).

CHARACTERS

A second important aspect of the analysis is the examination of the characters who populate a story. The close association between plot and character may be observed in the fact that it is the characters who generate the actions that make up the plot, thus leading to the famous statement from Henry James, "What is character but the determination of incident? What is incident but the illustration of character?" (qtd. in Chatman 112–13).

Characters are like real people in that we can know them only partially and never exhaustively. Our knowledge of real people comes through our experience of them in their actions and conversation. We learn about the characters of a story in much the same way—by their actions and by speech (both the speeches they make and those that are made about them).

Our understanding of a character is controlled and mediated by the narrator, who may even be one of the characters. The narrator may choose to reveal much about a character, in which case the character is complex or round; or the narrator may choose to tell us very little about a character, who is therefore flat. There are even some characters about whom we learn next to nothing. They appear to perform some specialized function in the plot and are simply agents (Berlin 31–32).

Other technical language that for some reason is not used as frequently in biblical studies, though it is more common in literary studies, is that of protagonist, antagonist, and foil. The protagonist is the main character of the story and the one through whose perspective we follow most of the action. The antagonist is the one who stands against the protagonist, blocking his or her desires. The foil is a character who serves as a contrast to other characters, most often the protagonist (Ryken 72).

Jonah is the protagonist of the Old Testament story. We are not sympathetic toward him, even though we may identify with him. God and the Ninevites (an unlikely pair) are Jonah's antagonists. The sailors on the boat on which Jonah tries to flee from God are a foil to Jonah, because, though they are pagans, they show respect and fear toward Jonah's God.

Jonah and God are round, complex characters, whereas the Ninevites as a whole constitute a single "corporate" flat character, and the king of Nineveh (or even the "great fish" for that matter) an agent.

Since Auerbach (3–23) and much later Alter (*The Art* 114–30), the biblical narrator's reticence about such things as character development is well documented. The biblical text does little by way of direct commentary and description of its characters. When details are given, they are therefore of special significance to the story. Thus Samson's hair, Saul's height, Bathsheba's beauty, and Job's righteousness are all crucial elements of their story. Most of our knowledge of a character comes indirectly through actions and dialogue.

Biblical narrative does not speak explicitly of the characters' personality or the motivations of their actions; therefore the reader is called upon to enter into the process and interpret the gaps of the narrative. This is not as subjective as it sounds. That David does not go out to war in the spring (2 Sam. 11:1) is clearly a negative statement about the king, a fact that becomes evident because his leisurely presence in Jerusalem leads to such catastrophic consequences (2 Sam. 11–12). Perhaps the best advice is Ryken's when he instructs Bible readers to "simply get to know the characters as thoroughly as the details allow you to" (75).

SETTING

The setting of a story is the space in which the characters perform the actions that constitute the plot. It is important to recognize, however, that setting performs more than one function in a narrative. Much of the narrative of the Bible is highly literary prose with a historical intention. It is therefore not surprising that biblical authors give us details about specific physical locations in which the action takes place. Thus the first important function of setting in biblical literature is that it imparts reality to the story. We can picture the action of the story in our minds as that action is related to well-known ancient settings. But setting contributes more to a story than providing a simple backdrop for the action. Other functions include generating the atmosphere or mood of a narrative and contributing to the story's meaning and structure. Let me illustrate these three functions of narrative with another brief look at the book of Jonah.

Although we are not told where Jonah is when he first hears the word of the Lord, we are told that he flees to the port town of Joppa. He is fleeing from Nineveh by setting sail on the Mediterranean. These locations are all historical places well known from antiquity. They are not the fabrication of the author's imagination. Their use in the narrative implies the reality of the story.

The book of Jonah further provides illustration of the other two functions of setting—generating atmosphere and contributing to the meaning of a story. God calls Jonah to go to Nineveh, and eventually he does go there. Important to the story is the fact that Nineveh was the major city of Assyria, the ruthless nation that oppressed Israel and many other small nation states for over a century. After receiving the call to go to Nineveh, Jonah flees in the opposite direction. His westward rather than eastward direction tells the reader much about Jonah's state of mind toward God without the need for direct authorial commentary.

Finally, in one of the most spectacular settings of any biblical story, Jonah speaks with God from the belly of a large fish in the depths of the sea. This setting shows God's control even over the sea and its monsters. The sea and its monsters are often found, especially in poetic settings, as representative of the forces of chaos and the absence of God. By having Jonah speak to God from the belly of the fish, the biblical author makes it clear that Jonah can find no place on earth to escape God (Ps. 139).

We must realize that in the historical narrative that dominates the narrative genre of the Bible, the author's choice of setting was usually restricted. Authors simply placed action where it actually occurred. Of course these authors controlled the selectivity of detail in the description of settings, requiring the reader to pay close attention to these textual signals.

POINT OF VIEW

This last narrative trait is closely related to the presence of a narrative voice in the story. The narrator is the one who controls the story. His is the voice through whom we hear about the action and the people of the narrative. The narrator's point of view is the perspective through which we observe and evaluate everything connected with the story. In short, the narrator is a device used by authors to shape and guide how the reader responds to the characters and events of the story.

Literary critics make some basic distinctions in point of view, starting with first- and third-person narrative. In first-person narrative, the narrator is also a character in the story. This kind of narrative appears infrequently in the Bible, but it may be illustrated by parts of Nehemiah and the "we" passages in Acts. By far the most frequent type of narrative is that of the third-person narrator, about whom Rhoads and Michie (36) comment thus:

> The narrator does not figure in the events of the story; speaks in the third person; is not bound by time or space in the telling of the story; is an implied invisible presence in every scene, capable of being anywhere to "recount" the action; displays full omniscience by narrating the thoughts, feelings, or sensory experiences of many characters; often turns from the story to give direct "asides" to the reader, explaining a custom or translating a word or commenting on the story; and narrates the story from one overarching ideological point of view.

As these and other authors have pointed out, such a narrative strategy gives the impression of an all-knowing mind standing behind the stories of the Bible—a mind that in the context of the canon must be associated with God himself.

Thus it is not surprising that the Bible knows nothing of the so-called unreliable narrator. In the words of Sternberg, "The Bible always tells the truth in that its narrator is absolutely and straightforwardly reliable" (51). As Sternberg also notes, the narrator, while telling the truth, often does not tell the whole truth, and this results in the characteristic brevity of biblical narration. This narrative reticence produces gaps in the story and thus both invites the reader into a participatory role in the interpretive process and protects the mystery of God and his ways in the world.

Narrative Style

There are many different ways of telling the same story. For instance, a scene in a novel could be presented by means of a dialogue or through a description by a narrator. These choices contribute to the style of a work. In the words of Leech and Short (19), "Every writer necessarily makes choices of expression, and it is in these choices, in his 'way of putting things,' that style resides. . . . Every analysis of style . . . is an attempt to find the artistic principles underlying a writer's choice of language."

The concept of narrative style may be expanded beyond that of an individual author, so that on a more general level we may speak of a cultural style. My purpose in this section is to examine biblical style in the spirit of Alter's methodologies. We will in turn look at the following narrative devices: repetition, omission, dialogue, and irony.

REPETITION

Repetition is a function of most literature, but it is particularly emphasized in biblical literature, where it occurs on a number of different levels: words, motifs, themes, and whole scenes (what Alter calls type scenes [see *The Art* 95–113]). While here we are most interested in repetitions that occur within a unified work, we must also keep in mind that some repetition, especially of motif and theme, occurs beyond a single work and even across the whole canon (see Longman 1982 for an example). Here is where literary study intersects with biblical theology.

Repetition provides a sense of coherence to a narrative. This coherence is denied even by some critics like Alter who prefer to think of the text as a "composite unity," thus providing a diachronic explanation for a synchronic phenomenon. That is, the repetition is taken as a sign that the text is the end result of a process in which several sources have been brought together over a period of time. Over against this approach, others argue that the repetition may provide the key to the meaning of a story (Ryken 83), as in 2 Samuel 7 where the repetition of "house" (*bayit*) indicates that the chapter is about the building of David's "house," that is dynasty.

OMISSION

Another characteristic trait of biblical narrative is its tendency to omit information that the reader might expect to find. I hinted at this above when I described the "reticent narrator" (Alter). This phenomenon has also been called gapping and is nicely described by Sternberg (235) as "a lack of information about the world—an event, motive, causal link, character trait, plot structure, law of probability—contrived by a temporal displacement."

DIALOGUE

In the context of telling a story, the narrator will often recount dialogue. Different literary traditions have various ways of handling dialogue. For instance, nineteenth-century English novels (e.g., those by Eliot) have considerable narrative exposition in relationship to dialogue. Biblical prose is the opposite, with a noticeable preference for dialogue, so much so that Alter (1981, 69) speaks of the Bible's penchant for "narration-through-dialogue."

While the narrative exposition of the Bible is important to convey necessary information, the reader's interest is often captured most readily by dialogue. It brings a vividness to the story, a sense of being present.

Alter (63–87) and Berlin (64–87) provide detailed examples of the conventions of dialogue in the Bible. These include such things as the predominance of two-character dialogues, the importance of the initiation of the dialogue, the manner in which dialogue will contrast two characters, and the way in which dialogue "conveys the characters' internal psychological and ideological points of view" (Berlin 64).

IRONY

Irony is a term that is hard to pin down because it is used to label a number of different, though related, textual strategies. Edwin Good, in one of the few full discussions of biblical irony in recent days, throws out a simple definition at which he scoffs: "To say one thing but mean another, generally the opposite—that is sufficient definition of irony for most people" (22). But then, again, he never finally arrives at a more sophisticated definition.

One of the clearest discussions of irony may be found in Wayne Booth's *Rhetoric of Irony.* Booth makes an important distinction between stable irony and unstable irony, of which only the former is found in the Bible. He describes stable irony as sharing four characteristics. First, it is *intended* by the author. The ironic author asserts "something in order to have it rejected as false" (Muecke 56). Of course, this view involves a hypothesis about an unstated intention of the author, but Booth points out that stable ironies are almost always easily recognized. Second, stable irony is *covert.* The implied author and narrator are silent about the ironic nature of a statement or passage. Ironies are "intended to be reconstructed with meanings different from those on the surface" (Booth 6). Third, biblical ironies are *stable* in that there is a limit to how deeply they displace the surface meaning of the text. Finally, such ironies are limited in terms of scope, treating only a certain part of the text as ironic. In Booth's terms they are *local.* Biblical narrative contains many examples of irony in both the Old and New Testaments. Turning again to the book of Jonah, we may cite, among many other ironies, the fact that an Israelite prophet disobeys God's command to preach repentance, while the hardened and notoriously violent Assyrians repent after a sermon that takes all of a verse (3:4) and simply announces judgment with no mention of the possibility of forgiveness.

Conclusion

The narratives of the Bible thus are both similar to and different from contemporary narratives. As the past few years have abundantly demonstrated, we may, as a result, benefit in our understanding of the stories of the Bible by taking a literary approach to them. In doing so, however, we must never lose sight of the other dimensions of the biblical text, notably its historical and theological significance. With this reminder, however, it is possible to bracket those functions for pedagogical purposes and to concentrate for the moment on the impressive narrative strategies of the individual books that make up the Bible. This is the task of the chapters to follow.

WORKS CITED

Abrams, M. H. *A Glossary of Literary Terms.* 4th ed. New York: Holt, Rinehart and Winston, 1981.

Alter, Robert. *The Art of Biblical Narrative.* New York: Basic Books, 1981.

———. "A Response to Critics." *Journal for the Study of the Old Testament* 27 (1983): 113–17.

Auerbach, Erich. *Mimesis.* Trans. Willard Trask. Princeton: Princeton UP, 1953.

Berlin, Adele. *Poetics and Interpretation of Biblical Narrative.* Sheffield: Almond, 1983.

Booth, W. C. *The Rhetoric of Irony.* 2d ed. University of Chicago Press, 1983.

Brooks, P. *Reading for the Plot: Design and Intention in Narratives.* New York: Vintage, 1984.

Chatman, S. *Story and Discourse.* Ithaca, N.Y.: Cornell UP, 1978.

Frye, Northrop. *The Great Code: The Bible and Literature.* London: Ark, 1981.

Good, Edwin M. *Irony in the Old Testament.* Rev. ed. Sheffield: Almond, 1981.

Leech, G. N., and M. H. Short. *Style in Fiction.* London: Longman, 1981.

Longman, Tremper, III, "The Divine Warrior: The New Testament Use of an Old Testament Motif." *Westminster Theological Journal* 44 (1982): 290–307.

———. *Literary Approaches to Biblical Interpretation.* Grand Rapids: Zondervan, 1987.

———. "Storytellers and Poets in the Bible: Can Literary Artifice Be True?" *Inerrancy and Hermeneutic.* Ed. H. M. Conn. Grand Rapids: Baker, 1988. 137–49.

Magonet, J. *Form and Meaning: Studies in the Literary Techniques in the Book of Jonah.* Rev. ed. Sheffield: Almond, 1983.

Muecke, D. C. *Irony and the Ironic.* Critical Idiom 13. London: Methuen, 1970.

Prickett, Stephen. *Words and the Word: Language, Poetics and Biblical Interpretation.* Cambridge: Cambridge UP, 1986.

Rhoads, D., and D. Michie. *Mark as Story: The Introduction to the Narrative of a Gospel.* Philadelphia: Fortress, 1982.

Ryken, Leland. *Words of Delight: A Literary Introduction to the Bible.* Grand Rapids: Baker, 1987.

Sternberg, Meir. *The Poetics of Biblical Narrative.* Bloomington: Indiana UP, 1985.

CHAPTER 5

Biblical Poetry

Tremper Longman III
Westminster Theological Seminary

The occurrence of poetry in the Bible is surprising to many. After all, the biblical writers are intent on communicating a message, and poetry by its direction and its heavy use of literary artifice seems to work against that goal.

Poetry, quite simply, is harder for most people to understand than prose. People today have less experience of poetry, since it is unlike everyday conversation and writing. It was for this reason that the Living Bible, one of the most popular dynamic-equivalent translations, chose to render the psalms in a prose format, collapsing much of the parallelism into simple prose statement. The implicit message is, If you want people to know what is being said in the psalms, get rid of its poetic structure.

Although it is hard to define precisely what distinguishes Hebrew poetry from Hebrew prose, this dichotomy must have existed in antiquity as well. One need only read the book of Kings and then contrast its style with that of the book of Psalms to recognize a difference that in modern terms is the difference between prose and poetry.

The history of research is marred with the false starts of attempts to define the difference by means of traits unique to poetry over against prose. Either these traits also appear in prose contexts (parallelism) or exist in neither Hebrew poetry nor prose (meter). The failure to achieve consensus has led to the radical position of James Kugel, who in other ways has contributed enormously to our understanding of biblical literature. Kugel rejects the traditional distinctions between prose and poetry, believing they are foreign to the culture of the Old Testament.

It is, however, much more in keeping with the distinction between a book like Kings and a book like Psalms to retain the poetry-prose distinction, while granting that the border between the two is not clear-cut and that the difference is not the result of the presence of unique trait(s) but of a heightened and intensified use of those traits (parallelism, imagery, terseness—to be described below).

A quick skim of the Bible reveals a considerable amount of poetic literature, especially in the Old Testament. Examples include major poems in the Pentateuch (for instance, Gen. 49; Ex. 15; Deut. 33) and the historical books (Judg. 5). The so-called wisdom books are almost exclusively in poetic format (Psalms, Job, Proverbs), as are, more surprisingly, vast tracts of the prophets. Indeed, if all the poetic portions of the Old Testament were gathered together, they would be longer than the New Testament.

The contrast with the New Testament is interesting to note but hard to explain. There are smaller poems in both the Gospels and the Epistles (e.g., Luke 1:46–55, 68–79; Phil. 2:6–11), but there is no single poetic book in the New Testament. This contrast, however, should not keep us from recognizing the poetic quality of much of the teaching of Jesus and the book of Revelation. While it is true that the terse, parallel lines of the Psalter, for instance, are present only in those passages noted above, the heavy use of figurative language by Jesus and the apocalyptic seer render their teaching essentially poetic.

The most productive way to explain the presence of such large portions of poetry in a book that intends to communicate a message is to remember that the Bible does more than simply feed the intellect with facts. The Bible is an affective book that communicates much of its meaning by moving the feelings and the will of its readers. Literary prose and poetry are equally appropriate media for the Bible. In their own ways, both of them inform, arouse emotions, stimulate the imagination, and appeal to a reader's will.

The biblical authors frequently utilize the poetic forms of their day. It therefore becomes incumbent upon readers of the Bible not to depoeticize its form but instead to familiarize themselves with its conventions in order to read it in the way that it was originally intended.

The Conventions of Biblical Poetry

While there is overlap even between ancient biblical and familiar Western poetry, there are also significant discontinuities. Each culture has its own poetic code. As a result, there are strange as well as familiar features awaiting the modern reader of the poetry of the Bible.

Our discussion of these traits will be in two parts. In the first place, we will examine the primary traits of biblical poetry. These traits are primary because they occur consistently, almost pervasively in the poetry. The secondary traits, to be discussed in the next section, are secondary only because they occur more occasionally.

The distinction between primary and secondary poetic conventions is a distinction of degree and not of kind. There is no single trait or cluster of traits that defines Hebrew poetry as over against prose. This explains why it is occasionally difficult (for instance, in some passages in Hosea or Jeremiah) to categorize a text as either prose or poetry. It used to be thought that meter was such a genre-identifying trait, but we will see how meter has proved to be an elusive category in the analysis of biblical poetry.

The most obvious trait of Hebrew poetry is its terseness. This characteristic leaps out at even the beginning reader of the Bible by virtue of formatting conventions of English translations. With very few exceptions, most English translations put a single poetic colon on a line. The result is a large amount of white space on the page.

The fundamental unit of Hebrew poetry is the line, not the sentence, as in prose. The line is composed of two or more short clauses that are often called cola (singular: colon) by biblical scholars. The most frequent line has two cola (a bicolon), each colon containing three words. Lines with one colon (monocolon) or three cola (tricolon) are not unusual, nor are cola with two or four words. It is, however, very rare to find a poetic line that consists of more than four words.

That the lines are short or terse is another way of expressing the fact that Hebrew poetry, like most poetry, is compact; it says a lot using few words. This compactness is the result of four features.

First, Hebrew poetry uses few conjunctions. Even the simple conjunction "and," the direct object marker, and the relative pronoun are only rarely used and are often suspected of being late prosaic insertions (Cross and Freedman). This feature is blurred a little in English translations, which will often add a conjunction to help the reader along. For instance, in Nahum 2:5:

He summons his picked troops,
yet they stumble along the way.

The conjunction "yet" is supplied and not in the Hebrew text.

The second characteristic of biblical poetry that leads to terseness is parallelism, which I will describe fully below. There is a definite tendency toward a rough isosyllablism in Hebrew poetry. By this I mean that cola within a parallel line will normally have an equal or near equal number of syllables.

Closely related is the third source of terseness, ellipsis. Ellipsis is the tendency to drop a major element out of the second colon of a poetic line with the expectation that the reader will carry over that element from the first colon. Ellipsis is most common with the verb and may be illustrated by Hosea 5:8 (Watson 303–4):

Blow the trumpet in Gibeah,
the horn in Ramah.

The last source of compact expression in the poetry of the Bible, also to be discussed fully below, is imagery. Imagery stimulates the imagination by embodying multiple meanings in concise form. An image not only triggers a train of thinking about a subject but also evokes an emotional response.

The second primary trait of Hebrew poetry is the verse form known as parallelism. The near repetition that characterizes the poetic line in Hebrew poetry has long been observed. It was named parallelism by Robert Lowth in the eighteenth century, the term borrowed from geometry to describe what he called "a certain conformation of the sentences" in which "equals refer to equals, and opposites to opposites . . ." (Lecture III, quoted in Berlin 1).

Since Lowth, parallelism has been recognized as the most telltale feature of biblical poetry. Also since Lowth, literary and biblical scholars have emphasized the equivalence between the related cola of a poetic line. This may be illustrated by C. S. Lewis's statement about parallelism that it is "the practice of saying the same thing twice in different words" (1961, 11). While Lewis did understand the parallel line to operate according to the principle "the same in the other," his emphasis was on the coherence of the cola, and handbooks on biblical poetry presented an even less balanced statement on the relationship between the cola than he did.

Parallelism has received intense scrutiny over the past few years from biblical and literary scholars (Kugel, Alter, Berlin, O'Connor, Geller, and others). The emerging consensus is that the parallel line is a more subtle literary device than previously thought. The new paradigm for understanding parallelism is development rather than equivalence. The biblical poet is doing more than saying the same thing twice. The second part always nuances the first part in some way. Kugel rightly refuses to replace Lowth's traditional three categories of parallelism (synonymous, antithetic, synthetic) with others. He simply argues that the second colon always contributes to the thought of the first colon, as suggested by his formula "A, what's more B."

The interpreter thus must pause and meditate on a poetic line like the well-known Psalm 1:1:

Blessed is the man
who does not walk in the counsel of the wicked
or stand in the way of sinners
or sit in the seat of mockers.

Isolating the verbs in their context, we clearly see a progression of thought in the way that Kugel suggests. All three verbs figuratively relate the person to evil. As he moves from "walk" to "stand" to "sit," the psalmist imagines an ever closer relationship to evil, in other words a more settled relation with it. In short, parallelism is based simultaneously on the logic of synonymity and the logic of progression; as we move from one line to the next, something is repeated and something is added.

Parallelism is the most frequently occurring literary device in poetry. We must keep in mind, however, that not all poetry contains parallelism and that some prose does (e.g., Gen. 21:1). Furthermore, though space does not allow a detailed description, recent studies have enlarged our understanding of parallelism beyond the semantic described above and into grammatical and even phonological dimensions (Berlin and Cooper).

The third trait of Hebrew poetry is imagery and figurative language. Imagery is not the exclusive province of poetry, but the frequency and intensity of imagery is heightened in discourse that we normally recognize as poetic. It is, after all, another way to write compactly, as well as to increase the emotional impact of a passage.

As M. H. Abrams points out, imagery is an "ambiguous" term (78). He goes on to quote C. Day Lewis, who speaks of imagery as "a picture made out of words." Such pictures are often the result of comparison, the two most common types being metaphor and simile. Simile, on one level, is not even figurative language; it is capable of being understood on a literal level. A simile is a comparison between two things and is marked by the use of "like" or "as." Song of Songs 4:1b is a clear example:

Your hair is like a flock of goats
descending from Mount Gilead.

Metaphor has long been considered the master image or even the essence of poetry by literary scholars since the time of Aristotle. Metaphor presents a stronger connection between the two objects of comparison and is truly figurative language, as in Song of Songs 4:1a:

Your eyes behind your veil are doves.

Metaphor catches our attention by the disparity between the two objects and the daring suggestion of similarity. The reader must ponder and reflect on the point of the similarity, and by so doing he explores multiple levels of meaning and experiences the emotional overtones of the metaphor. A well-known example comes from the first line of Psalm 23:

The LORD is my shepherd.
I shall not be in want.

What does it mean to compare the Lord to a shepherd? To read the image in context, we would immediately suggest that the poem speaks of God's protection, his guidance, and his care. We would stop short, however, if we did not remember that the shepherd image was a well-used royal image in the ancient Near East. Reading the text sympathetically, we would experience assurance and feel comfort even in the midst of danger.

Metaphor and simile do not exhaust the repertory of figurative language in Hebrew. E. W. Bullinger lists hundreds of categories of figurative language. Besides metaphor and simile, Leland Ryken treats the following five figures of speech and gives examples. The first is symbol. "A symbol is a concrete image that points to or embodies other meanings" (*How to Read* 97). Ryken's example is "Light is shed upon the righteous" (Ps. 97:11). A second category is hyperbole, "conscious exaggeration for the sake of effect" (*How to Read* 99):

With your help I can advance against a troop;
with my God I can scale a wall. (Ps. 18:29)

Then there is personification, which attributes personality to inanimate objects. The psalmist frequently uses this poetic device in order to demonstrate that all of creation and not just human creation is dependent upon God and owes him praise:

Let the sea resound, and everything in it,
the world, and all who live in it. (Ps. 98:7)

Ryken notes that the poets of Israel use apostrophe in order to express strong emotion. Apostrophe "is a direct address to something or someone absent as though the person or thing were present and capable of listening" (*How to Read* 98). He includes among his examples Psalm 2:10:

Therefore, you kings, be wise;
be warned, you rulers of the earth.

These representative figures of speech should not be taken as a mere list of categories. They are representative of the devices that were available to the Hebrew poet as he communicated his message with vivid freshness and concreteness. They lend richness of meaning to the poem and seek to evoke a strong emotional response from the reader.

Terseness, parallelism, and imagery are the three primary traits of biblical poetry. The acrostic form is a striking example of a secondary poetic device. It stands out because it is so noticeable in the original and because its existence entails an obviously artificial form of the language.

An acrostic is a poem in which the first letters of successive lines form a recognizable pattern. While in some poems from ancient times (such as some Babylonian poems) the name of a scribe who copied the text, or perhaps some hidden message, was spelled out in this way, the examples found in the Old Testament all follow the order of the Hebrew alphabet.

There are many examples of acrostics in the Bible. The two most famous are perhaps the so-called Giant Psalm (119), which is broken up into eight-verse stanzas by the acrostic, and the book of Lamentations. In the latter, the first two chapters follow a verse-by-verse acrostic whereas the latter two chapters group the letters into three-verse stanzas. One of the more interesting acrostic patterns is found in the first chapter of Nahum. The acrostic covers only half the alphabet and even then skips an occasional letter. Other acrostics in Hebrew occur at Psalms 9, 10, 25, 34, 37, 111, 112, 145; Proverbs 31:10–31; Lamentations 1–4.

The purpose of acrostic form may only be guessed. On the one hand, it may help in the process of memorization. On the other hand, acrostics also communicate a sense of wholeness. As Watson points out, “By using every letter of the alphabet the poet was trying to ensure that his treatment of a particular topic was complete” (Watson 198). I would expand this to include the idea that an acrostic imparts a feeling of wholeness to a text. Nahum’s first chapter confirms this. This disrupted acrostic occurs in a poem that extols God as the divine warrior who disrupts the normal created order. Thus, once again, form supports meaning.

A somewhat neglected secondary convention of Hebrew poetry is the use of stanzas and strophes. Most studies of biblical poetry have concentrated on the level of the parallel line. Little has been done to describe rhetorical patterns that encompass the whole poem. This neglect is due mostly to uncertainty about analysis on this level. Scholars often question if broader patterns exist in biblical poems.

There is no doubt that most poems are unified wholes, but the relationship between the parts is almost always described in terms of content. For instance, grief psalms share a similar structure, by which any individual psalm may be divided in separate parts. Thus Psalm 69 may be described in the following way:

Invocation and Initial Plea to God for Help (v. 1a)
Complaints (vv. 1b–4, 7–12, 19–21)
Confession of Sin (vv. 5–6)
Further Pleas for Help (vv. 13–18)
Imprecation (vv. 22–28)
Hymn of Praise (vv. 30–36)

Each of these sections is composed of at least one and usually more than one parallel line. The question arises as to whether or not it is legitimate to call these broader groupings stanzas and/or strophes. Watson (160–200) has one of the most extensive discussions of this issue, arguing that the answer to this question is affirmative as long as these terms are understood in the broad sense as "units within the poem." Furthermore, as Watson also points out, verse groupings above the level of the individual poetic line are occasionally possible by means of such devices as recurrent refrains (Pss. 42–43) and acrostic patterns (Ps. 119).

The significance of this discussion is to recognize that the reader can expect biblical poems to have a structure that goes beyond the individual line and encompasses the whole poem. This broader structure is most easily recognized on the level of content but is occasionally supported by elements of style.

Hebrew poets often play on the sounds of the language to achieve poetic effect. Rhyme, a phonological device well known to readers of English poetry, is nonexistent in Hebrew. Since verb, number, and gender endings are alike, it is too easy to do and therefore not prized as a literary device. Nonetheless, there are occasional sound plays in Hebrew verse, most frequently alliteration and assonance. Occasionally, the sound play supports the meaning of a verse, for instance in the alliteration of Nahum 1:10:

kî 'ad-sîrîm s^{e}bukîm ûk^{e}sāb^{e}am s^{e}bû'îm 'ukk^{e}lû k^{e}qaš yābēš mālē'

They will be entangled among thorns
and drunk from their wine;
they will be consumed like dry stubble.

As Cooper has suggested, the repetition of the *s* sound in this verse may actually parody the lisp of a drunk.

It is important to add a brief note about meter. The question of the existence of meter in biblical poetry has been much discussed since the church fathers. Many different schemas have been suggested, and none has convinced more than a handful of scholars. In recent years a consensus has grown that either the meter of biblical poetry is undetectable or else, as seems more likely, it is nonexistent.

Psalm 114

The danger of my foregoing description is that it gives the impression that biblical poetry is made up of a number of discrete traits. While it is possible to discuss these traits separately for pedagogical purposes, poetry is not simply the sum of all its component parts. A biblical poem is a result of the interplay of these and other traits that bind the meaning, the form, and the sound of the language together. The next step toward understanding biblical poetry is to undertake the analysis of a poem. I have chosen Psalm 114 as my example, though space does not permit a full explication of the poetic forms in this rich poem (see Geller, "The Language of Imagery"):

When Israel came out of Egypt,
the house of Jacob from a people of foreign tongue,
Judah became God's sanctuary,
Israel his dominion.

The sea looked and fled,
the Jordan turned back;
the mountains skipped like rams,
the hills like lambs.

Why was it, O sea, that you fled,
O Jordan, that you turned back,
you mountains, that you skipped like rams,
you hills, like lambs?

Tremble, O earth, at the presence of the Lord,
at the presence of the God of Jacob,
who turned the rock into a pool,
the hard rock into springs of water.

The psalm is characteristically terse and compact. There are few conjunctions and frequent ellipses, especially of the verb. The poem is composed of eight bicola, corresponding with the versification. Syntax and subject matter lend support to the division into four stanzas found in the NIV and other versions.

The relationship between cola within the line demonstrates the coherence and difference that I described above. I will use the first two verses as an example. These compose one stanza made up of two bicola, but when translated into English they are best rendered as a single sentence.

The first verse is really a dependent clause, which begins not with a conjunction but rather with a preposition prefixed to a verbal form. The first colon simply alludes to the Exodus by the traditional formula that "Israel came out of Egypt." The second colon uses a variant name for the whole of Israel and then uses a descriptive phrase for Egypt, "a people of foreign tongue." The latter heightens the strangeness of Egypt and therefore the greatness of the deliverance. The second verse is a bicolon that serves as the main clause of the sentence and begins in the first colon to identify Judah, the southern portion of the Holy Land, with a cultic term, *sanctuary*. This is appropriate, since the temple was built in Jerusalem. The second colon expands the perspective and speaks now of Israel, the whole of the land, and uses a political term, *dominion*. Throughout these verses and indeed throughout the poem we see such subtle differences within a basic coherence between cola.

My comments on the second verse lead immediately to a consideration of the imagery of the psalm. In the first colon of the second verse the Israelite conquest of Palestine is likened to the establishment of a home for God. The whole of the land in effect became holy ground, much like the temple itself. Palestine is identified with the temple. The similarity between the two is that God may be said to dwell in both, with the result that the land is holy.

The second picture offered by the psalmist is the result of personification. For the present purpose I will restrict my comments to the first part of the third verse:

Why was it, O sea, that you fled,
O Jordan, that you turned back?

Here the psalmist attributes human abilities and emotions to the Red Sea and the Jordan River. The historical books inform us (in Ex. 14 and Josh. 3) that God miraculously split these bodies of water to allow his people to cross through them. The psalmist creates a vivid picture of a conflict between God and the sea/river at this time, evoking a whole set of responses.

Indeed, the images in both verses 2 and 3 evoke a distinct emotional response because the content of the imagery, as with much imagery in the Bible, has its source in ancient Near Eastern religious texts. In the Baal texts known from Ugarit and the Enuma Elish from Mesopotamia, the warrior god (Baal/Marduk) struggles with the sea god and the monsters who support him (Leviathan, Rahab). The defeat of the sea leads to the creation of the world and more specifically to the building of the deity's home/sanctuary. This psalm is illustrative of the broader Near Eastern background of much of Old

Testament imagery. Biblical poets will often attribute to Yahweh the acts and qualities of foreign deities and in this way seek to denigrate their worship while promoting the worship of Yahweh.

The poets of the Bible often express themselves figuratively. Ryken is right when he says that without the imagery "their [the biblical poets'] utterances would lack the vividness, the experiential richness, the arresting quality that makes a statement worthy of attention and memorable, and the precision that metaphor confers on them" ("Metaphor" 22).

Old Testament Poetic Types

Four principal types of poems can be discerned in the Old Testament: lyric, epic, prophetic, and dramatic. These four types often overlap.

Ryken defines a lyric poem as "a short poem containing the thoughts or feelings of a speaker" (*Words of Delight* 227). The psalms are clear examples of biblical lyric, as is the Song of Songs. Both are personal expressions of deeply held emotions. Indeed, the psalms explore the whole emotional spectrum from the brightest joy to the darkest anger and grief, just as the love poems in the Song of Songs portray the full range of romantic sentiments. The psalms also subdue any specific historical reference, so that later readers find expression of their own feelings and can appropriate the psalmists' words as their own (Longman, *How to Read* 46–48).

Historical poems differ from lyric in that they recall past events, in particular the great acts of God. They are usually expressions of thanks to God for these events. Exodus 15 is a prime example as it recalls in loving detail the miraculous deliverance of Israel from the Egyptians at the Red Sea.

The poetry of the prophets has a lyrical quality in that it conveys deeply personal expressions. Prophetic poetry also has a historical dimension as it invokes past saving acts of God. But the prophets use poetry with a more intense appeal to the wills of their hearers. They seek to persuade and to convict, and to achieve this they use the heightened language of poetry.

As far as we know, drama did not exist in the ancient Near Eastern world. At least in one place in the Bible, however, we have poetry with a dramatic quality to it, though it is extremely unlikely that it was ever acted on the equivalent of a stage. The book of Job is, according to Ryken, "a 'closet drama'—intended to be read rather than acted" (*Words of Delight* 343).

Conclusion

The extensive occurrence of poetry throughout the Old Testament and its continued use in the New Testament remind us that the Bible is not simply an informational book. The biblical authors stimulate our imaginations as they fill our minds with images that give us an adequate, but partial, glimpse of the nature of God and of his relationship with his creatures.

WORKS CITED

Abrams, M. H. *A Glossary of Terms.* 4th ed. New York: Holt, Rinehart and Winston, 1981.
Alter, Robert. *The Art of Biblical Poetry.* New York: Basic Books, 1985.
Berlin, Adele. *The Dynamics of Biblical Parallelism.* Bloomington: Indiana UP, 1985.
Bullinger, E. W. *Figures of Speech Used in the Bible, Explained and Illustrated.* 1898. Rpt. Grand Rapids: Baker, 1968.
Caird, George B. *The Language and Imagery of the Bible.* Philadelphia: Westminster, 1980.
Cooper, A. S. "Biblical Poetics: A Linguistic Approach." Ph.D. diss. New Haven: Yale UP, 1976.
Falk, Marcia. *Love Lyrics From the Bible.* Sheffield: Almond, 1976.
Freedman, David, and Frank M. Cross. *Studies in Ancient Yahwistic Poetry.* Missoula, Mont.: Scholars, 1975.
Geller, S. A. *Parallelism in Early Biblical Poetry.* Missoula, Mont.: Scholars, 1979.
———. "The Language of Imagery in Psalm 114." *Lingering Over Words.* Ed. T. Abusch et al. Winona Lake, Ind.: Eisenbrauns, 1990. 179–84.
Hawkes, T. *Metaphor.* Critical Idiom 25. London: Methuen, 1972.
Kugel, James L. *The Idea of Biblical Poetry.* New Haven: Yale UP, 1981.
Lewis, C. S. *Reflections on the Psalms.* New York: Simon & Schuster, 1961.
Longman, Tremper, III. *How to Read the Psalms.* Downers Grove, Ill.: InterVarsity, 1988.
O'Connor, Michael. *Hebrew Verse Structure.* Winona Lake, Ind.: Eisenbrauns, 1980.
Ricoeur, Paul. *The Rule of Metaphor.* Toronto: University of Toronto Press, 1977.
Ryken, Leland. "Metaphor in the Psalms." *Christianity and Literature* 31 (1982): 9–29.
———. *How to Read the Bible as Literature.* Grand Rapids: Zondervan, 1984.
———. *Words of Delight: A Literary Introduction to the Bible.* Grand Rapids: Zondervan, 1987.
Watson, W. G. E. *Classical Hebrew Poetry.* Sheffield: JSOT Press, 1984.

PART 2

CHAPTER 6

The Literature of the Old Testament

Tremper Longman III
Westminster Theological Seminary

Imposing obstacles stand in the way of a literary appreciation of the Old Testament. Why, after all, do most readers go to the Old Testament? In many cases people turn to it to encounter God or to discover the past, and sometimes the theological and historical purposes are conjoined. It is of course legitimate to read the Old Testament for these reasons, but in so doing, one may be overlooking an important element. Readers often neglect the literary nature of the text.

Another reason why few readers make the effort to gain an appreciation of the Old Testament as a literary whole is that the Old Testament is a massive and, to many, a bewildering book. Upon first encounter it gives the impression of being a haphazard collection of stories, poems, laws, and prophetic utterances. Those who read through the Old Testament often lose sight of the unity of its plot, if not in the second half of Exodus, at least in Leviticus and Numbers.

English translations have in some ways militated against the possibility of literary appreciation. No one can gainsay the aesthetic value and literary beauty of the Authorized Version from the standpoint of the English language, but it does little to give the reader insight into the native conventions of the text, most notably by neglecting to format the poetry in a distinctive manner. Modern translations are a mixed bunch. The worst in terms of format is the New American Standard Version, which treats each verse as a separate paragraph in its attempt to be a "literal" translation. But even some of the best from a literary perspective (e.g., The New International Version, Jerusalem Bible, New English Bible, and New Revised Standard Version) are inadequate. Consider that the well-entrenched modern convention of inserting chapter and verse numbers cuts against the literary grain.

Biblical scholarship since the Enlightenment has only exacerbated the problem with its predominantly historical interests in the text. Texts that to "naïve" (precritical) readers seem beautifully constructed wholes are dissected under the scholarly microscope and taken to be hopelessly composite and contradictory weaving of disparate sources. Stephen Prickett shows how this scholarly mindset affected the fundamentals of university curriculum in the early nineteenth century so that biblical studies became effectively isolated from literary studies, a separation from which the field of biblical studies is just now beginning its recovery.

The Literary Quality of the Old Testament

A curious neglect of the literary nature of the Old Testament has existed in the guild of biblical scholarship and the church. But perhaps not in every part of the church. Young children are still taught the Bible and catch the wonder of such memorable stories as the Exodus, Samson and Delilah, and David and Goliath. Then, too, the literary nature of the Bible is reflected in the pervasive use of biblical plots, themes, and allusions in literature (see Ryken, ch. 35), even though present levels of biblical illiteracy have seriously hindered modern attempts to teach literature in the secondary schools and colleges of the Western world.

But in what way is the Old Testament literary? This question will be answered by demonstration in the chapters that follow, but here let me begin with definition. As Leland Ryken has stated (13), "The subject matter [of literature] is human experience, not abstract ideas. Literature *incarnates* its meanings as concretely as possible." Upon reading this definition, we immediately recognize its applicability to the Old Testament, where instead of encountering expository essays, historical treatises, and scientific or theological explanations, we find well-told stories and beautifully constructed poems.

An interesting illustration of this point is the biblical teaching on adultery. The Old Testament teaches in a number of different ways that to take another person's spouse is ethically wrong. One looks in vain, however, for a moral treatise that spells out this principle and its reasons. Rather, one encounters stories like the attempted seduction of Joseph by Potiphar's wife (Gen. 39). The narrator/author displays ethical principles by Joseph's example and speech as he reacts to the repeated attempts of Potiphar's wife to lure him into her bed: "How then could I do such a wicked thing and sin against God?" (Gen. 39:9). The book of Proverbs, though more directly didactic in tone, takes the same perspective in a highly imaginative poem in chapter 7. We have space enough to cite only the climactic last verses:

With persuasive words she led him astray;
she seduced him with her smooth talk.
All at once he followed her
like an ox going to the slaughter,
like a deer stepping into a noose
till an arrow pierces his liver,
like a bird darting into a snare,
little knowing it will cost him his life.

Now then, my sons, listen to me;
pay attention to what I say.
Do not let your heart turn to her ways
or stray into her paths.
Many are the victims she has brought down;
her slain are a mighty throng.
Her house is a highway to the grave,
leading down to the chambers of death. (vv. 21–27)

Consider, finally, the same teaching as it is given in the Ten Commandments: "You shall not commit adultery" (Ex. 20:14). Even here, in what is its most directly didactic statement, the principle is stated in the context of the story of Israel at Mount Sinai.

The Old Testament does more than inform readers' intellect with facts about God and history. It also arouses emotions, appeals to the will, and stimulates the imagination. It does so not only through its content but also by self-consciousness about its form of expression. The use of literary artifice has long been recognized in biblical poetry, but recent studies have made it clear that the same is true in its prose as well. Literary scholars have concentrated on books like Genesis and 1 and 2 Samuel, which are the most interesting prose books from a literary perspective. But even books like Leviticus and Numbers (discussed by Levine and Milgrom, and Baroody and Gentrup in this volume) display interesting literary characteristics (though they should not be overstated).

The Genres of the Old Testament

The Old Testament is not a monolithic book from a literary perspective. It is an anthology or collection of different genres. Recent studies of genre (Hempfer; Longman, *Literary Approaches* 76–83) have shown that the concept is a descriptive tool that exists at different levels of abstraction. Thus, one may speak of broad and narrow genres as well as admit that not only texts as a whole but also passages within a text are amenable to generic identification.

On one level, for instance, it is correct to say that the Old Testament contains stories and poems. These two categories encompass the whole of the Old Testament, indeed the entire Bible. I will not dwell here on these categories, however, since two chapters treat them fully (see chs. 4 and 5). I will rather survey what may be considered a second level of genre: history, lyric poetry, wisdom, and prophecy. This discussion will introduce topics that will be specified and refined in the chapters that follow in part 2.

HISTORY

We may begin with a description of history because so much of the Old Testament is devoted to the remembrance of the past that some readers come away with the impression that the Old Testament is a kind of history textbook. The books of Genesis through Esther, in spite of the differences among them, are bound together by a common interest in the past. They recount events from creation to the postexilic period.

To confuse the function of these books with that of modern history textbooks is a serious misreading. True, they are both concerned to inform their readers about past events, but much writing of history claims an unattainable neutrality of reportage that discourages literary presentation. The Old Testament, on the other hand, makes no pretense to neutrality; it displays the past as a testimony to God's judgment and grace. Thus Sternberg is right to describe the function of biblical narrative as historical, ideological (theological), and literary.

For instance, Genesis 11:1–9, in recounting a past event, does so in a way that shows the author's concern for literary style. Fokkelman has written a most illuminating literary analysis of this short text. He points out that "the narrator of Gen. 11:1–11 did his job within the square centimeter" (11) by making a careful use of each of the 121 words that make up the text. To accurately summarize Fokkelman's careful thirty-five-page analysis is impossible, but by noting word plays, alliterations, and the use of "the whole earth" as an inclusio, he is able to demonstrate a closely knit and linguistically based chiasm, which he describes in the following way (Fokkelman presents the structure of the passage in Hebrew; the translation is mine):

"the whole earth had one language" A (v. 1)
"there" B (v. 2b)
"to each other" C (v. 3a)
"Come, let us make bricks" (*lbn*) D (v. 3b)
"Let's build for ourselves" E (v. 4a)
"a city and a tower" F (v. 4b)
"And God went down to look" X (v. 5a)
"the city and the tower" F′ (v. 5b)
"which the sons of men built" E′ (v. 5c)
"Come . . . let's confuse" (*nbl*) D′ (v. 7a)
"each man, the language of his neighbor" C′ (v. 7b)
"from there" B′ (v. 8b)
"the language of all the earth" A′ (v. 8c)

According to Fokkelman,

> unity of language (A) and place (B) and intensive communication (C) induce the men to plans and inventions (D), especially to building (E) a city and a tower (F). God's intervention is a turning point (X). He watches the buildings (F′) people make (E′) and launches a counterplan (D′) because of which communication becomes impossible (C′) and the unity of place (B′) and of language (A′) is broken. (22–23)

Those conversant with recent secondary literature on the Old Testament know that many have proposed chiastic structures on slim or nonexistent evidence, but the strength of Fokkelman's analysis lies in the fact that it is based on related words and not the general thought of the units. His study also goes beyond mere description of an interesting structural form to an explanation of the relationship between form and meaning as he points out how fitting such a chiastic structure is in a sin/judgment context where the *lex talionis* comes into play. To further support his argument, he shows how this structure is present in other similar contexts (Gen. 9:6; Lev. 24:17–21).

It is true that Genesis 11:1–11 "occupies a special position in OT narrative art by the density of its stylistically relevant phonological phenomena" (Fokkelman 13), yet it stands as a witness to what is observed throughout the historical literature—a self-consciousness of literary presentation.

This partial analysis of Genesis 11:1–11 is simply an example of the type of literary impulses to be found in the historical books of the Old Testament. The following chapters will amply illustrate the many ways in which these books are rightly called literary. For instance, as we read the historical books we observe the authors telling us stories with vivid characters, and we encounter plot conflicts, not the mere recording of information in a documentary fashion. Fascinating plots, memorable characters, significant settings, and artistic structures all contribute to the artistic interest that we find in these books.

While biblical scholarship has downplayed the literary qualities of historical prose in the Old Testament over the past two centuries, the pendulum has swung in the opposite direction in the past fifteen years. The result has been an imbalance toward the literary nature of the text, expressed well by Robertson when he states, "Nothing depends on the truth or falsity of [the Bible's] historical claims" (548). More recently, however, scholars are calling for an interpretive approach that takes seriously both the Old Testament's historical assertions and its obvious aesthetic quality (Long).

LYRIC POETRY

As a special idiom and mode of discourse, poetry occurs throughout vast parts of the Old Testament. Its traits are discussed in the introductory chapter on biblical poetry. In the context of the present chapter it is appropriate to note lyric poetry as one of the "second level" genres of the Old Testament.

Lyric poems are reflective or affective poems that express the personal thoughts and feelings of a speaker. Emotion is especially regarded as the differentia of such poems. Lyric poems are constructed on a three-part principle of introduction–development–resolution, and their unity can be formulated in terms of theme and variation.

Two books of the Old Testament are almost completely collections of lyric poems. The book of Psalms is an anthology of songs intended at least in part for religious worship in the temple. It expresses the feelings of the believing soul. The Song of Songs is an epithalamion (marriage poem) consisting of a series of lyric poems and fragments.

But we can also find lyric poems scattered throughout the historical narratives. Famous examples include Moses' song of victory at the Red Sea deliverance (Ex. 15:1–18), the Song of Deborah (Judg. 5), David's elegy for Saul and Jonathan (2 Sam. 1:17–27), Job's poem on wisdom (Job 28), Hezekiah's psalm of praise when his life was spared (Isa. 38:9–20), and Jonah's prayer while he was in the great fish (Jonah 2).

We should also observe that the ancient Hebrews mingled poetry and prose in a way that is unfamiliar to us. As a result, we must be prepared to find lyric outbursts at virtually any point in the Old Testament. When God brings Eve to Adam, Adam responds with four lines of lyric response (Gen. 2:23). When Lamech kills a young man in vengeance, the event is recorded in the form of Lamech's lyric fragment celebrating his exploit before his wives (4:23–24).

WISDOM

The subject matter of wisdom literature differs markedly from that of Old Testament history. The latter is vitally concerned with the history of God's dealings with his people, the covenant, and formal worship. Wisdom literature is marked by a virtual absence of all three. In the place of these topics, the wise men of Israel found insight in meditation upon creation, nature, and the relationships between men and women. Wisdom literature imparts knowledge concerning how to live life and how to deal with some of its more difficult aspects (such as suffering and doubt). The history of redemption is only occasionally mentioned. The wise man observes the workings of God's world and gives insights for living.

As a result, wisdom literature is very practical. It is related to biblical law in that it often speaks in imperatives, giving its readers direction in how to live their lives. It does not impart a knowledge full of facts so much as a skill in living.

The books of Proverbs, Ecclesiastes, Job, Song of Songs, and certain psalms (most notably 1 and 119) are traditionally categorized as wisdom. The Song of Songs is wisdom because, as a series of love poems, it teaches us about the intimacy of human marital love. Job is wisdom because it encourages faith in the light of suffering in the present evil world. Ecclesiastes warns against doubt and directs the reader to a simple belief in God. Of course, proverb after proverb spins out helpful observations about life and also gives instruction on how to live obediently.

The wisdom books are predominantly poetical, perhaps because they are not historically specific and also because the wisdom teachers appeal more to the emotions and imagination than do the historical books. While chapter 5 describes the conventions of Hebrew poetry at some depth (terseness, parallelism, imagery), here we will emphasize the fact that these books are more obviously literary than are the prose sections of the Bible. Since poetry is a highly artificial language (that is, filled with artifice), no one doubts its literary nature.

PROPHECY

Most readers equate prophecy with prediction. That is, they understand the prophet's mission to be totally preoccupied with the future. While there is no question that prophets look into the future, their ministry is rooted in the present. When they address the future in terms of judgment and/or salvation, they do so with a burning concern for the present. They want their contemporary audience to do something now, usually repent and turn back to God.

In their appeal to the hearts of their listeners/readers, they, like the wise teachers of Israel, speak and write in poetic forms, a mode of communication anticipated by an early description of the prophetic phenomenon in Israel:

When a prophet of the LORD is among you,
I reveal myself to him in vision,
I speak to him in dreams. (Num. 12:6)

We should thus not be surprised to find some of the most memorable and powerful imagery in the Bible produced by the prophets of Israel:

In the last days
the mountain of the LORD's temple will be established
as chief among the mountains;
it will be raised above the hills,
and peoples will stream to it. (Mic. 4:1)

> "In my vision I looked, and there before me were the four winds of heaven churning up the great sea. Four great beasts, each different from the others, came up out of the sea." (Dan. 7:2–3)

The historians, lyric poets, wisdom teachers, and prophets of Israel wrote to inform their audience about God and his relationship with his people. For the most part and with different levels of intensity, they wrote with a marked self-consciousness about their language. They were concerned not only with what they said but how they said it; the latter explains why a literary approach is so natural to the study of the Bible.

The Plot of the Old Testament

The Old Testament at first overwhelms the reader with diversity. There is prose and poetry, wisdom and prophecy, love poems and poetry that expresses anger. It is easy to miss the overall story of the Old Testament in the maze of individual stories. But a holistic reading reveals a story line that has a beginning, a middle, and the anticipation of an end.

The opening chapters introduce the main characters. The scene is the Garden of Eden. The cast of characters includes God and Adam and Eve, dwelling in perfect harmony. But there is also a fourth character, the serpent. It is the latter who introduces tension into the story by tempting the human characters to rebel against God. This plot conflict between God and the forces of evil continues and provides a "unity" to the plot of the Old Testament (Ryken 179).

The plot conflict begins in earnest immediately following the disobedience of Adam and Eve, when God curses the perpetrators, particularly the serpent, in a passage that has rightly received much attention through the centuries:

> *And I will put enmity*
> *between you and the woman,*
> *and between your offspring and hers;*
> *he will crush your head,*
> *and you will strike his heel. (Gen. 3:15)*

The rest of the book of Genesis, the rest of the Old Testament, and indeed the rest of the Bible, may be understood to flow from this verse. Conflict abounds in the Old Testament: between Cain and Abel, Jacob and Esau, Moses and Pharaoh, Israelites and Philistines, David and Goliath, prophets and apostate kings. But behind all of the individual stories is the story of how God creates, punishes, and protects his people. Thus, the Old Testament begins with creation, narrates the Fall, and continues with restoration. The Old Testament, however, is a story without closure. When it comes to an end with books like Daniel, Zechariah, and Malachi, God has restored his people to their land, but they live under the rule of a foreign superpower. The final note of the Old Testament is a note of longing, a longing for God's intervention to free his people from oppression and to bring them to their former glory.

Beckwith points out that the Protestant canon takes its clue from the tradition of the cessation of the prophets (1 Macc. 4:46; 9:27) and argues that the canon of the Old Testament comes to a close sometime during the period of Persian oppression and with this note of future expectation (369–76). The Christian tradition believes that the narrative continues with the Gospel and comes to a definitive literary conclusion in the book of Revelation, which narrates the restoration of the conditions of Eden.

More memorable than the episodes of the Old Testament are its characters. Even novice readers come away with a strong impression of its leading actors. Noah, Abraham, Joseph, Moses, Joshua, Deborah, David, Jezebel, Nebuchadnezzar, Nehemiah, Jeremiah, Daniel—just listing their names evokes strong emotions and vivid memories. The following chapters will focus on certain of these characters to illustrate in more detail how they function within the context of the stories of the Old Testament.

The Themes of the Old Testament

The coherence of the Old Testament is not simply a result of unity of plot but also of certain important literary themes that connect the disparate writings. Biblical scholars often discuss these themes under the category of biblical theology (Vos; VanGemeren), but they may also be understood as literary themes that network the writings of the Old Testament by means of intertextuality.

At the center of the Old Testament stands God. The common intention of each of the books of the Old Testament is to reveal Yahweh, the God of Israel. To be more specific, though, the Old Testament never presents God abstractly. He is always spoken of in relationship with his people. Further, the Bible most often describes this relationship in concrete and vivid figurative language. For example, God relates to his people as king, and as a king he enters into treaties (covenants) with his servant subjects, Israel. It is thus not surprising that one of the most pervasive and unifying themes of the Bible is the covenant (Robertson). But there are many other themes of relationship as well. God is a father, a mother, a husband, a wise teacher to his people Israel, and more.

For purposes of illustration, I will briefly describe two such themes, God as deliverer and God as warrior. Exodus through Deuteronomy provides a literary account of the Exodus from Egypt and the forty years of wilderness wanderings. These historical events become a metaphor of God's deliverance and are applied to later deliverances. Most notable in the Old Testament is the use that the prophets make of this theme as they anticipate the Exile and the eventual restoration of God's people. Hosea, for instance, sees the Exile as a new wilderness wandering that will lead eventually to a new entrance into the land, an entrance marked with more hope (notice the play on the Hebrew word *achor,* "trouble" [see Josh. 7:26]) than the first entrance under Joshua:

> *Therefore I am now going to allure her;*
> *I will lead her into the desert*
> *and speak tenderly to her.*

There I will give her back her vineyards,
and will make the Valley of Achor a door of hope.
There she will sing as in the days of her youth,
as in the day she came up out of Egypt. (2:14–15)

This passage is merely representative of an extensive use of this theme throughout the prophets, a use that continues into the New Testament Gospels, which describe Christ's ministry in terms clearly reminiscent of the Exodus. The epistle to the Hebrews sees the present Christian pilgrimage as a wilderness wandering that will come to an end when Christians cross the Jordan into their heavenly promised land (Stock).

A different example of a theme that ties together many of the writings of the Old Testament is the imagery associated with God as a warrior (Longman, "The Divine Warrior"; Longman and Reid). The theme's first explicit occurrence appears in Exodus 15:3:

The LORD is a warrior;
the LORD is his name.

Moses led Israel in this assertion of praise in the context of Israel's deliverance at the crossing of the Red Sea. He saved his people and judged the Egyptians in the same act. The Red Sea crossing is just one of a large number of occasions in the Old Testament in which God is pictured as a warrior who fights against Israel's enemies and also against disobedient Israel itself (Lam. 2:5–6). Toward the end of the Old Testament period, the prophets no longer see God working as warrior in their midst but expect a day to come when he will once again intervene to free them from the bondage they were experiencing under the hands of the Babylonians and later the Persians (Dan. 7; Zech. 14). Nearly every book of the Old Testament in some way presents God as a warrior. Exceptions are mostly short books (Ruth, Jonah) or wisdom books (Ecclesiastes, Song of Songs). The theme continues into the New Testament, which pictures Christ's death and resurrection as a military victory over the spiritual forces of darkness (Col. 2:15) and anticipates his coming as the final divine warrior (Rev. 19:11–21).

Reading the Old Testament

The Old Testament is a fascinating anthology of writings produced over a millennium in a culture distant from that of the modern world. The contemporary reader must be flexible in reading strategy in order to interpret its different parts with integrity. The writers of the following chapters intend to explore and explicate the history, wisdom, poetry, and prophecy of the Old Testament from a literary perspective.

Even when we have read the entire Old Testament, however, a sense of incompleteness remains. Unlike the New Testament, with its book of Revelation, there is no sense of closure in the Old Testament. The Masoretic Text ends with the book of Chronicles, whose story line continues within the Hebrew Bible itself (Ezra–Nehemiah). The arrangement of the Christian canon (based on the Septuagint and Vulgate) concludes with Malachi and a look beyond the Old Testament:

> See, I will send you the prophet Elijah before that great and dreadful day of the LORD comes. He will turn the hearts of the fathers to their children, and the hearts of the children to their fathers; or else I will come and strike the land with a curse. (4:5–6)

WORKS CITED

Alter, Robert. "A Response to Critics." *Journal for the Study of the Old Testament* 27 (1983): 113–17.

Beckwith, R. *The Old Testament Canon of the New Testament Church.* London: SPCK, 1985.

Fokkelman, J. P. *Narrative Art in Genesis.* Assen/Amsterdam: Van Gorcum, 1975.

Hempfer, K. *Gattungstheorie.* Munich: W. Funk, 1973.

Kugel, James L. *The Idea of Biblical Poetry.* New Haven: Yale UP, 1981.

Levine, B. A. *Leviticus.* JPS Torah Commentary. Philadelphia: Jewish Publication Society, 1989.

Long, V. Philips. *The Reign and Rejection of King Saul: A Case for Literary and Theological Coherence.* Atlanta: Scholars Press, 1989.

Longman, Tremper, III. *Literary Approaches to Biblical Interpretation.* Foundations of Contemporary Interpretation 3. Grand Rapids: Zondervan, 1987.

———. "The Divine Warrior: The New Testament Use of an Old Testament Motif." *Westminster Theological Journal* (1982): 290–307.

Longman, Tremper, III, and Daniel Reid. *The Divine Warrior.* Grand Rapids: Zondervan, forthcoming.

Milgrom, Jacob. *Numbers.* JPS Torah Commentary. Philadelphia: Jewish Publication Society, 1990.

Preminger, Alex, and Edward L. Greenstein, ed. *The Hebrew Bible in Literary Criticism.* New York: Ungar, 1986.

Prickett, Stephen. *Words and The Word: Language, Poetics, and Biblical Interpretation.* Cambridge: Cambridge UP, 1986.

Robertson, O. Palmer. *The Christ of the Covenants.* Grand Rapids: Baker, 1980.

Ryken, Leland. *How to Read the Bible as Literature.* Grand Rapids: Zondervan, 1984.

Sternberg, Meir. *The Poetics of Biblical Narrative.* Bloomington: Indiana UP, 1985.

Stock, A. *The Way in the Wilderness.* Collegeville, Minn.: Liturgical Press, 1969.

VanGemeren, Willem A. *The Progress of Redemption: The Story of Salvation From Creation to the New Jerusalem.* Grand Rapids: Zondervan, 1988.
Vos, Geerhardus. *Biblical Theology: Old and New Testament.* Grand Rapids: Eerdmans, 1948.
Zerafa, P. P. *The Wisdom of God in the Book of Job.* Rome: Herder, 1978.

CHAPTER 7

Genesis

John H. Sailhamer
Trinity Evangelical Divinity School

The book of Genesis is the Bible's "book of beginnings," as its very title in the English Bible suggests. Structurally the book falls into two distinct and unequal parts. Chapters 1–11 are primeval history, beginning with the story of the regression of the human race from its creation and original perfection to its fall from innocence in Paradise. The downward spiral of evil subsequently reaches two climactic judgments from God—the Flood as a punishment for the moral corruptness of the human race, and dispersal after the folly at Babylon. Chapters 12–50 then proceed to tell the story of patriarchal history, which is at the same time the story of the origin of the nation of Israel. The key figures are Abraham, Isaac, Jacob, and Joseph.

The most obvious genre at work in Genesis is heroic narrative. In one sense, Genesis is a collection of hero stories—stories built around the representative and exemplary life of a protagonist whose experience reenacts the conflicts and celebrates the values of the community producing the stories. Heroes capture the popular imagination and focus a culture's self-awareness, and the heroes of Genesis are no exception. Martin Luther caught the heroic spirit of the book when he wrote that the patriarchs were "the heroes, as it were, of the entire world" (354). Each of the hero stories that constitute the book of Genesis has its distinctive emphasis and flavor. Adam and Eve are the prototypical parents of the human race and the archetypal sinners. Noah is a solitary person of integrity in an evil age and the agent of God's rescue for the human race. Abraham's story is the story of a quest for a son and a land and of the spiritual conflicts and growth that this quest generates. The story of Jacob tells of a self-reliant trickster's struggle to become a godly person. Joseph's life reenacts the pattern of the suffering servant whose personal misfortunes bring about redemption for others.

But the book of Genesis is more than an anthology of hero stories: it is also an epic. Tolstoy called it "the epic of Genesis" (452), and Erich Auerbach, comparing Genesis to Homer's *Odyssey,* regarded it as being "equally epic" (7). Genesis is epic because it is a story of national destiny, recounting the story of the ancestors of the nation of Israel. The plot recounts a familiar epic feat of the formation of a nation under divine providence. Equally epic is the way in which Genesis contains the early chapters in the overarching story of the Bible that biblical scholars have taught us to call salvation history—the history of God's providence, judgment, and redemption in his dealings with the human race.

Genesis is not, of course, a wholly typical epic. It substitutes a sequence of heroes for the single hero who usually unifies an epic. More important, it is a domestic and pastoral epic (Northrop Frye correctly speaks of "the pastoral era of the patriarchs" [170]). The great scenes of Genesis do not occur on the battlefield but in the family. Its heroes are not international figures but domestic ones. Hermann Gunkel noted that "the material of Genesis . . . contains no accounts of great political events, but treats rather the history of a family" (5). The heroes' quests are domestic and spiritual, not political.

A Monument to Our Humanity

Genesis illustrates to perfection G. K. Chesterton's view that "there is such a thing as the divine story which is also a human story" (246). Before we look at the theological orientation of the book, something deserves to be said about the sheer humanity of the stories we find in Genesis. Genesis is a book of elemental human experience. Its settings, for example, put us into an elemental world of hill and valley, stream and desert, rocks and grass, sky and stars. Vocation has the same elemental quality, with people reduced to such universal categories as tiller of the ground, shepherd, hunter, ruler, homemaker. The roles that characters fill also have a simplified primitive quality—husband, wife, parent, child, ruler, servant.

Everywhere we turn in Genesis, we find our own experiences highlighted. Perhaps this is why literary authors have taken more from Genesis than any other book of the Bible (Warshaw/Miller). Anyone who has taught these stories knows how strongly people resonate with them and how difficult it is to move beyond the book in a classroom survey of the Bible.

Part of the humanity of Genesis consists of what literary people call realism—the unexpurgated portrayal of human life at its sordid worst. Genesis is a shocking book. In it we find magnified images of sin—stories of sibling rivalry, family conflict, hatred, rape, incest, sexual perversion, deceit, and a host of other destructive behaviors. The characters of Genesis are portrayed as Cromwell wished to be painted—warts and all. Franz Delitzsch said about the patriarchs of Genesis that they are so deeply flawed "there is almost more shadow than light in them. . . . Their faults are the foil to their greatness with respect to the history of redemption" (275–76).

But we also find heightened images of virtue in Genesis. Half of the roll call of heroes of faith in Hebrews 11 comes from the pages of Genesis—worshipful Abel, righteous Noah, obedient Abraham, fruitful Sarah, and promise-expecting Isaac, Jacob, and Joseph. If the book of Genesis gives us memorable images of evil—the Fall, the corrupt earth destroyed by the Flood, Babel, Sodom and Gomorrah, a despised brother sold into slavery—it also gives us heightened images of good—the perfect creation, Paradise the perfect garden, covenant, altar, rainbow, Abraham's willingness to offer Isaac on a mountain, Jacob's being blessed by an angelic wrestler, Joseph's refusal to give in to sexual temptation, and his reconciliation with his brothers.

Genesis is more than a monument to our humanity, but it is not less. Writes one literary critic, "Genesis is not only the beginning of the Bible but the beginning of the biblical process: that record of our humanity at its worst, best, most mediocre, and most noble" (Roche 3).

But of course Genesis is more than a human story and more than an anthology of hero stories. It is a consciously composed and intricately structured whole in which language is used to portray the world from a specific religious perspective. The strategies employed by the author to create that world will occupy the rest of this chapter.

The Narrative World of Genesis

An essential feature of biblical narrative is its ability to "mimic" the real world, that is, to reproduce a real world in linguistic form. It is easy to overlook this characteristic by simply taking it for granted. Although the biblical authors were clearly interested in the "lessons" embodied in the stories they wrote, their first, more fundamental, concern was the depiction of a world in which those lessons made consummate sense. They were not merely depicting a view of the world. They were at one and the same time creating the world they were depicting. By representing reality in their narratives, they were defining its essential characteristics. This is surely not to say they were making it up. There is every reason to maintain that the world we find depicted in these narratives was, in fact, intended by them to be identified as the real world.

A biblical narrative text takes the raw material of language and shapes it into a version of the world of empirical reality. Its essentially linguistic structures are adapted to conform to events in everyday life—e.g., the limitations of time, space, and perspective--in order to present events and characters before the reader as happening *just as they happen in everyday life.* Readers thus look at the events in the narrative in much the same way as they would look on events in real life. Events happen in the text before one's eyes. As Emile Benveniste has put it, "The events are chronologically recorded as they appear on the horizon of the story. . . . The events seem to tell themselves" (Benveniste, quoted in White 7).

Most traditional Christians and Jews will be quite familiar with the world we find depicted in the Bible. Indeed it can be argued that until very recently the biblical world was the sole contender for the Western world's conceptualization of reality, at least in the popular mind. This very familiarity with the world presented in the Bible, however, can also be an obstacle to our appreciation of the role that the Bible has had, and indeed should have, in our world today. A fuller understanding of the literary strategies of biblical narrative can be of great service in this venture. It helps us to see not simply this or that lesson taught by the Bible; it also provides the means for appreciating and applying the basic structure of the biblical world to contemporary life. My interest in this chapter is not the lessons about God and people taught in the Bible. My concern is rather directed to aspects of the world depicted for us in the Bible.

Although there are many aspects of the narrative world presented to us in the book of Genesis that merit our attention, I will focus on two: divine causality and divine retribution. Not only do these two notions pervade the Genesis narratives; they are also the two aspects of these narratives that seem most out of place in the modern world.

Why does the Pentateuch begin the way it does? Why not begin with the list of laws given at Mount Sinai? Why begin with a narrative of God's creating the world? Rabbinical commentaries were particularly concerned with this question, in large measure because they saw the Sinai laws as central to the purpose of the Pentateuch. If the Torah was about law, why did it not begin with a discussion of the law? The answer given by Rashi shows remarkable appreciation for the role that these narratives play in the purpose of the writer: "If the nations of the world should say to Israel, 'You are thieves because you have stolen the land of the Canaanites,' they may reply, 'All the earth belongs to God. He made it and gives it to whomever he pleases'" (Shual 1–2). The purpose of the Creation narrative is not only to teach religious truth, though it allows for that, but also to establish a claim about the nature of the world and God's relationship to it. He made the world. It is thus his world, and he can do with it what he pleases.

Thus from the very beginning the narrative defines the nature of the real world it depicts. It is a world in which God is an active agent. It is his world, and one who lives in that world must reckon with him. Of course there is the possibility that people will fail to acknowledge the divine presence, and thus throughout the book of Genesis the reader is continually reminded of the consequence of failing to reckon with the presence of God in the world. A number of the stories in the book seem specifically directed toward establishing this fact: the fall of humankind (Gen. 3), the Flood account (Gen. 6–9), the confusion of languages in the city of Babylon (Gen. 11), and the destruction of the cities of Sodom and Gomorrah (Gen. 19).

We find in these narratives a virtual chain of events depicting a world governed by a God who holds the people of his world responsible for their actions. In this world, "chance" is just another way to speak of divine causality, as in the story of Abraham's servant seeking a bride for Isaac (Gen. 24:12). Literally the servant prays, "O Lord, cause a chance to happen today," and "before he had finished speaking" it happened (24:15). This is a world very different from the world of modern thought, but it is a world that the biblical narratives present to us and challenge us to accept as our own.

Narrative Technique and the Construction of "Reality"

Of many narrative techniques present in Genesis, I will concentrate on three: recursion, contemporization, and foreshadowing.

The narrative technique of "recursion" is the author's deliberate shaping of narrative events so that key elements of one narrative are repeated in others. The cumulative effect of such stories is the sense that the whole of the real world has a shape and order that is reflected in the shape and order of the biblical narratives. An example of recursion in the Genesis narratives can be seen in the way in which the story of the restoration of the land after the great Flood (Gen. 7:24–9:17) follows the same pattern and order as the earlier account of Creation in Genesis 1:

	Creation Account	*Flood Account*
1.	And darkness was over the face of the deep (1:2)	And the sources of the great deep were broken up (7:11)
2.	"And let the dry land appear" (1:9)	And the tops of the mountains appeared (8:5)
3.	"Let the land bring forth vegetation" (1:11–12)	There in its beak was a freshly plucked olive leaf (8:11)
4.	"They shall be for signs and seasons, days and years" (1:14)	On the first day of the first month . . . (8:13f.)
5.	And God said, "Let the land bring out the living creatures" (1:24)	And God said, . . . "And bring out the creatures" (8:17)
6.	And God blessed them saying, "Be fruitful and multiply and fill the land" (1:22)	And God said, "Be fruitful and multiply upon the land" (8:17)
7.	"Let us make man" (1:26)	And Noah came out (8:18)
8.	And God blessed them and said to them, "Be fruitful and multiply and fill the land" (1:28)	And God blessed Noah . . . and said to them, "Be fruitful and multiply and fill the land" (9:1)
9.	"And rule over the fish of the sea" (1:28b)	". . . and among all the fish of the sea, they are given into your hands" (9:2)
10.	And God said, "Behold, I give to you . . . for food" (1:29)	"To you it shall be for food" (9:3)

The implication of such similarities and recursions in narrative structure is that the world depicted by these narratives also has this same design and purpose. Furthermore, the fact that the author of the Pentateuch has appended to the Flood account the short narrative of Noah's drunkenness

(9:18–27) further suggests a divine design and plan to the events recounted in the narrative. It does so because the narrative of Noah's drunkenness closely emulates the earlier account of the Fall (Gen. 2–3), thereby becoming an example of recursion:

The Fall (Genesis 2–3)	*Noah's Drunkenness* (Genesis 9:20ff.)
1. And the Lord God planted a garden . . . and put the man there (2:8)	And Noah planted an orchard (9:20)
2. And she took from the tree and ate (3:6)	And he drank from the wine and became drunk (9:21)
3. And they knew that they were naked (3:7)	And he uncovered himself in the midst of the tent (9:21)
4. And they made clothing for themselves (3:7)	And they covered the nakedness of their father (9:23)
5. And their eyes were open and they knew that they were naked (3:7)	And Noah woke up from his sleep and he knew what his young son had done (9:24)
6. "Cursed are you" (3:14)	"Cursed is Canaan" (9:25)
7. Cain, Abel, and Seth (4:1–2, 25)	Shem, Ham, and Japheth (9:25–27)

These examples show that a major aspect of the meaning of the biblical narratives lies fundamentally in the patterns of divine purpose that they infuse into our understanding of the world. According to Hans Frei, the effect of these narratives on the readers of Scripture has been appreciated by countless generations of readers:

> Christian preachers and theological commentators, Augustine the most notable among them, had envisioned the real world as formed by the sequence told by the biblical stories. That temporal world covered the span of ages from creation to the final consummation to come, and included the governance both of man's natural environment and of that secondary environment which we often think of as provided for man by himself and call "history" or "culture." (1, 13)

A second narrative trait of Genesis is contemporization, meaning that the past is often portrayed in light of events and institutions of the present. For example, the narrative of Cain and Abel (Gen. 4:1–24), the first case of manslaughter in the Bible, is cast along the same lines as the last case, that is, the provisions for the cities of refuge at the end of the Pentateuch (Num. 35:9–34; Deut. 19:11–13). In each of these narratives God gives the same provision for protection against the "avenger of blood," that is, a city in which there is the rule of law. The writer would have us see that the same God is at work throughout all of history.

This same technique is surely at work in the portrayal of Abraham's battle with the four kings from the east in Genesis 14. As the details of the narrative show, when Abraham battles the kings of the East, he follows the provisions later laid down in Deuteronomy 20 for the conduct of war with nations afar off. Moreover, his response to the king of Sodom in the same chapter matches what would be expected of one from Deuteronomy 20 (Sailhamer 122ff.). The pattern of the narrative thus reinforces the reader's understanding of the world as itself in conformity with the plan and purpose of God. People who are like Abraham in walking with God find themselves at home in God's world.

Third, the narratives in Genesis recount events in such a way as to foreshadow and anticipate later events. This technique differs from recursion noted above in that foreshadowing anticipates fulfillment and not mere repetition of the past. By means of foreshadowing, central themes are developed and continually drawn to the reader's attention, with the result that a further sense of purpose is added to the reader's understanding of events. The sense of the biblical narratives is not only that God and his plan are at work in the history recounted in them but also that this history has a goal. The "first things" anticipate the fulfillment of the "last things."

For example, the account of Abraham's entry into the land of Canaan is notably selective. Only three sites in the land are mentioned, and at these sites Abraham built an altar—at Shechem (12:6), between Bethel and Ai (12:8), and in the Negev (12:9). As Cassuto has pointed out, it can hardly be accidental that these are the same three locations visited by Jacob when he returns to Canaan from Haran (Gen. 34–35), as well as the sites occupied in the conquest of the land under Joshua (Josh. 1–11). Jacob and Joshua built altars at these very same sites.

A small narrative segment that has attracted an extraordinary amount of attention over the years is the account of Abraham's visit to Egypt in Genesis 12:10–20. The similarities between this narrative and those of Genesis 20 and 26 are well known. Such similarities are best seen as part of the larger typological scheme of these narratives, intended to show that future events in God's world are often foreshadowed by events from the past. This can also be seen from a comparison between Genesis 12:10–20 and the large narrative unit that deals with the Israelites' sojourn in Egypt (Gen. 41–Ex. 12). The following chart suggests that the composition of Genesis 12:10–20 has been intentionally structured to prefigure or foreshadow the events of Israel's sojourn in Egypt:

12:10	There was a famine in the land	41:54	There was a famine in all the lands
12:11	When he drew near to go into Egypt . . .	46:28	When they came toward the land of Goshen . . .
12:11	He said to Sarai his wife	46:31	Joseph said to his brothers
12:11	"I know that . . ."	46:31	"I will go up and say to Pharaoh . . ."
12:12	"And it shall come to pass when the Egyptians see you, they will say . . ."	46:33	"And it shall come to pass when Pharaoh calls you, he will say . . ."
12:13	"Say . . ."	46:34	"Say . . ."
12:13	"That it may be well with me on account of you"	46:34	"That you may dwell in the land of Goshen"
12:13	And the officers of Pharaoh saw her and declared it to Pharaoh	47:1	And Joseph came and declared to Pharaoh . . .
12:15	And the wife was taken into the house of Pharaoh	47:5	And Pharaoh said, . . . "Settle your father and brothers in the best part of the land"
12:15	And Abraham acquired sheep and cattle	47:6	"Put them in charge of my livestock"
		47:27	They acquired property and were fruitful and increased greatly
12:17	And the Lord struck Pharaoh with great diseases	Ex. 11:1	"One more plague I will bring against Pharaoh"
12:18	And Pharaoh called to Abram and said . . .	12:31	And Pharaoh called to Moses and Aaron and said . . .
12:19	"Take . . . and go"	12:32	"Take . . . and go"
12:20	and sent them away	12:33	to send them away

13:1	And Abram went up from Egypt toward the Negev	12:37	And the sons of Israel traveled from Rameses toward Succoth
13:1	And Lot went with him	12:38	And also a great mixed multitude went with him
13:2	And Abram was very rich with livestock,	12:38	And they had very much livestock,
	silver, and gold	12:35	silver, and gold
13:4	(Returned to the altar and worshiped God)	12:11	(The Passover)

It seems clear that a "narrative typology" lies behind the composition of these texts. The author wants to show that the events of the past are pointers to those of the future.

The Joseph Narrative

There is no story in the Pentateuch more primed to show the work of God in the world than that of the Joseph narrative. Not only in the narration of the story itself, but also in the dialogue and conversation of the characters, the work of God in the world is the central topic. It is not that the story itself is intent on "teaching" this lesson as an item of dogma or religious knowledge. The purpose is rather to portray the world as the kind of place in which God's will is accomplished regardless of human efforts to the contrary.

As with our discussion of the Genesis narratives generally, two aspects of the narrative world of the Joseph story deserve special attention—divine causality and divine retribution. It is impossible to read the story without seeing that God is actively at work in the world he is depicting. This is brought out by four primary techniques of dialogue—thematization in dialogue, motivation in dialogue, summary in dialogue, and scripted dialogue.

Throughout the narrative, the dialogue of key characters gives expression to the notion of divine causality. This is thematization in dialogue. For example, Joseph says to Pharaoh, "The reason the dream was given to Pharaoh in two forms is that the matter has been firmly decided by God, and God will do it soon" (41:32). Joseph's steward says to the brothers, "The God of your father has given you treasure" (43:23). The reader knows that the steward's words cannot be taken seriously. There has been no mention of money given to the steward. Nevertheless, his words echo the thrust of the narrative and the major themes of the book.

Dialogue is also used to exhibit motivation, which sets the events of the story in motion and provides a guide to its plot and resolution. When key characters speak in the Joseph narratives, their words become programmatic of the events that follow. Jacob, sending his sons to Egypt, declares, "Go down there . . . so that we may live and not die" (42:2). As the story unfolds, these words prove definitive for the outcome of the narrative, as the lives of the sons of Jacob are spared in Egypt. The echo of Jacob's words can be seen in those of Joseph: "It was to save lives that God sent me" (45:5). Through such dialogue that attributes motivation to events the work of God is shown to be an essential part of the course of events recounted in the narrative.

Similarly, Joseph's brothers say to him in a fit of jealousy, "Do you intend to reign over us?" (37:8). Their words anticipate the central events of the narrative that follows. At the conclusion of the story we are brought back to the picture of Joseph's brothers bowing down to him (42:6), as we are told that at that moment Joseph "remembered his dreams about them" (v. 9).

Summary in dialogue occurs when key characters summarize the central thesis of the story. At the close of the story, Joseph says to his brothers, "It was to save lives that God sent me ahead of you" (45:5). Thus, though the brothers were responsible for Joseph's being sold into Egypt, and though they intended to do him harm, Joseph's words show us that God was ultimately behind it all and had worked it out for good (cf. 50:20).

We can also speak of scripted dialogue in the story. Throughout the story of Joseph, lesser characters speak lines that prove far more important than their sense in the immediate context. Their "off the cuff" remarks appear as if scripted for the larger occasion of the story. In the words of the cupbearer, for example, the reader's attention is redirected to the earlier event of Joseph's interpretation of dreams in prison. The cupbearer says of him, "Things turned out exactly as he interpreted them to us" (41:13). As it turns out, even the cupbearer's forgetfulness worked in Joseph's favor since, just at the opportune moment, he remembered Joseph and recounted his wisdom before the king. By drawing the reader's attention to the events of the previous passage, both the wisdom of Joseph and the divine causality of the events are expressed.

When we turn from the motif of divine causality to that of divine retribution, we find some of the same uses of dialogue, beginning with thematization in dialogue. The Joseph story shows that through Joseph's own schemes his brothers came to an awareness of their guilt and they were ready to acknowledge it. Toward the end of the story their utter frustration finds expression in their question, "What can we say?" (44:16). Then comes the expression of their guilt: "How can we show ourselves to be right?" Within the logic of the narrative, the rhetorical answer to these questions is an implied negative: "We have nothing to say, we cannot show ourselves to be right." Thus the conclusion that the brothers are forced to draw is, "God has found the iniquity of your servants" (v. 16).

Although we can clearly see that the brothers have only the immediate issue of the lost cup in mind, within the compass of the whole of the Joseph narrative their words take on the scope of the much broader confession of their former guilt as well. As readers we know that the brothers have not taken the cup and are thus innocent here. Joseph had it put into Benjamin's sack. We also know that the brothers know they did not take the cup. Thus when they speak of God's "finding out their guilt" (44:16), we are forced to generalize their sense of guilt within the context of the narrative as a whole. The author leads us to read their words with a broader significance than they might have intended on that occasion. We see the narrative interconnections that were not a part of their own understanding within the situation itself.

Divine retribution also emerges through scripted dialogue. The words of the brothers when they discover that their money has been returned to them in their grain sacks almost inadvertently expresses the notion of divine causality. When each saw his own money returned, he asked, "What is this that God has done to us?" (42:28). Whatever the brothers might have meant by it, in the logic of the narrative their words have an ironic ring of truth. Though we know it was Joseph who had the money put back into their sacks, their words point us to the work of God, serving to confirm the direction the narrative as a whole appears to be taking. God is at work in the schemes of Joseph, and we are allowed to see in this narrative a preliminary reminder of the ultimate theme: "God meant it for good" (50:20).

WORKS CITED

Auerbach, Erich. *Mimesis: The Representation of Reality in Western Literature.* Trans. Willard Trask. Princeton: Princeton UP, 1953.

Calvin, John. *Institutes of the Christian Religion.* Vol. 1. Philadelphia: Westminster, 1973.

Cassuto, Umberto. *Encyclopedia Biblica.* Vol. 1. Jerusalem: Bialik Institute, 1955.

Chesterton, G. K. *The Everlasting Man.* 1925. Rpt. Garden City: Image Books, 1955.

Delitzsch, Franz. *A New Commentary on Genesis.* Vol. 2. Trans. Sophia Taylor. Edinburgh: T. and T. Clark, 1894.

Frei, Hans W. *The Eclipse of Biblical Narrative, A Study in Eighteenth and Nineteenth Century Hermeneutics.* New Haven: Yale UP, 1974.

Frye, Northrop. *The Great Code: The Bible and Literature.* New York: Harcourt, 1982.

Gunkel, Hermann. *The Legends of Genesis.* Trans. W. H. Carruth. 1901. Rpt. New York: Schocken Books, 1964.

Luther, Martin. *Luther's Works.* Vol. 1. Ed. Jaroslav Pelikan. St. Louis: Concordia, 1958.

Roche, Paul, ed. *The Bible's Greatest Stories.* New York: Mentor, 1990.

Sailhamer, John. "Genesis." *Expositor's Bible Commentary*. Vol. 2. Grand Rapids: Zondervan, 1990.

Shual, Chaim Dov. *The Commentary of Rashi on the Torah* (in Hebrew). Jerusalem: Mossad Harav Kook, 1988.

Tolstoy, Leo. "What Is Art?" *Criticism: The Major Statements*. Ed. Charles Kaplan. New York: St. Martin's, 1975. 451–63.

Warshaw, Thayer S., and Betty Lou Miller. *Bible-Related Curriculum Materials: A Bibliography*. Nashville: Abingdon, 1976.

White, Hayden. "The Value of Narrativity in the Representation of Reality." *Critical Inquiry* 7 (1980): 5–27.

CHAPTER 8

Exodus, Leviticus, Numbers, and Deuteronomy

WILSON G. BAROODY AND WILLIAM F. GENTRUP
Arizona State University

The life of Moses, from his birth and early years in the opening of Exodus to his death and legacy at the close of Deuteronomy, provides the narrative frame for most of the Pentateuch. As distinguished from Genesis, which encompasses a human history of at least four thousand years, these four monumental books, after the first two chapters of Exodus, span a period of only forty years, from Moses' calling at age 80 until his death at age 120.

A marvelous collection of narrative and law is concentrated within this time frame. Nothing short of an epiclike birth and odyssey of a nation, achieved by the divine agency of spectacular miracles, is recounted here. Its whole legal and religious constitution is also included, a narrative strategy that is roughly equivalent to setting a country's legislative and theological principles within the biography of its founder. Through its fascinating combination of story and statute, these books, anticipating Horace, teach and delight simultaneously. The events of Moses' life and the emergence of Israel into nationhood are presented as a series of encounters and dialogues with God, whose main plan, through personal revelation in the form of miracles and laws, is to restore his people to the divine image and companionship of creation (Gen. 1:26–27; 3:8–9).

Literary critics with a background in Western literature tend to view these books, especially Exodus, as an epic (at least epiclike) and to compare them to the *Iliad,* the *Odyssey,* the *Aeneid,* and *Paradise Lost.* Richard Moulton, whose *Literary Study of the Bible* in its 1895 and 1899 editions can justly be regarded as the first major modern work emphasizing purely literary analysis of the Bible, is associated with this view. Its most persuasive advocate is Leland Ryken, who detects in Exodus the epic conventions of a journey and founding of a nation, supernatural intervention and machinery, a central national hero, a basis in history, the values and experiences of an entire society, and what he calls "type scenes" and "high style" (*Words* 127–35; see also *Literature*). As an epic hero Moses best parallels Virgil's Aeneas: both figures require divine persuasion to obey their calling to found a nation, both continually receive divine direction, and both perform religious worship. The most recent tendency, however, has been to follow Robert Alter's *Art of Biblical Narrative* (1981) in considering narrative without comparison to classical epic (see also Sternberg).

Both the Romans and the Hebrews were also known for their fully developed legal systems. A major difference, however, is that the national epic of the Romans is wholly narrative; its laws must be found in separate official documents, whereas the story of the founding of the Hebrew nation is replete with law, so much so that the traditional understanding of the Pentateuch as books of instruction (i.e., Torah) neglected its narrative features. It is the significant contribution of modern critics to have called attention to the literary quality of Hebrew narrative, which, nevertheless, some have regarded as primarily a framework for the presentation of law.

Narrative and Law

The books of Exodus, Numbers, Leviticus, and Deuteronomy certainly do constitute a marvelous unity of narrative and legislative genres, a fusion expressing indirectly the biblical axiom that principles and actions are inseparable. Earlier combinations occur in the creation and patriarchal accounts in Genesis, but the pattern is particularly developed in these latter four books, in which the juridical often predominates.

Literary critics of biblical and Jewish literature, such as Edward Greenstein (84) and Barry Holtz ("Midrash" 178–79), have increasingly recognized the interrelationship between these seemingly distinct genres. The point is perhaps more easily understood when Torah or law is translated "instruction" or "teaching." Joel Rosenburg describes how narrative is frequently "a didactic prop for the laws" and how laws often appear as "events" in the narrative (65). David Damrosch considers this mixture in the Pentateuch "the most important generic innovation of its age" (*Narrative Covenant* 35–37). This hybrid genre sometimes adds poetry (e.g., Ex. 15; Deut. 32) and prophecy (e.g., Ex. 34:11–17; Lev. 26:32–46; Deut. 18:15). Other scholars focus on distinct genres. Leland Ryken identifies Exodus 1–20 and 32–34, Numbers 10–14 and 20–24, and Deuteronomy 10 and 34 as the "main narrative sections" (*Words* 130). Leonard Thompson recognizes the acknowledged law codes as Exodus 20–23, 25–31, and 34:10–27, all of Leviticus, and Deuteronomy 12–26 (154).

EXODUS

Reflecting this broader pattern in the four books, there are two main parts to Exodus: the primary narrative (chs. 1–19) describing Moses' early life and calling, the ten plagues and subsequent liberation from Egyptian bondage, and the journey to Mount Sinai; and the legal material pertaining to the giving of the Ten Commandments and to tabernacle worship (chs. 20–40). Each part contains insertions of the other genre, mixing storytelling and lawgiving. J. P. Fokkelman outlines the major alternations of these (56–58).

The combination of the tenth plague and Passover is a clear example. The narrative first announces the certain deaths of the firstborn of humans and livestock (ch. 11), except of those who observe the elaborate instructions of Passover. YHWH's people must take an unblemished lamb one-year old and roast and eat it with unleavened bread and bitter herbs. On this first occasion, they must apply the lamb's blood to the doorposts and lintels of their dwellings and consume the meal after clothing and preparing themselves for immediate departure from Egypt. These and other details are to be observed in perpetuity (12:1–28).

The rest of the account shifts back to narrating the terrible fulfillment of the plague on the Egyptians and the Israelites' flight from the land (12:29–42) but returns briefly at the end to proscriptions against the participation of uncircumcised "foreigners" or "strangers" in the Passover. This is a logical digression, since for the first time in at least eighty years Israel was liberated from slavery to the uncircumcised. Laws for consecrating the firstborn follow, inserted here rather than being included with subsequent ones because the tenth plague was based on the value of the firstborn (13:1–2, 11–16). After the Passover account, the Exodus begins, signaled by a return to narrative. The pursuing Egyptians destroyed at the Red Sea, the miracle supplies of manna and water, the war with Amalek, the appointment of judges on Jethro's advice, and the arrival at Sinai are then recounted (chs. 16–19).

The second part of Exodus focuses on legal instructions, beginning when the Lord dispenses the Ten Commandments (20:1–20) and the "Book of the Covenant" (20:21–23:33), a series of laws that clarifies the Decalogue and begins and ends with prescriptions about worship that anticipate those related to the building and equipping of the tabernacle (25–31, 35–40). Within these passages there are also alternations between narrative and legislative material. Just as the primarily narrative first half of Exodus had been interrupted by the lengthy legislative Passover section, so, conversely, the primarily legal second half is relieved by the story of the idolatry of the golden calf (chs. 32–34).

The episode dovetails well with the material that precedes and follows it, namely, the instructions for proper tabernacle worship (chs. 25–31) and their later repetition in the construction narrative (chs. 35–40). The topic of true worship unifies each segment. Although the Hebrews have been liberated from Egypt and have experienced other miracles, they readily seek to worship another god. While Moses is on Mount Sinai receiving the instructions for the tabernacle, the people revolt and command Aaron, "Make us gods." Ironically, the gold and silver used for the image, part of the spoils taken from the Egyptians, were intended for the furnishing of the tabernacle (36:2–7). The jewelry specified, earrings, symbolizes the people's failure to use their ears properly in hearing YHWH's words as they promised (19:7–8).

In contrast to the detailed account of the tabernacle, Aaron makes the calf very quickly—in less than a sentence: "I cast it [the gold] into the fire, and there came out this calf" (Josipovici's translation, 97). (Aaron's passive posture and self-defensive tone, Gabriel Josipovici observes, recalls that of Adam blaming his fall on Eve [97].) The figure of the idol recalls the cattle that had such a prominent role in the conflict with Pharaoh, who refused to let the Israelites leave Egypt to sacrifice properly to YHWH (Ex. 3:18; 5:3–17; 8:8–29) and anticipates the calf idol of Jeroboam (1 Kings 12:25–33).

Although the account of the fashioning of the false image is terse, "the narrative lovingly lingers on every detail of the making of the Tabernacle" (Josipovici 96–97; see also his whole treatment of the subject, 90–107). The earlier call in Egypt to proper worship is consummated at the close of Exodus when the tabernacle has been built and the Lord's presence inhabits it. The account represents the lengthiest use of repeated description in the Pentateuch or any book of the Bible, rivaled only by the related one of the temple of Solomon, first commanded to David (2 Sam. 7; 17:1–15; 28:11–29; 1 Chron. 21:28–22:19) and later constructed by Solomon (1 Kings 5–8; 2 Chron. 2–7).

The description of the tabernacle moves from the interior to the exterior. First described is the Holy of Holies with its ark, tablets of the Ten

Commandments, cherubim, and mercy seat; then the features of the Holy Place, the table of shewbread, lampstand, and altar of incense; and finally the outer court with its bronze altar. When repeating all this information in the actual construction, the account switches to a narrative format (chs. 35–40). Thus, the repeated third-person perspective: "he [or, 'they'] did . . . as the Lord had commanded Moses." This second version has an exterior-to-interior organization. The building of the whole tabernacle is described first, then its smaller units, such as the inner sanctuary. This is, of course, the reverse of the original instructions, a pattern of repetition that results in a chiastic structure for chapters 20–40, the description of Holy of Holies–exterior courts–exterior courts–Holy of Holies.

By ending with the construction of the tabernacle, the book of Exodus concludes precisely in contrast to its beginning. Whereas in Egypt the Israelites were enslaved, with no opportunity to worship their God, now they are free and able to serve him. The penultimate words of the book fittingly encapsulate what has been the goal of all the building effort: "So Moses finished the work. Then a cloud covered the tent, and the glory of the LORD filled the tabernacle" (40:33–34).

Later readers have commonly associated the tabernacle of Exodus with creation, the ark of Noah, and Solomon's stone temple. The links are ancient; they are assumed at least as early as Philo and Josephus (Josipovici 95, 99–102). The New Testament book of Hebrews also features the tabernacle and portrays Jesus as fulfilling the sacrifice and priesthood systems of the Pentateuch.

LEVITICUS AND NUMBERS

While Exodus decrees the structure of the tabernacle and outfits the priesthood that functions there, Leviticus records YHWH's commands about the sacrificial system (chs. 1–7) and the ritual holiness he requires (chs. 11–17). The narrative passage between these two sets of laws unites them and serves to distinguish between true and false worship (chs. 8–10).

Here is recounted how Moses consecrates Aaron and his sons according to the divine directions of Exodus 29, after which Aaron properly offers sacrifice. Immediately, however, his two sons, Nadab and Abihu, offer the "strange fire" specifically prohibited in Exodus 30:9 and are themselves consumed by fire. Because the incident involves sacrifice, it relates to the content of the first set of laws, and because the mysterious sin of Aaron's sons reflects on their moral character, it also relates to the second set. The episode illustrates perfectly the overall role of law in the Bible. In Leviticus, Damrosch says, "the law is represented in its ideal, fully functioning form, the best model against which to assess the complicated uses and misuses of law by characters throughout Old Testament narratives" ("Leviticus" 66).

Although nearly all readers have seen this interlude as the book's only narrative, several scholars have recently examined laws that seem to share those generic features. For example, in his discussion of levitical burnt offerings, Damrosch suggests that the different kinds of sacrifices permitted, depending on economic status—bullock, lamb or goat, dove or pigeon—are "instances of narrative variety within the ritual order" ("Leviticus" 66–69). The tripart description of each type of offering and certain repeated phrases such as "sweet savour unto the LORD" confer even a lyrical and dramatic quality to these laws.

Numbers is a narrative and a supplemental lawbook between the sacramental lawbook of Leviticus and the social lawbook of Deuteronomy. It recounts the journey of the emerging nation from Sinai to the eastern side of Jordan, where it is about to enter the Promised Land. Here the mixed form of narrative and legal material is particularly striking and elaborate. The dozen major shifts back and forth, not counting the short passages of narrative implementation within the legal sections, are almost dizzying. Jacob Milgrom (xv–xvii) identifies the major alternations between narrative (N) and law (L) as follows: 1–10:10 (L); 10:11–14:45 (N); 15 (L); 16–17 (N); 18–19 (L); 20–25 (N); 26–27:11 (L); 27:12–23 (N); 28–30 (L); 31–33:49 (N); 33:50–56; 34–36 (L). The alternating sections entail two major topics—God's continuing elaboration of his principles and, despite his meticulous care, the sustained murmuring and rebellion of his people.

YHWH's additional statutes are decreed at major stations along the way, for example, at Sinai, where Passover is again observed (1–10:10), at Kadesh (chs. 15, 18–19), and at Moab (chs. 28–30, 34–36). Sometimes a new law is introduced to meet a specific need, as with the daughters of the deceased Zelophehad to insure their family inheritance (27:1–11), a provision later repeated in the closing chapter and applied generally to other heiresses (36).

Within Numbers the main narratives tell of rebellion, recalling the ones in Exodus. Those who resist YHWH and Moses include Miriam and Aaron (ch. 12), Korah (chs. 16–17), the elder generation of Israelites who refuse to enter the land (chs. 13–14), and the new generation who, just as they are about to enter it, worship Baal-Peor (ch. 25). The most significant episode is the refusal to enter this land of "milk and honey," figs, pomegranates, and grapes so huge that two men are needed to carry one cluster (ch. 13). The report that the present inhabitants are giants next to whom "we were in our own sight as grasshoppers" causes the congregation to reject the enthusiastic belief of Caleb and Joshua that they can win the land.

For this disobedience they are forbidden to enter it, and instead, ironically, their children, whom they claimed would die victims in the desert, will fulfill the national destiny.

In contrast to this dispiriting incident, successes are also recounted, such as the conquest of Sihon, king of the Amorites, and Og, king of Bashan (ch. 21), and the turning of the attempted curses of the prophet Balaam into blessings (chs. 22–24).

DEUTERONOMY

The fifth book of the Pentateuch follows the pattern of narrative and legal combination as Moses recapitulates to the new generation their salvation history (chs. 1–11) and then elaborates upon the social significance of the law (chs. 12–30). As Jacob Milgrom summarizes, "By the admixture of these two genres," Deuteronomy is "a parade example of this literary type" (xvi). After the people recite the detailed list of curses for disobedience and of blessings for obedience to YHWH (chs. 27–30), Moses commissions Joshua as his successor (ch. 31) and sings a song of celebration (ch. 32). Now 120 years old, he views the land from Mount Nebo, a land that he, like his generation, cannot enter, and then, like Jacob in Genesis, blesses each of the tribes (ch. 33). The final brief narrative records his death and eulogizes him, avowing that the people have finally learned to obey divinely appointed leadership in the case of Joshua (ch. 34).

The book does not proceed chronologically but in the reverse order of preceding material: from the wilderness journeys of Numbers back to the two presentations of the Decalogue in Exodus. This is an appropriate order for the new generation, its intended audience. Moses recalls their recent experience before charging them with the law and describing events before they were born. The structure of Deuteronomy presents itself in chiasmic relationship with the previous three books, particularly Exodus and Numbers.

Blessings and Cursings

The pattern of alternation between narrative and law throughout these four books is supplemented by a series of blessings and curses. These naturally culminate in Deuteronomy as the people are about to enter their land. Each book closes with a blessing that is dependent on right worship and the avoidance of idols and images, as Leviticus 26 makes clear. Otherwise, disastrous results are assured.

At the end of Exodus Moses blesses the nation for completing the tabernacle (39:43), and afterwards, the habitation of the Lord's glory within it furnishes a nonverbal blessing (40:34). Numbers begins with the blessing of the people by the priests (6:24–27) and concludes with the blessings of Balaam who was hired to curse Israel (chs. 22–24). The blessings of the narrative in Deuteronomy (chs. 7 and 11) include the promise that remembrance and obedience will bring about "the days of heaven upon the earth" (11:21). The most extensive blessings and curses occur after the law is restated and the nation is gathered on Mount Ebal and Mount Gerizim to repeat them responsively (chs. 27–28). After a song of Moses, longer than his celebration after crossing the Red Sea forty years before, the leader pronounces blessings on each of the tribes (chs. 32–33). These benefits are implementations of the priestly blessing commanded by YHWH himself:

> *The* LORD *bless thee, and keep thee:*
> *The* LORD *make his face shine upon thee,*
> *and be gracious unto thee:*
> *The* LORD *lift up his countenance upon thee,*
> *and give thee peace. (Num. 6:24–27)*

Stylistic Arrangements of Laws

The laws on a particular subject in Exodus, Leviticus, Numbers, and Deuteronomy are rarely codified in one place but appear in at least two books, often in three, or even all four. To find all that the Pentateuch has to say on a subject, the various particulars and details of a legal topic must be gathered together. In other words, the commands are not fully expounded in a logically arranged legal treatise. This lack of organization produces a pattern like a weaving or a tapestry.

The format of commandments is also relevant to their interpretation. They are structured according to two basic formulas, absolute or conditional, and the former varies additionally according to a negative or positive pattern, slightly similar to the parallelism of Hebrew verse, which amplifies statements through the means of complement, development, or antithesis.

The laws or teachings begun in Exodus and concluded in Deuteronomy, then, are of two kinds, absolute or apodictic ones, usually introduced by the contrasting formulas "Thou shalt" or "Thou shalt not," and conditional or casuistic ones, expressed in a narrative form, such as "If a man [does this], then [this will happen]." The Decalogue illustrates the apodictic kind in contrasting forms, three positive and seven negative. Although most of the Ten Commandments are stated negatively, the introduction and central laws uniting commitment to God and to the human family are stated affirmatively: "I am the LORD thy God, which have brought thee out of the land of Egypt, out of the house of bondage," "Remember the sabbath day to keep it holy," and "Honor thy father and thy mother." Then follow the remaining negations: not to kill, commit adultery, steal, bear false witness, or covet.

Brief commands of this kind are often embellished by a positive/negative pattern. For example, the prescription "Judges and officers shalt thou make thee in all thy gates" is a positive command requiring judges in all cities in all of the tribes to be "just," but this is followed by two negative warnings against favoritism and bribery and then by a final reminder to be "just" (Deut. 16:18–20). Thus, the law is given four times, developed by parallel negative statements in a parallel positive frame.

Other series of laws are usually arranged to achieve variety by alternating absolute and conditional forms. Sometimes the casuistic instructions are brief, and sometimes they treat a specific topic at length. Those found in Deuteronomy 22 are good examples. Observing the usual pattern, the passage starts with the absolute type of command (two in this case), followed by two conditional ones, then a series of absolute commands, and an even longer series of conditional ones; it concludes with a terse absolute command.

More specifically, the first precept combines a negative-positive (shalt not–shalt) formulation for variety: "Thou shalt not see thy brother's ox or his sheep go astray, and hide thyself from them: thou shalt in any case bring them again to thy brother." Then a number of conditional and absolute clarifications are added, such as if the unfortunate person does not live near or is unknown, one is expected to retain the lost goods until they are claimed (vv. 1–4). This rather lengthy command is succeeded by a briefer absolute one about distinctions between male and female dress (v. 5). Two conditional situations ensue: if a bird's nest is discovered and there are young in it, the mother bird must be spared for she is needed by her youth (vv. 6–7); and when building a new house, a battlement or railing must be built for the roof so that no one can fall from it (v. 8). A series of absolute laws then condemns other mixtures, like those against which the above gendered-dress codes were based, to represent the divine insistence against any kind of compromise with pagan practice and to reemphasize the divine distinctions of creation. Thus vineyards may not be planted with mixed seed, nor plowing be done with both an ox and an ass, nor wool and linen be combined in the composition of clothes (vv. 9–12). The last is combined with the absolute command that fringes or *tefillin* be worn on the borders of the garments. This is succeeded by a series of "if" conditions about marriage and chastity, concluding with the law that if a man has sexual relations with a single woman he is required to compensate her father and must marry her for a lifelong union (vv. 13–28). And there is a final absolute statement that no man shall abuse his father's wife (v. 30).

Scholars and critics have been puzzled by the seeming lack of logical or literary unity among various topics addressed in legal sequences and have found each other's explanations unsatisfactory. Victor Hamilton summarizes the attempts by Gerhard von Rad, Moshe Weinfeld, Norman Geisler, Calum Carmichael, and S. Kaufmann, for example, at configuring some sort of inherent order in the laws (415–18). But instead of solutions based on models outside of or elsewhere in the Pentateuch, as some of the above critics propose, the unity of a collection of laws might well be assumed. The juxtaposition of assorted commandments suggests a subtle relationship. Their miscellaneousness itself may be the unifying principle. Chapter 22 just discussed is such a passage.

An analogy to this type of organization is that of the great American poet Walt Whitman in section 15 of "Song of Myself." This section shares the structure and many of the same details as Deuteronomy 22. For example, in the first nine lines Whitman combines images of a contralto singing from the organ loft with a carpenter dressing his plank and singing with his plane, the married and the unmarried celebrating a festival dinner, the hunter of wild birds seeking his prey, deacons being ordained at an altar, spinning girls making clothes, and farmers observing their growing grain.

The subsequent lines in the section, and *Leaves of Grass* as a whole, achieve just what chapter 22 and the whole book of Deuteronomy do: they give insight into how unrelated elements may be associated. Both continually mix the obviously divine and sacred with the ordinary and common, the social hierarchy with the simplest occupations of each human being. Some of the elements in "Song of Myself" may even allude to Deuteronomy. Whitman refers to making a roof, to the one-year honeymoon, to various forms of sexual expression and, like the Bible, to the ideals of family life. Both proclaim the unity of life and the sanctity of every part and aspect of it. Walt Whitman's "I make holy whatever I touch" expresses the spirit of Deuteronomy. God's attention to the seemingly insignificant and disparate details of life sanctifies them. Together, they affirm the call of everyone and of every activity to be holy.

The commandments in Exodus, Leviticus, Numbers, and Deuteronomy develop, comment on, or expand the Decalogue. The tradition is that 248 are positive ("Thou shalt") and 365 are negative ("Thou shalt not"), thus making up 613 commandments. (Jesus reduces these 613 to two commandments in Matthew 22:37–39.) Any given topic may be expressed by what "thou shalt" or what "thou shalt not" do. For example, there are 53 positive commands about sacrifices offered to God and 69 negative ones, 19 mandatory commandments about the temple and 22 prohibitions. Food, festivals, agriculture, commerce, justice, and all personal and community activity receive similar parallel treatment (Wigoder 129–39). Such a lengthy list of laws on these subjects reflects the consciousness of the holiness of all of life.

Literary Devices

Repetition is the chief literary device of the Pentateuch, indeed of the entire Old Testament. The series of plagues upon Egypt and the pattern of repeated deliverance from them illustrate the method. So too does the series of rebellions, judgments, and deliverances during the journey of the Hebrews to the Promised Land, a pattern repeated in the book of Judges and in the prophets until the nation goes into captivity, as recorded in 2 Kings.

Robert Browning's *The Ring and the Book* and William Faulkner's *As I Lay Dying* provide analogues for repeating episodes or parts of a story from new or different perspectives. Both authors narrate the same events in these works from the points of view of different characters. Similarly and specifically, repetition in Deuteronomy gains in perspective from retelling material after forty years of wandering and from the contrast between the people's point of view and Moses'.

Three times in his opening address of Deuteronomy Moses tells the congregation, "The LORD was angry with me for your sakes" (1:37; 3:26; 4:21) due to their behavior recounted in Exodus and Numbers. They provoked YHWH "from the day that thou didst depart out of the land of Egypt, until ye came unto this place" and "ye have been rebellious against the LORD from the day that I knew you" (9:7, 24). The suggestion is that Moses feels his punishment at being forbidden to enter the Promised Land is not primarily due to his own failure but to his frustration brought about by them. In Numbers the emphasis is clearly on Moses' own culpability, on his harsh outcry at Horeb and his disobedience in striking, instead of speaking to, the rock to bring forth water, as he had done earlier at Massah in Exodus 17.

Through the device of repetition Deuteronomy provides other fresh perspectives and details on previously recorded actions. For example, Moses interceded not only for the people when the golden calf was made but also for Aaron, with whom the Lord was "very angry" (9:20; cf. Ex. 32). We discover for the first time that Moses, not only Joshua and Caleb, had addressed the people when they rejected their destination and had encouraged them to remember their miraculous deliverance out of Egypt and their divine preservation in the wilderness when God cared for them as a father cares for a son (1:21–23). Also new is the information that while heeding the advice of his father-in-law Jethro about appointing judges, Moses himself had anticipated this need and gave careful instructions to the appointees (1:9–18). We hear more of his activities, exhortations to obedience, and warnings, especially against idolatry.

We also hear more about YHWH in Deuteronomy and are given more commentary on earlier episodes. In the conquest of Sihon, king of the Amorites, a victory often recalled in the Old Testament, we learn that Moses himself sent messengers to that ruler, whereas in the account in Numbers only Israel the nation is mentioned. Israel's role in this event, presumed to be divinely ordained, is specifically ascribed to YHWH in Deuteronomy, and the conquest is associated with the deliverance from Egypt. Sihon's resistance is like Pharaoh's. The Lord "hardened his spirit, and made his heart obstinate," and he provided victory for the Hebrews over him (Deut. 2:26–37).

Another form of repetition involves codes of law. Sometimes they are briefly interrupted or slightly changed, as in the two receptions of the Decalogue and the two accounts of the tabernacle in Exodus. The most extended case is the two parts of Deuteronomy: the first, as already discussed, restates Israel's history, while the second, giving the book its Greek name, repeats the whole law, adding new provisions on specific subjects. In most cases the repeated version involves significant modifications, elaborations, and differences in focus from the first, and these help complete the sacred history and teaching. For example, there is a new emphasis on rejoicing in, not just obeying, YHWH (12:7, 12, 18; 14:26; 16:11, 14–15; 26:11; 27:7). Another form of repetition is a summary, and Deuteronomy is able, fittingly, as the final legal book, to encapsulate the whole law in the familiar *shema:* "Hear, O Israel: The LORD our God is one LORD: and thou shalt love the LORD thy God with all thine heart, and with all thy soul, and with all thy might" (6:4–5).

The legal material in Exodus and Deuteronomy has much in common, but it is arranged differently and the contexts are different. J. A. Thompson provides a list of parallel laws for the two books (25–30). Exodus, with its proximity to the tabernacle and Leviticus, emphasizes worship; Deuteronomy emphasizes personal and social relationships.

Other literary devices are *irony* and *reversal.* The abject slavery of the Hebrews and the decree for the deaths of male newborn as Exodus opens is the complete reversal of the great favor enjoyed by Joseph and Jacob and all his family at the close of Genesis. There is, however, the irony that the future deliverer of the people will be spared and even brought up in the household of Pharaoh by the intervention of his daughter. The self-efforts of the young Moses to help his people only result in his rejection and exile for forty years.

Ironically, only when he is thoroughly convinced of his inadequacies, which he exhibits by arguing against YHWH's call, can he lead the nation to liberty. A crueler irony perhaps consists in Moses' final failure. After his great patience with the rebellious Israelites for forty years and the three times he interceded with the Lord to spare their impending annihilation, the "meekest of men" loses his temper, and he, like the adult generation, misses the Promised Land.

Despite God's special miracles on their behalf, the daily supernatural manifestations of the daytime pillar of cloud and the nighttime pillar of fire, the presence of God in the tabernacle, and the daily provision of manna, the people still grumble, complain, rebel, and apostatize. The explicit irony involved consists of the comparison made between the ten occasions when Egypt's pharaoh rejected YHWH's demands in the account of the ten plagues in Exodus and the "ten times" his own nation rejected him (Num. 14:22).

Most ironic of all is the people's rejection of the real meaning of the central events of their history: the Creation and the Exodus. The first affirms their companionship with God by being created in his image. The second, the Exodus, proclaims the freedom of his people to be true worshipers of the only true God. The persistent underlying message of these four books is that human beings are the only ordained image of divinity. By rejecting the original "image and likeness" in themselves, human beings are doomed to seek in various forms of idolatry and false worship an image of God.

There are also, however, affirmative ironies and reversals. Thus, in Numbers 22–24 Balaam tries three times to curse Israel but instead blesses them. There is even a comic element to the story in the prophet's failure to perceive an angel blocking his path whom his donkey can see. Finally, God reminds his people, as in Deuteronomy, that they do not enter the Land of Promise because of their greatness or righteousness. They are indeed the least of peoples, selected to show God's glory, and have been most unfaithful, but the Lord loves them and wishes to fulfill his promises to their fathers (7:7–8; 9:4–8).

Themes

As Martin Buber and Abraham Heschel have observed, the major goals of the whole Old Testament are *the celebration of the human race and the realization of intimacy between God and humankind.* Even those who emphasize that the Pentateuch's primary concern is to reveal God's greatness, not man's, recognize that salvation is the "characteristic activity" of God (Cole 28). God wishes his people to enjoy him and to be his friends and stewards of creation. In Genesis the companionship theme is developed through individuals and families in the figures of Adam and Eve, Abraham, Isaac, and Jacob. In the next four pentateuchal books this concept is expanded to a whole nation.

YHWH's chief means of establishing this intimacy between himself and his people is the institution of laws and a system of worship. His deliverance of Israel from slavery (Ex. 1–15), the provision for his physical presence (chs. 25–40), his sustaining them (Numbers), and the declaration of his principles (Leviticus and Deuteronomy) exemplify this divine desire for relationship. Such intimacy requires, most of all, holiness. Through the law, *every detail of life is sacramentalized.* As YHWH states in Exodus 31:3 and over and over again in Leviticus, he intends to "make holy" this representative people. Victor Hamilton appropriately observes that even "Leviticus describes a holiness that applies to everyone," not just to priests, "a holiness within the reach of all, out of the reach of none" (245–46).

The main way God's people can show their loyalty and reciprocal desire for intimacy with him is through *the avoidance of idolatry.* One of the first commands of the Decalogue, spoken in YHWH's own voice (just as he spoke to Adam and Eve in the Garden) is "I am the LORD thy God, which have brought thee out of the land of Egypt, out of the house of bondage. Thou shalt have no other gods before me" and "Thou shalt not make thee any graven image or any likeness of anything . . ." (Ex. 20:2, 4).

So intense is the condemnation of idolatry that it engages much of Moses' later commentary on the first dispensation of the commandments (Deut. 5–9). To worship other gods will result in destruction "from off the face of the earth" (6:14–15) instead of the promised blessings, which include the absence of "all sickness" (7:12–16). False images must be destroyed by fire and no vestige retained, not even the silver or gold on them: "for it is an abomination to the LORD thy God" (7:25). Even if a prophet, family member, "or thy friend who is as thine own soul" suggests worshiping a false god, that person must be executed (ch. 13). Moses says of such worshipers that "they sacrificed unto devils, not to God" (32:17). (Milton's view of the false gods in *Paradise Lost,* books 1 and 2 especially, derives from passages such as this.) Prohibition of idolatry is just as strong a thematic interest in later biblical books.

Anticipating the New Testament's two greatest commandments, worshiping and obeying God must be concurrent with *love and care for others,* which may be summarized thus: "Thou shalt love thy neighbor as thyself: I am the LORD" (Lev. 19:17). This is the theme of the second half of the Decalogue, of some concluding commandments of Exodus and Leviticus, and especially of the second half of Deuteronomy.

Loving God is inseparable from loving others, which the numerous provisions for the poor, the widow, and the orphan affirm, as do the many allusions designating others as "brother" or "neighbor." The order to rescue and return any lost or endangered possession of another (22:1–4), the requirement to leave some of any harvest behind for those in need (24:19–22), the right to satisfy one's hunger in any field or vineyard but not to take more food than is needed (23:24–25), and the command not to embarrass by repossession (24:10–11) illustrate the biblical responsibility for others' welfare and reputation treated in these books. As Nahum Sarna observes, there is also a strong emphasis on caring for the stranger, usually accompanied by the statement "Remember you were once strangers in Egypt" (4–5). Because of these provisions, Thomas Henry Huxley, the champion of agnosticism, claimed that the code of Deuteronomy transcends the most humane considerations of modern law.

Conclusion

The mass of Scripture that comprises Exodus through Deuteronomy is traditionally read either for its legal content (Torah) or for its remarkable narratives, rarely both together. Later retellings of the Passover and the Exodus, for instance, testify to their inherent narrative appeal and historical applicability; in Dante's letter to his patron comparing the allegory of *The Divine Comedy* to an allegorical interpretation of the exodus from Egypt, in the American slave song "Go Down, Moses," and in the film *The Ten Commandments,* for example. On the other hand, the long tradition of Jewish commentary on the legal portions of these books testifies to their importance distinct from the narrative content. The literary approach taken here has attempted to give due attention to both genres and to consider their interrelationship. A literary approach to these books combines the traditionally Jewish focus on the law and the traditionally Christian concentration on the narrative parts that the New Testament especially allegorizes. A literary approach takes account of all that is there.

What is found in Exodus through Deuteronomy is a sophisticated patterning of both narrative and legal sections, which often serve each other as "breaks" or shifts. A mixing of genres seems to be the norm, unlike the neoclassical disdain for it. The combinations often follow either a chiastic or an A-B-A pattern, that is, a narrative passage relieved by a legal one and succeeded by another narrative text, or vice versa. Another organizational device operating in the arrangement of laws could be designated *discordia concors,* a harmony in disunity. The miscellaneous variety of these ordinances embraces all of human experience and calls all of it to the life of holiness. Every detail of life is sacramentalized.

It is these two elements of Exodus, Leviticus, Numbers, and Deuteronomy—the legal component, which addresses humanity's need for righteousness, and the narrative one, which describes the miraculous saving acts of God that give proof to the covenant on which that righteousness is founded—that together reveal YHWH's plan in these books to restore his people to the divine image and companionship purposed in creation.

WORKS CITED

Alter, Robert. *The Art of Biblical Narrative.* New York: Basic Books, 1981.
Alter, Robert, and Frank Kermode, eds. *The Literary Guide to the Bible.* Cambridge, Mass.: Harvard UP, 1987.
Buber, Martin. *I and Thou.* New York: Scribner, 1958.
Cole, R. Alan. *Exodus.* London: Inter-Varsity, 1973.
Damrosch, David. *The Narrative Covenant.* San Francisco: Harper & Row, 1987.
———. "Leviticus." *Literary Guide to the Bible.* Ed. R. Alter and F. Kermode. 66–77.
Fokkelman, J. P. "Exodus." *Literary Guide to the Bible.* Ed. R. Alter and F. Kermode. 56–65.
Greenstein, Edward L. "Biblical Law." *Back to the Sources.* Ed. B. W. Holtz. 83–103.
Hamilton, Victor P. *Handbook of the Pentateuch.* Grand Rapids: Baker, 1982.
Heschel, Abraham. *The Prophets.* 2 vols. New York: Harper & Row, 1962.
Holtz, Barry W., ed. *Back to the Sources: Reading the Classic Jewish Texts.* New York: Summit, 1984.
———. "Midrash." *Back to the Sources.* Ed. B. W. Holtz. 177–211.
Huxley, Thomas Henry. *Science and the Hebrew Tradition.* 1893. Rpt. New York: Appleton, 1913.
Josipovici, Gabriel. *The Book of God: A Response to the Bible.* New Haven: Yale UP, 1988.
Milgrom, Jacob. *Numbers.* Philadelphia: Jewish Publication Society, 1990.
Moulton, Richard G. *The Literary Study of the Bible.* Boston: Heath, 1899.
Rosenberg, Joel. "Biblical Narrative." *Back to the Sources.* Ed. B. W. Holtz. 31–81.
Ryken, Leland. *The Literature of the Bible.* Grand Rapids: Zondervan, 1974.
———. *Words of Delight.* Grand Rapids: Baker, 1987.
Sarna, Nahum. *Exploring Exodus.* New York: Shocken, 1986.
Sternberg, Meir. *The Poetics of Biblical Narrative.* Bloomington: Indiana UP, 1985.
Thompson, J. A. *Deuteronomy.* London: Inter-Varsity, 1974.
Thompson, Leonard. *Introducing Biblical Literature: A More Fantastic Country.* Englewood Cliffs, N.J.: Prentice Hall, 1975.
Whitman, Walt. *Leaves of Grass.* Philadelphia: David Mckay, 1891–1892.
Wigoder, Geoffrey, ed. *Encyclopedic Dictionary of Judaica.* Jerusalem: Keter, 1974.

CHAPTER 9

Joshua and Judges

KENNETH R. R. GROS LOUIS
AND WILLARD VAN ANTWERPEN, JR.
Indiana University

Historical Record or Literary Narrative?

Like the storyteller, who selects episodes and incidents from a variety of sources and weaves them together into a collection of tales, the historian must also make important choices about what to include, what to exclude, where to interrupt the historical narrative with personal commentary, and when to allow events to speak for themselves. The two Old Testament books of Joshua and Judges have both been read by various critics as history or as fictional narrative—as written historical documents outlining the development of a nation or as collections of oral tales about the exploits of individuals. The terms *history* and *fiction,* however, are elusive, and the distinction between "literary" and "nonliterary" often seems arbitrary. Still, the kinds of questions different readers ask as they come to a text differ in identifiable ways, shape their understanding of meaning, and help to determine the labels (though sometimes misleading) that are given to their various approaches.

Literary critics do not come solely to discover the character of individuals, either historical or fictional, or to trace the actual progression of events during a specified period of time. Rather, their approach assumes unity in a text and seeks to probe the themes and threads that hold a given work together, to understand what it is to be human, to live with individual history, but also to explore what it is to be part of a community. Ultimately, the literary approach we use involves asking the largest of human questions: What role does a divine being play in how we conduct ourselves? Are we basically good or evil? What do we mean when we call someone a good person? Is evil a separate force in the world? How do we organize ourselves into communities? What is the end or goal of life? How do we identify, individually and collectively, our heroes?

Curiously, perhaps counterintuitively, the answers to many of the largest of human questions are often found in the smallest details of a text. Repeated phrases and words give clues about what holds a work together; anomalies in particular passages suggest meaning that goes deeper than the surface; the presence or absence of characters in specific scenes shade and color our reading of various events. These, and many others, are the threads that hold a text together, help bring coherent meaning to any literary work, and point the reader toward the larger questions of human existence.

We might begin by looking at the books of Joshua and Judges in relation to two other ancient collections, the *Odyssey* and the *Anglo-Saxon Chronicles*. We assume that the Homeric poet had a number of stories about Odysseus to draw on, but that he judiciously selected those stories that went together to transform what might have been merely an elaborate travel tale into an epic that explores the dimensions and facets of a larger-than-life heroic character. The *Anglo-Saxon Chronicles,* on the other hand, while displaying some of the same elements as the *Odyssey* (it describes the character of important individuals in a national history), has none of the links and threads that hold the *Odyssey* together as a unit. Although the *Chronicles* is peppered with poetic devices and even contains several Old English poems, it emerges as a *historical* document that chronicles important year-by-year events from the time of Christ to the middle of the twelfth century. The point of this record is the events themselves. A literary text, on the other hand, with stories and tales intricately linked into a single unitary document, seeks to explain, to bring meaning and order to the paradoxical events of human experience. In this sense, Joshua and Judges approach the *Odyssey* more closely than the *Anglo-Saxon Chronicles.*

Pattern-Creating Events

In Joshua and Judges we are given in written form a series of episodes, possibly based originally on oral accounts of tribal heroes. The questions we ask—why these heroes? why these particular stories? why in this particular order?—are always implicit; for embedded in these books, as in the Homeric poem, are clues about why the authors included some events and excluded others. Repetitions and echoes, words and phrases, characters and action all form links that connect and unify the two books, that point us to common and contrasting attributes of individual leaders and to the nature of the Israelite community.

We should note first the overriding patterns that give surface unity to the two books, the patterns that suggest a theory of history. The book of Joshua opens with comforting words. Though Moses has died, the Lord makes it clear from the outset that Joshua will take his place and that he, the Lord, will speak directly to him and lead him:

> Moses my servant is dead. Now then, you and all these people, get ready to cross the Jordan River into the land I am about to give to them—to the Israelites. I will give you every place where you set your foot, as I promised Moses. . . . As I was with Moses, so I will be with you; I will never leave you nor forsake you. (Josh. 1:2–5)

Already here, however, we find the first hint of a tension, if not a pattern, that will arise throughout the book. "Be careful," the Lord continues immediately after his words of encouragement, "to obey all the law my servant Moses gave you; do not turn from it to the right or to the left, that you may be successful wherever you go" (1:7). This suggestion that the promise given to Moses may have been conditional implies a view of history. Perhaps the history of the nation will not emerge as an ever-progressing movement toward a final goal—the occupation of the Promised Land—but as a cyclical, perhaps even declining, pattern. Nevertheless, a first reading of the opening of Joshua indicates that Israel is in a position of great strength, and the people's insistence that they will be loyal (1:16–17) affirms the united agreement to serve only the Lord.

In contrast, the first chapter of Judges (despite remarkable similarities between its first verse and the first verse of Joshua) describes a very bad situation in which a number of Canaanite strongholds have not been taken by the Israelites. The enemy is all around and among the Israelites, an enemy difficult to defeat because it has iron chariots. Making what seems by itself not an unreasonable decision, the Israelites work out an amicable agreement with their enemies. With this situation of incomplete conquest and political chaos as a backdrop, the book of Judges imposes a pattern of history on ensuing events. This new pattern, however, compels the reader to return to Joshua and rethink the original optimism of that book.

Joshua 5 and 6, for example, tell the stories of several verbal encounters between Joshua and the Lord and between Joshua and an angel of the Lord near Gilgal (so named because of the Lord's promise to roll away the reproach of Egypt). The Israelites have renewed the covenant of circumcision and celebrated the Passover, and the Lord's previous promises are now made specific: "See, I have delivered Jericho into your hands along with its king and its fighting men" (6:2). The angel of the Lord also appears in Judges 2, but the words here force us to think differently about the message in Joshua. As before, the angel appears, but the narrative adds the seemingly needless detail that he went up from Gilgal to Bokim, from the place where "the LORD rolled away reproach" to a "place of weeping." A question immediately surfaces: Was that promise to Joshua merely temporary, elusive? How will it affect the history of the nation? If we recall the detail of place names, the message becomes ever more ominous:

> I brought you up out of Egypt and led you into the land that I swore to give to your forefathers. I said, "I will never break my covenant with you, and you shall not make a covenant with the people of this land, but you shall break down their altars." Yet you have disobeyed me. Why have you done this? Now therefore I tell you that I will not drive them out before you; they will be thorns in your sides and their gods will be a snare to you. (Judg. 2:1–3)

As we read Judges, the progressive quality of history in the opening of Joshua now seems ironic, even cynical, so that the most positive events of the book must be reconsidered on the grid of a different pattern.

The Progression of History in Joshua

Of all the individual stories in Joshua and Judges, modern readers may be most familiar with the story of Jericho. Like the stories of Samson, Jephthah, and Gideon, it is a popular source of artistic inspiration. It is important, however, not to detach the artistic and literary potential from the narrative as a whole. Taken by itself, for example, the figure of the prostitute Rahab might appear both as a type for the salvation of Israel and as a type for the salvation of the individual sinner. In the larger context of the narrative, however, it raises different questions. The story of Jericho follows immediately on the Israelites' insistence that they will be loyal and by their reiteration of the phrase repeated several times at the end of Deuteronomy and three times in the first chapter of Joshua: "Only be strong and courageous" (see also Josh. 8:1; 10:7; 11:6; 23:6). In this context, the opening lines of the story of Jericho are striking:

> Then Joshua son of Nun secretly sent two spies from Shittim. "Go look over the land," he said, "especially Jericho." So they went and entered the house of a prostitute named Rahab and stayed there. (Josh. 2:1)

This connection between the command to be strong and the entrance into the house of a prostitute raises questions about patterns that will follow. How reliable are the Lord's promises? How much should the Israelite leaders depend on their own ingenuity? Where are the lines between practical living and faith? Do the necessities or desires of individual action determine or undercut national history? Most important for the people of Israel, will the Lord's promises to Abraham, Moses, and Joshua be fulfilled, or will the inability of humans to live up to the conditions associated with them determine the future of the nation?

Despite these questions and portents of trouble, the action of Joshua happens on a large and majestic scale. Perhaps the drama of the destruction of Jericho is surpassed in the Old Testament only by the crossing of the Red Sea—the two events marking the most significant moments of the national history: the departure from Egypt and entrance into Canaan. In many ways most of what follows in Joshua and Judges must be read in the light of this gripping story: the seven priests carrying seven trumpets, the armed guard at the front and at the rear, the ark of the covenant, the entire assembly, the march seven times around the city, the shout and the blast of trumpets, the collapse of the walls, the slaughter that follows, the saving of Rahab, the burning of the city, the curse against whoever rebuilds the city, and the recognition of Joshua's fame throughout the land.

Then, stunningly and dramatically, the opening of chapter 7: "But the Israelites acted unfaithfully in regard to the devoted things; Achan son of Carmi, the son of Zimri, the son of Zerah, of the tribe of Judah, took some of them. So the Lord's anger burned against Israel" (7:1). Perhaps most striking in the two stories that follow is the presence (or absence) of the Lord. Whereas the Lord gives specific instructions in chapter 6 about the battle against Jericho, there is no indication at the outset of the conflict at Ai that Joshua or anyone else consulted the Lord. (With a tone of incredulity, the narrator comments specifically in chapter 9 that the men of Israel did not consult the Lord when meeting with the deceptive Gibeonites.) The spies who return from Ai report that the city will be easily overcome, so Joshua sends three thousand men; they are promptly routed. Only then does Joshua call on the Lord. Even his complaint is on a large scale—"If only we had been content to stay on the other side of the Jordan!" The turn-around from the victory at Jericho is nearly as dramatic as that victory itself, and the description of Achan's punishment is as elaborate as the description of the pillage that followed victory. The public punishment—the sorting through, tribe by tribe, clan by clan, family by family, and man by man, the public stoning of the entire family—is insufficient. Only after the burning of the family does the Lord turn from his anger.

It may be the hovering presence of the Lord throughout the book of Joshua that brings this sense of scale to the stories collected there. The stories of Judges, on the other hand, seem to focus more on individual people, and the events there lack the epic proportions of Joshua. Even the torches, shattered jars, and trumpets of Gideon, while reminiscent of the trumpets of Jericho, lack the imaginative impact of an entire nation circling a city. The punishment of Barak—that he would have to share the glory of victory with a woman—seems almost inconsequential when compared to the defeat at Ai and the stoning and burning of Achan. Similarly, the cunning of the Gibeonites may foreshadow that of many of the judges, but the action takes place on a larger stage and involves whole nations rather than only a few individuals.

The narrative view of history, the scale of character and action portrayed, all shape the reader's understanding of these texts, but each narrative is also carefully crafted. The leitmotif, "do not be afraid or discouraged," obviously affects our reading both of the victory at Jericho and the defeat at Ai, but it is better understood when seen in the light of other details of the stories. Chapter 8 begins another cycle of victory and defeat, and although the order is slightly altered, the same elements marking the story of Jericho are present—the reading of the commandment; the building of an altar; the sacramental observations; the passing on both sides of the ark; and finally, the tremendous victory at Ai, as at Jericho, ending with the reduction of the city to a heap of stones.

On first reading, the opening chapters of Joshua might strike us as a triumphant description of the success of Israel's initial forays into the land of the Canaanites. Another reading, however, one focusing on the patterns of the narrative, raises doubts that grow as we find out about the civil war of chapter 22, and they are multiplied many times in the pattern that emerges in Judges. For example, the leitmotif "all Israel prostituted themselves" marks the book of Judges, especially when read in the context of the numerous sexual activities described in the book. Jephthah's mother is identified as a prostitute, as is Samson's wife; the taking of non-Israelite wives is described in chapter 3; and the conflict between the Levite and his concubine described in chapter 19 ends with frightening stories of rape and forced marriages. All these may affect a second reading of the story of the prostitute Rahab and the spies and make us recall again our initial questions about the nature of good and evil.

Still, throughout the book of Joshua there remains a sense of the presence of the Lord that is missing in Judges. In chapters 10–12, the Lord is obviously the subject, the primary instigator of action in the battle against the five kings of the Amorites. As the narrative comments, "There has never been a day like it before or since" (Josh. 10:14). Consider the repeated action of the Lord throughout the chapter: the Lord said; the Lord threw them into confusion; the Lord hurled large hailstones down on them; the Lord gave the Amorites over to Israel; the Lord listened to a man; surely the Lord was fighting for Israel. These statements provide a context for the repetitions that follow in chapters 10–12. "Then Joshua and all Israel with him" is repeated six times in 10:29–43; the constant affirmation—Joshua subdued the whole region, Joshua took this entire land, Joshua waged war against all these kings, Joshua totally destroyed them and their towns, Joshua took the entire land just as the Lord had commanded—gives a sense of totality or completeness to the occupation of Canaan; and the long list of kings in chapter 12 implies absolute victory. This description, the presence of the Lord behind it all, underlines the feeling of inexorable progress in the Joshua story that is never present in the up-and-down stories of Judges. Furthermore, the simple statement at the end of chapter 11—"Then the land had rest from the war"—would seemingly be the end of the book, the final culmination.

Given this progressive context of the first twelve chapters, and the rise-and-fall context of Judges, what are we to make of the ensuing chapters on "inheritance"? Sad echoes? We read, "But the people did not drive out the people of Geshur and Maacah"; "Judah could not dislodge the Jebusites, who were living in Jerusalem"; "they did not dislodge the Canaanites living in Gezer"; "yet the Manassites were not able to occupy these towns, for the Canaanites were determined to live in that region." Or are all doubts overwhelmed by the seeming fulfillment of the great promise? After all, we read:

> So the LORD gave Israel all the land he had sworn to give their forefathers, and they took possession of it and settled there. The LORD gave them rest on every side, just as he had sworn to their forefathers. Not one of their enemies withstood them; the

> LORD handed all their enemies over to them. Not one of all the LORD's good promises to the house of Israel failed; every one was fulfilled. (Josh. 21:43–45)

Following these passages and the questions they raise, the conflict of chapter 22 is especially troubling. Verses 1–6 record Joshua's commendation of the Reubenites, the Gadites, and the half-tribe of Manasseh. They have completed their obligation to help the other tribes drive out the Canaanites and are free to go back across the Jordan to the land that they have chosen for their inheritance. Joshua's universal warning in verse 5 is hardly disconcerting in the context of this blessing. Notice, however, in verse 10 how quickly the feeling of goodwill disintegrates. The two and a half tribes build an altar at the Jordan River, and immediately the whole assembly of Israel gathers to go to war against them. Fortunately, Phinehas and the other priests are able to negotiate an understanding with the tribes, and civil war is averted (unlike at the end of Judges), but the precariousness of the Israelites' position has been underlined. The promises of the Lord are fulfilled; history has moved steadily forward to a seeming conclusion; what will happen next?

Prior to one final insistence from the people in chapter 24 that they will be loyal, Joshua gives his farewell. Full of numerous echoes of his address at the beginning of the book, it reminds all of Israel of the great acts of the Lord; his promises are fulfilled. Now, however, the warning becomes more direct and is accompanied by a curse: "If you violate the covenant of the LORD your God which he commanded you, and go and serve other gods and bow down to them, the LORD's anger will burn against you, and you will quickly perish from the good land he has given you" (Josh. 23:16). In fact, with history "completed" there seems to be no place to go, except, perhaps, to reconsider some of the ominous portents and overtones of previous events and to anticipate a new order, one in which the Lord is frequently absent, the scale of the human stage is lessened, the natural progression of history is changed, and the acts of individual leaders appear much more random and surprising than the neatly directed rule of Joshua.

Link-Creating Stories

Judges 1–3 provides a thematic link with Joshua, and the description of 2:12–21 underlines for us the changed order. The pattern described here is imitated throughout the accounts of the greater judges. Israel does evil, God is angry, he raises enemies to punish the Israelites, they repent and cry for help, a judge is chosen to save them, there is a brief period of peace, and the cycle begins again. The beginning of each major narrative is basically the same: "And the people of Israel did what was evil in the sight of the LORD." There is a certain futility about the alternation of glory and misery in Judges that, while not overwhelming in Joshua, certainly is presaged. There is not, however, anything aimless or meaningless about this futility, a sense we often get from the world of the Homeric poems, since here God comes repeatedly to Israel's aid, and his actions indicate a profound concern and affection for Israel. That affection is perhaps another unifying element. From God's perspective, after all, the Israelites are an ungrateful and hopeless lot, returning as they do again and again to the ways they should begin to realize lead only to disaster.

Chapter 1, with its long list of towns taken and not taken—reminiscent of the lists of Joshua—consists of only two brief narratives, but they are important in setting the tone of the whole book and are directly connected to previous narratives in Joshua. In 1:12 Caleb promises his daughter Achsah to the man who successfully takes the town of Kiriath-sepher. Othniel accepts and satisfies the condition. As he is about to go off with his bride-to-be, she urges him to ask her father for a field. She then makes the request to Caleb herself—"Give me a present"—and he complies. The same story was already told in Joshua 15; in fact, it was also told there in the context of the administrative allotment of land. Why the repetition, and word for word? We should be struck by the practical shrewdness of Achsah, as well as by her boldness in asking for the field. She seizes the opportunity to get something that neither her father nor her husband had considered. While such action seems out of place in Joshua, we will see that this kind of opportunism and shrewdness characterizes most of Judges. Additionally, in the context of prostitution, harlotry, and degrading treatment of women that develops in Judges, it may point to the benefits available within what both texts imply is an accepted covenant of marriage.

The second narrative is in 1:23–25: "When they [the House of Joseph] sent men to spy out Bethel (formerly called Luz), the spies saw a man coming out of the city and they said to him, 'Show us how to get into the city and we will see that you are treated well.' So he showed them, and they put the city to sword but spared the man and his whole family." Why the repetition of the same kind of story already told in Joshua? One reason seems to be to show that the following action will be on a smaller scale: a nameless man coming out of the city is hardly as intriguing as the prostitute Rahab; the parenthetical phrase—formerly called Luz—highlights that the city does not warrant the kind of curse placed on Jericho; and the simple description that they put the city to the sword cannot compare to the drama of trumpets, shouts, and walls falling down. Also, this decision, like Achsah's, is shrewd and opportunistic, but it is a decision that involves betrayal and treachery. Curiously, in a book that is full of sexual activity, rape, and mistreatment of women, there seems to be no hint of sexual impropriety at Bethel as there was in Joshua, which contains no other descriptions of sexual sin. Already in these opening chapters, the line between being shrewd and being a traitor, between being faithful and being enterprising, is perhaps hard to draw and may depend on the perspective of the draftsman. These lines become even more unclear as humans, rather than the Lord, begin to take center stage.

The Surprises of Judges

To exhibit a larger theory of the cycles of history, the compiler of Judges presumably had many stories from which to choose. We return, then, to our earlier question: Why these particular stories of these particular judges—of Ehud, Deborah, Gideon, Jephthah, and Samson? There must be other links here, other themes being developed in addition to a theory of history and God's great love of Israel. The stories, told with characteristically biblical honesty, are always dominated by an abiding faith that beneath the chaos there is a certainty, an order, if only Israel will be loyal enough to find it. Still, perhaps before it can accept that certainty and achieve that loyalty, Israel must understand and accept something about human experience, the limits of human capacities to interpret contemporary events, especially as questions about God's promises persist.

The book of Judges is full of surprising answers to questions about human experience. We know little about many of the judges, and they seem to have little in common. All we know of Ehud is that he is left-handed, Deborah is a prophetess who lives under a palm tree, Gideon is a poor farmer, Jephthah is the son of a prostitute, and Samson is a strong man whose strength resides in his hair. They do different deeds. They have, some of them, different kinds of blemishes. They plan their strategies differently. Ehud conceals his weapon and performs an act of individual assassination; Deborah prophesies that Sisera will be sold into the hand of a woman; Gideon plans a night mock attack; Jephthah makes a deal with God to ensure victory; Samson depends on the force of his arm.

About each, however, there is something memorable. What they have in common, if we can call it that, is their rich diversity. The book of Judges delights in surprises, in diversity of character and situation, in reversals of expectations. The hand of the Lord falls where it wills, often in unexpected places—on a southpaw, on two women, on the youngest son of a poor farmer in a weak clan, on the son of a prostitute, on the son of a barren woman. There is a delight here in the diversity of being, in the fullness of being, in the range of those chosen by God to save the people he loves. These are old-fashioned, country people—Deborah under her palm, Gideon on the farm, Jephthah and his daughter and the simplicity of the relationship, Samson the county fair bell-ringer. There is wonder here at the variety of people, at the value of every kind of person. Implicit in Judges is a conviction of the worth of different human gifts and human characteristics, a vast democracy of spirit, once this weak and worthless cast is transformed by God's Spirit. Even a characteristic such as human treachery is not all bad under certain circumstances.

Samson in a sense epitomizes the judges. He is, like Israel, a special child of God. He also is, like Israel, immature, opportunistic, rash. His weakness for women culminates in the loss of strength through the wiles of Delilah—like Israel, he has played the harlot once too often. He is enticed, as Israel is enticed; the source of his strength is taken from him, as God, the strength of Israel, removes himself to punish the Israelites; he is overcome, bound, and subdued, as Israel is sold into the power of her enemies and driven into the hills and mountains. Samson's blindness seems to symbolize the blindness of the people of Israel when they give in to temptation and weakness and do evil in the sight of the Lord. Samson suffers literally the darkness that the Israelites suffer figuratively when they turn away from God and are forced to live in caves and dens, when their highways are unoccupied, their villages empty. But as the strength and favor of God are renewed repeatedly to the Israelites, so Samson's God-given strength returns in a natural manner; indeed, so natural is the return—"The hair on his head began to grow again after it had been shaved"—that it suggests, like the coming of dawn after night, how natural it is for God to give Israel new strength against their enemies.

What ultimately unifies Judges is its delight in contradiction. It edifies because it describes for us in a series of swift, vivid narratives the paradoxical nature of human experience. Things are not always what they seem, as the characters of the judges exemplify. That is why the story of Abimelech is so central to the book. He is not a judge, but he could be. He is, after all, like Jephthah, an outcast, the son of a prostitute. The narrative of Abimelech establishes the whole background of the age, the tone and setting in which the judges operate. He is a military adventurer, a professional killer, able and entirely unscrupulous, very dangerous. He illustrates what Israel could become if it were not for the judges.

According to the book of Judges, people have a dual nature. Human experiences are therefore paradoxical. Eglon sends all away because he expects to receive a secret message, and the message is death; his servants do not enter for fear of angering him, and all the while he lies with Ehud's dagger buried in his fat belly; Sisera is delighted to find safety in Jael's tent, and she drives a nail into his temple; Gideon declines the kingship, takes the jewels instead, and they turn out to be a snare to him and to his people; Abimelech successfully burns down one tower, but when he tries the same thing a second time, he is killed; Samson toys and riddles with his women but then confides in them, at first only at the loss of a bet, and ultimately, at the loss of his eyes and life.

Paradox, History, and Human Experience

When considered in the context of Joshua, these contradictions become even more significant, because they point to larger paradoxes in Israel's history. The ending of Judges is especially striking when juxtaposed to the concluding verses of Joshua. When Samson, the last of the judges, dies, a new leitmotif is introduced: "In those days Israel had no king; everyone did as he saw fit" (Judg. 17:6; 18:1; 19:1; 21:25). The sentence, repeated four times in the midst of two curious stories, seems to emerge as the narrative's final comment on the sad state of Israel. Chapters 17 and 18 tell the story of Micah's theft of twenty-eight pounds of silver from his mother, their return, and the making of an idol for Micah's house: "Micah had a shrine, and he made an ephod and some idols and installed one of his sons as his priest" (Judg. 17:5). It is here that the leitmotif appears for the first time; it reappears seven verses later, after Micah hires a traveling Levite as his priest, insisting that the Lord will be good to him because he has followed the levitical law given to Moses. A careful reader, however, might recall the end of Joshua and that book's leitmotif: "Be strong and courageous." In 23:6 Joshua commands Israel to obey the law of Moses, not to associate with other nations, not to invoke the names of their gods. Superficially, perhaps, Micah follows this commandment; still the silver image is certainly troubling. Unlike the end of Joshua, where the altar erected by the two and a half tribes is built to the Lord and civil war is averted by the intervention of Phinehas the priest, the action at the end of Judges escalates into battle. Six hundred Danites not only convince Micah's priest to join them but also take his idols with them. Thus, after a brief encounter with Micah, they go to Laish, "a peaceful and unsuspecting people" (Judg. 18:27). "In those days," the narrative again reminds us, "Israel had no king."

The final three chapters of Judges tell a sordid story of another Levite from the hill country of Ephraim. It is a story of illegitimate sex, drinking, rape, murder, more conflict. This time, however, four hundred thousand people of Israel (not six hundred) gather to fight the Benjamites to avenge the murder of the Levite's concubine at Gibeah. (The narrative recalls Ehud by telling us that seven hundred of them are left-handed slingshot experts.) There follows a remarkable account of the battles. The Israelites inquire of the Lord who should fight; the Lord replies that Judah should go first. And yet the Benjamites rout the Israelites—twenty-two thousand are killed; on the second day, another eighteen thousand are killed. The Israelites then go to Bethel before the third day to inquire again. Parenthetically, the narrative notes that the ark of the covenant is in Bethel and Phineas is ministering before it. The Israelites now ambush the Benjamites, rout and kill twenty-five thousand of them. After more killing at Jabesh-Gilead, the civil war abruptly ends with an offer of peace, with the stealing of a few more wives for the Benjamites, with the return of all the tribes to their "inheritance." (Are we to think of the end of the book of Joshua?) The final verse of Judges is haunting: "In those days, Israel had no king; everyone did as he saw fit."

We should be struck that the conclusion of the narrative seems to focus on the lack of a king. Following the death of Moses, Joshua appears to possess the most kinglike attributes. He has proper lineage and power, and he acts both as an international statesman and as domestic leader, but the *book* of Joshua mentions nothing about a king. In fact, the very last verse speaks of the death of the priest, Eleazar, son of Aaron, father of Phinehas, buried at Gibeah in the hill country of Ephraim. Perhaps the narrative, so overwhelmed by the hovering presence of God, must emphasize, even at the end, the primacy of the priestly function over the kingly function, the divine over the human. The narrative of Judges, however, focusing on the actions of men and women, is almost oblivious to the presence of the Lord, whose instructions to the Israelites to fight the Benjamites, for example, lead to disaster on the first two days of battle and, for no apparent reason, are successful on the last day.

Joshua and Judges, read as a single literary unity, suggest paradoxical answers to some of the questions that trouble us: What role does a divine being play in our lives? What makes a good person good? How do we identify our heroes? At times the narrative view of history in the two books seems to identify a progressive pattern moving toward a final goal; at other times it seems cyclical, even declining. The promises of God are simultaneously conditional and unconditional. The presence or absence of God sometimes affects events in history, but often no relation is evident between his involvement and the outcome of what humans do on their own. The characters offer similar mixed messages: Samson kills more in his death than he does in his life; the Gibeonites deceive; Achsah is shrewd; civil war may or may not break out. More crucially, the king may or may not be more important than the priest; the story itself may be the chronicle of a nation called by God, or it may be a collection of tales about human heroes.

Perhaps, ultimately, the literary critic must conclude from Joshua and Judges that life is enigmatic and unpredictable and that our experience is, from a human perspective, paradoxical. Still, even given the contradictions, both books strongly imply that resolution lies in God: Israel, despite individual and national flaws, richly and honestly recorded, despite their inability to understand, repeatedly stressed and underlined, must continue to inquire of the Lord, must stop playing the harlot.

WORKS CONSULTED

Alter, Robert. *The Art of Biblical Narrative.* New York: Basic Books, 1981.

Gros Louis, Kenneth R. R. "The Book of Judges." *Literary Interpretations of Biblical Narratives.* Ed. K. Gros Louis et al. Nashville: Abingdon, 1974. 141–62.

Gunn, David M. "Joshua and Judges." *The Literary Guide to the Bible.* Ed. Robert Alter and Frank Kermode. Cambridge, Mass.: Harvard UP, 1987. 102–21

Josipovici, Gabriel. *The Book of God: A Response to the Bible.* New Haven: Yale UP, 1988.

Polzin, Robert M. *Moses and the Deuteronomist. A Literary Study of the Deuteronomic History, Part One: Deuteronomy, Joshua, Judges.* New York: Seabury, 1980.

Schaeffer, Francis A. *Joshua and the Flow of Biblical History.* Downers Grove, Ill.: InterVarsity, 1975.

Sternberg, Meir. *The Poetics of Biblical Narrative: Ideological Literature and the Drama of Reading.* Bloomington: Indiana UP, 1985.

Webb, Barry G. *The Book of Judges: An Integrated Reading.* Sheffield: Sheffield Press, 1987.

CHAPTER 10

Ruth

NANCY M. TISCHLER
The Pennsylvania State University

Wedged between the violent stories of the judges and the tragic drama of King David is a small jewel of a folk tale. The book of Ruth tells of two women, stripped of their men and their means of support, who seek to survive and to preserve the family—with God's blessing. The story begins and ends with a narrative history, establishing its role as a bridge between the more earth-shaking acts of earlier judges and later kings. Ruth is an elegantly wrought classic version of the rags-to-riches story, of hard work and proper reward, told from the point of view of women.

The Story

The shape of the narrative parallels Greek drama, with a prologue, a postlude, and five intervening acts. It has the same limitations on the numbers of characters who join in the dialogue, the choral presence for broad pronouncements, and the same patterns of thematic elaboration. (For alternative views on the book's structure and mode, see Campbell, Rauber, Smith, Sasson, Ryken, and Thompson.) Using the structure of the drama for our purposes, the book divides this way:

Introduction (1:1–5). A remarkably terse introduction sets the scene, telling of a family displaced by famine, partially assimilated into a new culture, deprived of its men, and then forced to reconstitute itself as a new family out of the survivors—all women.

Act 1: The Exodus (1:6–18). The tale quickly focuses on the conversation between Naomi and her daughters-in-law, firmly establishing the centrality of Ruth and revealing her unswerving loyalty. Within a few lines, we know the key characters, their major concerns, and their core of loyalty. The structure is established for the remainder of the book, using the simple alternation of narrative–dialogue–narrative.

Act 2: Bethlehem (1:19–22). The next scene transplants the women to Bethlehem, their ultimate home, where a chorus of women welcome Naomi back into their midst and listen to her bitter lament over God's behavior in stripping her of husband and sons. This scene, which repeats the pattern (narrative–dialogue–narrative) and speed of the first act, adds information regarding Naomi's bitterness and her quarrel with God, and it ties the women to the harvest and nature, providing a balanced contrast between Moab and Bethlehem.

Act 3: Boaz Introduced (2:1–23). Moving steadily in a rapidly rising action toward the real solution for these women, the narrative shifts to their human hope in the person of Boaz. This section begins with a prelude, a conversation between Naomi and Ruth; allows Boaz to spot the stranger in his field and to inquire about her background and character; and finally arrives at a climax in the confrontation of the two central figures. The words and actions become stronger through the scene: Ruth solicits his sufferance and he agrees, offering her even more help than she requested, finally making her his public guest by sharing his noontime food and drink with her. The seeds are now sown for the remaining actions. He has demonstrated his concern for her safety and her well-being, and she has specifically noted the importance of formal relationships (i.e., she is not his maidservant). Her concern with sharing her good fortune with Naomi foreshadows the conclusion of the tale.

This third scene is far longer and more complex than the earlier two. It introduces a key actor and provides hope, while continuing the earlier themes of nature, women, security, and the will of God. The concluding narrative section provides for passage of three months, to the end of both the barley and wheat harvests, rushing through the weeks at a pace faster than in the previous scenes, but somewhat more slowly than in the prologue.

Act 4: The Plan (3:1–18). In a beautifully balanced structure, Naomi and Ruth's opening dialogue this time fixes on the relationship of Boaz to the family. It leads neatly into the subsequent intrigue, designed to involve Boaz permanently and formally in their lives. The climax of the story then comes with the recognition scene on the threshing floor, in which Ruth's plot finds favorable resolution in Boaz's gentle and generous response. The earlier scene in the field had established his character, foreshadowing this congenial resolution. We are prepared for his orderly manner of arranging for her welfare and his carefully reasoned justification for such action. This scene, which is full of suspense, excitement, surprise twists, and relief, ends with rewards and vows. While it could have been a scene of lust and passionate exchange, it becomes instead a gentle, reasonable, and honorable arrangement, the basis for a new intrigue, this time between Ruth and Boaz.

This scene is as long and complex as Act 3 (ch. 2), providing means for intensifying the suspense. The climax is also a recognition scene, revealing the true nature of the redeemer as well as reinforcing our faith in Ruth's courage and resourcefulness.

Act 5: The Public Pronouncement (4:1–12). The following scene, which brings the lovers' relationship from dark into light, from private into public, reveals Boaz confronting his kinsman at the gate to settle the legal obligations. After a rhythmic alternation between dialogues involving Naomi and Ruth, and Ruth and Boaz, we now have a distinct break. Boaz meets with his kinsman, works through the law, proclaims his intent, and then joins with Ruth. Though also full of suspense and clever twists, the action is nonetheless part of the solution, the denouement. By now we know that Boaz will do as he has vowed. It is appropriate that the finale of this section is choral and public. Boaz turns to the elders and the people, the silent witnesses to the drama, who now join to celebrate the relationship of this ceremony to the history of Judah.

Postlude (4:13–22). The rapid narrative, moving at a pace like that of the prologue, certifies the consequences of renewed family—the birth of Jesse, whose line was to include David and Jesus. The conclusion returns to the opening, noting that the family lives, thus perpetuating the name of the dead and demonstrating that God has indeed blessed his people. Ruth, by reliving some of the same crises as did Rachel and Tamar, proves a stranger no longer, but a daughter-in-law worth seven sons. Naomi will be nourished in her old age by a God who cares about her and her family.

Ruth as a Woman's Story

Ruth is a woman's story in many ways. It is about women, for women—and perhaps even, in its earliest form, by women. Unlike almost any other narrative in Scripture outside of Genesis and the beginning of Luke, the book of Ruth focuses on women's concerns and makes them universal. Its characters, structure, actions, form, theme, and theology have a particularly—though certainly not exclusively—feminine perspective. No matter what the gender of the scribe who finally fixed the story in written form to save it for posterity, the story retains much of its original flavor.

Regardless of the arguments that continue to swirl about the text and the circumstances of composition, the literary critic and the common reader can find unique treasures in this pastoral interlude.

In the story, Ruth moves from wife to widow to sojourner to wife to mother. In fact, the story is remarkable for its range of terms for women. Naomi, for example, is an *'almarâ,* a woman who has lost husband, sons, and father (Sasson, "Ruth" 323). Ruth, who is a *nokriyyâ*—a foreign woman—is concerned with the roles of handmaiden, maidservant, concubine, and wife, though there is very little marital terminology in the story (Sasson, "Ruth" 321). Although the reader cannot escape the importance of the relationship to men in defining women, the central relationship is between two women not related by blood. These women form an unconventional family that ties together the two sets of husbands and sons, allowing the generations to continue. Ruth retains the archetypal role of stranger in the midst of God's covenant people until she finds a home with Boaz (Rauber 168). In a classic archetypal design, the women bracket the story in which the men live and die, serving as symbols of immanence and continuity. But even so, the story is basically about women who initiate the actions and take the risks in order to encourage the more phlegmatic men to the happy ending (Trible 161).

Unlike many modern feminists who find themselves in turmoil over mother-daughter relationships and the fetters of family obligations, the author of this story celebrates this voluntary bond between generations. Others watch the women together and applaud Ruth for her selfless devotion to her bitter but wise mother-in-law.

The contrasting Orpah takes the more conventional path, returns home to her own mother, and rejects the newly forged bond with the in-laws. Myth assigns her the role of progenitrix of Goliath, the antagonist for Ruth's David. By her choice of the safer path, Orpah underscores the risks in Ruth's courageous choices.

Naomi is a rare example of the older woman as a central figure. Authors, like most men, usually prefer younger women. Naomi herself recognizes that the woman past childbearing age is usually considered a bore and a burden. In this story, by contrast, Naomi is the image of bitterly won wisdom—like the female personification of Wisdom in Proverbs or the oracles of Greek literature. Like Job, she finds herself distressed, challenged, and blessed. At times, like him, she argues with God, but follows his laws and remains faithful to his ways, finding herself blessed with new hope. Ruth, whose nationality became synonymous with paganism, ironically becomes the human vehicle for her fulfillment.

Ruth, her daughter-friend, is the more gentle, attractive, and traditional heroine of the tale. Younger, sweeter, and probably more physically appealing (though not celebrated for her beauty), she draws our attention and interest. Although obedient and virtuous, she also proves to be strong, unfaltering, and courageous. More like a hero than a heroine, she abandons her own roots to adopt another family, another country, and another god. This is one of the most heroic acts in Scripture, rivaling even Abraham's travels to the Promised Land (Trible 168). In choosing to leave Moab, Ruth knows that Naomi cannot protect her, cannot produce another heir for her to marry, cannot provide for her most basic physical needs. (VanZyl describes the Moabite culture in considerable detail.)

Ruth accepts the role of provider, gleaning in the fields for long hours, facing the daily threat from other gleaners, bowing low before the landowner, bringing home scraps from her noontime meal. The story is full of hints of the degradation in this role—reminding us of another agricultural worker portrayed by Thomas Hardy almost three thousand years later—Tess of the d'Urbervilles. Although the symbolism of the story reinforces Ruth's ties to the land, reflecting the progress of the harvest, she is less of a creator of the earth than is Tess. Ruth is more like the frontier women celebrated by Willa Cather, not a fragile flower born to be crushed by cruel and godless men. She is, in some ways, the kind of woman that Ellen Glasgow loved, a woman with a "vein of iron."

Ruth also shows herself to be untraditional in her courting practices. Although the story has a faint hint of the Cinderella tale, with the change of clothing and the shrewd strategy for drawing the attention of the wealthy suitor, it is neither so focused on physical beauty nor so dependent on supernatural intervention. Ruth needs no fairy godmother; she has her mother-in-law, Jewish law, and the protection of Yahweh. Boaz may, on waking, believe her to be a Lilith, but he is not seduced by her beauty or her feminine wiles, though he does seem pleased that a younger woman could find an older man appealing. From his first view of her, he admires her behavior; his final decision is in response to her just claims.

If this is a love story, it is primarily the love between Ruth and Naomi. But these two women, stripped of power and in dire need of protection, are forced to use the tools in their possession. Although the story is charming, it has a core of grim realism. Ruth and her wily mother-in-law calculate the means for approaching the man they need for their security. Ruth follows Naomi's advice to bathe and perfume herself, and to approach Boaz after he has finished his food and drink. She accepts the role of aggressor in courtship with Boaz, perhaps because he is an older man who has no dream of a May-December romance. This would appear to be the ultimate risk for a woman, who chances everything when she makes herself sexually vulnerable—in uncovering him and lying beside him on the threshing floor. The story is silent regarding Boaz's marital status; we are given no hint whether he has wives or concubines. No matter what Ruth thinks she knows of him, he is nonetheless a stranger who presents a genuine threat as well as an opportunity. Her virtue, her reputation, her life are all threatened in this dangerous moment in the dark.

The Old Testament law is quite fierce in its treatment of unchaste women, though somewhat more relaxed when the woman is not a wife. Even though Ruth's homeland accepted cult prostitutes, we see no evidence here that she expects Boaz to treat her as a Moabite rather than an Israelite. And Naomi surely has warned Ruth of the fierce prohibitions of the Jewish law. She may have told her, however, of Tamar, who was celebrated for her courage and trickery in dressing as a prostitute and demanding her legal rights under levirate law. She may know of other women, less blessed, who are the objects of sexual violence. The story is silent regarding the motivation of the characters.

We do know that Ruth is delighted with Boaz's gracious response. She follows his orders, as she had previously followed Naomi's, and accepts his protection with apparent relief. In the story of Ruth, marriage and childbirth come from God as the special blessings dear to the woman. Ruth is explicitly willing to serve as handmaiden or as wife; she needs the protection of a man and the redemption of the family property. By contrast, the life of the handmaid is living hell for a modern author like Margaret Atwood, who has written a dystopia on this subject, *The Handmaid's Tale.* Subjected to man, reduced to the status of property, doomed to bear her master's children and to do his will, Atwood's fictional heroine loses her entire identity and sense of worth. Ruth, a symbol of the older view, sees such subjection as the fulfillment of her destiny. Her individual identity is subsumed in her family. In a sense, she is a true forebearer of Mary, who was to bow herself down at the Annunciation with the echoing words, "I am the handmaiden of the Lord."

Thus, the characters, their natures, their perils, and their rewards may be described as feminine rather than feminist. The ultimate reason for preserving the story—that it chronicles the genealogy of David—may be seen as masculine, but the form itself is not. In fact, David's descent from a Moabite woman appears to undercut the strong Hebrew claim to blood purity, usually evidenced in modern Israel by the mother's Jewish lineage.

This is, after all, not the story of Boaz, but of Ruth, who becomes a gentile antecedent for Jesus. Here the convert is a more attractive figure, for the Christian tradition is inclined to favor conversion and to rejoice in chosen family rather than blood relations.

Women in Scripture

In recent years, an imaginative band of feminist critics have explored a wide range of meanings in Scripture, digging into the neglected regions of ancient history and teasing fresh possibilities out of the familiar words. Some of these critics have a deep respect for Scripture, while others find they love suffering humans too much to be deterred by words that appear to thwart and diminish them. Both groups have focused attention on the unexplained silences of the Scripture, trying to understand the unspoken. Those of us who seek a middle course believe that the Scripture is inspired and does hold in itself the key to its own interpretation. We need not warp it to discover its riches for women as well as men. For such critics and readers, the effect of the feminist critics—even those with whom we disagree—is to open our ears that we may hear. We have grown more sensitive as a result of the fresh emphasis on this long-neglected point of view.

This feminine angle of vision that appears in Ruth is unusual in Scripture. Certainly the stories of the matriarchs, which we find in Genesis, are tales of women whose importance is determined primarily by the men they married or bore. They may be wayward tricksters or outspoken critics, but they seldom serve as more than accessories to the men who are the main event. Rachel, who like Ruth, had some ties with Bethlehem, is little more than the beautiful beloved, the justification for fourteen years of labor.

Some of the Hebrew women did show strength of character in ways parallel to Ruth's and Naomi's—Miriam was a rebel, Tamar was a risk-taker—but they were not the major figures in the tales. The man was the center of the narrative, as he was indeed the center of historical action at the time, not only in Israel but in most of the ancient world. Miriam was forbidden to lead; this was the job given by God to Moses. Her rebellion resulted in swift and firm retribution. (In point of fact, the actual leader was neither man nor woman, but God, the real center of the story.)

Nor do the women who appear in the stories of the Judges have quite the same role as Ruth. On the one hand, we see the alien woman as temptress. Delilah is the very antithesis of Ruth, enticing Samson to his mutilation and tragedy and bringing her people to defeat through her unscrupulous use of sexual power. Women are labeled virtuous or vicious, depending on their national loyalty rather than their private behavior. Other lands, and the women of other lands, are perceived as morally inferior, temptingly different, and ultimately threatening. Ruth is a heroine because she changed her allegiance and lived in accordance with Israel's principles of virtuous conduct. (See my *Legacy of Eve* and *A Voice of Her Own* for fuller discussions of these points.)

The warlike housewife Deborah is yet another contrast to Ruth. Here the woman rises to the needs of the hour and takes her chances as the leader of armies, assuming the role of the man when no men could do the job. As a judge and a warrior, Deborah is an Amazonian figure, unlike any other woman in Scripture. Naomi may have the wisdom of Deborah, and Ruth may have her courage, but both express these virtues within the more normal domestic terrain of woman. They are not grand public figures, not memorable except within the family they nurtured, the family that cherished them in return. They represent the more typical role of women in most of history, which has traditionally ignored the quiet and gentle part of human activity while it focuses on and celebrates the brassy violence of politics and war.

Neither a warrior nor a scarlet woman using her sexual power, Ruth is one of those modest, hardworking women usually loved and forgotten. She does not have either the extravagant display of Bathsheba nor the consequent illicit and tragic consequences. Nor does she use the trickery of Esther, who demonstrates far more the harem mentality and who acts on the orders of a man who wishes to use her as a tool to manipulate other men for the good of the Israelites. Ruth is more akin to the Bride and the Mother, those great archetypes of the book of Revelation, who stand in contradistinction to the Whore of Babylon. This is a great tribute to a Moabitess.

As noted earlier, in many ways this story is more closely parallel to Mary's than to the Old Testament stories. Like her ancestor, Mary rejoiced in her role as mother of the male child who would lead his people. Bethlehem was eventually the family home for both. Both relied on the advice of older women, who understood their concerns and comforted them.

Women and Authorship

Like Mary's story, Ruth's is the kind of "old wives' tale" kept alive by telling and retelling among families. It is a story that would have been exchanged at the many places women gather to draw water and to scrub clothes, to watch their children and to prepare their meals. It has that specifically feminine focus on the wonders that dwell beneath the surface of the practical life that women cherish. Like Eudora Welty's tales of Southern families, this story smacks of the fireplace or the kitchen table, the conversations shared when families gather on special occasions to remember who they are and where they came from. The unpretentiousness of its narrative ties the story of Ruth to the folk tradition and to all those stories attributed to "Anonymous." (Virginia Woolf insisted that Anonymous was a woman. In this case, she may be right.)

Although it may fit with either the tales of the Judges, which precede it, or the court narratives of David, which follow it, Ruth's story has a different flavor from either. While it may be said that this actually belongs to the stories of Bethlehem and the household of David, it is different from this group. Like the epics of the Greeks, also clustered around heroes and places, the songs and stories of the Hebrews might well have been recounted by bards as a form of entertainment. With the genealogy at the end, Ruth's story might have become part of the cluster of stories around David. Certainly other heroic cycles have tales of the forebearers and the birth of the hero. But others rarely focus on the life and pain of the women. We can see why the scribes chose to set the book apart from both collections in Scripture.

As noted earlier, controversy swirls about the authorship, the time, the text, and the purpose of the story. Regardless of their quarrels, the critics uniformly refer to the author by masculine pronouns. After all, women were unlikely to have the opportunity or the skill to become scribes. But, as demonstrated here, the point of view, the concerns, the vocabulary, and the treatment of character are clearly feminine. This is not to say that only women can speak or write knowingly of women and of women's concerns. We see throughout history the sympathetic narrative of women's stories by men—Richardson, Hardy, and many others have written sympathetically of poor young women who appealed to their more powerful and wealthy employers. And among the ancients, both Homer and Euripides write with genuine feeling about women's pain in widowhood and poverty. Nor are all women domestic and lyrical in their inclinations. Miriam's fierce war song, for example, is as bloody as that of Moses.

But this tale of Ruth has the quality of closely observed life that we have come to expect in women's literature, in the works of authors such as George Eliot or Eudora Welty. It touches on blessings and curses that are central to the life of women, of meals and menial labor, of strategies for survival, of dressing carefully to beg help, of kneeling before a powerful stranger, of rejoicing with the neighbor women in a marriage and a birth. We do not see them in the context of wars and powerful court intrigues; these are not important people. Like George Eliot's stories, the book of Ruth shares the spirit of Dutch genre paintings, dealing simply with common things, discovering the beauty in the ordinary. It has simple power. It is no wonder that so many have resonated to this work and to the vision of Ruth, standing in "alien corn."

It also has the beautifully wrought design we expect of those who love craftsmanship. Like Jane Austen, working with her two inches square of ivory, the writer of this story drafts her tale with elegance and precision. It has the quality of a beautifully designed dance, with careful parallels, balanced exchanges, turns and returns, and circular construction. Those who make baskets, decorate pottery, or weave garments would understand this kind of craft, the brackets within brackets that surprise and delight (Rauber 174).

Storytelling Technique

To demonstrate this deceptively simple formal beauty, let us take a small section of the story, the scene of decision that appears in the first chapter. The entire story is bracketed by a narrative voice, which sets the scene and explains why the story matters. In the opening, we find the time, place, and principal characters. Like Luke's homey tale of another birth in Bethlehem, this also informs the listener/reader of the greater world—which proves to be the lesser in the wisdom of time. Here it is in the days that the judges ruled, there in the reign of Caesar Augustus. Here a famine moves the family from Bethlehem to Moab; there the taxation enrollment moves them from Nazareth to Bethlehem.

In one brief paragraph, a family moves to another land, settles, marries off two sons to local women, spends ten years as settlers, and then experiences (without explanation) the death of all three males in the family—the father and both sons. The woman who came to Moab with three men is now facing life with two young women who would fare better without her. At this point the women assume names and step forward to make their own choices.

This sets the scene for the famous dialogue. The land of Judah, in a reversal, now has food, but Naomi has lost her hope. We see an example of the frequently repeated chiasmatic structure that also sets in motion the central conflict between Naomi and God. While the woman with the background in faith is angry with God, blaming him for her losses, her pagan daughter-in-law elects to enter into a lifelong walk of faith with him and his people. This prologue allows the author to attack the story at a late point in the family history and to shape the plot around Ruth as an unexpected blessing and source of hope. For all of the automatic use of vows, blessings, and references to God, Naomi needs to be taught that God has his people constantly in his care. Things do not just "happen"; they are brought about in the fullness of God's mysterious will.

The ironic twist here is characteristic of the style of the author, who relishes balanced contrasts and swift reversals. Two sons are replaced with two daughters. And then the daughters, being tested, find themselves to be contrasting types. They choose between two mothers, one a birth mother, one an adopted mother-in-law.

Naomi, in her blunt wisdom suggests the path they should clearly take: "Go, return each of you to her mother's house. May the Lord deal kindly with you, as you have dealt with the dead and with me. The Lord grant that you may find a home, each of you in the house of her husband!" (1:8–9a).

This gentle blessing, which derives from the daughters' behavior as well as the fondest wishes for women, provides a graceful closure for their life together. It balances the past, present, and future, the two sets of families, the two sets of husbands in a neat structure.

The response has some of the same tone of ritualized behavior: "Then she kissed them, and they lifted up their voices and wept" (v. 9b). Emotionally and formally, these are the proper actions, followed by their perfunctory refusals: "No, we will return with you to your people" (v. 10).

Having said this, they listened as Naomi reiterates her first blessing and expands upon her reasons for the orders she gave earlier:

> Turn back, my daughters, why will you go with me? Have I yet sons in my womb that they may become your husbands? Turn back, my daughters, go your way, for I am too old to have a husband. If I should say I have hope, even if I should have a husband this night and should bear sons, would you therefore wait till they were grown? Would you therefore refrain from marrying? No, my daughters, for it is exceedingly bitter to me for your sake that the hand of the LORD has gone forth against me. (vv. 11–14)

The second speech of Naomi sheds the good manners and strips away the sense of hope. She is blunt about her barren future and the physical needs of her daughters-in-law. The sardonic rhetorical questions have the power of poetic form to reinforce their cruel message. The parallelism and incremental structure underscore her rationale: A woman must be married; Naomi is too old to marry or to provide mates for these women. She has nothing left to offer them and therefore expects them to find someone more useful. Behind this tough, practical view of human relationships is the even more painful insistence that God himself is against her.

The neatness of the parallelism and the careful scrutiny of human behavior continue in the second response of the two daughters-in-law. Repeating the emotional outburst, thereby suggesting its stylized role and further reducing its sense of spontaneity and genuineness, the Scripture tells us: "Then they lifted up their voices and wept again," but this time with different actions. The words and the cries do not always reveal the heart: "Orpah kissed her mother-in-law, but Ruth clung to her" (v. 14). The one is affectionate, but not stupid; the other has a tragic quality of unswerving love. The contrasting verbs tell of two very different women—a powerful economy of means. Naomi spots the distinction quickly, seeing the impact of her words on pliant Orpah and the tenacious Ruth. Turning to the second woman, with a fresh determination she pleads, somewhat more gently and simply than before, for the third time: "See, your sister-in-law has gone back to her people and her gods; return after your sister-in-law" (v. 15). (In ballads and folk tales, three is usually the magic number for accomplishing the required action.)

After this rich prelude, we have the great message of Ruth herself, the first time she has spoken as an individual rather than as a type, joining her kinswoman in obligatory choruses. Now she asserts in her own firm, clear voice:

> *Entreat me not to leave you or to return from following you;*
> *for where you go I will go,*
> *and where you lodge I will lodge;*
> *your people shall be my people,*
> *and your God my God;*
> *where you die I will die,*
> *and there will I be buried.*
>
> *May the LORD do so to me and more also if ever death parts me from you. (vv. 16–18)*

Here we see an even stronger statement—more rhetorical and poetic—than Naomi's, picking up on both her themes and Orpah's. Ruth uses the parallel and (to the English-speaker) redundant use of infinitives ("to leave you or to return from following you"), which we know as a pattern of Hebrew poetry and formal speech. She follows this with a series of "where you . . . there I" speeches, going from singular to plural, from present to future, ending with God, death, and burial. The burial breaks the pattern of "You . . . I," providing both climax and closure. This forcefully responds to the earlier entreaties: she is not in quest of a husband, but settling for the present love of another woman; she is not interested in returning, like Orpah, to her people and her gods, but chooses Naomi, the Israelites, and Yahweh. The rhythmic parallels rise to a crescendo in the concluding oath, leaving Naomi speechless: "And when Naomi saw that she was determined to go with her, she said no more" (1:18).

The speeches are delightful for the characters they reveal, the moods they expose, the themes they present. In this brief set of exchanges, we have the indicators for the rest of the story: this will be the tale of returning together and living in love that forms a family, at least for the time being, without men or children or potential for the future. It will also be the tale of becoming a part of another people; and finally, it will be the tale of living with Naomi's God. The people and the God turn out to be a rich surprise for Ruth, who accepts pain and destitution, only to be blessed with affection and abundance. Naomi's surprise will be that, while she seeks blessing, she has already been blessed.

The gods of Moab become a part of Ruth's discarded past. She leaves a country whose very origin sounds like a smutty joke, whose gods demand the sacrifice of the firstborn sons and the prostitution of the daughters, and goes to Israel, where the fertility has been restored. She turns to a God who allows his people to suffer from famine, but who comforts them and redeems them. The ironic balance of fertility and sterility in the story suggest that these are central concerns of the storyteller. The family had left Judah because of famine, moving to the nearby Moab, a land that venerates fertility. But here the men die and the women remain barren. In returning to Bethlehem—the House of Bread—and casting their lot with the God of Israel, they find the abundant life. An older man, not the usual image of fertility, a gracious protector, offers to spread his wings over them and give them security. By a convoluted system of proxy marriage, Naomi finds her line restored, a child on her breast once again.

Conclusion

For the historical, feminist, legal, and formalist critics, this story is a treasure trove. But for the general Christian reader, the confusions of the law and problems of authorship are less important than the more central concerns: human need and divine protection. The redeemer motif here, as in Job, seems to be a shadowing forth of the great Redeemer we see in the New Testament. The gracious hero who reaches out to the foreigner in the midst of the people and raises up his helpless servant is an image of God's grace.

The request for help and the vow to respond form a central covenant in the story, reflecting the bracketing covenant vow between Ruth and Naomi and pointing to the larger vow that all the characters accepted with God himself when they became his people. Boaz takes Ruth under his wing as God has taken Israel, she is given the legal and public proclamation of her relationship, and the community celebrates the new life. Her choices are blessed by a loving and just God.

The tie that binds, the covenant, is here certified by the genealogy that concludes the story. The opening, with its emphasis on the family moving away from Israel, and the conclusion, which brings the family back into the lineage of David, give shape and meaning to the story of Ruth (for more, see Hals).

This is not the tale of a woman seeking adventure or wealth or romance, nor even the tale of a sentimental love for another woman, nor is it a trickster narrative about the niceties of the law. It is the story of one of God's people, from another land, who sought to become part of his people and his faith. As Paul would explain it, it is a foreshadowing of God's grace as he reached out in the gospel message to the whole world.

WORKS CITED

Alter, Robert, and Frank Kermode, eds. *The Literary Guide to the Bible.* Cambridge, Mass.: Harvard UP, 1987.

Campbell, Edward F. *Ruth.* Anchor Bible. New York: Doubleday, 1975.

Hals, Ronald M. *The Theology of the Book of Ruth.* Facet Books Biblical Series. Philadelphia: Fortress, 1969.

Ohlsen, Woodrow. *Perspectives on Old Testament Literature.* New York: Harcourt, 1978.

Rauber, D. F. "The Book of Ruth." *Literary Interpretations of Biblical Narratives.* Ed. Kenneth R. R. Gros Louis et al. Nashville: Abingdon, 1974. 1:163–76.

Ryken, Leland. *Words of Delight: A Literary Introduction to the Bible.* Grand Rapids: Baker, 1987.

Sasson, Jack M. *Ruth: A New Translation with a Philological Commentary and a Formalist Forklorist Interpretation.* Johns Hopkins Near Eastern Studies. Baltimore: Johns Hopkins UP, 1979..

Smith, Louise P. "Introduction and Exegesis, the Book of Ruth." *The Interpreter's Bible.* Ed. George A. Buttrick. Nashville: Abingdon, 1953. 2:829–52.

Thompson, Leonard. *Introducing Biblical Literature: A More Fantastic Country.* Englewood Cliffs, N.J.: Prentice-Hall, 1978.

Tischler, Nancy M. *Legacy of Eve: Women of the Bible.* Atlanta: John Knox, 1977.

———. *A Voice of Her Own: Women, Literature, and Transformation.* Grand Rapids: Zondervan, 1987.

Trible, Phyllis. "A Human Comedy: The Book of Ruth." *Literary Interpretations of Biblical Narratives.* Ed. Kenneth R. R. Gros Louis et al. Nashville: Abingdon, 1974. 2:161–90.

VanZyl, A. H. *The Moabites.* Leiden: E. J. Brill, 1960.

CHAPTER 11

First and Second Samuel

V. Philips Long
Covenant Theological Seminary

Superlatives abound whenever discussion turns to the literary qualities of the books of Samuel: "It would be hard to find anywhere a greater narrative"; the Samuel narratives are composed in "a prose which, for combined simplicity and distinction, has remained unmatched in the literature of the world" (H. G. Richardson and W. R. Arnold respectively; both quoted in Preminger and Greenstein 556–57).

Three basic traits of the Samuel narratives may be highlighted as contributing to their literary sophistication and appeal. The first is the *scenic* character of the narration. The books of Samuel tend to communicate more by "showing" than by explicit "telling." Much as a dramatic stage play calls on its viewers to exercise intellectual and moral judgment in making sense of the words and actions of the *dramatis personae,* so scenic narration keeps explicit commentary to a minimum and calls on the reader's powers of discernment and evaluation. The second trait of the Samuel narrative is its *succinct* character, by which it accomplishes its goals with a minimum expenditure of verbiage and with a consequent heightening of the importance and profile of the (fewer) words that are chosen. The third is the *subtle* character of the narration which, though constrained by a necessary (if sparse) framework of explicit commentary, conveys much of its message and perspective implicitly through a variety of story-telling techniques.

Scenic, succinct, subtle—is it any wonder that the Samuel narratives figure prominently in recent treatises on the poetics (i.e., workings) of biblical narrative (e.g., Alter; Bar-Efrat; Berlin; Licht; Ryken, *Words of Delight;* Sternberg)? And is it any wonder that the literature of 1 and 2 Samuel has for generations proved fascinating to a broad spectrum of Bible readers, from the simplest to the most expert?

The Samuel narratives have also held a literary fascination of a different sort for scholars whose chief interest may be described as diachronic, or "excavative." For these scholars, whose aim has been to detect and delineate the sources that presumably underlie the biblical narratives as we now have them, the books of Samuel have provided a favorite hunting ground. Cooper's reference to 1 Samuel 1–12 as "that *locus classicus* of source criticism" (68) is typical of the kind of comment that one frequently encounters in the scholarly literature on the books of Samuel.

In principle, of course, there is nothing objectionable in the assumption that 1 and 2 Samuel may have been composed in part from earlier source materials. One need only think of the numerous references in Kings and Chronicles to the sources used by their compilers to see the plausibility of such a hypothesis. The problem, however, is in the criteria sometimes adduced to "divide the text" when, as in the case of Samuel, the putative sources are no longer extant. Often the very same textual features isolated by traditional literary critics as indicating distinct sources can and have been explained in entirely different ways by literary scholars committed to giving the text a "close reading" on its own terms before resorting to diachronic explanations (cf. Moberly 22–27). Repetition within a narrative context, for example, is frequently cited by traditional literary critics as indicating a juxtaposition or commingling of two sources (Longman 95), but modern literary scholars often point to the very same feature as evidence of the narrator's rhetorical skill. In short, the criteria of division frequently employed by source-oriented literary scholars are sometimes undercut by the insights of more recent synchronic literary scholarship.

Peace within the scholarly guild has, so far, been maintained largely through polite noncommunication. Many scholars seem to prefer a deferential nod in the others' direction to the heated debate that would likely ensue were their competing and, in some instances, mutually exclusive conclusions to be compared. It may be hoped, however, that the future will see increased scholarly interaction, so that the quest for improved understanding of the Bible may proceed unburdened by outworn and, in the light of newer insights, often unfounded theories. It seems likely that open discussion would lead to a generally firmer conviction of the unity and coherence of the books of Samuel, whatever might have been their now largely unrecoverable textual prehistory.

In what follows, our aim will be to focus on those *literary* structures that contribute to the coherence and cogency of the Samuel narratives. Just as an admirer of the visual arts will tend to view a work of art first from a distance (to get a sense of the overall composition) and then up close (to appreciate the finer points of the artist's craft), so we will begin with a brief look at the larger structures and overall composition of 1 and 2 Samuel, and then turn to a sampling of smaller-scale strategies employed by the narrative artist(s) who composed Samuel.

Literary Composition: An Overview

PATTERNS AND PIVOTAL EVENTS

Even a cursory glance at the texts of Samuel will discover that, while the bulk of the material is presented in narrative prose, at certain significant junctures there is a shift from prose to poetry. Sometimes the heightened diction of poetry gives a stretch of text an emphatic character, as for example in Samuel's pronouncement of judgment on Saul in 1 Samuel 15:22–23. At other times it provides the appropriate medium for expressing deep emotion, as in David's lament over Saul and Jonathan in 2 Samuel 1:19–27. At still other times it may signal a special genre, as in the parable of Nathan to David after his sin against Bathsheba and Uriah (2 Sam. 12:1–4). In the latter instance, David, apparently missing the stylistic hint, interprets Nathan's story as a straightforward judicial case requiring judgment and as a consequence is entrapped by the parable and convicted by his own pronouncement (cf. Sternberg 429–30).

Of particular significance in terms of overall composition are two poetic sections that more or less frame 1 and 2 Samuel. The first is Hannah's prayer (1 Sam. 2:1–10). Described by Carlson (43–44) as one of two "pivotal passages" in the early chapters of Samuel, Hannah's prayer strikes thematic/theological keynotes that will reverberate throughout the narratives that follow. Like the Magnificat, which Mary, the mother of Jesus, would sing a millennium later, Hannah's song rejoices in the Lord's deliverance (v. 1; cf. Luke 1:46–48), extols his uniqueness and holiness (v. 2; cf. Luke 1:49–50), condemns proud boasting (v. 3; cf. Luke 1:51), cites reversal of human fortunes as a typical action of the sovereign Lord (vv. 4–8; cf. Luke 1:52–53), and expresses confidence in the Lord's faithful care of his own (v. 9a; Luke

1:54–55). These same themes of divine grace and sovereignty are revisited near the end of 2 Samuel in the poetic compositions ascribed to David (2 Sam. 22:1–23:7). Thus, the books of Samuel are framed fore and aft with poetic pieces providing thematic orientation for the reading of the intervening narrative episodes. Hannah's prayer also anticipates the coming of the "king," the Lord's "anointed" (1 Sam. 2:10), while the closing frame is ascribed to the king himself (2 Sam. 22:1; 23:1). This again is very much in keeping with a dominant concern of the books of Samuel: the issue of human kingship and how it should be exercised.

The second of Carlson's "pivotal passages" is the judgment speech delivered to Eli in 2:27–36. Here again the theme of reversal of fortunes is prominent. Although the point has been largely overlooked in scholarly discussion (but see Smelik 135–36, in addition to Carlson 44), it seems reasonable to suggest that the story of Eli's rejection functions programmatically in the books of Samuel to orient the reader to the themes of election, sin, and rejection. In other words, in terms of the overall composition of the books of Samuel, the story of Eli provides a "rationale for rejection" that should not be overlooked in seeking to come to terms with, for example, Saul's rejection.

PLOT, OR LOGICAL PROGRESSION

Turning now from these patterns and pivotal events, I will attempt to trace briefly the general plot, or logical progression, of the larger narrative. It has been customary to subdivide 1 and 2 Samuel into presumed source materials such as the Ark Narrative, the History of David's Rise, the Succession Narrative, and so forth. But even assuming that these component narratives once existed independently of their present context (which is not at all certain), they are now so well integrated in the larger narrative that their boundaries have proved notoriously difficult to delineate (cf. Gordon, *1 & 2 Samuel* 81–82 and passim). Our interest, at any rate, is in the flow of the narrative as it now stands.

The first seven chapters of 1 Samuel, coming as they do between the book of Judges and Israel's first experiment with royalty, serve two functions. They depict conditions existing at the end of the "judges period," and, more importantly, they describe events immediately preceding Israel's request for a king. The essential unity of 1 Samuel 1–7 has been defended by Willis in two essays appearing in 1971 and 1979. Willis contends that these chapters, taken together, follow a well-attested Old Testament pattern in which (1) the Lord prepares his man, (2) a crisis is described, and (3) the Lord's man successfully guides Israel through the crisis. In 1 Samuel the pattern might be something like this: chapters 1–3 describe the preparation of God's prophet Samuel, chapters 4–6 describe the crisis in which God's power is displayed, and chapter 7 draws the two preceding sections together by describing how God's power, working through God's prophet, delivers God's people from their enemy, the Philistines.

Against this backdrop of the sufficiency of Israel's God, the faithlessness of Israel in requesting a king appears in bold relief: "Give us a king to lead us, like all the nations" (8:5), one who will "go out before us and fight our battles" (8:20). Chapters 8–15 describe the Lord's concession, despite his displeasure, to the people's demand and the subsequent failure of Israel's first king. We will consider the rise and rejection of Saul at the end of this essay, so further comment is unnecessary here.

The emotional and psychological descent of Saul (after his definitive rejection in ch. 15) and the inversely related ascent of David are traced in 1 Samuel 16–31. Sensing that David is the one to replace him, the rejected Saul tries repeatedly to take David's life and, unable to do so, eventually takes his own (31:4). All the while, David is providentially, if circuitously, guided toward the throne, for, as the narrative often reminds us, "the LORD is with him" (16:18 and passim).

After Saul takes his life, the way is open for David to take the throne without lifting his hand against the Lord's anointed. In 2 Samuel 1:1–5:5 are recorded the steps by which David becomes king, first over Judah and then over all Israel. Although his enthronement over the former proceeds smoothly, blood is spilled before the way is clear for him to become king over the latter. The narratives are careful to make the point, however, that David is as innocent in relation to the deaths of Abner, Saul's former general, and Ish-Bosheth, Saul's surviving son, as he was in relation to the deaths of Saul and Jonathan.

With David finally on the throne of a united Israel, 2 Samuel 5–10 summarize the transactions, both political and theological, by which David's rule is established. Chapter 7 records the highly significant "Davidic promise," or "dynastic oracle," in which the Lord, after refusing David's offer to build him a "house" (temple), promises David that he, the Lord, will build David a "house" (dynasty) that will endure forever. This "Davidic promise" establishes, beyond all doubt, that the purposes of God for the house of David are sure. But it in no way implies that David or his descendants may not forfeit some of the temporal benefits of their privileged position if they fall into sin.

Chapters 11–20 depict the domestic and political chaos that follows in the wake of David's sins of adultery and murder (ch. 11). Although David genuinely repents when confronted by Nathan in chapter 12, and God immediately forgives, sin still has its consequences. With his ability to exercise proper authority apparently impaired (see, e.g., 2 Sam. 13:21; 1 Kings 1:6), David lives to see his own sins of murder and adultery replicated in the lives of his sons (e.g., 13:14, 28–29; 16:22). Not until he has experienced two rebellions, the first by Absalom and the second by Sheba, son of Bicri, does his reign regain a measure of equilibrium.

Chapters 21–24, which together form a kind of epilogue, provide thematic closure for the books of Samuel. At the heart of this symmetrically structured unit (abcc′b′a′) are two Davidic poems celebrating the two fundamental reasons for David's blessedness: (1) the Lord is his deliverer, and (2) the Lord has made an "everlasting covenant" with him (23:5). Framing this central core focusing on David's *divine* benefactor are two lists of Davidic champions, the *human* agents of David's success (21:15–22 and 23:8–39). Finally, the outside frame consists of two accounts of royal sinners—Saul (21:1–14) and David (ch. 24). These serve as a reminder that the distinction between Saul and David, between a rejected king and an accepted one, is not that one is a sinner and the other is not, for both are sinners. Rather, the distinction lies in the very different attitudes to faith and repentance displayed by the two and, at a deeper level still, in the sovereign election of the one, the "man of God's own choosing" (1 Sam. 13:14), over the other.

Literary Craft: A Sampling

Turning now to smaller-scale narrative techniques and strategies in the books of Samuel, we must be very selective, both in terms of the techniques surveyed and in terms of the number of examples cited for each. Our focus is particularly on those "modes of indirection" by which the "narrator" in Samuel seeks to persuade the "reader" to embrace certain ideological/theological perspectives on the persons and events described.

KEY WORDS AND WORDPLAYS

Since Buber's seminal essay of 1936 on *Leitwortstil* (key-word style), biblical scholars have become increasingly attentive to the ways in which the significant repetition of a word or root in the Hebrew of a biblical text (or complex of texts) can underscore an important theme, whether or not the theme is explicitly articulated. An oft-cited example from Samuel is the frequent recurrence in 1 Samuel 9–10 of derivatives of the root *ngd,* in keeping with the focus of this section on the designation of Saul as *nāgîd* ("prince, leader, king designate"; see, most recently, Edelman 44–45). Another example of the use of key words to emphasize a theme is the repetition in 1 Samuel 15 of the words "hear, harken to" (*šmʿ*) and "voice, sound" (*qôl*). At issue in this chapter is whether Saul will "harken to" the "voice" of God mediated by Samuel (v. 1). In the course of the story Saul claims to have done so (v. 13), but the "sound" (*qôl*) of the spared livestock that Samuel "hears" (*šmʿ*) indicates otherwise (v. 14). Saul has, in fact, "harkened" (*šmʿ*) to the "voice" (*qôl*) of the people rather than God (vv. 19–24; cf. Alter 93–94; Long, *Reign and Rejection* 148, 151).

A further example of *Leitwortstil* is the repetition of the root *kbd* in the early chapters of 1 Samuel. In both verbal and nominal configurations this root has to do with "weightiness, honor, glory" and the like. The root is introduced in 1 Samuel 2:29, where Eli is accused of (both figuratively and literally) "honoring/giving weight to" his sons above the Lord by "fattening" themselves on portions of the sacrifices that should have been the Lord's alone. In verse 30 the Lord declares, "Those who honor me [consider me *weighty*] I will honor [consider *weighty*], but those who despise me [think *lightly* of me; root *bzh*] will be disdained [considered *light*; root *qll*]." In the episodes that follow, the theme of "honor/weight" continues to resonate as the root *kbd* is repeated: Eli's death by broken neck is explained in 4:18 as resulting not only from his backward plummet but, ironically, from the fact that he was "old and *heavy* [*kābēd*]"; with the departure of the Ark of God from Israelite territory, Eli's grandson receives the birth name Ichabod (*'î kābôd*), "Glory/honor gone" or "Where is the Glory?" (4:21); during the ark's sojourn in Philistine territory the hand of the Lord *weighs heavily* (*watikbad*) upon the enemy (5:6; cf. v. 11); when the Philistines become desperate to be rid of their "captive turned captor," they prepare to send the ark back by exhorting one another to "give *honor/weight* [*kābôd*] to Israel's God" (6:5) and not to "*harden* [*tᵉkabbᵉdû*]" their hearts as the Egyptians and Pharaoh had "*hardened* [*kibbᵉdû*]" theirs (6:6). (For similar treatments, see Polzin 46–47, 56; Garsiel 61.)

While *Leitwortstil* (key-word style) involves a single root, wordplays (or puns) may involve distinct, yet similar-sounding roots. Puns today are often maligned as the lowest form of humor (though we might recall Edgar Allan Poe's remark: "Of puns it has been said that those most dislike who are least able to utter them"). In the Bible, at any rate, as in much ancient literature, wordplay is employed as a forceful rhetorical device. An example is Jonathan's commentary in 1 Samuel 14:24–29 on his father's curse (root *'rr*) uttered in the midst of a battle with the Philistines. While Saul had warned that anyone who should eat anything before the completion of the battle would be "cursed" (*'ārûr*), Jonathan finds that the result of eating is just the opposite—he is "refreshed," literally his "eyes are brightened" (root *'ôr*). Something of the same effect in English is conveyed by the following sentence: "By my father's word I should have been *stricken,* instead I have been *strengthened*" (further, see Long, *Reign and Rejection* 28–29).

IRONY

As the above discussion suggests, irony abounds in the closely woven fabric of the Samuel narratives. Rather than discuss some of the more obvious instances (such as the irony implicit in the description of both the boy Samuel and Eli's sons as "not knowing the Lord" [2:12; 3:7] or in the manifold ambiguities and ironies involved in the David and Uriah exchanges in 2 Samuel 11), let us look at two apparent difficulties that might be resolved by a greater sensitivity to irony. The first involves the question posed in 1 Samuel 10:11 by some acquaintances of Saul. Upon seeing Saul prophesying with a band of prophets (shortly after his anointing by Samuel), those who had formerly known Saul seem surprised: "Is *even* Saul among the prophets?" (For a defense of this rendering instead of the more common translation, "Is Saul *also* among . . . ," see Long, *Reign and Rejection* 208 n. 54.) The repetition of this same query in 1 Samuel 19:24 has given rise to the diachronic speculation that the two passages represent competing, mutually exclusive, etiologies. It has been plausibly suggested, however, that the second occurrence of the saying, in chapter 19, is a "satirical recapitulation" of the first (Jobling, "Jonathan" 10). That is to say, if in chapter 10 there is an openness to the possibility—however unlikely it may seem to Saul's acquaintances—that he might indeed have joined the prophets, chapter 19 discloses the full irony of such a thought: Saul prophesies "among the prophets" only as the Spirit of God overpowers him against his will.

The second example involves the theological, ethical difficulty presented by 1 Samuel 16:2. In this verse, God instructs Samuel to tell what appears to be a half-truth—"I have come to sacrifice to the Lord"—though the immediate context makes clear that Samuel's real business is to anoint a successor to Saul. But the broader context suggests something else as well, as Gordon has observed. Noting that in the immediately preceding chapter Saul twice excuses his disobedience in sparing the Amalekite livestock by claiming that they had been spared only "to sacrifice [them] to the Lord your God" (15:15, 21), Gordon asks:

> Is it possible, then, that when dealing with 1 Samuel 16:2 we should be looking the verse up under "irony" rather than "ethics"? That in this case the fool is being answered according to his folly, in a manner which recalls the "deceiver deceived"

> motif that appears elsewhere in the Old Testament? Perhaps we can occasionally be too solemn in our discussion of Old Testament problem texts. ("Simplicity" 80)

CHARACTERIZATION

While the Samuel narratives are not devoid of explicit characterizations—e.g., "Eli's sons were worthless men" (1 Sam. 2:12); Abigail "was intelligent and beautiful, but her husband was hard and mean in his dealings" (25:3)—the portrayal of character is most often achieved through a variety of implicit, or indirect, means. In 1 Samuel 13–14, for instance, the narrator does not subject Saul and Jonathan to explicit evaluation but, rather, presents the two in such a way that the actions of the one serve as oblique commentary on the actions of the other. Not only are Saul and Jonathan linked by virtue of their similar status (king and crown prince) and by the numerous epithets pointing to their relationship as father and son (12x in chs. 13–14), but also by the fact that they alone, among all Israel, are equipped with sword and spear (13:22). Encouraged by these indicators to evaluate the one in the light of the other, we discover that, contrary to majority scholarly opinion, Saul is depicted unfavorably throughout chapters 13–14 and not just in the Gilgal episode of 13:7b–15a (cf. Jobling, "Saul's Fall"). For example:

> Saul's general passivity (cf. 14:2) contrasts with Jonathan's activity; Jonathan initiates the action (e.g., 13:3; 14:1, 6), while Saul simply responds to it (e.g., 13:3b; 14:16–18). Jonathan succeeds in discovering Yahweh's will, even without access to oracular devices (14:9–10), while Saul is singularly unsuccessful on three occasions, and his commitment to the divine inquiry seems to deteriorate as the narrative progresses—viz., in 13:8–9 Saul waits until the last minute before taking matters into his own hands, in 14:18–19 he calls for the oracle but breaks off the inquiry in midstream, and finally in 14:36 he must even be reminded that divine inquiry is necessary. (Long, *Reign and Rejection* 41)

Perhaps most tellingly of all, Saul's excuse in 13:11 for having proceeded with sacrifices in Samuel's absence—"because I saw the army scattering from me"—is dealt an indirect but devastating blow by Jonathan's confession a chapter later: "Nothing can hinder Yahweh from saving, whether by many or by few" (14:6).

As these few remarks suggest, the narrator in Samuel is a master of indirect characterization through comparison and contrast. Sometimes even entire "episodes which may be basically unrelated are made to resonate with each other through the reprise in one of words or ideas which belong in the first instance to the other" (Gordon, "Simplicity" 76). For a fine example of this technique, called narrative analogy, see Gordon's essay on the function of the Nabal episode in 1 Samuel 25 in relation to the two sparings of Saul by David in 1 Samuel 24 and 26 ("David's Rise"; cf. idem, *I & II Samuel* 181–87).

"Saul's Rise" Through Literary Eyes: An Example

Because of space limitations, I have touched on only a few of the narrative techniques exhibited in the texts of Samuel. I have not discussed, for example, the narrator's use of verbatim or near verbatim *repetition* to achieve rhetorical objectives. And yet, since Muilenburg's seminal essay in 1953 drawing attention to repetition as a "major stylistic feature" in ancient Israelite narrative (100), increasing numbers of scholars have given serious attention to the significance of repetitive structures within the Bible (e.g., Alter ch. 5; Berlin 71–82; Licht chs. 3 & 4; Longman 95–96; Ryken, *How to Read* 59–60; Sternberg ch. 11). Alter, for example, has shown that close attention to the "small but revealing differences in the seeming similarities" (97) is often the key that unlocks the meaning of difficult passages (for an example illustrating this point, see my discussion of the disputed section of 1 Samuel 15:24–29 in *Reign and Rejection* 34–39).

Despite the necessary selectivity and brevity of my treatment, perhaps enough has been said to suggest something of the subtle virtuosity of the Samuel narrator. Making use of a variety of often *indirect* means, the narrator seeks to lead the reader into certain theological (or ideological) ways of thinking about the persons and events presented in the narrative. Greater sensitivity to the narrator's literary strategies will often yield a deeper understanding of the theological, and even historical, significance of the text. The aim of this final section is to illustrate how this is so by focusing on an important *crux interpretum* in 1 Samuel—one that has perplexed interpreters not only on the literary level, but on the theological and historical as well. I am speaking of the rise and rejection of King Saul.

SAUL AS VILLAIN OR VICTIM

The basic problem on the theological level is that Saul, having first been elected by Yahweh (1 Sam. 9–10) in response to the people's request (ch. 8), is very soon rejected (chs. 13, 15) for what most commentators perceive to be, at worst, minor infractions. The fervency with which Samuel pronounces judgment on Saul in 1 Samuel 13 has caused recent commentators to query the fairness of Samuel—and even of Yahweh himself. Brueggemann, for example, characterizes Saul's actions when confronted by Samuel in 13:10 as "properly and guilelessly deferential." Samuel, on the other hand, is "harsh, unresponsive, and accusatory"—and this despite the fact that Saul offers what "appear to be compelling and valid reasons" for proceeding to offer sacrifices before the arrival of the tardy Samuel (99). Brueggemann is particularly perplexed by Samuel's castigation of Saul in verse 13: "You have not kept the commandment of the LORD your God!" Brueggemann comments, "This is a remarkable statement because Samuel cites no commandment that has been broken, nor can we construe one" (100). According to Brueggemann's reading, the "posturing," "peevish" prophet Samuel plays a "daring, brutal game with Saul's faith, Saul's career, and eventually Saul's sanity." The result is that "the narrator invites us to wonder, as Saul must have wondered, about Samuel (who appears here to be unprincipled) and about Yahweh" (101). Such ponderings are reminiscent of an earlier work by Gunn, in which he concluded that "the 'Story of the Fate of King Saul' shows that God *does* have a dark side. David knows only one side of his God. Saul knows the other" (131).

On these readings, Saul is more victim than villain. But before we jettison such fundamental biblical-theological concepts as the goodness, holiness, and justice of God in favor of *Star Wars*-like notions of "light side" and "dark side," we would do well to look carefully again at the texts. Since it is Samuel's behavior in Gilgal in chapter 13 that has caused the greatest consternation among interpreters, we will begin there. Brueggemann is correct to ask what specific "command," or "charge" (*miṣwâh*), Saul has failed to keep (13:13), and indeed he is on the right track in suggesting that Saul's offense has something to do with Samuel's authority. Yet, until we come to understand the events leading up to the showdown in chapter 13, we can little appreciate the gravity of Saul's failure or the appropriateness of Samuel's rebuke: "You have acted foolishly" (v. 13). So we must look to the broader, antecedent context; and verse 8 of chapter 13 sends us in the right direction.

SAUL AS WE FIRST MEET HIM

The reference to "the *mô'ēd* [meeting, appointment] set by Samuel" in 13:8 clearly recalls 10:8. Unfortunately, the latter verse has generally been dismissed as secondary to chapter 10 on the supposition that its injunction that Saul go to Gilgal and wait for Samuel is in direct contradiction to what comes immediately before—viz., Samuel's charge to Saul to "do what your hand finds to do" (v. 7). This need not be the case, however, for verses 7 and

8 may in fact be read as complementary—the charge given in verse 8 being contingent on the fulfillment of the charge given in verse 7. If we ask what Saul's hand might have found to do, the context is again helpful. The dual charge of 10:7–8 is issued on the occasion of Saul's anointing by Samuel. It comes after the anointing itself (10:1) and after Samuel's prediction of three signs that will confirm Saul's election (10:2–6). In verse 7 Samuel explicitly tells Saul that it is *when the three signs have been fulfilled* that he is to *do what his hand finds to do.* The third sign will take place, according to verse 5, at Gibeah Elohim ("the Hill of God"), where, as Samuel tells Saul, there is a Philistine garrison (or governor). Commentators have puzzled over this apparently gratuitous mention of a Philistine presence on the site of the third sign (e.g., McCarter 182). But we must remember that, according to 9:16, Saul's chief responsibility as Israel's leader will be to deliver Israel from Philistine domination. Does it not seem that Samuel's explicit mention of a Philistine presence in the context of his description of the third sign constitutes a rather unambiguous hint as to what Saul's hand should find to do? Were Saul to attack the garrison, the result, of course, would be only to provoke the Philistines, not to defeat them. Thus, it makes sense that Samuel issues a second command in 10:8. Once Saul has provoked the Philistines by attacking the garrison, he must repair to Gilgal to await Samuel, who, when he has arrived, will consecrate battle by offering sacrifices and will give Saul further instructions regarding the ensuing battle.

If this interpretation is basically correct, it seems curious that chapter 10 records no aggressive action by Saul vis-à-vis the Philistines. We are left with only two explanatory possibilities. Either we must resort to diachronic hypotheses by which we postulate an earlier stage in the tradition in which Saul *did* respond to his first charge by doing what his hand found to do, or we must conclude that in chapter 10 Saul simply falters in the execution of his first assignment. Given the passive, hesitant Saul that we come to know in later chapters, we need not be too surprised to discover hints of these later deficiencies already at this early stage in his career. But if this is what our narrator wishes us to understand, why does he not come right out and tell us that Saul has faltered? Again, sensitivity to the sometimes subtle literary strategies employed by biblical narrators may help us.

In his *Poetics of Biblical Narrative,* Sternberg has argued that every literary work raises certain questions in the mind of the reader to which it does not give direct answers. Instead, the reader must infer the answers during the process of reading from hints within the text. In other words, a literary work such as the books of Samuel

> establishes a system of gaps that must be filled in. This gap-filling ranges from simple linkages of elements, which the reader performs automatically, to intricate networks that are figured out consciously, laboriously, hesitantly, and with constant modifications in the light of additional information disclosed in later stages of the reading. (186)
>
> In works of greater complexity, the filling-in of gaps becomes much more difficult and therefore more conscious and anything but automatic. (187)

I would suggest that Saul's apparent inaction in 1 Samuel 10 and the narrator's silence establish a gap that requires filling as the reading process continues. The legitimacy of any attempt to fill the gap will be measured by its "fit" with other elements within the narrative complex. If we assume, then, as I have suggested, that Saul falters in chapter 10 and fails to fulfill his first charge by doing what his hand finds to do (v. 7), how does this "fit" with the episodes that follow?

SAUL'S FALTERING IN ITS BROADER LITERARY CONTEXT

If the account of Saul's rejection has perplexed theologians, the account of his rise to the throne (1 Sam. 9–13) has proved no less vexing to literary critics and historians. The virtually universal consensus of scholars is that these chapters cannot be read as a convincing sequence of events. It is my contention, however, that once we recognize Saul's faltering in chapter 10, the subsequent episodes follow quite logically as necessary stages in Saul's progress to the throne. In the present essay, we are limited to the few brief comments that follow (for fuller discussion, see Long, *Reign and Rejection,* chs. 6 and 7; *idem,* "How Did Saul Become King?").

At the end of the anointing episode, where we would expect Saul's hand to be finding something to do, we find him instead in conversation with his uncle (10:14–16). When the uncle hears that Saul has encountered Samuel, he is naturally curious to hear what Samuel had to say. Saul speaks only of lost livestock that have been found but, as the narrator points out, says nothing of the kingship. Is he perhaps ashamed of his inaction, or fearful that his uncle, were he to hear what Samuel has said, might chastise him for not taking action?

Moving to the next episode (10:17–27), we read how Samuel convenes an assembly in Mizpah and casts lots to sort out the one whom the Lord has chosen to be Israel's new king. Since, on our reading, Saul has yet done nothing to distinguish himself publicly, it makes sense that Samuel should conduct such a procedure as an alternate means of bringing Saul to public attention. The lot falls predictably on Saul, but he is nowhere to be found. When the ever-reluctant appointee is finally dragged from his hiding place behind the baggage, it is with a measure of justification that certain troublemakers query, "How can this one save us?" (v. 27).

In chapter 11 Saul finally distinguishes himself by rescuing the citizens of Jabesh-Gilead from the Ammonites. Now, at last, all the people are satisfied; indeed they are overjoyed with Saul, and they hold a great celebration. Samuel, however, is not mentioned among the celebrants (v. 15), and in chapter 12 he adopts a solemn tone, warning the people that kingship can yet fail. It is almost as if there is a test of allegiance still to be stood. Might it be that Samuel has in mind the as yet unfulfilled "first charge" issued to Saul at the time of his anointing?

Against this background, it is not surprising that the very next episode (ch. 13) opens with Jonathan attacking a Philistine garrison (or governor) at Geba (possibly the same site as Gibeah Elohim). Here, at last, as various commentators have noted, *someone* finally does what Saul's hand should have found to do in chapter 10 (so, e.g., Stoebe 247). That it is Saul's son, and not Saul himself, who does the deed is passed over without comment by the narrator, though he does note (with irony?) that Saul sent out a report stating, "Saul has attacked the Philistine garrison" (v. 4). With stage one of his initial charge now, at last, fulfilled, it remains for Saul but to execute stage two. As we have already noted, however, in this regard he fails. He may have waited seven days, but he does not wait *until Samuel comes.* The timing of Samuel's arrival, just as Saul is in the middle of sacrificing, gives the appearance of an intentional testing of Saul, and that is precisely what the preceding context has led us to suspect. But why is this test so important? And why is Saul so severely judged for failing it?

SAUL'S FAILURE IN THE LIGHT OF ITS LITERARY CONTEXT

According to the text of Samuel as we have it, the events surrounding Saul's rise to the throne were set in motion by the people's demand to have a king "like all the nations" (8:5). The Lord recognizes in this demand a rejection of his own royal rule (8:7), but he is willing, nevertheless, to grant the people a king and even to bless him—but not a king of the sort they envisage. To be acceptable, the new king must be willing to submit himself to an authority structure whereby God's rule may continue. It is this authority structure that Samuel seeks to establish in 10:7–8. Whereas in the "judges period," for example, a hero-deliverer would typically both receive the Lord's instructions directly *and* carry out the assigned (military) task, with the inception of monarchy these two functions are divided. The reception and mediation of the Lord's instructions become the function of the prophet, while the king becomes the standing military agent. If God, the Great King, is to continue to rule, it is mandatory that the human king heed the voice of the prophet. Saul's first charge (10:7–8) seems designed to test Saul's ability to do just that. Saul's failure to take this charge seriously enough to wait for Samuel in chapter 13 should not be thought trivial, nor should Samuel's emphatic accusation (or lamentation) "You have acted foolishly" and his pronouncement that Saul's kingdom will not endure be regarded as a peevish overreaction. Some have likened Saul to a Greek tragic hero, and indeed there is an element of hubris in Saul's acts of disobedience, since "a decision against the divine . . . always implicitly elevates the decider above the divine" (Good 79). In the end, Saul, like Eli, is rejected for failing to give due weight (honor) to the Lord. Unlike Eli, however, Saul does not respond with "He is the LORD, let him do what is right in his own eyes" (3:18), but drives himself crazy (literally?) trying to maintain his grasp on a throne no longer rightfully his.

Conclusion

In the above discussion I have attempted to offer glimpses into some of the literary qualities of the books of Samuel and to suggest ways in which literary reading may be the pathway to improved theological understanding. Were space permitting, we might also pursue the idea that literary reading can enhance our understanding even of historical questions. In the case of Saul's rise, for example, the primary reason that the biblical record is adjudged historically unreliable is that the narratives are believed not to make coherent sense as a story (for fuller discussion of these matters, see Long, "How Did Saul Become King?"). At any rate, it should by now be recognized that a literary approach to the Bible is not a tangential aberration, though the literary enterprise is certainly not without its share of aberrant interpretations. In the scenic, succinct, and subtle narratives that constitute the books of Samuel, the danger of "overreading," of becoming overly subtle in interpretation, is ever-present, but so is the danger of "underreading." That which grounds literary study in rationality and a degree of objectivity is the discipline of poetics, or narrative criticism, and a desire on the part of the interpreter to develop an ancient literary competence whereby ancient texts can be read and interpreted on their own terms.

WORKS CITED

Alter, Robert. *The Art of Biblical Narrative.* New York: Basic Books, 1981.
Bar-Efrat, Shimon. *Narrative Art in the Bible.* Trans. D. Shefer-Vanson. Journal for the Study of the Old Testament Supplement Series 70. Sheffield: Almond, 1989.
Berlin, Adele. *Poetics and Biblical Interpretation.* Sheffield: Almond, 1983.
Brueggemann, Walter. "First and Second Samuel." *Interpretation: A Bible Commentary for Teaching and Preaching.* Ed. J. L. Mays et al. Louisville: John Knox, 1990.
Buber, Martin. "Leitwortstil in der Erzählung des Pentateuchs." *Werke.* München: Kösel-Verlag, 1964. 2:1131–49.
Carlson, R. A. *David, the Chosen King: A Traditio-Historical Approach to the Second Book of Samuel.* Stockholm: Almqvist och Wiksell, 1964.
Cooper, A. "The Act of Reading the Bible." *Proceedings of the Eighth World Congress of Jewish Studies* (1981), 61–68. Jerusalem: Magnes, 1983.
Edelman, D. V. *King Saul in the Historiography of Judah.* Journal for the Study of the Old Testament Supplement Series 121. Sheffield: JSOT Press, 1991.
Garsiel, M. *The First Book of Samuel: A Literary Study of Comparative Structures, Analogies and Parallels.* Jerusalem: Revivim, 1985 (Hebrew, 1983).
Good, Edwin M. "Saul: The Tragedy of Greatness." *Irony in the Old Testament,* 56–80. London: SPCK, 1965.
Gordon, Robert P. "1 & 2 Samuel." *Old Testament Guides.* Ed. R. N. Whybray. Sheffield: JSOT Press, 1984.
———. *I & II Samuel: A Commentary.* Exeter: Paternoster, 1986.
———. "David's Rise and Saul's Demise: Narrative Analogy in 1 Samuel 24–26." *Tyndale Bulletin* 31 (1980): 37–64.
———. "Simplicity of the Highest Cunning: Narrative Art in the Old Testament." *Scottish Bulletin of Evangelical Theology* 6 (1988): 69–80.
Gunn, David M. *The Fate of King Saul: An Interpretation of a Biblical Story.* Journal for the Study of the Old Testament Supplement Series 14. Sheffield: JSOT Press, 1980.
Jobling, D. "Jonathan: A Structural Study in 1 Sam." *The Sense of Biblical Narrative.* Journal for the Study of the Old Testament Supplement Series 7. Sheffield: JSOT Press, 1978. 4–25.
———. "Saul's Fall and Jonathan's Rise: Tradition and Redaction in 1 Sam 14:1–46." *Journal of Biblical Literature* 95 (1976): 367–76.
Licht, J. *Storytelling in the Bible.* Jerusalem: Magnes, 1978.
Long, V. Philips. "How Did Saul Become King? Literary Reading and Historical Reconstruction." In a forthcoming volume on ancient Near Eastern and biblical historiography. Ed. D. W. Baker, J. K. Hoffmeier, and A. R. Millard. Winona Lake, Ind.: Eisenbrauns.
———. *The Reign and Rejection of King Saul: A Case of Literary and Theological Coherence.* Society of Biblical Literature Dissertation Series 118. Atlanta: Scholars, 1989.
Longman, Tremper, III. *Literary Approaches to Biblical Interpretation.* Foundations of Contemporary Interpretation 3. Grand Rapids: Zondervan, 1987.
McCarter, P. Kyle. *I Samuel: A New Translation with Introduction, Notes & Commentary.* Anchor Bible. Garden City: Doubleday, 1984.
Moberly, R. W. L. *At the Mountain of God: Story and Theology in Exodus 32–34.* Journal

for the Study of the Old Testament Supplement Series 22. Sheffield: JSOT Press, 1983.

Muilenburg, James. "A Study in Hebrew Rhetoric: Repetition and Style." *Supplements to Vetus Testamentum* 1 (1953): 97–111.

Polzin, Robert M. *Samuel and the Deuteronomist. A Literary Study of the Deuteronomic History: 1 Samuel.* San Francisco: Harper & Row, 1989.

Preminger, Alex, and Edward L. Greenstein, eds. *The Hebrew Bible in Literary Criticism.* New York: Ungar, 1986.

Ryken, Leland. *How to Read the Bible as Literature.* Grand Rapids: Zondervan, 1984.

———. *Words of Delight: A Literary Introduction to the Bible.* Grand Rapids: Baker, 1987.

Smelik, K. A. D. *Saul, de voorstelling van Israels eerste Konig in de Masoretische tekst van het Oude Testament.* Amsterdam: Drukkerij en Uitgeverij P. E. T., 1977.

Sternberg, Meir. *The Poetics of Biblical Narrative: Ideological Literature and the Drama of Reading.* Bloomington: Indiana UP, 1985.

Stoebe, H. J. *Das erste Buch Samuelis.* Kommentar zum Alten Testament. Gütersloh: Gerd Mohn, 1973.

Willis, J. T. "An Anti-Elide Narrative Tradition from a Prophetic Circle at the Ramah Sanctuary." *Journal of Biblical Literature* 90 (1971): 288–308.

———. "Samuel Versus Eli: I Sam. 1–7." *Theologische Zeitschrift* 35 (1979): 201–12.

CHAPTER 12

First and Second Kings

G. MICHAEL HAGAN
North American Baptist Seminary

Chronological and Narrative Time

Paradox encompasses the two Old Testament books of Kings. Most people describe the books as biblical history, but they remember the colorful stories and characters—for example, Solomon exhibiting his wisdom with two prostitutes (1 Kings 3:16–28) and Elijah confronting the prophets of Baal on Mount Carmel (18). When asked about the content of Kings, readers focus on the primary structuring device hinted at in the title—the accounts of the kings. Yet prophets also play a substantial role in these accounts.

Literary aspects such as drama and character dominate most readers' experience of these books. Why? Because storytelling is the vehicle that the writer uses to recount the history of Israel from King Solomon to the downfalls of the divided kingdoms of the north (Israel) and south (Judah).

My aim in the discussion that follows will be to make the reader sensitive to the storytelling aspects of Kings. The implied question that governs my commentary is, What questions should a reader bring to Kings to experience it as literature and as narrative?

The content of Kings traces Israel's history from Solomon to the fall of

Jerusalem. It begins in a context of the last days of David. David passes to Solomon a united monarchy (1 Kings 1–2). Solomon's reign follows (3–11). He rules with David's and God's blessings (3:3–15), but in the end he fails by turning aside after other deities (11). His son inherits a troubled kingdom that soon divides into two separate states. The text follows the divided monarchy in a synoptic fashion until the destruction of Samaria and the northern state (1 Kings 12–2 Kings 17). Particular attention is directed at the dynasty of King Omri (1 Kings 17:1–2 Kings 10:31). After the destruction of the northern kingdom, the history of Judah continues until her own fall at the hand of the Babylonians (2 Kings 18:1–25:21).

Chronology frames the royal court narrative. Introductory and concluding formulas occur, beginning with Rehoboam. Introductory formulas follow this pattern: a king (personal name), son of the preceding king (PN), reigned in Judah. He was *n* years old when he became king. He reigned *n* years in Jerusalem (or other city name) and his mother's name was *y* (1 Kings 14:21). Concluding formulas follow this pattern: Now the rest of the acts of king (PN) are they not written in . . . ? And PN slept with his fathers and was buried with his fathers in the city. His mother's name was *y*. His son (PN) became king in his place (14:29–31). With Judah's kings the formulas are consistent in form and content. However, both are missing in Queen Athaliah's case (2 Kings 11). In the accounts of the kings of Israel, the introduction or conclusion, or both, are sometimes missing (2 Kings 9:22–28). The dating of kings places each in relation to the other in a relative manner, linking north and south synoptically.

It is characteristic of the books that chronological time interplays with narrative time (Nelson 9). For instance, *chronology* controls the narrative of 1 Kings 14:19–16:34 as it presents in succession the reigns of Rehoboam, Jeroboam, Abijam, Asa, Nadab, Baasha, Elah, Zimri, and Omri. In 1 Kings 17:1–22:40, the Elijah cycle, *narrative* time takes over. The events are organized by the things the author/narrator wants to present about Elijah, the so-called narrative constraints, rather than strict chronological order. For this reason, scholars wrestle with the actual time presented in the narrative of Elijah. The same phenomenon and subsequent chronological problems occur with the Elisha cycle (2 Kings 2:1–8:15).

In fact, wherever time slows down in the telling of Israel's history, it points to the importance that the author/narrator attaches to the material. For example, Solomon's story requires eleven chapters, spanning forty years. Similarly, the lesser-known dynasty of Omri—which includes the reigns of Omri, Ahab, Ahaziah, and Jehoram, the ministries of Elijah and Elisha, and the kings of Judah who interact with Omri's dynasty (Jehoshaphat, Jehoram, and Ahaziah)—spans forty-four years in nineteen chapters, more space than allotted to Solomon. Kings also slows down to recount the reigns of Hezekiah and Josiah.

If Kings slows at points of transition and in places of importance, it may be concluded that the reader should look carefully at Solomon, probably as paradigmatic to the overall direction of the books. The reader is asked to reflect over the dynasty of Omri and its confrontation with YHWH and his prophets. Attention should turn to the reign of Hezekiah and his reliance on God and on Isaiah. Care should be taken with the reforms of Josiah. Of course, the reader should not lose sight of the movement from peace and prosperity at the beginning of the books to the destruction at the end, reflecting a tragic pattern for the overall story.

It is precisely at this point that modern interpreters of Kings bog down in questions of chronology. Looked at through literary eyes, chronology serves a utilitarian role, providing a framework for viewing the lives of Israel's leaders, prophets, gods, and people as the nation spiraled downward to destruction. For this reason, much of Kings develops through parataxis (Long 25), a device in which stories are placed side by side without subordination or climax (Nelson 10). A clear example unfolds in the Elisha cycle (2 Kings 2–8), where each account displays little interconnection or interdependence with others. Each story opens a new world that gives insight into God's care of the common people in Israel through the prophet Elisha. If all sixteen stories are viewed together, then additional perspectives surface. This ever-expanding richness of perspective may explain the continuing relevance of the two books of Kings.

The Characters

Many characters inhabit the narrative world of these two books. Rulers take a major part, often balanced by prophets. Unifying the royal characters is the assessment of God, which occurs in the introductory and concluding formulas. Did the king live up to the standard required by God as epitomized in David or did he fall into the model of sin determined by the narrator and epitomized by Jeroboam? Determination is simple, with little ambiguity in categorization.

Manasseh demonstrates this tendency toward classification. In the text of Kings, Manasseh shows that he is an idolater and a murderer (2 Kings 21:1–9, 16). Although he reigns fifty-five years, eleven in coregency with his father, nothing positive comes from his rule. He epitomizes failure (21:2, 17–18). Unnamed prophets oppose him (21:10–15), predicting the condemnation of Judah because of him. Intriguingly, Kings leaves out a brief period of repentance that 2 Chronicles 33:11–17 presents. It did not fit the intention of the author/narrator, who spotlights Manasseh's sins.

The degree to which characters in Kings are elaborated varies widely. At one end of the continuum, we find a fully developed character who displays multidimensions of personality. In the middle we meet the character who shows only one dimension, a typical character. At the far end of the spectrum the agent appears. An agent serves as a device for the telling of the story. David, for example, is old and barely ruling as Kings opens. Abishag must keep him warm. He appears one-dimensional unless you add the descriptions in the books of Samuel. On the other hand, Bathsheba, Nathan, and Zadok the priest are presented more fully than in earlier narratives. Bathsheba, in fact, appears as the most developed personality in chapter 1.

The stories of Elisha display the same development. In one story Elisha looks like a grouch, calling down a curse from God that culminates in the mauling of forty-two lads by two female bears (2 Kings 2:23–25), while in another he travels some distance to revive a child (4:25–27). A full picture of Elisha is painted only after many stories. Each individual narrative account reveals limited qualities of character. Every major and minor character in Kings should be viewed in light of the whole collage of individual stories.

The court narrative as told in Kings fits Thomas Carlyle's statement that "history is the biography of great men." The books present person after person, each of whom acts a part, lives a moment in the monarchy, exhibits positive or negative traits or both, and then gives way to the next described person(s)—kings (Solomon plus nineteen in Judah, counting Queen Athaliah, and nineteen in Israel), prophets (some bearing names, others unnamed; some true to YHWH, others false to YHWH, others true to false gods), servants (with major and minor roles), adversaries (some from within the country and others from foreign nations), gods (true and false from the narrator's point of view), and an environment that takes on its own character at every turn.

Plot

Where is this conglomeration of characters going? The God of Judah and Israel binds it together. As R. D. Nelson says, "God is the central actor in the plot of Israel's history. God demands the total loyalty" (13). Lurking behind each event, each story or cycle of stories, looms the question of loyalty to YHWH.

Linked to this unifying force is the historical setting of the audience. Kings closes with the destruction of Jerusalem (2 Kings 25). Tied with this collapse of Judah is a crisis of faith. Why have God's people suffered so at the hands of a pagan people (cf. the theology of the prophets Jeremiah and Ezekiel)? The historical reasons surface as Kings meanders through the monarchical period. The audience is expected to know the traditions of Israel's salvation history, the ancient tribal system, the geography of Jerusalem, the exterior of the temple, the geography of the land, the theology of Deuteronomy, the history of Joshua-Samuel—in other words, be sufficiently well-informed to understand the direction of the books of Kings (Nelson 6–7). Babylonian exiles fit this picture best as the original audience.

Several overriding themes bolster the central question of loyalty to YHWH for the exiles. For example, the theme of apostasy and reform surfaces in several guises. Jehu destroys the idolatrous dynasty of Omri. Hezekiah and Josiah promote strong reforms during their reigns, one prompted by the prophet Isaiah and the other by the written word of YHWH. In Josiah's reign the extent of idolatry is striking (2 Kings 23). Progression of sin leads to the invasion of idolatry at every level of society. Elijah's famous question on Mount Carmel sounds the keynote: "How long will you waver between two opinions? If the Lord [YHWH] is God, follow him; but if Baal is God, follow him" (1 Kings 18:21).

One of the main plot conflicts growing out of the loyalty question is that of the king versus the prophet. The kings in Israel and Judah misused their roles. Consequently, YHWH confronted them through prophets. G. von Rad points out a prophecy-fulfillment pattern that emerges eleven times in Kings, often in royal contexts (78–81). Tension develops between human initiative and divine control (Savran 160). The books of Kings teach that God is in control of history.

This tension manifests itself in the temple. The temple is built by Solomon and is destroyed as described in 2 Kings 25. How ironic that Israel's symbol of relationship with YHWH could become one of the main reasons for her downfall.

The plot conflict of Baal versus YHWH also ties in with the overall theme of the books. Already seen in the great drama of Elijah on Mount Carmel (1 Kings 18), YHWH promises punishment for idolatry and does not turn away from his anger (2 Kings 23:26).

Techniques of Storytelling

Classification of the genre of Kings as a whole and of individual stories remains difficult (Long 30–31). As historical literature it manifests a historylike quality, developing lists, reports, stories, and historical cycles to present with purpose and intent the view of the author/narrator. History is brought alive by the narrative. Injected into the narrative are speeches by YHWH and miracles in different guises. Are these elements also historical? Literary analysis needs to remain in touch with the worldview of the original teller rather than work from a modern view of the miraculous. The author/narrator includes the miraculous alongside the political or historical (Zakovitch). This phenomenon could be described as naïve (Halpern 248) or "fictionalized 'telling'" (Long 30), but the text makes no such distinctions. Miracles do tend to group around the prophets (e.g., Elijah-Elisha stories).

Stylistic traits that are used by the court narratives vary considerably among the various stories. One device that is used in developing plot in many stories in Kings involves conflict resolution. Many accounts begin with naming a main protagonist and alluding to some fact that hints at the problem to follow (i.e., 1 Kings 21:1). Tension-developing dialogue clarifies the problem along with the main characters. This slow-telling through conversational interaction leads to a hurried, almost mad-rush reporting that culminates in the resolution. If the story varies from this pattern, it does so at the end, as though a neat and tidy conclusion is not the most important part of the account. An open-ended quality results. For example, Jehoram tries to bring Moab back under his control after it rebelled against his kingship (2 Kings 3). Israel pushes Moab back to its last stronghold, where the Moabite king sacrifices his son, evidently to change the course of battle. Israel withdraws, and the story ends with no resolution (3:27).

Another stylistic device used in Kings is foreshadowing. This suggestive "look-ahead" may take place in large scope or in small details. Solomon's story, when viewed as a whole, appears prototypical to Kings (Savran 155). Within the unfolding of his story, little hints occur that prove profound for the people of Israel and for Solomon himself. For instance, hidden in Solomon's prayer at the dedication of the temple is a foreshadowing of the Exile (1 Kings 8:46–53). Another example surfaces on the same occasion in the Lord's response to Solomon's prayer. The Lord reminds Solomon about his conditions for continued leadership. Solomon must obey God's commandments or else all Israel will suffer punishment (9:6–9). The unraveling of Solomon's greatness in chapter 11 opens up a view to Israel's future.

In a similar vein, Kings employs a prophecy-fulfillment pattern with twelve explicit cases where a prophet's word is fulfilled "according to the word of YHWH" (von Rad 74–91). Implicit fulfillment strengthens this element of foreshadowing. For instance, Elijah's threefold commission (1 Kings 19:15–17) unfurls without comment through Elisha and his disciples (19:19; 2 Kings 8:7–15; 9:1–10).

Also related to foreshadowing is a rich network of analogy used in the books (Nelson 10–11). Analogous pairs abound in Kings (e.g., two mothers and their sons, 1 Kings 3:16–28; 2 Kings 6:26–31). Some accounts appear so similar that they are considered the same story told twice (e.g., 1 Kings 17:17–24; 2 Kings 4:18–37), though they need not be. Often more important reasons may be deduced for their inclusion, such as the mirrorlike reflection of Elisha's ministry from Elijah's.

As typically seen in Rehoboam's inauguration (1 Kings 12), a point of view in Kings surfaces through the narrator/author, the character(s), and the reader(s). The omniscient narrator/author controls the direction of the stories, occasionally giving a direct word of explanation (as in 12:15). A character may reveal a point of view through words or deeds, as Rehoboam does (12:6, 9), though usually the character's point of view is most clearly presented by the narrator/author. The reader's point of view surfaces through transitional comments aimed at the reader, such as the time and location problem with Jeroboam (12:2–3), which assumes the reader's knowledge of Jeroboam's flight to Egypt (11:40), or the narrator's intrusion to make a comment that assumes a questioning reader.

Another stylistic trait in the storytelling of Kings pertains to presentation of characters. Usually only one character takes center stage at a time. The principal character in a story will interact with only one other person at a time. When a large group is involved, the speaker will address one person. If a helper or servant becomes involved, then the main protagonist relates to only one at a time.

Because of this focus on one character it remains difficult to ascertain a plot unity for the whole work. It is easier to do so for an individual story, though the connection with other accounts eludes the reader. In addition, character consistency slips because of this focus. In one scene a character may appear as a faithful servant, while in another he reeks with greed (e.g., Gehazi, 2 Kings 4; cf. 5:20–27). Still later, the same servant may appear in a neutral role (e.g., Gehazi, 8:1–6). Story takes precedence over character consistency. In real life, people are not as consistent as they are made out to be. But Kings reflects this disparity because of its storytelling conventions, which focus on a particular story apart from other accounts that also involve the character, not because of a lack of honest portrayal of the characters.

Yet another stylistic trait involves dialogue, which typically presents the main suspense and clarifies the direction of the story. Reporting balances dramatization by describing the subsequent events.

Some of these techniques are distinctive to Kings, while others occur in common with other biblical narratives. For instance, storytelling devices that fit with the prophets appear in these books (e.g., foreshadowing). New characters and situations change the specifics, but often patterns follow conventions.

An Example: The "Man of God" (1 Kings 13)

One of the most difficult chapters in Kings is the story of the "man of God" in 1 Kings 13, which proves to be an essential chapter for understanding the book as a whole because it gives a picture of a key theme: disobedience and punishment. Four scenes transpire: the "man of God" warns Jeroboam (vv. 1–10), an "old" prophet fools the "man of God" (vv. 11–19), the "man of God" dies (vv. 20–25), and the "old" prophet buries the "man of God" (vv. 26–32). In each scene the best entry point becomes character study.

The chapter begins by bringing the "man of God" to the altar at Bethel, where Jeroboam has set up a worship alternative and is present himself to participate in a feast (12:33). No name is given to the "man of God," though elsewhere this phrase always refers to a prophet and is corroborated by his words and the words of the old prophet (v. 18). The text tells us that he came from Judah at the instruction of YHWH (v. 1). He cries out against the altar "by the word of YHWH" (v. 2) and supports YHWH's word with a sign (v. 3). In verses 8 and 9 he reveals more of the word of YHWH by refusing to eat or drink in Bethel and by returning by a different way from the way he had come, "by the word of YHWH." YHWH's word is known by the proclamations of the "man of God." The narrator reports the fulfillment of the sign (v. 5) and the obedience of the "man of God" (v. 10). Both references reflect on his character.

In the first scene Jeroboam is the antagonist. He burns incense at the altar, an act associated with his other idolatrous practices (12:28–33). His actions place him where he hears the "man of God." The king exercises his authority when he orders the prophet seized (v. 4). No clues as to tone are presented in the text: Is he angry at the prophet's words? Is he anxious? He points his hand at the prophet, and it withers. The text does not indicate who ordered the fulfillment of the prophet's word against the altar, but it is knocked over (v. 5). Then, after prayer by the "man of God," the king's hand is restored (v. 6). In thankfulness or out of politeness, the king invites the prophet home for refreshment and reward (v. 7). The prophet refuses, declaring obedience to the instructions of YHWH (vv. 8–9).

What is missing from the first scene? For some reason the people are never indicated in the text, though they should be supposed as the prophet's audience and as the king's force to command.

Closure of the first scene paves the way for the second one. Several more characters surface in the second scene. An "old" prophet dwells in Bethel, but was not present at the cultic activities of scene one. However, his sons were there, and one describes the day's events to his father (v. 11). This description is merely reported instead of dramatized, since the first scene has already given the pertinent details to the reader.

Other than the age and family of the prophet, no indication of the character of the old prophet presents itself. He had sons, and they went to the festival, perhaps implying their apostasy. But why didn't the old prophet attend the festival? Was it because of his age, or because of a different view toward Jeroboam's deeds? Was he a prophet of YHWH or of a false deity or deities? The text does not tell us. When he meets the "man of God," a brief interchange takes place that gives some indication of his character. Indeed, the old prophet finds the "man of God who came from Judah" (v. 14). He invites him home with him; the "man of God" refuses, repeating the same reasons he had given to the king (vv. 16–17). The old prophet lies to the man, the narrator tells us (v. 18), telling him of a new revelation supposedly given to him by a messenger. Again, there is reference to the word of YHWH. The man of God returns with the old prophet and eats and drinks with him.

At this point the only indication that something is wrong is the comment of the narrator. If the old prophet lied, then surely the man of God will not be held accountable? Perhaps a new revelation has been given? Perhaps the instructions to the man of God came to him by a messenger in Judah, and this new word makes sense in that context? Scene two ends with disobedience, but with no sign of the punishment that will follow in the next scene. Tension pervades the close of scene two.

In the third scene the word of YHWH comes to the old prophet as they sit at the table. This time it is truly the word of YHWH. "Thus says YHWH": you have disobeyed by not keeping the commandment of YHWH (vv. 21–22). The earlier words spoken by the "man of God" to the king and the old prophet are repeated now by the old prophet. The man of God's own words condemn him.

The old prophet reveals new aspects of his character in this scene by voicing the words of YHWH and by providing a donkey for the prophet whom he has helped destroy (v. 23). But the generosity cannot assuage the wrong. He marches off like a condemned man. On the road home, a lion kills the man of God. The donkey survives (v. 25), according to a report by some witnesses who view the scene. Is there a connection between the man's death and his disobedience? No connection is made, except the silence of the man of God.

Just as the old prophet's sons and the men on the road fulfill agent roles in the story, so does the lion. He "meets" the man of God, as the old prophet had met him before, but he kills him and throws him into the middle of the road (v. 24). The lion metes out the punishment.

In the fourth scene the words of the old prophet draw the story to its conclusion. He identifies the disobedient "man of God" by the witnesses' description (v. 26). Then he goes out, retrieves the body, and buries the man in his own grave (v. 30). While mourning the death of his "brother," he voices to his sons the key words of the chapter. He instructs them to bury him next to the man of God when he dies. Why? Because the word of YHWH that he pronounced against the altar and the high places shall surely come true (vv. 31–32). Upon what basis can he make this assessment? Since YHWH's word through the old prophet proved true, so also the man of God's earlier words will come true.

In his final statement the old prophet expands the prophet's first pronouncement about Josiah (v. 2). The mention of Josiah by name is only the first of several miraculous elements in the text, including also the withered hand of Jeroboam, the death of the man of God but not of the donkey, and the nondeath of the old prophet who gets the body from the road in front of the lion. These words come true years later in the reign of Josiah, perhaps the most profound miracle in this story (2 Kings 23:17–18). Words predicted years before bind together the books of Kings.

The story of the "man of God from Judah" stresses the importance of the word of YHWH. Be obedient to his word or suffer the consequences of disobedience. This message summarizes Kings.

In addition, this chapter epitomizes many literary elements found in the books of Kings. There is dramatic confrontation and conciliatory pause, clarity and mystery. As characters, YHWH and his prophet stand against the king and his sin. Jeroboam typifies the kings that follow him. He becomes the measuring device by his sinful deeds. The people stand on the sidelines in passive pose. To whom should they listen? To further confuse the scene, an old prophet enters the story. Even the man of God mistakes his message for that of YHWH.

Speech clarifies the message of the man of God, the viewpoint of the king, and the result of not listening to YHWH. Action unfolds the wonder of the miraculous and the mystery of complete obedience. The narrator confirms the words and actions of the man of God and the old prophet by noting their significance for Jeroboam's reign (vv. 33–34). Every element comes together to deliver the message of the chapter.

Conclusion

The books of Kings exhibit paradox. On the one hand, they whisk us away to a strange world very different from our own. That is part of their nature as primitive documents, but it is also part of their charm and intrigue. On the other half of the paradox we find recognizable human experience. The drama that unfolds, the themes that surface, the people who are presented ring as loud today as they did in their original context.

The specifics may have changed, but the portrayals span the whole gamut of life, moving from the greatest to the least, from world politics to a moment in the life of a minor character, from the profound to the mundane. The contents of these ancient books continue to provide wisdom for today's reader, if we will listen.

A close reading of the text demonstrates that the literature of Kings is like a fine tapestry—it warrants analysis while at the same time showing by its existence that it should be simply enjoyed. Literary theory cannot do away with the subjective practice of reading, but it can provide a formal means for a more sensitive reading.

WORKS CITED

Halpern, B. *The First Historians.* San Francisco: Harper & Row, 1988.

Long, B. O. *1 Kings, with an Introduction to Historical Literature.* Grand Rapids: Eerdmans, 1984.

Nelson, R. D. *First and Second Kings.* Interpretation. Atlanta: John Knox, 1987.

Savran, G. "1 and 2 Kings." *The Literary Guide to the Bible.* Ed. Robert Alter and Frank Kermode. Cambridge, Mass.: Harvard UP, 1987. 146–64.

von Rad, Gerhard. *Studies in Deuteronomy.* Studies in Biblical Theology. Trans. D. Stalker. London: SCM, 1953.

Zakovitch, Y. "Rationalization of Miracle Motifs in Biblical Narrative," *Proceedings of the Ninth World Congress of Jewish Studies: Division A—The Period of the Bible,* 27–34. Jerusalem: World Union of Jewish Studies, 1986.

CHAPTER 13

First and Second Chronicles

RICHARD L. PRATT, JR.
Reformed Theological Seminary

As the chapters in this volume evidence, biblical interpreters have come to acknowledge the value of examining the literary features of Old Testament books. From one end of the theological spectrum to the other, scholars no longer treat literary art as insignificant ornamentation, but as a vital concern of responsible interpretation. The justifications for this hermeneutical shift are manifold, but one reason moves to the foreground in Old Testament studies. Here we deal with religious texts, books crafted to convey normative ideological perspectives for the community of faith. If for no other reason, therefore, we must concern ourselves with the literary qualities of Old Testament texts because they are the media of ideology.

In this chapter we will explore several links between literature and ideology in the book of Chronicles (1 and 2 Chronicles). Two factors make Chronicles particularly fertile ground for evaluating these interconnections: our knowledge of the chronicler's central outlooks, and the availability of his principal literary sources.

Recent studies have resulted in widespread consensus on the chronicler's major theological emphases. Different viewpoints on the specific date of the chronicler have resulted in various assessments of his purposes, but the prevailing acceptance of separate authorship for Chronicles and Ezra-Nehemiah has highlighted several major *Tendenzen* in Chronicles (Pratt 28–44). The chronicler wrote to encourage the postexilic community in three principal areas: the reunification and ordering of God's people under the Law of Moses, the renewal of temple personnel and services, and the restoration of the Davidic throne. From his point of view, these dimensions of life were essential ingredients for the full restoration of postexilic Israel.

Beyond this, interpreters can discern the chronicler's literary skills by comparing his work with the sources on which he relied. We do not have access to many sources the chronicler used (e.g., 1 Chron. 9:1; 29:29), but we possess his primary literary foundations: Samuel and Kings. When the complexities of textual traditions are taken into account (McKenzie 1983), comparisons with Samuel and Kings reveal the chronicler's distinctive literary achievements and display how skillfully he conveyed his views.

To explore the link between literary features and ideology in Chronicles, we will concentrate on characterization and plot in his narrative material. Chronicles begins with nine chapters of genealogies (1 Chron. 1:1–9:44) that contribute significantly to the development of the chronicler's central themes. In this study, however, we will concern ourselves with the narrative portions of Chronicles. This investigation will be limited, but it will touch on items representative of the entire book.

Characterization

If we define characterization as the display of a character's "habits, emotions, desires, [and] instincts" (Thrall and Hibbard 74), a cursory reading may give the impression that characterization is barely present in Chronicles. Along with most biblical writers, the chronicler gives few explicit details about the psychological dimensions of persons in his stories. Readers are usually left to infer for themselves the qualities of characters' inner lives. Nevertheless, Chronicles often presents striking profiles of characters' moral and religious dispositions. The chronicler skillfully orchestrated appearance, status, actions, speech, and authorial comments to help his readers understand, evaluate, and react to characters.

CHARACTERIZATIONS OF ROYALTY

Many persons appear in Chronicles, but royal figures occupy center stage. The kings of Judah serve as fenceposts along which the plot of the history runs. To understand how the chronicler characterized various kings, we will begin with an overview and then examine two specific kings—Manasseh and Solomon.

A survey of royal figures in Chronicles reveals three basic types of characterizations. First, a shadow of moral darkness falls over a number of kings. Jehoram (2 Chron. 21:4–20), Ahaziah (22:1–9), Ahaz (28:1–27), Amon (33:21–25), Jehoahaz (36:2–4), Jehoiakim (36:5–8), Jehoiachin (36:9–10), and Zedekiah (36:11–14) have few, if any, redeeming qualities. None of these characterizations, however, reflect the chronicler's unique perspectives; he basically adopted outlooks already appearing in the book of Kings.

A second class of royal portraits displays both negative and positive elements. Some of these mixed portraits follow Kings closely. Asa (2 Chron. 14:2–16:14) and Jehoshaphat (17:1–21:3) appear as mixed characters in Kings as well. Yet other examples of these portraits represent the chronicler's own hand at work. The reigns of Rehoboam (10:1–12:16), Joash (22:10–24:27), Amaziah (25:1–28), Uzziah (26:1–23), Josiah (34:1–36:1), and Manasseh (33:1–20) reflect more balanced presentations than those found in the book of Kings.

In his third class of royal characterizations the chronicler presented largely positive portraits of certain kings. By omitting failures recorded in the book of Kings and adding examples of positive accomplishments and divine blessings, he presented a number of kings as models of devotion and obedience. Chronicles offers extraordinarily positive pictures of David (1 Chron. 11:1–29:30), Solomon (2 Chron. 1:1–9:31), Abijah (13:1–14:1), Jotham (27:1–9), and Hezekiah (29:1–32:33). The profiles of David, Solomon, and Hezekiah are mixed in Samuel and Kings; the accounts of Abijah and Jotham are predominantly negative. Yet the chronicler exalted all these kings as positive models for his readers.

To illustrate some of the ways the chronicler used characterization, we will look at examples of the last two types of royal character profiles. Manasseh will represent a mixed presentation; Solomon will serve as an example of idealization.

MANASSEH

The chronicler fashioned a remarkable portrait of Manasseh (2 Chron. 33:1–20). His account depends to a large extent on 2 Kings 21:1–18 but diverges from it as well.

In the book of Kings, Manasseh is the miscreant of miscreants. From beginning to end he is a relatively flat character, displaying nothing but evil attitudes and actions. Two elements of the story develop this ominous portrait: Manasseh's actions as the protagonist and God's reactions as the antagonist.

In the first place, the account in Kings only records Manasseh's sins. He followed "the detestable practices of the nations" (2 Kings 21:2), introduced syncretism (vv. 3–6), and oppressed the people (v. 16). The book of Kings does not hint at a single redeeming quality in Manasseh's life. Even the regnal summary at the end of the account does not soften this extremely one-sided portrait (vv. 17–18). As far as Kings is concerned, Manasseh was a hardened apostate, vicious murderer, and merciless tyrant.

This negative profile finds confirmation in the actions, attitudes, and words of God. Several times the narrative mentions the grace of God toward Israel to highlight the severity of Manasseh's rebellion (2 Kings 21:2, 4, 7–9). Manasseh's actions were "evil in the eyes of the LORD" (vv. 2, 6, 15, 16). They were so abhorrent that God declared, "I will forsake the remnant of my inheritance and hand them over to their enemies" (v. 14). These divine reactions reveal the extent to which the writer of Kings portrayed Manasseh as a villain.

Second Chronicles 33:1–20 immediately reveals a drastically different portrait of Manasseh. A few scholars have suggested that Manasseh's reign appeared more balanced in the chronicler's *Vorlage* of Kings than it does in the book of Kings as we have it (McKenzie 250). A thorough discussion of this proposal is beyond the scope of our study. It must suffice to say that there is no compelling evidence in favor of the view. The chronicler's version of Manasseh's reign is so replete with his distinctive theological concerns that it most likely reflects an intentional divergence from his *Vorlage* (Williamson, "Review of McKenzie" 112–13).

How, then, did the chronicler characterize Manasseh? He developed Manasseh into a round character, forming a three-dimensional portrait. He acknowledged the severity of Manasseh's failures, but he also presented a drastic change in the king.

The negative side of the chronicler's characterization shows his heavy reliance on the book of Kings. With few insignificant exceptions 2 Chronicles 33:1–9 closely parallels 2 Kings 21:1–9, repeating the list of the king's sins.

Nevertheless, the chronicler's characterization of Manasseh also takes a different direction. He omitted the prophetic word against the king (2 Kings 21:10–15) and replaced it with an account of Manasseh's transformation (2 Chron. 33:10–17). Rather than threatening exile against the nation, God chastened the king himself by exiling him to Babylon. During this trial, Manasseh "sought the favor of the LORD," "humbled himself greatly," and "prayed to him" (vv. 12–13). This change of character is confirmed by God's response: "The LORD was moved by his entreaty and listened to his plea; so he brought him back to Jerusalem" (v. 13). As if to dispel any doubts, the chronicler informed his readers of Manasseh's inner conviction; he then "knew that the LORD is God" (v. 13).

The chronicler's characterization went one step further. Upon his return to Jerusalem the king became a reformer par excellence. He rebuilt the outer wall of the city (2 Chron. 33:14), reestablished Judah's military might (v. 14), removed the idols (v. 15), sacrificed to the Lord (v. 16), and instructed the people to serve God (v. 16). These acts of devotion stand out prominently in the chronicler's portrait of Manasseh.

Why did the chronicler present such a different characterization? The writer of Kings used Manasseh's reign to give a historical justification for the Exile. The chronicler, however, wanted his readers to see how Manasseh's life adumbrated their experiences. His readers had sinned against God, gone to Babylon, sought the favor of God, and returned to the land. Now they too were in the process of rebuilding the kingdom. If the king who sealed the fate of Judah demonstrated his repentance by reforming and rebuilding, how much more must they do the same?

SOLOMON

The chronicler's portrait of Solomon (2 Chron. 1:1–9:31) represents the third major type of characterization of royalty. He transformed a mixed view of Solomon in Kings into an idealized portrait. The length of material devoted to Solomon's reign will not permit a detailed comparison between Kings and Chronicles; I will simply summarize some of the more significant similarities and differences.

Solomon's reign in Kings consists of three major sections: Solomon's rise (1 Kings 1:1–2:46), his tainted glory (3:1–10:29), and his downfall (11:1–40). This format presents positive and negative outlooks on the king. The first section defends Solomon's actions as he struggled for control over the kingdom (McCarter 11–13). The middle portion of Solomon's reign concentrates primarily on positive aspects of Solomon's character. He attained wisdom from God (1 Kings 3:12, 28; 4:29–34) and demonstrated that wisdom in a variety of ways (3:28–10:29). This glorious picture is slightly marred by Solomon's marriage to Pharaoh's daughter (3:1–3) and his giving more time to his palace than to the temple (6:38–7:1). Yet the middle section is positive on the whole. The third section of Solomon's reign (11:1–40) offers a thoroughly negative assessment of the king. Solomon's many foreign wives led him into syncretism. As a result, God determined to divide the kingdom (vv. 11–13) and raised adversaries against him (vv. 26–40).

The writer of Kings presented Solomon as a round character. He acknowledged the greatness of Solomon but also revealed his failures. This two-sided portrait not only provided a realistic assessment of the king's reign, but it also fit well with the purpose of Kings by demonstrating the value of the Davidic line for Israel as well as the justice of the Exile.

The characterization of Solomon in Chronicles stands in sharp contrast to the balanced portrait in Kings. The chronicler reworked the material so that Solomon appears to have few, if any, flaws. To present his idealization of Solomon, the chronicler omitted material found in the book of Kings and included new information.

Four of the chronicler's omissions warrant mention. First, he modified Nathan's words to David about Solomon (2 Sam. 7:14; 1 Chron. 17:13). In the book of Samuel, Nathan conveyed God's promise, "I will be his father and he will be my son." But the prophet also warned, "When he does wrong, I will punish him with the rod of men, with human floggings inflicted by men." The chronicler maintained the positive word of the prophet, but omitted the warning because his characterization of the king had no room for failure.

Second, Chronicles omits the account of Solomon's struggle for power (1 Kings 1:1–2:46). The omission of this material portrays the transfer of kingship from David to Solomon as a smooth crescendo in Israel's history. In the chronicler's portrait, Solomon was never involved in a struggle for power.

Third, Chronicles omits the record of Solomon's Egyptian wife (1 Kings 3:1–3). Apparently, the chronicler felt that a detailed account of the king's relationship with Pharaoh's daughter would detract from his idealization.

Fourth, Chronicles completely omits Solomon's downfall (1 Kings 11:1–40). The chronicler did not hide the fact that Solomon had foreign wives (2 Chron. 8:11), but he omitted the lengthy discussion of it as found in Kings for fear that it might mar the king's character.

These omissions had a dramatic effect on the presentation of Solomon. As far as the chronicler's account indicates, Solomon did no wrong. Whatever flaws the king may have had, the chronicler considered them insignificant to his purposes. He lifted Solomon to the level of a royal paragon.

In addition to moral idealization, Chronicles portrays Solomon as an astounding political leader. This aspect of his characterization depended on the widespread support Solomon received. For example, within the chronicler's additional material (1 Chron. 29:22b–25) he depicted Solomon's overwhelming support from the nation. "All Israel obeyed him. All the officers and mighty men as well as all of King David's sons pledged their submission to King Solomon" (vv. 23–24). Similarly, the chronicler added an introduction to the story of Solomon's dream at Gibeon (2 Chron. 1:1–6), showing how he ruled over all the nation (v. 2).

Beyond this, Solomon is also idealized as a religious leader. With the omission of the king's political struggles and syncretism, the vast majority of Solomon's reign focuses on his building and organizing the temple. Six of the nine chapters given to Solomon report his cultic activities as demonstrations of his wisdom (2 Chron. 2:1–7:22).

The chronicler's characterization of Solomon formed a striking contrast with that of his source. Instead of a balanced, round figure, Solomon becomes a one-sided, ideal character. The chronicler viewed Solomon's reign as a golden era, a time when the people, the king, and the temple were in proper order. For this reason, he presented an idealized Solomon to provide his postexilic readers with a flawless model for their reconstruction efforts.

Plot

The chronicler's literary acumen also emerges in his handling of plot. Following Aristotle's simple definition of plot (*mythos*) as "the arrangement of incidents" (Aristotle 6.8), I will compare several aspects of material in Chronicles, Samuel, and Kings to see how the chronicler used plot to communicate his ideological point of view. I will illustrate the chronicler's skills in this area in three ways: by briefly surveying the overarching plot of his history, turning to his use of parallel plot structure, and exploring an important example of large-scale anticipation and recollection.

OVERARCHING FEATURES OF PLOT

The most obvious feature of plot in the chronicler's history is the centrality of royal figures. In this regard, his book follows the pattern of Samuel and Kings. They too structure the record of Israel's history according to the reigns of kings. This feature is so fundamental to Chronicle's structure that it is easily overlooked, but its significance must not be underestimated. The chronicler could have adopted any number of strategies toward Israel's complex history. He had the option to arrange his record according to strict chronological sequence, warfare, economic conditions, tribal rivalries, or theological motifs—to name a few possibilities. Instead, his purposes were served well by the pattern already established in Samuel and Kings.

The chronicler's concern with royal figures in Israel's past displayed his convictions concerning Israel's future. He had not given up hope in the institution of kingship. He was a royalist, propagating the importance of Jerusalem's throne to the postexilic community. He looked at Israel's future as he viewed her past. The nation's fate rested on the reestablishment of Jerusalem's dynasty.

Despite this similarity of his record with Samuel and Kings, the chronicler streamlined his plot by excluding significant portions of his sources. A comparison of the lengths of the histories reveals that the chronicler significantly abbreviated his account. Samuel and Kings comprise 101 chapters of material, whereas the chronicler's narrative amounts to 65 chapters. A thorough comparison of the chronicler's plot with that of Samuel and Kings goes far beyond the purpose of this study. Yet it will be helpful to comment on the principal way in which the chronicler's plot is simpler than his sources.

The primary way in which the chronicler simplified his plot was to omit those portions of his sources that focused on kings other than David and his descendants. Apart from a brief account of his demise (1 Chron. 10:1–14), Saul's reign is excluded from Chronicles. Similarly, there is no report of the competition between Solomon and Adonijah (1 Kings 1–2). On occasion, the chronicler acknowledged the activities of many kings in northern Israel (2 Chron. 10; 13:1; 16:1), but he consistently omitted large portions of the text of Kings that focused on events in the North. Whereas the writer of Kings constantly shifted back and forth between occurrences in the southern and northern kingdoms, the chronicler concentrated his record on the South, thus greatly simplifying his history.

The chronicler's exclusive concern for Judah results from his ideological purposes. In the postexilic period, restoration from exile had begun in Jerusalem, not Samaria. As a result, the chronicler concentrated his history on events in Judah. His chief concern was to draw attention to the positive and negative lessons that Judahites in his own day could learn from their past.

PARALLEL PLOT

Parallel plot structure may be defined as the arrangement of two or more sets of material into analogous patterns that draw attention to similarities and contrasts between events. The chronicler used this literary technique on a number of occasions, but I will restrict my discussion to his record of Asa's reign (2 Chron. 14:1–16:14).

From the outset it is apparent that the chronicler's record is considerably larger than that of Kings (1 Kings 15:9–24). Asa's reign in the book of Kings follows a simple outline: introduction (1 Kings 15:9–10), overview and evaluation (vv. 11–15), war with Israel (vv. 16–22), and Asa's death and successor (vv. 23–24). The chronicler omitted a small portion of his source (1 Kings 15:9–10), followed Kings with minor modifications elsewhere (compare 1 Kings 15:11–12 with 2 Chron. 14:2–3; 1 Kings 15:13–16 with 2 Chron. 15:16–19; 1 Kings 15:17–22 with 2 Chron. 16:1-6; 1 Kings 15:23–24 with 2 Chron. 16:11–14), and inserted two sections of new material (2 Chron. 14:4–15:15; 16:7–11). These additional elements expanded the sixteen verses of Kings to forty-eight verses in Chronicles.

The chronicler enlarged Asa's reign to form two contrasting parallel plots.

Asa's Early Years of Prosperity	14:1–7
Victory in War With the Cushites	14:8–15
Prophetic Approval and Royal Reforms	15:1–19
Shortcoming in War With Israel	16:1–6
Prophetic Condemnation and Royal Sin	16:7–10
Asa's Late Years of Sickness and Death	16:11–14

As this outline indicates, Asa's reign divides into two echoing sections (2 Chron. 14:1–15:19 and 16:1–14). These halves share several elements in common. Both sections contain descriptions of events in particular years of Asa's reign that form an *inclusio* around the material (14:1–7; 16:11–14). Both halves also report warfare (14:8–15; 16:1–6) and prophetic announcements along with Asa's reactions (15:1–19; 16:7–10).

The parallels between these sections form a pattern of striking contrasts. The first half displays Asa as one who sought God and relied on him; the second half presents him as one who refused to seek God and to rely on him. This contrast comes to the foreground in a number of ways. Early in his reign the land was "at peace" (2 Chron. 14:1, 5–6); Asa led the people in prosperity (14:7). At the end of his reign, however, Asa became ill and died because he did not seek God (16:12). In his first war, Asa routed the Cushites because he had relied on the Lord through prayer (14:8–15). In his second war, however, Asa fell short of complete victory because he relied on an alliance with Ben-Hadad of Syria (16:1–6). His first encounter with a prophet was positive (15:1–7); Azariah promised reward for the king and his nation (15:7). The second encounter was negative (16:7–9); Hanani condemned Asa to continuous war because he had not trusted God (16:9). Finally, Asa's first reaction to the prophetic word was to lead the nation to further reforms (15:8–19). His second reaction was to imprison the prophet and to oppress some of his subjects (16:10).

What ideological purpose did these symmetrical plots serve? The chronicler expanded Asa's reign into a pattern of contrasting parallels to set two options before his readers. If they trusted God and submitted to his prophets as Asa had done in his early years, they could expect the blessings of peace and prosperity in their day. If they trusted human alliances and resisted the prophetic word as Asa had done in his later years, they could expect only failure and hardship.

Anticipation and Recollection

The chronicler also used a number of large-scale plot structures to communicate his ideological outlooks. For instance, he closely connected the reigns of David and Solomon (Braun 503–16), used Asa as a model for the record of Jehoshaphat (Dillard 129–30), shaped Hezekiah into a second Solomon (Williamson, *Israel* 119–25), and formed the reigns of Amaziah and Uzziah according to the pattern of Joash (Williamson, *1 and 2 Chronicles* 327, 332).

One of the most impressive large-scale features of plot in Chronicles is the anticipation and recollection that takes place in connection with Solomon's dedicatory prayer (2 Chron. 6:12–42). The chronicler used Solomon's prayer at the dedication of the temple to heighten his readers' expectations as they continued reading his history. Moreover, he shaped his record of subsequent events so that they could be properly understood only in terms of the theological background of Solomon's prayer.

Before we turn to the chronicler's use of Solomon's prayer, I should say a word about the role of this royal prayer in the book of Kings. We may divide 1 Kings 8:22–53 into four parts: setting (v. 22), doxology (vv. 23–24), petitions for the Davidic dynasty (vv. 25–26), and petitions regarding the temple (vv. 27–53). The final portion of the prayer is particularly important for our purposes. Here Solomon elaborated on his hopes for Israel's future in a series of seven petitions (1 Kings 8:31–32, 33–34, 35–36, 37–40, 41–43, 44–45, 46–53). In these petitions the king described a number of situations in which the temple could serve as a place for effective prayer.

Solomon's hopes for future prayers in the temple raised significant dramatic tension. Were these hopes ever realized? Did the temple serve the function David's son expected? As we will see, the writer of Kings answers in the affirmative.

Three petitions in Solomon's prayer anticipate events that actually take place in the book of Kings. First, in 1 Kings 8:44–45 Solomon anticipated an event in Jehoshaphat's reign. He requested that God hear prayers offered in battle. In 1 Kings 22:1–37 Jehoshaphat joined Ahab in war against Syria.

When the Syrians threatened Jehoshaphat's life, he called out and escaped harm. The traditional Hebrew text of 1 Kings 22:32–33 suffers from haplography (*wyhwh . . . wyhy*) and should be emended in the light of LXX boc2e2 (*καὶ κύριος ἔσωσεν αὐτόν*) to read, "But Jehoshaphat cried out, *and the LORD helped him. God drew them away from him. . .*" (McKenzie 159–60). Just as Solomon had asked, God responded to the prayer of Judah's king in the midst of battle.

Second, 1 Kings 8:37–40 foreshadows the reign of Hezekiah. Solomon asked God to hear the prayers of the people "when an enemy besieges them in any of their cities" and when "a disease may come" (1 Kings 8:37). These two situations occurred in Hezekiah's day and gave rise to his two prayers. Hezekiah's first prayer was in response to the siege of Sennacherib (2 Kings 19:14–19); his second prayer was in response to his own mortal illness (20:1–3).

Hezekiah's actions show that Solomon's hopes for the temple were not in vain; they proved to be true in the critical days of Assyrian aggression against Jerusalem. Hezekiah was not simply a pious man rewarded by God; his prayers were endorsements and demonstrations of Solomonic ideals for prayer in and toward the temple.

Third, Solomon's final petition (1 Kings 8:46–53) moves to the foreground because it anticipates events in the life of Jehoiachin (2 Kings 25:27–30). Solomon's last request addressed the situation of exile. He asked God to hear the repentant exiles when they prayed toward the temple (1 Kings 8:48–49) and to "cause their conquerors to show them mercy" (v. 50). A recollection of this hope appears in the final scenes of Kings (2 Kings 25:27–30). Although repentance and prayer are not mentioned explicitly, Jehoiachin received kind treatment from his captors. Once again, the writer of Kings showed that Solomon's prayer did not fall on deaf ears.

Solomon's dedicatory prayer serves a similar function in the book of Chronicles (2 Chron. 6:12–42). For the most part, the chronicler's version of the prayer follows 1 Kings 8:22–53 closely; the greatest difference appears at the end of the prayer (compare 2 Chron. 6:36–42 with 1 Kings 8:46–53) (Pratt 246–50). Were Solomon's hopes in vain? Is there good reason for hoping in the temple as a place of prayer? The chronicler answered these questions by establishing a pattern of anticipation and recollection even more extensive than the threefold design in Kings.

The first examples of this expanded role for Solomon's prayer appear in the reigns of the first four kings of Judah. In each case, the kings faced a military threat, called out in prayer, and received God's blessing: (1) Rehoboam and the nobles of Judah uttered a prayer of repentance during the Shishak invasion (2 Chron. 12:6). In response, God blessed Judah with a reprieve from total destruction. (2) During Abijah's reign, the Judahites "cried out to the LORD" (13:14) in battle against Jeroboam and won the victory. (3) Asa offered a lament in his battle against the Cushites (14:11) and succeeded. (4) Jehoshaphat "cried out and the LORD helped him" (18:31) against the Syrians. He also offered a lengthy public lament before defending Jerusalem against the Moabites, Ammonites, and Meunites (20:5–12). All but one of these passages (18:31) came from the chronicler's hand. They represent his own effort to show how Solomon's prayer anticipated future events. The first four kings of Judah demonstrated that praying to God in and toward the temple had dramatic effects on Judah's history.

In addition to the prayers of these first kings of Judah, the chronicler recollected Solomon's prayer in the reign of Hezekiah. He mentioned Hezekiah's prayer during the Sennacherib invasion (2 Chron. 32:20; cf. 2 Kings 19:15–29) and his prayer for healing (2 Chron. 32:24; cf. 2 Kings 20:2–3), but only summarized them. The chronicler placed more emphasis on Hezekiah's prayer for the sick at his great Passover celebration (2 Chron. 30:18–19). In line with Solomonic expectations (2 Chron. 6:28), God heard Hezekiah's request and healed the people. This prayer held particular importance for the chronicler. In his view, Hezekiah's Passover celebration symbolically reunited Israel and Judah in worship as one people under their Davidic king (Williamson, *1 and 2 Chronicles* 350–51). As such, the event was a glorious prefiguring of the chronicler's hope for the full restoration of postexilic Israel. How did these grand circumstances come to fruition? Hezekiah followed the hopes of Solomon's dedicatory prayer. How may the chronicler's readers reach their goals? They must adopt Solomon's outlook on prayer and follow Hezekiah's example.

Finally, Solomon's prayer also anticipates the reign of Manasseh (2 Chron. 6:25; 33:12–13). In a scenario that recollects Solomon's prayer (6:25), Manasseh prayed in exile, and God returned him to the land. The connection with Solomon demonstrated the chronicler's ideological outlook. The full return of the scattered exiles could take place only as the postexilic readers applied Solomon's dedicatory prayer to their circumstances as Manasseh did.

From this brief overview it is evident that the chronicler used Solomon's prayer to establish a pattern of anticipation and recollection much like that of the book of Kings. However, he expanded this plot device and gave it a much more prominent role in his history. The chronicler returned many times to the theme of prayer. Prayer had brought God's blessing to Judah many times in the past. The hopes of the postexilic community rested on their attention to praying in and toward the temple as well.

I began this chapter with the proposal that literary art serves as a medium of ideology in the book of Chronicles. To be sure, we must not reduce the role of artistic elements in the Old Testament to this function; literary design has many other purposes as well. Even so, our investigation of Chronicles has made it clear that appreciating characterization and plot in Chronicles is essential to understanding the chronicler's ideological point of view. This study also suggests that a similar connection holds true for the rest of the Old Testament. Put simply, ideology and literary art go hand in hand in Old Testament interpretation.

WORKS CITED

Aristotle. *Poetics.*

Braun, R. "Solomonic Apologetic in Chronicles." *Journal of Biblical Literature* 92 (1973): 503–16.

Dillard, Raymond. *2 Chronicles.* Word Bible Commentary. Waco, Tex.: Word, 1987.

McCarter, P. Kyle. *II Samuel: A New Translation with Introduction, Notes, and Commentary.* Anchor Bible. Garden City: Doubleday, 1984.

McKenzie, S. "The Chronicler's Use of the Deuteronomistic History." Unpublished Ph.D. diss., Harvard University, 1983. Also published as *The Chronicler's Use of the Deuteronomistic History.* Harvard Semitic Monographs 33. Atlanta: Scholars, 1985.

Pratt, Richard L. "Royal Prayer and the Chronicler's Program." Unpublished Th.D. diss., Harvard University, 1987.

Thrall, William F., and Addison Hibbard. *A Handbook to Literature.* New York: Harper & Row, 1936.

Williamson, H. G. M. *Israel in the Book of Chronicles.* Cambridge: Cambridge UP, 1977.

———. *1 and 2 Chronicles.* New Century Bible Commentary. Grand Rapids: Eerdmans, 1982.

———. "Review of S. L. McKenzie, *The Chronicler's Use of the Deuteronomistic History.*" *Vetus Testamentum* 37 (1987).

CHAPTER 14

Ezra–Nehemiah

Douglas Green
Westminster Theological Seminary

Perhaps the most basic strategy in reading is determining where a story begins and where it ends. When a book is divided into sections, each with its own title, we need to know whether those divisions mark chapters in a larger unified work or discrete short stories in an anthology.

A similar problem occurs with sequels. The relationship between the two works must be understood. How closely are they bound together? Does the sequel have its own integrity so that it "makes sense" without reference to the earlier work, or is the connection so "tight" that the sequel would be incomprehensible without reading the first book?

Surprisingly perhaps, readers of Ezra and Nehemiah must answer such questions. Are Ezra and Nehemiah two separate short stories? Is one a sequel to the other? Or are "Ezra" and "Nehemiah" merely chapter titles in a unified work called "Ezra-Nehemiah"? What of their relationship to 1 and 2 Chronicles? Do they all share the same author? And if so, do they comprise a unified narrative from 1 Chronicles 1 to Nehemiah 13? Or is Ezra-Nehemiah to be understood as a sequel to Chronicles? How we answer such questions will influence our interpretation of Ezra and Nehemiah.

While it is generally accepted that Ezra and Nehemiah together form a unified narrative ("Ezra-Nehemiah"), a number of scholars have recently argued that the author of this work is not the author of Chronicles (see Japhet; Williamson; Eskenazi 14–36). My analysis will follow this approach, but I do not deny the possibility of reading Ezra-Nehemiah as a sequel to Chronicles. Even if the two works come from completely different hands, the repetition of 2 Chronicles 36:22–23 in Ezra 1:1–3a functions on a literary level as a signal that the two books can, and indeed should, be read together (Blenkinsopp 48–49; see also Ackroyd 199–201). On the other hand, arguments that Ezra and Nehemiah were originally two separate works (Talmon 357–58), as well as the early Christian tradition that divided Ezra-Nehemiah into two books, encourage readers to find independent narrative coherence in each book.

Thus, although I contend that Ezra and Nehemiah are best understood if read as a unified work separate from Chronicles, this does not rule out the possibility of differently nuanced readings that take into account the position and shape of the books in the Hebrew and Christian canons.

Major Themes

Ezra-Nehemiah is a story about the building of two walls: "Nehemiah's wall" and "Ezra's wall." The former is a visible wall that physically separates the "house of God" and its inhabitants from the unclean world of the Gentiles (Childs 633–34 and see, e.g., Neh. 13:15–21). The latter is the invisible, spiritual wall of obedience to the Law, by which Israel was to "separate themselves" from the unclean Gentiles (Niphal *bdl:* Ezra 6:21; 10:11; Neh. 9:2; 10:29 [EV 10:28]; see also Ezra 10:8; Neh. 13:3). Through their obedience, the people of God were meant to maintain a clear boundary between two realms.

This interest in boundaries is unveiled slowly. The narrative opens with the decree of Cyrus that the temple (literally, "the house") of the Lord in Jerusalem should be rebuilt (Ezra 1:1–4). That task is undertaken in the face of stiff opposition during the reigns of Cyrus and Darius. But eventually the work is completed and celebrations follow (Ezra 6:13–22). Because the goal set by the decree of Cyrus has been accomplished, there seems little reason for the narrative to continue. But the perceptive reader has already noticed that in the middle of the account of the opposition to the rebuilding of the temple during the reign of Darius the narrative shifts, both spatially and temporally. Ezra 4:6–23 recounts the attempts to prevent the rebuilding of the entire city of Jerusalem during the later reigns of Xerxes and Artaxerxes.

This apparent digression is best explained on the narrative level. The decree of Cyrus concerned the rebuilding of the "house of the Lord." It is clear that at the level of the event itself, Cyrus had nothing more in mind than the rebuilding of the temple. But by weaving together the two different accounts of Gentile opposition, the author effectively redefines Cyrus's intentions. The "house of God" includes the temple, but it is now more broadly defined (see Ezra 3:6–8); it extends to the city of Jerusalem itself (Ezra 4:12) (Eskenazi 55–56). Note also that the rebuilding of the city is described in terms of the restoration of its walls and foundations (Ezra 4:12–16). This is important for the development of the narrative because it creates the expectation that the "house of God" cannot be completed until those walls are rebuilt. That expectation will remain unfulfilled throughout the rest of the book of Ezra, while the other major theme—the building of "Ezra's wall"—is introduced and developed.

In Nehemiah 1–6 the focus once again falls on the city of Jerusalem and specifically on the reconstruction of its walls (Neh. 1:2–3). Despite intense opposition, "Nehemiah's wall" is soon finished, and once again the goal of the narrative—the rebuilding of the "house of God"—appears to have been attained.

Yet, again the narrative continues. In part, this is because the task of rebuilding "Ezra's wall" is still not complete. But there is more to be said about the narrative function of "Nehemiah's wall" too. As far back as Ezra 4, the narrative has drawn a dividing line between Jew and Gentile. When the surrounding nations ask to assist in the rebuilding of the temple, the rebuff from the Jews clearly distinguishes the two groups: "You have no part with us in building a temple to our God [literally, 'the house of our God']" (Ezra 4:3). This same note of separation echoes in the background when the narrative function of the city wall is gradually revealed. As soon as the wall and gates are rebuilt, the gates are locked during a part of each day (Neh. 7:3), and the residents of the city are appointed to guard duty. At this point the narrative is tantalizingly enigmatic. No reason is given for the locking of the gates, nor is it clear against whom this action is directed. Nevertheless, we note that immediately upon the completion of the walls and gate they begin to function as a barrier between two realms.

After hinting that "Nehemiah's wall" will function to physically separate different groups, a quest begins in order to find people who are qualified to live inside these reconstructed walls (Neh. 7:4). First they are drawn from the whole body of people who had confessed their sins and had separated themselves from the surrounding nations by promising to keep the Law of Moses (Neh. 9–10). More specifically, the people chosen by lot to reside in the city are a people set apart, being the nation's tithe to the Lord

(11:1). They are also referred as those who "volunteered" (Hitpael *ndb*) to live in Jerusalem (11:2). In Ezra, the Hitpael of *ndb* is used to refer to free-will offerings made to the Lord (3:5). Here the people themselves are the free-will offerings, not to build of the "house of God" but to populate it. Finally this special status of the new residents of Jerusalem is emphasized by the fact that they are "blessed" [*brk*] by the remainder of the people (11:2).

With a holy people now ready to take up residence, for the first time Jerusalem is called "the holy city" (Neh. 11:1). The broader goal of the narrative has been reached: the building of the "house of God," understood as the city where a people wholly devoted to the Lord lives.

In the final episode (Neh. 13:4–31), however, we see clearly that if "Nehemiah's wall" functions to encircle the holy people, it is also a boundary separating clean and unclean, a physical expression of the way Law-keeping was to keep Israel separate from the neighboring peoples. When Nehemiah shuts the gates to exclude Sabbath breakers from the holy city (13:15–22), two realms on either side of the wall are finally and ideally defined. Inside is all that is holy and clean (Neh. 11:1–3; 12:30; 13:22), outside are the wicked (13:17) and profane (13:18). "Nehemiah's wall" stands in the realm of the holy, but it is also the barrier that keeps the two separate. It is not merely a wall of defense but also a boundary defining the ideal community of the people of God over against all that is less than ideal or opposed to the ideal. It is both a physical wall of separation and a metaphor for the boundary of separation that adherence to the Law would erect.

Throughout the narrative, the stories of the two means of separation are intertwined. For example, Ezra's unannounced arrival on the narrative scene "during the reign of Artaxerxes" (Ezra 7:1) raises the expectation that he will recommence the building of the city walls brought to a halt under the injunction of that king (Ezra 4:23) (Eskenazi 71). We soon discover, however, that Ezra is not a builder but a "teacher well versed in the Law of Moses," devoted to "teaching its decrees and laws" (Ezra 7:6, 10). These laws are the tools of his trade, and the hearts and minds of the people of God are the materials he works with. As he goes about his work we see that he is building a wall of separation between Jew and Gentile, a wall broken down by intermarriage (Ezra 9:14; 10:2), a wall that could be rebuilt only by the people's renewed commitment to separating themselves from the "detestable practices" of the neighboring Gentiles (Ezra 9:11–12; 10:3, 11). By placing this account of Ezra's activities (Ezra 7:1–10:44) in the middle of the narrative of the rebuilding of the temple and city walls (Ezra 3:1–6:22; Neh. 1:1–6:16), the people's adherence to the Law and specifically their separation from foreign wives becomes an integral part of what it means to rebuild the "house of God." It suggests that the "house of God" will never be fully complete until a qualified people—separated from the foreign nations—is found to inhabit it.

As we noted, this quest for a separated people continues after Nehemiah's wall is completed. The ideal for the community is now expressed in terms broader than just rejection of intermarriage with Gentiles. Observance of feasts and Sabbaths is enjoined (Neh. 8:13–18; 10:32 [English version, v. 31]), along with attention to the proper functioning of the temple (Neh. 10:33–40 [EV 32–39]). But separation from the Gentiles remains the primary concern. The ones assembled to confess their sins are designated as those who "had separated themselves from all foreigners" (Neh. 9:2; also 10:29 [EV 28]). When they make their binding agreement, they first declare, "We promise not to give our daughters in marriage to the people surrounding us or take their daughters for our sons" (Neh. 10:30). Indeed, at the high point in the story, in that moment before the narrative begins its descent into the valley of the people's failures, the community responds to the Law and completes the spiritual wall of separation between Jew and Gentile: "they excluded [Hiphil *bdl*] from Israel all who were of foreign descent [literally, 'the mixed group']" (Neh. 13:3). Thus the second boundary, "Ezra's wall," is built.

Characters

It is evident that Ezra-Nehemiah has been composed from a variety of sources—official documents, personal memoirs, letters, and inventories—each written in a different setting, each for a different purpose. Under these conditions, authorial control over more precise narrative techniques such as characterization is diminished. The author-redactor is to a large extent bound by the choices made by the authors of his sources, so it is primarily in the *arrangement* of these sources that the narrative's coherence is to be found. It is for this reason that the structure of Ezra-Nehemiah is the key to understanding its meaning. Nonetheless, characterization in Ezra-Nehemiah clearly supports the main thrust of the plot.

The characters of the main actors are drawn with broad strokes. There is no ambiguity, no subtlety. To borrow Adele Berlin's definition, they are "flat characters" or "types," displaying a single dominant quality or trait (Berlin 24).

Ezra and Nehemiah are uniformly virtuous: Ezra a model of devotion to the Law (Ezra 7:6), Nehemiah equally as noble, with particular emphasis on his care for the welfare of the people (Neh. 1:2–11; 5:1–18). All their actions are consistent with these dominant traits.

Similarly, the narrative leaves no room for assessing the leaders of the surrounding nations in a positive light. When they ask Zerubbabel for permission to assist in the rebuilding of the temple, since they too are worshipers of Yahweh (Ezra 4:2), we might be tempted to see some good in these men. But the narrator has no intention of allowing us to yield to such a temptation. Even before these leaders make this request, they are characterized bluntly as the "enemies of Judah" (Ezra 4:1). There is no chance to assess the motivation behind the request, no opportunity to interpret their words as the first subtle elements in a complex characterization. By this method of direct characterization, "the whole personality gets crammed into one or two adjectives, with clear evaluative import but little else" (Sternberg 328). The narrator is not interested in a subtle portrayal of these leaders; he reduces them to a single epithet: "enemies." Such reduction to single traits is, however, extremely important to the development of the plot (Bar-Efrat 53). The narrative depends on this black-and-white portrayal of the characters for its vitality. The plot is built around a simple struggle between Good and Evil, with each side struggling to vanquish the other.

David Clines has explored how the strategy of narrating large sections of the story from Nehemiah's point of view shapes the characterization of Nehemiah and his enemies. For example, Clines notes that the enemies never really speak for themselves. We must accept Nehemiah's interpretation of their actions or simply stop reading. So when Sanballat invites Nehemiah to a meeting at Ono (Neh. 6:1–9), we must depend on Nehemiah's assessment of his opponents' intentions: "They were scheming to do me harm" (6:2). Yet Nehemiah presents no firm evidence that this is Sanballat's intention and, according to Clines, Sanballat's subsequent actions are not necessarily designed to injure Nehemiah's person. We know Sanballat's character only through Nehemiah's biased perspective (Clines 144–48). A complex, nuanced characterization of Sanballat is neither possible nor intended. Narrating a story from the perspective of one side of a conflict inevitably results in a black-and-white portrayal of the combatants.

Between the wicked leaders of the surrounding nations and the righteous leaders of Israel stand the people of Israel. Both collectively and individually they are neither completely wicked nor completely righteous. Sometimes they are one, sometimes the other. Sometimes they act ambiguously. Yet it is the very ambiguity of their characterization that makes them the most well-rounded and lifelike characters in the story. We have no doubt how the leaders will act. Tobiah will always be wicked; Nehemiah, righteous. Not so the people. The unpredictability of their reactions in any situation creates much of the narrative's tension. On whose side will they align themselves? Under whose influence will they fall? Will they qualify to meet the challenge God has set before them?

Through the first eight chapters of Ezra all the characters fall neatly into two opposing camps. In 9:1 a note of confusion is introduced: "The people of Israel . . . have not kept themselves separate from the neighboring peoples with their detestable practices." They are described in contradictory terms. They are the "people of Israel" and yet they act like Canaanites and other despised Gentiles. Even when they agree to separate from their foreign wives, they sufficiently qualify their commitment (Ezra 10:12) to prevent us from predicting with certainty how they will react to further challenges.

In Nehemiah, these ambiguities are even more pronounced. In 5:1–5 Jews oppress fellow Jews. In 6:17–19 members of the Jewish aristocracy are in league with Tobiah. In 13:15–22 the people violate the Sabbath, and in 13:23–28 they are still intermarrying with Gentiles. Moreover, individuals from among the people are portrayed as ambiguous characters. For example, Meshullam the son of Berekiah is numbered among those who support Nehemiah in rebuilding the wall (Neh. 3:4, 30), and yet his daughter was married to the son of Tobiah (6:18).

Ezra and Nehemiah and their enemies are single-trait characters; their actions are always consistent with those traits. But the people, both collectively and individually, are complex characters, fraught with contradictions and ambiguities. As "fully fledged characters," they look like "real people" (Berlin 23). They are the only actors with the potential for complex reactions to situations. Indeed, success or failure in building the "house of God" depends less on Ezra and Nehemiah or their enemies and more on the people. This is a shift in the nature of biblical narrative away from a focus on leaders to the community as a whole, from individual heroes to ordinary people (Eskenazi 2). Indeed, as we will see, it is this very complexity in the characterization of the people that permits the author to bring his narrative to its open-ended, ambiguous conclusion.

Style

We have already noted that Ezra-Nehemiah revolves around two major themes: the reconstruction of temple and city and the spiritual state of the people. This dual focus is also reflected in the structure of the narrative, which is divided into two distinct movements or "chapters." The first "chapter" (Ezra 1:1–Neh. 6:19) focuses on the building project, with the people's spiritual condition as a secondary motif. The second "chapter" (Neh. 7:1–13:31) flows out from this secondary motif to narrate the quest for a Law-observing people who will occupy the rebuilt "house of God." Each chapter is developed through five successive and parallel stages:

	"Chapter 1"	"Chapter 2"
	Ezra 1:1–Neh. 6:19	Neh. 7:1–13:31
Introduction	Ezra 1:1–2:70	Neh. 7:1–7:72a [EV 73a]
First Step	Ezra 3:1–6:22	Neh. 7:72b [EV 73b]–8:18
Second Step	Ezra 7:1–10:44	Neh. 9:1–10:40 [EV 39]
Climax	Neh. 1:1–6:16	Neh. 11:1–13:3
Subversion	Neh. 6:17–19	Neh. 13:4–31

The first "chapter" opens when "the LORD moved the heart of Cyrus" (*hēʿîr yhwh ʾet-rûaḥ kōreš*) to permit the Jews to return to Jerusalem to rebuild the "house of the LORD" (Ezra 1:1–4) and reaches its *ostensible* goal when the walls of Jerusalem are completed and the opposition of the surrounding nations collapses (Neh. 6:15–16). The second "chapter" narrates a new sequence of events, those occurring "after the wall had been rebuilt" (Neh. 7:1). Here, divine prompting again gives the narrative its direction. Nehemiah says, "My God put it into my heart" (*wayyittēn ʾĕlōhay ʾet-libbî*) to register the people so that residents for the newly rebuilt city could be found (Neh. 7:4–5). After these people have been chosen (Neh. 11:1–3) and the priests and Levites have purified them together with the city walls (Neh. 12:30), the narrative *apparently* reaches its goal with the people's decision to exclude from Israel, not just the foreign wives as had been the case earlier, but all who were of mixed descent (Neh. 13:3).

But in both cases, at the height of the nation's accomplishments—the completion of the building project and the final radical commitment of the people to separate from all Gentiles—the narrative subverts the success. At the close of the first "chapter" the wall is rebuilt and the enemy defeated—or so it seems. At this point the narrative reintroduces Tobiah, a leading Gentile opponent of the building project. The reader discovers two profoundly unsettling facts in this brief postscript to the first "chapter": Tobiah continues to have corrupting influence among the Israelite nobility and, in fact, he is related by his own marriage and the marriage of his son to this same nobility (Neh. 6:17–19).

This same subversive style can be seen in the conclusion to the second "chapter" (Neh. 13:4–31). Having reached the high point of the narrative—

the dedication of the city wall and the people's commitment to remove the foreigners (12:27–13:4)—Nehemiah 13:4–31 surprisingly narrates events from an earlier period. At first it is difficult to see how this final passage serves the overall structure of the story, and it is often taken as somehow separate from the main structure, as if trailing away as an afterthought (Eskenazi 123). But there are significant parallels between this section and the final verses of the first "chapter" (6:17–19). In both, Tobiah reappears as a deleterious influence on the Jewish establishment (6:17–19; 13:4–9), and the problem of intermarriage with Gentiles is emphasized (6:18; 13:23–28). These connections suggest that once again the author wants to subvert the reader's perception that the community has finally reached its goal.

It is no accident that the reader is left bewildered by Nehemiah 13:4–31, with its litany of failures juxtaposed to the obedience and the celebration of 12:27–13:3. Has this been a story of success or failure? Most, perhaps all, of the examples of failure occurred before the events described in Nehemiah 13 (see v. 4), so is not chapter 12 really the last word on Israel's achievements? Then why is the narration of failure left to the end of the story? As a flashback to scenes of previous failures, it raises doubts about the depth of the people's commitment to keeping the Law. Or is it perhaps really a record of Nehemiah's reforms, emphasizing his greatness? But the list of the actions of this one man are set in the context of a sorry inventory of the nation's failures, from high priest to ordinary people. Wherever we set the emphasis, the narrative ends in ambiguity and uncertainty.

What is the significance of this subversion? The reader rejoices that the restoration community has reached its goal but is left wondering how permanent that success will be. Will the community continue to move forward? Will it even hold the ground it has gained (McConville 211–12)? The allusion to Solomon (Neh. 13:26–27) succinctly illustrates the community's predicament. In effect, Nehemiah asks the people, "Will you be like Solomon—Solomon, who built the house of God, who began so well and ended so disastrously? Will you emulate him, destroying your good work by marrying foreign women?" The sin that wrought so much havoc in the preexilic community now crouches at the door of postexilic society. Who will be the master? The narrative ends ominously with unanswered questions and doubts about the reality of the people's commitment to Law keeping.

We noted at the outset that Ezra-Nehemiah is a story about two walls. In the end both walls have been reconstructed. The boundaries that defined the people of God over against the wickedness of the Gentiles are finally in place. But the author's "subversive" arrangement of his sources raises doubts about the quality and permanence of what the postexilic community has achieved. He leaves us with more questions than answers. Are these boundaries secure? Will the two worlds remain separate? It is as if "To be continued" has been written at the end of the work, challenging the original readers to make their own story a sequel in which they rise to the occasion and remove all doubts about the security and permanence of the house of God.

WORKS CITED

Ackroyd, Peter R. "Chronicles-Ezra-Nehemiah: The Concept of Unity." *Zeitschrift für die alttestamentliche Wissenschaft* 100 (1988): 189–201.

Bar-Efrat, Shimon. *Narrative Art in the Bible.* Bible and Literature Series 17. Sheffield: Almond, 1989.

Berlin, Adele. *Poetics and Interpretation in Biblical Narrative.* Bible and Literature Series 9. Sheffield: Almond, 1983.

Blenkinsopp, Joseph. *Ezra-Nehemiah: A Commentary.* Old Testament Library. Philadelphia: Westminster, 1988.

Childs, Brevard S. *Introduction to Old Testament as Scripture.* Philadelphia: Fortress, 1979.

Clines, D. J. A. "The Nehemiah Memoir: The Perils of Autobiography." *What Does Eve Do to Help? And Other Readerly Questions to the Old Testament.* Journal for the Study of the Old Testament Supplement Series 94. Sheffield: JSOT Press, 1990. 124–64.

Eskenazi, Tamara C. *In an Age of Prose: A Literary Approach to Ezra-Nehemiah.* Society of Biblical Literature Monograph Series 36. Atlanta: Scholars, 1988.

Japhet, Sara. "The Supposed Common Authorship of Chronicles and Ezra-Nehemiah Investigated Anew." *Vetus Testamentum* 18 (1968): 330–71.

McConville, J. Gordon. "Ezra-Nehemiah and the Fulfillment of Prophecy." *Vetus Testamentum* 36 (1986): 205–24.

Sternberg, Meir. *The Poetics of Biblical Narrative.* Bloomington: Indiana UP, 1985.

Talmon, Shemaryahu. "Ezra and Nehemiah." *The Literary Guide to the Bible.* Ed. Robert Alter and Frank Kermode. Cambridge, Mass.: Harvard UP, 1987. 357–64.

Williamson, H. G. M. *Israel in the Books of Chronicles.* Cambridge: Cambridge UP, 1977.

CHAPTER 15

Esther

Wilma McClarty
Southern College

The book of Esther troubles, an uneasy presence in the canon. Martin Luther wished it did not exist, lamenting its pagan indiscretions. Ancient Jewish teachers questioned if reading it would defile the hands. No allusions to Esther exist in the New Testament. In the story, the law and the covenant never merit mention. Nor is the book represented in the Dead Sea Scrolls. Today's women label the story chauvinistic.

And even if all of these objections could be glossed over, other puzzling ones persist: Why is there no mention of God? Why no reference to prayer? Why did Esther conceal her Jewishness? Daniel certainly did not. Why such revenge against Haman's *sons?* Why did a Jewess marry a pagan king in the first place? And what about the beauty pageant motif of the queen-selection process?

What should be said to a teenager who cites Esther as a model for Christian courtship behavior, claiming biblical precedent to justify secular relationships, a pagan lifestyle, or premarital sex?

Who might have written the tale? Did Esther write Esther? Did the erstwhile queen of Persia use her literary skills to record a feminine view of history—perhaps her-story? Probably not.

If she did not, then could some other Jewess have authored the narrative? A tantalizing hypothesis. But again, probably not. Of the Old Testament books whose authors *are* known, none is a woman. In her book *The Israelite Woman,* Brenner suggests why few women are seriously considered as authors of even small portions of the Old Testament: "One assumes that women, who are not inherently inferior to men from the aspect of literary potential, were so family-bound that their literary efforts (be they educationally or sociopolitically motivated) were either publicly unknown, or unrecorded by their male colleagues" (46). So what chance did women have to be coached in the craft of narrative to the literary heights evidenced in the Esther story? Understandably, Esther scholars automatically assume a *he* wrote the story.

Nevertheless, a literary analysis of the book of Esther reveals that its author—male or female—wrote with a strong feminine bias. This positive stance toward women reveals itself in the narrator's art, a masterful mix of content and craft. But a literary approach to the story does more—it answers many of the previously mentioned objections to the book. And most important, such an analysis reveals that the plot's development unfolds in the context of the roles played by its perceptive women, not just Mordecai.

Literary critics today associate the elements of plot, character, setting, point of view, and theme with the narrative genre, all elements that can be traced to biblical stories such as Esther. Edgar Allan Poe did not invent the short story. Credit can go to the Bible. In fact, narrative is the dominant genre in the Old Testament. In his analysis, one literary critic has stated that "the prominence of narrative as a biblical form arises from the Bible's view of God. The God of the Bible is, above all, the God who acts" (Ryken, *The Literature* 77). Consequently, for Bible stories to be read most comprehensively, they should be approached as literature and specifically as narrative.

So too with the Esther story. The complex interplay of narrative elements intrigues and informs: its fascinating plot, its psychologically interesting characters, its historically based setting, and its provocative themes (plus what it does *not* say)—all presented with an omniscient third-person profeminine point of view. Esther is in fact the Old Testament book that "has occasioned more antipathy from some readers, and more enjoyment for others" than any other (Fuerst 32).

Plot

A well-crafted plot does more than just tell what happens; its structure supports its theme. Such is the plot of Esther. Whether it is believed that

Esther is the heroine or that Mordecai is the hero does not affect the story's plot unity nor the plot structure's support of the theme of God's people delivered. But this time a woman is the agent of deliverance.

In an artistic plot, any rearrangement of episodes would negatively affect theme. But Esther is so structured that the episodes' sequence heightens the two themes of God's providence and the woman-as-agent.

First, the theme of God's providence is emphasized when the narrative starts in prosperity and then "descends into potentially tragic events, and quickly rises to a happy ending. Tension is built up and released. . . . The plot unfolds in three stages . . . prelude, struggle, and aftermath," with the ascending action describing "an account of how various obstacles to the deliverance of the Jews are overcome" (Ryken, *The Literature* 75). Likewise, the Bible begins in Genesis perfection ("and God saw that it was good"), goes on to depict the descent into the chaos of sin, and then ends with Revelation's picture of the Garden of Eden restored. Plot analysis, then, reveals how the story of Esther becomes a microcosm of the whole plan of redemption, a revelation that might help answer some objections to its being in the canon.

And second, the author's feminine bias reveals itself in the way Esther becomes increasingly significant as the story of final victory unravels. The plot is so ordered to emphasize her progressively complex role. From a dependent orphan, completely submissive to Mordecai's manipulations, she emerges at plot's end as confidently in control of her life—and a nation's.

Once storytellers determine the most supportive episode sequence, they have additional organizational options, such as conflict and suspense. In Esther, the conflicts ferment over deep-seated issues. Haman and Mordecai's confrontations have both personal and national dimensions. Haman, a personal enemy of Mordecai, is also an Agagite, and he therefore perhaps also participates in the longstanding conflict between Israel and the Amlekites. In addition, Vashti and the king clash over courtly matters, including the place of women in the kingdom.

Esther herself is involved with all conflict types, but more so. Her inner turmoil over what it might cost her to take charge intensifies until the "If I perish, I perish" decision is made.

Once the plot sequence sets these different conflicts in motion, the suspense naturally follows. The reader's eagerness to find out what will happen as these diverse conflicts play themselves toward resolution heightens the plot's tensions even more.

Character

The author's feminine bias reveals itself most convincingly in the narrative element of character, the way people are depicted. In the first place, the men in the story do not excel on their own in any desirable way. It is the women—Vashti, Zeresh, and Esther—who display the most commendable behaviors. These three women are more realistic, more crafty, more perceptive, and hence ultimately more in control than the men are. As one critic observes, "In Esther, unsubtle villains meet with brutal fates; proud partisans are fully vindicated; lovely heroines retain the affection of all; and stolid, dim-witted monarchs are there to be used by all" (Sasson 341).

VASHTI

The author's positive characterization of women is especially evident when juxtaposed to the story's characterization of its men—Vashti as a foil to the king, Zeresh as a foil to Haman, and Esther as a foil to Mordecai.

In addition to the providential theme, scholars agree that a main purpose of the Esther story is to provide a rationale for the Feast of Purim. Why, then, did the author include the story of Vashti—if not to make a woman look good? No major theme is advanced by the incident's inclusion. Again, why does Vashti's story need to be told at all? If background for Esther's becoming queen is necessary, why couldn't the story have started, "Since King Ahasuerus was without a queen, a search began throughout the land for a beautiful young virgin . . ."? Why do readers really need to know that the gorgeous Queen Vashti refused the king's command to display herself, whatever that displaying involved?

One reason suggested for Vashti's refusal to appear is that since only harem women and concubines stayed at the feast once the drinking began, Vashti did not want "to degrade herself to that level." Vashti was a "proud woman who refused to be manipulated by a man, even by a king." She "stands in stark contrast to the drunken, impulsive king and his fawning courtiers who magnify the event into a constitutional crisis" (Jones 174–75).

But the real issue is, Who is in charge in Persia, the men or the women? Feminists stress that Vashti's banishment resulted not because she disobeyed but because that refusal could upset the male-dominated status quo. Were Vashti not punished, "her decision could be the start of a major revolution. Other women might look to her as their model; her example would then empower them to rebel against the domination of their husbands." Vashti was vanquished "because she was an enormous threat to the patriarchal status quo. . . . [she] 'wins' by losing. She triumphs over patriarchal domination and control" (Laffey 214–15, 217).

KING AHASUERUS

By comparison, King Ahasuerus is characterized as a "bumbling, inept figure, the object of mocking by the Hebrew storyteller as he exchanges a gleeful wink with his audience." As a foil to Ahasuerus, Vashti remains "a moral norm that heightens the king's status as a playboy and dunce" (Ryken, *Words of Delight* 118). He may be king, but he is a puppet too, being easily manipulated by his chamberlains, never knowing quite what to do: "What shall we do unto the queen Vashti according to law, because she hath not performed the commandment of the king Ahasuerus by the chamberlains?" (1:15). Ironically, Vashti loses the queenship for *not appearing* when summoned; later Esther risks the same position *for appearing* when not summoned. Obviously, any person who threatens the king's "rules" threatens his fragile ego, for apparently he is ridiculously obsessed with power.

Later when Haman convinces him that "it is not for the king's profit to suffer them [the Jews]" (3:8) and Ahasuerus orders their destruction, the author depicts the king as an irresponsible playboy by recording, "And the king and Haman sat down to drink; but the city Shushan was perplexed" (3:15).

Easily angered, he never seems quite in control: "Therefore was the king very wroth, and his anger burned in him" (1:12), "When the wrath of king Ahasuerus was appeased . . ." (2:1), "And the king arising from the banquet of wine in his wrath . . ." (7:7). In addition, this anger made him impulsive and unrealistic. Seeing Haman upon Esther's couch, he asked, "Will he force the queen also before me in the house?" (7:8) and then impulsively commands, "Hang him thereon" (7:9). Had not the king's wrath blinded him to reality, he certainly would have known that sexual matters were at the moment the last interest in Haman's mind. Haman may have deserved to die, but certainly not for violating the queen!

ZERESH

Another contrasting pair revealing feminine bias is Zeresh and Haman. Zeresh appears only twice in the story, the first time giving advice to her husband Haman when he had called a group together to gloat over his recent royal favors: "Then said Zeresh his wife and all his friends unto him, Let a gallows be made of fifty cubits high, and to-morrow speak thou unto the king that Mordecai may be hanged thereon; then go thou in merrily with the king unto the banquet" (5:14). This recommendation needs to be judged in its context, not about what we as readers know *will* happen. From what *Zeresh knew,* she did give very realistic advice. To all those gathered to hear, Haman had boasted about his riches, his many children, his recent promotion, and his banquet invitations.

But the second time Zeresh speaks, she warns realistically and perceptively: "Then said his wise men and Zeresh his wife unto him [Haman], If Mordecai be of the seed of the Jews, before whom thou hast begun to fall, thou shalt not prevail against him, but shalt surely fall before him" (6:13). It is Zeresh, not Haman, who perceives prophetic significance in Haman's having had to lead Mordecai through the streets giving him honor. It is Zeresh, not Haman, who discerns the incident as being another link in the timeless rivalry between Jews and non-Jews, a son of Kish (2:5) and a son of Agag (3:1). It is Zeresh, not Haman, who analyzes the symbolism of Haman's recent humiliation.

Although Zeresh is neither a major nor a complex character, yet what the narrator does select to record about her reveals her to be a perceptive, realistic woman, a non-Jew capable of insightful observations.

HAMAN

One of three main male characters in the story, Haman does exhibit cleverness and control in his plot to destroy the Jews. However, "these qualities are overshadowed and destroyed by his blind hatred of Mordecai, which leads him to abandon his plan and seek a more immediate fulfillment of his ends," behaviors that lead "in turn to a rashness that climaxes in the beginning of his fall in ch. 6" (Humphreys, "Life-Style" 215). Proud of his connections to the king, Haman is "so insecure that he brandishes his *vita* even before those who must know it well (5:9–12)." In addition, Haman's "vanity turns him into a buffoon (6:6), so does his panicked reaction to Esther's accusation (7:8)" (Sasson 337).

In short, Haman is proud yet insecure, revengeful yet easily intimidated, aggressive yet quickly panicked, crafty but bumbling. By contrast, his wife Zeresh remains logical, controlled, perceptive—all characteristics the writer made even more noticeable by contrasting them to the traits of her husband.

MORDECAI

A third pair the storyteller places in contrast is Esther and her cousin Mordecai. At different points in the narrative, Mordecai is characterized as being proud, patriotic, solicitous, crafty, caring, revengeful, and visionary—a mixture of commendable and uncomplimentary traits.

Mordecai's actions get the whole Jewish people in trouble in the first place when he as a Jew refuses to bow or in any way give honor to Haman. Since his motive for not giving homage is not explicitly stated, the text's bald statement that "he had told them that he was a Jew" (3:4) could be interpreted several ways. Was it national pride, religious loyalty, a personal vendetta, or a mixture of all three? Not wishing to show reverence to someone other than God is, of course, the most worthy motive. But worthy or not, the potential genocide of the Jews was thwarted by Esther, not Mordecai. In summary, Mordecai got the Jews into trouble; Esther got them out.

But *any* of these motives presents a problem viewed in the context of Mordecai's dealings with Esther. Mordecai certainly let his Jewish connections, national or religious or both, be known, flagrantly violating the law: "Then the king's servants, which were in the king's gate, said unto Mordecai, Why transgressest thou the king's commandment?" (3:3). Mordecai "told them that he was a Jew" (3:4). Yet why did he not allow his adopted daughter the same openness? We read, "Esther had not shown her people nor her kindred: for Mordecai had charged her that she should not show it" (2:10). His charge to her is particularly troublesome if his motive for not showing honor to Haman was for religious reasons. Was he not forcing Esther to compromise her Jewish conscience, advising her to act in pagan ways in a pagan court?

And worse yet, if his motive for not bowing to Haman resulted from a personal vendetta (although the Haman issue had not yet arisen), did he feel that his own personal and political aspirations could be fostered by having a secret confidant in high places? A despicable reason, really, for cajoling an adopted daughter into national and/or religious identity loss!

ESTHER

But it is Esther after whom the book is named who intrigues us the most. "Of all the biblical heroines," one scholar has observed, "Esther has enjoyed greatest popularity among writers, artists, and musicians, representing feminine modesty, courage, and self-sacrifice" (Sasson 908). And from a literary analysis, Esther is the most complex character in the story.

To be complex, a character must grow as a narrative progresses. Jones credits Talmon with being one of the few to notice Esther's character growth: "In the course of events she ascends from the role of Mordecai's protegee to become her mentor's guardian." Esther "completely overshadows her uncle [rabbinic tradition calls him cousin] and outclasses his adversary Haman in the art of crafty planning and successful execution." Finally, "it is Esther's superior cleverness which saves the day. . . . It is clearly Esther who plays the decisive role in the development of events." From chapter 4 on, Esther is in control. She, not Mordecai, can save the Jews. By the end of the story, Esther's image has been changed from sex object to gifted sage (Jones 172–73, 176–77).

Scholars, however, continue to debate the question of whether Mordecai is the hero or Esther the heroine of the story. Moore would disagree with Talmon: "Between Mordecai and Esther the greater hero in the Hebrew is Mordecai, who supplied the brains while Esther simply followed his directions" (Moore lii). But evidence for Talmon's position becomes even more convincing when supported by specifics tracing Esther's growth as compared with Mordecai's. A literary analysis from the angle of character complexity and growth does not support the claim that Mordecai furnished the brains and "Esther simply followed his directions."

As convincingly as anywhere in the story, the narrator reveals a feminine bias in his treatment of the personal growth of the two leading characters. In chapter 2, Mordecai commands while Esther obeys: "Esther had not shown her people nor her kindred: for Mordecai had charged her that she should not show it" (2:10). Mordecai continues to be involved, walking "every day before the court of the women's house, to know how Esther did, and what should become of her" (v. 11). But by the year's end, Esther on her own, with no help from Mordecai, had "obtained favour in the sight of all them that looked upon her" (v. 15). Furthermore, "the king loved Esther above all the women . . ." (v. 17). Esther's native beauty may have won the king's heart, but her own attractive personality must have been the attraction to the rest of the court.

Even though she was queen, Esther's ties to Mordecai were still strong: "Esther had not yet shown her kindred nor her people; as Mordecai had charged her: for Esther did the commandment of Mordecai, as when she was brought up with him" (2:20). Her lifelong habits of obedience to Mordecai are not easily forgotten even though she is now in the king's palace. By the narrator's detailing her continuing allegiance to Mordecai's orderings, Esther's progressive independence becomes even more impressive as the plot unfolds.

But soon the Haman/Mordecai conflict intrudes on Esther's ideal world, and Esther begins to take charge. Mordecai cries out in sackcloth and ashes at the resulting decree. When Esther hears of his dismay, she sends new clothes, but he won't have them. She then sends Hatach, a king's chamberlain, to get details. Esther is beginning to act, to initiate, to take charge. A small act, admittedly, to send Hatach, but a beginning! The beautiful orphan is being transformed by ordeal, a literary archetype.

Hatach returns with Mordecai's charge that she "go in unto the king, to make supplication unto him, and to make request before him for her people." Esther responds by stating her reluctance to risk death, and she would indeed be risking death, since she had not been called to come to the king for thirty days. Mordecai answers, "Think not with thyself that thou shalt escape in the king's house, more than all the Jews. For if thou altogether holdest thy peace at this time, then shall there enlargement and deliverance arise to the Jews from another place; but thou and thy father's house shall be destroyed: and who knoweth whether thou art come to the kingdom for such a time as this?" (4:13–14).

Notice how this plea appealed to her Jewishness, her family ties, all in the context of an ominous prophecy, closing off with an ego appeal to the possibility of her being a person of destiny. Isn't it interesting that Mordecai had commanded Esther *not* to reveal her Jewishness, but now in trouble, he commands her to disclose her ties? Isn't it interesting that Esther had successfully kept her origins secret (why couldn't she indefinitely do so?), but now Mordecai threatens her with exposure?

For whatever reason, she took his bait, but she also took charge of her life, never giving it back to him. It was his last command to her, but not hers to him: "Go, gather together all the Jews that are present in Shushan, and fast ye for me, and neither eat nor drink three days, night or day: I also and my maidens will fast likewise; and so will I go in unto the king, which is not according to the law: and if I perish, I perish" (4:16). She thought up that plan; Mordecai hadn't. Esther is her own person at last. Divested of her origins by her adopted father's command, she accepts herself for what she is, a Jew, willing to take charge of her life and prevent a genocide in so doing. Intellectually aware of the risks of intervention, she nevertheless responds, "If I perish, I perish."

The role reversal is complete—commander becomes doer; doer becomes commander. Esther has been transformed from an obedient, dependent child doing Mordecai's commands to a commander herself ordering Mordecai's doings: "So Mordecai went his way, and did according to all that Esther had commanded him" (4:17). In fact, the prominent role Mordecai does continue to fulfill is due to Esther's direct influence. After Haman is hanged, the king gives Haman's house to Esther (not Mordecai). And with one generous move, Esther introduces Mordecai to the king as being her relative, and the expected perks follow: "And Mordecai came before the king; for Esther had told what he was unto her. And the king took off his ring, which he had taken from Haman, and gave it unto Mordecai over the house of Haman" (8:1–2). Had Esther not chosen to introduce Mordecai to the king, Mordecai's high political position might never have materialized:

"For Mordecai was great in the king's house, and his fame went out throughout all the provinces: for this man Mordecai waxed greater and greater" (9:4). Even though he had foiled an assassination plot, he had already been rewarded for that—and probably forgotten. There is no indication in the text that the king knew or cared about him as a person; he may not have even recognized Mordecai. Haman—not the king—had led Mordecai through the streets on the horse.

Although Mordecai waxed great, the king still turned to Esther for the "what to do": "And the king said unto Esther the queen . . . now what is thy petition? and it shall be granted thee: or what is thy request further? and it shall be done" (9:12). From that point on, Mordecai's involvement revolves around implementing Esther's ideas, not his own.

In summary, to survive in hostile times demands a plan. To survive requires being smarter than circumstances. And Esther showed herself capable of strategizing, executing, analyzing, and modifying a course of action, persevering in its fulfillment.

Did Mordecai, then, as has been asserted, possess the brains, and was Esther his puppet, a beautiful one admittedly, but still a puppet? No, definitely not, as a close literary analysis of character complexity shows.

And one more point: the title of the story *is* Esther, not Mordecai. It is, in fact, one of only two books in the whole Bible to be named after a woman.

The narrator of the Esther story left to literature six memorable characters, all easily associated with adjectives: the deposed but virtuous Vashti played against the bumbling playboy king; the realistically perceptive Zeresh compared with the rashly revengeful Haman; the courageous Esther contrasted with the conniving Mordecai. If the plot that weaves them all together were a boxing match, Vashti and Zeresh would have scored knockouts against their male counterparts, and Esther would have won in a unanimous decision, Mordecai having admittedly some desirable traits.

Setting

Setting, another narrative element, involves a story's time and place, a location in which the plot can happen. The author's feminine bias in the Esther story setting is more subtle, more indirect than in the story's character developments. Biblical scholars argue whether the narrative was historical or fictitious, but in either case the writer selected details of setting to emphasize the reality of the story, thus giving additional credibility to its characters and to the themes that develop.

Scholars agree that the author of the story had a remarkable knowledge of Persian court life. The writer includes historically accurate facts about the empire, artifacts, court practices, and customs. In chapter 1 alone, these details of time and place lend authenticity, thus providing a rich narrative texture for the following story of court intrigue, revenge, conflict, thwarted schemes, and final victory—for Esther and her people. Specimens include these: "from India even unto Ethiopia, over an hundred and seven and twenty provinces"; "in the third year of his reign"; "showed the riches of his glorious kingdom . . . an hundred and fourscore days"; "pillars of marble"; "vessels of gold (the vessels being diverse one from another)"; "drinking was according to the law"; "seven days . . . seven chamberlains"; "the seven princes of Persia and Media"; "king's decree . . . throughout all his empire."

Chapter 2 establishes Mordecai's and Esther's status as Jews in exile, a situation pregnant with potential trouble. Then little Hadassah, renamed Esther, loses her name and her mother and father, becoming as it were a double exile in this hostile land. But, we are specifically told, she is "fair and beautiful." The setting is now complete. We are ready for the upward climb of our heroine. Will she be chosen to replace Vashti? Will the king find out she is a Jewess? Will the fate of Vashti be hers?

Humphreys offers an excellent summary of the way in which setting contributes to the action of the story:

> From the outset the reader of this story is transported into a world that cannot fail to fascinate, a captivating world of wealth, the center of a vast empire, the locus of all earthly power. The setting is designed to grasp the intense interest of readers . . . [who] have always been drawn to accounts of intrigue in high places. . . . In these contexts power is to be had and used, and with it great wealth and honor. . . . It is a setting in which power, wealth, and honor are to be seized. . . . In this setting the deepest schemes and passions of men and women will be exposed. . . . It is a setting designed to reveal the essence of human life, a setting in which the risks are huge and the prizes larger than life itself. (Humphreys, "The Story" 100)

The author has succeeded. We as readers are hooked, snagged by the artistically recorded trappings of time and place. No reader yet ever had the fortitude to leave a gorgeous woman with an unknown fate, especially one in the intriguing setting of ancient court romance and power conflict.

Theme

Theme concerns the meaning of a story, whereas purpose is why the writer wrote it. And while scholars agree that the book's major purpose is to establish historical validation for the Feast of Purim (Childs 599), many stress that the book's *main* theme is God's providence. Here is a typical statement:

> Esther is unique among the Old Testament Scriptures in the way in which it deals with religious and moral issues. The writer certainly seems to have stressed the value of political intrigue and human intellectual acumen, and to underplay, if not actually to disregard, the possibility of divine intervention. At the same time, the literary skill of the author leaves the reader in little doubt that he is observing the operation of divine providence as the narrative proceeds, and that the indestructible nature of the Covenant People will ultimately be made evident. (Harrison 1098–99)

But the theme of providence is intertwined with the theme of a woman as the agent of providence. In the Esther story, a woman is highly honored to be the instrument of such deliverance. As I noted earlier, from chapter 4 Esther is on her own, making astute decisions, planning strategy, handling crises. The author's positive descriptions of Esther's courage, her determination, her "grace under pressure" (to borrow a Hemingway phrase) are all particularly impressive in light of the theme of God's providence, God seeing fit to use a woman when a whole nation's existence is at stake: "Providence seemed to have advanced her [Esther] on purpose for this work" (Clarke 801). As if in reversal of the Eve-got-us-into-trouble mindset, the reader now has the Esther-got-us-out-of-trouble emphasis.

Summary

The story of Esther is a literary entity in itself. Nevertheless its theme of divine providence puts it into the mainstream of the Bible in general—the ultimate victory of God's people, then and in the future. It becomes a mini-narrative of the Greatest Story Ever Told! Narrative analysis should eliminate major objections to the book's being included in the canon. Even the structure of the story is significant, the shape of the plot reflecting the shape of the entire biblical narrative, all sixty-six books: the Garden of Eden, the Fall, and Eden restored. And this time a woman looms large in the restoration.

One way a short story distinguishes itself from a sketch or tale is that it "has a definite formal development, a freedom from looseness in construction; however, it finds its unity in many things other than plot, although it often finds it there—in effect, in theme, in character, in tone, in mood, even, on occasion, in style" (Thrall and Hibbard 458). Esther was artistically crafted, as a literary analysis of its elements shows. And almost all of the questions raised at the beginning of this chapter could be partially or completely explained with a similar analysis geared to each issue. A careful literary analysis helps readers see not only what is thematically germane but also what is not. Hence a literary analysis becomes not optional but necessary:

> The Bible demands a literary approach because its writing is literary in nature. The Bible is an experiential book that conveys the concrete reality of human life. It is filled with evidences of literary artistry and beauty, much of it in the form of literary genres. It also makes continuous use of resources of language that we can regard as literary. A literary approach pays close attention to all of these elements of literary form, because it is through them that the Bible communicates its message. (Ryken, *How to Read* 30)

The content and the artistry form a symbiotic relationship that cannot be ignored without a loss to both.

But the book of Esther specifically has done all of the above with a very positive approach to women, at times displaying even a bias. The handling of character demonstrates this attitude best. The author could have presented all the Jews positively and all the pagans negatively, but such is not the case. Vashti and Zeresh are notable examples. Neither religion nor nationality seemed to figure in. But gender did, the three women—two minor characters and the major one—being exemplary but still believably human.

And one final response to a modern problem with the book—its being faulted for its chauvinistic attitudes. Those who feel such should read it again, this time more analytically. By dissecting the story to analyze its parts, the reader can then put the whole back together with increased awareness and subsequent appreciation. Close inspection will reveal the encouragingly positive feminine approach of its author. Or to state it another way, this same reading will prevent misreading, as for example, finding chauvinistic attitudes in the book of Esther when upon scrutiny the opposite exists. The culture was undeniably chauvinistic, but the narrator would have us notice what women were able to do in a stultifying environment where women were possessions, beautiful toys for men's entertainment; where queens were powerless, royal in name only; and where females in general were dutifully obedient, childlike, and unthreatening. At plot's end, Esther was none of these.

The book of Esther troubles, an uneasy presence in the canon. But a literary analysis reveals valid defenses for the book's inclusion in general and its modern relevance specifically. Esther has come to the kingdom for such a time as—now.

WORKS CITED

Brenner, Athalya. *The Israelite Woman: Social Role and Literary Type in Biblical Narrative.* Sheffield: JSOT Press, 1985.

Childs, Brevard S. *Introduction to the Old Testament as Scripture.* Philadelphia: Fortress, 1979.

Clarke, Adam. "Esther." *Clarke's Commentary.* Vol. 2. New York: Abingdon-Cokesbury, 1947.

"Esther." *Encyclopedia Judaica.* Vol. 6. Ed. Cecil Roth et al., 1971.

Fuerst, Wesley J. "Esther." *The Books of Ruth, Esther, Ecclesiastes, The Song of Songs, Lamentations.* The Cambridge Bible Commentary on the New English Bible. 66 vols. Ed. P. R. Ackroyd, A. R. C. Leaney, and J. W. Packer. Cambridge: Cambridge UP, 1975.

Harrison, R. K. *Introduction to the Old Testament.* Grand Rapids: Eerdmans, 1969.

Humphreys, W. Lee. "A Life-Style for Diaspora: A Study of the Tales of Esther and Daniel." *Journal of Biblical Literature* 92 (1973): 211–23.

———. "The Story of Esther and Mordecai: An Early Jewish Novella." *Saga, Legend, Tale, Novella, Fable: Narrative Forms in Old Testament Literature.* Ed. George W. Coats. Journal for the Study of the Old Testament Supplement Series 35. Sheffield: JSOT Press, 1985.

Jones, Bruce. "Two Misconceptions About the Book of Esther." *Catholic Biblical Quarterly* 39 (1977): 171–81.

Laffey, Alice L. *An Introduction to the Old Testament: A Feminist Perspective.* Philadelphia: Fortress, 1988.

Moore, Carey A. *Esther.* Anchor Bible. Garden City: Doubleday, 1971.

Ryken, Leland. *How to Read the Bible as Literature.* Grand Rapids: Zondervan, 1984.

———. *The Literature of the Bible.* Grand Rapids: Zondervan, 1974.

———. *Words of Delight: A Literary Introduction to the Bible.* Grand Rapids: Baker, 1987.

Sasson, Jack M. "Esther." *The Literary Guide to the Bible.* Ed. Robert Alter and Frank Kermode. Cambridge, Mass.: Harvard UP, 1987. 335–42.

Thrall, William F., and Addison Hibbard. *A Handbook to Literature.* Rev. and enlarged by C. Hugh Holman. New York: Odyssey, 1960.

CHAPTER 16

Job

Jerry A. Gladson
First Christian Church (Disciples of Christ)
Garden Grove, California

To enter the world of Job is to confront one of humanity's oldest, most baffling enigmas: the plight of an innocent person overwhelmed by inexplicable tragedy. Through simple narrative, elegant poetry, and climactic epiphany Job captivates readers as few books seem capable of doing. Job resembles a tranquil body of water. On the surface everything appears inviting, but beneath the surface powerful undercurrents sweep toward terrifying eddies and great, yawning abysses of uncertainty.

Is the book a drama, a poem with an implicit narrative, a narrative with poetical dialogue, or a lament? What is the nature of its structure? What essential message or messages did the author intend to convey? Did a single author write the work, or were additional writers or editors involved? When did the author write? What audience did he or she envision? What occasion stimulated the writing of Job?

Although we cannot address all these questions here, such issues make Job as difficult to access from the perspective of literary art as it is from those of theology and exegesis.

Genre

Since Job's literary genre differs from anything else in the Bible, it comes as no surprise that scholars have advanced a variety of proposals regarding its genre.

Job's disillusionment and constant search for divine respite remind one of the *lament,* a liturgical form common in the Old Testament, represented in many psalms (e.g., Pss. 22, 61) and the book of Lamentations. Since the structure of Job varies from the typical lament, which usually consists of an invocation, a complaint, a petition, an affirmation of confidence, and an acknowledgment of divine response, Westermann (1956) thinks it represents a "dramatization" of a lament. Job's initial lament (ch. 3) receives answer through the arguments of his friends in the dialogue (chs. 4–27) and concludes by another lament of Job (chs. 29–31). Similar is Gese's designation of Job as an "answered" lament based on its sequence of distress (chs. 1–2), complaint (chs. 3–37), divine response (chs. 38–41), and restoration (ch. 42) (Gese 1958).

Some laments appear to have functioned in a legal as well as liturgical context. Since the book often utilizes judicial metaphors, Richter identifies Job as the text of a *judicial process* (1959). Chapters 4–14, accordingly, represent an attempt at preliminary settlement, while chapters 14–31 are the formal legal settlement between Job and his friends and Job's prayer for a divine settlement. Gottwald, on the other hand, prefers to describe the dialogue between Job and his friends as a *disputation speech* (1985).

Moving away from the more liturgical or legal genres, we note an increasing tendency to identify dramatic elements in Job. Frye, Whedbee, and Urbock consider it a *comedy,* or seriocomedy: it represents a story of incongruity in which the hero finally arrives at restoration. As a comedy, the book of Job provides a microcosm of the entire Bible. Its extended poetry leads Neyrand (1922–24) to classify it as an *epic,* whereas Kallen and others, drawing for comparison on the Greek tragedies of Aeschylus, Sophocles, or Euripides, prefer the category of *tragedy.* That Job lends itself to the stage confirms the presence of such dramatic elements.

Cox (1986) retains the Hebraic category of the *mashal,* used widely by the Hebrew wisdom writers. The biblical writers apply the term *mashal* to a whole range of compositions, from a single proverb (Prov. 1:6) to a didactic poem (Isa. 14:4–21). Cox suggests Job constitutes a "bi-polar" *mashal* consisting of two panels. Leaving aside the prologue (chs. 1–2), the first panel (chs. 3–31) could be entitled "God as man sees him," while the second (chs. 38–42), minus the Elihu speeches (chs. 32–37), represents "God as he sees himself." The book thus contains, in *mashal* form, a double exploration of the divine nature. It proclaims the freedom of God beyond human comprehension.

As valuable as these emic and etic attempts to identify Job with liturgical, dramatic, and legal genres may be, none seems capable of accounting for the entire book. Because no single genre classification has gained widespread support among biblical or literary scholars, a number of scholars considered Job a *sui generis,* i.e., a unique composition (Crenshaw 1970). I am inclined to agree. At least no comparable literary form has yet emerged from the ancient Near East. It is possible, however, that either our knowledge of ancient wisdom genres is too narrow or ancient writers exercised much more flexibility in their use of conventional forms. Both these considerations, moreover, may have been operative. The Joban author, as is generally the case with any writer, has drawn from a variety of genres to create a distinct composition. Within the book there are several subgenres, e.g., narrative (chs. 1–2; 42:7–17), soliloquy (chs. 3, 29–31), a disputation (chs. 4–27), theophany (chs. 38–41), and a wisdom poem (ch. 28). Job participates in a variety of genres, none of which applied rigidly categorizes the entire book.

Unity, Theme, and Plot

Closely bound up with the problem of genre are the various literary elements within Job. Although one can identify the major elements of its literary structure, it has proven more difficult to show precisely how these elements function together within the book. What Job intends to say, however, grows out of its arrangement. Form and function go together. The problem of the inner function of the various components of the literary structure is inextricably tied up with the puzzle of its theme. It will be best, therefore, to examine both the structure and the content as indicators of the theme and plot.

Job contains a narrative shape, making it possible to trace the usual beginning, middle, and end of a plot and thus identify a thematic emphasis within the book. Two prose narratives (chs. 1–2; 42:7–17), which initiate and conclude the conflict, form an inclusion that frames Job. Because of the literary and thematic tensions between the prologue/epilogue and the poem, many scholars regard the former as an old folktale furnishing the author an occasion for the poem. The present form of the book, however, supplies a tension between the narrative and the poem that may be an intentional part of the literary strategy. The prologue/epilogue reflects the popular notion of retribution, that disaster overtakes the disobedient, which the poetical section then debates. The poetic dialogues (3–42:6), first between Job and his friends and finally between God and Job, advance, complicate, and eventually resolve the conflict. Since conversation carries the action forward, it often appears slow and monotonous to the narratee, or reader, like that in *Waiting for Godot*.

Using an omniscient point of view, the narrator makes the narratee privy to the divine viewpoint. Because the narratee sees the plot from God's perspective, sensing a positive outcome, it is difficult to identify fully with Job. On the other hand, the narratee cannot identify fully with God either, because he or she becomes impatient at the lengthy divine indifference to Job. This point of view creates a tension in the narratee that raises a key theme of the book: What is God like?

THE PROLOGUE

The conflict in the prologue centers on the character of human devotion to God. Characterized by a double structure, the prologue uses dialogue to set up this initial conflict. By a conspicuous absence of conversation in the silence of the friends after they had arrived to comfort Job (2:11–13), it catches the reader off guard when the poetic debate begins with Job's outburst (3).

Two conversations in the heavenly realm between Yahweh and Satan (literally, "the satan," or "the adversary") are based on the motif of satanic challenge and divine "bet." "Have you considered my servant Job," Yahweh boasts, "that there is none like him on the earth, a blameless and upright man, who fears God and turns away from evil?" (1:8; 2:3). "Does Job fear God for nought?" Satan retorts. "Have you not put a hedge about him and his house and all that he has. But put forth your hand now, and touch all that he has, and he will curse You to Your face" (1:9–10a, 11). Yahweh responds to the challenge, releasing Job into the power of Satan, who promptly destroys all Job's property and strikes him with a loathsome skin disease.

Does anyone serve God unconditionally, without ulterior motive? This is the human question. The divine behavior here, however, raises an even more profound difficulty: What kind of God would allow the faithful Job to become a hapless pawn in the hands of Satan? This is the problem of theodicy that has baffled theologians for centuries. It constitutes the divine question.

THE DIALOGUE AND THE ELIHU SPEECHES

The motif of theodicy now advances into the dialogue. The poem consists principally of three cycles of debate or dialogue between Job and his three friends—Eliphaz, Bildad, and Zophar (3–27).

The dialogue begins formally with Job's soliloquy lamenting his dire fate (3). Eliphaz, Bildad, and Zophar then follow, with Job responding in turn to each one (4–14). The second cycle repeats this same essential structure (15–21). Unfortunately, the third cycle (22–27) appears truncated in some way. Bildad's speech seems unusually short (25:1–6), while Job appears strangely to take up the friends' ideas against which he has previously argued vehemently (e.g., 27:13–23). Zophar has no speech at all. It is not clear whether this truncation was deliberate, intended for literary effect, perhaps to underscore the futility of the debate, or has occurred as the result of a dislocation during the early transmission of the text. The speeches of the friends tend to decline in strophic quantity toward the end of the cycles, however, lending support to the notion that the shortening is intentional.

Job's speeches in the first cycle are longer than those of the friends; in the second, about the same length; and in the third, they decrease in quantity like that of the friends. The ebb and flow of the strophic pattern in the cycles complements the structure of the entire book (Webster 1983), while the repetitive speeches of the friends and Job's lengthy rejoinders act noticeably to retard the plot.

On their part, the friends advocate a conventional answer that inextricably links one's deeds to the outward state of life. Job, who actually concurs with this basic position, complains that though his deeds have been virtuous, he has suffered like a sinful person. He addresses his plaint directly to the Source of justice and so begins to contend with God in addition to quarreling with the friends. Job's dispute with God is really a *quest* for God, however disguised by Job's mournful tone it may appear to be, and this quest gives a thematic unity to the entire work. When his attempt to break through to God flounders, the center of his relational world appears to disintegrate. "The hand of God has touched me!" he moans (19:21b). Yet, in each cycle Job's faith exhibits a progressively higher timbre. The fluctuation between despair and faith dominates; in the end, when God appears, faith wins out (Ryken 1987).

The hymn to wisdom (28), which appears to be an interjection of the poet and not a continuation of Job's speech in the third cycle (27), further delays settlement of these issues. This majestic poem points to a resolution found in God, or specifically, in divine wisdom, rather than one arising out of human contention or debate. The poem has enough ambiguity to make it difficult to interpret, but it seems to have a Januslike function. By separating wisdom from the human realm, it underscores the futility of the preceding dialogue with the friends (28:12–22). An equally forceful emphasis on the transcendence of wisdom points forward to the resolution found in the divine speeches (vv. 23–28).

Job's eloquent final defense (chs. 29–31) emphasizes, as one would expect, his side of the struggle, closing with a daring, dramatic challenge to God: "Here is my signature! let the Almighty answer me!" (31:35). At this point the reader expects a divine response, but instead the Elihu speeches (chs. 32–37), consisting of four or five poems (33:1–33; 34:1–37; 35:1–16; 36:1–25; 36:26–37:22), postpone the outcome still further. In his concluding reflection on the mystery of God (37:21–24), Elihu hints that justice may be found within the mysterious will of God. At the same time, while pointing the reader toward the resolution to be found in the divine speeches, he ironically identifies with the simplistic attitudes of the friends by warning Job: God "does not regard any who are wise in their own conceit" (v. 24).

THE DIVINE SPEECHES

When God dramatically appears on the scene in 38:1–41:34 after the poem has repeatedly spoken so passionately about him, the reader senses the climactic turn in the story. God *must* speak if matters are to be resolved. So the poet introduces God in the form of a spectacular theophany, accompanied by a roaring *seʿārâh,* whirlwind, or storm (38:1). This is the only theophany in the biblical wisdom literature, which was accustomed to discovering God indirectly in life's experiences rather than in a theophany.

God speaks majestically, yet in obscure, riddlelike discourse that seems at first glance to avoid Job's central concern. This obscurity can be understood as characteristic of an oriental preference for indirect, enigmatic speech (cf. the parables of Jesus [Mark 4:10–13]). There are two divine speeches, both introduced by a whirlwind (38:1; 40:6), paralleling the double structure of the prologue. The first (38:1–39:30) is followed by an interchange between God and Job (40:1–5), while the second (40:6–41:34) culminates with a second interchange between God and Job that constitutes the resolution of the book (42:1–6).

The expressive power of the poetry in the speeches represents an imaginative way of presenting God's speech in contrast with human language. As Alter has shown, the divine speeches poetically reverse Job's death wish in chapter 3, thus, in effect, nullifying the friends' debate and engaging Job directly (1984). The first speech reflects on creation and providence and highlights them by a metaphorical play on the themes of light and darkness

(38:2, 7, 12, 19–20, 24, 35; 39:9) and birth (38:8, 9, 21, 27–29; 39:1–4, 14–18, 30). In chapter 3 Job uses these same metaphors to speak of his crushing despair (3:1, 3–26); now God reframes them as symbols of life and renewal. Through the Behemoth (40:15–24) and the Leviathan (41:1–34), God portrays two creatures who live in a world beyond human comprehension. They seem to exist on the border between the natural and the supernatural world and hence have a mythic quality about them. The Behemoth and Leviathan evidently represent the inexplicable, dangerous, or sinister side of the created order. This, too, lies under Yahweh's sovereignty.

As overwhelming as the divine speeches appear to be, they are not intended to totally exclude any human understanding of God. Rather, in keeping with the wisdom view that creation has something to say that humanity needs to hear, the display of the wonders of nature suggests that all creation remains in the hands of God. Providence rules over all. The whole world is put back into the care and keeping of God. Job now recognizes, at least more keenly than ever before, that his destiny is "well protected by this mysterious God" (von Rad 225).

Job's double response to the divine revelation (42:1–6) resolves his conflict with God and, hence, with God's justice, not in terms of reason, but rather within experience. In the first response (40:1–5), Job admits his limited knowledge. The second divine speech evidently motivates him to abdicate his harsh charges against God (42:1–6). Job now discovers a living encounter and communion with God beyond the limits of conventional piety:

I had heard of You by the hearing of the ear,
but now my eye sees You.

His remorse in "dust and ashes" (42:6) recalls his initial condition where he "sat among the ashes" (2:8). Job's final words preserve a remarkable instance of assonance based on the sounds of the Hebrew letters *ayin* (ע) and *aleph* (א). Both letters, retaining an *-ah* or *-eh* sound, occur three times in the seven Hebrew words in 42:6.

ʿal-kēn ʾemʾas wᵉnīhamtî
ʿal-ʿāpār wāʾēper

Therefore I retract and repent
in dust and ashes.

With God's appearance and his acceptance of Job, the element of human conflict with God on Job's part recedes. The friends, who had ostensibly taken God's side, remain silent after God rebukes them (42:7–9). Satan is so completely vanquished he has vanished from the story. The stormy contest of the book now reaches equilibrium.

THE EPILOGUE.

The prose epilogue (42:7–17) functions, not as a resolution of the plot, but as a kind of poetic justice. In true U-shaped comedic fashion, it returns to the tranquil world of Job at rest, to the fullness (42:17b) he had known at the beginning (1:1–3). God restores to Job all his losses, often double, and Job lives to a ripe old age.

If irony perceives in things as they are an inconsistency, as Good suggests (1965), one can see in the whole of Job a profound irony, or even series of ironies. In their insistence that one's deeds are invariably reflected in the circumstances of life, the friends ironically never realize their orthodox view simply does not apply to Job's situation. While what they say may have theoretical validity in some instances, it is wide of the mark when it comes to Job. Job, meanwhile, grapples with his own ironies. In response to his plight, he turns on God, as though God were the source of his problem. The reader already knows, however, that God is not guilty of such a sadistic act. As Ryken points out, this ironic situation shows why God subtly rebukes Job at the end, and why Job "repents" (1987).

Perhaps the supreme irony is reserved for the reader. Beguiled by the omniscient point of view presented in the prologue (chs. 1–2), a reader begins by thinking he or she holds a distinct advantage over the characters, who are kept in ignorance of the heavenly agreement. The reader, maintaining this perspective throughout the poem, may even feel pity for the ignorance of Job and his friends. As the book concludes, however, the reader suddenly discovers he or she is just as ignorant about the relationship of suffering and divine justice as the characters. God remains a Mystery for character and reader alike.

The book of Job, if we may summarize, is about the problem of suffering in human experience and in the justice of God. The theme, plot, and literary arrangement of the book reinforce each other. We may outline the book as follows:

- Prose Prologue (1–2)
- Poetic Dialogue (3–42:6)
  - Job's Lament (3)
  - First Cycle (4–14)
    - The Speech of Eliphaz (4–5)
    - Job's Reply to Eliphaz (6–7)
    - The Speech of Bildad (8)
    - Job's Reply to Bildad (9–10)
    - The Speech of Zophar (11)
    - Job's Reply to Zophar (12–14)

- Second Cycle (15–21)
  - The Speech of Eliphaz (15)
  - Job's Reply to Eliphaz (16–17)
  - The Speech of Bildad (18)
  - Job's Reply to Bildad (19)
  - The Speech of Zophar (20)
  - Job's Reply to Zophar (21)
- Third Cycle (22–27)
  - The Speech of Eliphaz (22)
  - Job's Reply to Eliphaz (23–24)
  - The Speech of Bildad (25)
  - Job's Reply to Bildad (26–27)
- Hymn to Wisdom (28)
- Job's Final Defense (29–31)
- The Speeches of Elihu (32–37)
  - The First Speech (32–33)
  - The Second Speech (34)
  - The Third Speech (35)
  - The Fourth Speech (36–37)
- The Speeches of God (38–42:6)
  - The First Speech (38–39)
  - Job's Response (40:1–5)
  - The Second Speech (40:6–41:34)
  - Job's Response (42:1–6)

Prose Epilogue (42:7–17)

Style

By lavishing attention on seemingly insignificant aspects of the work, the author of Job has employed careful literary craftsmanship in arranging both the major and minor components of the book. Here we will be able to observe only a few of many examples of this literary elegance.

PARALLELISM

Since most of Job is poetry, one would expect to find here many of the various types of Hebrew parallelism. Examples of synonymous, antithetic, emblematic, repetitive, chiastic, and other types of parallels are replete within the book. A synonymous parallel that involves an adroit shifting between two Hebrew words for the verb "to come" is found in 3:25:

For the dread I dreaded also has come ['ātâ] *upon me,*
and what I feared come [bô'] *upon me.*

As M. O'Connor reminds us, no word in any language can be exactly paralleled with another (96), the use of two words meaning "come" here gives this bicolon an intensifying, focusing effect. By using the rarer verb *'ātâ,* found only in poetical texts and often depicting a hostile threat (30:14; Isa. 56:9; Jer. 3:22), the first colon draws attention to the anxiety of Job. The second colon resorts to the much more common *bô',* "come in, come" (Brown, Driver, and Briggs 97). While the difference between these two verbs is slight, the effect of using two different expressions has the seconding effect (Kugel 1981) of turning up the intensity (Alter 1985) and immediacy of Job's fear a notch, i.e., "(what is more) what I have feared [now] comes upon me."

Illustrating the author's grasp of an impressive, wide-ranging Hebrew vocabulary is the internal climactic parallel used to develop an external synonymous parallel between two bicola containing five different words for "lion" (4:10–11):

The roar of the lion ['aryēh],
the voice of the fierce lion [šāḥal],
the teeth of the young lions [k^epîrîm],
are broken.

The strong lion [layīš]
perishes for lack of prey,
and the whelps of the lioness [lābî']
are scattered.

The meaning here, to paraphrase, is that "the roar, voice, and teeth of the lions are broken, and what is more, even the strong lion and the lioness's cubs are scattered."

In Job's poignant appeal for someone to intercede between God and himself, we find an inverted, or chiastic parallel (16:19):

Even now, behold, (a) *in the heavens* (b) *is my witness,*
even (b') *my defender* (a') [*is*] *on high.*

Virtually the whole poem delights the reader in this manner. The parallels, shifts, and sudden twists give its poetry an elegance equaled by few other writers in the Old Testament.

FORMULAIC LANGUAGE

Artistry is especially evident in the author's use of conventional ancient Near Eastern formulas. In Job's soliloquy, his cursing of the night of his birth ("That night—let thick darkness claim it" [3:6]) sounds similar to a line from the Lamentation over the Destruction of Ur: "Let not that storm be given a place in the numbering" (Pritchard 1969, 463). In Job's first response to the friends an even better example occurs. Job, without alteration of a single word, but with an iconoclastic shift, transforms Psalm 8, a hymn about God's solicitous care of humanity, into a terrifying portrayal of an overprotective deity (7:16–21). With only the changing of one Hebrew word—"wicked" exchanged for "man"—he shifts the specific characterization of the wicked in Proverbs 10:28b ("the expectation of the *wicked* comes to nought") into a description of the entire human race ("You destroy the hope of *humanity*" [Job 14:19b]). In these instances, as Dion notes (1987), the author has used traditional formulas in the service of radical protest.

IRONY

As we have seen, irony pervades the book. The author's omniscient point of view permits the reader to approach the story on two levels, one representing the omniscient divine perspective, the other the limited view of Job and the friends, thus setting up an inherent irony. One example of this may be seen in Job's fear that God will kill him (13:14–15), so oppressive has his life become. Yet the reader knows this cannot happen because God has restricted Satan: "Only spare his life" (2:6).

Job and his friends also indulge in irony that is severe enough to be considered sarcasm. Job damns them with faint praise: "No doubt *you* are the people, and wisdom will die with *you*" (12:2, emphasis in the Hebrew), while Eliphaz backhandedly suggests that Job has "encouraged many" with his unrestrained, proud outbursts (4:3). Most impressive are the divine speeches, which are almost wholly irony. At one point, God challenges Job to take over the world if he thinks he can manage better (40:6–14)!

SIMILE AND METAPHOR

A master of metaphor, the Joban poet draws from flora, fauna, natural phenomena, and the human realm. Particularly noteworthy are the many botanical metaphors and similes used to depict the transience of human life (Pfeiffer 1948). Humanity is "like a flower" that withers, like an ephemeral shadow (14:2). In the end, humankind resembles a "tree . . . cut down" (vv. 7–12), for God terrifies them as the wind a leaf (13:25). The wicked, even more than others, are as insecure as blowing chaff on a threshing floor (21:18).

An especially colorful simile, taken from fauna, is the vivid comparison of Job's fleeting days of life to the swift flight of an eagle swooping down upon its hapless prey (9:26). In view of such finitude, Job's friends compete with each other for the most striking metaphor or simile to show the insecurity of the wicked. Humanity is a "maggot," a "worm" (25:6), declares Bildad. This distich, or couplet, a nominal sentence in Hebrew, is unusually terse and can be rendered as follows:

How much less humankind—maggot,
and humanity—worm!

Powerful wicked drive the poor off to work "like wild asses in the desert" (24:5), thus insulting common social morality. No wonder that what the wicked rely on, the friends think, is finally as insecure as a spider's web (8:14)!

Job, too, uses metaphors and similes to describe his frustration with God and the friends. The friends he likens to a dry, seasonal wadi or streambed (6:15–20), while he thinks God callously condemns humanity to long, lonely days of emptiness that are like a "slave who longs for the shadow" (7:2). God appears as an archer shooting arrows at him (16:12–13), or as an army battering at the walls of a city (v. 14). In defiance, Job appeals to the earth to divulge his plaint: "O earth, cover not my blood" (16:18). Yet the grave will still be his father and worms his mother and sister (17:14).

These are a few examples of the skill and beauty of Job. In order to grasp more completely the author's ability, it will be helpful to focus on a single passage: the hymn of Eliphaz in 5:9–16.

Taming the Inscrutable

An analysis of Job 5:9–16 will illustrate some of the literary qualities of the book as a whole. Although containing rhetorical questions, wisdom sayings, and a summary-appraisal, Eliphaz's hymnic poem in 5:9–16 exhibits characteristic wisdom style. A break (v. 8) introduced by *'ûlām,* "however," and an appeal in verse 17 frame the poem. This passage typifies the friends' case against Job and shows how they attempt to change his mind by theological and literary appropriation of traditional material.

He [God] does great things and unsearchable,
marvelous things without number:
he gives rain upon the earth
and sends waters upon the fields;
he sets on high those who are lowly,
and those who mourn are lifted to safety.

He frustrates the devices of the crafty,
so that their hands achieve no success.
He takes the wise in their own craftiness;
and the schemes of the wily are brought to a quick end.
They meet with darkness in the daytime,
and grope at noonday as in the night.
But he saves the fatherless from their mouth,
the needy from the hand of the mighty.
So the poor have hope,
and injustice shuts her mouth.

This hymnic poem forms part of Eliphaz's initial criticism of Job (chs. 4–5), which is a leading ingredient in the plot of the entire drama. It provides Eliphaz traditional support for his ethical imperative in 5:17–27 that Job submit to divine discipline.

The poem identifies God as a doer of wonders (v. 9). Using an external synthetic, or stairstep parallelism, composed largely of participial clauses, the poet skillfully refers to natural processes. Rain acts as a precursor of the divine work of social justice in the world (vv. 9–16). Verses 11 and 15, which concern God's compassion toward the oppressed, form an inclusio that uses the salvific activity of God for the disenfranchised to frame the central strophes of the poem.

The acts of Yahweh, as expected in wisdom, stand within the history of the individual rather than *Heilsgeschichte.* The parallel terms *gᵉdōlôt,* "great [things]," and *nīplā'ôt,* "wonders" (v. 9), appear together in other Old Testament passages (e.g., Pss. 106:22; 131:1; 136:4; Job 37:5). *Dāraš,* "to seek," belongs primarily to the recital language of the cult. These terms, set within the hymnic genre, join conventional literary form with an emphasis on the limits of human knowledge, permitting Eliphaz to enlist the divine mystery on the side of justice. In a trenchant personification of injustice (v. 16), the hymnic poem imagines injustice shutting her mouth in the face of divine support of the just.

This couplet in the Hebrew provides another good example of how the poet uses assonance: the last four words all end in an *ah* sound, giving the line a particularly pleasing effect on the ear. Yet Eliphaz does not voice the praise of God for its own sake (Westermann 1956). Divine activity, for him, supports conventional notions of human social order. He attempts to "tame" or exploit Mystery, originally rooted in an epistemic uncertainty (v. 9), to bring Job into submission (vv. 17–21). By such use of divine mystery, the Joban poet achieves a subtle irony that effectively characterizes the friends' basic view of inscrutability.

This brief example of literary art provides an example of how the poet throughout the book takes conventional forms and turns them around in unexpected ways to capture significant aspects of the conflict in the book. The entire book teems with exquisite literary strategems similar to Eliphaz's hymn.

The book of Job, in both its poetry and narrative, represents one of the Bible's superb examples of the symbiotic interaction of the beauties of language and the drama of the human encounter with God that lies at the core of the Judeo-Christian heritage.

WORKS CITED

Alter, Robert. *The Art of Biblical Poetry.* New York: Basic Books, 1985.

———. "The Voice From the Whirlwind." *Commentary* 77, no. 1 (1984): 33–41.

Brown, Francis, S. R. Driver, and C. A. Briggs. *A Hebrew and English Lexicon of the Old Testament.* Oxford: Clarendon, 1907.

Cox, Dermot. "A Rational Inquiry Into God: Chapters 4–27 of the Book of Job." *Gregorianium* 67, no. 4 (1986): 621–58.

Crenshaw, James. "Popular Questioning of the Justice of God in Ancient Israel." *Zeitschrift für die alttestamentlichen Wissenschaft* 82 (1970): 380–95.

Dion, Paul. "Formulaic Language in the Book of Job: International Background and Ironical Distortions." *Studies in Religion/Sciences religieuses* 16, no. 2 (1987): 187–93.

Frye, Northrop. *Anatomy of Criticism.* Princeton: Princeton UP, 1957.

Gese, H. *Lehre und Wirklichkeit in der alten Weisheit.* Tübingen: n.p., 1958.

Good, Edwin M. *Irony in the Old Testament.* Philadelphia: Westminster, 1965.

Gottwald, Norman K. *The Hebrew Bible: A Socio-Literary Introduction.* Philadelphia: Fortress, 1985.

Habel, Norman C. "The Narrative Art of Job: Applying the Principles of Robert Alter." *Journal for the Study of the Old Testament* 27 (1983): 101–11.

Hoffmann, Yair. "Irony in the Book of Job." *Immanuel* 17 (1983–1984): 7–21.

Kallen, H. M. *The Book of Job as a Greek Tragedy Restored.* 1918. Rpt. New York: Hill & Wang, 1958.

Kugel, James L. *The Idea of Biblical Poetry: Parallelism and Its History.* New Haven: Yale UP, 1981.

Neyrand, J. *Études bibliques* 59 (1922–1924): 129ff.

O'Connor, Michael. *Hebrew Verse Structure.* Winona Lake, Ind.: Eisenbrauns, 1980.

Pfeiffer, R. *Introduction to the Old Testament.* New York: Harper Brothers, 1948.

Pritchard, James B., ed. *Ancient Near Eastern Texts Relating to the Old Testament.* 3d ed. Princeton: Princeton UP, 1969.

Richter, H. *Studien zu Hiob.* Theologische Arbeiten 11. Berlin, 1959.

Ryken, Leland. *Words of Delight: A Literary Introduction to the Bible.* Grand Rapids: Zondervan, 1987.

Urbock, William J. "Job as Drama: Tragedy or Comedy?" *Currents in Theology and Mission* 8, no. 1 (1981): 35–40.
von Rad, Gerhard. *Wisdom in Israel.* Nashville: Abingdon, 1972.
Webster, Edwin C. "Strophic Patterns in Job 3–28." *Journal for the Study of the Old Testament* 26 (1983): 33–60.
Westermann, Claus. *Der Aufbau des Buches Hiob.* Tübingen, 1956.
Whedbee, J. W. "The Comedy of Job." *Semeia* 7 (1977): 1–39.

CHAPTER 17

Psalms

TREMPER LONGMAN III
Westminster Theological Seminary

Although literary approaches to the Bible are still considered something of a novelty, there is a long history of literary appreciation of the Psalms. This interest may be illustrated by the life and work of Robert Lowth, an eighteenth-century professor of English at Oxford whose work on the poetry of the Psalms is still important (Baker). Even earlier, Jerome, Augustine, and Josephus applied literary categories from their classical education to the understanding of the Psalms (Kugel).

The Psalms find a unity in their poetic form and in their expression of religious emotion and experience. They may thus rightly be described as lyric poetry (see below). The reader is first of all impressed, however, not by the unity that has drawn these poems together, but rather by the incredible diversity of the individual poems. They differ in date, length, mood, and content. Martin Luther best captured both the beauty and the diversity of the book in his well-known statement comparing the book to a garden:

> In the Psalms we looked in the heart of all the saints, and we seem to gaze into fair pleasure gardens—into heaven itself, indeed—where blooms in sweet, refreshing, gladdening flowers

> of holy and happy thoughts about God and all his benefits. (Cited in Longman 13)

While Luther's statement glosses over some of the harder emotions of the psalmist (sadness, anger, bitterness), he nonetheless has effectively captured the exquisite variety that we discover in the book.

Genre: Religious Experience and Its Forms

There is more agreement about the value of genre studies for the Psalms than for any other part of the canon. Perhaps this is because the individual psalms have only the most tenuous primary literary context, by which I mean that the psalms themselves are grouped in no apparent order, with some exceptions like the kingship psalms in the nineties, fifteen consecutively placed "Songs of Ascent" (i.e., pilgrimage psalms), and various minor groupings by author or cultic function.

Despite the absence of consecutive groupings within the Psalter, critics have categorized the psalms into subgroups since the time of Hermann Gunkel, the so-called father of form criticism. The lack of consensus in identifying the specific genres of the psalms can be explained partly by the fluid nature of genre and partly by different conceptions of the function of the Psalter during the Old Testament period. A general divergence exists between categories that emphasize subject and fixed form, and those based on mood or tone. In the classifications that follow, I have painted a broad picture of what both approaches do with the psalms.

If we approach the psalms in terms of familiar poetic types, they are obviously lyric poems (Ryken 109–14). A lyric poem is a brief poem expressing the thoughts or feelings of a speaker. Lyrics are thus personal and subjective and are reflective or affective. In lyrics we overhear the speaker, usually in a situation that stresses the private nature of the utterance. Lyrics are based on a principle of three-part construction: introduction (statement of theme), development (by repetition, catalog, association, or contrast), and concluding resolution. The most useful way to analyze the organization of a lyric poem is by the format of theme and variation.

Within the broad umbrella of lyric, the psalms yield further subtypes based on a combination of subject and structure. The largest category of psalms is the lament psalm, a fixed form consisting of as many as five ingredients that can appear in any order (invocation or cry to God, lament or complaint, petition or supplication, statement of confidence in God, and vow to praise God). Praise psalms, the next largest category, are also a fixed form, consisting of a formal call to praise, a catalog of praiseworthy acts and attributes of God, and a rounding off of the praise with a note of finality (often a brief prayer or wish).

Still other conventional types of psalms can be identified on the basis of content. Worship psalms, also known as "Songs of Zion," are recognizable by the implied situation of worshiping God at the temple and by consistent references to worship and pilgrimage throughout the poem. The Psalter has five nature poems (8, 19, 29, 104, 148) that invite comparison with the nature poetry that has made up such a huge segment of the world's poetry. The Psalter also contains examples of the encomium—a lyric form praising a character type according to prescribed formulas of praise (Ryken 119).

In keeping with the emotional content of the psalms, I turn next to another system of genres—that based on the moods or tone of the poems. The most frequently occurring psalms form a triad of encounter with God. The first is the hymn, noted for its exuberant mood, which calls upon the congregation to praise the Lord and also lists the reasons for praise. These are songs that are appropriate for those who feel right in their relationship with God. The lament, on the opposite end of the emotional spectrum, most often appeals to the Lord for help against the enemy. However, at times the psalmist recognizes that his problem is with himself or even with God. These songs are for those occasions when the people of God have a broken or clouded relationship with their Lord. Thanksgivings complete the triad. They have the emotional tone of the hymn, but are sung after the lament prayer is answered. They are songs that express the healing of relationship between God and the psalmist. Brueggemann provocatively labels this triad psalms of orientation, disorientation, and reorientation.

A smaller number of psalms fit into the pattern of four other genres—psalms of confidence, remembrance, kingship, and wisdom. Psalms of confidence or trust are most easily noted by their expression of crystal-clear calmness before the Lord. They are often short and have a striking metaphor that carries the theme (for example, Psalm 23, which presents variations on the theme that "the LORD is my shepherd"). Second, the remembrance of history plays a major role in the Psalter. Hymns joyously recall God's great past acts of salvation; laments evoke memories of God's presence in order to offset the hard realities of the present (Ps. 77). In a small group of psalms, however, remembrance provides the tenor of the whole poem (Pss. 78, 105, 106, 136). Kingship too, as a third genre, is an important concept throughout the book; many psalms implicitly are the words of the king. In a few psalms, though, kingship, either divine or human, is the explicit focus. These may extol or pray for the human king (Pss. 20, 21), or perhaps praise the divine kings (Pss. 24, 47, 93). A fourth psalm category is wisdom. We know wisdom from other biblical books such as Proverbs, Job, Ecclesiastes, and Song of Songs, and there are psalms that express the same special concerns as these books—an application of God's will to the nitty-gritty of life and concern about God's justice and love. The psalms in this category are few but noteworthy (Pss. 1, 45, 119), and wisdom motifs run throughout many other psalms.

Thus, though there are 150 separate poetic compositions in the Psalter, they may be grouped together into seven basic types. Each type encapsulates a particular religious experience and is specifically defined by the leading emotion expressed in the psalms: joy, grief, thankfulness, calmness, and reflection.

The Hymnbook of Ancient Israel

The Psalms have been compared appropriately to contemporary hymns. While the tradition of the historical titles indicates that the psalms were composed by individuals in response to some specific event, the psalms themselves were written in a way that subdued this reference. The psalm thus could be used by many individuals who share a similar, though not identical, experience with the psalmist. Psalm 51 was written by David when Nathan confronted him with his sin of adultery, but the psalm can be used by others who also must come to terms with their sins, even by those who are unaware of this historical background. In a similar way, we sing John Wesley's "How Happy Is the Pilgrim's Lot" without knowing that he was writing under horrible weather conditions while being persecuted by those who stood against him. Similarly, the psalms are a hymnbook that finds most frequent use in the midst of the congregation while engaged in public worship.

It is also correct to think of the psalms as literary prayers. What are hymns, but prayers set to music? The psalms of Israel are intimate and honest dialogue between God and his people.

A Literary Sanctuary

After the Fall (Gen. 3), men and women had to meet with God in special locations set apart for that purpose. Sin had created an immense barrier between God and his creatures. Thus we read in the Old Testament that, although God is everywhere, he is specially present for intimate dialogue only in certain places. These special places are sanctuaries, guarded by rituals of purity that protect God's holiness. The sanctuary takes different forms throughout the Old Testament (altars, tabernacle, temple), but it is always the place for intimate dialogue in the presence of God.

The psalms found their primary setting in the sanctuary. Their intimate and honest tone with God demonstrates that the psalmists knew that they were in the very presence of God. In many of them, it is as if God stands before the psalmist and we are overhearing their conversation. It is not surprising then that the psalms themselves may be thought of as a kind of literary sanctuary—an intimate expression of personal dialogue with God. This impression is strengthened as we look at the opening and closing of the book.

Psalm 1 functions as the doorkeeper to the sanctuary. While the book of Psalms as a whole has no obvious overarching structure, it appears that Psalm 1 was intentionally placed in its present canonical position in order to introduce the book. It is a unique wisdom psalm that contrasts the righteous person with the wicked. This contrast is achieved by description; it is up to the reader to identify with one or the other. As the physical tabernacle had many safeguards to its holiness, so Psalm 1 functions to keep out the wicked.

As at the beginning, so at the end. Five psalms are intentionally placed at the end to serve as the conclusion to the book (Pss. 146–50). These five are characterized by exuberant praise and in particular by the admonition "Praise the LORD!" The section is climaxed by Psalm 150, which contains exhortation to praise the Lord. The literary sanctuary that is the Psalms is thus concluded by an appropriate doxology.

The Workings of Hebrew Poetry

While much of the Old Testament is written in a poetic form, the Psalms are the prime example of Hebrew poetry. A literary approach to the Psalms must be sensitive to the ancient conventions of the biblical poet. These have been the subject of considerable debate, which I will not describe in this essay (see W. G. E. Watson). Instead, I will describe in a positive way the three most common characteristics of Hebrew poetry: terseness, parallelism, and metaphor. All three lead to an impressive compactness of expression. The Hebrew poet indeed said much in only a few words.

TERSENESS

Psalms are noted for their brief poetic phrases, usually containing three words in the Hebrew, rarely more than four. The effect of this technique is achieved in part by the repression of conjunctions ("like," "but," "or," "and," "therefore"). The result is a deeper engagement by the reader in the interpretive process, since he or she must supply the connections between a number of the phrases of the poem. A classic example is the opening line of Psalm 23:

The LORD is my shepherd,
I shall not be in want.

No conjunctions appear in the translation or the Hebrew original, though the implicit causal connection between the two parts of the verse (often called cola in biblical studies) would lead to an understanding of the verse as follows:

(Since) the LORD is my shepherd,
I shall not be in want.

A second type of omission that leads to terseness is ellipsis. Ellipsis occurs where the second part of the poetic verse assumes one of the parts of the first. Perhaps the most common type is when the first colon has a verb that serves for both, as in the following example:

You have put me in the lowest pit,
in the darkest depths. (88:6)

Ellipsis binds the two clauses more closely and also lends to the economy of expression.

PARALLELISM

Parallelism is perhaps the most familiar characteristic of Hebrew poetry (Alter, Kugel, O'Connor). It is the grouping of poetic phrases of nearly similar length and often of nearly similar meaning into a single verse:

Blessed is the man who does not walk in the counsel of the wicked
or stand in the way of sinners
or sit in the seat of mockers. (1:1)

On the surface, parallelism appears to be a function only of meaning, but closer analysis reveals a relationship between the phrases in grammar (Berlin) and sometimes even in sound (Cooper).

The near similarity of the lines causes the reader to consider the cola together and to interpret them in the light of one another. Their subtle differences require that the reader see progression from colon to colon. For instance, in Psalm 1:1 each colon intensifies the proceeding thought as it contemplates ever-increasing association with evil. The metaphor of walking with evil indicates an association with it that may be simply casual. To stand with evil is to take a more settled relationship with it, and to sit with evil is almost to be identified with it.

The principle, then, is to identify the parallelism on the basis of similarities between cola and verses and then to slow down and carefully meditate on the relationship between the phrases. How does the second part of a verse carry on, progress, repeat, or specify the thought of the first part?

IMAGERY

Although imagery is found in many different kinds of texts, it is particularly concentrated in poetic passages. Imagery is a concise way of writing, because an image conveys not only information but also evokes an emotional response (Caird, Keel). It is impossible to reproduce the effect of the first line of Psalm 23—"The LORD is my shepherd"—in a prose format, but even to attempt to do so would take many paragraphs.

An image compares two different things in order to teach something about one of them. In the example from Psalm 23, we interpret the image that compares God to a shepherd by unpacking it. That is, we ask ourselves in what way the Lord is like a shepherd (and in the process discover the dissimilarities as well). Indeed, the dissimilarities are what draw our attention to the image in the first place. It shocks us into interpretation. That is especially true of images where two very dissimilar things are brought together, as when the Lord is compared to a drunken man in Psalm 78:65:

Then the LORD awoke as from sleep,
as a man wakes from the stupor of wine.

As I said earlier, the three main characteristics of psalmic style are terseness, parallelism, and imagery. All three are compact ways of expressing thought. All three point to the need for slow and meditative reading of the Psalms. It is also significant to note that all three are capable of translation from Hebrew to another language at least to a certain extent. Parallelism is not lost in translation, especially if the translator is sensitive to the dynamics between poetic cola. It is, however, always better to work with the poetry in the original language, especially since many of the secondary poetic devices (see ch. 5) are observable only in Hebrew: wordplays, acrostics, and grammatical parallelism.

The Psalms as a Mirror of the Soul

Earlier we observed how the Psalms encapsulate human experience to the point that the genres of the psalms are best labeled by different human emotions. In this section we will reflect on the effect the psalms have on their readers. John Calvin noted this effect and used the analogy of a mirror to describe it:

> There is not an emotion of which anyone can be conscious that is not here represented as in a mirror. Or rather, the Holy Spirit has here drawn to life all the griefs, sorrows, fears, doubts, hopes, cares, perplexities, in short, all the distracting emotions with which the minds of men are wont to be agitated. (Calvin xxxvi–xxxvii)

Calvin here describes how the psalms work on the attentive reader. As we read a psalm, the psalm's emotional expression becomes a kind of foil to our own state of mind. We are struggling in faith and obedience and read, "Oh, how I love your law! I meditate on it all day long" (Ps. 119:97). We might feel the distance between the psalmist's faith and our own. Conversely, the psalmist could express the reader's feelings in a way far better than the reader could. In this way the psalms articulate our feelings and become a model prayer to us. They give us words by which we may address God.

The reader feels an immediacy with the psalmist and his emotional expression that is different from that of most other parts of the Bible. As noted above, the psalmists wrote out of a historical context (as indicated by the occasional historical title and some references within the historical books [1 Chron. 16:7]), but these historical references are subdued within the psalm itself. This may be clearly seen by way of contrast with some of the historical psalms found elsewhere in the canon (e.g., Ex. 15; Judg. 5). The psalmists wrote with the hope that others would use their compositions to express their own feelings before the Lord. The psalms themselves encapsulate human experience but subdue historical reference in such a way that the psalm is transferable to others. The psalms easily become mirrors of the reader's soul.

Intertextuality

The book of Psalms stands in the middle of the canon, and there is much cross-fertilization between it and the rest of the Bible. Occasionally one psalm (compare Ps. 113 with 1 Sam. 2:1–10) or an amalgam of a number of psalms (e.g., Nah. 1:1–8 and Jonah 2) is found on the lips of a biblical character or is utilized by a biblical author. Even more striking is the way in which the Psalter reflects the teaching of the rest of the Old Testament. It has long been observed that the Psalms are a "microcosm" of the message of the Old Testament. The fourth-century theologian Athanasius called the Psalms "an epitome of the whole Scriptures." Basil, the bishop of Caesarea in the fourth century, noted that the Psalms are a "compendium of all theology." Martin Luther aptly called Psalms "a little Bible, and the summary of the Old Testament." The great themes of the Old Testament are thus observed in the Psalter.

The Psalter also had a tremendous influence on the New Testament, being quoted more frequently than any other book with the exception of Isaiah. Jesus remarked that the Psalms, along with the rest of the Old Testament, anticipated his coming suffering and glorification (Luke 24:27, 44). It is thus not at all surprising that both Jesus and the disciples attribute laments to Jesus as they contemplate his suffering (Matt. 27:46; Luke 23:46) and also hymns as they celebrate his glorification (Matt. 22:42; 23:39). Jesus both takes the psalms on his own lips and applies them to himself (he sings the Psalms), and others attribute the psalms to him (we sing the Psalms to him).

Psalm 131

Psalm 131 epitomizes the Psalms and is noteworthy for its manageable style and fascinating content:

A song of ascents. Of David.

My heart is not proud, O LORD,
my eyes are not haughty;
I do not concern myself with great matters
or things too wonderful for me.
But I have stilled and quieted my soul;
like a weaned child with its mother,
like a weaned child is my soul within me.
O Israel, put your hope in the LORD
both now and forevermore.

The psalm's mood is obviously one of calm trusting in the Lord. It is not hard to identify it as an example of a psalm of confidence. The striking metaphor of God as a mother confirms this identification, an understanding that will guide our interpretation in the following paragraphs.

As we read the psalm slowly and meditatively, we should attend to the relationship between the poetic phrases of a verse. As mentioned above, we expect a progression, that is an "intensification" or "sharpening" (Kugel's terms) as the parallel line develops. As we study the first verse, we note that this is the case. The first phrase provides the basis for the rest when the poet denies pride in his heart. The heart in Hebrew conception is roughly equivalent to personality, the foundation of one's being. In fact, if the psalmist's heart had been proud, he could not have continued with the next two points. The first is that his eyes were not haughty. Literally, the Hebrew says "My eyes are not lifted up." In other words, his demeanor, or the way he presents himself to the world around him, is not arrogant. Lastly, he distances himself from pride in action. He stays within his limits. As we slowly reflect on the opening verse of the poem, we thus see progressive denials of pride in personality, attitude, and action.

Our next step is to unpack the rich imagery of the psalm, which leads us to focus on the second verse. An analogy is set up between the relationship of a weaned child to its mother and the psalmist's soul and God (implicit). What is most striking at first glance is the specificity involved in describing the child as weaned. More general terms were available to the psalmist, and this fact leads us to ask why he chose to describe the child in this way. The likely answer is that an unweaned child is anything but calm and satisfied in its mother's lap. It rather grasps for food at her breast. The weaned child on the other hand may calmly rest in its mother's protecting arms. The leading image of the psalm thus contributes to the confident mood of the psalm and brings us to the heart of the psalm's teaching about the nature of God and our relationship with him. God is compassionate and caring toward his people, and they should respond with confident trust and dependency upon him. The psalm serves as a mirror of the reader's soul by providing a model of trust against which readers compare their own relationship with God.

In keeping with the principle of intertextuality, Christian readers may read the psalm in the light of its expanded context, which includes the New Testament. In this case, the psalm is never explicitly cited in the New Testament, though the same thought is found in Jesus' demand of a childlike faith (Matt. 19:13–15).

Indeed, Jesus is the only one who can take this psalm upon his lips at all times and in every situation. David could not do so. One only has to think of the Bathsheba affair to realize that David was not a paragon of prideless submission throughout his life. Jesus, however, was. He most strikingly expresses the trust and submissive obedience to the Father described in the psalm when he accepts the cup of suffering that his Father gives him (Matt. 26:36–46). The psalm, as noted above, also has relevance to the Christian as a prayer that he or she may direct toward Jesus. The psalm in its Old Testament setting expresses heartfelt trust in and dependence on God. Indeed, the Christian can have and express an even deeper level of confidence in God after the ministry of Jesus Christ than before (Rom. 8:28–39), and Psalm 131 is an appropriate model for such a prayer.

WORKS CITED

Alter, Robert. *The Art of Biblical Poetry.* New York: Basic Books, 1985.
Baker, A. "Parallelism: England's Contribution." *Catholic Biblical Quarterly* 35 (1973): 429–40.
Berlin, Adele. *The Dynamics of Biblical Parallelism.* Bloomington: Indiana UP, 1985.
Brueggemann, Walter. *The Message of the Psalms.* Minneapolis: Augsburg, 1984.
Caird, George B. *The Language and Imagery of the Bible.* Philadelphia: Westminster, 1980.
Calvin, John. *Joshua. Psalms 1–35.* Rpt. Grand Rapids: Baker, 1981.
Cooper, A. *Biblical Poetics: A Linguistic Approach.* Unpublished Ph.D. diss., Yale University, 1976.
Gunkel, Hermann. *The Psalms: A Form-Critical Introduction.* Trans. T. M. Horner. Philadelphia: Fortress, 1967.
Keel, O. *The Symbolism of the Biblical World.* New York: Seabury, 1978.
Kugel, James L. *The Idea of Biblical Poetry.* New Haven: Yale UP, 1981.
Longman, Tremper, III. *How to Read the Psalms.* Downers Grove, Ill.: InterVarsity Press, 1988.
O'Connor, Michael. *Hebrew Verse Structure.* Winona Lake, Ind.: Eisenbrauns, 1980.
Ryken, Leland. *How to Read the Bible as Literature.* Grand Rapids: Zondervan, 1984.
Watson, W. G. E. *Classical Hebrew Poetry.* Journal for the Study of the Old Testament Supplement Series 26. Sheffield: JSOT Press, 1984.

CHAPTER 18

Proverbs

Raymond C. Van Leeuwen
Calvin College

At first glance it would seem difficult to say much about Proverbs as a literary work. Wolfgang Mieder, a leading proverb scholar has declared, "The proverb in a collection is dead" (Fontaine 54). And Proverbs itself is a collection of smaller collections, variously containing sayings, admonitions, and instructions. It was compiled over several centuries and bears the stamp of its diverse origins in the headings of its subcollections (10:1; 22:17; 24:23; 25:1; 30:1; 31:1).

But Mieder's dictum focuses on another, related problem. The usual contexts for proverbs are the face-to-face situations of daily life. A mother rouses her sluggard son with the maxim "The early bird gets the worm." A Nigerian father warns his teenage son, who is hanging out with the wrong crowd, "He who sleeps with puppies catches fleas." Peter Seitel has called such ordinary use of proverbs "the social use of metaphor." The proverb provides a metaphor that illuminates the essence of a problem or issue. It "hits the nail on the head." Yet it can do this from different points of view and with different implications. A young man from a wealthy family gets hired to a prestigious government post. He smirks to his buddies, "Money talks." But his better qualified, less connected rival, who was unjustly passed over for the job, may bitterly complain to his friends, "Money talks" (Kirshenblatt-Gimblett).

But this interactive, human context of meaning gets lost in a collection. In a book, isolated from life, compact sayings may seem to say not very much at all. Oral proverbs are highly dependent upon context and implicit cultural knowledge (What does "Carrying coals to Newcastle" mean?); they require an acute sense of situational "fittingness" (25:11, 12): "If the shoe fits, wear it." When properly used, a proverb makes its point perfectly (Carlston 88–89). But a collection of collections of fragments seems to lack all these interpretive essentials.

The sayings in Proverbs do not reveal their setting in life easily. Moreover, they seem helter-skelter, like mismatched beads on a string. Can this odd, multistringed necklace have any beauty? What wholeness unites these fragments of life? What knowledge might help us treasure these gems?

These very questions may provide the key to the use and appropriation of this proverb book. Perhaps our questions contain their solution. These collections were brought together by ancient scribes convinced that these sayings, for all their variety, belonged together as a repertoire of Israel's godly (and therefore also worldly) wisdom. With the conviction that Israel's one God was Creator and Lord of the *uni*verse (Prov. 3:19–20; 8:22–31), these various collections and sayings were brought together to form a universe of discourse, a multifaceted mirror and map to God's "inhabited world," a world itself indwelt with Wisdom and filled with delight (Prov. 8:31 RSV).

Some parts of Proverbs are carefully organized, some apparently less so. The wise reader must thus pay attention to immediate contexts (see on 26:1–12 below). Often we find "proverb pairs" (e.g., 25:16–17; 18:10–11). But long-distance contexts (and contrasts!) among proverbs are also crucial. The book is a treasury out of which the wise bring gems both old and new to fit the occasion (cf. Matt. 13:52).

For all its diversity of origin, genre, and point of view, and for all its brevity of expression, there is a significant coherence to Proverbs. In spite of the centrifugal tendencies of its tiny parts, there is a certain logic and coherence to its overall literary plan. As in any good book, "the whole is more than the sum of its parts." The tiny sayings, to change the image, are bits of tile, gathered into clusters and patterns of a mosaic whose colors, contours, and long-distance symmetries are worth pondering. The main structural components of this literary mosaic, usually signaled by titles, are these:

I. Title, Introduction, and Basic Principle (1:1–7)
II. Parental Instructions on Wisdom and Folly (1:8–9:18)

III. First Solomonic Collection of Sayings (10:1–22:16)
IV. "Sayings of the Wise" (Admonitions) (22:17–24:22)
V. Further "Sayings of the Wise" (24:23–34)
VI. Second Solomonic Collection of Sayings (25:1–29:27)
VII. Sayings of Agur and Numerical Sayings (30:1–33)
VIII. Sayings of King Lemuel (31:1–9)
IX. Heroic Hymn to the Valiant Woman (31:10–31)

Title and Introduction (1:1–7)

Like other ancient Near Eastern wisdom books, Proverbs begins with a title, followed by a brief statement of its purposes (1:1–6). This introduction culminates in a theological declaration that serves as the fundamental point of orientation for the entire book:

The fear of the LORD *is the beginning of knowledge,*
but fools despise wisdom and discipline (1:7; cf. 9:10).

Here God and humans, wisdom and folly, knowledge and sweat born of parental urging (cf. 1:8; 10:1, 4–5) are related in the tight space of eight Hebrew words. Life is caught between the pull toward God and the good and the pull toward folly and pseudogood. Faith is not opposed to reason but constitutes its possibility, its connection to reality (von Rad 53–73). More, the word "beginning" contains the hint, to be elaborated throughout the first nine chapters, that life is not static, but a journey whose end is found in its beginning (cf. T. S. Eliot, "East Coker" in *Four Quartets*).

Parental Instructions (Chs. 1–9)

Upon this foundation are built nine chapters of speeches addressed to "my son" by a mother or father (1:8–9). In genre and function, these speeches are akin to the Egyptian "Instructions," in which a father, king or vizier perhaps, left a testament of wisdom to his heir (cf. Lichtheim or *ANET* for examples). In later Jewish tradition a similar genre is the "Jewish Ethical Will" (Abrahams). Today, in Africa, in settings that function much as traditional rites of passage, there are churches that give similar instruction to young people about to enter adulthood (Barry Evans, oral communication).

But in their present *literary* context, these nine chapters, possibly the book's latest section, introduce us to the world within which the book and its parts find their meaning. Basic images of women, ways, and houses make explicit the worldview that the final author saw as the essential meaning context for chapters 10–31.

As speeches, chapters 1–9 consist of parental advice given to a young man about to assume the mantle of adulthood. This is parenesis, threshold wisdom, designed to prepare and guide the young as they step into the adult world with its problems and possibilities.

The advice is decidedly male in orientation. Much of it consists of warnings against the temptations of the "strange woman" who attracts sexually volatile young men with her verbal and physical blandishments. But the parent, as Wisdom's mouthpiece, offers an alternative. Turning to a mixture of metamorphic and literal language akin to the love poetry in the Song of Songs, he urges the youth to find delight with his wife:

. . . rejoice in the wife of your youth.
A loving doe, a graceful deer—
may her breasts satisfy you always,
may you ever be captivated by her love. (5:18–19; cf. 30:18–20)

The advice, however, is not only about women. Much of the parental talk concerns good and bad paths. In a pair of speeches used as background in Shakespeare's *Henry IV, Part 1* (I.ii; II.ii), the parent warns against temptation, while Wisdom herself warns the young of the consequences of ignoring her voice (1:20–33).

Specifically, the parental speech (1:10–19) warns against ancient "Falstaffs" who invite a young man to a nocturnal ambush. Together, these speeches, with their elaboration in chapters 2–9, establish the fundamental perspective for the wisdom collections to follow: Life is a conflict between wisdom and folly, good and evil. Wisdom and Folly are powerfully attractive "women" who issue contrary invitations to naïve young men, even employing the same language (9:1–6, 13–18). Like the love that pulls humans either to Augustine's City of God or toward the City of this World, so Proverbs 1–9 presents humans as pulled by *eros* for Wisdom or Folly.

Pervasively interacting with the imagery of love throughout chapters 1–9 is that of the "path." In contrast to the "way of sinners" (Ps. 1:1; cf. Prov. 1:15, 19), the first speech in chapter 2 invites the young to pursue Wisdom and the fear of the Lord. Wisdom

guards the course *of the just*
and protects the way *of his faithful ones. (2:8)*

As one reads through the speeches, the images of women and ways, foolish and wise, grow in mutual power and significance. And they come together, especially at the end of the journey (5:4–6; 7:24–27; 9:18).

Gradually it appears that more is at stake than moralistic advice against illicit sexual conduct and other wicked activities. For the seductress emerges as the image of folly, and the good wife (this old English word, like its Hebrew counterpart, signifies both wife and woman) as the image of wisdom. Wisdom is thrice personified as a woman who speaks to young men, in prophetic warning (1:20–33); to all humans as cosmic Wisdom (ch. 8); and finally to naïve young men, inviting them to a banquet whose goal is life (9:1–6) and whose mirror image is Folly's deadly feast (9:13–18).

These positive and negative images of women and ways constitute a symbolic representation of wisdom's worldview (Van Leeuwen, "Liminality"). Here, cosmos and culture are woven of one cloth, and cosmic order is the background for social order. Cosmos (8:27–29) and culture (5:15–19) are structured by divine limits within which freedom, life, and love flourish. As creatures of Yahweh, humans are naturally oriented toward Wisdom and the good. Yet they are constantly subject to the seductions of Folly, to disorientation by the pseudogood. As a young man's desire turns him toward one young woman or another, so human hearts are swayed by love toward Wisdom and life (3:16–18; 4:5–9; 8:35–36; 9:6) or toward Folly and death (2:16–19; 5:3–6; 7:21–27; 9:18).

The neighbor's wife (ch. 7) and folly, one must note, are not obviously bad; indeed, they are attractive. But they are forbidden fruit; a man's wife is sexually out-of-bounds for anyone not her spouse. As God set limits to the cosmic waters (8:29), so humans must limit their sexual "waters," keep them at home and out of the street (5:16).

Proverbs 1–9 signals the boundaries of life and death by paths, and by the parallel "openings" to houses (5:8; 8:34; 9:1, 4, 14, 16) and women's bodies (5:3; 9:16–17; Alter 181–82). Wisdom calls for life and love within limits, joy and freedom within form. Herein lies the essence of a wise, godly life, one that journeys in delight (8:30–31).

Other Sections of Proverbs (Chs. 10–31)

Although space precludes complete treatment, a few comments regarding several structural factors in the book's overall development beyond chapters 1–9 may be helpful to the reader.

The first Solomonic Collection falls into two subsections: Section A

(10:1–15:33) and Section B (16:1–22:16). Section A is almost entirely composed of "antithetical" proverbs in which line 1 is answered by a contrast or opposite in line 2. While chapters 1–9 focus on the opposition of wisdom and folly, chapters 10–15 emphasize the related contrast of righteous and wicked and the consequences attendant upon either lifestyle.

Indeed, this section of sayings is the most consistent in emphasizing the "act-consequence" or "character-consequence" relationship so often pointed out by scholars who think that the worldview of Proverbs is too simplistic: Is it always true, these scholars ask, that "the LORD does not let the righteous go hungry" (10:3)? This question can be generalized in a way that forces us to reflect on the very nature of proverbs, whether in oral or literary settings. Simply put, are proverbs true? For every proverb that promises a reward to the righteous and judgment to the wicked (e.g., 11:4, 6, 8), are there not countercases where bad things happen to good people, where the wicked prosper and vice versa? (Prov. 13:23; 22:16; 25:26; 28:6; cf. Job; Ecclesiastes; Ps. 73).

The first subcollection of sayings, Section A (chs. 10–15) emphasizes the way things usually are, the way they ought to go. Section B (16–22:16), on the other hand, has far fewer neat antitheses between righteous and wicked and presents far more exceptions to the rule, instances in which things do not go as they should. The literary sequence of sections A and B thus seems to embody a form of developmental pedagogy. Young persons need first to learn the basic rules of life—time enough later to learn its painful, mysterious absurdities. Faust's lament on his life of learning is inappropriate on the lips of a college freshman (Goethe, *Faust* 1:355–417, "Night"). Hard, timely work, for instance, is needed to succeed (10:4–5); crime does not pay (11:5, 21); honesty is the best policy (12:19), etc. We generally reap what we sow, and by such principles we ought to live. Of course life can bring injustice and irrational catastrophe. But one ought not on their account to abandon life and effort. Only a sluggard and a fool stays in bed for fear of "lions in the street" (26:13–14). As in language, so in life; we first learn basic rules and patterns, the exceptions come later. On returning from the country, my city-reared toddler excitedly told his mom, "We *seed* a cow!" He had mastered the past "ed" ending, but not the irregular verb.

It is typical of the proverb form to give expression to realities that may be ***true in general*** or ***usually true***. But by the very fact of their great brevity, proverbs do not express qualifications or exceptions to their rules. Instead, the wise user of proverbs will know when to use the more general proverb and when to use its exception-to-the-rule counterpart. We might call the more general proverb (that which describes what is most often the case) a "majority" proverb, and the exception to the rule a "minority" proverb. The wise person will know which proverb speaks to a particular situation.

Thus section B (16:1–22:16) presents many more instances in which things are beyond human control . . . but not beyond God's mysterious mastery of all (cf. 19:21; 21:30–31):

In his heart a man plans his course,
but the LORD determines his steps. (16:9)

Proverbs 16:9 moves from the innermost being of man, his heart (4:23), outward into the realm of action, a man's "way" of life, an image whose prominence in chapters 1–9 we noted. One's "course" may be as long as life; by contrast, a single step seems inconsequential. Yet "God is in the details." Some steps are fatal; others have lifelong significance. In his poem "The Road Not Taken," Robert Frost put it well:

Two roads diverged in a wood, and I—
I took the one less traveled by,
and that has made all the difference.

Again, while Proverbs generally reckons that blessings flow from righteousness (10:6) and that prosperity is both a divine gift (10:22) and a natural consequence of work and wisdom (10:4–5), section B and the following sections (16:1–29:27) recognize that things do not always work out this way. In this connection, the so-called "better . . . than" sayings let us know that in an upside-down world good things, like wealth and prosperity, may become tainted with evil. In the "better . . . than" form, we find juxtapositions that turn our "normal" associations, so common in chapters 10–15, upside down:

Better a little with righteousness
than much gain with injustice. (16:8)

Better a poor man whose walk is blameless
than a rich man whose ways are perverse. (28:6)

Chapter 31, the final chapter of Proverbs, contains sections VIII, Sayings of King Lemuel, and IX, The Heroic Hymn to the Valiant Woman. Like the Sayings of Agur in chapter 30, those of Lemuel appear to be a foreign import into Israel's canonical wisdom. Noteworthy is that they are the words of the queen mother, who occupied an important role also in ancient Israel (Andreasen). These "sayings" are actually of the royal Instruction genre, and concern wine, women, and justice for the poor (cf. Pss. 72, 82). Thus this penultimate section of the book corresponds to the Instruction genre found in chapters 1–9. There are also thematic affinities (women, royalty, justice; cf. 8:15–16).

The connection of 31:1–9 to chapters 1–9 is reinforced by the Heroic Hymn to the Valiant Woman (31:10–31; Wolters, "Proverbs XXXI"). For if chapters 1–9 elaborated cosmic Wisdom personified (1:20–33; 8), chapter 31:10–31 presents and praises wisdom incarnate in the form of an aristocratic, God-fearing Israelite wife. The valiant woman demonstrates her godliness precisely in the great variety and vigor of her "worldly" activities (Wolters, "Nature and Grace"), including a concern for the poor (31:20), which links her to King Lemuel. The poem is in the form of an acrostic based on the twenty-two letters of the Hebrew alphabet. The "valiant woman" ("of noble character," NIV) embodies human wisdom, as it were, from A to Z. (It is no accident that Ruth, whose book immediately follows Proverbs 31 in the Hebrew canon, is given this very epithet by her future husband Boaz [Ruth 3:11].)

Thus we may suggest that chapter 31 in its two parts combines with chapters 1–9 to form an "envelope construction" surrounding the shorter sayings, admonitions, and poems of chapters 10–30. Whereas Proverbs 1–9 invited young men to a love affair with cosmic Wisdom, Proverbs in its end presents a woman/wife—active and glorious in her own right—as wisdom, a divine gift (cf. 18:22) without whom life would seem incomplete. Wisdom's standing in relation to humankind as woman to man, and Yahweh's standing over against humankind/Israel as husband/wife, are metaphoric representations of reality whose depths remain unplumbed.

Meaning and Poetry in the Sayings

Sayings and admonitions in any language are famous for their eloquent brevity. When reading the sayings of Proverbs in English translation, it is easy to forget that we are reading the shortest *poems* in the Bible. But the Hebrew words are arranged like jewels in an exquisitely crafted setting (25:11–12), artful gems whose every verbal facet has been carefully chosen, matched, and polished to form a splendid whole. Although these two-part sayings have their roots in oral culture, the sayings of Proverbs, with their symmetry, polish, and purposeful juxtapositions, appear to be literary in character. Their artistry and richness of suggestion are all the more dazzling in view of their brevity. For the Hebrew sayings are incredibly compact. The synthetic nature of Hebrew words enables five to eight tightly bound Hebrew words to do the work of a dozen or more in English. Prefixes and suffixes combine in one-word meanings that require several words in English. Proverbs 28:11 contains seven Hebrew words, four in the first line and three in the second. But in English the verse stretches to a proselike eighteen words in the Authorized Version (KJV) and twenty in the NIV:

> *A rich man may be wise in his own eyes,*
> *but a poor man who has discernment sees through him.*

This saying revels in ironic reversal. In Solomon, the archetypal wise man, wisdom and wealth went hand in hand. But here wealth robs the wealthy of self-knowledge (cf. 26:12) as he confuses his wealth and status with what might produce them (8:18–19). Complacent expectations that connect wealth with wisdom and poverty with ignorance are here undone in the space of seven Hebrew words.

Essential to the poetry of Proverbs are the many devices of parallelism. Proverbs 11:22 by simple juxtaposition creates a figurative parallel of pig and person to unmask the vanity of beauty:

> *A gold ring in snout of hog . . .*
> *A woman both lovely and witless. (My translation)*

See 26:1–3, 11 for similar proverbs.

Many sayings, especially in chapters 10–15, create antitheses by an interplay of words and phrases in synonymous parallelism, intertwined with crucial contrasts. The parallels and contrasts (which may be considered antonymic parallels) are not used mechanically but employ subtle variations and nuances. The second line answers the first line but generally contains twists and surprises that provoke thought. In addition, the compression of words and the movement from line A to line B effects an "inter-animation of words" (Alter 165, citing Maynard Mack) so that the meaning of the whole is formed by the interplay of every part. Even when line B seems to say the same thing as line A "in different words," line B will present some intensification of thought, a greater precision, or a movement from the general to the specific. Synonyms are never completely synonymous!

Meaning and Contradiction in the Sayings

In some families, "Look before you leap" fits one son and "He who hesitates is lost" another! To ask *which* admonition is true simply misses the point. The proverb pair in 26:4–5 deliberately forces the reader to confront the problem of contradiction among sayings and admonitions:

Do not answer a fool according to his folly,
lest you be like him yourself.
Answer a fool according to his folly,
lest he be wise in his own eyes. (NIV *modified)*

In this contradictory pair, the wise person will know which proverb speaks to her particular situation, but the proverbs themselves do not resolve the dilemma for us. Far from providing absolute guidelines for every circumstance, proverbs require that we master a repertoire of sayings from which we can choose wisely, fittingly. Indeed, a proverb in the mouth of a fool is as useless as lame legs are for walking (cf. 26:7, 9). Worse, as the English proverb based on Matthew 4 has it, "The devil can quote Scripture for his own ends." A proverbial saying may be true but inappropriately delivered. To remark glibly to a widowed young mother that "in all things God works for the good of those who love him" (Rom. 8:28) may not be fitting, though the Pauline saying is true.

Another proverb pair highlights the ambiguity of silence: "A man of knowledge uses words with restraint . . ." but "even a fool is thought wise if he keeps silent . . ." (17:27–28). In his New Testament epistle James is keenly aware of the inconsistent, contradictory behavior of human speech (James 3:3–12; especially vv. 9–12). Proverbs distills this ambiguity into concise, potent imagery. A literal translation conveys the imagery, albeit awkwardly:

Life and death are in the tongue's hand;
He who loves her will eat her fruit. (18:21)

This proverb subtly plays on the feminine grammatical gender of "tongue" to give the saying an erotic tinge, reminiscent of the Song of Songs (cf. Song 2:3; 4:11–16), and to turn the hearer's thoughts to the powerful ambiguity of love, either for wisdom and life, or folly and death. This connection with the themes of Proverbs 1–9 is heightened by the following saying, in which love of wife parallels love of Lady Wisdom:

He who finds a wife finds what is good,
and receives favor from the LORD. (18:22; cf. 8:17, 19, 35)

The "better . . . than" form is also a way of rendering ambiguity or paradox; unexpected juxtapositions turn conventional judgments upside down:

Better is open rebuke than hidden love.
Faithful are the wounds of a friend,
false are the kisses of an enemy. (27:5–6; v. 6, my translation)

What is the upshot of all this? To use proverbs wisely, whether from the Bible or the sayings of contemporary America, one must have a proverb repertoire adequate to handle the complexities of life. If you know only, "You can't teach an old dog new tricks," and not also, "It's never too late to learn," you might commit a faux pas by using the wrong proverb! Goethe said of languages, "He who knows one, knows none" (*Wer nur eine Sprache kennt, kennt keine*). The maxim applies even more forcefully to Proverbs. Even in the Sermon on the Mount, Jesus presents sayings that on one level or another present conflicting advice (cf. Matt. 7:1 and 7:6, which require the reader to make judgments; cf. also 6:1 and 5:14–16). Rather than forcing us to erase or "harmonize" the ambiguities and "contradictions," biblical wisdom invites us to ponder the nuances and complexities of life; it invites us to become wise.

WORKS CITED

Abrahams, Israel. *Hebrew Ethical Wills.* Philadelphia: Jewish Publication Society of America, 1976.

Alter, Robert. *The Art of Biblical Poetry.* New York: Basic Books, 1985.

Andreasen, N. A. "The Role of the Queen Mother in Israelite Society." *Catholic Biblical Quarterly* 45 (1983): 179–94.

Carlston, Charles E. "Proverbs, Maxims, and the Historical Jesus." *Journal of Biblical Literature* 99 (1980): 87–105.

Fontaine, Carole R. *Traditional Sayings in the Old Testament.* Sheffield: Almond, 1982.

Kirshenblatt-Gimblett, Barbara. "Toward a Theory of Proverb Meaning." *The Wisdom of Many: Essays on the Proverb.* Ed. W. Meider and A. Dundes. 111–21.

Lichtheim, Miriam. *Ancient Egyptian Literature, Volume I: The Old and Middle Kingdoms.* Berkeley: University of California Press, 1973.

________. *Ancient Egyptian Literature, Volume II: The New Kingdom.* Berkeley: University of California Press, 1976.

________. *Ancient Egyptian Literature, Volume III: The Late Period.* Berkeley: University of California Press, 1980.

Mieder, Wolfgang, and Alan Dundes. *The Wisdom of Many: Essays on the Proverb.* New York: Garland, 1981.

Murphy, Roland E. *Wisdom Literature: Job, Proverbs, Ruth, Canticles, Ecclesiastes, Esther.* Forms of Old Testament Literature. Grand Rapids: Eerdmans, 1981.

O'Donovan, Oliver. *Resurrection and Moral Order: An Outline for Evangelical Ethics.* Grand Rapids: Eerdmans, 1986.

Seitel, P. "Proverbs: A Social Use of Metaphor." *Folklore Genres.* Ed. D. Ben-Amos. Austin: University of Texas Press, 1976. 125–43.

Taylor, Archer. *The Proverb and an Index to the Proverb.* Hatboro, Pa., and Copenhagen: Folklore Associates; Rosenkilde and Bagger, 1962.

Van Leeuwen, Raymond C. *Context and Meaning in Proverbs 25–27.* Society of Biblical Literature Dissertation Series. Atlanta: Scholars, 1988.

________. "Liminality and Worldview in Proverbs 1–9." *Semeia* 50 (1990): 111–44.

von Rad, Gerhard. *Wisdom in Israel.* Nashville: Abingdon, 1972.

Whybray, R. N. "Yahweh-sayings and Their Contexts in Proverbs, 10, 1–22,16."

La Sagesse de L'Ancien Testament. Ed. M. Gilbert. BETL. Gembloux: Leuven UP, 1979. 153–65.

Williams, James G. "The Power of Form: A Study of Biblical Proverbs." *Semeia* 17 (1980): 35–58.

Wolters, Al. "Nature and Grace in the Interpretation of Proverbs 31:10–31." *Calvin Theological Journal* 19 (1984): 153–56.

———. "Proverbs XXXI 10–31 as Heroic Hymn: A Form-critical Analysis." *Vetus Testamentum* 38 (1988): 446–57.

CHAPTER 19

Ecclesiastes

LELAND RYKEN
Wheaton College

Herman Melville called it "the truest of all books," and another American novelist, Thomas Wolfe, described it as "the highest flower of poetry, eloquence, and truth, . . . the greatest single piece of writing I have known" (quoted in Short ix). But biblical scholars have been less certain about the book of Ecclesiastes. A prevalent view is that the content of this wisdom book of twelve chapters poses a distinct problem in the canon and that its structure is an insoluble problem.

The content of the book, we are told, contradicts the general tenor of the Bible by being a nihilistic denial of meaning in the universe, or at least a statement of skepticism about life and God. Furthermore, surveys of attempts to identify the sequential structure of the book (e.g., Wright) reveal a litany of failures. Unable to find clearly marked units arranged in a meaningful order, most commentators have opted for viewing the book as a miscellaneous collection of proverbs, though variations continue to be made on the twofold scheme of a theoretical foundation (or observation of life) (1–6) and practical conclusions (7–12), surrounded by a prologue and epilogue.

By rendering the book of Ecclesiastes problematical, scholars have also rendered it inaccessible to modern readers. Yet the basic strategy of

Ecclesiastes is relatively simple, and literary analysis can provide clear pathways through the book. The theme of the book, far from being a problem, is a virtual summary of the biblical worldview: life lived by purely earthly and human standards is futile, but the God-centered life is an antidote. And far from being unstructured, the book of Ecclesiastes is one of the most tightly organized books in the Bible, confirming the writer's self-portrait as a person who lavished his time on "arranging proverbs with great care" (12:9).

The Dialectical Structure of the Book

The key to interpreting both the form and content of Ecclesiastes is to grasp the dialectical principle underlying the book. A contrasting set of opposites organizes the entire book.

There can be no doubt that Ecclesiastes expresses a grand contradiction. Life is said to be both futile and meaningful. The narrator is alternately negative and positive about life's possibilities. One moment he wallows in despair and the next moment he endorses the very activities of life that he had declared void of meaning. For example, after telling us for nearly two chapters that pleasure-seeking, acquisition of goods, and work are "vanity and a striving after wind" (2:11), the writer ends the first two chapters by declaring that "there is nothing better for a man than that he should eat and drink, and find enjoyment in his toil" (2:24). The right interpretation of the book is one that satisfactorily accounts for this system of contradictions. Viewing the book as organized on a dialectical principle meets this criterion.

It is no wonder, then, that critics have looked in vain for a logical progression in which things march sequentially from one unit to the next. Contrast, not sequence, is the organizing principle. The book itself presents a fluid movement back and forth, without transition, between the two types of material, one negative, the other positive.

Although the book is not structured as a story, a narrative framework nevertheless forms the subtext. By a series of recollections, reflections, and mood pieces, the speaker tells the story of his futile attempts to find satisfaction in life in all the wrong places. He also regularly balances this negative theme with assertions of an alternative to "life under the sun." This interpretation is not a new claim (readings of Ecclesiastes congruent with my own approach include those by Kidner, Eaton, Kaiser, and Ellul).

One of the common fallacies about Ecclesiastes is that it offers a positive antidote to the negative theme only at the end. But positive passages of affirmation occur throughout (beginning with 2:24–26). My own tabulation comes up with fifteen negative sections, thirteen positive ones, and three mixed ones (for amplification, see *Words of Delight* 320–26). The negative theme, which we might appropriately entitle "Life at Ground Level," gets much more space, outdistancing the positive passages by a ratio of three or four to one.

As our traveling companion through the text, the writer has given us plenty of help in differentiating the two types of material. The phrase "under the sun" or an equivalent occurs in twelve of the fifteen passages that are wholly negative in tone, but it occurs in only four of the thirteen positive passages. The positive passages, moreover, have something that is lacking in the negative ones—a conspicuous emphasis on God and a divine perspective to earthly life.

Since the latter claim is controversial, let me take time to explore a specimen passage from a midway point of the book:

> Behold, what I have seen to be good and to be fitting is to eat and drink and find enjoyment in all the toil with which one toils under the sun the few days of his life which God has given him, for this is his lot. Every man also to whom God has given wealth and possessions and power to enjoy them, and to accept his lot and find enjoyment in his toil—this is the gift of God. For he will not much remember the days of his life because God keeps him occupied with joy in his heart. (5:18–20)

The most obvious feature of this passage is that it is positive in outlook. It asserts the wisdom of enjoying life and implies that such enjoyment is possible. The common view of the Preacher as someone who denies life cannot be sustained by the text.

The second thing that strikes us about the passage is that God is conspicuously present in it. In fact, the passage is God-centered: "which God has given"; "to whom God has given"; "the gift of God"; "God keeps him occupied with joy in his heart." The passage ends with a powerful paradox—being diverted from life, not because it is anything less than joyful, but because God's joy in one's heart surpasses life's good things. According to the book of Ecclesiastes, there is an alternative to the weariness and emptiness of life under the sun. Readers who see the Preacher's outlook as totally negative cannot ask us to overlook passages such as the one I have quoted, nor should we minimize the degree to which God is absent from the negative passages and the focal point of the positive ones.

The positive passages are usually much briefer than the negative ones, but that is part of their effectiveness in serving as a foil. The unstated but controlling metaphor of the negative passages is the labyrinth or maze with its evershifting series of dead ends. By contrast, the positive passages come as a breath of fresh air. They leave us with the impression that something can be made of life if it is pursued in the right way. The brevity of the positive passages is not a sign of their unimportance but of the contrary: they decisively cut through the endless maze of frustration that prevails elsewhere.

What I have said already suggests that the archetypal quest underlies the collection of units, lending a narrative quality to an essentially lyric and proverbial book. The narrator steps forward as the archetypal quester who undertook, not a physical journey, but a journey of the mind and soul—a journey to find meaning and satisfaction in life. The transitions between units keep the quest motif alive as we read: *again I saw, then I saw, so I turned to consider, I have also seen, I turned my mind to know and to search out and to seek.* At the end of the book the narrator tells us that he has reached "the end of the matter" (12:13), reinforcing the feeling that a quest for understanding has attained its goal.

As we watch the quest unfold, we are continuously aware of the discrepancy between the narrator's present outlook and his futile search undertaken in the past. In effect, the narrator recalls the labyrinth of dead ends that he pursued from the safe position of someone who attained his goal and solved his problem. His restless past is recreated with full vividness, but when the narrator voices despair over the futility of life under the sun, he is not affirming this as his final answer to life's existence.

The book's double perspective ties in directly with its persuasive strategy. The success of most literature depends on the writer's ability to make the good attractive and to expose evil for what it is. In a variation of that strategy, the writer of Ecclesiastes has set for himself the task of making us feel the emptiness of life under the sun and the attractiveness of a God-filled life that leads to contentment with one's earthly lot.

In terms of space, then, Ecclesiastes presents a major theme and a minor theme. The major theme is the denial of meaning or satisfaction in life considered by itself. What spoils life in the negative passages of Ecclesiastes is the attempt to get more out of life—out of work, pleasure, money, food—than life itself can provide. The minor theme (in terms of space) is that meaning can be found in living earthly life as part of a bigger reality governed by the presence of God. The writer thus uses a very common literary strategy: he demonstrates at length the inadequacy of a common worldview and combines with this demonstration an alternate worldview.

Overall, Ecclesiastes exhibits one of the most basic of all literary principles—that form is meaning. The dialectical structure of contrasts—the alternating sections of despair and affirmation, the futile quest versus its successful conclusion—expresses the double theme of the book.

A brief look at the flow of the book will confirm the organization I have claimed. After a brief introduction to the narrator and theme (1:1–3), the writer unloads a collage of "under the sun" vignettes that protest the meaningless cycles of life on both natural and human planes (1:4–11) and the inability to find satisfaction in knowledge (1:12–18), pleasure and wealth (2:1–11), permanent achievement (2:12–17), and work (2:18–23). Then we get a long section of affirmation—of enjoyment as God's gift (2:24–26) and of time viewed from both a human perspective (3:1–8) and a divine perspective (3:9–22).

The same dialectical structure continues in the ensuing units. A section of satire against the futile quest to find meaning in the pursuit of wealth (4:1–8) is balanced by the ideal of human companionship (4:9–12). The fickleness of fame (4:13–16) is countered by a picture of the person as worshiper (5:1–7). A passage of satire that exposes the limitations of money (5:8–17) is followed by endorsement of life lived with God at the center (5:18–20). Assertions about the inherently tragic nature of life (ch. 6; 7:1–8) are followed by the assurance that there is a way for a person not be destroyed by these tragedies of life (7:9–14).

As we move beyond this midway point in the book, the units become smaller, the structure becomes more miscellaneous, and three mixed sections appear. In fact, chapter 10 is a collection of proverbs. The effect of these developments is to bring the two themes of the book into the closest possible tension. Here is life as we know it—of a mingled web, good and evil intertwined. The concluding positive affirmations are made in a context of realistic glances at life in the world (in fact, the portrait of the physiological symptoms of old age runs away with a section telling young people to enjoy life while they can). As in all great literature, the writer earns the right to make his affirmations by doing justice to the negative side of life. The narrator of Ecclesiastes is a realistic optimist. He rejects frivolous consolations (see especially 7:1–8) but not the Great Consolation.

The writer himself signals the two types of passages that make up Ecclesiastes with a pair of metaphors near the end of his collection. "The sayings of the wise," he tells us, "are like goads, and like nails firmly fixed" (12:11). The "under the sun" passages are goads that make us unable to settle down complacently with life lived on a purely earthly plane. The positive, God-centered passages are fixed points of reference.

Partial disagreement with details of my analysis should not be allowed to obscure the large measure of agreement that is possible among various interpretations of Ecclesiastes. While I have insisted on a positive counterpoint to the negative message of the book, there should be no doubt that the primary truth of Ecclesiastes is truthfulness to human experience at ground level. The speaker's major theme is the weariness and unfulfillment of life under the sun. At the heart of the book's vision is (to use Hamlet's famous statement) "the heartache, and the thousand natural shocks that flesh is heir to." Various interpretations can also find common ground in the dialectical structure of the book, even when they differ in how they define the contrast.

Literary Affinities

A recognition of the literary affinities of Ecclesiastes will clarify what happens in the book and at the same time suggest some of the literary richness that the author managed to compact into a brief work. We can begin with the nomenclature that biblical scholars have bequeathed—wisdom literature.

This amorphous genre implies something about both content and form. Wisdom literature is defined partly in terms of the stance of the narrator, who pictures himself as the wise person sharing observations about life and making exhortations based on them. Additionally, biblical scholars have lavished their attention on attempts to define the distinctive philosophy of life and theology of the wisdom writers (though this predominant ideational focus is the very reason that treatments of wisdom literature have so often been nonliterary in nature). Wisdom literature also implies a reliance on the proverb or aphorism as the basic form of discourse.

The book of Ecclesiastes meets these criteria of wisdom literature. The writer pictures himself as a wise man who has observed human life from every possible perspective. In keeping with the nature of wisdom literature as an instruction genre, the writer addresses himself especially to young people (11:9; 12:1). The writer's discourse also relies heavily on the proverb—not only the sentence proverb but bigger units such as the proverb cluster on a single theme, the brief narrative, and the portrait.

Wisdom writers of the Old Testament were, above all, observers of human life. They do not speak with the oracular authority of the prophets or the historical precision of the chroniclers. Rather, they are the photographers of the Bible (as Short's photographic commentary on the book vividly illustrates). The one irrefutable confirmation of the truthfulness of wisdom literature is a long, hard look at life around us. Wisdom literature is par excellence the voice of universal human experience as it exists anytime, anywhere, and this is the most basic touchstone of literature itself.

The book of Ecclesiastes also has affinities with an ancient genre known as fictional Akkadian autobiography (Longman 120–23). It adopts a fictional king as narrator/protagonist (conservative as well as liberal scholars accept the fictionality of the author as a persona) who engages in self-discourse. Ecclesiastes also shares with an Akkadian work such as the Cuthaean Legend the inclusion of both first-person narrative and first-person instruction.

In addition, the book of Ecclesiastes belongs to the domain of biblical poetry, a fact concealed by the prose format in which most of the book is printed in English versions. But even the prose sections are so saturated with parallelism that many of them meet the criteria of Hebrew poetry and could easily be printed in verse form. Equally characteristic of the poetic constitution of the book is the author's reliance on imagery and skill with metaphor. Futility, for example, is like trying to catch the wind. The transience and insubstantiality of life without God is like a vapor or mist. Human companionship is a threefold cord.

Ecclesiastes also has important affinities with lyric. Lyric is a subjective, personal utterance by a speaker who speaks directly in his or her own voice. The content of a lyric is either personal reflection or emotion. Lyrics are structured on a principle of theme-and-variation, which constitutes the best avenue for seeing the unity of individual passages in Ecclesiastes.

Ecclesiastes is essentially lyric in nature. It is filled with mood pieces in which the speaker reflects on life and makes us feel a certain way toward the subjects he discusses. Ecclesiastes is an affective book. Even the narrative sections are lyric in their effect as they make us *feel* the futility of the protagonist's latest quest for satisfaction. The persuasive strategy in Ecclesiastes is not to conduct a logical argument but to instill a feeling or mood that finally leads us to agree with the writer's verdicts on life.

Satire (the exposure of human vice or folly) also figures prominently in Ecclesiastes. This is not to deny that the speaker feels pain and regret over the failure of life to match its initial promise to satisfy human longings. To say that the book is satiric is only to say that it exposes the inadequacy of the successive lifestyles with which the speaker futilely experimented.

The negative sections of the book add up to an extended satiric exposure of the very things that dominate our own culture, making Ecclesiastes the most contemporary book in the Bible. Ecclesiastes is a satiric attack on an acquisitive, hedonistic, and materialistic society. It exposes the mad quest to find satisfaction in knowledge, wealth, pleasure, work, fame, and sex. Satiric portraits include the hedonist (2:1–11), the workaholic (2:18–23; 3:7–8), the devotee of money (5:8–17), the fool (7:1–8; 10:1–15), and the faithless woman (7:26–29). The satiric norm is the divine perspective that allows a person to avoid the dead ends that conspire against people when they limit their gaze to life under the sun. Above all, then, Ecclesiastes stands as a satiric "critique of secularism" (Hendry 570).

Another thing that makes Ecclesiastes seem contemporary is its status as protest literature. As in modern literature, the voice of protest or lament is never far from the surface in the mood pieces that make up Ecclesiastes. The overarching protest is against the failure of life to satisfy a person permanently and at the deepest level. Kidner comments that the speaker's protest suggests "something of a divine discontent" (35). The voice of unsatisfied desire, reminiscent of the great odes of English poet John Keats, dominates the negative sections of Ecclesiastes. In listening to that voice, we cover all the bases of life. As we accompany the speaker, we, too, protest the meaningless cycles of life; the failure of such things as knowledge, pleasure, wealth, and work to satisfy us; the tyranny of time; the oppression that the strong visit upon the weak; the failure of physical vitality; and the finality of death. It is easy to find parallels in ordinary literature, all the way from Macbeth's soliloquy about the meaninglessness of life to contemporary poetry.

In summary, we can trust the writer's own word for how he went about his task, "weighing and studying and arranging proverbs with great care" (12:9). At root the book of Ecclesiastes is a collection of proverbs. But the writer gave that collection a narrative thread, a lyric and poetic cast, and a strong element of satire and protest.

Style and Rhetoric

For all the scholarly disagreement about the structure and meaning of the book of Ecclesiastes, there has been agreement with the writer's self-portrait as a conscious stylist—as someone who "sought to find pleasing words" (or "words of delight") (12:10). The book contains two of the most famous passages in all of literature—the poem on time (3:1–8) and the metaphoric portrait of the physiological symptoms of old age (12:1–8). But the book is filled throughout with memorable and haunting statements. Four features are especially noteworthy about the style and rhetoric—rhythm, aphoristic tendency, repetition, and contrast.

The rhythms of the book are almost irresistible. They lend a haunting quality to the negative sections, where the repetitive monotony of the utterances finally weighs us down, especially if we read the passages aloud. The linear flow of the discourse is a great onward stream that keeps propelling us forward. Parallel constructions are doubtless the chief ingredient in this rhythm, but the fluidity of the sentences and the incipient narrative line provided by the quest motif also contribute. Miriam Lichtheim calls such writing "symmetrically structured speech" or the "orational style," standing midway between prose and poetry and activated chiefly by parallelism of members (11).

The aphoristic tendency is equally characteristic of the book. Since we do not generally share the ancients' fondness for aphoristic thinking, I need to say something about the form and purpose of a proverb (for more extended discussions, see Williams and Ryken, *How to Read* 121–26). The aim of a proverb is to make an insight permanent. It does so by being first striking and then memorable. In the words of Norman Perrin, a proverb "is a flash of insight into the repeatable situations of life in the world, and its aphoristic form not only represents insight but compels it" (296). What properties, then, lend this quality of striking memorability to a proverb?

Conciseness and compression are obvious factors. They help to produce the arresting strangeness that makes a proverb different from ordinary discourse. The self-containedness of the individual proverb enhances its ability to focus our attention. "To epigrammatize an experience," writes a literary critic, "is to strip it down, to cut away irrelevance, . . . to reduce it to and fix it in its most permanent and stable aspect, to sew it up for eternity" (Smith 208).

Furthermore, proverbs are often poetic by virtue of their use of imagery, metaphor, and simile. Sometimes the metaphoric quality of a proverb is concealed by the fact that the proverb is on one level a literal statement and becomes metaphoric only when we realize that the particular detail actually covers a whole category of similar experiences. When we read that "through sloth the roof sinks in" (10:18), we are aware that the writer is talking about more than a literal roof that leaks. He is talking about sloth as it appears in any area of daily living. Our metaphoric roofs leak whenever our inaction produces destructive results.

The striking memorability of a proverb is not a result of its form only. Content also helps to produce the effect. For one thing, great proverbs (as opposed to the trivialization of the form that is always on the scene) are high points of human insight. They fit James Joyce's definition of the moment of epiphany in a short story—a moment of intellectual or spiritual focus that brings an area of life into the clearest and most affecting light.

Proverbs are both simple and profound. On the one hand, they are short and easily grasped. Yet they penetrate life to its most profound level, and we never get to the end of their application. To be told that "if a tree falls to the south or to the north, in the place where the tree falls, there it will lie" (11:3) seems on the surface to be too simple an observation to warrant our attention. But as so often with aphorisms, the particular picture is simply a net whereby to catch something universal. The proverb about the tree is really a comment about the principle of finality that characterizes many aspects of our lives.

Proverbs are thus often paradoxically both specific and general, both particularized and universal. They may focus on a tiny aspect of life, but they express a general tendency in life, not a unique occurrence. Proverbs cover a whole host of similar events, and their application is openended. They follow a very basic principle of literature—the conviction that the universal can be expressed through the particular.

What is the effect of a proverb as we ponder it? Most emphatically, a good proverb is not designed to put an end to thought on a subject but instead to stimulate further thought and application. A proverb is a catalyst to reflection.

We must remember, too, that aphoristic thinking is part of the human urge for order. It enables us to master the complexity of life by bringing human experience under the control of an observation that explains and unifies many similar experiences. How many times have we not observed people whose compulsion was to make money and acquire possessions, only to find themselves dissatisfied? A proverb from Ecclesiastes brings all of these observed cases into focus: "He who loves money will not be satisfied with money; nor he who loves wealth, with gain" (5:10).

Being aware of the literary qualities of a proverb is essential to our enjoyment and understanding of the book of Ecclesiastes. Far too much commentary on the book has been preoccupied with the content of the book to the neglect of the thing that actually accounts for its power. Ecclesiastes is not a philosophic treatise. It is a highly artistic piece of literature, not an easy achievement for a work that is at its heart a collection of wisdom sayings and aphoristic reflections.

In addition to its rhythmic and aphoristic qualities, Ecclesiastes makes notable use of repetition as a rhetorical strategy. The very structure of the book, with its alternating negative and positive sections, lends a repetitive flavor to it. But so do patterns of imagery, phrases, refrains, and key words.

The most important of the repeated phrases is "under the sun." Either this phrase or an equivalent occurs more than thirty times in the book. It denotes life lived by purely earthly and human standards, without recourse to a supernatural order. Equally recurrent—and equally important in sounding the negative theme of the book—is the phrase "vanity of vanities." Modern translations are too quick to turn this phrase into an abstraction; in the original it means "vapor, mist, breath" (Gordis 204–5 et al.), with connotations of insubstantiality and fleetingness.

The unity of the book is heightened by additional phrases and words that are repeated throughout. Repeated formulas include "this also is vanity," "eat and drink," "toil," "enjoy" or "not enjoy," "striving after wind," "again I saw," and "I have seen." We are also continuously in a world of elemental images and activities, such as wind and water, eating and sleeping, life and death. Rhetorical questions are intermittent, lending unity of tone and reinforcing the affective nature of the book (since rhetorical questions are designed to move a reader to give assent to a statement).

If repetition is part of the book's deep structure, so is antithesis. I have already noted the contrast between life under the sun and life above the sun. But antithesis is as much a part of the book's texture as its structure. The juxtaposition of two worldviews and lifestyles is mediated through a whole structure of localized contrasts—between enjoyment and lack of enjoyment, wisdom and folly, change and permanence, youth and age, expectation and disappointment, human and divine perspectives. It is small wonder that the famous poem on "a time for everything" (3:1–8) takes antithesis as its chief structural principle.

The Eloquence and Wisdom of Ecclesiastes

To illustrate what I have said about Ecclesiastes, I have selected the following specimen passage (2:20–26a):

> So I turned about and gave my heart up to despair over all the toil of my labors under the sun, because sometimes a man who has toiled with wisdom and knowledge and skill must leave all to be enjoyed by a man who did not toil for it. This also is vanity and a great evil. What has a man from all the toil and strain with which he toils beneath the sun? For all his days are full of pain, and his work is a vexation; even in the night his mind does not rest. This also is vanity.
>
> There is nothing better for a man than that he should eat and drink, and find enjoyment in his toil. This also, I saw, is from the hand of God; for apart from him who can eat or who can have enjoyment? For to the man who pleases him God gives wisdom and knowledge and joy.

The most obvious feature is the juxtaposition of negative and positive passages, expressing the major and minor themes of the entire book.

The negative passage about the inability to find satisfaction in work is typical of other negative sections in the book. We note first the telltale phrase "under the sun." Repetition is prominent—in the key word *toil,* in the phrase "this is vanity," and in the parallel constructions in which the writer repeats a common idea (the futility of work) in different ways. The element of protest is strong in this satiric passage. The confirmation of the writer's observations lies deep within every reader's own experiences and observations of life on the block or in the office. The rhetorical questions in the quoted passage presuppose the reader's agreement.

Without transition, we are suddenly in a different world, but not a wholly different world. Like the preceding passage, the second one, too, speaks of eating and drinking and toil. The positive passages of Ecclesiastes, we should note, do not substitute another, "spiritual" world for the one in which we live. There is nothing escapist about the positive message of the book. Instead of escaping from the meaninglessness that he finds in earthly life by itself, the quester finds a way to import meaning and enjoyment *into* the earthly sphere.

How does he manage that feat? The second paragraph of the quoted passage shows us. First we notice the conspicuous emphasis on God: "from the hand of God," "apart from him who can . . . find enjoyment?" "God gives. . . ." This is in obvious contrast to everything that has preceded in chapters 1–2, where God is mentioned only once in passing. Earlier the protagonist had undertaken a human quest to find meaning and enjoyment, while here it is declared to be something that God gives. The shift in perspective from self to God, from human to divine, opens the possibility of what had earlier been denied, namely, enjoyment of earthly life. The common claim that the writer of Ecclesiastes was a nihilist is preposterous.

To sum up, it is regrettable that Ecclesiastes is considered an inaccessible problem book of the Bible. In contradiction of the stereotype, I hold up the book as one of the most enjoyable artistic books of the Bible, its content being close to lived human experience. The writer's self-portrait is accurate: he successfully "sought to find pleasing words, and uprightly he wrote words of truth" (12:10).

WORKS CITED

Eaton, Michael A. *Ecclesiastes: An Introduction and Commentary.* Downers Grove, Ill.: InterVarsity, 1983.

Ellul, Jacques. *Reason for Being: A Meditation on Ecclesiastes.* Trans. Joyce Main Hanks. Grand Rapids: Eerdmans, 1990.

Gordis, Robert. *Koheleth—The Man and His World: A Study of Ecclesiastes.* 3d ed. New York: Schocken, 1968.

Hendry, G. S. "Ecclesiastes." *The New Bible Commentary Revised.* Ed. D. Guthrie and J. A. Motyer. Grand Rapids: Eerdmans, 1970. 570–78.

Kaiser, Walter C., Jr. *Ecclesiastes: Total Life.* Chicago: Moody Press, 1979.
Kidner, Derek. *The Message of Ecclesiastes* (also published under the title *A Time to Mourn, a Time to Dance*). Downers Grove, Ill.: InterVarsity, 1976.
Lichtheim, Miriam. *Ancient Egyptian Literature: A Book of Readings.* Vol. 1. Berkeley: University of California Press, 1973.
Longman, Tremper, III. *Fictional Akkadian Autobiography: A Generic and Comparative Study.* Winona Lake, Ind.: Eisenbrauns, 1991.
Perrin, Norman. *The New Testament: An Introduction.* New York: Harcourt, 1964.
Ryken, Leland. *How to Read the Bible as Literature.* Grand Rapids: Zondervan, 1984.
———. *Words of Delight: A Literary Introduction to the Bible.* Grand Rapids: Baker, 1987.
Short, Robert L. *A Time to Be Born—A Time to Die.* New York: Harper & Row, 1973.
Smith, Barbara Hernstein. *Poetic Closure: A Study of How Poems End.* Chicago: University of Chicago Press, 1968.
Williams, James G. *Those Who Ponder Proverbs: Aphoristic Thinking and Biblical Literature.* Sheffield: Almond, 1981.
Wright, A. G. "The Riddle of the Sphinx: The Structure of the Book of Qoheleth." *Catholic Biblical Quarterly* 42 (1980): 313–34.

CHAPTER 20

Song of Songs

G. Lloyd Carr
Gordon College

In Dorothy L. Sayers's short story *The Vindictive Story of the Footsteps That Ran,* Lord Peter Wimsey remarks, "In my youth they used to make me read the Bible. Trouble was, the only books I took to naturally were the ones they weren't over and above keen on. But I got to know the Song of Songs pretty well by heart." Whether the Dowager Duchess was wise or not in monitoring her son's literary career is beside the point—at least she had a clear understanding of what the Song is all about.

This little book—only 117 verses, including the title—has been the object of a whole range of interpretive approaches. From the earliest traditions of the pre-Christian era through the centuries of the Middle Ages and the turmoil of the Reformation down to the present day, writers, both believing and skeptic, have argued divergent interpretations of the material.

The Song as Allegory

Allegory—"to say one thing but mean another"—as a *literary genre* has a long and honorable history. It is essentially an extended metaphor, often of book length, where the story is told with the explicit intention of having the elements and events represent something else. John Bunyan's *Pilgrim's Progress* is probably the best-known allegory in English literature. But allegory in this sense is clearly identifiable: the characters are obvious "traits" or "types"—Christian, Evangelist, Faithful, Hope, Pliable, Obstinate, Giant Despair—and the places are obvious representations—The Celestial City, The Slough of Despond, Doubting Castle, Vanity Fair—or the characters are talking animals as in C. S. Lewis's Narnia tales or Kenneth Grahame's *Wind in the Willows*. With these there is no danger in taking the story as being in any sense historical or anything more than a story—a story with didactic intent, but a fiction nonetheless.

Allegorizing is the use of allegory as an *interpretive method*. It first appears in the work of Theogenes of Rhegium, a Greek philosopher who lived about 520 B.C.E. Theogenes and his fellow philosophers used Homer's traditional stories of the gods and goddesses as vehicles for the new ethical and moral ideas the philosophical schools were attempting to inculcate into Greek society. Unfortunately, the old gods were even more corrupt than their devotees, so to make use of the ancient material it was necessary to "reinterpret the stories." To that end the philosophers developed an elaborate method of disregarding the apparent meaning of a passage and substituting another meaning more in keeping with their own concerns. In this way the original meanings are surpressed, and the new meanings superimposed on these traditional accounts so that the narrative is made to convey ideas not intended by the original author.

The allegorical method of interpretation found its way into Judaism primarily through the efforts of Philo, an Alexandrian contemporary of Jesus, and into the Christian community through the Epistle of Barnabas (c. A.D. 130) and the writings of Origen in the third century. Once introduced, the method took quick root and for many centuries became the dominant literary technique in dealing with biblical texts.

Since shortly after the time of the New Testament, by far the most common methodological approach in the interpretation of the Song among both Jews and Christians has been the allegorical. There are thousands of examples of the allegorization of the Song, but a few selected ones will serve to illustrate the point. Song 1:13 is a classic:

> *My beloved is to me a bag of myrrh,*
> *that lies between my breasts.* (RSV)

Traditional rabbinic interpretation (Rashi and Ibn Ezra) allegorizes the woman's breasts to mean the two cherubim that formed part of the "mercy seat" (the lid of the ark of the covenant), and the sachet of myrrh to refer to the Shekinah, the pillar of cloud symbolizing God's presence that stood between the cherubim in the Holy of Holies in the tabernacle (Ex. 25:17–22; 40:34–38; Num. 7:89).

Where Jewish allegory defines the relationship of Israel and Yahweh, Christian allegory frequently describes the relationship of Christ to the church. Here the same passage is taken to refer to the Scriptures of the Old and New Testaments, with Christ standing between them.

Another classic text is Song 7:2a:

> *Your navel is a rounded bowl*
> *that never lacks mixed wine.* (RSV)

A traditional high-church interpretation identifies this passage with the sanctuary of the church where the communion wine is always present. A similar view is that proposed by the nineteenth-century German Lutheran scholar E. W. Hengstenberg, who sees this passage as referring to "the cup from which the church revives the thirsty with its refreshing draught." And of course a glance at the page headings in any old edition of the King James Version of the Song will show example after example of how this book describes Christ's love for his church (Rowley).

I have acknowledged the allegorical interpretation of the Song, not because I think it is valid, but because of its persistent presence in the history of interpretation. The allegorical interpretation remains the backdrop against which more valid literary interpretations take their stand.

The Song as Drama

Origen (c. A.D. 250) argued that the Song was actually "a marriage song written by Solomon in the form of a drama." Not many ancient or medieval commentators followed Origen's lead, but since the mid-1800s a number of interpreters have picked up this suggestion. Franz Delitzsch's commentary was most influential in establishing the idea that the Song is a script for a dramatic or musical performance. In 1967 Calvin Seerveld published a version in oratorio format, complete with vocal assignments and a complete score (Seerveld). It has even been performed occasionally.

While the dramatic approach has wide support, there are insurmountable problems associated with it (Carr, "Drama"). At the most basic level there is the problem of the structure of the book. There is simply no plot. The story does not *go* anywhere. Only by gratuitous manipulation of the text can any sort of progress or plot development be introduced. Nor is there evidence of any character development. The characters are real enough, and the situations they find themselves in and the emotions they express among themselves are true to life, but by the time we have arrived at the last few verses of chapter 8 we have come full circle to recreate the atmosphere of chapter 1. The events and interchanges of these eight chapters do not move in a linear direction to a climax and resolution. Instead, in what some writers call "ring construction," they pivot around the central verses (4:16–5:1), with the last half of the book mirroring the ideas and even the specific vocabulary of the first half.

A second major problem with the dramatic theory is the difficulty of assigning speakers to the individual segments of the text. The suggestions range anywhere from twelve to forty-four separate text units, two (or three) major characters, several minor characters, a chorus of women from the city, a male chorus (the woman's brothers), and a mixed chorus of wedding guests. The roles and speeches of these last three groups are clear in some instances and murky in others, but it is the major characters who are the most difficult to identify with any certainty.

There is little problem identifying the woman. She is usually known simply as "Shulamith" or "the Shulammite" from the reference in 6:13. Those who identify the male figure in the poem as King Solomon usually link this name to "Abishag the Shunammite," David's last nurse/wife (1 Kings 1:3–4), who, presumably, then became Solomon's wife. Shulem may be an alternate for the name of Shunem, a small village in central Galilee, but apart from this passage in the Song, there is no evidence of this form of the name prior to New Testament times. Among the commentators there is broad general agreement as to which are the woman's speeches, though there is considerable variation in identifying their precise division and extent.

The major difficulty is with the male speeches. Those who argue for a dramatic approach generally attempt to establish a measure of conflict by dividing the male speeches between two individuals: King Solomon, who is endeavoring to add the Shulammite to his already extensive harem, and her long-term sweetheart from home to whom she remains faithful in spite of all the attention of the king. At first glance it would appear relatively simple to make this sort of distinction, but even Seerveld, after most careful consideration, is forced to admit that "the identification of voices and (interpretive) phrases . . . are admittedly careful precisions [*sic*] and imaginative extrapolations" (Seerveld 100). Whatever conflict the dramatic theory finds in the Song is contingent upon assigning these male speeches to the appropriate individuals, but in practice there is no clear or consistent division.

As noted above, there are several areas in the text where other groups or individuals speak. But again, there is no common agreement on who these people are, or exactly what the individual speech units include. Some (e.g.,

3:6–11, the description of the wedding procession coming up from the wilderness) are generally assigned to the woman's female companions, "the daughters of Jerusalem" (e.g., 1:5; 3:5), but the New International Version takes even this passage to be words of the woman herself.

Similarly, the unit describing the "little sister" (8:8–9) is variously attributed to the "daughters of Jerusalem," to the woman's brothers (as in 1:6b), verse 8 to the woman, and verse 9 to "Solomon." Some even assign the whole section 8:7b–12 to a group of political hacks. Even the limits of the passage are disputed. Do verses 8 and 9 stand as an independent unit (NIV, NEB, Dillow)? Is each verse a separate speaker (RV and ASV)? Is verse 10 included in the unit (RSV, the Rabbinic tradition, Falk, Seerveld, Exum, and Gordis)? Is the unit verses 8 to 13 (KJV), 7 to 12 (JB), or 6 to 12 (Delitzsch)? There is simply no scholarly agreement here.

But even if the speeches can be isolated, the dramatic approach still has major problems. There is an almost total lack of anything that could be called dialogue. The speakers, even when they are addressing each other, do not carry on conversation. The speech units are essentially monologues. Nor is there any indication of any direction for staging or stage business. These issues, along with the lack of developing plot line, would make a script of this sort fail miserably in a stage presentation.

The Song as Love Poetry

If neither the allegorical/typical interpretation nor the dramatic theory can be sustained, is there any other option available? It is here that an examination of other ancient literary texts proves fruitful. In its overall structure and content, the Song is one example of the universal genre of love poetry that runs from the songs of ancient Sumer to the one that was composed this morning.

The language of love is common parlance in all societies, and the ancient Near East is no exception. Examples of "love talk" are found in all these ancient literatures, but there are three extensive collections of love poetry extant from the ancient Near East—one from Sumer sometime in the middle period of the third millennium B.C.E. (Kramer, *Cuneiform Studies*), the second from Egypt about 1100 B.C.E. during the New Kingdom period (Simpson or White), and the third, much more fragmentary collection from Babylon in the middle of the first millennium B.C.E. (Lambert).

There are a number of similarities between these poems and the Song that we will examine below, but there are also a number of significant differences. The Sumerian material is primarily a New Year cult ritual celebrating the annual Sacred Marriage between the shepherd king Dumuzi and the goddess/priestess Inanna, whose primary responsibility in the pantheon was oversight of sexual love, fertility, and procreation. The story is preserved on more than twenty tablets, each of which is an independent composition, and many of which contain a colophon identifying the genre of the poem and its identification with Inanna. While these poems are obviously related to each other in the overall story, there does not appear to be any indication that they are a literary unit.

The Babylonian love poetry is similar. The texts that make up this collection are extremely fragmentary, and it is difficult to be absolutely certain of many details of the content or of the arrangement of the fragments (Lambert). What is certain is that there were various scribes involved in the copying of these texts, and that some of the accounts are preserved in more than one copy. One of the tablets appears to be a kind of "order of service" in which the "Regular Rites" are identified and first lines of the various other texts are quoted, often with stage directions for the participants. The other tablets contain a series of lyrics that describe in graphic detail the preparations for and the consummation of the sexual encounter of Marduk, the chief god of the city of Babylon, with his mistress, the chief goddess Ishtar. Marduk's consort Zarpanitum also plays a significant role in the account, reminding Marduk of her place as his wife and homemaker, but when he fails to heed her plea, she becomes extremely angry and stalks out of the house, leaving him to his rendezvous with Ishtar (Carr, "Drama").

The situation is somewhat different with the Egyptian love songs. There are at least nine different collections, each one with its own title, and some with the name of the scribe responsible for the writing. Many of the collections have a measure of internal consistency either of theme or structure, but apart from the love-song motif, there is not the unity that appears in the Sumerian and Babylonian collections. Some of these Egyptian songs have cultic overtones—appeals to the deities, activities in the various cult centers, some links to the funerary practices associated with the burial of the pharaohs, for example—but for the most part they are simple exchanges between lovers. There is little of the king/goddess element that is the core of the Mesopotamian material.

All of these collections share another common element: elaborate and often very specifically detailed descriptions of the physical attractions of parties. This form is often identified as the *wasf,* a term that in its narrow technical meaning is limited to poems composed and sung in honor of the bride or bridegroom as part of the wedding celebration, but is frequently used much more broadly to include any poem describing the adornment and physical charms of a woman. In preparation for welcoming Dumuzi into her bed, Inanna

... picks the buttocks stones, puts them on her buttocks,
Inanna picks the head-stones, puts them on her head,
She picks the lapis-lazuli stones, puts them on her nape,
She picks the ribbons of gold, puts them in her hair of the head,
She picks the narrow gold earrings, puts them on her ears,

The description of the ritual of ornamentation continues for several more lines as she chooses her veil and other garments, and the section concludes:

She picks a sweet "honey well" puts it about her loins,
She picks bright alabaster, puts it on her anus
She picks black willow, puts it on her vulva,
She picks ornate sandals, puts them on her feet....
In the "navel of heaven," the house of Enlil {the temple}
... Dumuzi met her. (Kramer, Cuneiform Studies)

In the Babylonian collection the material is somewhat more fragmentary, but there are two short excerpts preserved where Marduk speaks to Ishtar:

Zarpanitum is sleeping in the cella,
{but} ... you are my short silvery girl....
You are the mother, Ishtar of Babylon
The beautiful one, the queen of the Babylonians.
You are the mother, a palm of Carnelian,
The beautiful one....
Whose figure is red to a superlative degree. (Lambert 103, 123)

This final image probably indicates that Ishtar's skin has the rosy glow that comes with sexual arousal, and that Marduk recognizes her willing readiness.

And one of the Egyptian love songs, the first of the *Songs of the Orchard,* combines the nature imagery with the *wasf:*

The pomegranate says:
Like her teeth my seeds,
Like her breasts my fruit. (Simpson)

But this sort of material is not limited to ancient love poetry. John Donne is perhaps a little less direct, but just as deliberate:

Off with that girdle, like heavens Zone glistering,
But a far fairer world incompassing.
Unpin that spangled breastplate which you wear
That th' eyes of busie fooles may be stopt there....

Your gown going off, such beautious state reveals
As when from flowry meads th' hills shadow steales.
Off with that wyerie Coronet and shew
The haiery Diademe which on you doth grow;
Now off with those shooes, and then safely tread
In this loves hallow'd temple, this soft bed.

And e. e. cummings is even more explicit:

i like my body when it is with your
body. It is so quite new a thing.
Muscles better and nerves more.
i like your body. i like what it does,
i like its hows. i like to feel the spine
of your body and its bones, and the trembling
-firm-smoothness and which i will
again and again and again
kiss, i like kissing this and that of you,
i like, slowly stroking the, shocking fuzz
of your electric fur, and what-is-it comes
over parting flesh. . . . And eyes big love-crumbs,

and possibly i like the thrill

of under me you so quite new

Like other examples of the love-poetry genre, the Song shares such common motifs as nature imagery (horses, gazelles, goats, foxes, doves, gardens, apples, pomegranates, nuts, vines, palm trees, groves, mountains, pools), specific descriptions of the physical attractiveness of the lovers (hair, cheeks, breasts, thighs, feet, hands), perfumes (aloe, frankincense, cinnamon, nard, myrrh, saffron), ornaments (jewelry, necklaces, gold, silver, precious stones of various types), and such terms as prince, king, queen, lover, shepherd, and beloved. These are all common coin in love poetry.

Many of these elements are illustrated in the short unit that runs from 6:13 to 7:5 (Falk follows the numbering of the Hebrew text here, so identifies these as 7:1–6). The unit has all the marks of a classic *wasf* form: the wedding context, the presence of the guests and their active role in the celebration, the identification of the bride as "queen" or "princess," and most important, the specific, detailed description of the bride's physical attributes.

The section opens with a request by the wedding guests that the bride perform in "the dance of the two groups" (or "the counterdance"). It is probable that this was something like Salome's infamous "dance of the seven veils" in which the woman began the dance in a diaphanous costume and ended dancing naked before the onlookers. Her reply, "Why do you want to look at *me?"* does not imply prudery and an unwillingness to perform, but reflects the self-effacement she has already confessed in 1:6. We can almost hear her say, "There are lots of girls here who are prettier than I am." (Falk takes a slightly different tack, translating her question "What will you see as I move in the dance of love?" but the response is the same.)

The guests reply with a very specific and erotic description of why she is the center of their attention in this dance. Their gaze moves from her beautiful sandaled feet to her lustrous tresses, which ripple and shimmer as she dances for them. Her neck, her face, and her eyes are all described in terms that have been used earlier (e.g., 1:10, 15; 4:1, 4; 5:14), here modified and expanded. But the real focus of their attention is on the more intimate parts of her body. Her inner thighs are as beautifully crafted as the jewels used in the lovemaking that was part of the fertility rituals (cf. Hos. 2:13), the work of a master workman (v. 1). From the inner thighs, their look goes, not to the "navel" as many translations express it, but directly to her genitals. In the ancient literature, the two expressions used here appear frequently as descriptions of the vulva. The noun is used of the female genitalia in the Arabic literature and probably derives from a root meaning a valley or a place to be farmed, and the phrase "never lacking mixed wine" emphasizes the moist fertility of the valley. The imagery of "ploughing" as a euphemism for sexual intercourse is well attested in the literature (Kramer, *Marriage Rite,* and Lambert). The glistening skin of her lower abdomen is the soft color of ripening wheat encircled by the "lilies," another euphemism for her pudenda (2:16; 6:3). And the image of breasts like twin fawns has already been used in chapter 4.

Of course, a dominant theme in love poetry is the desire of the lovers to move to more intimate union. Loving banter, erotic descriptions of the beloved, secluded places where they may pursue their lovemaking, and a belief that the beloved is without fault, all marks of love poetry, find their expression in the Song (White).

The vocabulary of the Song reflects the whole love-song tradition of the ancient Near East, but there is one significant difference here. As we have already noted, many of the other ancient Near Eastern love poems have very specific references to the role of the king and the High Priestess in the fertility rituals associated with the Sacred Marriage (Kramer). But one significant item that runs counter to the view that the Song is primarily a theological allegory like these other poems is the fact that not a single one of all the major religious words in the Old Testament appears at all in the Song—not even the name of God (Carr, *Commentary* 42–44). The translation of Song 8:6 "the flame of Yahweh" in the Jerusalem Bible and the American Standard Version depends on taking the last syllable of the Hebrew word here as *yah,* an abbreviated form of the covenant name Yahweh. This is technically possible, but it is more likely that the syllable is functioning here as it often does, indicating a superlative. The Revised Standard Version's "a most vehement flame" correctly catches the force of the phrase (Gordis 26, 99). None of the terms related to sacrifice, worship, prophecy, election, covenant, blessing, sin, honor, law appears at all. There is no hint *anywhere* in the text itself that suggests any sort of cultic or religious application for this material.

But while the book is fairly straightforward, the language of the Song poses a very specific problem. Although the book is relatively short (117 verses), it contains an unusually high number of unusual words. As almost every verse has at least one of these words, it is difficult to be sure the translation of any given unit is correct. Very frequently an "educated guess" is about the best one can hope for. But that does not necessarily interfere with the sense of what is happening in the poem. The effect is much like reading T. S. Eliot's poem *The Waste Land*—many of the individual lines or stanzas are very obscure for most of us, and the arcane references listed in the Notes do not do much to illuminate the *meaning* of the poem. Nevertheless the poem still moves us.

And so it is with the Song. We may not always be certain of the precise meaning or exact connotation of a specific verse, but the flow of emotion and the excitement of the protagonists come across clearly as we listen.

The Problem of Structure

But is the Song one poem or an anthology of smaller poetic units bound together by theme and subject matter like the Egyptian collections? Many scholars argue that the Song is not a unit at all, but simply a collection of individual lyrical poems that share a common interest in human love. Robert Gordis, for instance, identifies twenty-eight "songs and fragments" classified under nine different motifs and patterns. And Marcia Falk, whose treatment is currently the most widely quoted literary analysis of the Song, breaks the text into thirty-one individual units, which, she declares, "had internal coherence and were not mere fragments" (Falk 108). She concludes this section with the observation that some of the sequencing of the poems "may be the result of an editorial juxtaposition" in which certain catchwords that appear in different poems "led a compiler to place certain poems alongside one another" (Falk 109).

In spite of such widely held arguments for an anthologized collection, however, a very strong case can be made that an examination of the whole book suggests otherwise. True, there are a number of individual units that can stand alone, but the composition as we now have it reveals a very careful arrangement of these units in a way that certainly forbids seeing it as a haphazard collection and almost as certainly precludes mere editorial arranging of some previously selected poems. Some of the units may have their origin elsewhere, but even if that is true, the final form of the Song indicates a single hand at work—and that hand the hand of a master craftsman.

It was argued above that the Song does not show any plot line—that is, a logical sequence through the piece from beginning to end with development of characters, progression from conflict through climax to resolution. Certainly there are specific episodes described, and some specific situations identified, but *progression* is not evident. The individual units seem to fold back on each other rather than moving the story forward. This element suggests that if we want to make some sense out of the arrangement of the individual units, some other structure must be sought.

The one formal structure that provides adequate understanding of the Song as we now have it is the form known as chiasmus. The term derives from the Greek letter chi which has the shape of the English letter X. Thus the adjective *chiastic,* "cross-shaped" is used to describe a literary unit, either longer or shorter, in which elements or ideas are expressed sequentially up to a central point and then expressed again in reverse order as the whole series unwinds. As suggested above, there is a rather orderly progression of themes and ideas in the first four chapters, then a pivot point in 4:16–5:1 and a subsequent unwinding of the themes and ideas in reverse order through the last four chapters. The match is not *strictly* exact, but it is extremely close, frequently even to the point of mirroring unusual vocabulary or inverting specific imagery. (For a detailed look at the chiastic structure of the Song, see Carr, *Commentary* 44–49, Exum, and Shea.)

It is important, therefore, in order to catch the sense of the Song to understand something of the chiastic structure of the book. Any division of the text is somewhat arbitrary, but the following arrangement appears fairly satisfactory to describe the broad outline and form.

I. Anticipation (1:2–2:7)
II. Found, and Lost—and Found (2:8–3:5)
III. Consummation (3:6–5:1)
IV. Lost—and Found (5:2–8:4)
V. Affirmation (8:5–14)

Three of the five sections (I, II, and IV) close with the refrain

Daughters of Jerusalem, I charge you
by the gazelles and the does of the field:
Do not arouse or awaken love
until it so desires.

(The closing verse of Section IV omits the gazelles line.) The third and fifth sections conclude with the common theme of consummation:

Eat, O friends, and drink;
drink your fill, O lovers. (5:1b)

and

Come away, my lover,
and be like a gazelle
or a young stag
on the spice-laden mountains. (8:14)

All five sections begin with one or both of the ideas of arousal (2:10; 5:2; 8:5) or the arrival of one of the lovers and the invitation of the other (1:2, 4; 2:8, 10; 3:6; 5:2; 8:5–6). The repeating cycle of invitation, exhilaration, and warning lends structure to the whole poem.

This becomes more evident in the detailed outline of the book:

I. Anticipation (1:2–2:7)
- A. The Beloved's first request (1:2–4)
- B. Her shy uncertainty (1:5–7)
- C. The Lover's gentle encouragement (1:8–11)
- D. The Beloved's soliloquy (1:12–14)
- E. The Lovers banter (1:15–2:2)
- F. The Beloved's second request (2:3–7)

II. Found, and Lost—and Found (2:8–3:5)
- A. The Lover's arrival (2:8–9)
- B. His first request (2:10–13)
- C. The Lover's intercession (2:14–15)
- D. The Beloved's response (2:16–17)
- E. The Beloved's search (3:1–5)

III. Consummation (3:6–5:1)
- A. A wedding song for Solomon (3:6–11)
- B. Beauty and desire (4:1–15)
- C. Consummation (4:16–5:1)

IV. Lost—and Found (5:2–8:4)

- A. The break (5:2–8)
- B. A leading question (5:9)
- C. A joyous response (5:10–16)
- D. A second question (6:1)
- E. A curious response (6:2–3)
- F. The Lover overwhelmed (6:4–10)
- G. The Beloved's excited anticipation (6:11–12)
- H. A request, a question, and a reply (6:13–7:5)
- I. The Lover's praise (7:6–9)
- J. Consummation—again (7:10–8:4)

V. Affirmation (8:5–14)

- A. Arousal (8:5)
- B. Commitment (8:6–7)
- C. Contentment (8:8–10)
- D. Communion (8:11–14)

A close examination of the text reveals numerous close parallels in vocabulary and theme in the related sections. For instance, 8:3 ("His left arm is under my head, / and his right hand embraces me") is an exact reprise of 2:6. Similarly, the beloved's invitation to her lover in 7:10–13 repeats many of the same expressions and thoughts he had directed to her in 2:10–15. This latter example demonstrates the care with which the author of the book deals with the ideas: not exact repetition—that would be too easy and obvious—but rather a series of fugal variations, elaborating and building a new movement from the block introduced earlier.

The question of structure is of more than technical interest, however. It plays a crucial role in facing up to the specifically erotic nature of the book. Human sexuality is a God-given gift to be celebrated and enjoyed. And the Song unabashedly celebrates that gift.

The problem, though, is that if the Song is arranged in a chronological way, there appears to be scriptural approval for premarital sexual encounters of the most intimate kind. The marriage celebration occurs in the fourth chapter, with the explicit exhortation to the couple to "drink [their] fill" of lovemaking climaxing the union in 4:16–5:1. Yet the language used in describing the relationship and its situations in the first three chapters make it absolutely clear that these two people are already sexually involved.

Much of the detailed support for this observation involves specific vocabulary common to the love poetry of the ancient Near East as we noted above, but two specific examples serve to illustrate the point. The exchange between the lovers in 1:12–17 includes the image of the lover lying between the beloved's breasts like a sachet of perfume (v. 13) while they are hidden away in a secluded grove of the forest (vv. 16–17). The passage in 2:3–6 also has specific erotic connotations. The traditionally pious reading of 2:4b, "his banner over me is love"—even frequently set to music and sung with great gusto by primary-age children to the huge delight of their teachers and parents—cannot be sustained. The verse is more accurately translated

He brought me to the house of wine (the tavern?)
and his intention was to make love to me.

Hardly the stuff of elementary school!

This understanding of the text is supported by the sixth verse, where the word translated "embrace" is actually the term "fondle" and is used in Proverbs 5:20 of sexual union. Helmut Gollwitzer puts it more bluntly: "There is no way around it. These two people are simply in love with one another, and are planning to sleep together without anyone else's permission, and without benefit of marriage license or church ceremony. And *that* is in the Bible!" (Gollwitzer 29).

Such a conclusion seems to cut across the whole biblical tradition of premarital chastity and postmarital fidelity. And it is primarily for that reason that the structure issue is so important. Recognizing that the whole book is a chiasmus solves the "chronological problem." The events described so graphically are not intended to be understood *sequentially.* They are *thematically* arranged around the central pivot point, her invitation in 4:16 and his response in 5:1 to consummate their marriage.

That perspective also helps clarify what is missing from this encounter. There are sweet and bittersweet episodes in the Song. There is joy and excitement in the presence of the beloved. There is the hinted as well as the overt eroticism in the descriptions of the physical attractions of the other. There is the tension of separation and the opposition of family and friends, but there is nothing in the Song that speaks of pregnancy or childrearing, nothing of the burdens and responsibilities of supporting a family, nothing of growing old together (or alone with only memories of a deceased spouse), nothing of (permanent) separation or personal disaster. Rather, the Song celebrates human sexuality as a fact of life, God-given, to be enjoyed within the confines of a permanent, committed relationship. This is no passing fling. What is celebrated here is total dedication to the beloved other, a permanent obligation gladly assumed. The Song is an extended commentary on those first recorded words of the human race—"This is now bone of my bones and flesh of my flesh" (Gen. 2:23). The promise of Eden is reflected in this relationship: two creatures, opposites, yet alike, "suitable" for each other, male and female made in the image of God, celebrating and fulfilling their

God-given desires. Freely and openly they give to each other, because they have been given freely.

WORKS CITED

Carr, G. Lloyd. "Is the Song of Songs a 'Sacred Marriage' Drama?" *Journal of the Evangelical Theological Society* 22 (1979): 103–14.

———. *The Song of Solomon. An Introduction and Commentary.* Tyndale Old Testament Commentaries. Ed. D. J. Wiseman. Downers Grove, Ill.: InterVarsity, 1984.

cummings, e. e. *100 Selected Poems.* New York: Grove, 1959.

Delitzsch, Franz. *Commentary on the Song of Songs and Ecclesiastes.* Edinburgh: T. & T. Clark, 1885.

Dillow, Joseph C. *Solomon on Sex.* Nashville: Nelson, 1977.

Donne, John. "To His Mistris Going to Bed." *The Complete Poetry and Selected Prose of John Donne.* Ed. Charles M. Coffin. Modern Library. New York: Random House, 1978.

Exum, J. C.: "A Literary and Structural Analysis of the Song of Songs." *Zeitschrift für die alttestamentliche Wissenschaft* 85 (1973): 47–79.

Falk, Marcia. *The Song of Songs: A New Translation and Interpretation.* Rev. ed. of *Love Lyrics From the Bible,* 1982. San Francisco: HarperCollins, 1990.

Ginsberg, H. L. "Ugaritic Myths, Epics, and Legends." *Ancient Near Eastern Texts Relating to the Old Testament.* Ed. James B. Pritchard. Princeton: Princeton UP, 1969. 129–55.

Gollwitzer, Helmut. *Song of Love: A Biblical Understanding of Sex.* Philadelphia: Fortress, 1979.

Gordis, Robert. *The Song of Songs and Lamentations.* 2d ed. New York: KTAV, 1974.

Lambert, W. G. "The Problem of the Love Lyrics." *Unity and Diversity.* Ed. Hans Goedicke and J. J. R. Roberts. Baltimore: Johns Hopkins UP, 1975. 98–133.

Kramer, Samuel Noah. *Cuneiform Studies and the History of Literature: The Sumerian Sacred Marriage Texts.* Proceedings of the American Philosophical Society. Philadelphia: American Philosophical Society, 1963. 107:485–515.

———. *The Sacred Marriage Rite.* Bloomington: Indiana UP, 1969.

Rowley, H. H. "The Interpretation of the Song of Songs." *The Servant of the Lord and Other Essays on the Old Testament.* 2d ed. Oxford: Blackwell, 1965. 197–245.

Seerveld, Calvin. *The Greatest Song.* Palos Heights, Ill.: Trinity Pennyasheet, 1967.

Shea, William H. "The Chiastic Structure of the Song of Songs." *Zeitschrift für die alttestamentliche Wissenschaft* 92 (1980): 396.

Simpson, W. K. *The Literature of Ancient Egypt.* 2d ed. New Haven: Yale UP, 1973.

White, John B. *A Study of the Language of Love in the Song of Songs and Ancient Egyptian Poetry.* Society of Biblical Literature Dissertation Series. Ed. Howard C. Kee and Douglas A. Knight. Missoula, Mont.: Scholars, 1978.

CHAPTER 21

Old Testament Prophecy

Richard Patterson
Liberty University

While earlier scholarship concentrated largely on Pentateuchal matters, since the end of the Second World War fresh interest in the prophets has blossomed to such an extent that one might well speak of the era since 1945 as the "flowering of prophecy" (Clements 51; Tucker, "Prophecy" 325). Contemporary scholarship has addressed numerous problems dealing with the study of prophetism and prophetic literature, such as the origins of prophecy, the nature of the prophetic office, the prophet's cultural context (social, political, cultic), and the literary criticism of the prophetic books, including the relation of prophecy to the Law, the relation of oral tradition to prophecy, the composition and compilation of the prophetic texts, the nature of Israelite prophecy, and the question of prophetic genre per se (Smith 986–1003; Tucker, "Prophecy" 326–56). The last of these will constitute the central focus of this article.

Building on B. Duhm's pioneering *Die Theologie der Propheten* (Bonn) and noting accounts of a prophet's unusual behavior (e.g., 1 Sam. 19:20–24), some scholars have suggested that prophecy is distinguished by its ecstatic quality. Others have pointed out the prophet's role as a preacher and, laying stress on the originally oral form of prophecy, have analyzed it in terms of various *Gattungen* (types) of prophetic sayings and/or speeches, such as threats, promises, and sayings.

The idea that prophecy could be defined in terms of its characteristic *Gattungen* (which became a guiding principle in the literary criticism of the Old Testament) received fresh impetus with the work of C. Westermann (98–128) who introduced new terminology into the system. Calling attention to instances of prophetic "messenger formulae," Westermann spoke of the prophet's role as a divine messenger to deliver Yahweh's words (see also Ross 98–107; Greidanus 242–43). Such messages were analyzed in terms of judgment speeches (whether to individuals or nations), accounts, and utterances (prayer, doxology), the first of which he considered the major component of prophetic genre. While all such studies have been defended or denied, the general principle that prophecy must be viewed in terms of various types and themes has come to be the dominant literary approach to prophecy.

While scholarly consensus has deplored finding any overarching criterion that distinguishes prophecy as a genre (Smith 1002), some have dared to hazard a specific literary nomenclature. Thus Richard Moulton (1388–93), laying stress on the prophet's role as a statesman for the opposition, suggested that prophecy, in a traditional sense, is spiritual drama, one that often takes the heightened form of rhapsody (e.g., Isaiah, Joel, Amos, Nahum, and Habakkuk). Leland Ryken (*How to Read* 166), calling attention to the location of the prophet's message in the mind or imagination as opposed to existing reality, tentatively puts forward the term "visionary literature." Such literature "transforms the known world or the present state of things into a situation that at the time of writing is as yet only imagined."

Neither of these suggestions, however, appears fully adequate to cover the spectrum of diverse genres found in the prophetic books. Indeed, no single rubric may prove to be totally sufficient. Perhaps the best approach may be to relate the literary productions of the prophet to his basic call and function. By far the majority of scholars have considered the prophet's commission to be a proclaimer of a God-given message (Friedrich, "Κῆρυξ" 701). The prophet is one who "regards himself as a messenger of Yahweh whose word he has to pass on" (Friedrich, "Προφήτης" 810; see also VanGemeren 76). Essentially, then, prophecy has to do with the proclamation of the divine message.

"Proclamation" has perhaps as adequate a claim as any as a designation for prophetic genre. Not only does it relate adequately to the various terms for prophet, but it also describes well his primary calling and various duties (Fee and Stuart 150–55; Greidanus 229). A prophet could be informed that he was set apart for God's service and called (Muilenberg 74–97) to proclaim his divinely entrusted message (e.g., Amos 7:14–15). Although not every prophet reports the circumstances of his call, each is conscious of the heavenly origin of his message. Very often the words connected with the communicating of that message carry the distinct sense of "proclaim" (e.g., *gĕrā'*: Isa. 40:2, 3; Jer. 2:2; 3:12; 4:5, 16; 5:20; 11:6; 34:17; Joel 3:9; Jonah 1:2; 3:4; Zech. 1:4, 14, 17; 7:7; *hašmîa'*: Isa. 41:22; 42:9; 43:12; 48:3, 5, 20; 62:11).

The oral nature of the larger part of prophetic communication reinforces the designating of prophecy as proclamation. While it is true that literary types such as law and historical narrative have been similarly viewed (Greidanus calls the whole Bible proclamation [20]), these may be better considered in terms of publication. For their designed end concerns the written record of God's holy standards and his dealings with humankind. Other proposed genres such as wisdom and psalmic material likewise lack the sermonic quality of prophecy.

Indeed, it is this feature that most characterizes prophecy. The prophets were the preachers of Old Testament times. To read prophecy, therefore, is to enter the world of the spoken word, a word that can be fully understood only by the exercise of the whole person. The reader must be attentive to the effect of the message not only on mind and eye but also on ear and heart. Thus readers of Micah 1:10–16 will fail to appreciate the full force of the prophet's words unless they understand something of the play on sounds and meanings in the words of judgment (e.g., "In Beth Ophrah [house of dust] roll in the dust" [*'āpār*], v. 10). Likewise, the effect of Nahum's proclamation of Nineveh's destruction (2:10) is greatly heightened by the striking assonance in the prophet's doleful dirge, "*bûqâ ûmĕbûqâ ûmĕbullāqâ*—destroyed and despoiled and denuded."

When we think of prophecy as being "sermonic" we must not, however, think of the tightly ordered exposition of Scripture that was born of Greek rhetoric at the hands of the early church fathers and, having been transformed into a sacred discourse via the medieval church, reached artful elegance in seventeenth-century England and France. Rather, Old Testament prophecy is more in the nature of a homily, a familiar discourse that, while proclaiming God's intentions, admonishes/encourages (whether directly or indirectly) its hearers to respond to the divine message.

Thus the nature of the prophet's call and task and the manner and form of his message point to prophecy as proclamation. Whether in speaking, writing, or the performance of his duties, the prophet's whole life was to be a sermon (cf. Jer. 1:5–19), a proclamation of the word, works, and will of God (Friedrich, "Προφήτης" 812; Greidanus 3).

Guides to Understanding Prophecy

Although readers of prophecy are thus to come with an appreciation of the sermonic quality of what they are about to read, they are nonetheless confronted with what often appears to be formidable roadblocks to their understanding. Even a trained biblical scholar like Douglas Stuart can lament that "the prophetical books are among the most difficult parts of the Bible to interpret or read with understanding" (Fee and Stuart 149). In the page of prophecy one meets many strange names. Some play major roles on the stage of earth's history (e.g., Nebuchadnezzar, Cyrus the Great); others have a more modest part (e.g., Hezekiah, Gedaliah). Long-departed people (e.g., Assyrians, Philistines) and ancient cities (e.g., Nineveh, Thebes) dot the prophetic landscape. While all of this is no more of a problem for prophecy than for other types of biblical literature (e.g., historical narratives, poetry), the very fact that the prophets deal with real people and the problems of the ancient world assures readers that their quest will be a rewarding one. Prophecy is designed to be relevant to everyday life. Moreover, the principles resident in the prophetic record are those that are applicable to the needs of every reader. In cases where a prophecy stands fulfilled (e.g., Isa. 37:33–37; Hos. 1:4), the reader is further assured that God is in control of all of earth's history, including the life of each individual person.

A more serious problem is the seemingly bewildering variety of literary forms one meets in prophecy. At first sight, the larger prophecies (e.g., Isaiah, Jeremiah, Ezekiel) in particular appear to contain such a kaleidoscope of material that the reader could despair of seeing any unity or structural arrangement to the book. Some have even suggested that the prophetic books are little more than collections of loose bits of material that somehow came together in tradition complexes devoid of inherent unity or structure. Nothing could be further from the truth.

As for matters of unity and structure, each book customarily has a basic authorial perspective and one or more dominant themes (e.g., the judgment of Nineveh [Nahum] or Babylon [Habakkuk], the Day of the Lord [Joel, Zephaniah]). Some prophecies show evidence of a bifid structure (Jeremiah, Nahum, Zephaniah) by which the two halves of the book answer to one another in deliberate design. Topics within a book are carefully arranged into units joined together via association of words, expressions, and ideas. These elements, often appearing toward the end of a unit and reappearing early in the following one, serve as a technique whereby the author stitches his various sections together. Thus Nahum's opening hymn to the sovereign God who defeats his foes who plot against him (1:3–10) is linked to the following application to Nineveh (1:11–15) by means of the idea of plotting. Similar literary hooks and key words stitch each portion of the prophecy. Even longer books such as Jeremiah and Ezekiel give evidence of this unifying technique (Patterson, "Bookends" 116–18).

The boundaries of the author's arranged material can be determined through such devices as headings, standard opening and closing formulae, refrains, and the use of bookending words/ideas to form an inclusio. Some otherwise independent units capture the emphases of the two sections on either side of them and therefore act as a literary hinge. These may form a single verse (Nah. 3:4), a full chapter (Jer. 36), or even an extended section (Isa. 36–39).

Unity and development of basic themes are thus formed by the careful placement of material in accordance with matters of association. The application of these common Semitic compositional techniques enables the reader not only to discern major units of a prophetic book but also to catch something of the author's emphases and overall intention.

Equipped with this information, readers can then turn their attention to the types of literature found in the prophecy. They soon realize that the pages of prophecy, far from being a homogeneous body of predictions (as so often popularly supposed), are filled with a seemingly endless variety of forms. Indeed, one needs to approach a prophetic book with the understanding that that book contains an anthology of the prophet's life and work—oracles that comprise many subgenres.

Announcements of Judgment

Although many (e.g., Tucker, "Speech" 27–40) have modified Westermann's basic threefold terminology for prophecy (speeches, utterances, and accounts), his concentration on the prophetic speech as most characteristic continues to carry the day (e.g., Tucker, "Role" 170; Greidanus 242; VanGemeren 76–79). Some declare it to be the basic form "which the prophets used more frequently than any other to deliver their messages" (von Rad 37). Because of the vast size of the body of prophetic judgment speeches, it is probably best to treat such oracles separately and designate them "announcements of judgment." Such oracles are built around two elements: (1) accusation, giving the reason for the Lord's judgment, and (2) announcement proper. Often these will be accompanied by some statement indicating the divine origin of the message. Consider, for example, Amos 4:1–2: accusation ("You women who oppress the poor and crush the needy and say to your husbands, 'Bring us some drinks!'"), messenger formula ("The Sovereign LORD has sworn"), announcement ("The time will surely come . . .").

Announcements of judgment may be delivered against (1) foreign nations or (2) God's covenant people. In both cases they may be directed against individuals, cities, or countries. In the former case, Isaiah condemns the king of Babylon (Isa. 14:3–20), Ezekiel pronounces God's judgment against Pharaoh (30:1–7) and the ruler of Tyre (28:1–19), and Daniel announces God's humbling of Nebuchadnezzar (4:19–27). Foreign cities, particularly capitals, are singled out for special denunciation: Babylon (Jer. 51:1–14, 54–58), Damascus (Jer. 49:23–27), Nineveh (Nah. 2–3) or Tyre/Sidon (Ezek. 26–27). In many instances the announcement of judgment against the foreign king and capital city can blend almost imperceptibly into an oracle against the country itself.

In addition to Israel's neighbors, extended prophecies detail the denunciation and doom of the major powers around which the complex international events of the seventh and sixth centuries B.C. revolved: Assyria, Babylonia, and Egypt. In most cases these announcements of judgment have been brought together in distinctive sections that are usually arranged in geographic orientation (Isa. 13–21; 23; Jer. 46–51; Ezek. 25–32; Amos 1:3–2:3; Zeph. 2:4–15).

The announcement of judgment is also used against Israel/Judah, whether against individuals such as kings (Jer. 36:29–31) and political and religious leaders (Jer. 23:9–40), or the cities of the land (e.g., Ezek. 16; 23), or the covenant nation and its people. The latter kind of messages appear ubiquitously in the prophetic books and characteristically emphasize Israel's infidelity to the Lord and the ethical standards of the Torah for which God's people must be judged (see, e.g., Jer. 2:1–3:5).

Such announcements are often delivered in the form of a woe oracle (e.g., Zeph. 3:1–7). These denunciations characteristically employ the elements of invective, criticism, and threat. Thus in the fourth of five woes proclaimed against the Chaldeans, Habakkuk (2:15–17) begins with an invective expressed in the form of a metaphor that blends into allegory. The Chaldean is a man who gives his neighbor (the nations) strong drink first to inebriate and then to denude him. As invective turns to threat, the allegory goes on to depict the giver of the drink (the Chaldean) being forced to imbibe his own drink and himself suffer a disgraceful exposure. The threat is further heightened by the use of two well-known biblical motifs: the cup (judgment) and the right hand (emphasis): "The cup from the LORD's right hand is coming around to you" (v. 16). In the criticism that follows, the Chaldeans' bent for violence (a key word in Habakkuk) against man, animal, and the natural world is condemned and assigned as a primary reason for their judgment. In a very real sense, then, the Chaldean has shown himself to be that false friend in the allegory. Everyone and everything that he touches is violently exploited to his own selfish ends so that only a judgment in kind can properly satisfy the demands of justice.

Kingdom Oracles

Kingdom oracles give details concerning the establishment of Israel's final kingdom. They consist of two types: (1) an announcement of universal judgment and (2) a promise of ultimate blessing (Vos 307–18). The former genre also functions as a type of the announcement of judgment oracle but has as its distinctive feature the judgment that stands at the culmination of the judgment series and serves to introduce the final era. The scope of the judgment is universal and encompasses such features as international warfare, terrifying events in the natural world, and widespread devastation on the earth (Joel 3:9–17). Thus Zephaniah (1:14–18), drawing upon a vocabulary and themes found in Joel 2:1–11, affirms that the great Day of the Lord's judgment will be a time of unprecedented warfare and be punctuated by supernaturally introduced dark clouds that bring about a pervading gloom and terrible distress. In the "great day of the Lord," "a day of wrath" (v. 14), "the whole world will be consumed" together with "all who live in the earth" (v. 18).

Scholars have largely followed Westermann in terming the promises of blessing "salvation oracles." Such oracles customarily contrast Israel's present chastisement with its future deliverance and restoration to the land to enjoy the Lord's everlasting favor. They often stress the absence of fear and give promise of worldwide peace and felicity (e.g., Isa. 43:1–7). At times these messages are tied to a new covenant that gathers up and fulfills all the promises in the Abrahamic and Davidic covenants. It is a covenant mediated through a shepherd who is at once divine and David's heir (Ezek. 37).

It is instructive to note that these oracles of judgment and hope are often juxtaposed or stitched together to form one fabric of future design (e.g., Isa. 59:15b–21). The blending of universal judgment and hope can at times take on a tone that approximates the apocalyptic literature of the intertestamental period with its stress on a revelation to a human recipient, otherworldly beings, cosmic dimension, and sudden drastic divine intervention brought together in a setting of ultimate eschatological salvation.

Although Old Testament kingdom oracles do foresee a time of

cataclysmic upheaval and earthly destruction coupled with the hope of universal peace and happiness (e.g., Zeph. 1:14–18; 3:8–20), the realization of all of this is tied to God's teleology (e.g., Dan. 2; 7). Accordingly, while Old Testament kingdom oracles partake of elements that will one day emerge in full apocalyptic fervor (e.g., 2 Enoch; 3 Baruch), they are considerably removed from apocalyptic as such.

Instructional Accounts

Although a great variety of prophetic material may be termed instructional (e.g., Hag. 1:5–11), several genres are used to provide specific information aimed at motivation. One may note first the covenant lawsuit (e.g., Isa. 3:12–4:1). In this genre God is often "portrayed imaginatively as the plaintiff, prosecuting attorney, judge, and baliff in a court case against the defendant, Israel" (Fee and Stuart 160). While warning of judgment, such oracles are intended nonetheless to instruct God's people with a view to changing their ways so as to avoid it. Lawsuit oracles can contain such distinctive elements as (1) witnesses (Mic. 6:1–2), (2) charges (Isa. 1:2b–4), (3) indictment (Isa. 41:21–24), and (4) sentencing (Isa. 3:18–14:1; see VanGemeren 400–2).

At times the related form, the disputation, occurs (e.g., Ezek. 18). Typical elements include declaration, discussion, and refutation. Malachi uses this genre well, crafting his argument by skillfully keying it to several short disputations. Illustrative is Malachi 1:6–14, where the priests' disrespect for God is at issue. The priests protest their innocence, but God charges them with offering ceremonially defiled sacrifices. Thus he who is a greater king is treated in a way that men would not treat mere earthly kings. The disputation is followed by an admonition to give God proper honor lest the Lord of the covenant levy the penalties written in the covenant upon them (Mal. 2:1–9).

The desired effect in both the covenant lawsuit and disputation speeches is to leave the opponent devoid of further argumentation and resigned to the divine decision. This is well illustrated in Habakkuk, which in a sense can be viewed as a long disputation of the prophet with his God. Habakkuk's objections based on his perception of divine activity (1:2–4; 1:12–2:1) are met by God's answers (1:5–11; 2:2–20) so fully that, following his prayer in which he considers the glory of God (3:1–15), he can only cast himself upon God alone (3:16–19).

Another important instructional genre is the exhortation or warning. Exhortations are usually built around (1) an imperative or volitional statement (e.g., come! hear! listen! return! etc.) and (2) a motive clause detailing the reasons for the command. Additional matters of content or description may be added. The exhortation can serve as a warning (Zeph. 1:7–13) as well. The exhortation/warning is often juxtaposed with the announcement of judgment in a stirring challenge to avoid the coming disaster. Thus, following an extended oracle of judgment, Zephaniah (2:1–3) urges his hearers, "Seek the LORD, . . . seek righteousness, seek humility; perhaps you will be delivered in the day of the LORD's anger."

Several other types can be viewed as instruction. Among these are the many examples of wisdom expressions found in such forms as admonitions (Hos. 14:9) and proverbial sayings (Isa. 10:15; 29:16; Ezek. 18:2). Several scholars have suggested an origin in traditional wisdom for many of the metaphors, similes, numerical sayings, and literary expressions found in the prophetic books, especially where the pericope is an extended one (e.g., Hos. 7:4–16; 9:10–11:12).

If the previous suggestion that the uniqueness of the prophetic office made both the prophet's words and his work to be media of divine communication, then the biographical (e.g., the majority of Jer. 26–29, 34–45) and autobiographical (e.g., Ezek. 24:15–27) notices in the prophets may also be viewed as instructional. To these may be added the occasional "confessions" of the prophet, whether for himself or vicariously for all Israel/Judah (e.g., Jer. 11:18–12:6). Particularly instructive are those instances of distinctive call to be a prophet together with a reminder that God's claim was upon his prophet's life and ministry (e.g., Jer. 1). Significant too are the accounts of symbolic acts performed by the prophets, again aimed at instructing God's people as to the divine will and purpose (e.g., Ezek. 4, 5). It appears that the reason for the inclusion of such material is not solely to supply interesting details concerning the prophet but also that the reader may see and be instructed through God's working in the life of his messenger.

Miscellaneous Genres

Several other minor genres may be noted. One such is prayer, a genre skillfully employed by several prophets and especially Jeremiah (e.g., Jer. 14:7–9, 19–22). Hymns and songs appear within the prophetic corpus (e.g., Isa. 42:10–13) as well as laments (e.g., Ezek. 19:1–14). One hymn of praise—Habakkuk 3:3–15—takes on epic proportions (Patterson, "Psalm" 178–85). That this twofold psalm belongs to the corpus of Hebrew epic may be seen in that, like the Mediterranean and Near Eastern epics that appear in the ancient literature from Rome to India, it is an extended narrative poem that recites the exploits of the hero—God himself. Like other ancient epics, it is nationalistic in tone. In typical fashion, it is filled with static epithets and phraseology drawn from an earlier age—the grand exodus and conquest era.

I should also mention satire, with its characteristic features of satiric vehicle and tone, object(s) of attack, and a satiric norm by which criticism is conducted. While whole books can be analyzed in terms of satire (e.g., Amos, Jonah; see Ryken, *Words of Delight* 334–40), satire is found within other genres such as lament or woe (e.g., Ezek. 19:1–14; 24:3–5). Nahum employs it with particular skill as a typical Near Eastern taunt song (2:11–13; 3:8–13, 14–19), attacking Nineveh through the use of metaphor, simile, and irony in a biting criticism of the Assyrian capital for its pride, rapacity, and cruelty (Patterson and Travers 441–42).

Vision reports also constitute a genre (e.g., Ezek. 1; 8–11). Often such visions project the future and take on a cosmic scope in which supernatural beings play a strong role, a heavenly mediator is present (Daniel, Zechariah), and the prophetic message has an eschatological perspective. All of this makes vision a suitable vehicle for the Old Testament's emergent apocalyptic form.

Stylistic Concerns

Prophecy also encompasses a literary richness far beyond the mere consideration of thematic unity, structure, and genre. Within its pages one may find both major literary vehicles—prose (particularly narrative) and especially poetry. While prose was utilized most frequently with biographical, autobiographical, and historical accounts (e.g., Jer. 37–44; Ezek. 24:15–27) and where God's speeches to his prophet (including vision reports) are recorded (e.g., Ezek. 8–11), poetry was used to convey God's message through his prophet to audiences. Alter suggests that the reason why so great a preponderance of prophecy is expressed in poetry lies in the fact that "poetry is our best human model of intricately rich communication, not only solemn, weighty, and forceful but also densely woven with complex internal connections, meanings, and implications. [Thus] it makes sense that divine speech should be represented as poetry" (141).

It may be said, then, that "most of the prophets were poets and their oracles were delivered and have been preserved in poetic form" (Freedman 18). This means that one may expect that all of the major genres with the exception of some types of instructional accounts will take on the heightened speech, literary richness, and urgency of tone and message that so characterized poetry. Exceptions occur, as in Haggai 1:5–11; however, even here the rendering of the passage in prose may be due to editorial choice despite the presence of many poetic elements.

It may be added that most of the familiar literary features occur with great frequency. Since poetry forms so great a part of prophecy, due to the very nature of poetic utterance with its reliance on the world of imagery and figures to heighten the effect of its material, one not unexpectedly encounters the free use of such literary features as simile, metaphor, synecdoche, irony, and various types of parallelism. Likewise, poetry lends itself well to the development of themes and motifs. Among the many that may be cited may be noted those of the shepherd (Jer. 23:1–8; Ezek. 34:11–31), the vine and the vineyard (Isa. 5:1–7; Hos. 9:10), the father and the son (Jer. 3:19; Mal. 1:6), and the husband and the wife (Isa. 54:1–8; Jer. 3:14; Hos. 1–3).

Old Testament prophecy, then, rather than being a disjointed, jumbled maze that bewilders those who enter it, may be viewed as a lovely stained-glass window. Its many genres and literary features, like individual panels with their variegated hues and themes, lend such color to the theme of the whole that those who view it are awed yet inspired by its vividness.

One example may serve to illustrate the literary quality of the genre. Within the short prophecy of Zephaniah one may find all three subgenres. (1) There are announcements of judgment both against foreign nations (2:4–15) and Judah (1:4–6), and against the city of Jerusalem (3:1–7). (2) Kingdom oracles of both types are present—not only announcements of universal judgment (1:2–3, 14–18), the latter taking on emergent apocalyptic proportions, but also a double promise of ultimate blessings (3:9–13, 14–20), the latter being almost hymnic in nature. (3) Instructional accounts built around warnings and exhortations also appear (1:7–13; 2:1–3; 3:8). Moreover, the whole prophecy is skillfully crafted in a familiar Semitic bifid structure (1:1–2:3; 2:4–3:20) that not only displays symmetry of design but also shows the deliberate use of stitch-words to thread together its major sections and its subunits. The effect of the whole is to give the reader a carefully reasoned proclamation of the Lord's purposes for Israel and all people that is easily understood and moves them to respond in humble acquiesence to the righteous standards of a holy God.

Something of Zephaniah's poetic skill and style may be displayed in 3:1–7:

1. *Woe to the city of oppressors,*
   rebellious and defiled!

2. *She obeys no one,*
   she accepts no correction.

She does not trust in the LORD,
she does not draw near to her God.

3. *Her officials are roaring lions,*
her rulers are evening wolves,
who leave nothing for the morning.

4. *Her prophets are arrogant;*
they are treacherous men.
Her priests profane the sanctuary
and do violence to the law.

5. *The LORD within her is righteous;*
he does no wrong.
Morning by morning he dispenses his justice,
and every new day he does not fail,
yet the unrighteous know no shame.

6. *I have cut off nations;*
their strongholds are demolished.
I have left their streets deserted,
with no one passing through.
Their cities are destroyed;
no one will be left—no one at all.

7. *I said to the city,*
"Surely you will fear me
and accept correction!"
Then her dwelling would not be cut off,
nor all my punishments come upon her.
But they were still eager
to act corruptly in all they did.

Having pronounced the judgment of the nations surrounding Judah (2:4–15), Zephaniah proceeds with a message of judgment against Jerusalem. This oracle is cast in the form of a woe. Moving from invective (v. 1), Zephaniah turns to criticism (vv. 2–4), citing the reasons for his people's punishment. Negatively, they have neither responded to God's chastisement nor placed their trust in God (v. 3). The positive declaration uses distinctive metaphors in describing Jerusalem's civil officials as roaring lions and evening wolves whose ravenous greed knows no bounds (v. 4). Her religious leaders, prophets and priests, are no better. Being carried away with their own arrogant and selfish ambitions, they have violated the sanctity of God's law and his house.

Moving on to threat (vv. 5–7), Zephaniah concludes the woe oracle with a vivid contrast between God and Jerusalem's leaders. He who in righteous concern has judged many nations hoped that such judgment would serve as a warning to turn Jerusalem from its unrighteous ways. But alas, unlike God, whose justice is dispensed with a regularity like that of the dawn of every new day, Jerusalem's citizenry arose early (v. 7) to corrupt their way still further. The implied threat is clear: Jerusalem must learn the lessons of a just God or suffer severe judgment.

The woe oracle itself thus serves as a culmination to Zephaniah's pronouncements of judgment. As in an earlier instance (1:2–6, 7–13), the judgment oracle gives way to instruction that exhorts its hearers to wait for the God who even now has convened his court to serve as both witness and judge of his people (v. 8). Woe oracle and admonition alike, however, carry with them a veiled hope. If God's people would but wait in believing and expectant trust for God's judicial process to accomplish its work, they could yet realize their ultimate destiny of restoration, renewal, and perfect rest (3:9–20).

Conclusion

Approaching Old Testament prophecy from a literary perspective, then, both liberates readers from the temptation of seeing every text as some sort of coded blueprint for the future that must somehow be decoded and equips them to approach a given passage in a balanced manner. This study has emphasized that Old Testament prophecy was primarily intended as the proclamation of God's revealed will in sermonic (or homiletic) fashion. Thus readers must come to the text with their whole person being attentive to the total effect of the passage.

Granted the usual constraints of grammar, history, theology, and context, a few basic literary guidelines for interpreting prophecy may serve in applying the information discussed above. (1) Read the whole book/passage carefully. (2) Discern the author's theme, tracing its development. (3) Look for the author's use of structural indicators such as bookending, hinging, and stitching devices and look for opening and closing formulae. (4) Identify the literary genre(s) employed and observe its elements. (5) Determine whether the passage is poetry or prose and apply the normal rules integral to each. (6) Be alert (especially in poetry) to the author's use of literary figures and motifs. (7) Reread the passage for full understanding, effect, and application.

WORKS CITED

Alter, Robert. *The Art of Biblical Poetry.* New York: Basic Books, 1985.

Clements, Ronald E. *One Hundred Years of Old Testament Interpretation.* Philadelphia: Westminster, 1976.

Fee, Gordon D., and Douglas Stuart. *How to Read the Bible for All Its Worth.* Grand Rapids: Zondervan, 1982.

Freedman, David N. *Pottery, Poetry and Prophecy.* Winona Lake, Ind.: Eisenbrauns, 1980.

Friedrich, Gerhard. "Κῆρυξ." *Theological Dictionary of the New Testament.* Ed. Gerhard Kittel. Vol. 3. Grand Rapids: Eerdmans, 1965. 683–717.

———. "Προφήτης." *Theological Dictionary of the New Testament.* Ed. Gerhard Kittel. Vol. 6. Grand Rapids: Eerdmans, 1968. 781–861.

Greidanus, Sidney. *The Modern Preacher and the Ancient Text.* Grand Rapids: Eerdmans, 1988.

Moulton, Richard G., ed. *The Modern Reader's Bible.* New York: Macmillan, 1914.

Muilenburg, James. "The 'Office' of the Prophet in Ancient Israel." *The Bible in Modern Scholarship.* Ed. J. P. Hyatt. Nashville: Abingdon, 1965. 74–97.

Patterson, Richard D. "The Psalm of Habakkuk." *Grace Theological Journal* 8 (1987): 163–94.

———. "Of Bookends, Hinges, and Hooks: Literary Clues to the Arrangement of Jeremiah's Prophecies." *Westminster Theological Journal* 51 (1989): 109–31.

Patterson, Richard D., and Michael E. Travers. "Nahum: Poet Laureate of the Minor Prophets." *Journal of the Evangelical Theological Society* 33 (1990): 437–44.

Ross, James F. "The Prophet as Yahweh's Messenger." *Israel's Prophetic Heritage: Essays in Honor of James Muilenburg.* Ed. B. W. Anderson and Walter Harrelson. New York: Harper & Row, 1962. 98–107.

Ryken, Leland. *How to Read the Bible as Literature.* Grand Rapids: Zondervan, 1985.

———. *Words of Delight: A Literary Introduction to the New Testament.* Grand Rapids: Baker, 1987. 334–40.

Smith, Gary V. "Prophet; Prophecy." *The International Standard Bible Encyclopedia.* Ed. G. W. Bromiley. Vol. 3. Grand Rapids: Eerdmans, 1986. 986–1004.

Tucker, Gene M. "Prophecy and the Prophetic Literature." *The Hebrew Bible and Its Modern Interpreters.* Ed. Douglas A. Knight and Gene M. Tucker. Chico, Calif.: Scholars, 1985. 325–68.

———. "Prophetic Speech." *Interpreting the Prophets.* Ed. James Luther Mays and Paul J. Achtemeier. Philadelphia: Fortress, 1987. 27–40.

———. "The Role of the Prophets and the Role of the Church." *Prophecy in Israel.* Ed. D. L. Petersen. Philadelphia: Fortress, 1987. 159–74.

VanGemeren, Willem A. *Interpreting the Prophetic Word.* Grand Rapids: Zondervan, 1990.

von Rad, Gerhard. *Old Testament Theology.* Trans. D. M. G. Stalker. Vol. 2. New York: Harper & Row, 1965.

Vos, Geerhardus. *Biblical Theology.* Grand Rapids: Eerdmans, 1948.

Westermann, Claus. *Basic Forms of Prophetic Speech.* Trans. Hugh Clayton White. Philadelphia: Westminster, 1967.

CHAPTER 22

Isaiah

William F. Gentrup
Arizona State University

The most quoted, the most poetic and dramatic, the most messianic and evangelical, the most universal, the most apocalyptic. Many superlatives can be attached to the first book of the latter prophets, the book of Isaiah. Its appeal has been pervasive and diverse.

In Isaiah the universe is addressed. The scope of the book extends beyond the usual covenant relationship of God and his people to the rest of humanity and all of nature. At the very start, heaven and earth are called upon as witnesses, and, at the end, the *new* heavens and *new* earth celebrate the restoration of the divine-human relationship (Isa. 1:2; 65:17–25; 66:22–24). Not only God, his messengers, and his people, but all nations of the earth (chs. 13–20), all animals and plants, are brought into the conversation. The lion shall eat straw like an ox and lie down with the lamb (11:6–9). Instead of the thorn and thistle there shall be the myrtle tree and the fir tree (55:13); even the desert shall be filled with water and blossom like the rose (35:1–7).

The most frequently quoted prophetic book in the New Testament and in the Jewish Mishnah, Isaiah is used so extensively by Luke and Paul that it has been called a fifth gospel (Schmitt 7, 16; Seitz 123). The patristic commentator Eusebius also described its writer as an evangelist because he "proclaims the Son of God in different ways" (cited in Schmitt 16). The fascination with Isaiah's eschatological content is evident from the book's careful preservation by the Dead Sea Qumran community, making it the oldest surviving manuscript of a complete Bible book.

Writers from other eras of apocalyptic fervor, such as the French Revolution and its aftermath, have also been drawn to Isaiah. M. H. Abrams emphasizes how important the apocalyptic passages of Isaiah (along with the book of Revelation) were to the Romantic movement (38–39). In particular, Isaiah was one of Shelley's favorite biblical books. According to Mary Shelley, it was one of the poetical texts (including Psalms and Job) that were his "constant perusal," "the sublime poetry of which filled him with delight" (Abrams 33, 485). He was immersed in the language and imagery of the book, borrowing from it for *Prometheus Unbound,* especially Act 4. Indeed, the words of Isaiah have inspired other artists, providing, for example, the text for some of the sublime choruses and arias of Handel's *Messiah.*

This influence is due in large measure to Isaiah's literary quality. Everywhere there is evidence of that "marriage of nobility of language to nobility of thought that is characteristic of Isaiah" (Ginsberg 16). The book contains masterful uses of all forms of wordplay and imagery: alliteration, assonance, anaphora, repetition, paronomasia, metaphor, simile, personification, allegory, and even puns. And despite its dissection into three large sections by diachronic critics, there is great artistry in the harmonizing of its structure, a conscious effort to unify all sixty-six chapters. Further, Isaiah makes good use of literary allusion and borrowing in references to Genesis, Exodus, and Micah, and in the duplication of several chapters from 2 Kings. Isaiah's lofty themes of social justice (1:16–17); YHWH's everlasting power over worldly empires, armies, and gods (8:1–4; 40:15–24; 44:6–20); and judgment and redemption on a cosmic scale (e.g., chs. 24, 54) also contribute to the book's exalted status.

Approaching Isaiah

The uninitiated reader may encounter difficulties when first reading Isaiah. Prophetic books do not normally achieve a narrativelike coherence (though there are exceptions like Jonah). Because of its length, Isaiah, more than other prophetic books, will probably seem like a miscellaneous collection of doom-and-gloom judgments and ecstatic promises of blessing. There are several basic strategies readers can employ to avoid getting lost in the book. First, since Isaiah wrote for real people involved in real events, it is obviously helpful to familiarize oneself with the historical background, to know that chapters 1–39 speak to the threat of an Assyrian invasion into Judah and Jerusalem and that Isaiah's answer to this threat is for Israel not to panic and seek foreign alliances but to trust God and let him defeat the enemy; and that chapters 40–66 promise the return of Israel from Babylonian captivity and contain moving reconciliation passages between Israel and her God.

But a historical awareness is not always essential for a literary appreciation of Isaiah. As Robert Alter points out, what allows many biblical prophecies to speak to us thousands of years after they were uttered is the fact that, though addressed to a concrete historical situation, they quickly shift to an "archetypal" level (146–47). One needs to be sensitive and attentive to this archetypifying momentum in order to fully appreciate one of the most salient qualities of biblical prophecy, especially that of Isaiah—its visionary character. By universalizing and expanding through hyperbole the scope of reference beyond the original circumstances, the prophet not only manages to make his words relevant to later generations but also to move outside of mundane reality and into that realm of conceptualization that can only be described as visionary.

Alter illustrates this hyperbolic development in a passage describing a potential military threat from Assyria (5:26–30). What begins as a fairly literal account of an approaching army intensifies to the level of a cosmic cataclysm. The familiar battle sounds of horses' hooves and chariot wheels are transformed to the din of a "whirlwind." The cliché of likening a war cry to the roar of a lion is heightened to the unquenchable growling of the sea. The passage ends in an apocalyptic image of utter chaos, a cosmic darkness enveloping the light (Alter 151–52). We have moved quite beyond the initial scenario.

Similarly, in a later prophecy of consolation (49:14–23), YHWH's straightforward assertion that he will not forget his people any more than a mother can forget her child is elaborated through images of splendiferous fecundity. Israel, pictured as a woman who has lost both husband and children, is promised more offspring than she can count, which will adorn her like jewels on a bride. Expanding on these images of biological bonds, Isaiah declares that the destruction and desolation of exile will be transformed into a dignified return: kings will be the nursemaids and queens the wet nurses of Israel's new progeny (Alter 158–60). Awareness of this poetic of intensification provides one key to unlocking the literary artistry of Isaiah.

Even if one knows the historical background and can relate to the universal element in individual prophecies, it is still sometimes difficult to follow a train of thought between them. Why are they in this particular order, and does their juxtaposition mean anything? As von Rad acknowledges, the "abrupt juxtaposition of predictions of doom and predictions of salvation . . . raised so many misgivings in the minds of more than one generation of scholars" (233).

This problem of coherence is resolved to a degree by the verbal connections or catchwords between discrete prophecies, especially at the end and the beginning of passages. A kind of coherence is achieved by the recurrence of the same word. For example, Sodom and Gomorrah function as a simile at the end of 1:7–9 to describe a pillaged Israel. This usage is followed by a demand of "you rulers of Sodom" and "you people of Gomorrah," sardonic references to Israel, to stop their hypocritical ritual sacrifices (1:10). The allusions to Sodom and Gomorrah have completely different contexts in these two prophecies but are a connecting link between them. Similarly, 4:2 ("the Branch of the LORD will be beautiful and glorious, and the fruit of the earth will be the pride and the *adornment* of the survivors of Israel") continues the clothing motif introduced at the end of the previous prophecy cataloguing the gaudy accoutrements of the proud "daughters of Zion" (3:16–26). Again, there are two different contexts, but a shared vocabulary or point of reference helps to make the transition. A unity is thus imposed on what sometimes seems to be a collection of detached oracles (see McKenzie 248).

Genre

The real challenge of a literary approach to reading Isaiah is to find a unifying strategy for the whole book, all sixty-six chapters, and not merely for individual passages. (Christopher Seitz has done excellent work on this topic.) Various types of structural frameworks or literary genres have been suggested as ways of reading Isaiah as a unified book. Some have viewed Isaiah as a drama because it contains an abundance of "dialogue" between God and his people/prophet and because its themes tend to be universal. A cosmic drama in which, as stated above, all nature as well as man is addressed (Moulton) or a cosmic "Vision" played out in twelve acts and many more scenes (Watt) describes certain aspects of the book. But in its overall structure Isaiah cannot be considered a drama in the usual sense of a conflict between characters who somehow grow or change through the action. Despite warnings, the people of Judah and Jerusalem do not repent. Furthermore, in prophecy the dialogue is one-way. Most of the time YHWH speaks *to,* not *with,* his interlocutors; he addresses but is not usually addressed.

As suggested above, beginning readers of Isaiah should not come to it with expectations of finding it a traditional narrative, which promises a sequential storyline. Except for chapters 36–39, Isaiah has no sustained narrative. Although one detects a clear effort at making connections between the discrete prophecies, usually by means of "catchwords," so that each prophetic unit leads into another, Isaiah does not have the chapter-by-chapter coherence of a novel.

The classification "visionary poetry" helps us come to grips with much that is alien and fascinating in Isaiah. Its beautiful millennial descriptions and powerful apocalyptic passages (e.g., 11:1–10; 34; 35) illustrate much of the book's basic character and important content (see Ryken). Yet the visionary description of alternate worlds, worlds of utopian peace or cataclysmic destruction, is only a part, albeit an important part, of Isaiah. Other prophecies relating to the political or national context (e.g., the Assyrian threat, Judah's social injustices) constitute a substantial portion of Isaiah and are also representative of it.

Perhaps the literary genre that most closely approximates the features of the book of Isaiah is the sermon. Speaking on God's authority, the sermonizer addresses an audience and, for example, warns of dire consequences for sin or consoles with promises of forgiveness and restoration, or both. (Like a good preacher, Isaiah provides hope of redemption, not only judgment.) The "vocative," confrontational tone of sermons is characteristic of prophecy in general and of Isaiah in particular. Even though it may be written down, it is essentially a spoken art form. All of these attributes can be found in Isaiah if viewed as a series or collection of sermons.

However, a sermon is not generally written in poetic form as most of Isaiah is. Moreover, a sermon traditionally explicates a text, but this is not a regular function of prophecy. Nor, usually, does a sermon suddenly shift from a mundane level to a visionary one as do some biblical prophecies. The sermon, then, does not work as a generic counterpart to prophecy either. As a literary genre, biblical prophecy, Isaiah being the supreme example, is *sui generis*. It is neither drama, narrative, vision, or sermon, though it may contain elements of each. The only generic convention we can be sure Isaiah follows is that of poetry.

Although there seems to be no single, identifiable generic counterpart to Isaiah as a whole, portions of it contain their own inherent unity. Diachronic critics and commentators generally agree that certain large sections form thematic or topical units. For example, they recognize the following divisions: "oracles against foreign and domestic enemies" (chs. 13–23), the "Isaiah Apocalypse" (chs. 24–27), oracles dealing with Judah's intrigue with Egypt (chs. 28–32), a collection of eschatological prophecies (chs. 33–35), and a "historical appendix" (chs. 36–39; see Ohlsen 207–8). Furthermore, critics agree on several topical units in chapters 40–55, such as the four Servant Songs (42:1–7; 49:1–7; 50:4–9; 52:13–53:12). How all of these independent sections relate to one another or function together with the rest of Isaiah is not a concern. But if we are to understand the literary design of the whole book, it is necessary to grasp the function of certain parts as well as to determine the overarching framework under which these disparate segments may be subsumed.

The Unity of Isaiah

Because some critics think of Isaiah as a collection of fragments of prophecies ranging over several centuries, the question of the book's unity is important to a literary approach. Although not a few Bible scholars believe that Isaiah has more than one author, an increasing number recognize that, despite that assumption, it contains a great degree of thematic and structural coherence. Thus the issue of *authorial* unity, while important theologically because of its repercussions regarding the supernatural predictive capacity of prophecy, becomes moot when Isaiah is approached from the perspective of synchronic literary criticism. The book as it now exists has been designed to stand as a whole.

Structurally, there is a general alternating pattern of prophecies of judgment and prophecies of redemption. What John McKenzie calls "a pleasing alternation of promise and rebuke" within chapters 40–48 also accurately describes the book as a whole (249). On the largest scale, this pattern corresponds to chapters 1–39 and 40–66. But, the configuration can be detected even in smaller sections. The first two chapters of Isaiah epitomize much of the book in this way. In chapter 1 the nation made up of "rulers in Sodom" and "people of Gomorrah" is judged as wounded, sick, and putrefying "from the sole of the foot even to the head" (1:10, 6). But immediately the assurance and invitation of redemption are given: "Come now, and let us reason together, says the LORD, though your sins are as scarlet, they will be as white as snow. . . . You will be called the city of righteousness, a faithful city" (1:18, 26).

Chapter 2 continues with the redemptive pattern in the much hoped-for promise that "in the last days" God's judgments will create an environment in which all people will "hammer their swords into plowshares, and their spears into pruning hooks" (2:4). The chapter ends on a note of "reckoning against everyone who is proud and lofty," a time in which people will flee into caves and holes in the ground before the "terror of the LORD" (2:12, 19).

The pattern here is just one of the ways in which the whole book achieves a unity. In general, Old Testament prophetic books warn their audience of the dire results of conduct that excludes the consciousness of God, but they also promise magnificent restoration. For example, the first chapter of Joel describes the wasteland resulting from abandonning God. But chapter 2 immediately declares a restoration, the most glorious springtime imaginable, a reversal symbolic of the outpouring of God's Spirit "on all mankind" (v. 28), and promises that "whoever calls on the name of the LORD will be delivered" (v. 32).

This simple pattern of warning and promise is also developed at length in Isaiah. Even though some scholars read Isaiah as a collection of fragments, this kind of structure occurs throughout the book and justifies reading it as a unity. The ubiquitous judgments described in chapters 1–39 are relieved by promises of blessing. In chapters 40–55 these positive affirmations increase in number in proportion to the judgments until there is mainly jubilation at the close of the book (chs. 56–66). Judgment is only briefly but appropriately applied to whatever had opposed the optimal dialogue of humanity and God, of heaven and earth.

The structure of the entire book of Isaiah is a "progression" of this intertwining of judgments and blessings (Lichtenstein, Thompson). The negative is never allowed to dominate. In a similar perception of its basic structure, David Rosenberg, the poet-translator of Isaiah, discovers a "serial" building up or "architecture" of "passion and vision" (ix).

Isaiah is also organized around two geographical poles. Prophecies about the imminent threat of Assyria dominate the first half of the book (1–39), while those that celebrate the liberation from Babylonian captivity two centuries later permeate the second (40–66). A few chapters in 1–39 anticipate, and thus create a sense of cohesion with, 40–66 (i.e., the oracle against Babylon in chapter 13; the millennial chapter 35). There is a careful balance to the overall structure that pivots nicely on chapters 36–39, its central historical prose section.

At first glance such a structure seems to emphasize the traditional division in Isaiah. Yet the two halves are sewn together so well by the central prose section (36–39) that, if not seamless, the result is at least as cohesive as the tragic and comic sections of Shakespeare's *Winter's Tale* or as structurally whole as Dante's *Divine Comedy* despite the vast distances between the various locales of the three cantos.

The Winter's Tale analogy is instructive and may be pursued further. Nearly the first three acts of Shakespeare's late romance are tragic in tone and action: Leontes, the king of Sicily, wrongly suspecting his wife of committing adultery with his best friend, the king of Bohemia, destroys (by III.ii) his marriage, his honored friendship, the trust and service of his best counselor, his son, and, so it seems, his daughter and his wife. Most of these lives and relationships are restored to him sixteen years later in the second part of the play, after his repentance. What unites this wintry and sad first half with the pastoral and redemptive second is an odd, brief scene (III.iii) that yokes together the heterogenous elements of violent death (crew of sailors drowned, man eaten by a bear) and providential rescue of innocent life; as the play puts it, of "things dying" and of "things new born." The scene manages to be a synecdoche for both parts of the play and also works as an anticipation of the second, which is set many years later, as Isaiah's second part is.

Although it does not contain necessarily any other generic feature of drama, Isaiah does resemble a tragicomedy in structure, at least the one described above. (In its broadest outlines the whole Bible is a tragicomedy.) Isaiah's central prose section, chapters 36–39, functions similarly to the pivotal scene in *The Winter's Tale* (III.iii). Chapters 36–37 allude to or sum up, through their focus on the threat of an Assyrian siege against Jerusalem, many of the prophetic warnings or judgments of doom, due to the sins of the nation, found in chapters 1–35. Furthermore, chapters 38–39 anticipate, through their shift in geographical reference to Babylon, the captivity assumed in chapters 40–66 and from which Israel will ultimately be delivered.

It is worthwhile to recall that chapters 36–37 report the invasion of Judah and the unsuccessful siege of Jerusalem by Sennacherib, king of Assyria, in the person of his general Rabshakeh. The threats and taunts of the Assyrians, who have conquered all the neighboring countries and their gods (36–37:13), are answered by the prayer of Hezekiah and the prophecy of Isaiah that the Lord will put his hook in the nose of the enemy and will "turn [them] back by the way which [they] came" (37:29). Chapters 38–39 center around a mortal illness from which Hezekiah is delivered. But because he foolishly exposes all the contents of the national treasury to a Babylonian delegation sent with letters and gifts to comfort him in his illness, YHWH uses this incident to foretell the eventual captivity in Babylon when all these treasures will be carried away.

Underscoring the pivotal or "hinge" function of these chapters and their apparently deliberate (and thus artistic) placement is their oddness in relation to the rest of Isaiah. No such historical prose chronicle exists anywhere else in the book, nor is there such a case of direct literary borrowing. Except for 38:9–20, the whole narrative is taken almost verbatim from 2 Kings 18–20. Thus "we are moved to ask why this section appears where it does, and what it is trying to say" (Seitz 110–11). Its unique properties seem to draw attention to its function in context, which, I have been suggesting, is to serve primarily as a bridge or link uniting the two main parts of Isaiah. The fact that the two events recorded in chapters 36–39 occurred, as well as can be determined, in reverse chronological order, i.e., the Assyrian invasion threat transpired after Hezekiah's illness and the treasury incident, also highlights the connecting role these chapters play in uniting the two "halves" of Isaiah (Wolf 41; Heschel 69, 75). Their reversal stresses the fact that the respective chapters pertain to the corresponding segments.

Themes and Allusions

As just discussed for chapters 36–39, Isaiah's prophecy makes deft use of borrowing from other sources. Like T. S. Eliot's *The Wasteland,* it is liberally sprinkled with literary allusions, in Isaiah's case to other biblical books, and like Eliot's poem, its allusions serve to develop its themes. Gerhard von Rad has shown in detail how Isaiah makes use of various motifs from Genesis, Exodus, Psalms, and Davidic history, particularly Exodus, to underscore the themes of waiting for and trusting in YHWH's protection and deliverance. It is interesting that these references to Exodus appear in chapters 1–39 as well as chapters 40–66 and substantiate another unbroken thread between the two parts. Intertextuality is a very common literary device in the Bible (surprisingly, we lack a full scholarly study of the technique), and it is pointedly effective in Isaiah. Like Milton, Isaiah was a politically conscious poet, in contrast to his contemporaries Hosea and Micah, and, like Milton, whose biblical allusions were used to expound on the political crises of his day, Isaiah looked back to events in Israel's past to comment on those of his own.

Isaiah's references to the Mosaic Law and to the image of hardening the heart (6:8–12; 8:17; 29:9–14; 30:8–14) in the first part of his prophecy are appropriate to the theme of judgment for the nation's injustice and exploitation of the weak. The terms "righteousness" and "justice" have a central function in Isaiah's preaching, and his concern for divine law cannot be overstressed (von Rad 149). This emphasis complements the more specific echo of Exodus and Davidic history in the act of deluding or the image of hardening the heart (Ex. 9:16–17; 11:10; 14:4, 17; 1 Sam. 16:14), a condition that justified the harsh judgment on both Pharaoh and Zion. The concept of hardening the heart is an inherited outlook, and its application in

Isaiah matches that in Exodus: through it God works out his far-reaching purposes in history (von Rad 154).

The promised return from exile in the latter part of Isaiah is also viewed in the perspective of the great antecedent Exodus in Israel's history. The prophet envisions a second Exodus with all its wonders: protection from the elements, springs of water in the desert, and miraculously provided sustenance (49:10). The thematic burden of this analogy to the first Exodus is that there is a divine plan and that YHWH's word does not fail (55:10–11). Israel is invited to "be still," "look to YHWH," and have "faith"—concepts Isaiah borrows from Exodus—to do nothing but take up a stance of obedience and to watch and see what the Lord will do (7:4; 30:15–18; see Ex. 14:13–14). He delivered his people before and will do so again. Yet Isaiah affirms that this is not a repeat of an old demonstration of God's power when he "makes a way through the sea" and "brings forth the chariot and horses," but "something new" (43:16–21). This stress on newness culminates in the later promise of a new heaven and new earth (chs. 65 and 66). Although he alludes to the past, Isaiah is the most forward looking of the prophets; in the future lies Jerusalem's salvation, a perspective that suggests the reason why Isaiah is the most frequently cited Old Testament prophet in the New Testament (Seitz 123; von Rad 175). Paradoxically, this new thing has been planned "long ago" (14:24–27; 37:26). Isaiah's allusions, then, serve to express one of his great themes to which he returns again and again: YHWH's control of universal history and his unthwartable purpose to deliver Zion within the context of great world empires "proudly strutting about on [the] stage of history" (von Rad 162).

The Narrator

Except for chapters 6 and 7 and a few verses from chapter 8, which describe, respectively, Isaiah's spectacular calling and the symbolic naming of his children, we learn almost nothing about him as a personality. The point of view of the book is omniscient, but the prophet himself, his relationships with others, his tribulations or afflictions, or any other biographical or personal information are not included. Other than brief references in historical passages (chs. 7, 36–39), the only other mention of him is to the "vision" or "word" or "oracle" that "Isaiah the son of Amoz saw." How remarkable this is in fact is shown by its contrast to the narratorial presence of the other major prophets, Jeremiah and Ezekiel, in their works. In them we learn many more details about the prophets' lives than in Isaiah, and to a larger degree the Lord speaks directly to them rather than to the people. Isaiah, however, focuses more on the dialogue between YHWH and his people than on that between YHWH and his prophet.

The significance of Isaiah's near "absence" in respect to the unity of the book is, as Seitz points out for those readers who accept a First and Second Isaiah, that the joining of the two parts is easily and unobtrusively done because of the lack of a strong Isaianic presence in either part (116–20). The larger artistic purpose of the retracted narrator in Isaiah transcends the issue of unity, however. This narrative technique is simply the most functional and dramatic choice for the audience and period of Israel's history that Isaiah addresses. In Isaiah's time there is still hope, still time for Zion to repent, to trust YHWH rather than foreign alliances to protect them against the Assyrian threat, whereas in Jeremiah and Ezekiel's times virtually the only ones YHWH can speak to are his prophets, since the people are so apostate and the time of their judgment is closer at hand (see, e.g., Jer. 25:4–7; Ezek. 3:7).

Isaiah's hidden narrator also creates more dramatic irony. The reader's attention is on the reactions of the people of Judah and Jerusalem. Just as the gospel of Mark, whose narrator is likewise hidden, starts off with the plain statement that Jesus is God and follows this immediately with vignettes in which various individuals (and the reader) are challenged to believe this, so Isaiah declares his "gospel" of YHWH's power to save from human destruction and his desire to forgive. Instead of individuals, however, it is Zion that is invited to have faith. The people of Judah and Jerusalem as a whole are confronted with the prophet's message, and their reaction is described in the third person by Isaiah, not, as in Mark, in their own voice.

Poetic Features

In addition to its structural artistry, Isaiah is also justly famous for its verbal and syntactical artistry. Isaiah contains several outstanding examples of paronomasia and onomatopoeia. The former device is illustrated by 5:7b, which plays on the antithetical meaning of words that sound similar in Hebrew: "Thus He looked for justice [*mishpat*], but behold, bloodshed [*mispāḥ*]; / For righteousness [*ṣᵉdāqâ*], but behold, a cry of distress [*ṣᵉʿāqâ*]." In only a slightly free translation, G. H. Box retains the alliterative soundplay of the original: "For measure he looked—but lo massacres! / For right—but lo riot" (41). An earthquake described in an eschatological section (24:19–20) evokes an appropriate topsy-turvy display of onomatopoeia, which Luis

Alonso-Schökel and his translator from Spanish, Jacqueline Mintz, have rendered into a rough English equivalent: "the earth shivers and staggers, stumbles and tumbles, quivers and quavers and quakes, jars and jerks and jolts" (182). As Schökel points out, these onomatopoeic clusterings are rare in classical Hebrew texts, and so it is difficult to determine how successful this example is; but it is clear that a consciousness sensitive to the aural potential of literary art is at work.

The beginning chapters of Isaiah also illustrate a developed scheme of balance and antithesis. The literary effect is akin to the intensity of the symmetrically opposite pairings in Shakespeare's "Sonnet 144" ("Two loves I have of comfort and despair"). The poet syntactically arranges these contrasting terms—e.g., comfort/despair, better/worse, man/woman, saint/devil, angel/fiend—for greater rhetorical effect. In chapter 1 of Isaiah a similar technique is used. Heaven versus earth (v. 1), animal versus human (literally "sons," vv. 2–3), Sodom/Gomorrah versus Zion/Jerusalem (vv. 8–9, 21–27), false worship versus true (vv. 10–17), and field/land versus city (vv. 7–9) have a rhetorical purpose comparable to Shakespeare's sonnet in both creating a clearly defined arrangement of ideas and heightening the antithetical gap between YHWH's standard and the people's behavior. In other words, the pairs structurally echo the predominant theme of obedience versus rebellion.

In chapter 2 the pattern continues in implicit contrast to chapter 1. Whereas in the first chapter the foreigners attack Israel and strip the fields (1:7) as the instrument of God's judgment, in the second they come to learn of his ways (v. 3). Instead of leading a military campaign, they will come in peace, beating their swords into plowshares and spears into pruning hooks (v. 4). Whereas in 1:10 the word of God was addressed to rebellious Israelites, here Gentiles seek to obey it (2:2–4). The rest of the chapter works on a series of antitheses respecting the debasement of human pride and the elevation of God's power (see, e.g., vv. 11, 20–22). Grogan goes into more detail on this pattern in both chapters (28–39). Not inappropriately, therefore, the New Open Bible refers to Isaiah as "the Shakespeare of the prophets" (770).

Isaiah's Legacy

Isaiah's legacy depends mostly on the genius and power of the variety of ways it describes a millennial age or peaceable kingdom: the lion shall lie down with the lamb (11:6), the desert shall blossom like a rose (35:1), mountains will shout and trees clap their hands (55:12), obstacles shall be removed and straight paths or highways set up (40:3–4), men will beat spears into pruning hooks and swords into plowshares and will not learn war anymore (2:4). Isaiah's imaginative capacity provides dozens of such edenic or utopian pictures. He is a prophet of hope and a source of some of the greatest visions of a Hopkinslike restored nature filled with God's grandeur and joy.

Is it any wonder, then, that later poets went to Isaiah to describe their hope of a future golden age? To take just one example, in *Prometheus Unbound* Shelley's appreciation of Isaiah is remarkably apparent in the following passage, which imitates Isaiah's familiar technique of personifying the natural world as an expression of millennial fulfillment.

Bright clouds float in heaven,
Dew-stars gleam on earth,
Waves assemble on ocean,
They are gathered and driven
By the storm of delight, by the panic of glee!
They shake with emotion,
They dance in their mirth. . . .
The pine boughs are singing
Old songs with new gladness,
The billows and fountains
Fresh music are flinging,
Like the notes of a spirit from land and from sea;
The storms mock the mountains
With the thunder of gladness. . . . (IV.40–54)

Isaiah deserves his reputation as the most poetic of the prophets. Like Milton, he capitalized on intertextual resonances to speak to the political realities of his day. Like Eliot, he also used a highly allusive technique to develop universal themes. His ecstatic personifications of nature glorifying God rival Hopkins' Welsh sonnets. His extended vocabulary (larger than that of any other Old Testament writer), gifted wordplay, rhetorical skill, and structural composition compare with Shakespeare's. His ability to envision idyllic, golden worlds rivals Shelley's invention. Much of what we admire about his prophecy corresponds to the aesthetic concept of the "sublime." Its celestial and terrestrial scope, its inclusiveness of all creation within its range of dialogue, its vision of the power of God to transform a desert into a garden, will inspire millennial hopes and poetic imaginations for generations to come.

WORKS CITED

Abrams, M. H. *Natural Supernaturalism: Tradition and Revolution in Romantic Literature.* New York: Norton, 1971.

Alonso-Schökel, Luis. "Isaiah." *The Literary Guide to the Bible.* Ed. Robert Alter and Frank Kermode. Cambridge, Mass.: Harvard UP, 1987. 165–83.

Alter, Robert. *The Art of Biblical Poetry.* New York: Basic Books, 1985.

Box, G. H. *The Book of Isaiah.* London: Isaac Pitman, 1908.

Clements, Ronald E. "The Unity of the Book of Isaiah." *Interpretation* 36 (1982): 117–29.

Ginsberg, H. L. "Introduction." *The Book of Isaiah: A New Translation.* Philadelphia: Jewish Publication Society of America, 1972. 9–24.

Grogan, Geoffrey W. "Isaiah." *The Expositor's Bible Commentary.* Ed. Frank E. Gaebelein. Vol. 6. Grand Rapids: Zondervan, 1986.

Heschel, Abraham J. *The Prophets: An Introduction.* Vol. 1. New York: Harper & Row, 1969.

Lichtenstein, Murray. "Biblical Poetry." *Back to the Sources.* Ed. Barry W. Holtz. New York: Summit Books, 1984.

Moulton, Richard G. *The Literary Study of the Bible.* London: D. C. Heath, 1899.

McKenzie, John L. "Literary Form and Structure." *Perspectives on Old Testament Literature.* Ed. Woodrow Ohlsen. 248–51.

The New Open Bible: Study Edition. Nashville: Thomas Nelson, 1990.

Ohlsen, Woodrow, ed. *Perspectives on Old Testament Literature.* New York: Harcourt, 1978.

Rosenberg, David. *Lightworks: A Poet's Bible.* San Francisco: Harper & Row, 1978.

Ryken, Leland. *How to Read the Bible as Literature.* Grand Rapids: Zondervan, 1984.

Schmitt, John J. *Isaiah and His Interpreters.* New York: Paulist, 1986.

Seitz, Christopher R., ed. *Reading and Preaching the Book of Isaiah.* Philadelphia: Fortress, 1988.

Thompson, Leonard. *Introducing Biblical Literature: A More Fantastic Country.* Englewood Cliffs, N.J.: Prentice-Hall, 1975.

von Rad, Gerhard. *Old Testament Theology.* Vol. 2. New York: Harper & Row, 1965.

Watt, John. *Isaiah.* 2 vols. Waco, Tex.: Baylor UP, 1987.

Wolf, Herbert M. *Interpreting Isaiah: The Suffering and Glory of the Messiah.* Grand Rapids: Zondervan, 1985.

This essay is dedicated to Bill Baroody, my friend and mentor, who spread hope and love, and who taught me "how good and how pleasant it is for brothers to dwell together in unity."

CHAPTER 23

Daniel

JAMES H. SIMS
The University of Southern Mississippi

The book of Daniel is perpetually fascinating to readers, perhaps because of its mysterious nature. It combines tautly dramatic narratives with a historically factual tone in its first half and uses vividly enigmatic visions to portray a certain and hope-filled future in which Israel's enemies are suddenly destroyed by divine intervention in its second half. Yet chapters 7 through 12 reflect largely historical events swirling around the same hero, and chapters 1 through 6 include calamities divinely visited upon pagan rulers and regimes to vindicate the faith of God's people.

The chief protagonist appears to be the same righteous man paralleled with Noah and Job in Ezekiel 14:14 and praised as the knower of dark secrets in Ezekiel 28:3, but he is no less mysterious, indeed he is more so, for these brief references. Like the Daniel of the Apocrypha (Song of the Three, Susanna, Bel and the Dragon), Ezekiel's Daniel is noted for righteousness and practical wisdom, not for seeing and interpreting apocalyptic visions. Yet the Daniel of the book that bears his name clearly exhibits the virtues of Ezekiel's and the Apocrypha's Daniel, though he is fully developed as a divine seer, while still very human.

While this literary analysis of the book of Daniel may serve to increase some of the mysteries of the work, its intention is to summarize some of the light already shed by others on the book's genre, chronology, historicity, and literary unity, and to provide some new insights into these topics as well.

Genre

Daniel is not included with the prophets (*n^ebî'îm*) in the Jewish Tanak but with the miscellaneous "writings" (*k^etubîm*), between the books of Esther and Ezra-Nehemiah. In most Christian Bibles, however, the book of Daniel is grouped among the prophets, although its apparently discrete narrative section, its unconditional predictions of the end-time coupled with specific though "sealed" time-tables, and its full-blown apocalypticism are recognized by most Christian scholars as features unlike those of other prophetic books. As we will see, the narrative section is not as distinctly separate as has been thought, and there is precedent in other prophecies for the inclusion of narratives about the prophet.

Perhaps the primary reason for the Jews' exclusion of Daniel from the prophetic books is the late date for the book's promulgation, since it came into circulation after prophecy was believed to have ceased. According to the Talmud, the men of the "Great Synagogue," including Haggai, Zechariah, and Malachi, wrote (compiled or edited) both the books of Daniel and Ezekiel: the traditional belief that only in the Holy Land could Scripture be written required that prophets who spoke or wrote in Exile must have their works written within the land of Israel. The final form of Daniel, then, would have been reached between 450 and 400 B.C., even if its composition occurred as early as the sixth century, contemporary with Daniel's career in Babylon (Slotki, "Introduction").

The modern consensus of biblical scholarship determines a date much later, between 167 and 163 B.C. (Eissfeldt 520–22). According to one critic, "Daniel is not prophetic literature nor is its hero to be counted among the prophets of the Old Testament tradition" (Newsome 214). In *The Hebrew Scriptures,* however, Samuel Sandmel discusses Daniel "with the Prophets because the book is more nearly related to them than to the Hagiographa [the writings]" (226). Certainly the book of Daniel has affinity with the literary prophets: while no immediate national crisis occasions the visions and predictions and no conditions are specified within which judgment may be avoided, there is the concern shared by all the Hebrew prophets with the long-range destiny of God's people and the same stress on the individual Jew's responsibility to conduct himself or herself appropriately during times that try people's souls. It may be that, as Norman Porteous has argued, "certain of the alleged differences between the book of Daniel and the great prophets of Israel are actually developments of the prophetic teaching adapted to a later time" (15).

Many prefer, following the principles of form criticism, to categorize Daniel as an apocalypse to be grouped with books like Enoch, 2 Esdras, the Assumption of Moses, the Testaments of the Twelve Patriarchs, Baruch, and Jubilees (Collins; Rowland; Kvanvig, *Roots;* Wilson; Porter). One critic explains *apocalypse* as a "sub-type of the larger literary category of eschatology" and sees in Daniel *"eschatology . . . dramatically amplified in a cosmic direction"* (Towner 10–11, italics his), quoting an epigram from Hermann Gunkel: "Apocalyptic is . . . mythological eschatology" (12). Another who disagrees, opposing the view that "most biblical apocalyptic [was] a foreign import," hypothesizes "apocalyptic groups [whose] social and religious background [determined] the *shape* of [their] religion and literature" and sees Daniel as evidence of such Qumranlike communities in Israel (Wilson 80, 93, italics his). But whether apocalyptic is a subgenre of eschatology, a native Hebrew development, or simply a phenomenon Israel shared with Persian, Akkadian, and other Near Eastern cultures, *apocalyptic* is the most widely agreed-upon genre for the book of Daniel.

There is no necessary contradiction, however, in designating Daniel both prophecy and apocalyptic. Earlier books of prophecy include such apocalyptic characteristics as oracular pronouncements that history is governed by and will be ended by God and bizarrely frightening visions explained only with divine help (Ezek. 1–2; 8; 38–39; Zech. 1–8; 12–14; Joel 3; Isa. 6:24–27); and some also include first- and third-person-narrated stories about the prophet (Isa. 36–37; Jer. 36–38; Amos 7:10–17). While the narratives about Daniel and his friends are less clearly interrelated with the prophetic visions and more extensively developed in characterization and plot than the narratives in other prophetic books, the evidence of verbal and thematic interlocking between the narrative and apocalyptic parts of Daniel works against the view that the book consists of two distinct genres unequally yoked together. On balance, the best generic classification of the book is apocalyptic prophecy.

Problems of Chronology and Historicity

The organization and handling of time in Daniel are particularly interesting and puzzling. Beginning as though a straightforward chronological sequence will be followed, keying events to certain years of certain kings' reigns, the book from its opening verses raises serious questions about its accuracy. Yet in the book's second half (chs. 7–12), the events apocalyptically portrayed as predictions are essentially accurate history in proper chronological order, a fact noted early by Porphyry, the third-century neo-Platonic philosopher, who argued for a second-century date for Daniel on the basis of its symbolic account of Antiochus IV of Syria (Collins 69). Daniel 1:1 states that Nebuchadnezzar besieged Jerusalem and captured Judah's king in "the third year of the reign of Jehoiakim," while 2 Kings 24 reports that Jehoiakim was dead and that his son, Jehoiachin, was already in the eighth year of *his* reign when Nebuchadnezzar (actually Nebuchadrezzar) seized him and "all the treasures of the house of the LORD" (24:8–15).

Surely an author who knew Jeremiah's prophecies so well (cf. Dan. 9:2 with Jer. 25:11; 29:10) must have also known the principal characters and time periods of the Kings account. Events as traumatic and with such extensive ramifications for the nation as the siege of Jerusalem and the captivity of Jehoiachin and the cream of Judah's noble youth could hardly be inaccurately represented without both author and reader recognizing the errors. To place these events in the third year of Jehoiakim's reign when they had actually occurred after his eleven-year reign and death is roughly equivalent to setting the scene for a book about an American held in a Japanese prisoner-of-war camp by referring to the attack on Pearl Harbor as having happened during the presidency of Herbert Hoover. And if such a book claimed to predict in substantially accurate detail the war in Korea, clothing the details in apocalyptic symbolism, and did not come to light before, say, A.D. 2300, readers could not be blamed for assuming the book to represent *prophetia ex eventu,* prophecy after the fact.

Such has been the fate of the book of Daniel. The consensus of modern biblical scholarship is that the book was composed in the second century B.C., that it is a pseudonymous work, and that it is indeed an example of prophecy after the fact. Certain assumptions underlie these conclusions, among them that accurately predictive prophecy is always prophecy after the fact and that the period in which a book describes historical events most accurately must be the period of the book's composition (Eissfeldt 520–22, Towner 115). Sandmel comments after considering just such problems as discussed here that Daniel, in spite of the "edifying tales in the first half of the Book [is so flawed in its attempt at prediction that it] can have little more than an antiquarian interest for us" (238). (Sandmel is disagreeing with Rowley, who had argued that apocalyptists see "more that is fundamentally true than all that is false" [Rowley 152].) The continued relevance of apocalyptic, particularly Daniel, for our time and for the future is strongly supported by Kvanvig ("Relevance of Biblical Visions" 44–46).

On the other hand, conservative scholars argue that even if Daniel's prophecies can be shown to reflect past historical figures, as in the case of the identification of Antiochus IV as the "little horn" of Daniel 7 and 8, these symbolic revelations can also be prophecies to be fulfilled beyond the horizon of known history, as the New Testament writers believed (cf. 1 Thess. 2:4 with Dan. 11:36; Rev. 13:1–7 with Dan. 7:3–12, 21, 25). Baldwin, for instance, explains Daniel 11:29–45 as applying to Antiochus but not exclusively so; she uses the metaphor of "telescoped" prophecy, that is, the conflation of past or present phenomena with future prediction, to indicate that the ultimate fulfillment of Daniel 11 may still be in the future (199–203). Another scholar, after exposing the supposed inaccuracies of Daniel, claims to raise no question about "the sacredness, authority, and inerrancy of the Book" (Hartman 53–54); in effect he embraces both horns of the dilemma—Daniel is inaccurate, yet Daniel is inerrant—on the grounds that an ancient writer should not be held to the canons of modern critical history.

I suggest instead that Daniel's "inaccuracies" are an integral part of the book's literary technique—that is, that a careful craftsman with an artistic as well as a theological purpose disregards chronological order and succession, for instance, to emphasize his theme of a divine sovereignty so magnificently transcendent as to nullify human concepts of time and political power. Thus the writer of Daniel deliberately confuses times and persons in the first half of the book (chs. 1–6), where Daniel's explanations of dreams and visions are prompt, perfectly accurate, and speedily fulfilled; and, just as deliberately, he thinly veils historical persons and events in apocalyptic metaphors in his substantially accurate second half (chs. 7–12), where Daniel, far from the poised young wise man of the narratives, is troubled and perplexed by the visions and must depend on angelic interpreters who never completely satisfy his curiosity (indeed, crucial meanings are sealed from him), faints, falls ill, and finally has visions replaced by angelic narrative (chs. 11–12), as though he is incapable of sustaining the strain of viewing the astounding images themselves.

The writer appears to be setting the two halves of the book against each other in genre (narrative versus apocalyptic), nature of the protagonist (third person strong wise man versus first person weak *naif*), and credibility of the work (erroneous history and clearly revealed mysteries versus mostly accurate though metaphoric history and mystifyingly incomplete revelations). At the same time, the author skillfully unifies the two halves by such devices as connecting themes with diverse imagery (four earthly kingdoms replaced by a divine kingdom in chs. 2 and 7), repeating similar literary forms (a psalm in ch. 2 and a prayer in ch. 9), anticipating the beast-rulers by a ruler-beast (chs. 4 and 7–8; see Burkholder 48), flashing back to past reigns for the timing of visions (chs. 6 and 7–8, 9, and 11), foreshadowing a vision in Cyrus's reign by early references (chs. 1, 10), and bridging the Hebrew of 1:1–2:4a and 8–12 by the Aramaic of 2:4b–7:28.

The apparently achronological order of the narratives in chapters 1–6 (the first year of each of the reigns of Nebuchadnezzar, Belshazzar [or Belsharusar, coregent with Nabonidus, not successor to Nebuchadnezzar], Darius, and Cyrus, approximately 604–485 B.C.), is replaced by the chronological order of the visions in chapters 7–12 (*seriatim,* the early years of Belshazzar, third year of Cyrus, and first year of Darius). Yet this contradictory tension pulling apart the book's two halves, though deliberately developed, is powerfully counteracted by unifying devices, as we have seen. Clearly each half shares some features of the other: the narrative half includes dream-visions, and the visionary half includes narrative. Indeed what is commonly referred to as the "fourth vision" in chapters 10–12 is actually a brief vision initiating a long narration.

The effect on the reader of the writer's art is a reinforcement in form of the book's overarching message: "The most high God [rules] in the kingdom of men, and . . . he appointeth over it whomsoever he will" (Dan. 5:21); the true sovereign is God, and human rulers pale into insignificance—even disappear as though they had never existed or appear and sit on thrones they never occupied in life—in the great panorama of Yahweh's cosmic rule. Again the reader's grasp is made sure on the theme that time, whether represented by divisions of "years" or "weeks" or "times," whether unfolding according to historical memory or creative fancy, is under the control of him whose kingdom "shall stand for ever" (Dan. 2:44); even "what shall come to pass hereafter" (Dan. 2:45b) can be shown by the eternal Lord as though it had already passed. Daniel's psalm speaks of the Lord's sovereign control over both time, as evidenced in nature's flux, and human rulers, whether humanely benevolent, blasphemous and cowardly, or bestially rapacious:

> *Blessed be the name of God for ever and ever:*
> *For wisdom and might are his:*
> *And he changeth the times and the seasons:*
> *He removeth kings, and setteth up kings. (Dan. 2:20–21)*

Here Daniel directly challenges the fatalism of Babylonian astral religion (Slotki xiv) and asserts that day passes into night, winter to spring, and so on, because of the Lord's constantly sustaining nature's phenomena, not because of a deterministically ordered universe. Time, both in the blessings and the sorrows it brings, and human kingdoms, whether comparatively gold, silver, or metals of lesser worth, seem to be supremely important from the human point of view, but from the divine overview, both time and principalities are "like the chaff of the summer threshing floors" (Dan. 2:35), gone with the wind before they come into being. In a book so filled with significant periods of time and overwhelming powerful forces that affect human life—past, present, future—the only abiding reality is God and his mysterious kingdom, the only proper concern of man to be loyal and obedient to him. Regardless of whether or not loyalty and obedience bring temporal deliverance, one may through them triumph over time and worldly pomp (Dan. 3:17–18; 12:1–3). "Time is telescoped into the lived moment. . . . The instant fills the whole horizon . . . a new world *has* to come, God's world. [W]hen the kingdom seems farthest off—it is closest" (Lacoque 252).

FIGURE 1

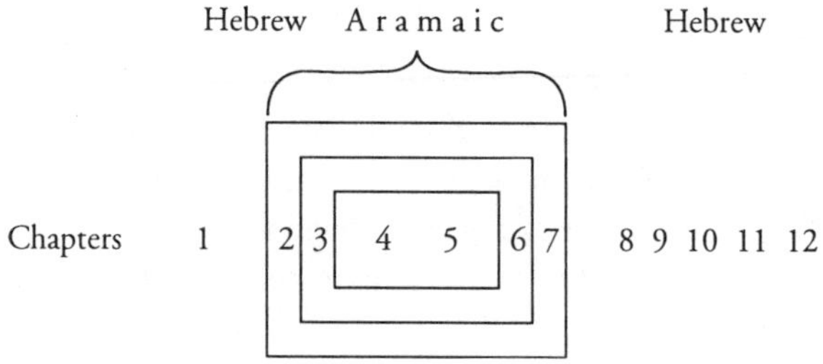

Literary Analysis: The Book as a Whole

Whether composed by one author or by such a group as the Great Synagogue working with older materials, the book of Daniel is a sophisticated literary unit, bound together in a final shape that is aesthetically satisfying, thematically clear, and yet, finally, open-ended and mysterious. Although the book appears to fall naturally into two very different halves, it paradoxically maintains its unity as a literary whole by creating both centripetal forces (motifs and images shared by both halves) and centrifugal forces (clear visions and confused history followed by clear history and puzzling visions). Chapter 7 has been widely recognized as the structural link between the two parts, so strongly binding the two that efforts to separate them are futile (e.g., Lacoque 13, Raabe 267, Porteous 95).

Some scholars propose a system of concentric chiasmi binding chapters 2–7 together as further evidence of the author's skillful linkage: word, theme, and imagery connect 2 and 7 to form the outside frame, 4 and 5 the center, and 3 and 6 the intermediate tier (Lenglet, Casey, Raabe, Davies; see Fig. 1).

Davies concludes that this chiastic structure is part of a design to draw the reader into ever closer contact with the figure of Daniel. First a third-person object of narration (1–6), Daniel next addresses the reader directly as first-person speaker (7–12:8), and finally an angel dismisses first Daniel (12:9) and then the reader (12:13) from the book.

Each of the six narratives is virtually self-contained, though the same Hebrew characters figure throughout: Daniel and his three friends—Shadrach, Meshach, and Abednego—in chapters 1–2; the three without Daniel in chapter 3; and Daniel without the three in chapters 4, 5, and 6. Talmon sees in the four young men one example of many in the book of "an ascending numerical pattern of 3 + 1, observable in other Near-Eastern literatures" and in other Bible books (347–48). In each narrative the pagan monarch is centrally important—Nebuchadnezzar in 1, 2, 3, and 4; Belshazzar (and, uniquely among the stories, the queen) in 5, and Darius in 6. But despite the continuity of characters from story to story and their chronological order, one narrative never depends on another, though, as we have seen, some careful interlinking is evident (e.g., Nebuchadnezzar's bringing vessels from the temple to Babylon prepares for Belshazzar's sacrilegious feast [1:2 with 5:2–4, 23] and Belshazzar is reminded of Nebuchadnezzar's bestial humiliation [4:33 with 5:21]; Nebuchadnezzar's decree that an image be worshiped is supplanted by a decree honoring God, and Darius's decree that only he may be petitioned is replaced by a decree that all his subjects tremble before Daniel's God [3:4–6, 29 with 6:7–9, 25–27]).

Even though they are not in the chronological sequence of the narratives, the visions of the second half of the book of Daniel are linked by expository narrative (7:1, 28; 8:1–2, 15–18, 27; 9:1–27; 10:1–4, 7; 12:13). One's first impression in reading chapters 7–12 is of chronological order because of the opening verses of each chapter (except 12), but upon comparison one finds that not only does chapter 7 revert from the reign of Cyrus (6:28) to that of Belshazzar, after chapters 7–10 have progressed from Belshazzar to Darius to Cyrus, chapter 11 suddenly flashes back to Darius's first year as Daniel's divine instructor encourages him with the intelligence that he and Michael have carried on their struggle against evil earthly forces all through Daniel's career and will continue to do so until the final triumph of good (12:1).

Since the narrator informs the reader at the beginning that "Daniel continued *even* unto the first year of king Cyrus" (1:21), one is surprised to find that Daniel's final vision and narration begin in the *third* year of Cyrus (10:1). Although "Daniel prospered in the reign of Darius, and in the reign of Cyrus the Persian" (6:28), perhaps Daniel's status as the primary wise man consulted by successive monarchs is diminished after the first year of Cyrus; if so, his mourning, fasting, and weakness in the last half of the book may result in part from a sense of being neglected. Such a circumstance may also explain the especially tender concern and complimentary approach of his divine visitor: he is touched, told to stand upright, addressed as "greatly beloved," and strengthened to receive the final vision-narration (10:2–19) with its assurance that Heaven continues to work for the vindication and blessing of the wise like Daniel. Even though earthly developments give no hint of the coming victory for the saints, "thy people shall be delivered" (12:1). Danna Fewell suggests convincingly that Daniel has political aspirations and is so changed in the last part of the book because, not having been able to sustain his courtly influence as successfully as earlier, he fears that the ultimate victory will come only after his death (159–60).

The absence of introductory links for the six narratives and the abrupt beginning of each has contributed to the scholarly theory that these stories constitute a collection of originally independent anecdotes about the Jewish intellectual and moral elite in the courts of pagan kings (see, e.g., Wills 144–203). The apocryphal stories in the Septuagint are similarly related only by their having to do with Daniel, though they are quite different in kind from the canonical narratives. It has even been suggested that Susanna and Bel and the Dragon are early forms of the detective story (Lasine). One can understand how the stories of Daniel have been read as midrashic tales, even as specimens of the distinct genre of "Diaspora Novel" (Talmon 353), as stories intended to illustrate general truths or abstract principles rather than to relate actual occurrences involving historical persons. However, careful comparison of the narratives and the visions of the book of Daniel strengthens one's impression of the interrelatedness of the whole and works against seeing the book as an editorial compilation with a sequence that results from "the (mistaken) historical reconstruction of the book's editor" (Zakovitch 113).

Much more important to the author of Daniel than convincing historicity in the narratives is an artistic arrangement calculated to give maximum effect to the moral and theological message embodied in the stories; indeed, as indicated by her subtitle, Fewell sees the six stories as "A Story of Stories" about sovereignty. The deliberate sequencing of the narratives reflects Daniel's and his friends' growth in the knowledge of the Lord, the effectiveness of worshiping him in pagan surroundings, and an awareness of the involvement of Yahweh in the direction of the whole world; by extension, through these stories, any faithful believer is encouraged to grow through loyalty and obedience in these areas of thought, devotion, and influence. Seen in this light, the six narratives constitute six oppositions of the human and the divine, with the divine always triumphing and human beings either recognizing and rejoicing in that triumph or being humiliated or destroyed by their failure to acknowledge it. Each story builds on the effect of the preceding one, and the visions of chapters 7–12 further illustrate and extend into the future and throughout the cosmos the lessons learned.

The young Hebrews learn, or test their prior knowledge of, the superiority of divine over human nurture (ch. 1) leading to the gift of superior wisdom (1:17); this divine wisdom exemplified in Daniel himself (ch. 2) soon triumphs over the combined human wisdom of Babylon's sages of whatever school (2:27–28); such wisdom, now exemplified in the three friends (ch. 3), dictates their willingness to die for the worship of the true God rather than to participate in idolatrous worship, no matter how grandly staged and powerfully enforced (3:14, 16–18). Divine nurture, divine wisdom, and divine worship are further developed into recognition of divine sovereignty (ch. 4) and the dependence upon it of human rule (4:25), of the divine judgment on blasphemous kings who fail to acknowledge that dependence (ch. 5), and of divine deliverance for the faithful and destruction for their malicious enemies (ch. 6).

These divine manifestations of sovereignty, judgment, and deliverance, so effectively proclaimed in story, are now illustrated in the visions of the four kingdoms (ch. 7) and in an even more startling view of the fourth kingdom (ch. 8). Repeating a pattern similar to that in chapters 1 and 2, divine nurture from the Scriptures leads to wisdom that enables Daniel to understand Jeremiah's past prophecy of the seventy weeks and to prophesy the future seventy sevens of years (weeks), the last seven years (one week) to be projected beyond history's horizon (ch. 9).

Daniel's final revelations (chs. 10–12) come after a period of abstinence from all human, physical nurture (10:2–3); yet the divine, spiritual nurture of a vision very like Ezekiel's (10:4–6, 10; Ezek. 1:26–2:2) brings supernatural strength (10:18–19) and wisdom (v. 21) to receive knowledge of the distant future. Although not to be understood by Daniel nor, therefore, by the reader, the prophetic foreview of chapters 10–12 illustrates divine rule, judgment, and deliverance (reminiscent of chs. 4–6); the perversion of divine worship into blasphemy (11:36–39); and judgment on the wicked and deliverance for the righteous, even for those who have died, all brought about by the Lord who alone rules not only the world's history but the entire cosmos (12:1–3, 10–13).

Figure 2 graphically represents the relationship of parts to the whole of the book of Daniel as perceived in the foregoing discussion.

Daniel closes with a promise of resurrection for both righteous and unrighteous (12:2), indications that the book is not intended to be clearly understood by those contemporaneous with its publication or for a long time

FIGURE 2

The Book of Daniel

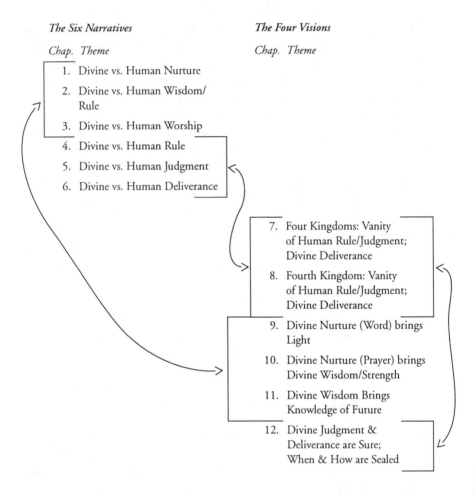

The Six Narratives

Chap. Theme

1. Divine vs. Human Nurture
2. Divine vs. Human Wisdom/ Rule
3. Divine vs. Human Worship
4. Divine vs. Human Rule
5. Divine vs. Human Judgment
6. Divine vs. Human Deliverance

The Four Visions

Chap. Theme

7. Four Kingdoms: Vanity of Human Rule/Judgment; Divine Deliverance
8. Fourth Kingdom: Vanity of Human Rule/Judgment; Divine Deliverance
9. Divine Nurture (Word) brings Light
10. Divine Nurture (Prayer) brings Divine Wisdom/Strength
11. Divine Wisdom Brings Knowledge of Future
12. Divine Judgment & Deliverance are Sure; When & How are Sealed

afterward (12:4, 9), mysterious and enormously intriguing references to numbers of days (12:11–12; cf. 8:14), and a quiet assurance to the character Daniel, and to all who share his faith in the ultimate victory of God and good, that rest and an appropriate standing in God's grace will be his, and theirs, "at the end of the days" (12:13), regardless of when that may be and how many events must yet intervene. As George Eliot wrote, the author of the book of Daniel "is entitled to the praise that he was the first who grasped the history of the world, so far as he knew it, as one great whole, as a drama which moves onward at the will of the Eternal One" (quoted in Levine 27).

WORKS CITED

Baldwin, Joyce G. *Daniel: An Introduction and Commentary.* Downers Grove, Ill.: InterVarsity, 1978.

Burkholder, Byron. "Literary Patterns and God's Sovereignty in Daniel 4." *Direction* 16 (Fall 1987): 45–54.

Casey, Maurice. *Son of Man: The Interpretation and Influence of Daniel 7.* London: SPCK, 1979.

Collins, John J. *The Apocalyptic Imagination: An Introduction to the Jewish Matrix of Christianity.* New York: Crossroad, 1984.

Davies, Philip R. *Daniel.* Sheffield: JSOT Press, 1988.

Eissfeldt, Otto. *The Old Testament: An Introduction.* Trans. Peter A. Ackroyd. New York: Harper & Row, 1965.

Fewell, Danna Nolan. *Circle of Sovereignty: A Story of Stories in Daniel 1–6.* Bible and Literature Series 20. Sheffield: Almond, 1988.

Good, Edwin M. "Apocalyptic as Comedy: The Book of Daniel." *Semeia* 32 (1984): 41–70.

Hartman, Louis F., and Alexander A. DiLella, eds. *The Book of Daniel.* Anchor Bible. Garden City: Doubleday, 1978.

Kvanvig, Helge S. "The Relevance of the Biblical Visions of the End-Time: Hermeneutical Guidelines to the Apocalyptical Literature." *Horizons in Biblical Theology* 11 (1989): 35–58.

———. *Roots of Apocalyptic: The Mesopotamian Background of the Enoch Figure and of the Son of Man.* Wissenschaftliche Monographien zum Alten und Neuen Testament. Neukirchen-Vluyn: Neukirchener Verlag, 1988.

Lacocque, Andre. *Le Livre de Daniel.* Commentaire de L'Ancien Testament. XVb. Paris: Delachaux et Niestle, Editeurs Neuchatel, 1976. Trans. David Pellauer. *The Book of Daniel.* Atlanta: John Knox, 1979.

Lasine, Stuart. "Solomon, Daniel, and the Detective Story: The Social Functions of a Literary Genre." *Hebrew Annual Review* 11 (1987): 247–66.

Lenglet, P. "La Structure littéraire de Daniel 2–7." *Biblica* 53 (1972): 172–90.

Levine, George. "George Eliot's Hypothesis of Reality (Derived from Daniel)." *Nineteenth-Century Fiction* 35 (1980): 1–28.

Newsome, James D., Jr. *The Hebrew Prophets.* Atlanta: John Knox, 1984.

Porteous, Norman W. *Daniel: A Commentary.* Philadelphia: Westminster, 1965.

Porter, Paul A. *Metaphors and Monsters: A Literary-Critical Study of Daniel 7 and 8.* Coniectanea Biblica, OT Series 20. Uppsala: CWK Gleerup, 1983.

Raabe, Paul R. "Daniel 7: Its Structure and Role in the Book." Biblical and Other Studies in Memory of S. D. Goitein. Ed. Reuben Ahroni. *Hebrew Annual Review* 9 (1985): 267–75.

Rowland, Christopher. "Apocalyptic Literature." *It Is Written: Scripture Citing Scripture.* Ed. D. A. Carson and H. G. M. Williamson. Cambridge: Cambridge UP, 1988. 170–89.

Rowley, H. H. *The Revelance of Apocalyptic.* London: Lutterworth, 1944.

Sandmel, Samuel. *The Hebrew Scriptures: An Introduction to Their Literature and Religious Ideas.* New York: Knopf, 1963.

Slotki, J. J., ed. *Daniel.* The Soncino Bible. London: Soncino, 1950.

Talmon, Shemaryahu. "Daniel." *The Literary Guide to the Bible.* Ed. Robert Alter and Frank Kermode. Cambridge, Mass.: Harvard UP, 1987. 343–56.

Towner, W. Sibley. *Daniel.* Atlanta: John Knox, 1984.

Wills, Lawrence M. *The Jew in the Court of the Foreign King: Ancient Jewish Court Legends.* Harvard Dissertations in Religion 26. Minneapolis: Fortress, 1990.

Wilson, Robert R. "From Prophecy to Apocalyptic: Reflections on the Shape of Israelite Religion." *Semeia* 21 (1981): 79–95.

Zakovitch, Yair. "U and ∩ in the Bible." *Semeia* 32 (1984): 107–14. (A response to Edwin M. Good.)

CHAPTER 24

Amos

LELAND RYKEN
Wheaton College

The part of the Bible that gives literary critics most difficulty is the prophetic and apocalyptic books. The reasons are multiple. Although biblical prophecy has exerted an *influence* on writers like John Milton and William Blake, prophecy in the biblical sense is not a common *genre* in literature at large. When judged by classical standards of unity, moreover, prophecy is too miscellaneous in structure and content to seem manageable. Literary critics look in vain for the superstructure that will provide a unifying impression of a prophetic book of the Bible. Richard Moulton viewed biblical prophecies as cosmic or spiritual dramas (1392), but while this suggestion has much to commend it, this classification, too, finally emerges as too amorphous to impose a firm unity on the prophetic books.

When faced with a book like Amos, therefore, literary critics confront a dilemma: should they abandon their familiar literary categories in deference to the foreign ones that biblical scholars use for biblical prophecy, or should they apply their familiar categories? Both approaches are defensible, and both are open to objection. Other chapters in this book treat biblical prophecy in the conventional terms of biblical scholarship. This chapter takes the alternate approach, with a view toward showing that if something is lost when we apply familiar criteria to unconventional biblical material, something is also lost when we fail to apply those criteria.

The book of Amos is conventionally classified under the rubric of prophecy, but this classification yields more to biblical scholars than to general readers, for whom Old Testament prophecy remains largely a closed book. It would be fruitless to deny that the book of Amos exhibits the conventional traits of biblical prophecy. The author, for example, steps forward as the one who speaks God's word to people with a voice of authority. As in prophecy generally, judgment and accusation dominate, and as we expect with Old Testament prophecy, there is the recantation at the end, with its vision of redemption, mercy, and restoration. The specific subgenres that make up the book are also familiar to biblical prophecy: oracle of judgment, oracle of salvation, wisdom saying, "woe" statements, report of visions, kingdom oracle, hymn, and lament.

The book possesses the familiar prophetic content and forms. But the conventional description of the book leaves it a collection of fragments, as well as a document that strikes a modern reader as unlike other writing and therefore remote. What superstructure can counteract the bewilderment that modern readers are likely to experience with the book of Amos and conventional descriptions of it?

In place of the customary classification, I propose to look at this remarkable book through the lens of a familiar literary tradition known as satire. Satire is an attack on human vice and folly. The ingredients of satire are four: object(s) of attack, a satiric vehicle that embodies the attack, a satiric norm (the standard by which the criticism is conducted), and a satiric tone (either biting or laughing). The essential differentiating feature of satire is the element of attack or exposure. Humor is not a necessary part of satire.

By itself, satire is not inherently literary, since the exposure of vice or folly can occur in expository or persuasive writing as well as literary writing. Satire becomes literary when the controlling purpose of exposure is combined with a literary method (such as fiction, narrative, character portrayal, metaphor). The aim is positive (the reform of people), but the technique is mainly negative, consisting of an attack on characters and actions. Satirists often distort, oversimplify, or exaggerate to make their points.

A standard literary definition of satire is "an attack by means of a manifest fiction upon discernible historical particulars" (Rosenheim 31). We might substitute the phrase "discernible literary technique" for "manifest fiction," but otherwise the definition stands. The fact that satire is an attack on historical particulars means that the reader of satire usually needs scholarly help in reconstructing the assumed social context—the economic, political, religious, or social conditions that the satirist attacks.

The Traditions of Satire

We can profitably begin, not with Amos, but with satire as a literary phenomenon. Satire falls into two main styles or traditions—the sophisticated and the informal.

Sophisticated satire is a polished work of literature. Its style is accomplished, and the work itself is distinctly literary in form (usually narrative). The satirist is more than a person denouncing vice in direct rebuke. He or she is also the maker of a literary work. The resulting satire is characterized by indirectness and subtlety. The sophisticated satirist is usually a private observer of society, not the spokesperson for a cause or a social group. The satirist is completely submerged in the story, and the tone is more likely to be light than bitter. Within the Bible, the book of Jonah and the satiric parables of Jesus are the obvious examples of sophisticated satire.

The informal tradition, also known as the plainspoken tradition, is very different. Plainspoken satirists are much less interested in literary craft than the formal satirist is, being preoccupied instead with content, at least ostensibly. They are less likely to tell a well-designed story than to employ direct rebuke and invective. The structure of informal satire is loose, its style direct and simple.

This literary naïveté corresponds to the moral and social simplicity of the informal satirist, whose stance is that of a plainspoken person of simple piety, humility, and even poverty. The plainspoken satirist is likely to be the representative for a cause or group, rather than a private person observing society. Informal satire is motivated by a sense of urgent involvement. It is not the product of a detached observer reflecting on what he or she sees in the surrounding society. Rather, it is a literature of religious or social protest. The object of attack is likely to be public evil or a corrupt social group, not the private evil of individuals. The tone of informal satire is rather consistently serious, moralistic, and sharply condemnatory, not light and humorous. To use Alvin Kernan's formula, the writer of informal satire is "the plain [person] with plain morals addressing plain people in plain terms on plain matters" (*Cankered Muse* 43).

It is apparent at once that Amos is par excellence the Bible's example of informal satire. Amos steps forward as a man of simple piety, humility, and social obscurity. He provides his own self-portrait as a someone "who was among the shepherds of Tekoa" (1:1), "a herdsman, and a dresser of sycamore trees" (7:14). He even eschews the title of prophet: "I am no prophet, nor a prophet's son" (7:14). As a shepherd figure, Amos evokes the innocent associations of pastoral literature, and we might note in passing that pastoral has always proved a ready vehicle for satire. The best literary analogue to the book of Amos is the medieval English satire *Piers Plowman* (which is, however, a much longer work). Howard Moss calls Amos "the prototype of the populist who springs out of nowhere to condemn a civilization. . . . There is something of Swift in the rigor of his attack, and something of the innocent who finds himself in the palaces of corruption" (210).

Like most informal satirists, Amos is a man of religious indignation and prophetic zeal. His tone is serious, moralistic, and practical. Fired by a spirit of religious outrage, he uses invective and rebuke to convey this tone. The object of attack is public, consisting of religious, social, and political vice. Amos champions the cause of a whole group, the socially oppressed, and he does so in the name of God. He is especially concerned with the greed, injustice, luxury, and moral callousness of those who professed to be models of righteousness. Political and ecclesiastical satire dominate the book.

Satiric Strategies in Amos

To read a satiric work like Amos, one needs first to identify the objects of satiric attack. Scholarly reconstruction of social context will often deepen our understanding of exactly what is happening, but the more literary a piece of satire is, the more likely it is to contain the help that we need to get the basic point. I will cite two specimen passages, beginning with part of the oracle against Israel (2:6–7):

Thus says the LORD:

"For three transgressions of Israel,
and for four, I will not revoke the punishment;
because they sell the righteous for silver,
and the needy for a pair of shoes—
they that trample the head of the poor into the dust of the earth,
and turn aside the way of the afflicted;
a man and his father go in to the same maiden,
so that my holy name is profaned. . . ."

Amos begins with the usual prophetic stance of invoking divine judgment against evil. Then he proceeds to catalog specific offenses in vivid imagery—slavery, oppression of the poor, legal injustice, sexual immorality, and/or participation in pagan fertility rituals with cult prostitutes. The satiric vehicle is the oracle of judgment, which in Amos has the overtones of a formal courtroom trial (Sinclair). The satiric norm (the standard by which the criticism is conducted) is God himself and his law and covenant as an extension of his nature. The satiric tone is biting.

My second specimen repeats the usual satiric format and is an attack on the wealthy women of Samaria (4:1–2):

> *Hear this word, you cows of Bashan,*
> *who are in the mountain of Samaria,*
> *who oppress the poor, who crush the needy,*
> *who say to their husbands, "Bring, that we may drink!"*
> *The LORD God has sworn by his holiness*
> *that, behold, the days are coming upon you,*
> *when they shall take you away with hooks,*
> *even the last of you with fishhooks. . . .*

The vehicle here is direct vituperation, beginning with the denigrating metaphor that compares wealthy women to cows (Bashan was a grain-producing region capable of producing fat livestock). The specific objects of attack are an affluent and self-indulgent lifestyle coupled with indifference to the suffering of the poverty-stricken. The scornful invective merges with the prophetic formula of predicting woe for the guilty, with the prediction itself becoming part of the attack. Again it is the character of God (specifically his holiness) that provides the norm by which the satire is conducted, and the tone is biting.

This analysis of two brief excerpts shows the kind of interpretive activities that a satiric book like Amos constantly requires of readers. We must be adept at identifying the objects of satiric attack and the satiric norm, we must be receptive to the satiric tone, and we must pay attention to the specific literary devices that the satirist employs.

Satiric Structure in Amos

In general, the organization of the book of Amos matches the naïve stance of the satirist that I noted earlier. The form is an encyclopedic accumulation of fragments. The plot of the book fits Kernan's description of the usual satiric plot: "It is clear that satire never offers that direct, linear progression which is ordinarily taken as plot. Instead, we get collections of loosely related scenes and busyness which curls back on itself. . . . Disjunctiveness and the absence of change" are the chief ingredients of a satiric plot (*Plot* 100). Of course this structure matches what we can infer about the process of composition and circumstances of oral proclamation that produced the Old Testament prophetic books.

The rapid-fire shifts that characterize the book of Amos are also part of its rhetoric of subversion. Satire is a subversive genre, and Amos heightens this tendency. The aim of the book is to assault our deep structure of perception and our complacency that life is essentially all right as it is. The staccato structure of the book contributes to this subversive strategy. As the writer keeps shifting topics and harranguing the audience, we begin to feel disoriented and assaulted.

The mixture of subgenres enhances the fragmentation of effect. Within the umbrella of satire, we find a virtual anthology of prophetic forms, including the proverb or saying, the oracle of judgment, the oracle of redemption, vision (including predictive visions of the future), doom song, taunt, pronouncement of woe, narrative, dialogue, descriptive vignette, and even occasional flashes of lyric.

The fragmentation that I have identified as the organizing principle of the book requires a major qualification. For all the author's disclaimers to literary sophistication, he manages to arrange his material into an artful fivefold pattern: (1) introduction to the book (1:1–2), (2) oracles against the nations (1:3 through ch. 2), (3) denunciation of Israel (chs. 3–6), (4) five visions of coming judgment (7:1–9:10), and (5) an oracle of salvation (9:11–15).

Most impressive of all is the intricate structuring of the oracles against the nations. Each oracle follows a common pattern that consists of five ingredients: (1) an opening formula ("Thus says the LORD"); (2) a balanced pair of clauses ("For three transgressions . . . and for four"); (3) a set formula for judgment ("I will not revoke the punishment"); (4) a statement of indictment; and (5) a list of judgments, beginning with the refrain "So I will send fire upon. . . ." The deeds that Amos cites are excessive cruelty in warfare, stealing people for the slave trade, and desecration of the dead—in brief, military atrocities.

In these oracles against the nations Amos obviously uses a technique of climax, creating a sequence of increasing urgency that culminates in the oracle against Israel, the main object of attack in the book. But there is more than this at work. The very arrangement of the oracles is clever and subversive. If we plot the nations on a map, we find that they crisscross each other to form a circle of despised pagan nations, and then, after the trap has been set, the circle suddenly turns inward and pounces on Judah and Israel. Edwin M. Good comments on the irony of the situation thus:

> With a map we can observe the geographical progression of the oracles from the periphery to the center. . . . We can imagine the xenophobic listeners nodding in happy agreement as the

> prophet's doom moves across one enemy after another, the very piling up of oracles lulling them to a doze until suddenly, with the characteristic prophetic shock, they are jerked awake. . . . The oracles are so adroitly arranged as to appear haphazard, satisfying the hearers' desire for destruction on their enemies, while all the time the doom circles closer and closer. The irony lies in the shock of the climax, which is surely not intended to be noticed until too late. (34)

In plainspoken satire like the book of Amos, we find an art that conceals itself.

Satiric Imagination in Amos

The literary imagination of Amos is most noteworthy, not in the structure of his book, but in his skill with smaller literary techniques. There is a lively imagination at work in the book of Amos, and it is best seen in such individual techniques as imagery, metaphor, simile, epithet, poetic parallelism, rhetorical question, proverb, paradox, and sarcasm. Most impressive of all is the parody present in the book—echoing literary or ecclesiastical form with inverted effect, in this case, satiric effect.

Much of the literary power of the book of Amos resides in its metaphors. Oppressors are described as trampling the head of the poor into the dust of the earth (2:7). God is a lion that roars (3:8). Samaria stores up "violence and robbery in their strongholds" (3:10). Wealthy women of Samaria are "cows of Bashan" (4:1). Israel is a forsaken virgin (5:2), the "day of the LORD" is darkness (5:18), and righteousness is "like an everflowing stream" (5:24). Here, in short, is a satirist with the gift of bold, energetic metaphor.

As Exhibit B, consider Amos's skill with a common formula of wisdom literature (3:3–6)—the proverb cluster on a common topic:

> *Do two walk together,*
> *unless they have made an appointment?*
> *Does a lion roar in the forest,*
> *when he has no prey?*
> *Does a young lion cry out from his den,*
> *if he has taken nothing?*
> *Does a bird fall in a snare on the earth*
> *when there is no trap for it?*
> *Does a snare spring up from the ground,*
> *when it has taken nothing?*

Is a trumpet blown in a city,
  and the people are not afraid?
Does evil befall a city,
  unless the LORD *has done it?*

The most obvious element of artistry is the strict parallelism. In each pair of lines, the first line describes a common situation from everyday life, while the second ascribes an obvious result or cause to the situation.

These parallel cause-effect observations are phrased as rhetorical questions, and this is part of the persuasive cast that Amos gives to his assertions. The purpose of a rhetorical question is not to elicit information but to awaken assent. Having assented to six obvious conclusions, the reader is trapped into agreeing with the climactic question as well, which is nothing less than the satiric point that adversity is God's judgment against sin.

The passage illustrates not only the poetic and rhetorical skill of Amos, but also the convergence of genres that we find in this encyclopedic work. As a collection of folk sayings based on everyday occurrences (chiefly in nature), the passage takes its basic strategy from wisdom literature. Everywhere, though, Amos adapts his conventional materials to his satiric purpose of sounding an alarm and subverting complacency.

Nowhere is the imaginative energy of Amos more striking than in his skill with literary parody—inverting the effect of conventional literary and liturgical formulas. Consider the inversions in this early passage (2:13–15):

Behold, I will press you down in your place,
  as a cart full of sheaves presses down.
Flight shall perish from the swift,
  and the strong shall not retain his strength,
  nor shall the mighty save his life;
he who handles the bow shall not stand,
  and he who is swift of foot shall not save himself,
  nor shall he who rides the horse save his life. . . .

Amos begins this portrait of unavoidable judgment by inverting the idealized associations of pastoral literature. A cart full of sheaves is supposed to be an image of abundance, a pastoral version of the good life, yet here it becomes an image of torture. The rest of the passage refutes the entire tradition of heroic and epic literature, where it is an axiom that the mighty are victorious and the warrior gains his ends with battlefield skill. The main point of this ironic reversal is satiric in nature, inasmuch as the passage increasingly makes the reader feel the futility of thinking that judgment can be avoided.

Such shocking parodies occur in big and small ways throughout the book of Amos. Whereas the conventional psalm of praise catalogs the blessings of God on his people, Amos gives us a catalog of God's acts of disaster visited on his people as a judgment for sin (4:6–11). Obituaries ordinarily announce an individual's death after it has occurred, but in a passage that James Luther Mays calls "funeral rites for the nation" (84), Amos composes an obituary for a personified nation before any demise has occurred (5:2). The effect is Swiftian—reading one's own obituary in the newspaper. It should also be noted that some of the elements of parody that I have been tracing belonged to the subversive tradition of satiric prophecy itself and were not original with Amos. Catalogs of chastisement and the lament-before-the-fact are found elsewhere in the Old Testament.

Rescue stories are a favorite with the human race, but Amos gives us a version of rescue that inverts the usual effect of both pastoral and rescue story: "As the shepherd rescues from the mouth of the lion two legs, or a piece of an ear, so shall the people of Israel who dwell in Samaria be rescued, with the corner of a couch and part of a bed" (3:12).

Amos does similar things with some of Israel's cherished liturgical and theological clichés. The conventional priestly exhortation to worship is turned on its head with his parody (4:4):

Come to Bethel, and transgress;
to Gilgal, and multiply transgression.

Again, the call to attend religious festivals and offer sacrifices was deeply ingrained in the Hebrew consciousness, but it gets the shock treatment when we hear Amos quote God thus (5:21–22):

I hate, I despise your feasts,
and I take no delight in your solemn assemblies.
Even though you offer me your burnt offerings and cereal offerings,
I will not accept them,
and the peace offerings of your fatted beasts
I will not look upon.

Similarly, the coming "day of the Lord" was envisioned by the Old Testament faithful as a time of vindication against national enemies. But the satirist Amos paints an opposing picture (5:18–20):

Woe to you who desire the day of the Lord!
Why would you have the day of the Lord?
It is darkness, and not light;
as if a man fled from a lion,
and a bear met him;
or went into the house and leaned with his hand against the wall,
and a serpent bit him.

Is not the day of the LORD darkness, and not light,
and gloom with no brightness in it?

In short, the satiric imagination of Amos paradoxically refutes his own disclaimers. Claiming not to be a prophet, he nonetheless delivers prophecies with all the customary forms. As the plainspoken person of simple piety, he displays a lively imagination and mastery of poetry, metaphor, and parody. Claiming only to speak "words" (1:1), he actually composes a work that conforms to all that we expect in a piece of satire.

Satire in the Bible

My purpose in treating Amos as a satire instead of as a conventional prophecy is partly to highlight the satiric strain in the Bible as a whole. The Bible is one of the most satiric books in the world, but because it contains few books that are wholly satiric (Amos and Jonah being the notable exceptions), the satiric element usually gets obscured.

Satire appears in every part of the Bible. It shows up in the stories, where wholly idealized characters are virtually nonexistent and where the character flaws of people are repeatedly exposed. Usually this results in a satiric coloring to stories that do not strike us as predominantly satiric, but the Bible has its share of satiric characters—the trickster Jacob, the tyrant Pharaoh (see Ackerman for some excellent commentary), King Ahasuerus and Haman in the book of Esther, and the ignominous prophet Jonah.

Satire is equally prominent in the proverbs of the Bible: "Like a gold ring in a swine's snout is a beautiful woman without discretion" (Prov. 11:22); "the sluggard buries his hand in the dish, / and will not even bring it back to his mouth" (Prov. 19:24). The book of Proverbs is filled with brief sketches of character types held up to satiric rebuke—character types like the lazy person, the drunkard, the miser, the loose woman, the nagging spouse, the fool. A satiric strain makes an appearance in the Psalms as well, where we encounter taunt songs directed against the worshipers of idols and portraits of the speaker's enemies in the lament psalms.

The largest repository of satire in the Bible is the prophetic books. This is not surprising, since their main ingredient is denunciation of the prevailing situation and the announcement of coming woe. The two basic prophetic forms are the oracle of judgment and the oracle of redemption or salvation. The best literary approach to the oracle of judgment is satire. These passages always have a discernible object of attack, a standard by which the judgment is rendered, and a vehicle of attack (consisting at its simplest of a statement of indictment and a prediction of calamity).

The second largest repository of satire in the Bible is the Gospels. A main part of the narrative strategy of the gospel writers is to hold up the opponents of Jesus (chiefly the teachers of the law and Pharisees) to satiric ridicule and censure (Boonstra). Jesus himself was a master of satire (Ryken 331–34). Some of his satiric discourses are in the tradition of the plainspoken satirist (his denunciation of the Pharisees in Matthew 23 being a model of informal satire). But Jesus' satiric parables (like those involving the rich farmer who built bigger barns, the self-righteous Pharisee who despised the tax collector, and the rich man who ignored Lazarus at his gate) are polished stories in which the satire is completely embodied in the details of a carefully crafted story.

The satiric impulse is never far from the surface in the Bible. Satire was a natural ally to the speakers and writers who gave us this book preoccupied with evil and its judgment. The effect of this pervasive satire on us as readers is that we are continually reminded that the Bible is an essentially subversive book, no matter how familiar we might become with it.

WORKS CITED

Ackerman, James S. "The Literary Context of the Moses Birth Story." *Literary Interpretations of Biblical Narratives.* Ed. Kenneth R. R. Gros Louis et al. Nashville: Abingdon, 1974. 74–119.

Boonstra, Harry. "Satire in Matthew." *Christianity and Literature* 29, no. 4 (Summer 1980): 32–45.

Good, Edwin M. *Irony in the Old Testament.* Philadelphia: Westminster, 1965.

Kernan, Alvin. *The Cankered Muse: Satire of the English Renaissance.* New Haven: Yale UP, 1959.

———. *The Plot of Satire.* New Haven: Yale UP, 1965.

Mays, James Luther. *Amos: A Commentary.* Philadelphia: Westminster, 1974.

Moss, Howard. "Amos." *Congregation: Contemporary Writers Read the Jewish Bible.* Ed. David Rosenberg. New York: Harcourt, 1987. 210–21.

Moulton, Richard G. *The Modern Reader's Bible.* New York: Macmillan, 1895.

Rosenheim, Edward W. *Swift and the Satirist's Art.* Chicago: University of Chicago Press, 1963.

Ryken, Leland. *Words of Life: A Literary Introduction to the New Testament.* Grand Rapids: Baker, 1988.

Sinclair, Lawrence A. "The Courtroom Motif in the Book of Amos." *Journal of Biblical Literature* 85 (1966): 351–53.

CHAPTER 25

Jonah

BRANSON L. WOODARD, JR.
Liberty University

Unique among the Minor Prophets is the book of Jonah, a highly unified, four-chapter prose narrative. In compact and clearly structured episodes, the author summarizes Jonah's foolish flight, miraculous deliverance, dangerous mission to Nineveh, and quiet defeat by compassionate Yahweh. The four settings—the stormy Mediterranean, the belly of the great fish, Nineveh, and the eastern side of the city—coalesce through the powerful interplay of terse, vivid commentary and lively, penetrating dialogue. Chapter 1 provides minimal background followed by a brief but telling confrontation between the ship's crew and Jonah, the frightened seamen then casting him overboard. In chapter 2 an anguished rebel faces the gracious God. All of the events lead to Jonah's prophecy to Nineveh (ch. 3) and his subsequent complaint when God has mercy on the contrite residents (ch. 4).

This well-known story, however, has a deceptively simple literary character. Even a casual reading soon becomes a formidable interpretive challenge as a number of basic but difficult questions arise. For example, can the protagonist be regarded as a prophet even though he is not called such within the book? Is the plot historical, purely imaginary, or in some sense both—mostly nonfictional, with some occasional exaggeration? If both, which part is fiction, which part fact? and what criteria serve as the basis for making such a distinction? Was the book written before or after the Exile? Is the highly poetic second chapter part of the autograph? Each of these questions carries weighty implications for the others, and we have yet to address what may be the crucial issue—the genre that best describes the book. Even the satiric vein in which the entire story is cast, according to modern scholarship (see Good, Holbert, Ackerman, Ryken), is not used nearly as extensively in the other books of the Twelve.

Is satire the only, even the primary genre present? Commentators who answer in the affirmative offer many valuable insights, but the thesis of the discussion that follows is that the book more thoroughly resembles another genre, Hebrew tragedy. The text of Jonah, examined on its own terms and in relation to various earlier sources known to its author, is a tragic narrative, the structured plot enlivening Jonah's character in a way that satire never could. The influence of tragedy, in turn, demands a careful use of history in reading the book (Stek) and a reconsideration of tragedy in ancient Hebrew writing, this writing then compared to Near Eastern satiric literature. Ultimately, the book of Jonah is shown to have a more sophisticated literary vision than modern criticism has found thus far, cause enough to suppose that tragedy and satire have more rhetorical similarities than either literary or biblical scholars have shown.

The Book of Jonah as a Satire

Perceiving Jonah as the satire of a haughty, overzealous Hebrew is not peculiar to this century, though much criticism along those lines has appeared since 1900. J. A. Bewer called the book a "prose poem[,] not history" (4), an assumption used by several other commentators (e.g., C. S. Lewis, Miles, Burrows) to describe the story as playfully humorous. Accordingly, the plot offers a persuasive illustration of divine love that transcends the obstinacy of a foolish zealot who would rather die than lead an ancient city to repentance. The narrator's focus on Jonah's incredibly harsh spirit has led some critics to set aside the issue of history and to regard the book as a postexilic satire published long after the fall of Nineveh in 612 B.C. (Ackerman 234). Many striking details in the story are thereby seen as either pure fiction or intentional exaggeration of historical events, to show Hebrew readers that God's covenant grace extends to Gentiles too. While the satiric nature of the book is debatable, its basis in fact is not; the book is historical.

Satire debunks a protagonist through either bitter invective (the Juvenalian tradition) or tongue-in-cheek narration (associated with Horace). The latter is said to pervade the Jonah story (Ryken, *How to Read* 161), highlighting the seemingly outlandish events and Jonah's ludicrous actions. This reading, with its impressive display of rhetorical analysis, proceeds as follows. Jonah, son of "truth" ("Amittai"), wishes to avoid truth at all costs—including the loss of his own life. He flees from the Truth, Yahweh's message, and loathes to speak it to the despicable Ninevites, though from the start (see 4:2) he well knows that Yahweh is merciful and gracious, not simply judgmental and punitive.

As for Jonah's relationship to truth, his shyness toward it (despite his father's name) seems as ridiculous as the suggestion that someone could sleep through a storm strong enough to dash a cargo ship to pieces (1:4, 6). This last detail is made all the more comical through wordplay. As Yahweh "hurls" a ferocious storm at the ship, so the crew "hurls" the cargo overboard (Holbert 65). While the tempest rages, no less, and the sailors fear for their lives, somehow they have the time and inclination to interrogate Jonah about his vocation, birthplace, homeland, and culture (1:8)—hardly the typical behavior of pagans trying to stay alive (Good 44–45). Moreover, their rebuke of him seems preposterous, even laughable, and other developments prompt heartier chuckles or broader smiles. For example, while the unregenerate sailors balk at the idea of throwing Jonah to certain death, *he* later displays no mercy at all toward Nineveh, apparently hoping to witness its destruction at the hand of Yahweh (4:5). Also, the sudden change in Jonah's character, from proud zealot (ch. 1) to humble servant (ch. 2), especially given the questionable sincerity of his statement "Salvation comes from the LORD" (2:9), is too fantastic to be factual, though a textual issue surfaces here, i.e., whether chapter 2 is part of the original composition or a later interpolation. If it is part of the autograph (Landes), the narrator's juxtaposition of pride and humility stands as artful construction of plot; if chapter 2 is extraneous, however, the "fish story" could be taken as imaginary, or primarily so, and other passages in the book could be argued more convincingly as fictitious too. Either way, the narrative would fit neatly into the rhetorical context of satire.

Yet a third example of bizarre contradiction occurs in chapter 3, as the violent, brutal Ninevites show such contrition for their sins that they fast and don sackcloth—even as their king puts on similar material, sits in the dust, and decrees that all city inhabitants (including the animals!) wear sackcloth as well. Everyone is commanded also to pray (3:5–8). Despite these realistic details, history does not confirm such a massive conversion in this gigantic fortress of the ancient world, and some ambiguity remains about the size of

Nineveh itself (see 3:3) and the length of time required for Jonah's trip (Burrows 82–83). Therefore, chapter 3, like the fish narrative that precedes it, is interpreted as deliberate overstatement, designed to amaze everyone, including Jonah himself (Good 48–51).

The finale to this wild turn of events is likewise fertile with incongruity that further degrades Jonah. A Hebrew messenger, commissioned to preach divine judgment, becomes irate when the recipients of his message repent. He is so irritated, in fact, that he wishes he were dead and makes his way outside the city to sulk. Again, though, he encounters divine intervention that further reveals his depraved nature. As Yahweh offers a disarming rhetorical question (i.e., Is anger the proper response to Nineveh's repentance?), the awfulness of Jonah's stubbornness and selfish heart is obvious. Of course, the familiar vine that has sprung up suddenly dies, at which the grumpy missionary again becomes angry (4:9). Once more Yahweh resorts to a rhetorical question: Should I not be concerned about the 120,000 souls in Nineveh, that great city, besides their many cattle? An ending with this literary device underscores the powerful irony that seems to make the issue of historical accuracy a moot point. Exaggeration, comic tone, fictional artifice, dissociation of protagonist from the historical Jonah (see 2 Kings 14:25)—these qualities build a compressed, forceful debunking of proud, bigoted Hebrews who thought Gentiles beyond the reach of divine mercy and love.

Hebrew Tragedy in the Book

Reading the book as a satire obviously has its strengths but overall seems inadequate. Although such a reading allows us to adhere closely to the text as a self-contained unit and finished product, it fails to account adequately for earlier Old Testament texts that were familiar to the author and, combined with other factors, shaped the genre and narrative structure of Jonah. The following explication shows the influence of Hebrew tragedy on the book, all of which requires a reconception of tragedy and a fresh interpretation of Jonah himself. Because Old Testament tragedy has reliable narrators, historical purpose, and factual details, my approach to the book presumes a reliable (though sophisticated) narrator, a historical (though perspectival) account, and a factual (though imaginatively constructed) plot. All in all, the main character displays a seriousness beyond the comic story, deepening the reader's awareness of the folly and frustration inherent in disobeying God.

Requisite to further analysis of the book's genre is an awareness of an important qualification about tragedy and the Old Testament. Readers of Jonah should not expect the book to conform neatly to an explicit literary genre called tragedy: "It is all but universally agreed that formal tragedy is not to be found within the literary repertoire of ancient Israel or early Judaism" (Humphreys 1). Even so, Hebrew tragic narrative does exhibit certain characteristics that—with caution—can be applied to Jonah. The first is a six-phased plot; the second, a tragic flaw within the protagonist that elucidates his own heroic status. Again, though, readers should anticipate a less rigid application of the literary form that would apply to, say, *Antigone, Medea,* or other formal Greek tragedies written centuries after Jonah.

With this limitation in mind, we notice in the book an orderly and clear display of the six phases of Old Testament tragedy—dilemma, choice, catastrophe, suffering, perception or realization of one's error, and death (Ryken, *Words of Delight* 145). Jonah's dilemma is the divine commission to prophesy to Nineveh and to do it *there,* unlike the commissions given other Hebrew prophets, who proclaimed their messages from the safe distance of their homeland. Jonah's choice, then, is to deliver God's message or to rebel. He rebels, perhaps in part due to his own nationalistic pride but due also to the threat of Ninevite brutality. No bodily harm ever comes to him in Nineveh, but he does experience a catastrophe, i.e., the storm at sea—in particular, some anxious moments in the Mediterranean after the crew throws him overboard. From all indications, his death is certain.

Before leaving the catastrophe on the ship's deck, we might notice the effect of this new genre analysis on the other important characters, the Gentiles, and the larger setting of the entire story. The literary importance of the non-Israelite sailors (1:5–17) and the Ninevites (3:4–10) lies in their interaction with the Hebrew prophet, the theological tension building as the plot unfolds. Whether the book is a tragedy or a satire, these Gentiles function as a corrective norm relative to Jonah's arrogant nationalism. However, in both situations these non-Hebrews are part of a larger calamity, the impending destruction by God, that deepens the reader's understanding of Jonah as a tragic figure.

The larger calamity, in turn, keeps the focus of the story not on Jonah's interaction with the Gentiles but on his own spiritual decline. The sudden religiosity of both the crewmen and the Ninevites, which seems genuine enough, clashes with the callousness of Jonah, revealing his alienation from God, which was first reported by the narrator early in chapter 1. From that point on, Jonah's fundamental problem becomes more clear: he struggles with his own identity as a Hebrew *and* his responsibility as a prophet to express God's merciful warning to the *goyim.*

This Hebrew-Gentile conflict can serve not only to satirize but also to develop a tragedy, the author using the struggle to reveal a character's *hamartia* or tragic flaw. Jonah's flaw differs from Samson's fleshliness (Judg. 13–16) and Saul's impulsiveness (1 Sam. 9–31): Jonah despises Gentiles. This contempt would be intensified if the crewmen's reaction to the storm were typical of other Mediterranean people. Interestingly enough, recent research of fourteen Hittite prayers found that these prayers, like the sailors' prayer in Jonah 1, "are made from the basic conviction that a transgression against the deity will be punished by a visitation; conversely, a blow which falls on a community or an individual indicates a wicked action which has been committed recently or even longer before" (Beyerlin 166). The crew on Jonah's ship may not have been Hittites, but as Gentiles they would receive no kindness from the Hebrew. In the larger context, however, the divinely sent gale serves a dual role: it exposes the crew's sensitivity to a supernatural order of law and reveals Yahweh's anger at the spiritual rebellion within Jonah. In this scene, as in Shakespeare's tragedy *King Lear* (see 3.1 and 3.2), a calamity in nature points to a crisis in the protagonist.

Following the dilemma, choice, and catastrophe, the author reports Jonah's suffering, three days and nights inside the fish, and either his tragic realization or an effective transition to it. Engulfed in darkness, perhaps nauseated by the stink within this fleshly tomb, a lonely and despondent Jonah experiences the same dissociation from divine mercy that his rebellion has prolonged for the Ninevites. But does he realize his error? The text allows two different answers, and both explain the larger narrative using the same phases of tragedy in the same order. Each answer deserves mention, though the second seems the more likely explanation.

Jonah's realization may take place inside the fish. Self-examination and the resolve to mend one's ways seem inherent in the final words of his psalm of thanksgiving: "What I have vowed I will make good. Salvation comes from the LORD" (2:9). Moreover, as if to remind readers of God's mercy on penitent hearts, the narrator reports that under divine command, the fish vomited Jonah on dry ground. Then off went the prophet to Assyria. If his words in 2:9 are sincere, at least for a while, his departure for Nineveh shows his commitment to the divine will. Further support for this reading comes from the parallel sequences of repentance and deliverance—Jonah's in chapter 2 and the Ninevites' in chapter 3. Of course, his complaint about Yahweh's sparing the city suggests that his earlier confession was mere heartless orthodoxy, intended only to appease God. Nevertheless, that Jonah's commitment is, like Nineveh's, temporary indicates even more parallelism in the two chapters and more evidence that a tragic perception, or a foreshadowing of it, has occurred.

But tragic perception also may happen later, interwoven in the final phase of tragedy—death. After Yahweh spares the city, Jonah asks to die (4:2–3), an utterance that in a comic genre such as satire may sound like a childish pouting; but if spoken by a protagonist in a tragedy, these words are more grave. In short, they reveal Jonah's tragic perception. He wants to die, says Adele Berlin, not because Nineveh has been spared but because he cannot reconcile his understanding of divine grace with his own responsibility as a prophet to "forthtell" Nineveh's doom, a "prophecy" that of course had not come true. From the very beginning, Berlin continues, Jonah assumed the risk that his message about Nineveh's coming devastation could prove inaccurate, his identity as a prophet consequently called into question—hence his initial flight (231–33). From this perspective, 1:1–2 assumes a concrete seriousness quite different from the supposed humor that some commentators have perceived in these verses. This same propensity for the serious and the concrete appears in many Old Testament stories about protagonists, especially in their relationships with Yahweh:

> Moses, Jonah, and many of the Old Testament heroes and prophets argued with Jehovah, questioned his judgment, criticized his harshness or (as with Jonah) his leniency, in actual dialogue. . . . Ideas, or truth, were not regarded apart, as abstractions or final causes. They were ideas-in-action, lived out and tested by men of flesh and blood. (Sewall 13–14)

This worldview, in turn, suggests that Jonah's flight to Tarshish, a direct challenge to God, and his response to Nineveh's deliverance are not as exaggerated as they have been depicted. With Nineveh spared, Jonah has no recourse; his only escape, he believes, is death.

What then of death? In this story no one actually dies, so how could it be read as a tragic narrative? Although death is absent, images of it appear throughout the account, too many to be incidental and inconsequential to the story. The downward movement typical of tragedy occurs from the first chapter, almost from the opening verse. Jonah goes down into the ship; later he is thrown overboard into an apparent watery grave; the fish is a symbol of the grave, as Jonah remarks (2:2–6); the protagonist himself twice utters a death wish (4:3, 8); and later, the vine dies. With these details is the author's use of the Hebrew root for "deep sleep," a state of dormancy so intense that it resembles death. According to Magonet (67), the word occurs only eleven times in the Old Testament, once in 1 Samuel 26:12, which is part of the tragedy of Saul (see 1 Sam. 9–31).

This use of tradition criticism, moreover, yields other significant details about the presence of Hebrew tragedy in the book of Jonah. Specifically, the author has borrowed phrases from Genesis 1–3, a passage introducing the spirit of tragedy to biblical narrative and serving as the "source and model of all later tragedies" (Ryken, *Words of Life* 147). As Holbert has shown (65), the "deep sleep" is found also in Genesis 2:21, as are two rhetorical questions (Jonah 1:8 with Gen. 3:11; Jonah 1:10 with Gen. 3:13). At the least, then, the author of Jonah shapes his own account by using language from two Old Testament passages that convey a strong tragic sense.

Jonah: A Tragic Hero?

Perhaps the most serious challenge to the argument that Jonah is a tragic narrative lies in the methodology of interpreting the protagonist himself. Again, formal tragedy and, more generally, the concept of literary genres originate in Greek thought, not Hebrew, so that modern English readers must keep the history of tragedy in clear perspective and thereby avoid westernizing the Old Testament, a Semitic text. The tragedies of Euripides, Sophocles, and Aeschylus were produced in the third century B.C., by my estimation some five hundred years *after* the book of Jonah was written. The protagonists created by these Greek tragedians have grandeur and stature; and each plot has various stages, including the inevitable death of the hero, such fate eliciting deep sympathy from the audience who always know beforehand the impossible circumstances facing this superhuman. Does Jonah possess grandeur and stature? I believe that he does, but not by the standards of Greek tragedy.

Whatever grandeur appears in Old Testament tragic heroes is clearly limited, contextualized in a larger heroism belonging to no one but God. Only prelapsarian Adam is given some special position, due presumably to his sinlessness. He, as well as Eve, is created in the divine image and given rule over all the earth. His naming Eve and later the animals, in turn, may enhance his stature. But throughout Genesis 1, where he is introduced, Adam is clearly subserviant to God himself. The narrative dwells not on Adam's thoughts and actions but on God's. The repetition in 1:27, in particular, emphasizes God's creative activity, not the human product.

The grandeur of other tragic figures in the Hebrew Bible is tempered as well. Samson's introduction in Judges 13, for instance, includes some supernatural elements. An angel announces his birth; he will be a Nazirite and will accomplish the feat of leading Israel out of Philistine bondage. Before long, though, the strong man is flaunting his carnality before family and friends, hobnobbing with the very enemies of Israel. And Saul, though much taller than his companions and highly promising as a leader, is not said to have

God with him, a detail that reminds the reader of Absalom and adds significance to Saul's unfamiliarity with Samuel. As Humphreys notes, "Even as we are introduced to this young man of such heroic potential, a discordant subtheme emerges to haunt otherwise high expectations" (29). Consistently, then, Old Testament heroes have clear limitations placed on whatever larger-than-life proportions they reflect.

However restricted their stature, these protagonists are divinely appointed to special tasks, as is Jonah. His great mission requires courage, boldness, and obedience. Certainly his cowardly flight and incredible attempt to hide from Yahweh create intense dramatic irony, i.e., the difference between what a character says or does and what the reader knows to be true. Obviously, no one can hide from God (Ps. 139 treats the notion as an ironic impossibility). But his task makes him a special man, not the sinless father of humanity or the Nazirite strong man, or even the Benjamite who is a head taller than the others, but a Hebrew prophet with a command from God.

This command, carried out in chapter 3, provides the context for Yahweh's silencing of Jonah in chapter 4. In this climactic portion the author highlights the paradoxical nature of divine redemption: while finite and fallible human wisdom seeks its own destruction, a plant (supernaturally given) sustains the death seeker in the desert sun. Nevertheless, as Yahweh explains, the now-withered vine is no more Jonah's property than is Nineveh. Further, the voice of God, speaking graciously through rhetorical questions, not oppressively through imperial decrees, gently silences the confused and desperate Jonah. That he remains alive hardly diminishes the effect of many powerful images of death throughout the book, underscoring the proud nature of the prophet and the tragic narrative about him—tragic in both the literary and theological senses of the word.

Reviewing, then, we recognize the sequence of events that leads from dilemma, choice, and catastrophe, to suffering, perception, and death. All the while, Jonah's tragic sense becomes more apparent; if the fish story seems humorous, smiles fade quickly by the time the Ninevite king calls the city to prayer and God spares these penitents. Suddenly, Jonah is caught between his own depraved wish to see them destroyed, as justice demands for misdeeds, and his spiritual sensitivity to the higher law of grace—all of this compounded by the fact that his announced but unfulfilled message of destruction has contradicted his own identity as a spokesman for God. A more pitiable circumstance is difficult to imagine and counters the satiric cast of the book.

Conclusion

Satire and tragedy both criticize a protagonist's failure to realize high but reachable ideals, involving the reader in a moving story that mixes scornful looks and smiles. Somewhere within that tension lies the overpowering rhetoric of a brief account in the Minor Prophets about nonsensical attempts to escape transcendent order and control, the painful but purifying chastisement that follows, and the stubborn disregard of divine grace upon even the most vile. How splendidly Jonah serves to illustrate Alexander Pope's well-known description of man as the "glory, jest, and riddle of the world." That he could be the glory at all gives the prophet a great but unfulfilled potential. Here lies the spirit of tragedy used so deftly by the author of Jonah, whose literary gifts make his narrative amuse and oppress simultaneously—as does much of life itself.

WORKS CITED

Ackerman, James. "Jonah." *The Literary Guide to the Bible.* Ed. Robert Alter and Frank Kermode. Cambridge, Mass.: Harvard UP, 1987.

Berlin, Adele. "A Rejoinder to John A. Miles, Jr., with Some Observations on the Nature of Prophecy." *Jewish Quarterly Review* 66 ns (April 1976): 227–35.

Bewer, J. A. *The International Critical Commentary on . . . Jonah.* Edinburgh: T. & T. Clark, 1912.

Beyerlin, Walter, ed. *Near Eastern Religious Texts Relating to the Old Testament.* Trans. John Bowden. Philadelphia: Westminster, 1978.

Burrows, Millar. "The Literary Category of the Book of Jonah." *Translating & Understanding the Old Testament.* Ed. Harry T. Frank and William L. Reed. Nashville: Abingdon, 1970. 80–107.

Good, Edwin M. *Irony in the Old Testament.* 1965. Rpt. Sheffield: Almond, 1981.

Holbert, John C. " 'Deliverance Belongs to Yahweh': Satire in the Book of Jonah." *Journal for the Study of the Old Testament* 21 (1981): 59–81.

Humphreys, W. Lee. *The Tragic Vision and the Hebrew Tradition.* Philadelphia: Fortress, 1985.

Landes, George. "The Kerygma of the Book of Jonah." *Interpretation* 28 (1967): 3–30.

Lewis, C. S. "Modern Theology and Biblical Criticism." *Christian Reflections.* Ed. Walter Hooper. Grand Rapids: Eerdmans, 1967.

Magonet, Jonathan. *Form and Meaning: Studies in the Literary Techniques in the Book of Jonah.* 2d ed. Sheffield: Almond, 1983.

Miles, John A. "Laughing at the Bible: Jonah as Parody." *Jewish Quarterly Review* 65 (1975): 168–81.

Ryken, Leland. *How to Read the Bible as Literature.* Grand Rapids: Zondervan, 1984.

———. *Words of Delight: A Literary Introduction to the Bible.* Grand Rapids: Baker, 1987.

Sewall, Richard. *The Vision of Tragedy.* New Haven: Yale UP, 1959.

Stek, John. "The Message of the Book of Jonah." *Calvin Theological Journal* 4 (1969): 23–50.

PART 3

CHAPTER 26

The Literature of the New Testament

Leland Ryken
Wheaton College

The main literary issue governing the New Testament can be simply stated: Is the New Testament literary in the ordinary sense of the term? This general question spawns more specific ones. Is it correct to speak of the New Testament's "formlessness . . . by classical standards" (Shaffer 66)? Is the New Testament literary but in such a unique way as to render "Greek and traditional humanist categories . . . inadequate as measuring rods" (Wilder 36)? Or should we claim, more radically, that "we must assume unliterary beginnings" for the New Testament, with the result that we will "look in vain for analogies in literature proper" (Dibelius 39)? Moving in the other direction, is the New Testament simply a mingling "of convention and innovation, of the familiar and the new" (Ryken, *Words of Life* 14–15)? Or is it, in fact, so similar to familiar literary genres and techniques that in discussing it we can use exactly the same critical terms that we apply to ordinary literature (e.g., Pervo)?

The primary question about literariness can be supplemented by secondary ones. One is the question of genre: Is the ostensible uniqueness of New Testament genres (gospel, acts, epistle, apocalypse) only apparent, or is it real? A second point of debate concerns stylistics: Do the vocabulary and style of the New Testament writings warrant the verdict that the New Testament "is not a work of literary art" (Lewis vii), or, contrastingly, does virtually every page of the New Testament display sophisticated rhetorical patterns, either Hebraic (Lind, Bailey) or classical (Kennedy)? The third issue concerns the unity of the material: Is the organization "rather scrappy" (Dodd 2)—possessing the organization of "a cycle, . . . piecemeal, traditional, inconsistent" (Shaffer 79)—or is it a subtly woven tapestry (the current scholarly consensus)?

To these contradictory claims we should add the truism that most readers simply find it difficult to think of the New Testament as literature. The New Testament is usually felt to be less literary than the Old Testament, though upon analysis it is hard to substantiate this impression. Yet when a group of contemporary writers of imaginative literature produced a book of responses to the New Testament, the volume almost entirely avoided literary analysis (Corn).

While the picture I have painted might seem confusing, it actually points us in the right direction. When judged by ordinary literary standards, the New Testament is both familiar and unfamiliar. Its uniqueness has a great deal more to do with its content than with its forms, and with the encyclopedic combination of its forms than with those forms themselves.

In the discussion that follows, I have chosen to talk first about how the New Testament is unlike ordinary literature and then how it is literary by conventional literary criteria. This is the chronology in which most people actually experience the matter. When the early church father Augustine first read the Bible as a Christian believer, it struck him as too lacking in literary intention to be considered literary by ordinary criteria (*Confessions* 3.5). But once he got beyond its deviations from familiar literature, Augustine found all kinds of eloquence and rhetorical sophistication in the texts (*On Christian Doctrine* 4.6–7). Many readers can attest a similar evolution in their experience of the New Testament.

An additional insight from Augustine is similarly helpful: Augustine surmised that the examples of eloquence in the New Testament Epistles "seem not so much to be sought out by the speaker as spontaneously to suggest themselves" (*On Christian Doctrine* 4.6). The New Testament writers, notes Augustine, "possess but . . . do not display" their eloquence (7), by which Augustine apparently meant that the writers do not flaunt their eloquence. The New Testament is folk literature—"a Book of the people," as Adolf Deissman pronounced it earlier in this century (quoted in Ryken, *New Testament* 20). On the surface, such literature can appear amateurish. But the mistake of much scholarship earlier in this century was to assume that folk literature of the type we find in the New Testament could not be genuinely and even subtly artistic. Equally destructive of literary appreciation of the New Testament has been the religious impulse to be singlemindedly preoccupied with a search for *what* the New Testament says, to the neglect of inquiring into *how* it says it.

Subsequent chapters will explore the literary features of the individual books and genres of the New Testament. In this introductory chapter I have avoided covering the same terrain and have focused instead on features that underlie the New Testament as a whole.

First Glimpses: Why the New Testament Seems Unliterary

It is not hard to see why the New Testament initially strikes us as being unlike familiar literature. One reason is the combination of three impulses that converge in these texts. Like the Old Testament authors, the New Testament authors combined historical, theological, and literary intentions. In the New Testament narratives, for example, we regularly sense a documentary impulse to get the historical facts about characters and events in front of the reader. Even more pervasive is the religious impulse of the writing—a didactic concern to impart both theological ideas and moral imperatives.

These informational purposes are so evident that only upon conscious analysis does it dawn on us that relatively little of the material is straightforward expository prose. Instead we find a preponderance of literary genres and subtypes, along with the presence of surprisingly subtle stylistic effects. Figurative language abounds. Appeals to the imagination (our image-making capacity) are continuous.

Reinforcing the unconventional mingling of literature with nonliterary material is the authors' encyclopedic tendency to combine diverse literary genres. The mixed-genre format is one of the most important literary distinctives of the New Testament and perhaps the leading reason that scholars through the centuries have been unable to agree on what kind of literature the New Testament is (or whether it is literature at all). The Gospels, for example, are collections or "cycles" consisting of such recognizable genres as narrative, poetry, proverb, satire, parable, and drama. The book of Acts combines narrative, travelogue, oratory, sermon, and courtroom forensics. The Epistles mix theological exposition, moral exhortation, travelogue, epistolary conventions, and lyric poems. The book of Revelation is a collage of genres—epistolary, visionary, poetic, narrative, dramatic.

The encyclopedic nature of the New Testament is accompanied by an organizational tendency toward disjointedness, an effect heightened by the way in which the New Testament writers show the same preference for the brief unit that we find in the Old Testament. Virtually no New Testament story or discourse extends beyond an individual chapter in English versions, and the overwhelming number of chapters consist of multiple units. Even a discourse like Jesus' so-called "sermon" on the mount is a collection of separate poems, discourses, exhortations, and parables.

The fact that much of the New Testament consists of cycles of collected anecdotes and teachings can be related to another feature, namely the oral roots of the New Testament. Most of what we read almost certainly existed first in oral form. Jesus himself wrote nothing of what we find in the New Testament. Oral forms such as addresses, sayings, and dialogues dominate the narrative parts of the New Testament. The Epistles, though written, reflect many conventions of oral rhetoric, being for the most part orally dictated and intended for public reading. A beatitude embedded in the opening salutation of the book of Revelation promises, "Blessed is he who reads aloud the words of the prophecy, and blessed are those who hear" (1:3). Amos Wilder correctly comments regarding the New Testament that "oral speech is where it all began" (40).

An additional reason for the initial impression that the New Testament is unliterary is its plainness. Its original language, for example, was *koiné* or common Greek, not refined classical Greek. The style is correspondingly unembellished and brief. The world portrayed is likewise ordinary and realistic. Erich Auerbach describes it as "a world which is . . . entirely real, average, identifiable as to place, time, and circumstances" (43).

The New Testament also possesses a confrontational quality that makes it seem different from ordinary literature. When we read Shakespeare or Dickens, we are at various times participants and spectators of the action, but we rarely if ever feel that we are being urged to make a commitment. Not so with the New Testament, which is a literature of encounter and confrontation that presupposes response as a condition of reading it. Auerbach noted the prevalence, without parallel in other ancient literature, of face-to-face dialogues in the New Testament (46).

Also without parallel are the unconventional genres by which the sections of the New Testament are named. The traditional nomenclature, inherent in the New Testament text itself, is fourfold: gospel, acts, epistle, apocalypse. We will find only one of these—epistle—in standard anthologies of English or American literature, and even there the letter will be a minor form, not the major form that it is in the New Testament, where twenty-one of the twenty-seven books are letters.

It is of course true that many of the literary features that I have described as making the New Testament seem unusual are also characteristic of the Old Testament. But one way in which the New Testament is unique is its Christocentric focus. The consistent focus of the Gospels is the person and work of Christ, who is the protagonist of the narratives. The book of Acts and the Epistles picture the world-changing impact of the life of Christ in the early church. And the book of Revelation begins by announcing as its epic theme "the revelation [unveiling] of Jesus Christ."

In summary, then, the New Testament first strikes us as unlike ordinary literature. Its structure is kaleidoscopic and encyclopedic, its ostensible purpose is the plain telling of the truth, its style is unpretentious, and its content is too relentlessly religious and didactic to be considered literary.

A Closer Look: The New Testament as Literature

A closer look reveals that there is much about the New Testament that is literary in the conventional ways, beginning with genre. The conventional fourfold classification noted earlier successfully divides the New Testament into the groupings of books as we find them, but in other ways this nomenclature is misleading. It makes the material appear more unfamiliar than it really is. It conceals the high degree of unity that exists across the board in the New Testament. Conversely, it makes the individual books or sections seem more unified than they really are. And the attempt to differentiate between the Gospels and the book of Acts on narrative grounds is unconvincing.

In place of the conventional genres, therefore, we could as well list the literary types that appear *within* the New Testament books: story, poetry, discourse or oratory, drama (dialogues in specific settings), proverb, satire, parable, encomium, and visionary writing. The moment we use this list, the New Testament suddenly looks a great deal more like ordinary literature. This list, moreover, shows some of the literary unity of the New Testament, since most of these forms appear throughout the New Testament. And it confirms the hybrid nature of the New Testament books, where it is the combination of ingredients that is unique, not the forms themselves.

Other features of the New Testament confirm its literary quality. It is a convention of literature to incarnate its meaning in the form of images, characters, and events. The aim of literature is not to state ideas but to recreate experiences. Literature fulfills this aim by appealing to the understanding through the imagination (our image-making and image-perceiving capacity). Because the New Testament storytellers usually write in short narrative units, it is easy to overlook how many appeals to the imagination these stories actually contain. Descriptions are brief but specific. Directly quoted speeches predominate over summarized narrative. The discourses embedded within the narratives tend to be poetic and imagistically rich rather than abstract:

> No one after lighting a lamp puts it in a cellar or under a bushel, but on a stand, that those who enter may see the light. Your eye is the lamp of your body; when your eye is sound, your whole body is full of light; but when it is not sound, your body is full of darkness. Therefore be careful lest the light in you be dark. (Luke 11:33–35)

The book of Revelation is similarly imagistic, representing what Austin Farrer termed "a rebirth of images." G. Wilson Knight correctly says regarding the New Testament that "its subject is incarnation; its technique is also incarnation" (49).

The part of the New Testament that may seem not to share this impulse toward incarnational embodiment instead of abstraction is the Epistles, but they are less of an exception than they appear to be. For one thing, the Epistles are occasional letters written on specific occasions and dealing with specific situations that had arisen in the lives of a church group or individual. They are rarely systematic treatises on a theological issue (though they do presuppose the narrative shape of the Gospel as a backdrop). Like literature generally, the Epistles give us pictures of daily life—in this case, the life of the early churches. Beyond that, the very language of the Epistles is frequently imagistic and metaphoric: "The tongue is a fire. The tongue is an unrighteous world among our members, staining the whole body, setting on fire the cycle of nature, and set on fire by hell" (James 3:6).

Literature is also definable by its concentrated use of special resources of language. Figurative language is the most obvious example. Whenever a writer uses metaphor, simile, symbol, hyperbole, apostrophe, personification, allusion, paradox, pun, or irony, we ascribe a literary quality to the discourse. The New Testament continuously exhibits these resources of language, even in the predominantly expository parts.

The New Testament is also literary by virtue of its self-conscious artifice. Individual narrative units and discourses that initially look random and miscellaneous repeatedly turn out to be subtly patterned, as recent literary analysis has convincingly shown. Many prose passages are so intricately patterned and display such a high incidence of parallelism that they could be printed as Hebrew poetry. Chiasm or ring construction (in which the second half of a passage repeats the elements of the first half in reverse order) is common. We also find such rhetorical devices as repetition, rhetorical questions, question-and-answer constructions, and imaginary dialogues.

Finally, a text is recognizable as literature whenever it makes major use of literary archetypes—master images that recur throughout literature, the building blocks of the imagination. These archetypes fall into three categories—images (such as light and darkness), plot motifs (e.g., quest or initiation), and character types (such as the villain or hero). The New Testament is a book filled with literary archetypes (Ryken, *How to Read* 187–93).

In summary, a book is literary if it invites a literary approach. The New Testament not only invites but requires such an approach. It asks us to pay attention to concrete details and images. Its material is expressed in recognizable literary genres (unconventionally mingled) and in distinctly literary language. And once we train ourselves to look for literary artistry and a reliance on archetypes, we will find them continuously. As with literature generally, we cannot fully comprehend the "what" of New Testament writings (their religious content) without first paying attention to the "how" (the literary modes in which the content is embodied).

Convention and Innovation in New Testament Literature

Considered as literature, then, what most characterizes the New Testament is the mingling of literary convention and innovation, beginning with the Gospels. The primary form in the Gospels is narrative, with setting, plot, and character as the basic elements. Wherever we turn, we find plot conflicts moving to resolution, reversals of action, turning points, and moments of epiphany. Familiar archetypes fill the pages—heroes, villains, refusers of festivity, outcasts, journeys, miraculous transformations, ordeals, happy endings, feasts, storms, and many more.

But along with these familiar narrative contours, we find unexpected features in the landscape. Only half of the content of the Gospels is narrative material. The rest is sayings, discourses, parables, and didactic conversations in which Jesus imparts truth to someone. Even in the narrative sections we encounter a host of subgenres that only partly parallel the stories we are familiar with: annunciation and nativity stories, calling or vocation stories, recognition stories, witness or testimony stories, encounter stories, conflict or controversy stories, pronouncement stories (in which a saying of Jesus is linked to an event that illustrates or explains it), miracle stories, passion stories, and mixtures of these. Where else in our reading experience do we encounter this combination of ingredients?

A similar mingling of convention and innovation emerges from the role that Jesus plays in the Gospels. He is recognizably the protagonist of the accounts, and the Gospels themselves are hero stories (stories built around the life of an exemplary person who is held up for admiration). The literary purpose of the Gospels is obvious: they exist to portray the life, teachings, and significance of Jesus. In these accounts Jesus appears "silhouetted against a world of formalized religion, hypocrisy, envy, evil and suffering" (Knight 169). No matter how futile the long scholarly quest to find ancient predecessors and parallels to the Gospels has been (for surveys see Talbert 1–23 and Tolbert 55–59), it has at least served the function of proving that the gospel stories about Jesus have affinities with other ancient narratives.

But here, too, the Gospels keep setting up resistance to conventional expectations. The hero is known to us as much by what he says as by what he does. Discourses are as important to the story as are events. Some of the things ascribed to this literary protagonist are unconventional—the ability to forgive sins, simultaneous humanity and divinity, a substitutionary death that is efficacious for others, and resurrection from death. We expect heroes to be earthly rulers, but Jesus initiates people into a spiritual kingdom.

The structure of the story likewise combines the typical and the atypical. The general pattern is chronological, as the storytellers follow Jesus from either birth or the beginning of his public ministry through his death and resurrection (the climax of all four Gospels). Like other stories, the Gospels put the protagonist in the center of the action and then arrange a series of other characters around him—the disciples, the Pharisees, the crowd of ordinary people (sometimes a nameless mass, at other times represented by particular characters). Individual episodes are often dramas in miniature.

But the narratives also violate a principle of plot construction that has been regarded as normal in Western literature since Aristotle—a beginning–middle–end sequence in which each event builds on its predecessor, forming a seamless chain of cause and effect. The Gospels are much less unified than this. They are organized partly by the dynamics of human memory, which recalls broad outlines, remembers single incidents, and strings together certain sequences of events.

The Gospels have episodic plots, not a single sustained action. The closest they come to a single action is a growing movement toward the Cross. The virtues of an episodic plot as the vehicle for telling the story of Jesus are obvious. The apparent randomness effectively portrays Jesus in his manifold roles. The kaleidoscopic variety of scenes, events, and characters captures the nature of the life that Jesus actually lived during his years as a traveling teacher and miracle worker. Jesus traveled, preached, led a group of disciples, performed miracles, engaged in dialogue with people, defended his actions and beliefs in open debate, and was finally put on trial and crucified. No wonder the Gospels possess the form and content that they have.

Sometimes the episodic nature of the Gospels is made even more acute by the writers' preference for the narrative fragment—the one-paragraph summary of an event, for example. As a result, we will find the usual density of meaning and artistry, not in individual units, but in the collage or mosaic of stories (something overlooked by commentators who claim undue simplicity for the stories of the New Testament when compared to those in the Old Testament).

To take a typical specimen, in Luke 9:28–62 we find this series of fragments: the transfiguration of Jesus (eight verses), Jesus' exorcism of an unclean spirit that the disciples could not cast out (seven verses), Jesus' foretelling of his death (three verses), the disciples' argument about who would be greatest (three verses), Jesus' rebuke to his disciples for wanting to prevent a nonfollower from performing miracles (two verses), the rejection of Jesus by a Samaritan village that the disciples wish to consume with fire (six verses), and Jesus' discourse on the requirements for following him (six verses). Can this collage of apparently unrelated events be the product of conscious narrative artistry? Certainly not in the conventional sense.

But the collage of fragments possesses a pattern that unfolds itself once we begin to look for it. To begin, the very abruptness of the format has the virtue of precise focus on specific things. Beyond this, the interrelatedness of the fragments shows that the writer viewed his materials as forming a mosaic. The overall configuration in these verses is the greatness of Jesus in contrast to the failings of the disciples (who are the reader's representatives in the story). We are given the "underside" of discipleship—an ever-expanding vision of how ignominiously followers of Jesus can behave. Silhouetted against the power and compassion of Jesus we see the disciples' lack of faith, jealousy, obtuseness, pride, bigotry, spirit of vengeance, and impulsiveness. What initially seemed to be a loose collection of journalistic entries turns out to be carefully patterned, but the density that we expect from stories depends here on our ability to view the fragments, not as isolated units, but as parts of a collage.

A distinction that Northrop Frye made long ago in his *Anatomy of Criticism* is helpful here. The Bible, said Frye, can be viewed from an Aristotelian viewpoint "as a single form" or from a Longinian point of view "as a series of ecstatic moments or points of expanding apprehension" (326).

The narrative structure of the Gospels encourages the second approach, but behind the self-contained units we can see interconnections. These interconnections will be more apparent if we are aware that the diverse material in the Gospels falls mainly into four categories: what Jesus did, what Jesus taught, the responses of people to Jesus (with the growing faith of the disciples and growing hostility of the religious establishment constituting two prominent motifs), and Jesus' dialogues, debates, and encounters (a hybrid between action and teaching).

One further thing strikes us as odd about the Gospels: they do not give a single story of Jesus but four complementary stories. The total effect has been described in terms of an analogy to television sports coverage:

> In these replays the action can be dramatically slowed down so that one is able to see much more than one was able to see in the action as it actually occurred. If one is given the full treatment—close-up, slow-action, forward-and-reverse, split-screen, the same scene from several perspectives, and with the verbal commentary and interpretation of an expert superimposed—one has a fair analogy of what the evangelists do. . . . One might add to the significance of the analogy by pointing out that the true significance of certain plays can only be known after the game is over. (Hagner 34)

Individual Gospels have their own characteristic ideas, images, settings, and emphases, while sharing a common core of material. As for alleged discrepancies among the accounts, we must remember not only that the story is told from four different perspectives, but also that as a traveling teacher and miracle worker Jesus said and did similar things in a series of different places. Even the parables may have been related differently as Jesus spoke to different audiences.

The book of Acts is as much a mingling of the familiar and unique as the Gospels are. Its genres are familiar, dominated by narrative, drama, and oratory. The story has all the narrative features and excitement of an adventure story, replete with voyages, arrests, riots, rescues, persecution, escapes. The progressive structure of this episodic plot is a narrative structure, as the Christian movement expands in waves outward from Jerusalem to Rome. The book even has its own repeated type scene: Christian leaders arise and preach the Gospel; God performs mighty acts through them; listeners are converted and added to the church; opponents begin to persecute the Christian leaders; God intervenes to rescue the leaders or otherwise protect the church.

Along with these familiar narrative features we find familiar archetypes: imprisonment, attack, rescue, journey, quest, trial, sea voyage, city. With literature we expect to find living situations, not abstract data, and again the book of Acts meets our expectations. It is not an ecclesiastical history filled with names and dates but rather a gallery of character portraits and memorable events.

But along with these conventional literary features we find much that is unusual. The very title of the book suggests its lack of a single protagonist. The affinities of the book with epic are well known, but no other epic has as an epic protagonist either a community (in Acts it is the Christian movement) or the Holy Spirit. At many points in Acts we are reminded of biography (Peter dominates the first half of the book and Paul the second half), but the book of Acts as a whole is not biographical.

If the form of the book possesses unique characteristics, so does the content. The book of Acts is filled with unique, once-only events, different from the more universal or representative occurrences that most literary narratives present. The history of the early church by eyewitnesses is a unique subject for a story, lending a distinctive flavor to the book.

If the Gospels and the book of Acts thus show a mixture of convention and innovation, so do the Epistles. They possess many of the same features that other letters of the Greco-Roman world do (Doty). They convey information and maintain personal acquaintance. They begin with a salutation (sender, addressee, greeting), devote most of the space to the body, and end with greetings and final wishes. Some are addressed to individuals, while others are "open letters" to groups. Like letters in general, they are occasional in nature and refer to implied social contexts or the specific arguments of opponents or supporters.

But other features depart from prevailing conventions of letter writing. The content of the Epistles is almost completely theological and moral (and in this sense the Epistles are reminiscent of the Gospels). The conventional Greek formula for the salutation ("Greetings!") becomes the theologically charged "grace and peace." The Epistles have an oral cast and are, in fact, homiletic and oratorical in tone and style. Most innovative of all are two additions to the list of usual components in the tradition of Greek letter writing, namely, a section of thanksgiving (a liturgically formulated statement of thanks and praise for spiritual blessings) and a section of *paraenesis* (lists of proverbial wisdom, of vices and virtues, of commands—in each case on moral issues).

When we turn to the book of Revelation, we again find much that is familiar—epic qualities, visions of another world, prophecies of future events, satire, hymns, dramatic pageants, even epistles. But the combination of these ingredients is unexpected, their arrangement exceedingly mixed, and their focus Christocentric in a way that is unmatched in parallel writings.

Qualities of Discourse

Something needs to be said, finally, about what can loosely be called the quality of discourse in the New Testament. The New Testament is a very poetic book, for example. Jesus is one of the world's best-known poets. He spoke naturally in image and metaphor. Much of what he said is so rhythmic that it can be printed in the form of Hebrew parallelism. While the Epistles are less consistently poetic, figurative language and parallel clauses abound there, too. The poetic element in the Epistles is enhanced by interspersed lyrics and liturgical fragments (for examples, see Ryken, *Words of Life* 107–16). The book of Revelation is essentially poetic in the sense that it uses figurative images to symbolize spiritual realities.

New Testament discourse is also very aphoristic or proverbial. The sayings of Jesus possess this quality in abundance (Tannehill), appearing in both his conversations with people and his discourses (where they sometimes carry the whole discourse, as in the famous beatitudes). Furthermore, one of the narrative subtypes in the Gospels is the pronouncement story, in which an event is paired with a proverb. Many of Jesus' parables are likewise accompanied by aphorisms. This same tendency toward aphorism is found in the Epistles and the Apocalypse.

Furthermore, the New Testament is a thoroughly dramatic book. If we open randomly to the Gospels, for example, we are likely to find directly quoted dialogue and characters encountering each other in a definite setting, sometimes with accompanying "stage directions" about gestures, entrances, and exits. Nearly 75 percent of the book of Acts consists of speeches (dialogues, sermons, addresses, courtroom defenses), with accompanying attention to the setting, circumstances, and audience. And the book of Revelation is built so thoroughly around dramatized scenes and pageants that it is plausible to believe that the writer adapted conventions from classical drama for an original audience accustomed to the theater (Bowman).

An underlying symbolism is also evident throughout the New Testament. On one level, no matter where we are in the New Testament, we find ourselves rooted in a physical world of sowing and baking, light and darkness, eating and drinking. It is a world that is entirely tangible. But by some mysterious transformation these realistic images from everyday life point beyond themselves to spiritual realities. The sensory world continuously opens into a spiritual world. The New Testament is preeminently a literature of "second meanings" in which there is almost always more than meets the senses (on symbolism as a feature of New Testament discourse, see the three relevant essays in Knight).

Another feature of New Testament discourse is its subversive nature, often expressed in a rhetoric of paradox. Jesus himself announced the coming of a new age in which the first are last and the last first, in which to lose one's life is to gain it, in which grace accounts for everything and human notions of merit count for nothing. The rhetoric of the Epistles is similar, as we are told, for example, that God "chose what is foolish in the world to shame the wise" (1 Cor. 1:27). At nearly every turn we catch a similar flavor of earthly values reversed and the invisible spiritual world declared to be more important than the ordinary world of human preoccupations.

The New Testament is thus a revolutionary book that announces a reversal of values and lifestyle. Its tone is everywhere one of exuberance and confidence. The writers are convinced that they are dealing with world-changing events and truths. *New* is one of the charged words of the New Testament. The world of the New Testament, writes Erich Auerbach, is on the one hand entirely real and average, but on the other hand it is a world that is "shaken in its very foundations, is transforming and renewing itself before our eyes" (43). G. Wilson Knight notes a similar tone, commenting, for example, that the apostle Paul in his writings "works for one end only: he would have all men see and enter the radiance and the glory that awaits their birth in Christ" (144).

As the New Testament unfolds, the scope of this transformation keeps expanding. In the Gospels we see the events that are themselves epoch making, along with their impact in the lives of individuals. In the book of Acts and the Epistles the transformation is more communal as it engulfs the church. The Apocalypse broadens the scope still more, as the whole cosmos is transformed by the power of Christ.

Linked with this conviction that the world is being transformed is the New Testament assumption that it is the fulfillment or completion of what preceded it in the Old Testament era. The New Testament is not a self-contained volume. It has a retrospective orientation that continually asks us to look backward to the Old Testament, whose events, prophecies, and rituals are regularly viewed as premonitions that have now come to fulfillment. The New Testament presupposes the Old Testament as a condition of understanding it. In the words of Northrop Frye, New Testament references to the Old "extend over every book—not impossibly every passage—in the New Testament; and some New Testament books . . . are a dense mass of such allusions, often with direct or oblique quotations" (79).

Finally, the rhetoric of the New Testament incorporates a frequent note of mystery. Much remains elusive as we read. We move between mingled clarity and mystery. Loose ends remain as we mull over what we have read. We often find ourselves needing the help of traditional interpretations of difficult material.

Reading the New Testament

The New Testament is a unique anthology of writings that calls for its own ways of reading. The big pattern is a narrative pattern, and we should above all read the New Testament as telling the story of Jesus and his followers. Even the Epistles contribute to this story by showing us the life and thought of the early churches. The book of Revelation contains the concluding chapters in the story and brings it to definitive closure.

With this big narrative pattern as the context, reading the New Testament requires constant alertness because of its piecemeal organization. Individual books are a mixture of genres and styles. Even the narrative parts show a tendency toward small, self-contained units. Reading the New Testament does not allow us to settle down comfortably with a steady stream of similar material. Instead it offers us a kaleidoscope of shifting units. The New Testament is in this sense a very demanding book to read.

But there are reassuring elements to counterbalance our potential bewilderment. The main focus is always in view, consisting of the person and work of Jesus and what those mean in the life of the individual believer, the believing community, and ultimately the cosmos. The claims of Jesus and the implications of following or rejecting him are the materials from which the mosaic of the New Testament is built. Another common theme is the need to live simultaneously in two worlds—the tangible world of everyday reality and the unseen spiritual world.

The New Testament is a paradoxical book that invites multiple levels of reading. It has a surface simplicity that makes it akin to folk literature. At the level of individual units anyone can catch the plot line, the characters, the big theological ideas, and the morality. At a more sophisticated level we start to piece together the fragments into bigger patterns. We also begin to sense nuances of meaning beneath the ostensibly simple surface. At yet another level we can see the artistry of the individual books and of the individual passages within them.

WORKS CITED

Auerbach, Erich. *Mimesis: The Representation of Reality in Western Literature.* Trans. Willard R. Trask. Princeton: Princeton UP, 1953.

Augustine. *Confessions* and *On Christian Doctrine. Great Books of the Western World.* Ed. Robert M. Hutchins. Vol. 18. Chicago: Encyclopaedia Britannica, 1952.

Bailey, Kenneth E. *Poet and Peasant: A Literary Cultural Approach to the Parables in Luke.* Grand Rapids: Eerdmans, 1976.

Bowman, John W. "The Revelation to John: Its Dramatic Structure and Message." *Interpretation* 9 (1955): 436–53.

Corn, Alfred, ed. *Incarnation: Contemporary Writers on the New Testament.* New York: Viking, 1990.

Dibelius, Martin. *From Tradition to Gospel.* New York: Scribner, 1935.

Dodd, C. H. *About the Gospels.* Cambridge: Cambridge UP, 1950.

Doty, William G. *Letters in Primitive Christianity.* Philadelphia: Fortress, 1973.

Farrer, Austin. *A Rebirth of Images: The Making of St. John's Apocalypse.* 1949. Rpt. Gloucester, Mass.: Peter Smith, 1970.

Frye, Northrop. *Anatomy of Criticism.* Princeton: Princeton UP, 1957.

———. *The Great Code: The Bible and Literature.* New York: Harcourt, 1982.

Hagner, Donald A. "Interpreting the Gospels: The Landscape and the Quest." *Journal of the Evangelical Theological Society* 24 (1981): 23–37.

Kennedy, George A. *New Testament Interpretation Through Rhetorical Criticism.* Chapel Hill: University of North Carolina Press, 1984.

Knight, G. Wilson. *The Christian Renaissance.* London: Methuen, 1962.

Lewis, C. S. "Introduction" to *Letters to Young Churches,* by J. B. Philips. New York: Macmillan, 1947. vii-x.

Lind, Nils Wilhelm. *Chiasmus in the New Testament.* Chapel Hill: University of North Carolina Press, 1942.

Pervo, Richard. *Profit With Delight: The Literary Genre of the Acts of the Apostles.* Philadelphia: Fortress, 1987.

Ryken, Leland. *How to Read the Bible as Literature.* Grand Rapids: Zondervan, 1984.

———. *The New Testament in Literary Criticism.* New York: Ungar, 1984.

———. *Words of Life: A Literary Introduction to the New Testament.* Grand Rapids: Baker, 1987.

Shaffer, E. S. *"Kubla Khan" and the Fall of Jerusalem.* Cambridge: Cambridge UP, 1975.

Talbert, Charles H. *What Is a Gospel? The Genre of the Canonical Gospels.* Philadelphia: Fortress, 1977.

Tannehill, Robert C. *The Word of His Mouth: Forceful and Imaginative Language in Synoptic Sayings.* Philadelphia: Fortress, 1975.

Tolbert, Mary Ann. *Sowing the Gospel: Mark's World in Literary-Historical Perspective.* Minneapolis: Fortress, 1989.

Wilder, Amos N. *Early Christian Rhetoric: The Language of the Gospels.* Cambridge, Mass.: Harvard UP, 1971.

CHAPTER 27

Matthew

Amberys R. Whittle
Georgia Southern University

The Genesis-like opening verses of the gospel of John led Northrop Frye to think that the gospel of John was intended to appear as the initial book of the New Testament (207), but in fact the gospel of Matthew has served the purpose very well. As the gateway to the New Testament, Matthew's gospel stresses Christ as the promised Messiah and King.

This gospel is memorable for the genealogy and infancy narrative of its first two chapters, its matchless rendition of the Sermon on the Mount, and the Olivet Discourse with its prophecy of the end of time and the last judgment. Matthew has also been the church's major gospel for purposes of teaching because of the magnificent discourses it contains.

Unity and Structure

Scholars have long divided Matthew's gospel into units ranging in number from three (e.g., Kingsbury, *Matthew as Story* 40–42) to five (Perkins 210) to as many as thirteen (Harris 274). David Bauer's book *The Structure of Matthew's Gospel* summarizes many of these analyses.

The three-part structure sees a division at 4:17 (immediately after the temptation in the wilderness and at the beginning of Jesus' ministry) and at 16:21 (after Peter's recognition that Jesus is "the Christ" and Jesus' prophecy of his death, and shortly before the Transfiguration). These divisions are marked by the phrase "From that time Jesus began. . . ." As Fujita explains, this particular analysis "has the advantage of underscoring the passion, death, and resurrection of Jesus—undoubtedly the culmination of Jesus' career. The theme of Jesus the Messiah emerges more clearly from this view as well" (130).

The most obvious facet of the book's organization is that it alternates between sections of narrative and sections of discourse. Matthew begins with the story of Jesus' birth and childhood (chs. 1–2) and ends with his death and resurrection (chs. 26–28). The five blocks of discourses, each followed by a variation on the statement "and when Jesus finished these sayings. . . ," include the Sermon on the Mount (chs. 5–7), the missionary discourse (9:35–10:42), the parables (13:1–52), the duties of discipleship (ch. 18), and the eschatological discourse familiarly known as the Olivet Discourse (chs. 23–25).

Ramsay comments that "probably from the first century to the twentieth, students have memorized the outline of Matthew by counting off the five discourses on the fingers of one hand" (quoted in Ryken, *The New Testament* 244). While some have seen the discourses as interrupting the narrative that contains them, Kingsbury has argued that

> each speech can be seen to be appropriately situated within the story's plot. . . . Intended to be heard and internalized, the great speeches of Jesus have as their chief purpose to bring the life of the disciple, or the implied reader, into conformity with the shape of Jesus' own life, which is one of single-hearted devotion toward God and loving service toward the neighbor. (*Matthew as Story* 113)

It is commonly suggested that the five discourses in Matthew are intended to parallel the first five books of the Bible, traditionally ascribed to Moses, and that the Sermon on the Mount in particular presents Jesus as a new Moses, giving a "new law" or final interpretation of the law. But as Perkins has observed, "Jesus is greater than Moses. He does not give Torah but embodies the Wisdom of God, which is Torah in its most primordial and cosmic form" (211). Via perhaps resolves some of these issues with his suggestion that "Matthew foregrounds the three-fold Christological structure and backgrounds the five-fold legal one. . . . In the distant past God spoke in prophets . . . and law. . . . The real intention of the law has been brought to light . . . in Jesus" (quoted in Ryken, *New Testament* 244).

The question of the audience for which Matthew intended his gospel is easily resolved. The book is addressed to a multiple audience—the disciples, new Christians to whom the gospel was read, and readers of any subsequent time. In each case the gospel's main purpose is the same: to prove that Jesus Christ was the long-promised Messiah.

The disciples are usually the immediate audience whom Jesus addresses in his discourses. Certainly the disciples as Matthew portrays them are more capable of learning from Jesus' teaching than they are in Mark's gospel. But as Kingsbury has observed, in this gospel Jesus often "speaks past" his immediate audience (*Matthew as Story* 107). In fact, Matthew is the only gospel to mention the "Church" (Harris 281). There is even a passage that explains how the church as a body of followers is to deal with unresolved conflict among its members (18:15–18).

The rhetorical aspects of this gospel were rightly emphasized in Pasolini's 1964 classic movie "The Gospel According to St. Matthew." By using a variety of camera angles and close-ups, the movie presents a preaching Jesus whose compassionate call to sinners is balanced by his powerful denunciation of those who oppose his mission.

The New Testament gospels are actually composed of many subgenres, such as sayings, miracle stories, parables, teachings, and many more. Despite these subgenres, which create an episodic impression, the gospel writers were able to unify their works primarily by keeping the principal focus on the ministry, death, and resurrection of Jesus.

Since Jesus' ministry involved considerable travel in Palestine (especially in Galilee, Samaria, Judea, and Perea), and since the Gospels reveal Jesus as one who journeyed from heaven to earth, ascended to heaven, and will return again to earth, the journey motif is especially important in Matthew. It is one of the chief means by which the gospel is unified and perhaps explains why an early name for Christianity was the "Way"—a metaphor for both the journey of life and the manner of living that Christ urged. The journey, of course, is one of the great archetypes of literature, from Homer's *Odyssey* through Bunyan's *Pilgrim's Progress* to Bellow's *Henderson the Rain King.*

From the beginning of his ministry in Galilee until his death, Jesus traveled to bring the message that the kingdom of heaven "is at hand" (in his person) and "to come" (at the "last day"). His journey also incorporates the motif of the quest, since his ultimate goal is the salvation of humankind. The action of Matthew's gospel develops during the journey toward a seemingly tragic climax in Jerusalem as Jesus confronts the religious and political authorities there.

Rhoads and Michie's comment about Mark's gospel that "there is a sense in which the primary opponent becomes death itself" (100) is also true of Matthew. During the Passion section of the story, Jesus takes on the archetypal role of the suffering servant (Ryken, *Literature* 290). The ultimate outcome of the story, however, is not tragic but rather "good news" because of Jesus' resurrection, which gives the gospel a "comic" plot like that of the Bible as a whole.

Literary Techniques

In addition to unifying his story around the journey motif, Matthew employs such literary devices as irony, paradox, and inversion. The controlling irony is perhaps the way in which the Son of God came into the world only to be rejected by those to whom he had been sent, including the religious establishment of the day. That irony is deepened by Jesus' being accepted by only a few of the "lost sheep of the house of Israel," whereas the Gentiles were more responsive to him. Furthermore, at the heart of the gospel and the Christian faith itself is a great paradox—the Son of God nailed to the cross like a criminal.

Inversion is also prevalent in this gospel, as it is in the Bible's view of life more generally. Put quite simply, from God's perspective the world has the wrong expectations and values, especially with its stress on power and materialism. Old Testament examples of such inversion include the choosing of Saul and David over more "likely" candidates for the throne. In the Gospels, Christ is born in a manger instead of a palace, the Messiah turns out to be the "prince of peace" instead of a conquering warrior-king, and emphasis is placed on the value of the meek and the poor, as well as women and children.

Further examples of ironic inversion include the choice of the disciples, most of whom were quite ordinary men, the difficulty for the rich to enter into the kingdom of heaven, and the concept that "many that are first will be last and the last first" (19:30). ("Whoever would be great among you must be your servant" [20:26].) Inversion is also reflected in the radical ethics of the Sermon on the Mount, where we are told that we must love our enemies, that it is virtuous to turn the other cheek when struck, and that we should not resist evil, even when provoked, for the sake of the soul.

Symbolism also abounds in this gospel. Kingsbury notes examples of "place symbolism" (*Matthew* 19–20), especially the mountain (e.g., the Transfiguration scene), Jerusalem (where Jesus' chief enemies are found), and the temple (which, because it has been defiled by the present religious leaders, will be replaced by the risen Christ). Matthew has Jesus deliver his most famous sermon on a mountain rather than on a plain (as in Luke), perhaps as a parallel to the Exodus experience on Mount Sinai.

Image patterns also figure prominently in Matthew. Particularly important is the imagery of judgment, especially trees, fruits, fire, and the gathering and burning of chaff. Jesus declares, for example, that "every tree that does not bear good fruit is cut down and thrown into the fire" (7:19). In the parable of the weeds in the wheat, the owner of the field tells his reapers, "Gather the weeds first and bind them in bundles to be burned, but gather the wheat into my barn" (13:30). Several times Jesus tells how in the punishment to come "men will weep and gnash their teeth" (e.g., 22:13). Matthew has emphasized this aspect of his story to reflect his theology, which serves to alert us to the fact that each of the gospels tells the story of Jesus and his teaching from an interpretive angle. Luke's gospel, by comparison, places little emphasis on punishment.

Images relating to hearing and seeing are also important in this gospel. For example, when the disciples ask Jesus why he speaks to the people only in parables, he answers, "Because seeing they do not see, and hearing they do not hear, nor do they understand. . . . But blessed are your eyes, for they see, and your ears, for they hear" (13:13, 16). Jesus' quotation from Isaiah here (Isa. 6:9–10) makes it clear that spiritual blindness and deafness are a willful thing. Furthermore, there is an implication in Matthew that a reader who is unsympathetic to Christ's message will not hear, that is, understand it. The broader principle is that in Matthew's gospel, as in the others, metaphor and symbol are the customary means for revealing spiritual reality.

The Discourses of Jesus

The Gospels are encyclopedic genres. Narrative is the big pattern, but within that framework as much space is given to discourse material as to action or plot.

Matthew's hero, Jesus, proves a master of literary expression. He was a great teacher, not only because he had an important message to deliver to the people, but also because he knew how to present truth in a mode that makes a vivid impression on the imagination. We should note in passing that the social context of these discourses was an oral one. Jesus apparently wrote nothing.

His hearers were ordinary people. On one level, therefore, his discourses and parables were easy to grasp. His parables and sayings, frequently anecdotal, appeal to the folk imagination as it exists at any time and place.

It is also apparent that Jesus knew the difference between "telling" and "showing." In order to make his ideas forceful, he drew striking word pictures with images that cling to the memory. For example, he explains, "When you give alms, sound no trumpet before you, as the hypocrites do in the synagogues and in the streets, that they may be praised by men" (6:2). The hyperbole here renders hypocrisy forever memorable. Or who can forget the character sketch of the hypocrite who magnifies another's faults while remaining blind to his own: "Why do you see the speck that is in your brother's eye, but do not notice the log that is in your own eye?" (7:3). Another hyperbole concerns spiritual priorities: "And if your right eye causes you to sin, pluck it out and throw it away; it is better that you lose one of your members than that your whole body be thrown into hell" (5:29). Here is the subversive rhetoric of Jesus that is a hallmark of the Gospels.

Jesus is equally adept with illuminating comparisons. In the Sermon on the Mount, he calls his followers "the salt of the earth" and "the light of the world" and warns those who would live a spiritual life, "Do not be anxious about your life. . . . And why are you anxious about clothing? Consider the lilies of the field, how they grow; they neither toil nor spin; yet I tell you, even Solomon in all his glory was not arrayed like one of these" (6:25, 28–29). Such passages reveal not only an astonishing poetic gift but also a heightened sensitivity to the beauty of the world.

Jesus also had at his disposal more elaborate methods of teaching that reveal an even more sophisticated artistry. The tightly balanced parallel structure in the Beatitudes is a good example. As Leland Ryken has pointed out, what emerges from the Beatitudes is an example of an ancient genre known as "the character," in this case a portrait of the follower of Jesus (*Words of Life* 120), and the genre of the beatitude itself is of distinguished literary ancestry. The elaborate parallelism of the passage renders it poetic.

Similar subtlety of patterning is evident from the way in which the parables in Matthew relate to the broader narrative. Mary Ann Tolbert has demonstrated the extent to which selected parables in Mark's gospel function as plot synopses with foreshadowing effect (125). The same is true in Matthew. The parable of the sower illustrates the results of Jesus' message in the story world of Matthew, as does the parable of the wicked tenants, which even predicts Jesus' crucifixion. Jesus' stories thus not only explain his message to his immediate audience of disciples and hearers but also signal to the reader the outcome of the narrative being read.

Characters

Characterization in Matthew is quite different from what we find in Western literature of the past several hundred years. Modern writers devote a good many words to the physical traits of the characters—traits that may indeed suggest something of their inner natures. By contrast, Matthew is virtually silent about the physical appearance of his characters, with the exception of a few suggestive words about the diet and dress of John the Baptist (though even here we are told nothing of the *personal* appearance of John). Not even Jesus, the hero of the book, is described physically.

The gospel writers were able to make us imagine the characters by suggesting *spiritual* traits instead of physical ones, primarily by careful selection of details relating to action and speech. In the case of Jesus, balance and realism are achieved by presenting not only a compassionate healer and savior but also one capable of displays of righteous indignation, as when Jesus chases the money-changers from the temple.

Matthew contains a number of characters whose essential traits are rendered briefly but so vividly that they forever remain in our imagination. They range from Herod early in the gospel to Pilate near the end. Herod schemes above all else to maintain worldly power, trying to deceive the wise men and slaughtering innocent children in the process. Pilate gives some indication of being a fair man, but his crafty pragmatism causes him to wash his hands of the matter of Jesus' death while carrying out the will of the people. These two are typical of Matthew's characters, who are at once figures from history and universal types.

The primitive simplicity of John the Baptist, "the lamp and not the light" (Culpepper 133), dressed in animal skins, contrasts with the formality of official Judaism. This fearless denouncer of corruption "prepares the way of the Lord" by calling the people to repentance. His unwillingness to compromise with evil eventually leads to his death, his head being served on a platter as reward for a young woman's dance. This horribly ironic foreshadowing of Jesus' own fate highlights an important literary feature of the Gospels—the cruelty and tragedy that we see displayed.

Then there is Peter, "the Rock," who walks on water in imitation of Jesus until his faith fails, who is so carried away with enthusiasm at the Transfiguration that he misses the point of it, who emphatically denies that he will ever deny his Master and then does so extravagantly, who weeps bitterly in the wake of his denial. These and others, such as the Canaanite woman whose faith and wit Jesus admires and rewards, ring true to human nature and add much to the literary realism of this gospel.

The Contending Forces and the Dynamics of Plot

The heart of plot is conflict. Matthew's gospel abounds with it. After an opening genealogy that connects Jesus to the Patriarchs (thereby showing that history reflects God's purpose), the alternating blocks of narrative and discourse both serve to advance the plot conflict. First John and then Jesus denounce the Pharisees, scribes, Sadducees, and "elders of the people." In his first discourse (the Sermon on the Mount), Jesus declares, "Unless your righteousness exceeds that of the scribes and Pharisees, you will never enter the kingdom of heaven" (5:20). The religious leaders respond by plotting to entrap Jesus, to arrest him, and to kill him. They even attribute his power to the devil. As Jesus' ministry continues, the conflict between these forces intensifies—a conflict between the "vipers" (a term used originally by John and then by Jesus) and the "fishers" of souls (Jesus and his disciples).

What is the exact nature of the conflict? Although Jesus claims from the start that his mission is to seek the "lost sheep of the house of Israel" (15:24) (Matthew's gospel is the most Jewish of the four Gospels), he sets himself against its religious leaders. The core of his antagonism is expressed in this rebuke: "You shut the kingdom of heaven against men; for you neither enter yourselves, nor allow those who would enter to go in" (23:13). These leaders have forgotten the spirit of true religion and "neglected the weightier matters of the law, justice and mercy and faith" (23:23). Satire is pervasive in Matthew's gospel (Boonstra).

Increasingly the temple is a symbol of all that is wrong with Judaism as Jesus found it. Jesus tries to cleanse it, foretells its destruction, and compares his resurrected body to a rebuilt temple. He declares, "I tell you, something greater than the temple is here" (12:6). At his death on the cross, the curtain of the temple was torn in two, symbolizing humankind's union with God through Christ alone.

The conflict in Matthew is thus between Jesus and what the temple symbolizes. The Transfiguration scene, about halfway through the gospel, is a revelation (epiphany) of the holiness and supremacy of Jesus, who will replace the temple. Eventually Jesus turns to the Gentiles who believe in him (foreshadowed in his praise of the faith of both the centurion in Capernaum and the Canaanite woman), telling his opponents, "The kingdom of God will be taken away from you and given to a nation producing the fruits of it" (21:43). The Gospels are proclamations of the Christ who announces humanity's new and very different relationship to God, with that very newness producing conflict.

Were it not for a miraculous event—the Resurrection—this conflict in

Matthew would end in tragedy, as the dynamics of the narrative just described hint. The plot is foreshadowed subtly in the opening genealogy, consisting of three sets of fourteen generations running from Abraham to David (greatness), to the Exile (humiliation), to the birth of Christ (greatness restored). The defining event within the gospel proper is the attempt of Herod to destroy the newly born king of the Jews, later echoed in Satan's offer of the kingdoms of the world and their power, an offer that if accepted would convert Jesus to a Herod figure.

The complication of the plot occurs in chapter 9, where the scribes say that Jesus blasphemes and the Pharisees attribute his power to the prince of demons. Jesus' opponents mistake the light for darkness. The crisis occurs in chapter 26 with the conspiracy among the chief priests, elders of the people, and the high priest "to arrest Jesus by stealth and kill him" (v. 4). The logical outcome of the action is the Crucifixion, but the curtain does not fall here. The turning point may be said to be the resurrection of Jesus, and the resolution consists of the commissioning of the disciples to spread Christ's message into the entire world.

The Matter in Question

Perhaps in no other literary work do questions function so importantly as they do in the gospel of Matthew. These questions raise some of the most significant issues of the book. They also create an air of suspense and lead the reader to provide his or her own answers to the questions. The most important question is, Who is Jesus? The disciples ask, "What sort of man is this, that even winds and sea obey him?" (8:27). From prison John inquires, "Are you he who is to come?" (11:3). Jesus asks his disciples, "Who do men say that the Son of man is?" (16:13). And again, "Who is my mother, and who are my brothers?" (12:48).

Elsewhere the questions focus on the heavenly kingdom—its value, its nature, and the way to enter it. The rich young man wants to know, "What good deed must I do, to have eternal life?" (19:16). Jesus asks regarding it, "What will it profit a man, if he gains the whole world and forfeits his life?" (16:26). The disciples ask, "Who is the greatest in the kingdom of heaven?" (18:1).

Questions serve to advance the plot conflict. The Pharisees ask Jesus questions "to entangle him in his talk." They ask, "Is it lawful to pay taxes to Caesar, or not?" (22:17). "Which is the great commandment in the law?" (v. 36). They also want to know why Jesus eats with tax collectors and sinners. When Judas appears for the purpose of betraying Jesus, Jesus inquires, "Friend, why are you here?" (26:50). Pilate interrogates Jesus: "Are you the King of the Jews?" Jesus responds, "You have said so" (27:11), confirming a modern linguistic discovery that our answers flow from our questions. These questions in the gospel help create considerable emotional intensity and a marked tone of spiritual urgency.

The Plot in Miniature

Chapter 12 of the gospel of Matthew epitomizes the gospel as a whole, especially the conflict between the "brood of vipers" (the scribes and Pharisees) and Jesus. Its literary methods include the mingling of narrative and discourse, allusion, foreshadowing, metaphoric language, and of course incessant questioning.

The very content of the chapter demonstrates the encyclopedic mixture of material that makes up the gospel of Matthew. The chapter opens with two brief stories of controversy, the first involving the disciples' foraging for grain on the Sabbath and the second recounting Jesus' healing on the Sabbath. A generalized comment about Jesus' healing ministry is then accompanied by the writer's assertion that Jesus fulfills "what was spoken by the prophet Isaiah" (12:17). Narrative then gives way to discourse as Jesus replies to promptings from the hostile scribes and Pharisees.

We find here in microcosm what the gospel as a whole repeatedly presents. Most prominent of all is the plot conflict between Jesus and his adversaries. This plot is advanced partly by the familiar rhetoric of interrogation. When confronted with the Pharisees' complaint about the disciples' behavior, Jesus asks, "Have you not read what David did when he was hungry? . . . Or have you not read in the law. . . ?" (12:3, 5). When asked, "Is it lawful to heal on the sabbath?" (v. 10), Jesus counters with a question of his own: "What man of you, if he has one sheep and it falls into a pit on the sabbath, will not lay hold of it and lift it out?" (v. 11). Later the people ask, "Can this be the Son of David?" (v. 23). And Jesus' subsequent discourse features still more questions.

In the discourses that fill the second half of the chapter, Jesus uses other techniques that characterize Matthew's gospel. He alludes to David, to the Old Testament Law, to Jonah, to Solomon. We find metaphor when he compares people to houses, human behavior to the fruit of a tree and to treasure, and his followers to sisters and brothers. The parabolic method is prominent, as Jesus tells metaphoric stories of binding a strong man to plunder his house and of an unclean spirit that leaves a man and then reinhabits him. And of course Jesus' gift for aphorism is apparent: "the tree is known by its fruit" (12:33); "the Son of man is lord of the sabbath" (v. 8); "every kingdom divided against itself is laid waste" (v. 25).

The chapter also echoes other parts of the gospel. In keeping with the prominence of the temple in Matthew, Jesus claims, "Something greater than the temple is here" (12:6). In keeping with Matthew's main theme, Jesus is presented as the culmination of the Old Testament—as the one who fulfills prophecy, who is greater than Jonah and Solomon, as the Son of David. Underlying all of these allusions is the implied superiority of Jesus to the traditions of Israel. Foreshadowing also appears, as the story of Jesus' coming death and resurrection is hinted at in the prediction that Jesus will be "three days and three nights in the heart of the earth" (v. 40).

This analysis shows why the gospel of Matthew invites a literary approach and why a traditional approach is inadequate. The gospel does, indeed, teach about Jesus. But it does so by literary means, including narrative, rhetorical devices, and metaphor. The story that Matthew tells, moreover, is not a series of self-contained units but a coherent whole. The final effect is to unfold to the discerning reader the meaning of who Jesus is and what he taught.

WORKS CITED

Bauer, David R. *The Structure of Matthew's Gospel.* Sheffield: Almond, 1988.

Boonstra, Harry. "Satire in Matthew." *Christianity and Literature* 29, no. 4 (1980): 32–45.

Culpepper, R. Alan. *Anatomy of the Fourth Gospel.* Philadelphia: Fortress, 1983.

Frye, Northrop. *The Great Code: The Bible and Literature.* New York: Harcourt, 1982.

Fujita, Neil S. *Introducing the Bible.* New York: Paulist, 1981.

Harris, Stephen L. *Understanding the Bible.* 2d ed. Mountain View, Calif.: Mayfield, 1985.

Kingsbury, Jack Dean. *Matthew.* Philadelphia: Fortress, 1977.

———. *Matthew as Story.* 2d ed. Philadelphia: Fortress, 1988.

Perkins, Pheme. *Reading the New Testament.* New York: Paulist, 1978.

Rhoads, David, and Donald Michie. *Mark as Story.* Philadelphia: Fortress, 1982.

Ryken, Leland. *The Literature of the Bible.* Grand Rapids: Zondervan, 1974.

———. *Words of Life: A Literary Introduction to the New Testament.* Grand Rapids: Baker, 1987.

Ryken, Leland. *The New Testament in Literary Criticism.* New York: Ungar, 1984.

Tolbert, Mary Ann. *Sowing the Gospel: Mark's World in Literary-Historical Perspective.* Minneapolis: Fortress, 1989.

CHAPTER 28

Mark

John H. Augustine
Pierson College, Yale University

Mark's historical narrative links together a series of brief stories in a broad mosaic, arranged generally by varying geographical settings. Moving rapidly from one event to another in a paratactic style, the narrative begins with the baptism of Jesus by John the Baptist and continues with a varied ministry of miraculous deeds and teaching in Galilee. A number of journeys outside Galilee end with a journey to Jerusalem that culminates in a final series of events in Jerusalem, including Jesus' entry upon a colt into the holy city, the cleansing of the temple, the confrontation in the treasury, and the passion. The narrative traces a series of conflicts between Jesus and his opponents, including Satan, demons, Jewish authorities, and even the disciples who take the role of enemies on occasion (Kingsbury). These conflicts often center around the nature of Jesus' identity.

The episodic plot depicts the protagonist, Jesus, struggling to initiate his followers into the mysteries of the kingdom of God. An examination of one aspect of Mark's thematic structure—that of Jesus' initiation of the disciples—within the context of a broader discussion of certain literary elements in Mark will demonstrate one type of literary approach to Mark's gospel. An analysis of certain key literary elements in the text itself and a consideration of its rhetorical strategies will be followed by a discussion of the motif of the disciples' initiation in Mark.

Literary Form

A literary genre provides a set of expectations that shape a reader's interpretation of a text. A number of literary critics have attempted to describe the genre of the gospel in terms of traditional literal categories. Like a biography, Mark's gospel describes events in the life of Jesus, but, unlike a biography, which lists chronological events in a subject's life, this gospel does not primarily describe the course of Jesus' life from birth to death; instead, Mark's narrative alters this format by paying more attention to the various responses of Jesus to the disciples, religious authorities, and the crowds (Talbert). Gilbert Bilezikian's *Liberated Gospel,* still the finest close reading of Mark as a literary work, compares the gospel of Mark to the genre of Greek tragedy because it follows the Aristotelian pattern of complication–crisis–denouement.

Many literary critics have recently attempted to show that the gospel of Mark represents a new or unique genre. For instance, Werner Kelber claims that the parables in chapter 4 provide what he calls a parabolic hermeneutic (219). Kelber is not referring to parable as a literary form in a historical sense. Rather, he is calling the gospel a parable in the metaphorical sense of a paradoxical, open-ended story that invites an individual reader's participation. Mary Ann Tolbert suggests that an adequate generic formulation of Mark's gospel would combine the elements of aretalogy, with its focus on miracle-working; biography, with its concern for the character of Jesus; and memorabilia, in its depiction of the teaching process between sage and disciple (59).

The Gospels have attracted the most literary critical attention to date of any section of Scripture (Moore). This is particularly true of Mark's gospel. At least since the appearance of Erich Auerbach's discussion of its verisimilitude and Helen Gardner's essay on its poetry, the gospel of Mark has consistently attracted the attention of literary critics. More recently, biblical scholars have paid closer attention to plot development, characterization, point of view, irony, style, genre, and other explicitly literary matters in Mark's gospel (Rhoads and Michie, Wilder).

A number of studies use Mark as a springboard for discussing issues related to literary criticism, particularly narrative criticism. Prominent among these works is Frank Kermode's *Genesis of Secrecy.* Kermode uses Mark to illustrate what he calls the "enigmatic and exclusive character" of narrative (33). He distinguishes between what he calls "outsiders," who read but do not understand, and "insiders," who read and interpret but whose interpretations are manifold.

Point of View

Another literary feature of Mark is the way in which the narrative develops simultaneously at several different levels. Norman Peterson examines the complex, shifting relations between various points of view in Mark that enhance our understanding of Mark as a carefully integrated narrative ("Point of View"). He contrasts the divine and human viewpoints represented in Mark, showing how all events are measured by the ideological standard shared by the narrator and Jesus. The most explicit example of the contrast between viewpoints is contained in Mark 8:31–33. Jesus foretells his coming death and resurrection only to be reprimanded by Peter, who expects the Messiah to triumph over his enemies on this earth. In response Jesus sharply criticizes Peter for thinking in human terms.

Gilbert Bilizekian traces the use of dramatic and nondramatic irony in Mark's gospel (121–24). Akin to a drama of mistaken identity, the gospel shows the Son of God moving unidentified amidst the crowds, his confused disciples, and plotting enemies in a story pervaded with increasing ironic intensity because of this split between appearance and reality. Of course, Mark's dramatic irony reaches its fullest expression in the religious authorities' desire to destroy Jesus, which, when fulfilled, actually accomplishes his mission as Messiah (122).

The writer of Mark's gospel also uses nondramatic irony, which takes the form of Jesus' use of esoteric language, or sayings that are understood by the audience or select characters but not by the characters addressed. Much of Jesus' teaching falls into this category, for he often spoke in parables or employed difficult sayings intended to keep their true meanings partially hidden until after the Resurrection, when proper understanding would become possible. Another form of irony that has been the subject of a number of recent literary treatments of Mark occurs when expectations are overturned or paradoxical sayings are uttered (Donahue, Tannehill). The shattering of expectations about the identity of the Messiah constitutes the greatest irony, but there are other examples of people's changing perceptions of Jesus and of his character as portrayed in his paradoxical teachings. Clean is considered unclean (7:1–23); the first shall be last (10:42–45); the disciples are often blind while the blind see (8:22–26; 10:46–52). The ironic tension and paradox in Mark combine to create a sense of mystery, strangeness, and indirection that has captivated the attention of literary critics, who seek to make sense of it by uncovering its rhetorical strategies.

The Initiation Motif in Mark

The character of Jesus is the primary, heroic figure of Mark's narrative. Mark's prologue (1:1–13) describes the earthly ministry of Jesus, beginning with his baptism (vv. 9–11), and his narrative ends with an account of Jesus' death and resurrection (chs. 14–16). As Donahue observes, Jesus is the constant initiator of action and the subject of the narrative's verbs until his arrest in 14:43. After that point, he is passive and becomes the object of the verbs in Mark (379). In an event fraught with situational irony and paradox, the suffering hero's death on the cross indicates the culmination of Mark's story and is the key to Jesus' identification as the Son of God (15:39). Rather than acting to establish an earthly kingdom as expected by many of his followers, the Son of God conquers his enemies through his death and resurrection in order to establish a spiritual kingdom.

The primary objects of Jesus' attention in his role as initiator of the kingdom of God are his disciples. The puzzling and complex relation between Jesus and the disciples has been the subject of much debate (Tannehill, Tolbert). Perched on the threshold of understanding, yet still mystified by the person of Jesus and by his teaching, the disciples struggle for comprehension. In watching their difficulties in grasping a paradoxical truth, we can identify with their distress and can also share in their dawning sense of understanding.

Initiation, a term most often used in cultural anthropology, describes the process of introducing the initiate into human society and into the world of spiritual and cultural values. It can be used to describe the transition from childhood or adolescence to adulthood, as in Shakespeare's *Henry IV;* entrance into a secret society, as in Mark Twain's *Huckleberry Finn;* or revelation of a new religious order, as recorded in the Gospels. Initiation is characterized by a series of tasks and events that test the initiate's commitment or development; it is often accompanied by a sense of isolation or physical withdrawal, and it usually involves explicit instruction, or in Mircea Eliade's anthropological terms, "indoctrination in secret tribal beliefs" (2). The disciples' series of perplexing encounters with Jesus and his teaching about "the secret of the kingdom of God" (4:11) often appear to follow the initiatory structure but also in some sense to subvert the initiatory pattern.

An important turning point in the narrative, which can be illuminated by seeing it as an initiation story, is the recognition scene at Caesarea Philippi (8:27–30), where Peter, on behalf of Jesus' followers, identifies Jesus as the Messiah. However, Jesus undercuts the importance of the recognition scene when he charges the disciples to keep silent. The initiates have just begun, in Mark's terminology, to understand the unique identity of Jesus and the nature of his mission. And in fact Jesus focuses on increasing their understanding. From that point forward, miraculous healings become rare, and the emphasis in the text falls more on Jesus' teaching to his disciples, often done in private. He is now embarking on the next phase in their initiation.

Jesus' success in miracle working and in debating in the first half of the narrative leads to his apparent failure—in his own death and his followers' misunderstanding—in the second half. Yet, just as Jesus gradually enables the blind man of Bethsaida to regain his sight and to see "everything clearly" (8:22–25), so also Jesus gradually initiates his followers into the secret of the kingdom of God. However, the disciples achieve only an uncompleted initiation at this point, for the narrative concludes abruptly with three women followers of Jesus—Mary Magdalene; Mary, the mother of James; and Salome—fleeing from the empty gravesite trembling and afraid. Although there are indications in the narrative that his followers will eventually see the risen Jesus and comprehend the meaning of his life and death (cf. 9:9–13; 14:26–31; 16:6–7), the indeterminate ending calls attention to the preliminary, initiatory character of the narrative as a whole.

Initiatory Tests of Faith and Recognition

As Werner Kelber points out in *The Oral and Written Gospel,* describing individual character development is not the strength of an orally based narrative such as Mark (69). However, the disciples' developing relationship with Jesus does provide continuity in the Markan narrative. The depiction of the disciples' relations with Jesus at the beginning of Mark is remarkably immediate. There is no lag, it appears, between his introduction to them and his securing of their confidence. Eager yet uncomprehending, the disciples abandon their former ways of life to follow Jesus. The spontaneity of their response is emphasized by the repetition of the word *immediately* in 1:18, 20, as well as by the simple but realistic depictions of their responses: Simon and Andrew drop their nets, James and John desert their father in his boat, and Levi leaves his seat at the tax office to follow Jesus. Jesus' early invitations to follow him, combined with the disciples' obedient responses, establish a basis for evaluating the behavior of the disciples throughout the narrative. The disciples' responses seem to measure up to their initiator's expectations—at least initially.

Early on, Jesus appoints twelve to serve as his closest associates; he gives them special responsibilities (3:13–19). Paralleling Mark's emphasis on Jesus' "authority" to teach (1:22) and to command "even the unclean spirits" (1:27) in chapter 1, Jesus imparts his own "authority" to these twelve disciples "to be sent out to preach" and "to cast out demons" (3:13–15). This appointment of twelve disciples foreshadows their actual mission described in 6:7–13. Specifically charging the disciples to take nothing on their initiatory journey except a staff, he then lists the items they are to exclude—bread, bag, money in their belts (6:8)—as if to emphasize the mission's urgency. Jesus also sends them out under his authority (6:7). The disciples followed Jesus' instructions; they "preached that men should repent"; they "cast out many demons"; and they "anointed with oil many that were sick and healed them" (6:12–13). Although Jesus warned them of opposition, there is no indication that any obstacles prevented the twelve disciples from accomplishing the task set before them. They met the challenges of their journey of initiation.

In another early test of faith, the initiates have more difficulty. Few initiates are not sorely tested. While journeying across the Sea of Galilee in a boat accompanied by Jesus, the disciples encounter a storm (4:35–41). The disciples wake a sleeping Jesus; after calming the sea, he asks the disciples, "Why are you afraid? Have you no faith?" (4:40). Ironically, although having seen the repeated miracles that Jesus had performed, the disciples nevertheless fail to understand his true identity, wondering, "Who then is this, that even wind and sea obey him?" (4:41). Their failure to understand is further emphasized by the ironic juxtaposition of the storm story with the narrator's observation that although Jesus spoke to the multitudes in parables, "privately to his own disciples he explained everything" (4:34). The initiates remain at the threshold of understanding, still unable to recognize the identity of their instructor even though they receive his added interpretations of his message.

Similarly, directly after describing Jesus' miraculous feeding of the five thousand with five loaves and two fish, the narrator describes how the disciples saw Jesus walking on the sea and were terrified. Once Jesus joined them in the boat, the wind ceased. Not learning to recognize his abilities from previous miraculous events, the disciples were "utterly astounded" by Jesus' power over nature, for "they did not understand" (6:52) the implications of the feeding miracles. The disciples' movement from acceptance to fear is not depicted in the terms of a modern novel, which might trace it by attributing it to a complex net of psychological factors. Rather, after describing their fear, the narrator bluntly comments that the disciples did not understand because "their hearts were hardened" (6:52).

The disciples' exclusive relationship with Jesus contrasts sharply with that of the crowds who seem to surround him constantly—yet without the same privileged access that they enjoy. Because of their position as initiates (4:10–11), the disciples often receive Jesus' explanations of the meaning of parables that the crowds cannot comprehend (4:33–34). At times, the writer even delivers a silent rebuke to the disciples by contrasting the crowds' recognition of Jesus with that of the disciples who ought—by means of their privileged position—to be able to comprehend better than they do. For instance, as if to emphasize this ironic development, Mark follows the story of Jesus walking on the sea and the disciples' inability to recognize or to understand him (6:45–52) with a description of the crowd "immediately" recognizing him (6:54). At the same time, the crowds' frequent enthusiastic response of amazement or astonishment can actually constitute an expression of incomprehension. In the end, they side with the religious authorities against Jesus; Pilate placates the crowds by delivering Jesus to the soldiers for crucifixion (15:15) while the crowd blasphemes Jesus as he hangs on the cross (15:29–30).

In contrast to the ubiquitous crowds, a number of minor characters serve as foils to the developing but uncompleted initiation of the disciples by exhibiting their faith and understanding of Jesus' true identity. These individuals demonstrate that they have overcome obstacles in their own initiatory tests of faith. Having completed their initiation of faith, their experience sometimes points the way for the disciples. Included in this group are the leper who asks Jesus to heal him (1:40–45); the people who bring the paralytic to Jesus for healing (2:3–5); Jairus, who pleads with Jesus for his daughter's life (5:21–24, 35–43); the woman with a hemorrhage who touches Jesus' clothing, trusting that she will be healed (5:25–34); the Syrophoenician woman who asks Jesus to exorcise the demon from her daughter (7:25–30); the father who brings his son to Jesus in order to have an unclean spirit removed (9:14–29); and blind Bartimaeus, who asks Jesus for mercy (10:46–52). Each one's simple faith and resultant healing followed by acceptance is in direct contrast to the disciples' wavering faith.

Jesus also refers to other exemplary figures in direct contrast to the disciples. For instance, to counter the disciples' desire for status, he points to the example of children (9:33–37; 10:13–16); to counter their desire for power, Jesus points to himself (10:42–45) as well as to a poor but generous widow (12:41–44). In an important foreshadowing of the disciples' eventual, more complete understanding of Jesus' true identity, the Roman centurion, a minor character, who observed Jesus breathe his last breath on the cross, recognizes the crucified and dying Jesus as "truly the Son of God" (15:39). This provides what may be the most dramatically moving and significant recognition of Jesus the Messiah. No disciples are ever reported to have experienced such a significant revelation of their understanding of the true identity of Jesus. They provide an ironic juxtaposition with the centurion, given that he understands the true nature of Jesus with only limited exposure, whereas the disciples with maximum exposure still express their doubts.

The first portion of Mark portrays the disciples undertaking their first initiatory steps, highlighted by the successful completion of their mission in chapter 6. Jesus himself establishes their exalted position as initiates in Mark 4:11. In the words of William Barclay's translation, Jesus told the disciples, "To you there is given the knowledge of the kingdom of God which only the *initiated* can know. To those who are outside, everything is expounded by means of parables" (90, emphasis added). Still, this teaching is followed by the quieting of the storm passage, where Jesus criticizes the disciples for their lack of faith (4:40) and their inability to understand his power over nature (v. 41).

Incidents of the disciples' inability to comprehend Jesus' identity as he probes and tests their commitment and understanding begin to multiply after their successful mission of preaching and healing in chapter 6. The third boat scene, in 8:14–21, is particularly disastrous for the disciples; the scene serves as a disappointing climax to the first half of the gospel in terms of their development as initiates. Although Jesus has now twice fed the multitudes, the disciples are concerned about a lack of food. In response, Jesus criticizes them for their lack of faith; in a torrent of no fewer than eight pointed, rhetorical questions he accuses them of the same blindness, deafness, and lack of understanding as the "outsiders" discussed in 4:11–12. As we follow the course of the narrative, the privileged initiates still appear to remain outside the circle of understanding, short of initiation. Consequently, their guide, probing with pointed questions, continues the initiatory process of opening their eyes through certain tests of recognition.

Jesus' Instruction on the Duties of the Initiate

A major ingredient of the Gospels—Jesus' teaching—can also be understood within the initiatory framework. Unlike the crowds, the disciples have been given "the secret of the kingdom of God" (4:11). Nevertheless, the distinction between the uninitiated public and the disciples is not absolute, for, as we have seen, the disciples fail to understand fully the secret with which they are entrusted. A progression is evident in the private instruction to the disciples. Step by step, Jesus introduces his disciples to the responsibilities of being the disciples of a suffering and resurrected Christ. In chapters 1–3 the disciples are called (1:16–20; 2:14) and appointed as the Twelve (3:13–19); they are then set apart as a select group of initiates who receive the secret of the kingdom. They are given private interpretations of public teachings or events: in 4:14–20 they are given an interpretation of the parable of the sower; in 4:21–25 they are told of revelations to come; in 7:14–17 they receive an interpretation of the parable on defilement given to the crowd. They are then given three passion predictions not given to the crowd at any time (8:22–38; 9:30–37; 10:32–45) and witness the vivid illustration of the fig tree parable and the temple-cleansing episodes.

Finally, these select initiates are given a detailed revelation about the future in the Olivet Discourse, in which Jesus remarks, "But take heed; behold, I have told you all things beforehand" (13:23). The private discussions between Jesus and the disciples from that point to the Passion center around Jesus' coming death: he is anointed for burial (14:3–9); Judas the betrayer is exposed (v. 17); Jesus predicts that the disciples will be scattered (v. 27); and, most important, he promises, "After I am raised up, I will go before you to Galilee" (v. 28), implying completion of their initiation after the Resurrection.

In chapters 8–13 the most significant instruction given to the disciples occurs in the form of private conversations held while they are withdrawn from the crowd. Although Jesus knows that the disciples will neither fully understand nor accept his instruction until after the Passion and Resurrection and their completed initiation, this exclusive instruction in the "secret of the kingdom" as well as insight into the end times insists on his identity as suffering Son of Man and resurrected Messiah (8:31–38; 9:12, 31; 10:33–34) whose initiates will accept suffering, opposition, and even martyrdom as a requirement of their authentic discipleship and completed initiatory status (8:34–38; 9:33–37; 10:28–31, 35–45; 12:43–44).

The disciples' recognition of Jesus is incomplete or partial, despite their exclusive times of private instruction with Jesus (6:52; 8:17). As we have seen, their uncompleted initiation is based on their misunderstanding of the nature of Jesus. Consequently, they are often told by Jesus to be silent (1:23–25, 34; 3:11–12; 5:6–7; 9:20).

Whether or not one accepts William Wrede's conception of the "messianic secret" as an interpretation of the commands to silence, the private instruction of the disciples (7:17; 9:30, 33; 10:10), and the parable theory (4:11–12), these elements of the narrative, taken together, do constitute a long-recognized secrecy motif. However, the disciples' partial state of initiation is due to their misunderstanding of the nature of Jesus and not properly part of an intended messianic secret motif. They fall short of understanding Jesus' true nature as the suffering and resurrected Messiah. However, the narrative alludes to a time after the Passion and Resurrection when they will comprehend the nature of Jesus more fully as full-fledged initiates (13:9–13; 14:28).

Mark: The Story Without an Ending

The gospel of Mark ends without a formal conclusion just as it begins without a nativity story. For the disciples, too, the ending seems incomplete. Still unclear about Jesus' identity and unable to comprehend the instruction about Jesus' suffering and death, they do not follow Jesus when his enemies come to take him, despite their firm assurances to the contrary (14:31); one even betrays him (v. 45), another denies him (v. 72), and they all abandon him (v. 50). Still, Mark suggests that the disciples will eventually fully understand when they see the resurrected Jesus in Galilee (16:6) as he promised earlier (14:28). Nevertheless, the text does end on a note of disappointment, fear, and sadness. The failure of the disciples to show courage and compassion at Jesus' death is matched by the women's failure at the Resurrection to tell the disciples of their meeting with Jesus (16:8). It is only from the standpoint of the Cross (as in the view of the Roman centurion) and Resurrection that they will be fully initiated into the secret of the kingdom that they had not before fully understood (9:9–13; 14:27–31; 16:6–8).

As Norman Petersen reminds us in his discussion of the allusions to post-Resurrection meetings between Jesus and the disciples in Mark, "The end of a text is not the end of the work when the narrator leaves unfinished business for the reader to complete, thoughtfully and imaginatively, not textually" ("When Is the End Not the End?" 153). The text thus points forward to a point of reconciliation when Jesus' conflicts with the disciples are resolved and his true nature is both understood and embraced by them.

The initiation motif—in New Testament language—the theme of true discipleship, provides a key to understanding the purpose and development of Mark. In fact, initiation rites were prevalent in the mystery religions and in Judaism at the time of the writing of the gospel. These rituals made the initiates eligible to participate in the life of the community. The gospel of Mark may be intended to perform the same function as it initiates the reader beyond the disciples' own understanding through the way the narrative unfolds. It enables the reader to catch up and go beyond the disciples, despite their seeming privilege as direct initiates of Christ.

WORKS CITED

Auerbach, Erich. *Mimesis: The Representation of Reality in Western Literature.* Trans. Willard R. Trask. Princeton: Princeton UP, 1953.

Bilezikian, Gilbert G. *The Liberated Gospel: A Comparison of the Gospel of Mark and Greek Tragedy.* Baker Biblical Monograph. Grand Rapids: Baker, 1977.

Donahue, John R. "Jesus as the Parable of God in the Gospel of Mark." *Interpretation* 32 (1979): 369–88.

Eliade, Mircea. *Rites and Symbols of Initiation: The Mysteries of Birth and Rebirth.* 1958. Trans. Willard R. Trask. New York: Harper & Row, 1975.

Gardner, Helen. "The Poetry of St. Mark." *The Limits of Literary Criticism: Reflections on the Interpretation of Poetry and Scripture.* Oxford: Oxford UP, 1956. 20–39.

The Gospel of Mark. Trans. and introd. William Barclay. Daily Study Bible Series. Rev. ed. Philadelphia: Westminster, 1975.

Kelber, Werner H. *The Oral and the Written Gospel: The Hermeneutics of Speaking and Writing in the Synoptic Tradition, Mark, Paul, and Q.* Philadelphia: Fortress, 1976.

Kermode, Frank. *The Genesis of Secrecy: On the Interpretation of Narrative.* Cambridge, Mass.: Harvard UP, 1979.

Kingsbury, Jack Dean. *Conflict in Mark: Jesus, Authorities, Disciples.* Minneapolis: Fortress, 1989.

Moore, Stephen D. *Literary Criticism and the Gospels: The Theoretical Challenge.* New Haven: Yale UP, 1989.

Peterson, Norman R. " 'Point of View' in Mark's Narrative." *Semeia* 12 (1978): 97–121.

———. "When Is the End Not the End? Literary Reflections on the Ending of Mark's Narrative." *Interpretation* 34 (1980): 151–66.

Rhoads, David, and Donald Michie. *Mark as Story: An Introduction to the Narrative of a Gospel.* Philadelphia: Fortress, 1982.

Talbert, Charles H. *What Is a Gospel? The Genre of the Canonical Gospels.* Philadelphia: Fortress; London: SCM, 1977.

Tannehill, Robert C. "The Disciples in Mark: The Function of a Narrative Role." *Journal of Religion* 57 (1977): 386–405.

Tolbert, Mary Ann. *Sowing the Gospel: Mark's World in Literary-Historical Perspective.* Minneapolis: Fortress, 1989.

Weeden, Theodore J. *Mark: Traditions in Conflict.* Philadelphia: Fortress, 1971.

Wilder, Amos N. *The Bible and the Literary Critic.* Minneapolis: Fortress, 1991.

Wrede, William. *The Messianic Secret.* 1901. Trans. J. C. G. Greig. Cambridge: James Clarke, 1971.

CHAPTER 29

Luke

Michael Travers
Mississippi College

Give honor unto Luke, Evangelist;
For he it was (the aged legends say)
Who first taught Art to fold her hands and pray.
Dante Gabriel Rossetti

Accustomed as we are to the gospel stories of the life of Christ with all of their episodes leading to the climax of the Crucifixion and the Resurrection, we often do not pay conscious attention to the fact that they are organized as narratives, not propositional theology. The effect of ignoring the narrative structure of the Gospels is to desensitize ourselves to the impact that narrative form has on our responses. Narrative form depends on the satisfaction of expectations. In Luke, narrative establishes and then fulfills its own expectations. This recognition is the starting point of a literary analysis of the Gospels, for they are narrative in form. In Kenneth Burke's formula, "We have clinched the arrows of [our] expectancy" (343) as we read Luke's gospel.

A literary approach will help to complete the picture of what the Gospels say and how they say it. In *The Great Code,* Northrop Frye reminds us that the Bible's "emphasis on narrative, and the fact that the entire Bible is enclosed in a narrative framework, distinguishes the Bible from a good many other sacred books" (198). When we read the Gospels, no less than when we read Genesis and Exodus, we are reading narrative. If we expect to be accurate interpreters of the Gospels, we must appreciate the influence of their narrative form on our understanding of their theology.

Narrative Theology in Luke

Although the Bible is narratively framed, the primacy of narrative in the Gospels should strike us as particularly significant when we consider how much of the New Testament is not narrative. James M. Robinson states that "the prominence of non-narrative forms of primitive Christian writing, such as the Pauline letters. . . , makes it clear that the emergence of the narrative Gospels is not to be taken as a matter of course" (98). It is safe to assume that when the evangelists wrote in narrative form, they made a deliberate choice among many forms of writing available to them. Until recently this seems to have been minimized by biblical scholars. Such interests as the oral transmission of the Gospels and the sources from which editors redacted in order to pass on a tradition to the next writer have dominated biblical scholarship for years (cf. Ryken, *Words of Life* 31; Perkins; Vorster 87–89, 92; Alter 3). Even those scholars who have attempted to grapple with the effects of the narrative genre on the theology of the Gospels have found it difficult to identify a specific genre for the Gospels with any confidence—and with good reason, for the Gospels are mixed writings.

C. H. Talbert characterizes the Gospels as "ancient biography," by which he means "prose narration about a person's life, presenting supposedly historical facts which are selected to reveal the character or essence of the individual often with the purpose of affecting the behavior of the reader" (*What Is a Gospel? The Genre of the Canonical Gospels,* 17). In *Words of Life,* Leland Ryken writes of the Gospels as more narrative than discourse (29–34), and Tremper Longman identifies them as narrative in *Literary Approaches to Biblical Interpretation* (111). Recent scholarship has so overwhelmingly found the Gospels to be narrative that, as early as 1983, W. S. Vorster could say, "It has been proved beyond doubt that the Gospels are narratives" (91).

All of this recent commentary should encourage us to begin at the beginning—the genre of narrative in the gospel of Luke. Narrative forms the basis for theology in Luke; to put it another way, theology is reified—made real, concrete—in narrative in Luke. In Kenneth Burke's terms, narrative shapes the expectations in which Lukan theology is communicated. There is no theology in Luke—no ideology—apart from narrative form.

When we speak of Luke as primarily narrative in genre, it should be understood that we do not have in mind some superficial literary "decoration" to theology. Rather, the narrative structure of Luke gives shape to the theology itself. Luke gives us "told truth," or "narrative theology"—truth told in place and time. Specifically, Luke tells the "story" of his protagonist Jesus Christ. ("Story" here should be construed to mean true history and biography in narrative form, not fiction.) Christ lives his life entirely in narrative contexts. Even his discourses and parables are contextualized narratively, often spoken to his disciples in order to teach a particular lesson that the immediate events occasion. Word and action are narratively framed. As Vorster states,

> The world (reality) created in a narrative is a narrated world even if and when the narrator makes use of events that really happened. . . . It is not a presentation of "reality"; it is narrated reality. (91)

It is with these "eyes" that we must see Luke; we must understand that truth is communicated primarily in narrated form in the gospel of Luke, not in theological propositions. First of all, then, we are not searching for "sources" of the gospel, whether they be Mark or "Q"; we are not looking for evidences of redaction; we are not even looking for Luke's *Sitz im Leben*. Rather, we are examining Luke for the significant influences that the narrative form has on the ideological content of the gospel, its theology.

The close link between narrative and theology forms the basis for what Paul Ricoeur calls "interpretative narrative." By "interpretative narrative," Ricoeur means the close "interweaving of theology and narrative, ideology incorporated into the very strategy of the narrative itself" (237). Although Ricoeur applies the term "interpretative narrative" specifically to the Passion narratives in the Synoptic Gospels, the gospel of Luke at large can be considered under the same rubric. Luke synthesizes his two most important themes—soteriology and its attendant claims on our social responsibility—with his narrative throughout his account. This fusion helps create a unified text as the basis for literary analysis along narrative lines, revealing as it does the two main themes of Luke's gospel: salvation to all who will believe, and the responsibility of believers to the socially disenfranchised.

The Plot

Luke's gospel is a well-crafted narrative. With careful predetermination (Luke 1:1–4), Luke recounts the events surrounding Christ's earthly life, beginning with the angelic visits to Elizabeth and Mary, and ending with Christ's ascension. Luke continues the narrative in the book of Acts, the sequel story of the early church, which is, from a literary as well as a theological perspective, the natural outworking of the story of Christ's earthly ministry. Because of the change in protagonists from Jesus Christ in the gospel to Peter and Paul in Acts, it is helpful to think of Luke and Acts as separate stories told by the same writer. We will understand the structure of the gospel if we think in terms of the characteristics of a narrative, not history or biography. A narrative tells a story by focusing primarily on events (plot) in the life of the protagonist. In Luke, Jesus Christ is the protagonist, and he is unique because he is divine as well as human. The protagonist must face conflict in the story. In Luke, the main opposition to Christ comes from Satan himself (e.g., 4:2–13) and the religious leaders of Israel (e.g., 7:30; 11:37–54; 12:1–5; 16:14–18; 20:1–47; 22:63–23:38). At times, even the disciples become antagonists to Christ (9:46–56; 22:21–30). And in Gethsemane Christ appears to be engaged in a psychomachia, or internal debate, about the imminent Crucifixion (22:41–45). It is the action (plot) and its agents (characters), then, that shape a narrative.

The plot of the gospel of Luke is an archetypal quest story. In a quest, a hero sets out in pursuit of a goal, with the action moving, against conflict and opposition, to the successful completion of the quest. Innumerable pieces of literature follow this pattern. Perhaps the most famous "religious" quest story is Bunyan's *Pilgrim's Progress,* in which the protagonist sets out in search of the heavenly city (cf. Drury 55). In Luke, Christ's mission is to die at Calvary and to rise again, thereby offering salvation to all people, Jew and Gentile alike (e.g., 2:31–32; 3:6; 4:18–21; 7:1–10; 24:47). On his way to Jerusalem, Christ is pictured as repeatedly satisfying the temporal needs of the people he meets. This macrostructure should not obscure the fact that the plot of Luke is quite circuitous by modern Western standards. Christ appears to wander here and there, stopping to heal or teach, finally setting his sight on Jerusalem only when the end is imminent. Although there are many theological outlines for the gospel of Luke, the following is a narrative outline: introduction (1:5–4:13); complications (4:14–9:50); crisis (9:51–53); falling action (9:54–22:46); and conclusion (22:47–24:53).

Establishing the setting of the events in Nazareth (1:26) and Jerusalem (1:5), the author introduces the protagonist through a nativity narrative and the testings in the Judean wilderness (1:5–4:14). Something of Christ's character is suggested here in his visit to the temple at age twelve and in the answers to Satan's temptations. At the end of this section in the temptation scene, Satan is introduced as the primary antagonist to Christ. The principal conflict is clearly established as that between Jesus and Satan, though the extent of that conflict is not clear until later in the story.

With characteristic narrative economy, Luke begins the rising action (complications) of his story with an incident that produces sharp conflict. In Nazareth, Christ reads from Isaiah and announces that he is the fulfillment of the Old Testament prophecy (4:18–30), incurring the wrath of all who hear. This early incident points up a significant motif of the gospel of Luke, namely Christ's frequent pronouncements of salvation and/or healing rejected by people who are not inclined to accept his offer. The complications section continues to the end of the Galilean Ministry, with Jesus characteristically teaching, healing, and inviting, and people variously accepting or rejecting his gifts.

The crisis—understood as the turning point that precipitates the conclusion—occurs with Christ's decision to "turn his face" toward Jerusalem. While John Drury cites the parallel events of 9:1 to 10:20 (the sending of the Twelve as paralleled by the sending of the seventy, as well as a number of other minor parallels in the two chapters) as the turning point, it is possible that a smaller, more defined action is the crisis—namely Christ's emphatic resolution to turn toward Jerusalem (9:51, 53). It is with this decision that he begins to move toward the city of his death and resurrection, and it is with this determination that Luke begins his unique middle section (9:51–19:27), in which he characterizes Christ with his own emphasis on the temporal ministry of the protagonist to the "fringe" people (and to the "up-and-outers" as well). The crisis is particularly important in the Gospels because it underscores the humanity of the protagonist who, in this case, is divine as well.

The falling action, or the events that follow logically from the crisis decision and lead to the conclusion, begins with the journey to Jerusalem (9:54) and ends with Christ's personal agony in Gethsemane (22:46). With incisive narrative instinct, Luke fills this section of the narrative with irony. For example, Christ is proclaimed by the masses on Palm Sunday as the Messiah but is cruelly betrayed a few days later by a kiss from an insider. In this section, opposition to Christ's ministry, both temporal and eternal, increases sharply. Take, for instance, the Pharisees' reaction to Christ's scathing indictment of their hypocrisy:

> And as he said these things unto them, the scribes and Pharisees began to urge him vehemently, and to provoke him to speak of many things: laying wait for him, and seeking to catch something out of his mouth, that they might accuse him. (11:53–54)

In this section, too, Luke incorporates much of the data which the other gospel writers do not include, such as the parables of the Good Samaritan and the Prodigal Son, and also the visit with Zacchaeus. The length of this section in Luke underscores the author's emphasis on Christ's concern with people's temporal needs.

The conclusion of the gospel of Luke brings the story to closure with a clear sense of resolution, leaving the reader with a sense of order. Luke's handling of this most consequential of all stories is magnificent. With great economy, Luke recounts the betrayal (22:47–53), death (23:26–48), resurrection (24:1–49), and ascension (24:50–51). There is no pathos here (Tinsley in Ryken, *The New Testament* 212–13), no tragedy (Tasker in Ryken, *The New Testament* 212); there is only action. Yet in these thirty verses (23:26–24:1), the reader is moved from despair to jubilation, from the prospect of hell to the promise of heaven.

In the plot of Luke's gospel, then, there is a clear structure. The narrative moves methodically to a conclusion and is patterned in such a way as to make that conclusion inevitable. Within this framework, however, the modern reader finds a number of self-contained stories incorporated within the larger action of Christ's earthly life.

Zacchaeus: The Gospel of Luke in Microcosm

Just as the gospel of Luke is one great story, so too there are a number of smaller, self-contained incidents that demonstrate the ways in which narrative elements work together to produce particular effects on the reader. One such incident is the story of Zacchaeus (19:1–10). Here is a brief, unified, and complete narrative comprised of a structured plot, a developed protagonist, and an implied theme.

The plot of this incident is carefully crafted with an exposition (vv. 1–3), complications (v. 4), crisis (vv. 5–6), falling action (v. 7), and resolution (vv. 8–10). In the exposition, the writer introduces the reader to the setting (Jericho) and the protagonist (Zacchaeus). The initial conflict of the story is present in these first three verses as well: Zacchaeus, "a wee little man," wishes to see Jesus but cannot because of the crowd ("for the press"). The reader's interest is piqued by this brief exposition. We are curious to find out if Zacchaeus will actually see Jesus, and if he does, what will happen. This is a classic narrative exposition: the reader meets the protagonist, discovers his dilemma, and desires to read on.

The complication in the story is extremely brief. Ignoring his social pride because of his overwhelming desire to see Jesus, Zacchaeus climbs a sycamore tree, thereby resolving his initial conflict. As a sidelight, it is significant that the author "paints" such a vivid picture here. The picture of the crowd and a diminutive adult in a tree is permanent in our minds. The stage is set for the crisis meeting as Jesus passes under Zacchaeus's tree and draws the crowd's attention to the man in its branches.

With the dialogic interchange between Zacchaeus and Jesus (vv. 5–6), the plot reaches its crisis. Calling him by name, Christ summons Zacchaeus to descend and host him that very day in his own house. Zacchaeus's immediate and willing obedience is the crisis of the story because it is the decision that changes his life, as his later pronouncements make clear. Zacchaeus's inner conflict, implied in part by his earlier intense desire to see Jesus, is immediately resolved here in his response to the Lord's request. Note the intense focus foregrounded in these verses on the one-to-one meeting of Jesus and Zacchaeus against the backdrop of the crowd, which despised the tax collector. Note too the appropriate use of dialogue, rather than action alone, to point the personal contact of the two important characters.

The author follows the crisis with the crowd's "murmur" about the social unsuitability of Christ's feasting with a "sinner" (v. 7). In this brief note, the author establishes another conflict, that of the crowd versus the individual, and suggests that social pride not only belittles a person, but excludes significant interaction with the Savior. This conflict is shown in the irony of situation in which the "sinner" Zacchaeus is converted and the self-righteous bystanders remain unchanged at the end of the story.

The resolution to this incident is a triumph for the protagonist. Willingly recompensing his fiscal dishonesty, Zacchaeus shows his changed character. The writer includes Christ's approbation of Zacchaeus's radical change in the concluding imprimatur: "This day is salvation come to this house, forsomuch as he also is a son of Abraham" (19:9). The story is "comic" in structure in that the conclusion is happy for the protagonist. Here the resolution is even triumphant. Despite his dishonesty and unpopularity, Zacchaeus is gloriously transformed by his visit with Jesus. The plot, then, is carefully structured to demonstrate the important change in the protagonist; it is driven by the sequence of conflicts that Zacchaeus must work through in order to be converted; and it is enlivened by the quoted dialogue at the most important points in the story. The resolution also provides the theme of the incident: Jesus Christ can change even the most sordid and lonely lives into lives of integrity.

The Portrait of the Protagonist

Without doubt, the gospel of Luke is unified primarily by the presence of the protagonist. Referring to the gospel in the books of Acts, Luke summarizes his presentation of Jesus Christ: "God anointed Jesus of Nazareth with the Holy Ghost and power; who went about doing good and healing all that were oppressed of the devil; for God was with him" (Acts 10:38).

Luke shows Christ's humanity (in his healing ministry among the people of Israel) and his divinity (for the Holy Spirit gives him "power" as "God was with him"). The reader learns about Jesus by typically narrative methods: what others say about him, what he himself says, and what he does. We learn of Christ from what others say in the early chapters because his public ministry had not yet started and Luke was not there to report events. Significantly, we come face to face with Christ in his public ministry, where we come to know him by what he says and does.

At the outset of Christ's ministry, the reader observes and hears him in action. In the discourse at Nazareth (4:16–32), Luke establishes a concrete and specific narrative setting for the incident: in his home town, on the Sabbath, and in the synagogue, Jesus takes the scripture of Isaiah 61:1 as his text and preaches himself as Savior to his countrymen. The choice of text is important, for it deals with the poor, the brokenhearted, the captives, and the blind (this last not found in Isaiah). Luke draws our attention to the humble subjects of Christ's soteriological mission and emphasizes Christ's compassion for the "down-and-outers" of his day by quoting the protagonist directly and showing the people's reactions to him, not by theological polemic.

We learn of Christ from his own words again at the dinner with the "chief Pharisee" in Galilee (14:1–24). Not often written about, this incident affords us a view of Christ with the "up-and-outers" rather than the poor. Fitting his conversation to his audience, Christ turns the dinner into a lesson on social responsibility. After he heals one sick with "dropsy" (14:4), Christ teaches two lessons to the socially established people present, using parables in both cases. (As this incident suggests, parables are more than a means of communicating a complex truth to an illiterate populace, because here Christ is speaking to the educated elite.) First, Christ teaches against pride in the well-known parable of the wedding invitations (vv. 7–14). The ironic impact of this lesson could not have been lost on his audience, no doubt all of them seated according to social position at the time of the telling.

Christ's second lesson relates to the "great supper" to which those invited decline to come. In this parable, Christ makes it clear that none of his auditors is so important that he cannot be displaced from the kingdom.

Cunningly undermining the Pharisees' pride at their own feast, Christ teaches social responsibility and an eternal perspective on this life. This incident, not outstanding as gospel encounters go, points up Luke's unifying consistency in his portrait of Jesus, presenting concretely and in narrative structure Christ confronting the errors of the wealthy and distinguished and calling the converted to social responsibility.

When we turn to the parables that Luke alone presents, Luke's portrait of Christ becomes even clearer. Two justly famous parables are those of the Good Samaritan (10:25–37) and the Prodigal Son (15:11–32). These uniquely Lukan parables present a portrait of Christ that is consistent with the two motifs of responsibility and salvation that characterize Luke's picture of his protagonist throughout his narrative. In the parable of the Good Samaritan, Christ clearly relates social responsibility to the kingdom of God. When the lawyer tempts Christ with his "loaded" question about eternal life (v. 25), Christ immediately turns his attention to temporal responsibilities to the unfortunate—in this case, of course, the wounded traveler. In concrete narrative form, Luke presents an account of the Samaritan actually doing what Christ teaches. There is no telling here, just showing of the lesson.

Luke presents the parable of the Prodigal Son in a similar manner, using concrete narrative action and characters to suggest an eternally significant theme. In the Prodigal Son, the themes are repentance (15:18) and forgiveness (vv. 22–24). In his gospel, Luke shows us the son brought to his nadir and finally repentant, and the father graciously and unequivocally forgiving the son. Who of us does not know the events of the story by heart? Here are repentance and forgiveness with "flesh" on them. Both of these parables are intense, concrete incidents that teach doctrine and reflect the character of Christ in Luke's twofold emphasis on soteriology and compassion. Luke is a master storyteller at his best in these parables, presenting a portrait of his protagonist that has become an important part of Western culture; all of us know the plot of these two parables by heart.

Conclusion

There is a case to be made that humans think primarily in narrative, not propositional forms. In *Human Communication as Narrative,* Walter Fisher suggests:

> Humans are essentially storytellers. . . . Rationality is determined by the nature of persons as narrative beings—their inherent awareness of *narrative probability,* what constitutes a

> coherent story, and their constant habit of testing *narrative fidelity,* whether or not the stories they experience ring true with the stories they know to be true in their lives. (64)

Fisher thinks of humans as *homo narrans,* a fact attested by the universal presence of story in all cultures and at all levels of society. Hayden White agrees with Fisher when he writes, "Far from being one code among many that a culture may utilize for endowing experience with meaning, narrative is a metacode, a human universal . . ." (6). Northrop Frye concurs in *The Great Code,* arguing, "The first thing that confronts us in studying verbal structures is that they are arranged sequentially, and have to be read or listened to in time" (31). Frye goes on to elaborate three "phases" of narrativity—the metaphoric, metonymic, and the descriptive—each more complex than the previous one, but his point is that *all* expression is narrative in one way or another (cf. "Myth II" in *The Great Code* 169–98). Logical, propositional thinking is a learned skill, honed with much discipline over an extended period of time, but narrative is a natural structure for speaking and listening.

If in fact we do think in narrative forms, there are important implications for analysis of all narratives, nonbiblical and biblical alike. When we consider the claims of the Bible to authority in all matters, the biblical narratives take on great significance as normative theology *ipso facto.* It becomes apparent that systematic theology is a second-order method for understanding the Gospels, not the substance of the Gospels themselves. The essence of Luke is "narrative theology" with flesh on its bones and sandals on its feet; it is Christ, the God-man, living redemption and compassion among his disciples and the multitudes and dying to rise again. The gospel of Luke is the poetry of Mary, Simeon, and Zechariah as they celebrate the advent of their Messiah. Luke is the Samaritan traveler reifying compassion for an injured Israelite; it is the forgiving father embracing his fallen son and restoring him to his proper position in the family. The gospel of Luke is Zacchaeus sitting in a tree and later promising fourfold restitution to those he has wronged. It is Peter's tears when he betrays Christ late that Thursday evening; it is the intense, concentrated account of the Crucifixion, compelling attention and assent. The gospel of Luke is the meeting on the road to Emmaus, when the disciples' hearts burned within them as the risen Savior revealed himself to them.

This is the theology of Luke—doctrine so integrated into narrative that we "see and hear" it, as it were. And isn't this the gospel message? Emmanuel, God with us—the Word become flesh and dwelling among us. Isn't this the way we should read the canonical accounts of Jesus Christ's earthly life and death? Through the gospel's own narrative structure, in careful, informed study of the details of the account, and with a sensitivity to its implications for us as Christians today.

WORKS CITED

Alter, Robert. "Introduction to the Old Testament." *The Literary Guide to the Bible.* Ed. Robert Alter and Frank Kermode. Cambridge, Mass.: Harvard UP, 1987. 11–35.

Burke, Kenneth. *Philosophy of Literary Forms: Studies in Symbolic Action.* Berkeley: University of California Press, 1973.

Drury, John. *The Gospel of Luke: A Commentary on the New Testament in Modern English.* New York: Macmillan, 1973.

Fisher, Walter R. *Human Communication as Narrative: Toward a Philosophy of Reason, Value, and Action.* Columbia: University of South Carolina Press, 1987.

Frye, Northrop. *The Great Code: The Bible and Literature.* New York: Harcourt, 1982.

Longman, Tremper, III. *Literary Approaches to Biblical Interpretation.* Grand Rapids: Zondervan, 1987.

Perkins, Pheme. "Crisis in Jerusalem? Narrative Criticism in New Testament Studies." *Theological Studies* 50 (1989): 296–310.

Ricoeur, Paul. "Interpretative Narrative." *The Book and the Text: The Bible and Literary Theory.* Ed. Regina Schwartz. Cambridge: Basil Blackwell, 1990. 237–57.

Robinson, James M. "The Gospels as Narrative." *The Bible and the Narrative Tradition.* Ed. Frank McConnell. New York: Oxford UP, 1986. 97–112.

Ryken, Leland. *The New Testament in Literary Criticism.* New York: Ungar, 1984.

________. *Words of Life: A Literary Introduction to the New Testament.* Grand Rapids: Baker, 1987.

Talbert, C. H. *What Is a Gospel? The Genre of the Canonical Gospels.* Philadelphia: Fortress, 1977.

Vorster, W. S. "Kerygma/History and the Gospel Genre." *New Testament Studies* 29 (1983): 87–95.

CHAPTER 30

John

Marianne Meye Thompson
Fuller Theological Seminary

Several assumptions undergird the approach to the gospel of John taken in this essay. First, the gospel constitutes a literary whole, from beginning (1:1) to end (21:25). Many Johannine scholars believe that chapter 21, as well as other passages, were added after the gospel was substantially in its present form (see Brown). But here we will study the text as a unity. Second, one can study the text as a whole precisely because it makes good sense and reads well if analyzed in the form in which we now have it (Culpepper; Ryken, "Fallacies"). And third, it is assumed that the author of the gospel, while interested in both history and theology, is nevertheless also interested in presenting these in a readable and artistic fashion. One can call attention to the gospel's literary features because the author used standard literary conventions in order to make his gospel interesting and lively. In no way does the use of literary criticism suggest that his gospel is "only" a story; but it is no less than that.

Thus the gospel of John is in part a deliberately crafted and artistic story about Jesus. In modern terms, one might compare the gospel to a dramatized documentary ("docudrama"; Stanton). The docudrama makes use of historical data and material, but presents it in such a way as to engage the viewer's attention and interest, while presenting the director's unique interpretation of the events recorded. Some incidents, persons, or themes may be treated in great detail; others can be glossed over more quickly. Events need not be recounted in strict chronological order, although at some point an overview of significant incidents leading up to a main event or grand finale will probably be included. The end product, if well done, will be carefully and deliberately crafted, shaped by the director's interests as well as by the subject matter and form, with the hope that it will inform, entertain, and involve the viewer.

Like a docudrama, the gospel of John uses historical data and material, sifted through the sieve of the author's viewpoint, the readers' interests and concerns, and the standard conventions that govern the particular form of art or literature. It is not created out of whole cloth, any more than a docudrama is. But creative freedom is exercised in telling the story. The gospel writer has been selective in his use of material (20:30; 21:25), arranging it in a broadly chronological framework with interpretative freedom. The book makes explicit its retrospective vantage point; that is, it interprets the story of Jesus, already knowing how that story ends, and in light of the events that follow after Jesus' death and resurrection (2:22; 7:39; 13:7). Ultimately, like the docudrama's intent to engage its viewers, the point of the gospel is to engage and involve its readers. From beginning to end, the gospel is not merely narrating "what happened then," but what can and does happen now.

Theme, Plot, and Unity of the Gospel

The theme of the gospel of John is "life." To be more precise, the gospel presents Jesus Christ as the one through whom God brings life to a dying world (Moule; Thompson). In the very first verse of the gospel, we are introduced to the "Word," who has been with God from all eternity. The Word always lives. The world was brought to life through this Word (1:3), because the Word is the one "in whom there is life" (1:4; 5:26). Jesus of Nazareth, the incarnate Word, subsequently speaks of the gift of life that he brings (5:25, 40; 6:27, 33, 51, 58; 10:10) and even of himself as life (11:25; 14:6). And when John summarizes his purpose for having written the gospel, he writes of his desire that those who read the book might believe in Jesus Christ, and so "have life" (20:31). From beginning to end, unity is provided to the gospel by the recurring theme of the life that is offered by and in Jesus, life that comes from the source of all life, the living God (6:57).

The story of how this life is offered to the world, and is sometimes received and sometimes rejected, forms the plot of the gospel as a whole. (For more on plot, see Culpepper; on structure, see Brown; Dodd; Ryken, *Literature.*) That plot is contained in miniature in John 1:10–13:

> [The Word] was in the world, and the world was made through him, yet the world knew him not. He came to his own home, and his own people received him not. But to all who received him, who believed in his name, he gave power to become children of God; who were born, not of blood nor of the will of the flesh nor of the will of a man, but of God.

Each episode of the gospel subsequently tells of encounter with the Word and of reception or rejection of the Incarnate Word's gift of life (Dodd). As each character in the story comes face to face with Jesus, the reader assesses the encounters through the lens of the words cited above (John 1:10–13). Will Nicodemus, one of Jesus' "own," receive him? Will the woman at the well welcome and believe in him? Will the man born blind become a child of God? As some characters fail to see who Jesus is and reject what he offers, the reader knows the dimensions of the tragedy, for here is God's incarnate Word dwelling among human beings. But as others receive Jesus, the readers know that it is not just a Jewish rabbi from Palestine who has made yet another disciple, but the Word of God who has brought to birth yet another child of God. And, at the end of the gospel (20:30–31), readers are faced with the question that has challenged each character in the story: Have they encountered and recognized Jesus? Do they welcome him, so as to be counted as the children of God?

The struggles to understand and recognize Jesus create the main conflicts in the gospel. Individuals battle their own misunderstandings (e.g., 2:18–20; 3:1–12; 4:7–26) and short-sightedness (e.g., 9:13–24; 11:45–53), their limiting presuppositions (5:10–18; 6:15; 7:40–52) and in-grown prejudices (8:39–59), and their fears of the scorn and ridicule of others (12:42–43). They struggle with Jesus' claims, including such claims that he offers the only way to life (6:44, 51; 11:25; 14:6), that he is the Son of God sent from the Father in heaven (6:42; 10:33–39), that he has the right to break the Mosaic Law (5:17–18; 9:13–16), and that only he can free them from bondage to sin (8:34–36). And there is conflict between believers and unbelievers (7:25–31; 9:1–40; 10:19–21), and even among unbelievers themselves (11:45–53), with respect to Jesus' claims and person. In short, all the conflicts arise from the struggle to understand, recognize, and believe in Jesus. The recurrence of this conflict throughout the gospel—especially because the conflict takes many shapes and recurs in various episodes—gives unity to the gospel. And the gospel continues to affect modern readers because the struggles to understand Jesus have not changed very much.

In addition to the unity given to the story by the recurring and overarching conflicts of recognizing Jesus and by the theme of life, other features combine to bring unity to the story as well. The narrator provides a chronology for the gospel by using the Jewish religious calendar, consistently referring to various festivals (2:13; 5:1; 6:4; 7:2; 10:22; 13:1; see Brown). What Jesus says or does is understood as the true interpretation and intention of the celebration of one of the Jewish holy days. The regular mention of feasts gives us one clue about what we need to know about Jesus, as well as providing continuity to the story.

Further structure is given to the story by the references to Jesus' "hour." Early in the gospel it is said that this hour has not yet come (2:4; 7:8, 30) or that the hour is coming (4:21; 5:25), and finally that it has come (12:23, 27; 13:1). The anticipation of Jesus' hour provides suspense to the story, and the decisive announcement of its presence ties together beginning and ending.

Interspersed throughout the gospel are various signs (miracles) that Jesus did (Brown; Dodd; Smalley; Wead). While the other gospels recount numerous miracles, John tells but a few. But precisely because they are few in number, the miracles become an even more important structural feature in John. Often the miracles in John are paired with a discourse in which Jesus expounds on the miracle, elaborating it in such a way that it becomes a symbolic pointer (hence, "sign") to who Jesus is. Similarly, in John there are seven "I am" sayings (6:35; 8:12 and 9:5; 10:7, 9; 11:25; 14:6; 15:1). Although they are not placed as regularly throughout the gospel as are the signs or feasts, by the regular inclusion of these formulas of self-revelation John depicts Jesus' progressive manifestation of the fullness of his identity. In essence the gospel is a series of epiphanies. Each saying stands on its own and yet in conjunction with the others paints the complete portrait of the protagonist of the gospel, Jesus, the Word become flesh.

The Movement of the Story

We may briefly trace the way the story unfolds (see also Ryken, *Literature*). In chapter 1 Jesus is presented to the reader with a host of messianic appellations: he is the Son of God, the King of Israel, the Messiah, and the one promised in the Scriptures. He is also designated as the one who will baptize with the Holy Spirit and "the Lamb of God, who takes away the sin of the world" (1:29). Jesus will bring life when on the cross he takes away the world's sin, which leaves the world mired in death, and releases the life-giving Spirit. Once the main character has been introduced, the action begins; and each deed or action of Jesus is as revealing of who he is as is the list of titles that has been produced in chapter 1.

The changing of over 120 gallons of water into choice wine at a wedding feast in Cana symbolizes the abundance of life and blessing that is available in the messianic age of fulfillment ushered in by Jesus (2:1–11). Ritual purification will no longer be needed by those who live in his presence. In the following story of Jesus' driving the money-changers out of the temple, we again see the important motif of the proper worship of God. Such worship depends not on a place, but on a person. The risen Lord, and not the sanctuary in Jerusalem, becomes the "temple of God"—that which mediates the presence and blessing of God to the people.

Having set the stage with these two episodes, the gospel then introduces a series of characters who encounter Jesus in a variety of settings. To each is presented the challenge of recognizing and receiving Jesus. Nicodemus appears first, offering an initial, cautious assessment of Jesus as a "teacher come from God." In the typically Johannine dialogue that ensues, Jesus takes the role of teacher and revealer, and his partner in conversation assumes the role of the misinformed and somewhat slow-witted questioner. Nicodemus's failure to understand is underscored by the readers' knowledge of Jesus' ultimate origins and of the summary of his message already provided (1:10–13)—that Jesus is the one who brings new birth by the power of the Holy Spirit. But the reader is left hanging, for it is not clear whether Nicodemus moves out of his confusion and misunderstanding to an acceptance of Jesus' claim. He will appear twice again in the story (7:50; 19:39–42), but for the moment he fades from the picture. The gospel's skillful weaving of Nicodemus in and out of the story adds to the gospel's unity, suspense, and drama.

In contrast to Nicodemus, the Samaritans in the next chapter come almost at once to a fuller understanding of who Jesus is. Jesus first meets a woman of Samaria at a well, drawing water. Her initial statement that Jesus must be a prophet (4:19) and her guess that he may be the Messiah (4:29) are eclipsed by her townsfolk's far more encompassing confession that he is the Savior of the world. This chapter also picks up the twin themes of the Holy Spirit and true worship, themes that have been found in chapters 1, 2, and 3 already. Here they are intertwined as Jesus says explicitly that God seeks "true worshipers." True worshipers are not confined to the walls of a particular place—such as the Jerusalem sanctuary—or to certain ceremonies of purification. They worship through the Holy Spirit, symbolized by the living water that Jesus promises to the woman. While the scenes and characters have changed, the unity of the story is clear, as John weaves together themes of worship, the Spirit, new birth, and their embodiment in the main character of the story, Jesus himself.

At the end of chapter 4, with the healing of the official's son, and on through the end of chapter 11, with the raising of Lazarus from the dead, the theme of life is dealt with most fully and explicitly (Dodd; Thompson). The healing of the official's son and of a man at the pool of Bethesda in Jerusalem who had been ill for thirty-eight years demonstrate Jesus' ability to restore physical wholeness with a word. Furthermore, these acts reflect the actions of the Father, who creates and sustains life, prerogatives now given to the Son as well (5:25–26). Jesus speaks the life-giving word of God, because he is the incarnate and living Word of God. In the following chapter (ch. 6), the feeding of the five thousand, coupled with the discourse on Jesus as the heaven-sent bread who gives true life, again points to the unifying theme that Jesus brings life to all who come to share in his feast. This is the heart of both the message and story of the gospel.

With chapter 5, the conflict between Jesus and his opponents escalates. Even some of his own disciples abandon him (6:66). In chapters 7–10, the hostility becomes palpable, and yet the response to Jesus is not monolithic. For while there is outright rejection and unbelief (7:48–52; 8:48, 59; 9:24, 29; 10:20, 31, 39; 11:45–53, 57), there is also tentative faith (7:26, 31) and glad assent, such as that manifested by the man born blind (9:35–38). He receives his sight, but he also comes to the insight of recognizing Jesus as Lord and Son of man, the emissary of God's grace and mercy.

A parabolic discourse about Jesus as the shepherd who protects his own sheep to the point of death (10:1–18) wraps up this long segment (chs. 7–10) and provides the transition to Jesus' climactic act in the first part of the book: the raising of Lazarus from the dead (11:1–44). Here one sees Jesus' life-giving power in all its fullness: into a world of death and decay, Jesus brings life that endures (Moule). Yet there is tragic irony in the fact that it is the deed that most fully manifests Jesus' life-giving power that also elicits the most decisive and hostile response—the authorities' decision to put Jesus to death (11:45–53, 57).

And now the shadow of the cross looms ever more darkly over the gospel. Jesus speaks of his imminent death in parable (12:24) and symbol (12:32, 35–36), finally prefiguring this ultimate act of sacrificial giving in washing his disciples' feet at his Last Supper with them (13:1–17). This last meal is then followed by four chapters that comprise Jesus' words of farewell, exhortation, and promises to his disciples. These "farewell discourses" are a typical feature of many biblical and ancient writings, and it is often in the words of a dying person that one learns what is dearest and most crucial to him (Brown). Jesus here promises that despite his departure, his presence with his disciples will continue: they will not be without his life-giving work. Indicative of the kind of work Jesus will continue to perform on their behalf, Jesus prays for them and for their steadfastness in the faith (ch. 17).

Following the supper, Jesus is arrested, tried, crucified, and buried. But he appears alive again to his disciples on several occasions. The last appearance to them takes us full circle to the beginning of the gospel. For just as we began with the calling of the disciples, here we have Jesus again alone with some of his disciples. And his call to them remains unchanged: Follow me (1:43; 21:19, 22).

Characters and Settings

One meets all kinds of people in the gospel of John (for more on character, see Culpepper). The full range of the cast of characters and the differences in the ways they are presented and developed contribute to the dynamic flavor of the gospel and prevent it from becoming monotonous. Not all characters are treated in equal depth. Some appear once (the Samaritan woman, the blind man), and some reappear several times (Mary, Nicodemus, the disciples, Caiaphas). There are esteemed Jewish religious leaders (Nicodemus, the Pharisees, Caiaphas, Joseph of Arimathea), ordinary folk (disciples, the crowds, Mary and Martha, a maid by the fire), those considered outcasts among society (the Samaritan woman), an enigmatic Jewish prophet (John the Baptist), Roman officials (the arresting soldiers, Pilate). This is the world of first-century Palestine. But almost any reader can find himself or herself in one of the characters of the gospel.

Women figure prominently in John. They are the key witnesses to Jesus' first sign (the changing of the water to wine), his climactic deed (the raising of Lazarus), and his being "lifted up" to God in the Crucifixion. To a woman Jesus announces that he is the Messiah, and it is a woman who anoints him for burial. And a woman, Mary Magdalene, is the first to see the risen Jesus. In contrast to the elite and powerful religious authorities and leaders, who are almost always portrayed in adversarial roles to Jesus, women—those not credited with religious understanding or roles—are usually shown coming to faith.

There are people whom Jesus heals: the official's son, the man at the pool of Bethesda, the man born blind, Lazarus. There are unnamed wedding guests for whom Jesus provides, crowds whom Jesus feeds, throngs whom he teaches, and some who come out to welcome his entry into Jerusalem. But not all are recipients of mercy and healing: some surprised merchants feel the wrath of his whip of cords in the temple as he drives them out.

There are Jesus' own disciples, some named, and some unnamed. Although at times they see correctly and affirm who Jesus is, at other points they puzzle about his teaching and desert him (6:66). There is reserved in the gospel of John a special horror for disciples who defect and fall away, and Judas is the representative of them all. Thus those who remain steadfast and loyal are praised all the more, and the chief representative here is the enigmatic and unnamed "beloved disciple." It is enough to know him as a model disciple, faithful in following Jesus, ready to believe in him. When measured against him, other disciples are shown to be lacking. He is the touchstone of faithfulness and love to Jesus.

These characters are shown in the full range of human activity: celebrating weddings, attending religious feasts and ceremonies, drawing water from a well, experiencing hunger and thirst. They experience the full gamut of human emotions: from sorrow to joy; from suffering and illness to hope and healing; from frustration, misunderstanding, and puzzlement to clarity of vision, trust and loyalty; from waffling, desertion, and giving up to dogged determination to stick with Jesus, earnestness, and sincerity; from hostility and anger to love and exuberance; from alienation and rejection to acceptance and peace. All these are the common stock of human experience. And the imagery of the gospel comes from the world of their experiences as well: weddings, childbirth, family, friendship, eating and drinking; tending sheep and vines, catching fish; teaching and learning; suffering; the elements of light, water, and bread; the experiences of living and dying.

As diverse as the characters are, and as wide-ranging as their experiences and emotions are, there is a common thread that unites them: they are people who seek life in a world of death. They seek to be fed, healed, enlightened; they seek to live. For they are part of a world in which death and illness are common—not easily accepted, but part of their experience. Out of that world comes the longing to live. Every experience of alienation, hostility, and illness is in reality a bit of death. But the protagonist of the story, Jesus, comes to bring healing, joy, and life to overcome that death. All the characters are measured by their response to the main character of the story.

The gospel ranges over the landscape of Palestine, from Judea, to Samaria, to Galilee. Jesus can be found at the river Jordan with the Baptist, at a wedding in Galilee, in the temple and its precincts in Jerusalem, at home with his family, in the home of friends, and at dinner with his disciples. What is striking is that the farther Jesus gets from the center of Judaism, from Jerusalem and its temple, the more likely he is to find faith and a following. It is the authorities who do not believe. But in alien territory such as Samaria he finds glad acclamation. Thus the movement in and out of Jerusalem corresponds roughly to the alternation of unbelief and belief.

Contrasting settings and characters are used to great effect in the change of scene from chapter 3 to chapter 4. In chapter 3, Nicodemus, an esteemed Jewish leader, member of the Sanhedrin, and learned teacher, comes to Jesus at night, apparently indoors. By contrast, in the next chapter, an unnamed woman, of the despised Samaritan religion, probably even of low standing among her own people, comes to Jesus in the full blazing sun, outdoors, at a well. The change of scenery is used as a backdrop to contrast effectively Nicodemus's tentativeness and the woman's boldness.

The Role of the Narrator and Literary Features

An omniscient narrator guides the reader through the gospel (on the role of the narrator, see Culpepper; Duke; Wead). In the opening verses, the reader is given a vantage point to understand the story that the characters of the gospel do not share. Throughout the gospel, the narrator continues to interject comments that enable the reader to know how to interpret the events of the gospel (Culpepper). For example, after recounting the episode of Jesus' cleansing of the temple, the narrator comments that Jesus spoke of his own body, but that even the disciples would not understand this until after Jesus' own resurrection (2:22). There are also times when the narrator intrudes to offer a corrective, such as in 4:2, where he notes that "Jesus himself did not baptize, but only his disciples." By means of such comments, the reader is reassured that the narrator is a reliable guide through the events of Jesus' life and death.

At other places the narrator offers no explicit commentary, but by skillful narration allows the events to speak for themselves. He does not, for example, explain the significance of the changing of water to wine. But by calling attention to the six stone jars of the Jewish rites of purification, and to the vast quantity of wine that was made out of the water, he underscores the abundant provision Jesus offers. And in chapter 9 he allows the witness of the healed man to contrast sharply with the hostile challenges of the Pharisees. Here little explicit commentary is required. The dialogue speaks for itself.

Variety of narrative style characterizes the gospel. Some stories, such as the changing of water to wine, the cleansing of the temple, and the healing of the official's son, are narrated briefly and with little explanatory comment. They receive fuller meaning from the contexts in which they are found. Other stories, such as the healing of the man at the pool, the feeding of the five thousand, and the healing of the man born blind, follow a distinctively Johannine pattern of a brief narrative followed by explanatory discourse focusing on the claims and person of Jesus. And, finally, sometimes dialogue and events are inextricably interwoven, such as in the healing of the man born blind and the raising of Lazarus. By employing a variety of approaches to each incident he chooses to narrate, the narrator keeps the story moving and engaging, avoiding tedious repetition. And although each story can stand on its own, together the stories build the whole gospel and gain further meaning from what precedes and what follows.

The gospel of John is noted for its peculiar stylistic and literary features. We may call attention to the gospel's use of symbolism, irony, misunderstandings, and use of words with double or ambiguous meanings.

John uses basic elements of life, such as water, light, and bread, and imagery from the world of human beings and nature, such as cultivating vines, tending sheep, and giving birth, as images to explain Jesus' work on earth (on symbolism, see Brown; Culpepper; Dodd; Wead). Water, an Old Testament and Jewish symbol of cleansing and purification, is used as a figure for the cleansing work of the Holy Spirit. The light of day symbolizes the illumination that Jesus brings to those who follow the path he charts. Bread, the staff of life, serves as an image of the very essence of Jesus' gift of life.

But often the symbolic function of Jesus' actions and discourse is not understood, and this gives rise to one of the features most characteristic of the gospel, namely, the repeated misunderstandings on the part of the characters who encounter Jesus (Brown; Culpepper; Wead). The Samaritan woman thinks that Jesus' offer of living water will save her the long and dusty trips to the well (4:15), just as crowds to whom Jesus promises "the bread of God which comes down from heaven and gives life to the world" think that he is speaking of bread that will satisfy their physical cravings and hunger (6:33–34).

With each misunderstanding, Jesus corrects the blatant miscomprehension on the part of the character in the story. By reading the gospel from beginning to end, the reader has the benefit not only of Jesus' correcting and explanatory words each time, but also of the cumulative affect of these various correctives. Thus with each subsequent misunderstanding, the reader learns that to hear Jesus aright one must ask about the deeper meaning that his words hold. For the true significance of what he says and offers is to be found not in some thing, but in his very presence among them. In short, the Johannine misunderstandings teach the reader how to read the gospel, for they show the reader what mistakes not to make if Jesus is to be understood correctly.

Some of the misunderstandings arise from the gospel's use of words that have more than one meaning. For example, the word typically translated "again" in the phrase "born again" can mean either "anew" or "from above." Nicodemus clearly hears Jesus telling him that he must be born again, a second time. But Jesus speaks of a rebirth that is "from above," that is, initiated by God's own power and not by human will or desire. "Lifted up" describes Jesus' crucifixion, but to those who understand it speaks of his "lifting up" and return to his previous glory with God in heaven.

The gospel also uses irony, by which a character in the story says something in innocence, not understanding the deeper or fuller level of what he or she says (Culpepper; Duke; Wead). At one point the high priest Caiaphas explains to the council, "It is expedient for you that one man should die for the people, and that the whole nation should not perish." The narrator points out the irony in these words, for Jesus did indeed die "for the people," not as Caiaphas meant, as a political sacrifice to appease the Romans and avert possible military intervention, but rather as a means whereby all those who would truly be "children of God" might be gathered together as one people.

A Brief Analysis of John 9

The story of the healing of the man born blind is one of John's most masterfully crafted narratives (Brown; Dodd; Duke; Resseguie). Various literary techniques are used to great effect. There is an interweaving of scenes and of action and discourse. Jesus' proclamation in 8:12 that he is the light of the world is followed by an explanation of that statement. In 9:5 the statement "I am the light of the world" is repeated, this time to be illustrated by the healing of the blind man, rather than explained in monologue or dialogue. And the narrative will be followed by another explanatory discourse, as Jesus compares his actions to those of a good shepherd who seeks and cares for his own sheep. Together Jesus' words and deeds comprise a unity, pointing to Jesus as the one who enlightens, who leads to life, and who gives his own life to safeguard the life of "his own." The narrative of the healing of the blind man will demonstrate who has come to follow the Light, the Good Shepherd, and so who can truly be called Jesus' own.

The story opens simply with the healing of the blind man. Following that action, various characters appear, manifesting a variety of responses. The man's neighbors are dubious and puzzled (9:8–9), ironically failing to recognize the healed man himself and of course failing to recognize the healer, Jesus! The Pharisees are hostile, sarcastic, and scornful. The man's own parents are fearful of what this healing will mean for them. But the man himself expresses an increasingly "enlightened" understanding of who his benefactor, Jesus, truly is. A wide range of human emotion is depicted, with the readers encouraged to see the story through their own "healed eyes," such as the blind man has received.

A number of literary features are used to create drama. There is an effective use of symbolism, for "sight" symbolizes the "insight" of faith, just as blindness symbolizes a failure to come to faith. There is a fine bit of Johannine irony as the Pharisees try to prove to the healed man that he was in fact never blind! And so there is also a great reversal in the story, as those who start out seeing end up blind, while the blind man alone ends up with true sight.

Drama is also provided through the use of questions. The neighbors ask, "Is this the man?" And a series of questions in rapid-fire succession follow: "How were your eyes opened?" (9:10). "Where is he?" (v. 12). "How can a man who is a sinner do such signs?" (v. 16). "What do you say about him?" (v. 17). "Is this your son?" (v. 19). "What did he do to you?" (v. 26). "Would you teach us?" (v. 34). "Are we also blind?" (v. 40). The healed man poses his own counter-questions. "Why do you want to hear it again? Do you too want to become his disciples?" (v. 27). "Who is he, sir, that I may believe in him?" (v. 36). And, finally, Jesus asks only one question, but it is the climax of the whole story, the point to which all other questions are building: "Do you believe in the Son of man?" (v. 35). This use of questions effectively builds drama and draws the reader inevitably into the story. For the questions are posed not only to the characters in the story, but to the reader as well. Is the reader blind, or seeing? Does the reader wish to become one of Jesus' disciples? Does the reader believe in the Son of man?

Another way in which the author builds to the climax of the story is by titles for or assessments of Jesus that are on the lips of the blind man. Jesus is first confessed as prophet (9:17), then as one who comes from God (v. 30) and to whom God listens (v. 31), and finally as Son of man and Lord (vv. 35, 38), whom the blind man worships (v. 38). By contrast, the Pharisees see Jesus as a sinner (vv. 16, 24) and of unknown origins (v. 29). They refuse to follow him (v. 28) because they do not see who he is (vv. 40–41).

This narrative epitomizes the conflicts, plot, and theme of the gospel. For those who see Jesus only on the physical, human level, as "Jesus the son of Joseph," will in the end fail to grasp his importance at all. But those who are led to understand that in the ministry and person of Jesus the Word of God was enfleshed among us see him for who he really is.

WORKS CITED

Brown, Raymond E. *The Gospel According to John.* Anchor Bible. 2 vols. Garden City: Doubleday, 1966 and 1970.

Culpepper, R. Alan. *Anatomy of the Fourth Gospel: A Study in Literary Design.* Philadelphia: Fortress, 1983.

Dodd, C. H. *The Interpretation of the Fourth Gospel.* Cambridge: Cambridge UP, 1953.

Duke, Paul. *Irony in the Fourth Gospel.* Atlanta: John Knox, 1985.

Moule, C. F. D. "The Meaning of 'Life' in the Gospel and Epistles of St. John. A Study in the Story of Lazarus, John 11:1–44." *Theology* 78 (1975): 114–25.

Resseguie, James L. "John 9: A Literary-Critical Analysis." *Literary Interpretations of Biblical Narratives.* Ed. Kenneth R. R. Gros Louis et al. Nashville: Abingdon, 1982. 2:295–303.

Ryken, Leland. *The Literature of the Bible.* Grand Rapids: Zondervan, 1974.

———. "Literary Criticism of the Bible: Some Fallacies." *Literary Interpretations of Biblical Narratives.* Ed. Kenneth R. R. Gros Louis et al. Nashville: Abingdon, 1974.

Smalley, Stephen S. *John: Evangelist and Interpreter.* Exeter: Paternoster, 1978.

Stanton, Graham. *The Gospels and Jesus.* Oxford: Oxford UP, 1989.

Thompson, Marianne Meye. "Eternal Life in the Gospel of John." *Ex Auditu* 5 (1989): 35–56.

Wead, David. *The Literary Devices in John's Gospel.* Basel: Friedrich Reinhardt Kommissionsverlag, 1970.

CHAPTER 31

The Parables

JOHN W. SIDER
Westmont College

Strategies for Interpretation

Whatever an interpreter's ruling interest in the parables, the first focus of literary analysis should be the texts we have. The texts of the Synoptic Gospels require the kind of thorough analysis often reserved for hypothetical "texts" of Jesus' original words or voice (e.g., Breech, 7). The scholarship of reconstruction assumes that the parables in their present form are fragments of early and later tradition stitched together so inexpertly that often the seams are obvious. But one reader's patched garment is another's seamless robe. Usually the conclusions are based on too cursory literary observations that do not acknowledge how well the elements of the text cohere.

Thus some scholars reject the authenticity of allegorical features in the belief that parable and allegory do not mix in Jesus' teaching. Some constrict the meaning of complex parables on the theory that a parable makes only one point. Some discount the interpretive commentaries on the unsafe grounds that "the speaker who needs to interpret his parables is not master of his method" (Cadoux 19; but see Beavis). Some assume that Jesus' "matchless mastery of construction" (Jeremias 12) never fails, though in fact the version that makes the better story (Cadoux 60) may be less original, since Jesus sometimes sacrificed compression, symmetry, or coherence as well as realism in order to point his analogy.

These problems—and others, of evidence and logic (Palmer; Sider, "Rediscovering the Parables")—make it seem unlikely that speculative reconstructions of the traditions behind the gospel texts of the parables will very soon deserve to be called assured results of scholarship. To make them the basis of one's initial literary study would be, in Hunter's words for another choice altogether, "a quite monumental preference for the inferior evidence" (222).

Interpreters should note their own literary preconceptions and test them by the texts. This is easier said than done; Jeremias warned against invoking "an alien law" for the parables (20), yet his segregation of parable and allegory is just that (Blomberg).

The best place to begin an inductive theory is with the function of analogy—the most significant common denominator in all the *parabolai.* Although the ancient Greeks used *analogia* for "resemblance," their common word for "analogy" was *parabole.* So too the evangelists'. Like the Old Testament *meshalim,* Jesus' *parabolai* vary from proverb (Luke 4:23), question (Luke 6:39), and taunt (Luke 14:8–11) to simile (Matt. 13:52), metaphor (Luke 5:36), riddle (Mark 7:14–17), and other types. But unlike *mashal* (or *parabole* in the Septuagint), *parabole* as a label for particular sayings is reserved in the Gospels exclusively for instances of those various forms that embody analogy. The common denominator of all the parables is not one rhetorical structure, nor even any characteristic of content such as realism or kingdom theology, but a particular form of thought.

This logic of analogy is explicit and overt in some sayings (e.g., Mark 13:28–29): "Now learn this lesson from the fig tree: As soon as its twigs get tender and its leaves come out, you know that summer is near. Even so, when you see these things happening, you know that it is near, right at the door." The rhetoric may be different in most of the sayings of Jesus labeled with the word *parable,* but the implied logic is identical: As soon as the seed falls along the path, the birds come and devour it. So also, when some hear the word, Satan immediately comes and takes it away. Some parables make just one analogy; but the Sower (Mark 4:3–9, 14–20) and some other stories consist of several analogies linked by a common theme (Sider, "Proportional Analogy").

The common definition of *parabole* as "story" is as misleading as other half-truths. Many are not stories in any accepted sense; the rest are not ordinary stories, but narratives put to the service of analogy. Scholarly equations of "parable in the strict sense" with "imaginary story" (Lambrecht

130) are not universal (cf. Kistemaker xiv). But they are a common mistake, perhaps based on the idea that *parabole* typically denoted "story" in Greek until the evangelists—influenced by the Septuagint rendering of Hebrew *mashal* as *parabole*—extended its field of meaning to subnarrative forms such as the proverb of Luke 4:23. The reverse is true. The word had always denoted "analogy." The evangelists may actually have been the first to broaden its meaning to include analogies elaborated into narrative.

The great achievements of this century's parable studies would be greater still if scholars had not so often taken the parables primarily as stories, and as analogies only incidentally, if at all. If they had not done so, the dichotomy of parable and allegory could hardly have arisen. (The *essence* of allegory is elaborated analogy—not, as Jülicher and others have said, pervasive symbolism, thematic obscurity, lack of verisimilitude, or conventional meaning. Certain allegories have all these features; many have only some, or none.) Although Jülicher rightly saw the logic of analogy in the "similitude" (1:70ff.), he failed to note that every "story-parable" is an analogy that becomes a story by means more or less allegorical. Thus a simple analogy on the father-son relationship (e.g., Matt. 7:9–11) is elaborated into a narrative cluster of analogies in the Two Sons (Matt. 21:28–32) and a still larger one in the Lost Son (Luke 15:11–32).

With his theory that allegory makes many points but parable only one, Jülicher overreacted to the abuses of allegorizing interpreters. Thinking of a parable primarily as a story encourages one to look for only one point, and to take part of a complex idea for the whole. Thinking of a parable first as an analogy prepares one to find several complementary points—as in the many-faceted poetic comparisons of John Donne.

Defining parable as "story" has also hindered structuralist studies (e.g., Patte), which focus on the deep structure of narrative. More work on the deep structure of analogy is needed before we can tell what alterations the structures of narrative may undergo when a parable of Jesus subordinates story to the purposes of analogy.

Likewise, interpreters who treat parables as narrative metaphors (while neglecting their function as analogy) sometimes privilege the sort of metaphor that is most untranslatable, equate the parables with this special type, and declare them untranslatable (e.g., Crossan 1979). But the rational structure of the analogy should be our first concern with a parable.

The Parable: An Image in a Text

The idea of "literary approaches" to the Bible is not new. Scholars have generally realized that "in the study of scripture . . . secular literature helpeth much" (Thomas More, *Dialogue Concerning Heresies,* 1529, I.22). What is new is substituting literary theories for broad, firsthand experience of literature. The more "theory" dominates criticism, the easier it may be to depend on deductions from theories rather than on comparison of the parables with suitable analogues in other literature. Yet any single "literary-critical model" will distort most literature, for there is more in the world of literature than is dreamed of in one philosophy.

Where should we look in literature to find the most useful analogues for the parables—replications of the whole combination of literary entities that combine with the pictorial and narrative images of Jesus' analogies? A simple parable such as the Thief in the Night (Luke 12:39–40) is very like an analogy of Oliver Goldsmith's from one of Samuel Johnson's conversations in Boswell's *Life of Johnson.* Jesus' parable is one element of a Lukan collage that begins with a request from the crowd (Luke 12:13) and is unified by one theme—the urgency of guiding earthly concerns from the perspective of the spiritual. Goldsmith's analogy is one element in a discussion that began with a remark of Boswell's and that is unified by the subject of religious toleration (538, 540).

The Occasion of the Discourse: A Remark by a Listener

Someone in the crowd said to him, "Teacher, tell my brother to divide the inheritance with me."	[Boswell] introduced the subject of toleration. . . .

The Vehicle of the Comparison: A Hypothetical Pictorial Image

If the owner of the house had known at what hour the thief was coming, he would not have let his house be broken into.	If I see a man who had fallen into a well, I would wish to help him out; but if there is a greater probability that he shall pull me in, than that I shall pull him out, I would not attempt it.

The Tenor of the Comparison:
An Application to a Discursive Argument

You also must be ready, because the Son of Man will come at an hour when you do not expect him.	So were I to go to Turkey, I might wish to convert the Grand Signor to the Christian faith; but when I considered that I should probably be put

to death without effectuating my purpose in any degree, I should keep myself quiet.

Both discourses are framed by narrative descriptions of the situation, which in turn are framed by the whole work—gospel or biography—in a combination of enveloping literary structures.

Gospel ⇨ episode ⇨ discourse ⇨ analogy ⇨ pictorial image + application

Biography ⇨ episode ⇨ discourse ⇨ analogy ⇨ pictorial image + application

The meaning of each image is defined partly from within, but partly by other literary components: application, analogy, discourse, and episode. It would be an obvious mistake to try to gather the full meaning of either image in isolation from its cooperative function in a larger literary structure. It is equally misleading to interpret the narrative images of Jesus' story-parables without accounting for their functions in larger literary structures. Close analogues for these more elaborate parables, too, may be found in biographical writing, such as Usher's reminiscence of Lincoln (96–97), whose analogy parallels Jesus' story of the Persistent Widow (Luke 18:1–8) in both context and internal structure.

Narrative of a Situation Involving a Response in Story-Analogy

Then Jesus told his disciples a parable to show them that they should always pray and not give up.

A short time before the capitulation of General Lee, General Grant told [Lincoln] that the war must necessarily soon come to an end, and wanted to know of him whether he should try to capture Jeff[erson] Davis, or let him escape from the country if he would.

The Vehicle of Comparison: A Narrative Image

He said: "In a certain town there was a judge who neither feared God nor cared about men. And there was a widow in that town who kept coming to him with the plea, 'Grant

He said: . . . "I told him the story of an Irishman who had taken the pledge of Father Mathew. He became terribly thirsty, and applied to a bartender for a lemonade, and me justice against my adversary.' For some time he refused. But finally he said to himself, 'Even though I don't fear God or care about men, yet because this widow keeps bothering me, I will see that she gets justice, so that she won't eventually wear me out with coming.' "

while it was being prepared he whispered to him, 'And couldn't ye put a little brandy in it all unbeknown to meself?' "

The Tenor of the Comparison: Application to the Subject of Discussion

And the Lord said, "Listen to what the unjust judge says. And will not God bring about justice for his chosen ones, who cry out to him day and night? Will he keep putting them off? I tell you, he will see that they get justice, and quickly."

"I told Grant if he could let Davis escape all unbeknown to himself, to let him go. I didn't want him."

Good parallels to the elaborated story-parables can be found in ancient fables: "Not fantastic stories, but . . . ordinary human characters and situations . . . religious or ethical themes . . . realism . . . [and yet] an element of extravagance" (Beavis 480). Other analogues abound in various forms: from More's analogy of Seneca in comedy (*Utopia* 28–29) and Shakespeare's "vicious mole" (*Hamlet* 1.4.17–38) to Lincoln's borrowed proverb on the crisis of the Union: "A house divided against itself cannot stand" (Lincoln 429) and the Lord High Executioner's song of "Tit Willow" in *The Mikado* by Gilbert and Sullivan (395–96). All of these instances are analogies with pictorial or narrative images, put to the service of discourse set in the context of some larger story.

Such parallels to Jesus' parables will help us more than freestanding "parables" of Kafka, which are not thus structurally enveloped. We may profit, of course, by studying the operation of any metaphor—or symbol, story, etc.—and the methods of critics who discuss them. But we must constantly ask, "How is this metaphor (or this way of understanding it) different from that found in a parable, where it functions in a story, in an analogy pointed for a particular occasion, and in other literary forms?" And it will be hard to find much practical criticism to use as a precedent for taking account, *all at once,* of the image of a parable and its complex interaction with the point of an analogy, the discourse for which it is invoked, and the gospel narrative that frames the discourse. For critics have not often paid that sort of attention to Lincoln's anecdotes, or Johnson's.

My intent thus far is to describe, perhaps more fully than hitherto, the peculiar situation that narrative has in the parables—but certainly not to downplay its significance. No other collection of such brief sayings has ever inspired so widespread and powerful a response from readers of all sorts. This unique phenomenon can be explained only partly as a product of the keen interest in anything so closely connected with Jesus Christ. Why has no comparable corpus of narrative analogies attracted a similar concentration of intense literary analysis, of a sort usually reserved for much more elaborate stories? Because none has come close to Jesus' parables in the subtlety and power of so many narrative features and techniques—such as vivid realism, unforgettable characters, archetypal motifs, striking contrasts, patterned repetition in language and events, memorable touches of the unusual or downright marvelous, skillfully exploited narrative points of view, and the like. These qualities of story deserve not less attention than in the past, but even more.

The rest of this essay, therefore, illustrates the possibilities for narrative analysis by reference to just one of the connections between Jesus' stories and their framing literary structures. How may the meaning of a parable be identified and clarified by the interplay of two interlocked narratives—Jesus' parable-story, and the evangelist's story of Jesus' discourse? For many other important literary topics in the parables I must refer the reader to other sources: various aspects of the parabolic image in itself (e.g., Via, Ryken), the functions of analogy (e.g., Sider, "Proportional Analogy"; Blomberg), and the relationship of Jesus' images to his discourses and the evangelists' theology (e.g., Drury; Donahue).

Image and Text in Interplay

Some of the connections between Jesus' stories and the evangelists' are obvious. The contrasting behavior of the "righteous" and the "sinners" who followed Jesus bears directly on the parables of the Two Sons (Matt. 21:28–32) and the Two Debtors (Luke 7:41–47)—Jesus says so himself. Luke says the same about other parables: expressly for the Pharisee and Publican (Luke 18:9–14) and implicitly for the Lost Sheep, Lost Coin, and Lost Son (Luke

15:1–2). So too more than once Jesus' enemies "knew he had spoken the parable against them" (Mark 12:12).

Yet it is easy to miss the interplay of image and text. Is the satiric object of the Rich Fool, for instance, nothing other than covetousness in general, as has been suggested? The context of Jesus' discourse does, indeed, identify the universal vice as part of his meaning (Luke 12:15, 21): "Be on your guard against all kinds of greed; a man's life does not consist in the abundance of his possessions. . . . This is how it will be with anyone who stores up things for himself but is not rich toward God." Yet in Luke's episode a historical particular is the inspiration for the image, and part of its satiric object (12:13): "Someone in the crowd said to him, 'Teacher, tell my brother to divide the inheritance with me.' Jesus replied, 'Man, who appointed me a judge or an arbiter between you?'" As at other times, his first response challenges the man's assumptions; but the story conveys his actual reply. God's question to the rich fool touches the man's inheritance very nearly, for the dead parent is powerless to execute his own will: "Then who will get what you have prepared for yourself?" And in possession the son's case would be the same. The man in the crowd—and the crowd too—knew that Jesus had spoken the parable against him.

Likewise the text surrounding the image of the Wicked Tenants develops two foci of meaning, complementary but distinct. The immediate context emphasizes Jesus' conflict with the authorities (Mark 12:12): "Then they looked for a way to arrest him." But throughout Mark's gospel the murder of the son has reverberations that make his death the real climax of the parable. Very near the beginning of the gospel (2:20) is a veiled prophecy of Jesus' death, and the intent to kill him surfaces soon after (3:1–6). Near the middle he openly predicts his destiny (8:31), and thereafter we are reminded of it over and over (9:9, 31; 10:33–34, 45; 14:8, 21, 24) until it brings the gospel to *its* climax. Fully to feel the force of Jesus' story, we need the whole of Mark's story.

Such examples only begin to illustrate the interplay of Jesus' stories with the evangelist's in *plot* and *character.* In the rocky soil of the Sower (Matt. 13:20–21) the spiritual dangers of "trouble or persecution" derive a haunting significance from Jesus' reaction to the death of John the Baptist (14:11–13): "His head was brought in on a platter and given to the girl, who carried it to her mother. John's disciples came and took his body and buried it. Then they went and told Jesus. When Jesus heard what had happened, he withdrew by boat privately to a solitary place."

Another kind of irony invests Jesus' image of the Children in the Marketplace, which points out his opponents' perverseness (Luke 7:33–35): "For John the Baptist came neither eating bread nor drinking wine, and you say, 'He has a demon.' The Son of Man came eating and drinking, and you say, 'Here is a glutton and a drunkard, a friend of tax collectors and "sinners."' But wisdom is proved right by all her children." For in Luke's narrative a Pharisee promptly provides a case in point, when a "sinful" woman anoints Jesus (7:39): "He said to himself, 'If this man were a prophet, he would know who is touching him and what kind of woman she is—that she is a sinner.'"

So too the meaning of the image of the Vineyard Laborers (Matt. 20:1–16) is underscored very soon after by the disciples' own heedlessness of Jesus' point. They replicate the laborers' selfish anger (v. 12: "You have made them equal to us"), when James and John are nominated for the highest places of honor in the kingdom (v. 24): "When the ten heard about this, they were indignant with the two brothers." Likewise Jesus' image of himself as the sinners' physician (e.g., Mark 2:17) is illuminated by his ministry as physical healer; and in his home town the two are merged (6:5–6): "He could not do any miracles there, except lay his hands on a few sick people and heal them. And he was amazed at their lack of faith."

The power of a parable frequently depends partly on Jesus' choice of an *archetype,* which may resonate with other archetypal images in the text. Thus in Mark 4, symbols of flourishing life reinforce one another: the Sower, the Growing Seed, the Mustard Seed. In all these, moreover, the divine qualities of the kingdom stand out more sharply against the demonic archetypes of chapters 3 and 5: the diseases of shriveled hand and hemorrhage (3:1; 5:25), the evil spirits (3:11; 5:1), destruction by drowning (4:38; 5:13) and the horror of a child's death (5:35). When Jesus invokes the analogy of David and the consecrated bread (Mark 2:25–26) to defend his disciples' violation of the Sabbath law, we find complementary archetypes of kingship: the historical image of Israel's great king, and the kingdom image of the Son of Man as Lord of the Sabbath.

Echoes of a parable's *language* can unfold its meaning. The parable of the Hid Treasure (*thesaurous,* Matt. 13:44) is illuminated by the "treasure (*thesaurous*) in heaven" of the Sermon on the Mount (6:20). (In Luke, "where your treasure is . . ." comes after the rich fool's "plenty of good things laid up for many years"—12:19, 34.) The "beloved son" who comes last to the wicked tenants (Mark 12:6) reminds us of the voice from heaven at Jesus' baptism and transfiguration (Mark 1:11; 9:7). Phrases from the parable of the Waiting Servants connect the Day of the Lord with present occasions when the disciples' vigilance fails:

Mark 13:35–36:	*Mark 14:72, 37:*
Keep watch because you do not know when the owner of the house will come back—whether in the evening, or at midnight, or when the rooster crows, or at dawn.	Immediately the rooster crowed the second time. Then Peter . . . broke down and wept.
If he comes suddenly, do not let him find you sleeping.	Then he returned to his disciples and found them sleeping.

At the very start of the parable of the Wicked Tenants (Mark 12:1), strong *connotations* set the mood: "A man planted a vineyard. He put a wall around it, dug a pit for the winepress and built a watchtower." This description carries all the threatening overtones of divine judgment expressed in Isaiah's image of the vineyard of Israel (5:1–7). These associations tie in both with "He will come and kill those tenants" (Mark 12:9) and with the beginning of Mark 13:

> As he was leaving the temple, one of his disciples said to him, "Look, Teacher! What massive stones! What magnificent buildings!"
>
> "Do you see all these great buildings?" replied Jesus. "Not one stone here will be left on another; every one will be thrown down."

Whereas the *point of view* of a free-standing story usually depends on the narrator's stance alone, Luke's story (15:1–2) provides Jesus' story of the Lost Son with two finely contrasted points of view: of the tax collectors and "sinners" who gathered to hear him, and of the Pharisees and lawyers who muttered: "This man welcomes sinners and eats with them." All through the parable, the two audiences of "righteous" and "sinners" sustain contrary perspectives on both sons—poignantly in the conclusion (15:30, 32):

> This son of yours . . . has squandered your property with prostitutes.
>
> This brother of yours was dead and is alive again.

Settings too can play off each other. They enrich the meaning of several parables in Luke 14 and 15, where Luke's literary design includes no fewer than eight meals, real, hypothetical, and symbolic: Jesus' Sabbath meal with a Pharisee (14:1ff.), his fellow-guests at a future wedding feast (14:8–11), a future meal given by Jesus' host (14:12–14), the messianic banquet (14:15), the feast of the kingdom here and now (14:16–24), Jesus' meals with "sinners" (15:2), the prodigal's husks (15:16), and the gracious father's celebration (15:23–32). This collage gives intricately complementary expressions to a single theme—the Pharisees' self-seeking pride, which keeps them from entering into the merciful fellowship of God's kingdom (cf. Luke 11:42, 52).

The Image and Text of the Good Samaritan

The ideal interpretation of a parable would weigh (alongside many other considerations) the combined force of all such features of narrative in their diverse connections. So Jesus' story interacts with Luke's in the parable of the Good Samaritan (10:25–37). The second great commandment makes the lawyer uneasy; so does the parable. Without telling him what to think and feel, Jesus' story invites him to recognize genuine charity for what it is. By more complex literary effects, Luke's story invites the reader too.

Beyond the parable's archetypal journey into danger is the framing *archetype* of Jesus' journey to Jerusalem and the Cross (9:51–19:38); his own unconditional love gives conclusive credibility to the Samaritan's deeds. The secure *setting* of Jesus' talk with the lawyer sets off the perils of the road to Jericho. Luke's *characterization* of this teacher of the law—as intent on circumscribing love—helps define Jesus' meaning in his portrayal of the priest and the Levite. The story's progress first unites and then divides the double *audience perspective,* of Jesus' audience and Luke's.

Both audiences can foresee the traveler's calamity; both are let down by the priest. And though the victim hopes for help from the Levite, the narrative "rule of three" (a feature of *plot structure*) might prompt both audiences to guess that the rescuer will be the third passerby. But this expectation is fulfilled in such ironic fashion that the two audiences' perspectives suddenly diverge. The rescuer's identity would be a coarse shock to Jews like the lawyer: against all expectations a Samaritan renders all possible aid under the least favorable conditions imaginable. But any Gentile reader of Luke might well take an ironic view of the lawyer's surprise.

Both audiences will marvel as the *climax* of the rescuer's identity begins a string of surprises. The man not only stops to help; he spends his own oil and wine, takes the victim to safe shelter, tends him there, stays with him till the next day, leaves a laborer's two-day wage (cf. Matt. 20:2) for expenses, and assumes liability for all unforeseen costs whatsoever. The meaning of the parable's climax is in the climax of the lawyer's story. His question about the second great commandment is "How much should I give?"

but Jesus simply asks him: "How much have you got?" In the *language* of Luke's story the lawyer's usage of "neighbor" defines his fellow human beings; but "neighbor" in Jesus' concluding question defines the lawyer himself.

And the double *point of view*—of Jesus' story and Luke's—points up the lawyer's moment of choice. The parable is governed throughout by the point of view of the presumably Jewish victim: he expects the priest and Levite to help; maybe he would sooner die than accept a Samaritan's help. As the primary audience of Jesus' story, the lawyer naturally identifies with the victim; but as actor in Luke's story, he is pressed against his will to adopt the point of view of the Samaritan in his marvelous dedication.

Everything contributes to this marvel. The setting by itself would make most folks pass by on the other side. If the priest and Levite can find excuses, a layman more. Most important, why would a Samaritan help a man who may curse him just for being a Samaritan? He is merciful despite an array of obstacles that might seem like a humorous exaggeration, but for the urgent seriousness of the story. Forced to compare himself with the Samaritan, the lawyer has no good excuse to avoid his neighbor.

Thus the interplay of story with story in archetypes, settings, characters, audience perspectives, plot structure and climaxes, language, and points of view can help us find in the parable more of what is there. It can also keep us from finding too much. By itself the image might seem like a general defense of Samaritans, or a general attack on the cult establishment. But the surrounding literary structures belie a structuralist interpretation (Patte 82–83) that sets true religion at odds with the Jewish religion:

> The semantic effect of the parable deeply challenges the traditionally religious: as long as they do not venture outside of their religiously ordered world and become irreligious, they cannot be symbolically identified with the truly religious person—they do not belong to the kingdom—and consequently they cannot act as a truly religious person. As long as they remain priest and Levite (and Jew) they cannot help the wounded man in the ditch.

Stopping for the wounded man would not make either priest or Levite irreligious even by conventional standards. Likely the Levite was not under ceremonial restrictions against touching a corpse (Jeremias 203–4); and since the man was alive, he was not untouchable to the priest (Lev. 21:1–4). The religious could have helped him without being irreligious.

The story outside the story makes it clear that the priest and Levite are important rather for their affinity with the teacher of the law, showing that despite good intentions he may mistake the form of the second great commandment for the substance. Jesus did object sometimes to the Jewish practice of religion (e.g., Luke 11:45–52); but this parable urges the lawyer to act in the spirit of the law.

Likewise the identity of the outcast Samaritan is important to strengthen the call to love in action—indefinitely extrapolated. The lawyer's respect for the law is not inimical to true religion and undefiled; nor are Samaritans specially qualified. But this is an antipastoral parable, undercutting idealizations of rural life and of its simplified social relationships. It throws official representatives of society into asocial chaos, giving more edge to the ostracized Samaritan's exemplary social role.

Conclusion

The interplay of image and text is so complex and subtle that for a long time to come any interpreter of the parables has excellent opportunities for fresh literary discoveries. Despite the subjectivity of literary judgments, the most promising future for the study of the parables is in mapping the full extent of their literary forms and functions. In this enterprise it is useful to remember that though our readings are tentative and sometimes reversible, Christians are fully justified in pursuing a stable meaning in the texts of the Bible. Of other texts the deconstructionist may be right to assert that stable meaning is a chimerical fancy. But the influence of deconstructionism in parable studies (e.g., Crossan, *Finding* 94) is regrettable. For the Presence behind the biblical text guarantees its stable meaning (though now we see it darkly) and promises to guide us eventually into all of its truth.

LITERARY WORKS CITED

Boswell, James. *Life of Johnson.* Oxford: Oxford UP, 1953.

Gilbert, Sir W. S., and Sir Arthur Sullivan. *The Complete Plays.* New York: Modern Library, 1936.

Lincoln, Abraham. "Speech Delivered at Springfield. . . ." *The Life and Writings of Abraham Lincoln.* Ed. Philip Van Doren Stern. New York: Random House, n.d. 428–38.

More, Saint Thomas. *A Dialogue Concerning Heresies.* London, 1529.

———. *Utopia.* Trans. and ed. Robert M. Adams. New York: Norton, 1975.

Shakespeare, William. *The Riverside Shakespeare.* Boston: Houghton Mifflin, 1974.

Usher, J. P. *Reminiscences of Abraham Lincoln by Distinguished Men of His Time.* Ed. Allen Thorndike Rice. 8th ed. New York: North American Review, 1889.

STUDIES CITED

Beavis, Mary Ann. "Parable and Fable." *Catholic Biblical Quarterly* 52 (1990): 473–98.
Blomberg, Craig L. *Interpreting the Parables.* Downers Grove, Ill.: InterVarsity, 1990.
Breech, James. *The Silence of Jesus.* Philadelphia: Fortress, 1983.
Cadoux, A. T. *The Parables of Jesus.* London: James Clarke, 1931.
Crossan, John Dominic. *In Parables.* New York: Harper & Row, 1973.
———. *Finding Is the First Act.* Philadelphia: Fortress, 1979.
Donahue, John R. *The Gospel in Parable.* Philadelphia: Fortress, 1988.
Drury, John. *The Parables in the Gospels.* New York: Crossroad, 1985.
Hunter, Archibald M. "Recent Trends in Johannine Studies IV." *Expository Times* 71 (1960): 219–22.
Jeremias, Joachim. *The Parables of Jesus.* 2d rev. ed. Trans. S. H. Hooke. New York: Scribner, 1972.
Jülicher, Adolf. *Die Gleichnisreden Jesu.* 2 vols. 1899. Rpt. with vols. reversed. Tübingen: Mohr, 1910.
Kistemaker, Simon J. *The Parables of Jesus.* Grand Rapids: Baker, 1980.
Lambrecht, Jan. *Once More Astonished.* New York: Crossroad, 1981.
Palmer, Humphrey. *The Logic of Gospel Criticism.* New York: St. Martin's, 1968.
Patte, Daniel. *What Is Structural Exegesis?* Philadelphia: Fortress, 1976.
Ryken, Leland. *How to Read the Bible as Literature.* Grand Rapids: Zondervan, 1984.
Sider, John W. "Proportional Analogy in the Gospel Parables." *New Testament Studies* 31 (1985): 1–23.
———. "Rediscovering the Parables: The Logic of the Jeremias Tradition." *Journal of Biblical Literature* 102 (1983): 61–83.
Via, Dan Otto, Jr. *The Parables: Their Literary and Existential Dimension.* Philadelphia: Fortress, 1967.

CHAPTER 32

Acts

CAREY C. NEWMAN
Palm Beach Atlantic College

At first blush, the book of Acts reads simply as a history of the earliest church. Full of chronological and geographical textual markers, Acts narrates how the church, through the tireless efforts of two apostles (Peter and Paul), made its way from Jerusalem to Rome in thirty short years. To construe the book as merely sermons framed by travelogue is to decline the true invitation of Acts. Acts bids the reader to join the sometimes chaotic, sometimes apocalyptic, but always marvelously expanding world of Jesus' earliest followers. Throughout this wonderful account, Acts consistently resolves any suspense concerning the reason for progress: expansion is to be explained by supernatural intervention rather than random, uncanny chance.

Genre

The wonderful features of Acts, no less than the historical ones, have clouded the issue of genre: Just what kind of literature is Acts anyway? Answers range from history or legal defense to Christian preaching or theology to popular literature or fanciful legend (cf. Ramsay, Haenchen,

Hengel, and Pervo). Unfortunately, such attempts to classify typically run roughshod over one of Acts' generic features—be it history, theology, literary architecture, or some combination thereof. Since Acts demonstrably shares some conventions of most, if not all, of the genres, the struggle to press Acts into (only) one classification has been especially difficult.

I suggest that "documentary" is an applicable generic classification, for documentary gathers up what are sometimes seemingly irreconcilable characteristics. Ostensibly, the "subject" of Acts is what happened—the *praxis,* the activity. As opposed to a work of fiction, Acts presents itself as a record of what occurred, arousing an expectation of authenticity. However one today judges the story's historical veracity, Acts attempts to mirror textually the events it narrates.

That Acts engages in observation does not imply, however, that Acts does not betray a purpose or a point of view. Acts is indeed "saying something"—every document(-ary) does. The objectives could range from cognitive (to inform, interpret, apply, analyze) to affective (to engender sympathy, acceptance, commitment). That Acts triggers any number of transformational outcomes rests on documentary's capacity to realize many aims simultaneously. Although traditionally charged with excessive staging, Acts selectively orders the spontaneous events it narrates. Editing in no way (necessarily) compromises the actuality of the events themselves. In summary: reading Acts as documentary does justice to the historical markers, the selective ordering, the claims for accuracy, and the entertaining value that characterizes the work.

Acts can therefore be compared favorably to a television documentary like *60 Minutes* or a work of New Journalism like Tom Wolfe's *The Right Stuff.* Like *60 Minutes,* Acts presents a selective account of what took place—both profit from significant editing; like *60 Minutes,* Acts strives for accuracy—to be caught in mispresenting the facts would result in grave social repercussions; and, like *60 Minutes,* Acts seeks to be entertaining—both have stood the test of time by attracting a wide and diverse audience.

Acts also can be viewed as an ancient precursor of New Journalism. Truman Capote's *In Cold Blood* or Norman Mailer's *Armies of the Night* depend on the reporter's aggressive gathering of details—novelistic details; this is no less true of Acts. Acts reports the story with techniques and devices normally associated with nonfiction literature. Like the works of New Journalism, Acts demonstrates that nonfiction (memoirs, autobiography, news reports, history) is a serious artistic form. When Tom Wolfe claimed that "there is a tremendous future for a sort of novel that will be called a journalistic novel or perhaps documentary novel, novels of intense social realism based upon the same painstaking reporting that goes into New

Journalism" (Wolfe 35), he was probably not thinking of Acts. Acts nonetheless can be read as a first-century docudrama (accurate yet nuanced), thereby benefiting from the momentum latent within realism. Indeed, Acts appears to revel in the joy and power of realism.

Whatever decision is made about the precise generic classification, a decision that may well be impossible to render with absolute certainty, generic properties are not mutually exclusive: Why shouldn't an accurate record of the wonderful exploits of Jesus' earliest followers be transformative and at the same time provide readers, both ancient and modern, with immense delight? Ultimately, the failure in generic labeling neither dulls the realistic luster nor assays the miraculous richness of Acts.

The Contexts for Reading Acts

Generic riddles can be solved, in part, by reading Acts within its two primary literary contexts—the Jewish Scriptures and the gospel of Luke. First, Acts signs within the narrative horizon generated by the Jewish Scriptures. Acts' use of divine-agency language—Holy One, Righteous One, Name, angel, voice, Glory, Son of Man, Prophet—contributes to the apocalyptically charged characterization of Jesus and his witnesses and blends their activity with that of the God of Jewish Scriptures.

The sermons contained within Acts resonate with echoes of their Old Testament subtexts. The forty-two clear citations of the Jewish Scriptures situate the events of Acts in the long line of God's deeds. Such intertextual linkages freely invoke the salvific archetypes of creation, exodus, covenant, kingship, suffering, and prophetic hope, images so dominant in the Jewish tradition, to explain the continued praxis of God recorded in Acts.

Although the Jewish Scriptures contain prefigurations of dramatic, divine visitations to earth and mysterious, human ascents into the heavens, Acts brings into relief that which before was only partially articulated. Acts tells how a particular story about a very particular person—the promised coming, life (words and deeds), death, exaltation, present activity, and future return of Jesus—rippled through the first century, creating an eschatological community of believers *ex nihilo*. By using words, phrases, images, and stories that already possessed referential power, Acts not only echoes the great acts of God in the Jewish Scriptures but also invites a comparison that ultimately demands narratological revisioning.

The second, more immediate, context for reading Acts is provided by its prequel, the gospel of Luke. Although the relationship of the two works can be debated on different levels—i.e., authorship, language, purpose, themes, theology, characters (see Tannehill)—by beginning with a reference to the "first word" (1:1), Acts renews the plot first started in the Gospel: "In the first book, O Theophilus, I have dealt with all that Jesus *began* to do and teach" requires "I will now tell you, O Theophilus, all that Jesus *continued* to do . . ." (Marshall 55–56). Acts thus forms the narrative sequel to all that Jesus began to do and teach.

Acts is therefore very much like Luke's gospel, for it records the activity of Jesus on earth. Unlike the gospel, Acts is not an account of the *earthly* deeds of an *earthly* Jesus, but rather the *earthly* activity of the *heavenly* Jesus. Jesus' exaltation from earth to heaven distinguishes Acts from the gospel and emerges as the precipitating event for the ensuing narrative.

The exaltation of Jesus also invites a comparison between Acts and Revelation. Like Revelation, Acts records an almost unrestricted access to the heavens: communication and information pass from heaven to earth through visions, dreams, angelophanies, and Christophanies. Whereas Revelation records the *future* deeds of an *exalted* Jesus, Acts records the *present* deeds of an *exalted* Jesus. While the difference in point of view between the gospel of Luke and Acts is spatial (earth to heaven) and between Acts and Revelation is temporal (present to future), all three works unite their textual voices to speak of the dramatic events surrounding the praxis of Jesus.

Whatever it is (and the debate is still open), Acts signs in light of and in conjunction with the narrative of the Jewish Scriptures and the story of Jesus. The words, phrases, images, archetypes, and intertextual linkages tether Acts to the way in which the earthly deeds of an exalted Jesus fit within the overarching narrative of the Jewish Scriptures, a story that reaches from "beginning" (creation) to "end" (kingdom of God). The complex web of analeptic and proleptic associations positively situates Acts in a larger story (Jewish Scriptures) whose "end" (resurrection) has already begun to be unfolded.

Structure in Acts

Acts employs any number of structuring devices. At first glance, the giant figures of Peter and Paul organize the text. The first half of Acts revolves around Peter and his exploits, while the second half coheres in the deeds and words of Paul. But the cast of Acts is not limited to just two players; the text introduces some ninety-five different characters, with Stephen, Philip, Barnabas, James, and Silas taking center stage at times.

Geography also shapes narration (Conzelmann). In the simplest sort of geographical structure Acts 1:8 serves as a paradigm: the Christian movement spread from "Jerusalem" (chs. 1–5) to "Judea and Samaria" (chs. 6–12), and even to the "ends of the earth" (chs. 13–28). A more complex geographical division arranges the text into six successive waves of expansion: (1) 1:1–6:7 recounts the birth of the movement in Jerusalem; (2) 6:8–9:31 covers the extension of the gospel to other parts of Palestine (Judea and Samaria); (3) 6:32–12:24 narrates the spread of Christianity to Antioch; (4) in 12:25–16:5 the focus shifts further west to Asia Minor and Cyprus; while (5) in 16:6–19:20 the gospel is preached in Macedonia and Europe; and, finally, (6) 19:21–28:31 chronicles Christianity's trek to Rome.

The sermons in Acts also help structure the narrative. Even the sermons themselves betray a common structure: in the coming of Jesus, the promises of God made in the Scriptures have been fulfilled; Jesus of Nazareth went about doing good, performing miracles by the power of God; this Jesus was crucified, raised from the dead and exalted to God's right hand; this same Jesus will come again to judge the world and restore the kingdom (Dodd 7–35). When considered together with the framing narratives, the sermons account for a significant portion of the total text and often function as the focal point of an episode (Bruce 34–40).

Acts also betrays a repeated cycle of experience (see Goulder): (1) God chooses witnesses who then (2) engage in preaching and/or mighty works; (3) a reaction to the praxis of God through the witnesses soon follows—on the one hand conversion, and on the other hand rejection, opposition, persecution, and even martyrdom; (4) despite opposition, new opportunities arise for the witnesses. The cycles begin as short episodes in Jerusalem, grow fuller in the expansion chronicled in Judea, Samaria, Asia Minor, and Europe, and finally end with a prolonged, single episode of Paul. Through protagonists, geography, sermons, and similar experiences, the text itself mimes the spiral of progress and expansion.

The Plot of Acts

The continued earthly activity of the exalted Jesus provides the basis for the episodic plot of Acts. Although taking many forms—spirit invasions, deeds accomplished in the name of Jesus, dreams, visions, angelophanies, Christophanies, miracles, sermons—the miniapocalypses all disclose key information to key characters at key junctures in the narrative, divinely emboldening the human agents to do the exploits of the exalted Jesus. The apocalypses guide and propel the newly formed community of followers in an ever outwardly spiraling adventure of progress and expansion, an adventure that ultimately stretches from Jerusalem to Rome.

The divine interventions yield marvelous consequences. At various stages of narration, Acts pauses to celebrate textually the apocalyptic tranquility infused by the continued activity of Jesus (e.g., 1:12–14; 2:41–47; 15:35; 28:30–31). By such summaries, Acts chronicles the deeds performed by believers (preaching, teaching, healing, praying), their future-worldly character (peace, unity, sharing, grace), and their unprecedented record of growth (multiplication, increase).

But the progress that Acts chronicles is not without significant detours. Throughout Acts a dark cloud hangs over the movement, for running alongside remarkable success is any number of threats. External forces repeatedly hinder progress: those who perform their activity under the aegis of Jesus suffer social marginalization, persecution, imprisonment, and even martyrdom. There are attempts to (con-)fuse the Jesus movement with Hellenistic, Samaritan, or traditional Jewish religious expressions. Internal deficiency, strife, and deceit plague the apocalyptic character of the community. On occasion, the pace of expansion presses the community of believers to the limits of their collective wisdom in facing the question, Can new converts be assimilated, and, if so, how?

Despite the external and internal threats—events forming the subplot of Acts—the various subgenres (dream-vision reports, miracle stories, sermons, conflict stories, devotional/hymnic material, theophanies, and apocalyptic summaries) work to secure progress. In fact, Acts transforms external and internal opposition into further expansion. By means of the recurrent apocalypses and revelations, Acts skillfully weaves the various subgenres to demonstrate the continued, progressive activity of the exalted Jesus.

The Story of Paul's Christophany (Acts 9:1–22)

An examination of the apostle Paul's encounter with the exalted Jesus (Acts 9:1–22) reveals how the subgenre of Christophany, an earthly appearance of the exalted Jesus, when read in contexts of the Jewish Scriptures and the gospel of Luke, contributes to the plot of progress and expansion. The fact that Acts repeats the account twice (Acts 22:4–16; 26:9–18) only serves to underscore the connotative power inherent in the story.

In both form and function, the appearance of Christ to Paul echoes the great "call" passages of the Bible (Gen. 15:1–6; Ex. 3:1–4:16; Josh. 1:1–11; Jer. 1:1–10; Ezek. 1:1–3:15; Isa. 6; 40:1–11; 49:1–6). The formal similarities are striking: like those of the prophets, Paul's Christophany contains an introductory word (9:1–3a), the report of divine confrontation (9:3b–4), an objection (9:5a), a commissioning (9:5b–6, 10–18), and a sign of reassurance (9:9, 18–19). The form also links the event with the many divine interventions contained within the gospel, especially the baptism and transfiguration of Jesus. The "call" passage form incorporates Paul into the list of venerable servants who have been commissioned at the hands of the living God.

Authorized by the resurrection appearance of Jesus, Paul continues the drama of salvation begun in the Jewish Scriptures and amplified in Jesus. The "chosen instrument" (9:15), Paul fills the role of the servant of Isaiah (49:1) who is to bring light/salvation to the nations. The Christophany also unites Paul with Jesus. Through suffering, Paul's life acquires the cruciformic shape of cross and resurrection, the very pattern of Jesus' life. Jesus continues his life in and through Paul's apostolic exploits.

Often overlooked is the apocalyptic character of the Christophany. Acts reports that Paul saw a "light out of heaven" (9:3; 22:6; 26:13) and heard the "voice" (9:4; 22:7; 26:14) of the One who "appeared" to him. Paul is called to be a witness to all that he has "seen and heard" (22:15; 26:16) and of what the risen Christ will yet "reveal to him" (26:16). Transformed by this "heavenly vision" (26:19), Paul obediently engages in missionary activity. The use of apocalyptically charged language places the Christophany squarely within the "throne vision" tradition of early Jewish apocalypses. Paul's apocalyptic vision of Jesus as the end-of-time revelation of God signals that the long-awaited kingdom of God was present in the exalted Jesus.

The Christophany dramatically advances the plot of Acts. The text first introduces Paul as a threat to progress and expansion. Present at and consenting to the murder of Stephen (8:1), Paul himself, through religious and political means, sought the physical dismemberment of the church (8:3). In Paul, Christianity faced the possibility of organized, effective, and passionate persecution (9:1–2). The divine intervention of the exalted Jesus baptizes the threat Paul posed, transforming threat into the very means of continued growth and expansion. Paul's mission to the nations, his message of Jesus as the apocalyptic "Son of God," and his suffering life are all consequences of his Christophany. As if ironic commentary on the will of God, the Christophany converts the one who persecuted into an object of persecution, a transformation of Paul from impediment to catalyst.

The Artistry of Acts: Resolution Without Closure

Acts sustains the emplotment of progress and expansion to the very end: the last picture is that of a hospitable Paul, in Rome, living at his own expense, engaging in preaching and teaching (28:30–31). Although under house arrest, Paul preaches without restriction (28:31). Despite Paul's imprisonment, the movement remains unshackled and unhindered.

The ending of Acts provides a sense of closure. Paul's preaching of the "kingdom of God" circles back to the beginning of Acts where Jesus preached the "kingdom of God" to the disciples (1:3). Paul's persistent testimony to the exalted Jesus recalls the pronouncement of Jesus: "You shall be my witnesses"—even to the ends of the earth (1:8). The unrestrictedness of Paul's mission, despite arrest, parallels the many times within Acts when the movement prospered in the face of disaster. Circularity and parallelism provide Acts with the sense of an ending, not only for the narrative begun in 1:1, but also for the gospel.

Through omission of key information, Acts also tenders a sense of openness and ambiguity. The reader is never told whether Paul successfully defended the charges raised against him. The reader is left in the dark concerning further expansion: What finally qualifies as "the ends of the earth"? Most importantly, the disciples' initial question concerning the "kingdom of God" remains unanswered: When will the kingdom be fully restored (1:7)? The textual muteness on this key question demonstrates that the ending fails to connect with the beginning completely. Acts therefore requires yet another narrative for successful completion—a narrative depicting the arrival of the "kingdom of God," the final apocalypse of Jesus, an apocalypse that overcomes all subversive hurdles once and for all and brings to exponential fullness both growth and expansion.

Textual openness and ambiguity introduce suspense to the act of reading. Positioned between exaltation and future apocalypses, the reader is left to wonder about expansion and growth. The failure of Acts to recapitulate fully its own beginning, however, does not leave the story unresolved. Acts documents the reason for expansion: the wonderful praxis of an exalted Jesus.

Acts therefore betrays something of a narrative paradox: the text reads with a sense of eschatological humility, not knowing when the "end" will fully occur, all the while boldly proclaiming the apocalyptic means for the arrival of the "end"—divine empowerment from heaven. The reader, too, becomes suspended and transfixed by resolution without final closure.

Reading Acts should not be (only) an exercise in early church theology or Greco-Roman historiography. The carefully crafted story generates a narrative world of divine intervention and identification in human affairs. This narrative world captivates and captures its readers today as successfully as it did those who first read it long ago. As documentary on the first collective steps of the empowered witnesses, Acts prods the reader today to surprise, discovery, and examination. The gaping hole in the sky, ripped wide open by the exaltation of Jesus, endows the text with a narrative power to which the reader can bear witness even today.

While the text awakens the reader to divine empowerment, only identification with the continued intervention of Jesus qualifies the reader to witness. By aggressively documenting the continued acts, the text mimes for the reader the activity of witnessing. In doing so, the text is only following the lead of its subject, for the exalted Jesus is the true and faithful witness and therefore the only qualified editor of the ongoing activity of his followers. Although the hole in the sky remains open yet today, the text fills that (w)hole with a faithful word of witness and invites the reader to do the same.

WORKS CITED

Bruce, F. F. *The Acts of the Apostles: The Greek Text With Introduction and Commentary.* 3d ed. Grand Rapids: Eerdmans, 1990.

Conzelmann, Hans. *The Theology of St. Luke.* Philadelphia: Fortress, 1961.

Dodd, C. H. *The Apostolic Preaching and Its Developments.* London: Hodder & Stoughton, 1936.

Goulder, M. D. *Type and History in Acts.* London: SPCK, 1964.

Haenchen, Ernst. *The Acts of the Apostles: A Commentary.* Philadelphia: Westminster, 1971.

Hengel, Martin. *Acts and the History of Earliest Christianity.* Philadelphia: Fortress, 1980.

Marshall, I. Howard. *The Acts of the Apostles.* Tyndale New Testament Commentaries. Grand Rapids: Eerdmans, 1980.

Pervo, Richard I. *Profit With Delight: The Literary Genre of the Acts of the Apostles.* Philadelphia: Fortress, 1987.

Ramsay, W. M. *St. Paul the Traveller and the Roman Citizen.* London: Hodder & Stoughton, 1897.

Tannehill, Robert C. *The Narrative Unity of Luke-Acts: A Literary Interpretation.* 2 vols. Minneapolis: Fortress, 1986, 1990.

Wolfe, Tom. *The New Journalism.* New York: Harper & Row, 1973.

CHAPTER 33

The Epistles

William G. Doty
The University of Alabama / Tuscaloosa

When we must arrange for an extended visit, or deal with a business problem in a town we have just visited, or seek to correct a misunderstanding among friends, most of us just pick up the telephone or FAX a communication. Hence it may well strike us as odd that so many of the New Testament writings dealing with such issues appear in epistolary form: some twenty of the twenty-seven books in the canon are referred to as letters, and letters appear as well in Acts and the Apocalypse to John. In order to comprehend fully the sorts of contents we can expect to find in the New Testament letters, we need a sense of their literary type (genre). What literary features characterize New Testament letters and the Greco-Roman Hellenistic letters that were their primary prototype?

Letters in the Greco-Roman Literary World

In the social world in which the early Christian writings appeared, letters were one of the most important media with which to communicate: almost anything could be (and was) shared in letter form, all the way from simple instructions for household workers, to invitations to family celebrations such as weddings, to the sort of reflective or meditative essays that today would be published in literary journals, and even to sermons and religious tracts. What to us is an ephemeral form that has by and large been replaced by the telephone and now the facsimile machine was in the Hellenistic Greek and Roman world a very frequent and important type of literature.

Anyone who has had an elementary school education knows that there are certain formulas one uses in writing a letter: "Dear Sir or Madam"; "Yours truly"; "the favor of a response"; "with reference to your FAX of 18 March." Such literary conventions are typical of every national literature, and indeed thousands of Greek and Latin letters from the Hellenistic world start off with a formal greeting or *salutation;* have a main *body* in which information is conveyed or a request is made, a command given, news shared; and conclude with *greetings* and goodbye wishes. The middle part, or body, of Greco-Roman letters was often very brief in informal or business letters; however, it could be quite long in communications between religious or philosophical communities, so much so that we might call such writings "letter-essays" (and therefore we need not worry about technical distinctions, such as those between "letters" and "epistles").

It is no surprise, then, when the Christian letter format typically moves from the traditional epistolary *salutation,* to the *body* (the place where the main subject of writing is treated, however formally defined in terms of literary characteristics or phrases), to the closing *greetings.* Along the way there are a number of modifications to the stereotyped conventions of Hellenistic epistolary language and literary subforms, and a number of instances in which the Christian writer follows Jewish custom and expands the basic structure to include an expression of thanksgiving or gratitude to God.

Look at the first letter to the Thessalonians for instance; there Paul is so grateful for the results of his initial work with the Christian community in Thessalonica that the typical declaration of thanksgiving is given three times! Knowing something about the typical style helps us understand a letter in its particular historical and social context. In this case we realize that Paul did not just forget and repeat himself, but he let the repetition of the thanksgiving unit emphasize his relief and gratitude that his early missionary endeavors among the Thessalonians were reaping rewards.

Aware that the thanksgiving-unit usually comes right after the salutation, we will not expect it at the end of the letter. We do not anticipate closing greetings at the beginning; and when we find Paul repeating the standard "I appeal to you, brethren" or "I beseech you" in one letter, we can explore how it is tailored to the local issues of a particular community, since it is used in seven letters in all. One subform returns again and again (only

Philemon lacks it) to the themes of *knowing* or *not being ignorant of*—often associated with the motif of *being ashamed* (in Romans, Philippians, and 2 Timothy). The phrase "I want you to know" is known well from the pre-Christian papyri, but that is about like saying that the Greeks spoke Greek! You might examine the use of these traditional formal units with these questions in mind: Is the writer seeking to convey new information in them? Does he wish to maintain an ongoing contact that seems threatened? Is he attempting to correct a position with which he disagrees?

Careful study of the literary features of the epistolary literature can inform our recognition of the ways the early Christian founders went about their business. It gives us an orientation to reconstructing the "typical" early Christian letter, and when we are confronted with the eighteen or twenty fragments of Paul's letters that technical analysis discloses in Romans, 1 and 2 Corinthians, Galatians, Philippians, 1 Thessalonians, and Philemon (more conservative analysts include additional materials as authentically Pauline), we have some basis for evaluating proposed reconstructions before we make judgments about theological contents.

Attention to the literary shapes and the language of the epistles will highlight their repetition and revision of Hellenistic rhetorical language and the correspondingly dynamic adaptation of the epistolary forms of the Mediterranean environment. It will recognize early Christian diversity: there is no one "Christian letter form" any more than there is any one "Christian language." And recognizing literary features used in the production of the Epistles helps us to appreciate the aims of the New Testament writers in light of the writing tools available to them. Every traditional genre has formal characteristics, and only if we are aware of what they are and how they function can we interpret accurately what is, for instance, "just a matter of speaking," and what is truly the metaphoric speaking forth of a whole new apperception of the meaning of life.

The Letter Genre and Subsequent Early Christian Literature

The choice of communicative genre is seldom made self-consciously; today, for instance, few would question that an attempt to influence the American public would obviously be pursued best by means of television programming or newspapers, since these are the media most frequently heeded. Paul's choice of the letter to communicate with persons and communities he had previously visited was surely just as natural, although getting those letters to the recipients was much more chancy than it would be today. The Roman Empire finally established a fairly trustworthy system of roadways and postal service, but for ordinary working people like the early Christian writers one still had to find a colleague willing to carry along messages and letters when undertaking a business or family trip.

Once determined, however, the choice of the letter as the literary genre used by Paul came to exert an extraordinary influence on all subsequent Christian literature. Throughout the later period of Christian beginnings, even writings that are more appropriately called essays or sermonettes or religious tracts than "letters" were shaped outwardly into epistolary form. The letter to the Hebrews, for instance, is a formal theological tract concerning the significance of the Christ that the author refers to as a "word of exhortation." But the sense that anything other than a "gospel" must be an "epistle" led both to the tract's epistolary closing in 13:22–25 and to the fact that the work is entitled "The *Epistle* to the Hebrews" in the New Testament canon.

Paul's own letters include materials apparently dictated at white heat, as in the shortest, Philemon, as well as carefully composed logical arguments, as in Galatians and Romans. But Paul always wrote with the situation of the recipients in mind and in tension with aspects of the situation that he thought needed correcting. Watch a person who is a careful arguer and you will see one of the traits involved: the speaker (in this case, the letter writer) picks up part of the vocabulary of the person opposed and takes it over. We wonder how much of what became normative Christian language was originally language stemming from positions opposed at the time or later (*mystery? salvation? spiritual?*—even the terms *gospel* and *ecclesia* were "baptized" into Christian usage from their pre-Christian origins).

Although later Christian letters were not always written in a furious give-and-take of ideas and problems and arguments and even name-calling, as were some of Paul's, the dominance of the epistolary form continues. In such letters, in addition to the formal units I have already named, we can identify lists of good and bad ethical behaviors, fragments of ceremonies and hymns, and some very early traditions about the Eucharist and Baptism that had been passed along orally in the preliterary Christian communities. Warnings against false teachers appear as Christian orthodoxy develops.

Often the later "letters" of the New Testament are what we would call today theological treatises, or ecclesiastical or religious instructions, such as the Letters of John or James, or the post–New Testament episcopal letters by which early church officials (bishops and popes) conveyed the correct date to observe Easter or elaborated some theological point. These letters do not follow the epistolary outline of most of Paul's letters, but then already in the

New Testament letters appeared in a wide range of epistolary formats. See, for instance, the slanderous denunciation of the enemy in the "Epistle" of Jude; the epistle conveying the supposed decree of the Apostolic Council, in Acts 15:23b–29; or the visionary, angel-dictated letters to the seven churches, in the Apocalypse.

But if subsequent Christian letters will take on all sorts of contours, what can we say about Paul's own "innate" epistolary style? Since Paul is adapting customary usage of the day for his own purposes, the reader ought to keep asking: What seems most traditional or stereotypical? Where are Paul's modifications of Jewish teachings most likely to be located? How does the overall configuring of any particular letter differ from that of others? Are certain parts of the letters more likely to carry the most important teachings, or are the letters more truly occasional, so that importance is determined by the haphazard arrangement of subjects to which the writer responds, rather than by their relative location in any particular letters?

Paul's Letter Form and Its Influence

As Paul began to develop his understanding of the Christian religion, he adapted, apparently single-handedly, the Hellenistic letter type found in both Jewish and non-Jewish communities. For instance, to begin his letters he took the Greek greeting *Charis!* and combined it with the Jewish wish for peace and health, *Shalom!* resulting in the phrase "Grace to you and peace!" that is found in Romans, 1 and 2 Corinthians, Galatians, Ephesians, Philippians, Colossians, 1 and 2 Thessalonians, and Philemon.

Before reading further in this section, the reader might profitably scan the Pauline letters in the *Pauline Parallels* compiled by Francis and Sampley, paying careful attention to the specific formal markers introduced by the editors and noting references to the writing process. For any particular formal element the *Parallels* provide a readout that illustrates at a glance how Paul had a sense of "the right way" to begin a letter, to move into the thanksgiving, to make an appeal, or to conclude.

In addition to these major structural elements there are several formal subunits typical of the Pauline materials, some of which, incidentally, refer to the epistolary situation itself. In them Paul commends someone (often the bearer of the letter) as worthy of the receiver's regard, or he mentions his own plans to follow up the letter with a personal visit (we see repeatedly that he considered letters makeshift substitutes for his actual presence), or he indicates that he is jotting down a note in his own handwriting after the secretary to whom he has dictated the letter has finished—the common office practice of the day, as indicated in six of his extant letters.

Other regularly appearing elements include various sorts of ethical teaching—he and subsequent New Testament letter writers regularly utilized the lists of vices, virtues, and duties popularized by the Hellenistic philosophical schools—and information about practices of the Christian communities such as baptism, prayer, the Eucharist, ascriptions, hymns, and teaching materials. Knowing the typical literary contours of these units, we can often gain insights into the particular historical situations that a New Testament letter-writer faced, and we can see how such a writer reached out for guidance to contemporary ethical teachings that might be brought alongside traditional Jewish morality.

Paul for his part always writes in conversation with the recipients of his letters. Sometimes he speaks out in anger about specific information concerning the community to which he is writing. On occasion he even refutes his religious competitors and critics, those who considered him the great heretic or the end-time antichrist! I do not think it can be emphasized strongly enough that Paul always operates in a dialogic context: he responds to gossip and to requests for information and teaching in letters sent to him. He sends his fellow workers to find out what is going on and then refers to their reports. And he makes it quite clear that he is out of patience with people who disagree with his own unique development of the new Gentile-positive Christian Judaism.

Thus letters often represent something like half the scene. We have the portions that come from one of the sides, and frequently it is difficult to figure out just what religious positions on the opposing side Paul is confronting! Apparently he quoted the language of opponents in order to refute or refine it; so we must recognize a certain defensiveness that caused Paul to use opponents' terms that he might not otherwise have wished to recognize or discuss. The later New Testament letter tradition will make it clear just who is causing what trouble: the pastoral and catholic letters do not pull any punches about who the schizmatics or heretics are and how such and such teachings will ruin a locally favored interpretation of Christian doctrine for ever and ever. But we must try to read even the Pauline letters with the question of the "other side" constantly in mind: Would Paul have come down so hard on so many positions if he had not been pushed hard by opponents arguing just the opposite? Can we locate points at which Paul seems less arbitrary than we may have thought at first reading, if we recognize that he may be overreacting to a particular position that we have not seen portrayed? (After all, extroverted reactive writers just start lashing out, reacting, rather than first carefully summarizing their opponents' views.)

Rhetorical Features

Hellenistic rhetorical training was found in any school, where pupils learned both to imitate the popular attorneys and orators and to write letters and essays in the style of the masters. Rhetorical tropes referring to the sphere of male sports such as those found in Philippians would have been familiar throughout the Mediterranean basin where Greek culture had spread, but imagine talking today about heading down the field for a Christian touchdown! Yet that is the sort of language Paul uses when he refers metaphorically to the relay races in Philippians 3 and 1 Corinthians 9. He also reflected the language usage of the courts of law in Galatians, and everyday colloquial Hellenistic Greek (the "common" or *koinê* Greek) when he referred to the socioeconomic and philosophical arenas of his own day. Colossians reflects speculative religious cosmology, and 2 Peter echoes contemporary apocalyptic; some analysts argue that Ephesians even uses Paul's own writings as a source of imagery and quotation.

And why not? since naturally New Testament writers would have used the literary genres and the rhetorical styles of their contemporaries if they were to be intelligible to all. One question literary analysis of the letters brings forth is this: In what modes of contemporary communication would such a religious enterprise be conveyed today? Obviously the classical "epistle" form would not be utilized—by the late Renaissance, in fact, a painting of a woman receiving or reading a letter ciphered a whole story of gender and privilege in itself, namely, a story of male intrusion into female territory. And in the later development of the epistolary novel, the letter became a form designating "unreality," an author's self-conscious "fiction," rather than a normal mode of everyday communication. Would the contemporary equivalent of the letter be the television commercial? What does the Christian do with the epistolary novel of today such as John Barth's *Letters: A Novel* (1979) or Alice Walker's *The Color Purple* (1982)? Just to ask such questions seriously indicates that we now appreciate the structural *functions* of literary forms as well as the contents that the biblical writings convey.

A fresh literary reading of the letters also discloses the rich *rhetorical* coloring reflected in the New Testament letters. While we are told that Paul's speaking in person was more impressive than his writing—and sometimes we wonder if he has not lost control of the logical development of a passage—nonetheless Paul was a powerful rhetorical imagist. He brought to his dictation the involved and creative phrases of a person who experienced the world with emotions bared; hence his anger, but hence also his striking creative freedom with respect to language.

Imagine telling the little group of Christians in somebody's household in Corinth, men and women who have finally come around to accepting Paul's revisionist religious teachings as authentic Christianity, that their smell is like a divine deodorizer! But in the same passage he goes on to prefer them as living epistles to sacred communiques cut mechanically onto stone message-posts: "We are . . . the aroma of Christ. . . . You yourselves are our letter, written . . . not on tablets of stone but on tablets of human hearts" (2 Cor. 2:15; 3:2–3). I am not sure either of those tropes would appeal to the strictly literary writer of our own era, but they are surely powerful images from the oral teaching and preaching of primitive Christianity.

Authorized Authors of the Christian Communities

An attentive reader can often gain useful insights by addressing straightforward questions to the epistolary texts: For instance, why does Paul stress apostolic authority so much? It is helpful to remember that the first "historian" of the early church, Luke in the Acts of the Apostles, does not even consider Paul an official apostle, since he limits that term to those who accompanied the historical Jesus. But Paul's own self-designation—"Paul, a servant of Jesus Christ, called to be an apostle" (Rom. 1:1)—represents a claim that Paul's authority is from the God who calls, or elects, certain prophetic groups and individuals to do his will and to exert religious authority.

Along with our attempt to reconstruct the other side of the issues to which epistle writers respond, then, it is important to reflect on the ways in which the writers' thought was shaped repeatedly by their sense of exerting apostolic authority, by their inspiration with respect to Christian beliefs that ought to become the norms for churches everywhere. Such authors did not write as "individuals" in the modern sense, but as ecclesiastical officials, and hence they name supporting coauthors in the letter salutations. Many of the letters that have survived (keep in mind how many were lost!—we even have references to some of the lost epistles) were self-consciously written in the mode of the authorial ecclesiastical plural ("*we* give thanks to God for you all") with public oral recitation by the recipient Christian group, most often in worship services, constantly in mind. A large number of early Christian letters address issues of authority in the churches, and the tradition that Christian letters are to convey instructions and commands from an ecclesiastical authority can be traced in four of the important apostolic fathers, as well as in the subsequent letters from popes and/or bishops ("encyclicals") that are still promulgated today in Roman Catholic, Eastern Orthodox, Episcopal, and Methodist Christianity.

The terminology of the epistles largely determined how the Christian communities would refer to their own members: the beloved of God, saints, brethren, the body of Christ, the church in ____, the exiles of the Dispersion. For the hearers among the small groups of Christians whom Paul gathered from among his business contacts, their friends and families, and then for those who received the later New Testament catholic, pastoral, and Johannine Letters, these epistolary writings were always conceived of as being read out loud, much as someone today may share with a gathering of friends a postcard from an admired colleague who was present at the opening of the Berlin Wall.

Although they were not "sacred literature" yet, and the types of small Christian affiliation-groups varied enormously, the New Testament epistles were often the founding documents by which the early household churches were established, and hence they were copied and passed around because they possessed almost scriptural importance from the very beginnings. As you read them, you will notice how they include portions of the ongoing services of worship, particularly those stemming from the baptismal liturgy that so prominently contrasted one's new Christian life with one's pre-Christian life.

The New Testament letters combine elements of traditional Jewish, Greek, and Roman letters with the sort of violent confrontational immediacy of the street preachers who were beginning to transform Greek and Roman philosophy from being an activity of the elite academy to being a matter of the folks on the street corner. As late as his final attempt in Romans to organize his religious beliefs systematically, Paul utilized the public soap-box speech (*diatribē*) of the wandering Cynic and Stoic philosophers. Probably the letters of James and Peter likewise reflect oral genres (sermons, catechesis, baptismal instruction), and later liturgically shaped hymns and phrases also become part of the rich *written* inheritance of Christianity that supplanted the oral transmission as much as a century or more later.

Reading the Letters

Paul's practices were not always followed by subsequent letter-writers, but we may summarize here some features that were often shared by later Christian letter-writers. Keeping these features in mind when reading the New Testament letters will help one correlate literary analysis with analysis of theological content.

1. As we have seen, Paul responds to particular situations, using the terms of the opponents and of those who agree with his own reformulations of Judaism; later New Testament epistles will augment Paul's own theological teachings, and others such as the letters of John probably were intended to augment and correct the theology of the fourth gospel. From a literary standpoint we must recognize how extensively the New Testament letters were influenced by these debate-and-correct or admonish-and-revise impulses. When reading these letters it is always important to seek their contexts: the occasion, the assumed audience who will read the letter, the adversaries addressed, the common positions of the Christian communities, the creative developments of this particular author, and so forth.

2. Often Paul develops a historical or theological point, sometimes citing traditions passed on to him such as those about the Eucharist, or Last Supper. But remember that Paul is the earliest New Testament writer we have, writing just twenty-five to thirty years after Jesus' death, and he may not have been familiar with many of the biographical traditions and the collections of what Jesus did and said that appeared in the Gospels several decades after his own letters were written. He is not concerned yet with the many questions about the definition of the "nature" of the Christ, or about the extent and institutional organization and hierarchy of Catholic Christianity, issues that move to center stage in the later, post-Pauline letters. Note how the book of James, in epistolary format, uses just that literary form to balance, if not correct, Paul's own earlier ethical teachings! When reading the letters, we must always remain alert to the relative stage in early Christian religious development they represent, and even to the question of development within the career of any one writer.

3. In considering the anticipated goal and end of all things (Christian eschatology), Paul considered the highly charged character of his own day as a time of realizing ancient promises: "Now!" Paul argued, "Christians can have the religious *experience* long promised in the Scriptures of Israel!" Paul's Spirit-filled religiosity was such that he spoke about his "own gospel" or his brand of Christianity in the mythical terms of the Garden of Eden: it was "a new creation," of as much importance for humankind as the fact that in the symbolic figure of the first human, Adam, sin entered the world, overcome only now generations later in the Second Adam, namely the resurrected Christ, literally known as a present being (*kyrios,* Lord) in communal Christian worship. Watch for the ways the early Christian letter-writers expressed their understanding of the "new utterance," the "treasure in earthenware vessels": language itself was transformed just as we have seen that the literary genre of the epistle was transformed, and even in translations we can sense the deep religious experience and enthusiasm that is given literary expression.

4. Fairly often Paul and other writers interpret passages of Scripture, arguing that they have been realized now in new ways, or allegorizing them. As one who was originally an observant Pharisaic Jew, Paul frequently refers to his own Jewish biblical heritage. In Romans 4 he repeats Genesis 15:6 no fewer than three times as he explains carefully how Christianity and Judaism realize different aspects of God's promises in his covenants with Abraham and Moses. Likewise 1 Peter reviews scriptural references to Christian holiness and righteousness, and elsewhere common Jewish symbols were freely reinterpreted: a good example is the famous existentializing or spiritualizing of the temple, so that instead of being a physical entity, it becomes an interior, experiential aspect of the Christian communities: "Do you [plural] not know that you are God's temple and that God's Spirit dwells in you? If anyone destroys God's temple, God will destroy him. For God's temple is holy, and that temple you are" (1 Cor. 3:16–17 RSV). Watch for other instances where traditional symbols and metaphors are transformed in early Christian epistolary diction, which will include liturgical fragments and religious songs and poetry quoted by letter writers.

5. Consistently Paul moves from a theological statement directly into a section featuring ethical admonition (*paraenesis*). Pauline theology and Pauline ethics are always two sides of the same coin, and he never remains on the abstract level for very long before applying a particular theological concept to the specific moral or ethical issues troubling his addressees. Letters provided an especially useful literary medium for working out the details of Christian ethical teachings, just as the epistolary *responsa* served to guide Jewish communities in the Diaspora. Letters continued to provide a flexible arena in which to develop early Christian thought, and the attentive reader will be able to sight instances where this development has structured the literary style and rhetorics of the letters.

Almost any New Testament epistle will be understood more clearly if some of the literary features we have explored here are kept in mind as the letter is read. It is helpful to watch for the broadest "paragraph" or unit of material in terms of the parts of the letter form, since the chapter and verse divisions now incorporated into Bibles were added centuries after the letters were written and sometimes break up the sequential flow of the actual epistolary units. Cross-references to situations mentioned in other letters and other early Christian writings ought to be kept in mind. And the reader must frequently learn to bracket out contemporary meanings of words that have taken on subsequent theological weight that they did not bear in the periods during which the New Testament was written; we soon realize, for instance, that the New Testament refers to several types of baptism, and that the ways in which Christianity was related to the mother religion, Judaism, vary even within the work of one figure such as Paul.

While our focus here on "letters" has been on materials from about two thousand years ago, we are looking at a phenomenon still alive in many ways. Of course there is that power of receiving a letter notifying one of a college fellowship or an award of some sort; and likewise there is the awful experience of learning of a death, or hearing some other tragic news. But also the reconstructive power of epistolary communication can still be experienced directly today: the "Letter from a Birmingham Jail" written by Nobel Peace Prize winner Martin Luther King, Jr., mobilized the entire Civil Rights movement and helped Christians and non-Christians alike to remember the ancient message about freedom that was proclaimed already in the epistle to the Galatians but needed to be revoiced in terms of twentieth-century America.

WORKS CITED

Francis, Fred O., and J. Paul Sampley. *Pauline Parallels.* Foundations and Facets. 2d ed. Minneapolis: Augsburg Fortress, 1984.

A most useful workbook that prints out side-by-side passages related formally or thematically. Seeing all the thanksgiving passages laid out at once, or recognizing from the printout just how similar all the liturgically shaped closings are, will develop the reader's perception of literary forms and rhetorical styles.

Ryken, Leland. *The New Testament in Literary Criticism.* New York: Ungar, 1984.

Two sections are especially useful in this context: "Epistle as a Literary Form," 66–77, presents extracts from a number of scholars representing different viewpoints about the "literariness" of the New Testament letters, their basic form, and the types of materials incorporated. "Paul as a Letter Writer," 273–81, surveys stylistic features and their free combination in the Pauline letters. In some of my earlier publications cited there I argue more strongly than I would today for the relevance of understanding New Testament epistles on the basis of formal literary parallels with non- and pre-Christian letters.

Doty, William G. *Letters in Primitive Christianity.* Guides to Biblical Scholarship, New Testament Series. Minneapolis: Fortress, 1973.

Dated now, but a widely used summary of epistolary literature in Hellenism and the various formal elements of New Testament letters.

Aune, David E. *The New Testament in Its Literary Environment.* Library of Early Christianity. Philadelphia: Westminster/John Knox, 1987.

Almost a quarter of this useful book is devoted to "Letters in the Ancient World" (ch. 5) and "Early Christian Letters and Homilies" (ch. 6).

White, John L. *Light From Ancient Letters.* Foundations and Facets. Minneapolis: Augsburg Fortress, 1986.

Stowers, Stanley K. *Letter Writing in Greco-Roman Antiquity.* Library of Early Christianity. Philadelphia: Westminster/John Knox, 1986.

These books help students to analyze actual samples of non- and pre-Christian letters. Together they form a comparative basis for a study of subsequent Christian adaptations.

Petersen, Norman R. *Rediscovering Paul: Philemon and the Sociology of Paul's Narrative World.* Minneapolis: Fortress, 1985.

A long book on Paul's shortest letter, but it exposits the social world *behind* all the letters, as it were, and represents a state-of-the-art survey of what we know about terms such as "my brother," or "friend," Paul's relationship to the political state, and so forth.

Altman, Janet Gurkin. *Epistolarity: Approaches to a Form.* Columbus: Ohio State UP, 1982.

The epistolarity novel was so popular that by the eighteenth century it accounted for about a fifth of all fiction published. While there are any number of works studying the genre, Altman's seems to me to raise some of the most interesting questions that we might use to read back to the New Testament traditions *through* the later traditions; her excellent bibliography will lead either to the fictional works themselves or to secondary critical studies.

Derrida, Jacques. *The Post Card: From Socrates to Freud and Beyond.* Trans. Alan Bass. Chicago: University of Chicago Press, 1987.

The very nature and status of knowing and "truth" are challenged today; so we should not be surprised to find a radical questioning of the communicative tradition represented by epistles or postal cards. Derrida's work explores all the philosophical soft spots, sometimes parodying, sometimes reflecting on technical matters, but always reflecting on the dream of perfect communication ("the old dream of the complete electro-cardio-encephalo-LOGO-icono-cinemato-bio-gram" [68]).

CHAPTER 34

Revelation

Leland Ryken
Wheaton College

The book of Revelation is the most thoroughly literary book in the Bible. It everywhere prefers the imaginative to the propositional. It incarnates its meanings in images, events, and visions. No book of the Bible has been more influential as a literary model, with Milton and Blake heading the list of those influenced by it.

The book of Revelation is not only a literary masterpiece. It is also an accessible book—a work of folk literature with close ties to "underground" literature like the political cartoon (Wishart 459; Beasley-Murray 16–17) and to children's literature with animal characters and marvelous events.

Five Fallacies

Modern readers approach the book of Revelation through a cloud of misconceptions that pose obstacles to a literary enjoyment and understanding of the book. Five of these are particularly important.

1. One fallacy is that the book of Revelation is a totally unique book, totally unlike familiar literature. There is, of course, much that is unfamiliar

about Revelation, but the book will yield most of its meanings if it is approached in terms of the two most familiar literary categories—story and poetry.

On the narrative side, the book is structured around a central plot conflict between good and evil, God and Satan, angels and demons. Christ is the protagonist of the action, the victorious warrior. Against him are arrayed forces of evil and chaos. This action has the sense of progression and climax that we associate with stories, with the conquest of evil occurring in incremental stages until it is finally and totally complete.

As in all stories, events are placed in settings that correlate with the action and characters. The individual episodes of Revelation will fall readily into place if we simply apply the usual narrative questions of setting (*where* does the action occur?), character (*who* are the actors or agents?), plot or action (*what* happens?), and outcome (what is the *result* of the action?).

Along with narrative, poetry forms the basic substance of the book of Revelation. To understand what is happening, we need to know how to respond to concrete images like blood and crown and water. Austin Farrer christened the book of Revelation "a rebirth of images," proposing "to introduce into the field of scriptural divinity a known method of poetical analysis" (20). Being poetic, the book requires us to apply all that we know about metaphors (e.g., a woman "drunk with the blood of the saints") and similes (the sun becoming "black as sackcloth"). As I will note shortly, symbolism constitutes the basic mode of Revelation, and here, too, the book of Revelation belongs to the familiar literary form of poetry.

2. What I have said already helps to dispel a second fallacy that surrounds the book of Revelation—the view that it portrays future events only. If we operate on this premise, the material naturally seems remote from our everyday lives. It is true that the prologue to the book announces that it will show "what must soon take place" (1:1), but this time reference is ambiguous. For one thing, New Testament writers regard the entire era from the incarnation of Christ as "the latter times."

Even more important is the open-ended nature of the visions of the book of Revelation—so open-ended, in fact, that there have historically been four main interpretations of the book. The most common approach in the twentieth century has been the futuristic interpretation, which holds that virtually all of the prophecies in the book will be fulfilled at some future date immediately preceding the end of history. But in earlier centuries interpreters were prone to regard the book as forecasting the whole of human history from the time of Christ to his return, or as a picture of what is true of human history and God's actions at every point in history. To interpreters weary of speculative interpretations, the view that the prophecies of Revelation were fulfilled in the early centuries after Christ has held a perennial appeal.

The metaphoric mode of the book allows us to see an element of truth in all of these interpretations. Images and symbols *are* open-ended and subject to multiple applications. If the picture of the whore of Babylon would have reminded the original audience of its surrounding Roman society, it also reminds us of what we see around us. The visions of cosmic collapse in Revelation have been recognizable to every generation of readers, but they have even more relevance to an age of environmental pollution and nuclear capabilities. In short, the literary mode of Revelation means that its visions are perpetually up to date, while the eschatological cast of the book means that its visions will be climactically realized at the end of history.

What virtually all of the rival interpretations have in common is that they implicitly agree that the book is metaphoric in the sense that the details in the text stand for something else, or need to be related to something else. The professed literalist who applies the visions of Revelation to contemporary events is busy searching for the referent, just as surely as the interpreter who sees the details as the embodiment of universal principles.

3. A third fallacy is that the book of Revelation is a book of esoteric symbols that only the initiated can hope to master. The truth is that for the most part the images and symbols of Revelation are universal. Revelation is one of the most overtly archetypal books in the Bible—so much so that Northrop Frye calls it a "grammar" of archetypes (141). Its images are those of our waking and sleeping dreams—blood, lamb, dragon, beast, water, sea, sun, war, harvest, bride, throne, jewels. Its color symbolism is equally universal—light for goodness, darkness for evil, red for bloodshed and perverse passion. Heaven is high, as we have always known it to be, and hell is low and bottomless.

The last half of the book is a spiritualized version of familiar folktale motifs: a woman in distress who is marvelously delivered, a hero on a white horse who kills a dragon, a wicked prostitute who is finally exposed, the marriage of the triumphant hero to his bride, the celebration of the wedding with a feast, and the description of a palace glittering with jewels in which the hero and his bride live happily ever after. The book of Revelation does not require a guidebook to esoteric symbols. It requires a keen eye for the obvious and a childlike receptivity to folktale patterns. "The purpose of symbols," writes Farrer, "is that they should be immediately understood, the purpose of expounding them is to restore and build up such an understanding" (20).

4. A fourth fallacy that can mislead us is a widespread theory that the book of Revelation must be interpreted literally. I need to guard against

possible misunderstanding here. I do not mean to imply that the characters and events portrayed in Revelation do not represent characters and events that are historically real and actual. The question is how these real events are pictured. Most of the time they are portrayed symbolically.

At the beginning of chapter 12, for example, we read about a woman in travail who gives birth to a son who is to rule all nations with a rod of iron, a red dragon who tries unsuccessfully to devour the child, and the miraculous ascent of the child into heaven. Here is one of the hermeneutical keys within the book of Revelation. It is not hard to discern the historical facts behind this symbolic picture, namely, the birth and incarnate life of Christ, followed by his ascension. A good question to keep asking as we read this book is this: Of what historical event or theological event or event in salvation history does this passage seem to be a symbolic version?

Another such hermeneutical key comes at the beginning of chapter 6. Four horse visions portray the increasingly destructive nature of warfare and accompanying famine and death. It is a symbolic picture of Christ's prophecy in the Olivet Discourse that at the end of the age "you will hear of wars and rumors of wars. . . . For nation will rise against nation, and kingdom against kingdom, and there will be famines and earthquakes in various places" (Matt. 24:6–7). Even in the letters to the seven churches (chs. 2–3), which we commonly think of as the most historically rooted or realistic section of Revelation, we find a barrage of symbols that cannot be literal pictures of the reality they portray—symbols such as a tree of life and Satan's throne in an earthly city and people's receiving the morning star and Christ standing in front of a metaphoric door and knocking to enter so he can eat supper. If there is this much symbolism already in the historically realistic letters to the churches, how much more may we not expect in the fantasy that follows, replete with a red horse and a dragon who sweeps down a third of the stars of heaven and a lamb who can unfold a scroll?

5. A final obstacle that makes Revelation a closed book to many modern readers is the belief that it is a bewildering collection of fragments, too formless to grasp at once. This impression is created partly by the brevity of the individual units that make up the procession or pageant of visions. But the writer worked overtime to insure that this kaleidoscope of individual units would not be chaotic. With a book containing so many individual units, numerous structural schemes can be successfully applied, but the most convincing one—the one advertised within the book itself—is the one that sees the book as organized around patterns of seven, enveloped by a prologue and an epilogue (for details, see Ryken, *Words of Life* 147–63).

Specifically, the fourfold prologue in the opening chapter consists of a statement of theme and source (vv. 1–3), a formal salutation (vv. 4–8), introduction of the narrator (vv. 9–11), and a presentation of the hero (vv. 12–20). This is followed by sections devoted to the letters to the seven churches (chs. 2–4), the seven seals (chs. 5–7), the seven trumpets (chs. 8–11), seven great signs (chs. 12–14), the seven bowls of wrath (chs. 15–16), and seven events of final judgment and the consummation of history (17:1–22:5). The epilogue returns us to the epistolary rituals of the prologue, as the narrator addresses the audience on the urgency of the message he has written.

In contrast to prevailing assumptions, then, the book of Revelation stands as an accessible book dominated by familiar conventions of narrative and poetry, a book that tells us as much about the current scene as about the future, a book that uses symbols to portray recognizable events, a book of archetypes and universal images, and a carefully structured book in which virtually everything falls into patterns of seven.

Literary Genres

If we ask what makes Revelation a literary book, one of the immediate answers is the convergence of literary genres that we find there. The author could scarcely have known that he was penning the conclusion to the canonical Bible, but there can be no doubt that his document nonetheless is a virtual compendium of biblical genres. Books of the Bible are always tending toward a mixed-genre format, but nowhere so prominently as in its final book.

We might begin with the genre that the author himself affixes to his book, namely, prophecy. Prophecy is first of all visionary in content in the sense that it portrays scenes, characters, and events that either belong to a different order from ordinary reality or that have not yet occurred (Ryken, *How to Read* 165–75). Such literature transports us to visionary realms—realms that are sometimes transcendent, at other times earthly but with ordinary conditions so altered and reversed as to be strange by ordinary standards. Events tend also to be temporally remote, usually projected into the future.

This element of otherness or strangeness extends also to the scenes and agents in prophetic literature. The setting is cosmic, extending to whole nations and even the whole earth. In the book of Revelation we alternate in a regular rhythm between heaven and earth. Filling this cosmic stage are actors that transcend ordinary visible reality—God and angels, "living creatures" with six wings and "eyes all around" (4:8), and imaginary beasts. Forces of nature also become leading actors.

This visionary content naturally produces its own rhetoric and tone

(Wilder; Collins). It is a rhetoric of fantasy that makes no pretense of limiting itself to empirical everyday reality as we actually observe it. The atmosphere is frequently surrealistic, with ordinary aspects of creation distorted into sinister and threatening forms—water turned to blood, for example, or the heavenly bodies falling from the sky, or apocalyptic locusts that attack people with scorpionlike tails. Apocalyptic rhetoric might also be called subversive, inasmuch as a leading strategy is to undermine usual assumptions, such as that what we see physically is all that exists or that the world will continue approximately as it is now. More than anything else, visionary rhetoric mingles the familiar and the unfamiliar. The result is a combined sense of mystery and reality.

Prophetic writing possesses a distinctive structure as well as rhetoric. It progresses as a series of visions, as in a pageant. The best model for the book of Revelation is modern cinematic effects—a kaleidoscopic sequence of pictures, sounds, images, and events, always shifting and never in focus for very long. Not only do the individual units keep shifting, but they consist of a range of diverse material, including visual descriptions, speeches that the visionary hears and records, dialogues, monologues, brief snatches of narrative, direct discourses by the writer to an audience, letters, prayers, and hymns. This pageant or phantasmagoria is dreamlike, confirming the accuracy of the conventional literary label "visionary."

If the overriding genre of Revelation is prophecy, other genres are also important. One of these is drama. In fact, the book may show the author's awareness of the conventions of classical drama (Bowman). Revelation is filled with dramatized scenes and pieces of dialogue. Characters and events are often placed in elaborately embellished settings. Instead of encountering smooth narrative transitions, we confront a sequence of abruptly shifting scenes. Characters often move in ritualistic fashion, as though stage managed.

There is also much that is epiclike about Revelation, and anyone familiar with classical epic or Milton's *Paradise Lost* is on native ground when reading Revelation. The style is an epic style, replete with epic similes, epithets, copia or fullness, allusions, and grandeur. The content of the book is also epiclike, with such motifs as supernatural characters, marvelous events, cosmic sweep, catalogs, heavenly councils preceding events on earth, warfare, conquest, empire, and visions of the future.

The portal through which we enter the book of Revelation is, however, much humbler than we might expect from what I have said thus far. The first thing we meet is the conventions of the epistle, leading someone to claim that "Revelation is, in fact, the first book to show the influence of the collected and published letters of Paul" (Goodspeed 201). We find much in Revelation that reminds us of the New Testament epistles—a formal salutation in the opening verses, two chapters (2–3) dominated wholly by the conventions of letter writing, concluding admonitions, and a final benediction.

Lyric poems also make the last book of the Bible read like a compendium of what has preceded. Scattered among the visions, these brief interludes display the parallelism characteristic of biblical poetry and possess the singing quality of lyric. Their subject is usually adoration, and their context is ordinarily heavenly worship. It would not be hard to place the poetic fragments of Revelation alongside such Old and New Testament counterparts as creation hymn, psalm of worship, doom song, and Christ hymn.

A final genre that will help to classify what happens in the book of Revelation is apocalypse (literally "unveiling"). Traits of this biblical genre include dualism (with the universe decisively divided into good and evil), eschatological viewpoint (preoccupation with events at the end of history), visionary mode, messianic focus, presence of angels and demons, animal symbolism (use of animals to represent human characters, events, or movements), and numerology (use of numbers with symbolic meanings). Apocalyptic writing tends to be a vision of judgment, with the writer denouncing an existing system of values and predicting its miserable end. Satire (an attack on human vice) naturally looms large.

One particularly helpful interpretive strategy for the book of Revelation is to read it in the light of Jesus' eschatological discourse in Matthew 24–25. When asked by his disciples what "the close of the age" would be like, Jesus outlined a sequence of five events: (1) wars, earthquakes, famine, and false teachers (24:5–8); (2) persecution of Christians (24:9–22); (3) false Christs and false prophets (24:23–28); (4) natural disasters, the appearance of Christ, and the harvesting of the elect (24:29–31); and (5) final judgment (24:32–25:46). This is the background against which we can measure the events described in the book of Revelation.

The book of Revelation, then, stands as a collection of biblical genres. As we read the story that it tells, we hear echoes of such diverse genres as prophecy, apocalypse, drama, epistle, epic, and lyric poetry.

Style and Rhetoric

Cutting across all the genres of Revelation is the basic literary mode of symbolism. This means that images and events are constantly used to represent something else. When we read about a lamb or lion or warrior, we understand that these represent Christ, the hero of the book. A dragon stands for Satan. The details are not literally true or actual, though they bring actual persons and events to mind.

Although the book of Revelation is strongly sensory and even visual (in the sense that we visualize images and symbols), it is not predominantly pictorial. The harder we try to visualize what is described, especially as a composite picture, the more incomprehensible and grotesque things become. Symbolic writing, comments Richardson, "does not paint pictures. It is no pictographic but ideographic. . . . The skull and crossbones on the bottle of medicine is a symbol of poison, but not a picture. . . . The fish, the lamb, and the lion are all symbols of Christ, but never to be taken as pictures of him" (16). "When we try strenuously to visualize" many of the scenes, writes Kiddle, "we find many details . . . which are intellectually but not pictorially comprehensible. . . . We must therefore take it that John is using a metaphor so familiar that its pictorial quality does not appear" (70–71; see also selected excerpts in Ryken, *New Testament* 315–25; Farrer 304–5).

The effect of this impressionistic style is a tremendous sense of mystery and transcendence. In praising the power of biblical apocalyptic, J. H. Gardiner observed that when we compare the serenity of the Greek representations of the gods with the visions of Revelation, "the latter at first may seem confused and turgid. Then as one thinks it over, the very clarity and definiteness of outline in these wonderful marbles stand out as a limitation: in comparison with these vague and mystical imaginings of the Christian seers the representations of Greek art are impotent," being essentially "a glorified and idealized man. The visions of the apocalypse, on the other hand, transcend once for all the limitations of human nature" (272).

Allusiveness is another feature of Revelation. There are 350 allusions to the Old Testament (Tenney 101–16), as well as many references to the redemptive life of Christ and New Testament eschatological passages. Farrer rightly claims that the author "is always doing something with the Old Testament," adding that the images "have an astonishing multiplicity of reference" (19). I said earlier that the symbolic mode of Revelation requires the reader to constantly make connections with familiar theological realities and events in salvation history. Familiarity with biblical prophecy and the New Testament is a prerequisite for interpreting the book of Revelation, which is in no sense a self-contained book.

In the original, Revelation is stylistically distinctive for its violation of normal syntax and grammar. Translator J. B. Phillips describes "the tumultuous assault of words" in this way: "Revelation piles word upon word remorselessly, mixes cases and tenses without apparent scruple, and shows at times a complete disregard for normal syntax and grammar" (xi). Beardslee theorizes that although the New Testament generally eschews a special religious or "sacred" language, the book of Revelation "approximates such a special diction, a special artistic language. It does so by imposing Hebrew or Aramaic language patterns on Greek in such a way as to produce what has been called the most sustained body of violation of the rules of Greek grammar that exists anywhere. These are not mere violations of ignorance. . . . The intention, brilliantly successful, is to produce a hieratic speech" (59).

The dominant rhetorical strategy in Revelation is repetition, which forms the basic compositional device of the book. Not only does one vision follow another in repeated pattern; the visions are consistently arranged into sevenfold patterns. These sevenfold units, in turn, are arranged in a cyclic manner, so that we get the impression that we are retreading similar material as we progress through the book. Yet it is not a simple repetition, being instead incremental ("growing") repetition, as in the old ballads. As the conflict between good and evil becomes more and more intense, and as judgment becomes increasingly severe, we move from visions involving a fourth of the earth (6:8) to those involving a third of the earth (8:7–12) to those involving the entire earth (15:1). What we find, then, is a spiral of sevenfold visions that recapitulate and intensify each other and end with a tremendous sense of final judgment and redemption.

Another element of repetition is that each of the sevenfold units shows the same general chronology. The early visions in each unit focus on fallen human history, with its attendant evil and judgment. As the units continue to unfold, the focus shifts to the end of history and the glorification of believers in heaven. In the vision of the seven seals (chs. 6–7), for example, we begin with four horse-visions symbolizing warfare and famine, followed by the cry of the martyrs, the vanishing of the earth, and a vision of the glorified saints in heaven. From earth to heaven, from history to its consummation—this is the recurrent movement in the units that make up the book of Revelation. No matter where we dip into the book, we can know where we are.

The themes of the book, too, are constantly being restated as we progress through the book. The big ideas of Revelation include the fact of spiritual conflict between forces of good and evil, the degenerative effect of evil in human history, the judgment of God against evil, the eventual triumph of the good and salvation of believers, the supremacy of Christ, and the theme of the two worlds—the simultaneous existence of a spiritual world and the visible earthly world.

To bring the literary quality of the book of Revelation into focus, I have selected for analysis the first eight verses of chapter 12:

> And a great portent appeared in heaven, a woman clothed with the sun, with the moon under her feet, and on her head a crown of twelve stars; she was with child and she cried out in her pangs of birth, in anguish for delivery. And another portent appeared in heaven; behold, a great red dragon, with seven heads and ten horns, and seven diadems upon his heads. His tail swept down a third of the stars of heaven, and cast them to the earth. And the dragon stood before the woman who was about to bear a child, that he might devour her child when she brought it forth; she brought forth a male child, one who is to rule all the nations with a rod of iron, but her child was caught up to God and to his throne, and the woman fled into the wilderness, where she has a place prepared by God, in which to be nourished for one thousand two hundred and sixty days. Now war arose in heaven, Michael and his angels fighting against the dragon; and the dragon and his angels fought, but they were defeated and there was no longer any place for them in heaven.

We notice first the genres. This is visionary literature in which the writer pictures characters and events remote from everyday reality. The mode is equally epic, with its motifs of supernatural characters, celestial battle, and cosmic setting. The emphasis on action shows the narrative bias of the book as a whole. And such features as the dualism of good and evil, the visionary mode, the messianic focus on Christ, animal symbolism, and numerology show the affinities of Revelation with apocalyptic writing.

The symbolism of the passage is also apparent. In fact, the writer signals his symbolic mode by speaking twice of a "portent" (RSV) or "sign" (NIV), as distinct from a literal fact. If we interpret the symbols in light of biblical predecessors and archetypes, it is not hard to piece the story together. The woman in travail is Israel, an identification strengthened by the association of the woman with the dreams of the patriarch Joseph (references to the number twelve and to the sun, moon, and stars). The child who is to rule all nations is Christ, and the dragon is identified within Revelation itself (20:2) as Satan. The inability of the dragon to destroy the child, who is taken into heaven, symbolically reenacts the redemptive life and ascension of Christ.

The passage thus mingles the familiar and the strange. If much suggests mystery and transcendence, the details also remind us of familiar events in salvation history. The passage awakens universal feelings: we have known from childhood that a dragon means trouble and that in color symbolism red is often a sinister color. The imaginative world of Revelation itself supplies the meaning of some of the symbols. Thus the seven heads of the dragon make it a demonic parody of the lamb with seven horns (5:6), and the dragon's ten horns symbolize the power of evil.

The passage also refutes common misconceptions. For all its surface strangeness, the passage is not unique; instead, it employs common strategies of narrative and poetry. Nor is Revelation completely futuristic, since the quoted passage, considered chronologically, is a flashback from the main action of Revelation. The symbols, moreover, are not primarily esoteric but tend to be either familiar biblical allusions or universal archetypes. And from start to finish the passage is symbolic rather than literal, though it brings actual events to mind.

The End of the Biblical Story

Part of the literary significance of the book of Revelation is its status as the conclusion to the Bible as a whole. The total shape of the Bible is an important part of its literary power. Northrop Frye describes it as "a single archetypal structure extending from creation to apocalypse" (315). The overall movement is a U-shaped story, beginning with the creation of the world and the placement of two humans in a perfect garden. This is succeeded by a fall from innocence and expulsion from the garden. By a tortuous route, fallen human history winds its way back to the perfection of the beginning, with the return signaled partly by the reappearance of paradisal imagery in the last chapter of Revelation (22:1–2).

This circle of stories is framed at both ends by similar material. At the outset we are surrounded by associations of creation and new beginnings. At the end we likewise move in the atmosphere of a new heaven and a new earth. The first two chapters and the last two portray a perfected universe. Satan enters the story in the third chapter and exits in the third chapter from the end.

A further sense of completeness emerges from the contrast between the simplicity of the opening and the luxurious abundance of the conclusion. Roland M. Frye notes that the perfection of the universe at the end of Revelation "is conveyed through rich and luxuriant symbols of dimensions, design, and decorations." This "symbolic opulence," he notes, "is set in sharp contrast . . . with the stark simplicity of the opening verses of the Bible," thereby bringing "the Biblical epic . . . to its incomparable close" (xxv). The Bible's story begins in a garden and ends in a city.

I said at the outset of this chapter that the book of Revelation is the most thoroughly literary book in the Bible. Its enjoyment and understanding depend on our ability to bring literary expectations to it. Primarily this means an ability to interpret narrative and symbolism, an awareness of the intricate structuring of the book around patterns of seven, a sensitivity to literary genres like epic and prophecy, and an ability to complete the metaphoric mode of Revelation by linking its surface details to familiar theological realities or events in salvation history and human history.

WORKS CITED

Beardslee, William A. *Literary Criticism of the New Testament.* Philadelphia: Fortress, 1970.

Beasley-Murray, G. R. *The Book of Revelation.* London: Marshall, Morgan, and Scott, 1974.

Bowman, John W. "The Revelation to John: Its Dramatic Structure and Message." *Interpretation* 9 (1955): 436–53.

Collins, John J. "Introduction: Towards the Morphology of a Genre." *Apocalypse: The Morphology of a Genre. Semeia* 14 (1979): 1–19.

Farrer, Austin. *A Rebirth of Images: The Making of St. John's Apocalypse.* London: Dacre, 1949.

Frye, Northrop. *Anatomy of Criticism.* Princeton: Princeton UP, 1957.

Frye, Roland M. "Introduction." *The Bible: Selections from the King James Version for Study as Literature.* Boston: Houghton Mifflin, 1965. ix-xxxix.

Gardiner, J. H. *The Bible as English Literature.* New York: Scribner, 1927.

Goodspeed, Edgar J. *How to Read the Bible.* Philadelphia: Universal Book and Bible House, 1946.

Kiddle, Martin. *The Revelation of St. John.* New York: Harper, 1940.

Phillips, J. B. *The Book of Revelation.* New York: Macmillan, 1957.

Richardson, Donald W. *The Revelation of Jesus Christ: An Interpretation.* Richmond: John Knox, 1939.

Ryken, Leland. *How to Read the Bible as Literature.* Grand Rapids: Zondervan, 1984.

———. *The New Testament in Literary Criticism.* New York: Ungar, 1984.

———. *Words of Life: A Literary Introduction to the New Testament.* Grand Rapids: Baker, 1987.

Tenney, Merrill. *Interpreting Revelation.* Grand Rapids: Eerdmans, 1957.

Wilder, Amos N. "Apocalyptic Rhetorics." *Jesus' Parables and the War of Myths: Essays on Imagination in the Scripture.* Ed. James Breech. Philadelphia: Fortress, 1982. 153–68.

Wishart, Charles F. "Patmos in the Pulpit: A Meditation on Apocalyptic." *Interpretation* 1 (1947): 456–65.

PART 4

CHAPTER 35

The Literary Influence of the Bible

LELAND RYKEN
Wheaton College

Not only is the Bible itself a work of literature—it is also the major source and influence for Western literature. No sharp distinction can be made between the Bible *as* literature and the Bible *in* literature. A symbiotic relationship exists between the Bible and Western literature: our acquaintance with imaginative literature influences how we talk about the Bible as literature, and the Bible itself has influenced Western literature since the Middle Ages.

In an oft-quoted statement, Northrop Frye noted that the Bible is "the major informing influence on literary symbolism. . . . Once our view of the Bible comes into proper focus, a great mass of literary symbols from *The Dream of the Rood* to *Little Gidding* begins to take on meaning" (Frye 316). The Bible, writes someone else, "becomes one with the Western tradition, because it is its greatest source" (Henn 258). Even in the present century many writers acknowledge their indebtedness to the Bible (Kehl 5).

The starting point for any discussion of the Bible as a presence in imaginative literature remains C. S. Lewis's landmark monograph *The Literary Impact of the Authorized Version.* It was here that Lewis bequeathed the distinction between the Bible as a literary source and a literary influence: "A source gives us things to write about; an influence prompts us to write in a certain way" (15). The survey that follows attempts no more than to provide an anatomy and history of how writers have used the Bible, accompanied by a minimum of illustrations.

The Bible as Literary Source

At the simplest level, writers have used the Bible as a source of titles for their works. Of course the Bible lends itself to such use by being an aphoristic book. A title taken from a phrase in the Bible at once supplies an aura of evocativeness and eloquence. In addition, writers use such titles to suggest an interpretive framework for their works.

Our own century has produced the most titles taken from the Bible, with novels heading the list. Specimens include *Go Down Moses* (Faulkner), *Absalom, Absalom!* (Faulkner), *East of Eden* (Steinbeck), *The Fall* (Camus), *The Sun Also Rises* (Hemingway), *Go Tell It on the Mountain* (James Baldwin), *The Power and the Glory* (Graham Greene). But poets also continue to find the Bible an attractive source for titles. A random dip into the collected poems of Edwin Arlington Robinson discloses such titles as "The Valley of the Shadow," "Peace on Earth," "Many Are Called," and "If the Lord Would Make Windows in Heaven."

Writers also draw upon the Bible for the names of fictional characters. In Hawthorne's *Scarlet Letter,* the ostracized Hester (a variant of Esther) names her illegitimate child "Pearl." Echoing "the pearl of great price" in Jesus' parable, the name suggests both the worth of the child and the way in which she cost her mother everything in terms of social standing in the Puritan community.

The most important way in which the Bible serves as a source for literature is that it supplies the subject matter of poems, stories, and plays. There are so many such works by both major and minor authors that they make up a small library. The range of ways in which authors treat biblical material is immense.

At one level, the writer's impulse is simply to imagine a biblical character or event in an attempt to make it come alive. The English Romantic poet Lord Byron, for example, writing in fast-moving anapestic meter, captured the swift decisiveness of the nighttime death of the Assyrian army (2 Kings 19:35 and Isa. 37:36). The third of six stanzas conveys the flavor of the poem:

For the Angel of Death spread his wings on the blast,
And breathed in the face of the foe as he pass'd;
And the eyes of the sleepers wax'd deadly and chill,
And their hearts but once heaved, and for ever grew still!

The aim here is to recreate the biblical event as vividly as possible, with no attempt to interpret it.

Even in such instances, though, writers do more than retell a biblical story. In recreating a biblical event, Byron used his imagination to embellish the details that appear in the spare style that characterizes biblical narrative. Byron's poem also illustrates another typical feature of such literature—the tendency to retain some of the stylistic qualities of the King James Bible, seen here in the abundance of "and" coordinates that contribute a sense of fluidity to the movement of the story line.

Most writers go beyond the impulse to recreate a biblical event or character and offer an interpretation of the biblical material as well. The following poem entitled "The Dreamer," by William Childress, is an example:

He spent his childhood hours in a den
of rushes, watching the gray rain braille
the surface of the river. Concealed
from the outside world, nestled within,
he was safe from parents, God, and eyes
that looked upon him accusingly,
as though to say: Even at your age,
you could do better. His camouflage
was scant, but it served, and at evening,
when fireflies burned holes into heaven,
he took the path homeward in the dark,
a small Noah, leaving his safe ark.

At the literal or descriptive level, the poem makes the event of Moses in the basket of rushes come alive in full sensory detail as we picture the rain falling on the water, the enclosed nature of the basket, and the evening setting in which the infant returned to his mother's care.

But by means of allusions to other heroes of biblical literature, the poet also offers an interpretation of the role of Moses in biblical history. The title of the poem links Moses with the youthful Joseph, who became a patriarch of the nation of Israel. When the basket in which Moses was placed is metaphorically called a den, we perceive Moses as another Daniel, a hero of faith and courage. At the end of the poem, Moses is linked with Noah, preserver of life. We might also note in passing that in the original Hebrew text the word used to describe the basket in which Moses was placed in the

Nile River is the word for ark, and that the only other place in the Old Testament where the word appears is the story of Noah.

What I have illustrated in microcosm appears on a grander scale in plays and full-length stories based on biblical material. Here writers use the Bible for their plots and characters, showing the same range that I have noted in brief poems. One option is historical fiction, in which a storyteller attempts to remain true to the settings, customs, and institutions of the ancient world. Thomas Mann's tetralogy *Joseph and His Brothers* is an example, though this tradition consists mainly of an enormous quantity of generally second-rate fiction.

More appealing to major writers has been the practice of transposing biblical characters and stories into the writer's own world, thereby telescoping the remoteness of the ancient text into everyday immediacy. Robert Frost, for example, put the biblical prophet Jonah into a mid-twentieth-century New York milieu in his play *A Masque of Mercy.* In Wolf Mankowitz's play *It Should Happen to a Dog,* the events of Jonah's life are placed in a modern setting, as Jonah becomes a traveling salesman type who complains about his lot.

Any full-length retelling of a biblical story becomes an interpretation of the material. There is, however, a range of intention evident among writers who write plays and stories on biblical material. At one end of the spectrum we get the impression that the author wished to remain as faithful as possible to the Bible. As we move across the continuum, writers feel free to reinterpret a biblical character or event, and at the far end of the spectrum we sense that the writer was attracted to the biblical material not for its own sake but as the best possible vehicle for expressing his or her own vision of life.

Milton's closet drama *Samson Agonistes* is an example of a work in which the writer chose a biblical story not primarily for its own sake but as a framework that would allow him to achieve his own literary purpose. It is true that Milton used every possible shred of data that the Bible and Christian commentary offered on the life of Samson. And like the Old Testament story, Milton's drama is both a temptation story and a tragedy.

But Milton's Samson is much more than the Samson we meet in Judges 13–16. The Old Testament story is almost exclusively a story of external physical action. Milton transformed that story into a psychological and spiritual drama in which the crucial action occurs within Samson. An equally important shift is that Milton made the progress of Samson a story of patient suffering, repentance, and salvation. In other words, Milton's portrayal of Samson was influenced by the biblical depiction of the suffering Job (Radzinowicz, *Samson Agonistes* 227–60) and the hero of faith in Hebrews 11. Milton also modeled some of Samson's speeches on the biblical lament psalms (Wall).

Milton's play typifies how writers can use a story and characters from the Bible as an outline for their own story. In the process of writing a long story or play, Milton found it necessary to amplify and imagine episodes in greater detail than the Bible does, or to invent totally new episodes. Even here, though, Milton's aim was to remain true to the overall content of the Bible.

Sometimes writers use the Bible only as a point of departure and reinterpret biblical material in light of their own viewpoint. A famous twentieth-century example is Archibald MacLeish's play *J.B.,* which occasioned a storm of critical debate (for specimens, see Bartel 344–78). MacLeish borrowed his characters and the story of exceptional calamity from the Old Testament, transposing the action into a modern setting. But the meaning of the story diverges from the biblical source. In the biblical version, Job's climactic moment of epiphany is an encounter with God in his simultaneous transcendence and immanence. In MacLeish's play, the climax is an affirmation of human love between the protagonist and his wife.

Biblical Allusions in Literature

Literary allusions form a natural transition from the Bible as a source to the Bible as an influence for writers. It is customary to speak of the Bible as a source of allusions, but we hardly mean that when writers allude to the Bible they are using it as a source in the way they do when they take their story material from the Bible. Perhaps we can rightly view the Bible as providing the writer's language (broadly defined) on these occasions. Alternately, we might regard the Bible as an influence on how writers develop a subject taken from a source other than the Bible.

In simple or straightforward allusion, writers refer directly to the Bible as a pre-text in such a way that our understanding or construing of a statement depends on our knowledge of the relevant biblical passage(s). John Donne, for example, begins a sonnet with the apostrophe "At the round earth's imagined corners, blow / Your trumpets, angels." What trumpets and angels are in view? The statement remains a mystery until we link it with the apocalyptic visions in the book of Revelation, where we read about "four angels standing on the four corners of the earth" (Rev. 7:1), as well as seven angels with trumpets who herald events at the end of history (Rev. 8).

In complex allusion, the reader needs to go beyond simply making a connection between a passage and its biblical pre-text and interpret *how* a detail in the text relates to a biblical precedent. In such interpretation, we may have to choose some potential connections and discard others. In Milton's sonnet on his blindness, for example, the poet speaks of "that one talent which is death to hide." Milton's talent is his poetic ability. By linking himself with the one-talent, unprofitable servant of Christ's parable of the talents (Matt. 25:14–30), Milton expresses the depth of his despair and fear over the inactivity forced on him by his blindness.

But Milton does not make a simple equation between himself and the slothful servant of the parable. He is only partly like the wicked servant: the servant *chose* to be unprofitable, while Milton's blindness forced him to be inactive. Milton pushes us toward such an interpretation by the very next statement in his poem: "though my soul [in implied contrast to the wicked servant in the parable] more bent / To serve therewith my Maker."

Sometimes writers add depth-of-field with biblical allusions. Here we do not need to catch the allusion in order to construe the passage, but identifying and interpreting the allusion sharpens a statement that would otherwise remain vague and one-dimensional. For example, when Milton begins his sonnet on his blindness with the comment, "When I consider how my light is spent," we do not need to link the statement to anything in the Bible in order to sense that the poet is talking about his lost eyesight. But the statement means something much richer if we identify its biblical allusions. In the background, for example, is Jesus' evocative description of blindness in Matthew 6:22–23: "The eye is the lamp of the body. So, if your eye is sound, your whole body will be full of light; but if your eye is not sound, your whole body will be full of darkness. If then the light in you is darkness, how great is the darkness!" Equally evocative is a statement of Jesus in the story of the healing of the man born blind (John 9): "I must work the works of him that sent me, while it is day: the night cometh, when no man can work" (v. 4 KJV). In other words, Milton's blindness is not only a physical handicap but also a spiritual state, a lack of service to God. This is reinforced by the way in which the parable weaves in references to the parable of day-workers in the vineyard (Matt. 20:1–16), where darkness likewise represents an end to the opportunity to serve the master.

Biblical allusions can also signal an interpretive framework for either an entire work or a specific aspect of it. Often such allusions appear in titles or names. In *Great Expectations,* Dickens names the criminal who is the protagonist's benefactor Abel Magwitch. Like the innocent biblical character martyred by his evil brother, Dickens' character is portrayed as a sympathetic victim unfairly killed by an unjust judicial system. When William Faulkner wrote a novel about the death of a person's dreams and of Southern culture, he entitled the book *Absalom, Absalom!* By thus alluding to David's fatherly lament over the loss of his son in the Old Testament story of death, violence, and tragic betrayal, Faulkner draws attention to the elegiac nature of his own story—a story that Robert Alter in his discussion of the biblical element in the novel calls "a story about primal sin, the tainting of an inheritance, the loss of a promised land, the violent twisting of the fraternal bone" (124; cf. also 123).

In addition to putting interpretive allusions into titles, writers weave them into the texture of their story or poem. At the end of Tolstoy's *Death of Ivan Ilych,* the protagonist undergoes a great change in attitude. Many critics treat this moment of epiphany in humanistic terms as the hero's coming to self-understanding, but if we pay attention to the pattern of allusions to the Gospels, we can see that Tolstoy intends us to interpret the experience as Christian conversion. Ivan's turnabout comes at the end of three days of terrible suffering during which "time did not exist for him." His mental anguish is caused by his awareness "that he cannot save himself." After falling through a black sack into light, Ivan cannot find his former fear of death, asking (in echo of 1 Cor. 15:54–55), "Where is it? What death? There was no fear because there was no death." And just before his actual death, Ivan hears someone say, "It is finished," thereby repeating Christ's last utterance from the cross.

A further category is ironic allusions that reinterpret biblical material in such a way that we are aware of how a writer has revised the biblical source. William Butler Yeats pinned the title "The Second Coming" on an apocalyptic poem expressing his view of the collapse of the Christian civilization of the past two thousand years and its replacement by something approaching anarchy. Yeats did not believe in the biblical version of Christ's second coming. Instead his allusion is a metaphoric reinterpretation of the biblical image of Christ's return.

Closely akin to biblical allusions in literature are biblical archetypes. An archetype is a recurrent plot motif, character type, or image. The Bible is the most familiar and a definitive version of the archetypes of literature. Northrop Frye calls it "a grammar of archetypes"—the place where we can find them in their most systematic and complete form (135). This is why critics appeal to the Bible as a helpful interpretive framework even when a writer does not insist on it.

There is ample reason to believe that writers frequently model their works on biblical versions of an archetype, even when they do not signal that connection by way of allusion. Novelist Joyce Cary, when asked whether he based his fictional characters on real people, replied, "You can't. . . . They aren't simple enough. Look at all the great heroes and heroines. . . : They are essentially characters from fable" (Cowley 52). The need to impose a discernible universal pattern on human experience leads writers to model their characters, stories, and poems on archetypes, especially as we find them in the Bible.

Often writers use devices of disclosure that invite us to connect their archetypes with the Bible. Charles Dickens' novel *Great Expectations* is based on the archetypal journey of a discontented young man away from home to a life of indulgence based on inherited money that finally brings disillusionment, followed by a return to the protagonist's home. This is obviously a reenactment of the archetype of the prodigal son, as Dickens hints when he tells us late in the story that Pip "felt like one who was toiling home barefoot from distant travels, and whose wanderings had lasted many years." Similarly, when Dylan Thomas wrote a poem about his fall from childhood innocence in a pastoral poem that recalled his youthful visits to an uncle's farm in Wales, he linked his experience with the biblical archetypes of early Genesis with the single assertion that "it was Adam and maiden."

The Bible as Literary Influence

An influence, said C. S. Lewis, shows a writer how to write on a given subject. One of the most important ways in which the Bible has influenced storytellers is in the development of characters and plots. Thomas Hardy did not get his story material for his novel *The Mayor of Casterbridge* from the Bible; he took it straight from his observations of life in rural England. But in inventing the shape and details of this story of generational conflict in which a younger man supplants an older man, Hardy drew upon the Old Testament story of Saul and David (Moynahan; Aschkenasy).

The Bible has also influenced style, including language, syntax, and imagery. William Wordsworth begins a famous sonnet of social criticism with this pair of lines:

The world is too much with us; late and soon,
Getting and spending, we lay waste our powers.

When Wordsworth speaks of "the world" having infiltrated our lives with the acquisitive spirit, he is echoing New Testament vocabulary for a worldly lifestyle: "the cares of this world, and the deceitfulness of riches, choke the word" (Matt. 13:22); "love not the world, neither the things that are in the world" (1 John 2:15); "be not conformed to this world" (Rom. 12:2). We also catch in Wordsworth's lines the parallelism of biblical poetry ("late and soon," "getting and spending"), as well as an echo of the military picture of "the destruction that wasteth at noonday" from Psalm 91:6.

Biblical imagery has been a dominant influence on English and American poetry. William Blake's resolve to combat the forces of industrialism is an example:

Bring me my bow of burning gold!
Bring me my arrows of desire!
Bring me my spear! O clouds, unfold!
Bring me my chariot of fire!

The feeling is the poet's own, but the imagery is coming from the Old Testament prophets. Isaiah, for example, envisions that "the LORD will come with fire, . . . to render . . . his rebuke with flames of fire. For by fire and by his sword will the LORD plead with all flesh" (66:15–16). Jeremiah provides further images: "Behold, he shall come up as clouds, and his chariots shall be as a whirlwind" (4:13). To these prophecies can be added the story of Elisha at Dothan, where "the mountain was full of horses and chariots of fire" (2 Kings 6:17; see also 2:11–12).

The Bible can also influence how a writer uses a given literary genre, even when the genre does not come from the Bible. The epic form in which Milton wrote *Paradise Lost* came from the classical tradition, but the modifications that Milton introduced were modeled on several books of the Bible (Ryken). In replacing heroic, military values with pastoral and domestic ones, Milton found a model in the book of Genesis. In writing an epic that chastises the people portrayed in the story instead of celebrating their exploits, Milton followed the lead of the epic of the Exodus. And in spiritualizing such epic motifs as warfare and conquest, Milton imitated what he found in the book of Revelation.

The Bible in Literature: A Brief History

The Bible was present in English literature from its beginning. The oldest extant piece of English literature is a nine-line lyric poem by Caedmon. Celebrating God's creation of the world, it takes its subject from early Genesis and its style from the parallelism of Hebrew poetry. From Caedmon there flowed a tradition of Old English poetry that used the Bible as a source for its content. We find, for example, narrative poems entitled *Genesis* and *Exodus* that retell the stories of patriarchs and Moses. Similar poems narrate events in the life of Christ. Overall, biblical poetry accounts for over a third of surviving Old English poetry (Shepherd).

The other option for Old English writers was to use the Bible as an influence and source of allusions when they wrote about story material drawn from other sources. The epic poem *Beowulf* represents a whole tradition of heroic poems influenced by the Bible. The plot comes from folklore, but this heroic myth is set within the overall biblical story of creation and providence, judgment and hell (Lee). Allusions link the monster Grendel with Cain.

In the Middle Ages, the tradition of using the Bible as a source for content lived on especially in the dramatic tradition. Cycles of plays known as mystery plays depicted events from the Bible from creation through the final judgment. Similar use of the Bible as a source occurred in poetry. Lyric poems were often imaginative relivings of events in the life of Christ (e.g., "I Sing of the Maiden" on the virgin's conception, and "Sunset on Calvary" on the tragic sorrow of the crucifixion). Longer narrative poems sometimes did similar things: *Purity* incorporates the stories of the Flood, the destruction of Sodom and Gomorrah, and Belshazzar's feast, and *Patience* encourages the virtue announced in the title by means of negative example when it retells the story of the impatient Jonah.

The Bible served as influence as well as source in medieval literature. The rhetoric of transcendence in the vision of heaven in *Pearl* is modeled on pictures of heaven in the book of Revelation. William Langland's encyclopedic *Piers Plowman* defies all literary classifications, but it shows the influence of biblical prophecy and apocalypse (Bloomfield). A 450-page book discusses biblical allusions and influence in Chaucer (Besserman).

The practice of theorizing about the literary use of the Bible began with the Renaissance and the Reformation. This has been most fully documented in Barbara Lewalski's book *Protestant Poetics and the Seventeenth-Century Religious Lyric.* Lewalski uncovers a wealth of evidence showing that writers and readers alike regarded the Bible as a model for literary genres, a source of imagery, and an influence on style. The result was the greatest flowering of biblical influence in the whole history of English literature, seen on the grandest scale in such writers as Christopher Marlowe (Sims, *Dramatic Uses;* Cornelius) and Edmund Spenser (Baroway; Hankins; Shaheen, *Faerie Queene*).

Shakespeare of course looms as a major figure, and *Macbeth* can stand as a typical specimen. The plot for the play comes from Holinshed's *Chronicles*. But as the story develops, we are reminded repeatedly of parallel actions and characters in the Bible—of Jezebel's urging, planning, and helping to execute a crime to gain something for her husband, of Pilate's futilely washing his hands in false innocence, of Herod's slaughter of the innocents, of King Saul, a doomed king near death consulting a witch. Throughout the play we move in a world reminiscent of Old Testament histories of kings whose evil could taint a whole nation, and of the pictures of moral and natural collapse in the book of Revelation (Jack). Macbeth's famous

"Tomorrow, and tomorrow, and tomorrow" soliloquy is a mosaic of biblical allusions (Milward 153–54; Shaheen, *Shakespeare's Tragedies* 172).

The practice of using the Bible as a source continued to flourish in a tradition known as "divine poetry" (Campbell), with the major works of Milton—*Paradise Lost, Paradise Regained,* and *Samson Agonistes*—standing as the climax of the movement (Radzinowicz; Sims). The Bible was even more prominent as an influence than as a source during the sixteenth and seventeenth centuries. Chana Bloch's state-of-the-art analysis of George Herbert's lyric poetry illustrates the range of ways in which the Bible served writers during two centuries when the Bible was the assumed frame of reference for every writer and reader.

The next great flowering of biblical influence occurred during the Romantic movement of the early nineteenth century. As with the Renaissance, the literary influence of the Bible coincided with an appreciation of the Bible *as* literature. But one major change is apparent: for most writers of the Romantic movement, the Bible was only a work of literature, not a book whose religious doctrine was believed as it had been by Renaissance writers. The truth that Romantic writers saw in the Bible was the truth that they found in other works of literature—truthfulness to human experience, especially human feelings.

Romantic interest in the Bible was rooted in the primitivism of the movement (Roston, *Prophet and Poet*). The Bible was admired as an ancient and oriental book rooted in nature. Its imagery was the stuff of elemental human experience, and the very style of the Bible was invoked as a model of simplicity. Paradoxically, the Bible also appealed to Romantic writers for its sublimity and majesty. The Romantics sensed mythological power in the Bible, especially its poetry.

With the renewed interest in the Bible in the early nineteenth century, writers used the Bible in the full range of possibilities. Sometimes they used the Bible as a source for their material, as in Byron's collection of lyrics entitled *Hebrew Melodies* or his drama *Cain.* Biblical allusions pervade the poetry of such poets as Emily Dickinson (Capps 27–59), Shelley (Weaver), Keats (L. N. Jeffrey), Byron (Looper), and Poe (Forrest). In the apocalyptic poetry of the Romantic movement we often catch the strains of the prophetic voice of the Bible (Abrams; Tannebaum), and Walt Whitman's prosody is indebted to biblical parallelism (Allen).

In nineteenth-century American literature it is the storytellers who show the most influence of the Bible. Herman Melville's *Moby Dick* is the most famous example (Hoffman; Holman; Stout; Wright). The Bible served as the mythological universe and informing metaphor for writers in the New

World, with the story of early Genesis providing the expressive symbols that writers used to portray their vision (R. W. B. Lewis).

While biblical influence waned during the second half of the nineteenth century in America, it continued to flower in England. Robert Browning is the towering figure (Machen; McClatchey), especially in his four poems on biblical subjects—*Karshish, Cleon, A Death in the Desert,* and *Saul.* Poets like Tennyson (Robinson) and Christina Rossetti (Jimenez) exhibit an abundance of biblical allusions, and the fiction of Dickens illustrates both direct allusion (Stevens) and ironic or revisionist allusion (Larson).

The prominence of the Bible in twentieth-century literature is all out of proportion to its relatively meager influence in a secular society. In terms of sheer quantity, biblically derived and influenced literature in the twentieth century rivals that from any other century.

Most surprising of all is the quantity of literature that takes a biblical character or event as its subject. Poets continue to write poems on biblical material (Douglas C. Brown's anthology *The Enduring Legacy: Biblical Dimensions in Modern Literature* provides typical specimens). The best poem on the nativity of Christ belongs to the twentieth century—T. S. Eliot's "Journey of the Magi." A dramatic tradition of plays based on the Bible can be traced in our century (Roston, *Drama* 233–321; de los Reyes), and the volume of fictional narrative is immense (for specimens, see Blacker and Blacker).

Nor has biblical allusion dropped out of sight. "I will arise and go now," begins one of William Butler Yeats' poems, echoing the moment of the prodigal son's resolve in Christ's parable. When T. S. Eliot's unfortunate J. Alfred Prufrock muses to himself what it might have been like to break out of his world of phony social trivialities, he imagines that it would have been like saying, "I am Lazarus, come from the dead, / Come back to tell you all." This is a double allusion—to the story of Lazarus' coming back from the dead, and to the parable of the rich man and Lazarus, in which the rich man begs Abraham to send Lazarus back to his brothers to warn them about hell. We see the Bible in the poetry of poets from Edwin Arlington Robinson (Fussell) to Dylan Thomas (Kidder; Moynihan).

Lacking a publicly accepted standard of truth, modern writers forge their own mythology. In doing so, they draw eclectically on a wide range of private and traditional sources, including the Bible. Samuel Beckett spoke for many a modern writer when he said, "I am aware of Christian mythology. . . . Like all literary devices, I use it where it suits me" (Bair 18–19). As the phrase "like all literary devices" suggests, the use that most modern writers make of the Bible is a purely literary phenomenon, divorced from religious belief.

It is small wonder, then, that modern writers have felt even freer than earlier writers to reinterpret biblical material without regard to its original meaning. William Butler Yeats, writing about how every "fine thing" in human experience "needs much laboring," entitled the poem "Adam's Curse," not because he had religious belief in the biblical story of the Fall, but because it provided a convenient and universal metaphor for his theme. As Yeats contemplates the nature of the coming civilization, he wonders exactly what "rough beast . . . / Slouches towards Bethlehem to be born." Yeats does not literally expect the new age to begin in Bethlehem, which is for him simply a metaphor for new beginnings.

Major novelists, too, continue to find the Bible important to their work. They include Faulkner (Bjork; Coffee; Malin), Steinbeck (Crockett; Rombold; Slade), Conrad (Purdy), and Joyce (Moseley). And on the dramatic scene, a major work like T. S. Eliot's *Murder in the Cathedral,* even though its subject comes from English ecclesiastical history, is thoroughly rooted in the Bible in its modeling of the hero on such biblical figures as Job and Christ, in the indebtedness of the choral speeches to the penitential psalms and psalms of praise, and in its allusions ("Here is no continuing city"; "Until the grinders cease / . . . And all the daughters of music shall be brought low").

From Caedmon's "Hymn" to contemporary fiction, poetry, and drama, the Bible has been a continuous presence in Western literature (D. L. Jeffrey). Usually the story of biblical influence on literature has resembled the history of Western literature itself, from Renaissance belief in the Bible as a religious authority, through the Romantic glorification of primitivism, to the modern impulse to create one's own mythology from a synthesis of diverse sources and casually to reinterpret biblical material.

WORKS CITED

Abrams, M. H. *Natural Supernaturalism: Tradition and Revolution in Romantic Literature.* New York: Norton, 1971.

Allen, Gay Wilson. "Biblical Analogies for Walt Whitman's Prosody." *American Literature* 6 (1934): 301–15.

Alter, Robert. *The Pleasures of Reading in an Ideological Age.* New York: Simon & Schuster, 1989.

Aschkenasy, Nehama. "Biblical Substructures in the Tragic Form: Hardy, *The Mayor of Casterbridge;* Agnon, *And the Crooked Shall Be Made Straight.*" *Biblical Patterns in Modern Literature.* Ed. David H. Hirsch and Nehama Aschkenasy. Chico, Calif.: Scholars, 1984. 85–94.

Bair, Deirdre. *Samuel Beckett: A Biography.* New York: Harcourt, 1978.

Baroway, Israel. "The Imagery of Spenser and the *Song of Songs.*" *Journal of English and Germanic Philogy* 33 (1934): 23–45.

Bartel, Roland, ed. *Biblical Images in Literature.* Nashville: Abingdon, 1975.

Besserman, Lawrence. *Chaucer and the Bible.* New York: Garland, 1988.
Bjork, Lennart. "Ancient Myths and the Moral Framework of Faulkner's *Absalom, Absalom!*" *American Literature* 35 (1963): 196–204.
Blacker, Irwin R., and Ethel M. Blacker, eds. *The Book of Books: A Treasury of Great Bible Fiction.* New York: Holt, Rinehart and Winston, 1965.
Bloch, Chana. *Spelling the Word: George Herbert and the Bible.* Berkeley: University of California Press, 1985.
Bloomfield, Morton. *Piers Plowman as a Fourteenth-Century Apocalypse.* New Brunswick, N.J.: Rutgers UP, 1962.
Brown, Douglas C., ed. *The Enduring Legacy: Biblical Dimensions in Modern Literature.* New York: Scribner, 1975.
Campbell, Lily B. *Divine Poetry and Drama in Sixteenth-Century England.* Cambridge: Cambridge UP, 1959.
Capps, Jack L. *Emily Dickinson's Reading 1836–1886.* Cambridge, Mass.: Harvard UP, 1966.
Coffee, Jessie M. *Faulkner's Un-Christlike Christians: Biblical Allusions in the Novels.* Ann Arbor: University of Michigan Research Press, 1983.
Cornelius, R. M. *Christopher Marlowe's Use of the Bible.* New York: Peter Lang, 1984.
Cowley, Malcolm, ed. *Writers at Work: The Paris Review Interviews.* London: Secker and Warburg, 1958.
Crockett, H. Kelly. "The Bible and *The Grapes of Wrath.*" *College English* 24 (1963): 193–99.
de los Reyes, Marie. *The Biblical Theme in Modern Drama.* Quezon City: University of the Philippines Press, 1978.
Forrest, William M. *Biblical Allusions in Poe.* New York: Macmillan, 1928.
Frye, Northrop. *Anatomy of Criticism.* Princeton: Princeton UP, 1957.
Fussell, Edwin S. *Edwin Arlington Robinson: The Literary Background of a Traditional Poet.* Berkeley: University of California Press, 1954.
Hankins, John E. "Spenser and the Revelation of St. John." *Proceedings of the Modern Language Association* 60 (1945): 364–81.
Henn, T. R. *The Bible as Literature.* New York: Oxford UP, 1970.
Hoffman, Daniel G. "Moby Dick: Jonah's Whale or Job's?" *Sewanee Review* 69 (1961): 205–24.
Holman, C. Hugh. "The Reconciliation of Ishmael: *Moby Dick* and the Book of Job." *South Atlantic Quarterly* 57 (1958): 477–90.
Jack, Jane. "*Macbeth,* King James, and the Bible." *English Literary History* 22 (1955): 173–93.
Jeffrey, David L., ed. *A Dictionary of Biblical Tradition in English Literature.* Grand Rapids: Eerdmans, 1992.
Jeffrey, Lloyd N. "Keats and the Bible." *Keats-Shelley Journal* 10 (1961): 59–70.
Jimenez, Nilda. *The Bible and the Poetry of Christina Rossetti: A Concordance.* Westport, Conn.: Greenwood, 1979.
Kehl, D. G., ed. *Literary Style of the Old Bible and the New.* Indianapolis: Bobbs-Merrill, 1970.
Kidder, Rushworth M. *Dylan Thomas: The Country of the Spirit.* Princeton: Princeton UP, 1973.
Larson, Janet L. *Dickens and the Broken Scripture.* Athens: University of Georgia Press, 1985.

Lee, Alvin. *The Guest Hall of Eden.* New Haven: Yale UP, 1972.

Lewalski, Barbara K. *Protestant Poetics and the Seventeenth-Century Religious Lyric.* Princeton: Princeton UP, 1979.

Lewis, C. S. *The Literary Impact of the Authorized Version.* Philadelphia: Fortress, 1963.

Lewis, R. W. B. *The American Adam.* Chicago: University of Chicago Press, 1955.

Looper, Travis. *Byron and the Bible.* Metuchen, N.J.: Scarecrow, 1978.

McClatchey, Joe H. "Browning's 'Saul' as a Davidic Psalm of the Praise of God: The Poetics of Prophecy." *Studies in Browning and His Circle* 4 (1976): 62–83.

Machen, Minnie G. *The Bible in Browning.* New York: Macmillan, 1903.

Malin, Irving. *William Faulkner: An Interpretation.* Stanford: Stanford UP, 1957.

Milward, Peter. *Biblical Influences in Shakespeare's Great Tragedies.* Bloomington: Indiana UP, 1987.

Moseley, Virginia. *Joyce and the Bible.* De Kalb: Northern Illinois UP, 1967.

Moynahan, Julian. "*The Mayor of Casterbridge* and the Old Testament's First Book of Samuel: A Study of Some Literary Relationships." *Biblical Images in Literature.* Ed. Roland Bartel. Nashville: Abingdon, 1975.

Moynihan, William T. *The Craft and Art of Dylan Thomas.* Ithaca: Cornell UP, 1966.

Purdy, Dwight H. *Joseph Conrad's Bible.* Norman: Oklahoma UP, 1984.

Radzinowicz, Mary Ann. *Milton's Epics and the Book of Psalms.* Princeton: Princeton UP, 1989.

———. *Toward "Samson Agonistes": The Growth of Milton's Mind.* Princeton: Princeton UP, 1978.

Robinson, Edna Moore, *Tennyson's Use of the Bible.* Baltimore: Johns Hopkins UP, 1917.

Rombold, Tamara. "Biblical Inversion in *The Grapes of Wrath.*" *College Literature* 14 (1987): 146–66.

Roston, Murray. *Biblical Drama in England.* Evanston, Ill.: Northwestern UP, 1968.

———. *Prophet and Poet: The Bible and the Growth of Romanticism.* Evanston, Ill.: Northwestern UP, 1965.

Ryken, Leland. "*Paradise Lost* and Its Biblical Epic Models." *Milton and Scriptural Tradition: The Bible into Poetry.* Ed. James H. Sims and Leland Ryken. Columbia: University of Missouri Press, 1984. 43–81.

Shaheen, Naseeb. *Biblical References in Shakespeare's Tragedies.* Newark: University of Delaware Press, 1987.

———. *Biblical References in The Faerie Queene.* Memphis: Memphis State UP, 1976.

Shepherd, Geoffrey. "Scriptural Poetry." *Continuations and Beginnings: Studies in Old English Literature.* Ed. Eric Gerald Stanley. London: Nelson, 1966. 1–36.

Sims, James H. *Dramatic Uses of Biblical Allusions in Marlowe and Shakespeare.* Gainesville: University of Florida Press, 1966.

———. *The Bible in Milton's Epics.* Gainesville: University of Florida Press, 1962.

Slade, Leonard A., Jr. "The Use of Biblical Allusions in *The Grapes of Wrath.*" *College Language Association Journal* 11 (1968): 241–47.

Stevens, James S. *Quotations and References in Charles Dickens.* Boston: Christopher, 1929.

Stout, Janis. "Melville's Use of the Book of Job." *Nineteenth-Century Fiction* 25 (1970): 69–83.

Tannebaum, Leslie. *Biblical Tradition in Blake's Early Prophecies: The Great Code of Art.* Princeton: Princeton UP, 1982.

Wall, John N., Jr. "The Contrarious Hand of God: *Samson Agonistes* and the Biblical Lament." *Milton Studies XII.* Ed. James D. Simmonds. Pittsburgh: Pittsburgh UP, 1980. 117–39.

Weaver, Bennett. *Toward the Understanding of Shelley.* New York: Octagon, 1966.

Wright, Nathalia. *Melville's Use of the Bible.* Durham, N.C.: Duke UP, 1969.

CHAPTER 36

The Novelist and the Bible

CHAIM POTOK
Novelist

The *novelist* and the *Bible?* Dare we pen those words in the same sentence?

A novel—at its most mediocre: a frivolity; a fleeting artifact; an entertainment; candy for an airplane ride; puffery for a lazy summer afternoon or a long winter night. And at its best: an iconoclastic and often Gnostic vision of the world in carefully coded language; a cry of the heart in story form; an elitist word game.

The Bible in relationship to a form of *entertainment?* Or to even the most sober and sophisticated of *stories?*

Are we not mixing categories here? Toying with apples and oranges?

In the New York world of my childhood—the decade of the Depression and dark birth of Nazism—school and home were of a single mind with regard to the Bible.

We never called it "the Bible" but "the Torah"—the Teaching, the Law—and we meant by that a book of books: any or all of the Five Books of Moses, that is, the Pentateuch, or the entire canon of sacred Scriptures: Pentateuch, Prophets, and Writings. And when we used the word "Torah" without the definite article, we were referring to *the act of study,* to an educational process that encompassed all the millennia of Jewish religious learning: Scriptures, as well as classical, medieval, and contemporary rabbinic texts. One held in one's hands *the* Torah; one read *the* Torah; but one *studied* Torah. Each of us, fine-tuned to the subtleties of the tradition, could detect instinctively the nuances of that term.

This we knew with consummate conviction: The Torah—in its meaning as the Five Books of Moses, the written Law—was the word of God revealed at Sinai to the children of Israel some while after the Exodus from Egypt. We were told that the oral Law, too, was revealed at Sinai, and many centuries later shaped into the Talmud, but not many of us really understood what that meant, the Talmud seeming so vast and formless. But the Torah was ultimate authority, immutable, dense with sanctity, suffused with inexhaustible significance. As much tamper with its sacred words as alter a law of the cosmos; as much wear out its meaning as dry up the oceans.

And the narratives in the Torah—the sin of Adam and Eve; the murder of Abel by Cain; Noah and the Flood; Abraham and the laughter of Sarah; the binding of Isaac; the cunning of Rebekah; the cry of Esau; the flight of Jacob; the selling of Joseph—sacred history parading before my eyes in classrooms, in the synagogue, at home. I dreamed of Joseph and his resplendent coat. I suffered with the enslaved children of Israel. I stood at Mount Sinai. I marched in the wilderness. I witnessed the passing of Aaron and wept at the death of Moses. I entered the Promised Land with Joshua. I fought in the armies of the Judges and King David. I gazed in awe at the oriental splendor of the court of King Solomon. A panoply of heroes and ordinary people—and, astonishingly, their weaknesses were never concealed from me. The Torah did not mask the pitiless truths about the dark side of humankind.

If I had questions about those stories, there were ready rejoinders by teachers and commentators. At times their replies might contradict one another. But we understood that the great sages of the past—the creators of law and the writers of commentary—had the right and the wisdom at times to disagree with one another over this or that sacred text, whereas we, their descendants, were obligated to follow the decisions of contemporary teachers, those ordained to carry on the ancient chain of tradition begun with Abraham and Sarah; we were charged with the covenantal obligation to obey the Law given at Sinai and interpreted throughout the generations by those in rightful authority.

The Five Books of Moses told of the purpose of creation, the responsibility of humankind, and the specific burden to be borne by the people of Israel. The very book itself was sacred: its printed words, its paper, its binding. If you dropped a copy of the Five Books of Moses, you quickly picked it up and put it to your lips in a reverential kiss. If you placed a copy of the Five Books of Moses on a table, you were not to place any other sort of book on top of it; ultimate sanctity was not to be demeaned by serving as a prop for any works of lesser consequence.

Torah in both its narrowest and broadest sense mirrored the numinous sacred soul of the world.

And literature? What was literature?

During my early years in high school—a religious high school in which were taught the secular subjects mandated by the State of New York—literature consisted of Shakespeare, Robert Louis Stevenson, Sir Walter Scott, and similar others. Dramas and stories. It never occurred to me to relate those tales to Torah. *Treasure Island* and Genesis? *Ivanhoe* and Exodus? *Hamlet* and a tractate of the Talmud? Any venture at connectedness between those two realms was so beyond thought as to make it unnecessary for me even to consider erecting a defensive wall between them. How could one conceivably equate man-created tale with God-given Word?

When I was sixteen years old, I read quite by chance, and not because it was required by the English studies curriculum, a serious contemporary adult novel: *Brideshead Revisited* by Evelyn Waugh. Soon afterward I read *A Portrait of the Artist As a Young Man* by James Joyce.

To this day, I do not understand that sudden youthful resolve to explore serious adult fiction. Those two novels were my introduction to literature.

Catholic English aristocracy and Oxford in *Brideshead,* Catholic Irish poverty and Jesuit schooling in *Portrait*—and my Orthodox New York Jewish world. Cultural antipodes.

And yet—I felt myself somehow linked to those strange and distant cultures and their confrontations with modernity, to their struggles to cling to old truths in the teeth of new realities. I was mesmerized by the way the writers had used story-telling to shape the churning inchoate conflicts between the inner world of faith and the outer world of secularism. Could I, too, use language one day to map the landscape that was my own dark arena of confrontation with the secular world?

I began to read hungrily. And I began to write.

All during those embryonic years of writing—from about sixteen to twenty—literature and Torah remained unrelated realms. Isaiah and Melville; Jeremiah and Faulkner; Ezekiel and Kafka. It simply never occurred to me that they could in any way encroach upon one another.

Then, in one of those singular brushes with chance that often shape the life of a writer, I attended, during my last year in college, a required class in the third book of the Torah, Writings.

The teacher was a pious scholar, a man in his late fifties, a family man. He taught The Song of Songs.

The Song of Songs is part of the Scriptures; it is a sacred work. He taught it in the traditional manner, as an allegory, using the Midrash, which sees the book as a dialogue between God and the people of Israel:

> "Oh, give me of the kisses of your mouth, / For your love [*dōdêkā*] is more delightful than wine." The words of the Torah are like one another, they are close companions (*dôdîm*) to one another.
>
> "Your cheeks are comely with plaited wreaths." These are the Rabbis. "Your neck with strings of pearls." These are the disciples who strain their necks to hear the words of the Torah.
>
> "Ah, you are fair, my darling, / Ah, you are fair." Behold you are fair in the performance of the commandments. Behold you are fair in deeds of kindness.
>
> "My beloved is mine, / And I am His." He is my God, and I am His nation.

He sat behind the large darkwood desk, a stocky man, brown mustache on his pallid features, gray fedora on his head, reading aloud The Song of Songs and quite methodically neutralizing its sensuality. And I accepted it as it was presented: sacred poetry.

Related somehow to the poetry of Wordsworth, Coleridge, Keats, Shelley, Browning, Tennyson, whose work I was then studying as an English major? Unthinkable. And I didn't think it.

Then fortune intervened.

Graduating from that fundamentalist college, I entered the Jewish Theological Seminary of America—a traditional rabbinical school with a nonfundamentalist modern scientific approach to biblical and rabbinic sources.

The first book of the Bible I studied in that seminary was The Song of Songs.

The professor, a noted scholar of the Bible, spent the entire first class lecturing on the language and historical background of The Song of Songs.

The book, he said, was a collection of love songs very much like other such songs in the ancient Near East. In those songs descriptions of physical beauty were typically rendered through exaggerated sensuous language.

The Song of Songs, he said, is entirely a sensuous book: God is neither alluded to nor invoked. Its songs celebrate marriage and were no doubt sung in ancient Israel from time immemorial, the verses undergoing changes as the language evolved.

The version we have, the professor went on, probably dates to the third century Before the Common Era (B.C.E., the traditional Jewish way of dating, to avoid the term "Before Christ"). Because marriage was ordained by God in the Hebrew Bible and sex was not seen to be intrinsically shameful, and also because the book was attributed to King Solomon, The Song of Songs was accepted into the canon in the year 90 C.E., even before it was allegorized. Later generations of Rabbis, seeking to dilute its eroticism and ensure its sanctity, put it through the process of allegorization, and the book became an account of the history of the early relationship between God and the congregation of Israel.

That and more I learned during that first class in The Song of Songs.

I walked out of the class with my head spinning. Erotic love songs! Marriage songs! Living people singing at exalted moments in their lives. A book of the Bible positioned in the context of the history of language. Suddenly a text nuanced and textured; it occupied space; it filled a niche *in time.*

Teacher after teacher in that seminary focused the new scholarly apparatus .of modern scientific analysis—philology, history, grammar, surrounding parallel cultures, archaeology, structure, imagery, metaphor, metonymy, synecdoche, allusion, and so much more—on the Bible's poetry and prose. Hosea, Amos, Jeremiah, Isaiah, Psalms, Job, and others. The books were alive!

After four years in that seminary the notion of reading and understanding the Bible as literature—truly remarkable literature articulating God's efforts to dialogue with man and man's search for God—was as obvious to me as it had once been unthinkable. I could not conceive it otherwise.

But there were problems.

Literature in our time is by and large the creation of iconoclasts, breakers of images, themselves as dubiously moral as the rest of us, outrageous rebels who infuriate us and challenge societal stability by laying bare the small and large weaknesses and hypocrisies that bedevil our inner and outer lives.

Devout Christians, Jews, and Muslims tend to regard literature as a hazard to piety. Dictatorships of the right and left see it as a threat to the state.

Viewing the Bible through the prism of literature seems at first glance a distortion and diminishment of the sacred.

Literature also has attached to it the notion of facts falsified by the fires of the imagination. Indeed, only the fatuous go to literature for truths of history, whatever those may be. One does not read *War and Peace* for a true account of the Napoleonic invasion of Russia. Are we to say then of the Bible that it is literature and does not give us historical truths?

And what are we to make of the Revelation at Sinai, that moment when, we are told, the infinite God encountered finite man and the destiny of our species was forever changed? Is the biblical record of the Revelation literature?

And, to press the matter further, what is the Bible, really? A work of infinite perfection? If so, what are we to make of the sophisticated new discipline of textual criticism born about two hundred years ago in the universities of Germany and France? What are we to do with the truths given us by that new discipline? And if the Bible is less than perfect, if it is not the creation of God, then whose creation is it? The creation of men and women? Why should we commit our lives and destinies to a book that is a human creation, to a work of literature? How many would go to the barricades for Homer, Sophocles, or Shakespeare?

The notion of the Bible as literature is particularly grievous, even dangerous, to very religious Jews, because all of Jewish law depends on the fixed nature of the biblical text. One wonders what might transpire in the arena of American constitutional law if the text of the Constitution were subjected to change. Rabbinic law is built upon the assumption of the absolute sanctity of the biblical text, of the potential legal nuances and resonances in each sacred word, indeed in each holy letter, of the Five Books of Moses.

And so we have come down to these questions: Can we look upon the Bible as literature and still regard it as a sacred work? And, What if anything can a contemporary novelist learn from this ancient work?

The Hebrew Bible is a vast collection of various kinds of writing: narratives, laws, mores, genealogies, tales, tribal lists, histories—the canonical remains of nearly a thousand years of oral and written traditions transmitted by people who shaped the world mainly through words because image-making was largely forbidden to them.

Theirs was a sacred covenantal history. They received and recounted their vision of reality only through words, all the time filled with the conviction that those words touched that sacred history at its core. And at that core was their God, his covenant with his people Israel, and his direction of their destiny.

When I say that the Bible can be seen as literature, I make no comment on the nature of God, covenant, and Jewish destiny. Nor do I pass judgment on the events of Sinai. The notion of the Bible as literature does not necessarily impose humanist orientation on the contents of the Scriptures. It only tells us that the Bible has been formed in a certain way, and that if we read it through the categories and discipline of literature, we will achieve a clearer understanding of its words. Whether God or man fashioned the Bible, the fact is that much of it has the feel, the look, the resonance of literature. It is by and large a *shaped* text. Someone (or some One) who deeply loved language, cared about form, was sensitive to literary structure and not averse to the sheer delights of wordplay passed a hand over the text and crafted it in certain ways. And now that we know what to look for, we can perceive the hand moving, molding, sculpting the language.

One brief example. King Saul, in a sudden rage, has tried unsuccessfully to kill David. A bewildered and fearful David asks Jonathan, the king's son, "What have I done? What is my crime and what is my guilt against your father that he seeks my life?" (1 Sam. 20:1). At first glance, the repeated "what" seems awkward, and points to an exhaustion of language. (Indeed, in the New Jewish Publication Society Translation of The Holy Scriptures [NJPS], the authorized Bible for English-speaking Jewry, published in 1985, the third "what" is omitted.) But Professor Robert Alter, who has written much and well about the Bible as literature, views those repetitions as a quite deliberate literary use of the oratorical figure of speech known as anaphora. As in Psalm 23:

He makes me lie down in green pastures;
He leads me to water in places of repose;
He renews my life. . . .

And Matthew 5:3:

Blessed are the poor in spirit. . . .
Blessed are they that mourn. . . .
Blessed are the meek. . . .

And Shakespeare's *King John* 2.1.561:

Mad world! Mad kings! Mad composition!

And Shakespeare's *Richard II* 1.1.40:

This royal throne of kings, this sceptered isle,
This earth of majesty, this seat of Mars. . . .
This blessed plot, this earth, this realm, this England. . . .

The meticulous analyses of biblical stories—the Creation story, the Flood story, the Joseph story, the Moses story, the story of Jephtha's daughter, to name a few—found in the work of prominent contemporary scholars (see, for example, *The Art of Biblical Narrative* and *The World of Biblical Literature* by Robert Alter; *The Narrative Covenant* by David Damrosch; *The Poetics of Biblical Narrative* by Meir Sternberg; *In Potiphar's House* by James L. Kugel), are further instances of the keen use of literary exegetical tools on the Bible itself as well as on the interpretive process to which it has been subjected through the centuries.

We know more about the nature of literature today, in the wake of Dante, Shakespeare, Milton, Jane Austen, Flaubert, and Joyce, than we ever did. We can read the Bible as we rarely could before; we have come to realize how sophisticated, how *literary,* is its writing. Further, we can now discern clearly the Bible's own quite distinctive writerly voices—from the sublime beginnings of the book of Genesis to the communal sensuality of The Song of Songs to the awesome final section of the book of Job.

Often, textual problems in the Bible tend to be resolved either by emendation or some fortunate archaeological find.

Examples of the former are plentiful in NJPS, where suggestions for emendations of difficult passages may be found in the footnotes throughout the pages of the Prophets and the Writings—but are deliberately avoided in the Pentateuch, the core book of Judaism. Most contemporary Bible scholars, however, would not hesitate to suggest emendations to the text of the Pentateuch.

As for archaeology, systematic excavations and accidental finds have returned to us much of the ancient world in which the drama of the Bible was set. Beams of light have been thrown upon many previous dark regions of the biblical text. The spiritual and physical landscapes of the Bible are now accessible to us in ways that were unimaginable two hundred years ago.

One of the most extraordinary archaeological discoveries of our century occurred in 1928, at the site of the ancient city of Ugarit, in northern Syria. Royal tombs, two temples, numerous artifacts, a library. In the library were found many inscriptions in familiar Near Eastern languages and in one previously unknown Semitic language. Scholars deciphered it and named it Ugaritic.

Several hundred Ugaritic texts, among them three major epics, have in the past decades helped scholars recover the literary and cultural background of the Hebrew Bible. One of those texts forced a strange destiny on a familiar phrase in Psalms: ". . . the valley of the shadow of death" (23:4).

The Septuagint read it that way because the Alexandrian Jewish scholars who translated the Hebrew saw *ṣ-l-m-w-t* in the text, did not know what to make of it, and broke it into two Hebrew words they did know, *ṣal māwet,* "shadow of death." "Shadow of death" journeyed from the Septuagint to the Vulgate to King James. But we now know that *ṣ-l-m-w-t* is a Ugaritic word, *ṣalmût,* and means "deepest darkness." The line in Psalms should read, "a valley of deepest darkness." And, indeed, that is the way NJPS renders it.

Many texts once thought capable of elucidation only through emendation or archaeology are now clarified through the contemporary perception of the nature of biblical literature. Further, careful literary analysis enables us to see unity in texts where previous scholars saw only the results of ancient editors' vain attempts to bring together disparate tribal traditions. Robert Alter's *World of Biblical Literature* offers an instance of literary analysis at work on the tasks of unity and clarity:

The text of 2 Samuel 5 reads, in Alter's translation:

> All the tribes of Israel came to David at Hebron and said, "Here, we are your bone and flesh. Long ago, when Saul was king over us, you were Israel's leader in battle. And the Lord said to you:
>
> *"You shall shepherd my people*
> *and you shall rule over Israel."*
>
> All the elders of Israel came to the king at Hebron, and King David made a covenant with them in Hebron before the Lord, and they anointed David king over Israel.

Rather than viewing this passage as an instance of two traditions, tribes and elders, ineptly spliced together by an editor, Alter offers it as a paradigm of the biblical literary stratagem now known as *resumptive repetition:* whenever a narrative is interrupted by a digression—here, a quote from the Lord—the writer resumes the narrative by repeating the statement made before the interruption.

Today, we can realize a clearer understanding of the intent of many biblical texts by reading them through the prism of literature: dialogue, character development, word repetition, resumptive repetition, economy of language, the use of rhythms, symbols, imagery, the deliberate arrangement of words for their sheer musicality.

But what about the problems?

I mentioned earlier that I preferred not to deal here with difficulties about the nature of the Bible, its sanctity, what really happened at Sinai, the relationship of rabbinic law to a suddenly fluid text. Indeed, most scholars who use this literary approach to the Bible are interested only in what is found in the text as we have it. Few literary scholars possess the technical skill needed for text-critical analysis of the Bible.

Still, the problems are very much with us. And they confront

Christians and their Bible as well. Hard challenges arise from the findings of scientific Bible scholarship, the discovery of the Dead Sea Scrolls, the ongoing attempts to date the Gospels and fix the historicity and specific culture context of Jesus.

My own experience with contemporary biblical scholarship has enabled me to understand these quandaries and provided me with the subject matter for a number of my books. *The Chosen, The Promise, In the Beginning* are about culture confrontations at the cores of conflicting cultures. Much that is in those books centers around the problem of the Bible in the modern world.

It has been a very long journey for me, this passage from my deeply religious New York world, where the Bible was frozen sanctity, to this time in my life when I am able to see it as a work pulsing with vitality and contemporary meaning. I have tried to record the tension and excitement of that journey in my novels. I have used modern secular literary techniques to write about the contemporary coming-to-terms with an ancient sacred literature.

That has been my way of bringing together the novelist and the Bible. The journey, I hope, is not yet ended.

WORKS CITED

Alter, Robert. *The Art of Biblical Narrative.* New York: Basic Books, 1981.
———. *The World of Biblical Literature.* New York: Basic Books, 1991.
Damrosch, D. *The Narrative Covenant.* San Francisco: Harper & Row, 1987.
Kugel, J. L. *In Potiphar's House.* San Francisco: Harper & Row, 1990.
Sternberg, M. *The Poetics of Biblical Narrative.* Bloomington: Indiana UP, 1985.

CHAPTER 37

The Bible Through a Poet's Eyes

GENE WARREN DOTY
University of Missouri–Rolla

Reading the Bible as a Child

Reading the Bible begins for me as a child, with Sunday school and Vacation Bible school. The first Bible I remember owning was covered in black imitation leather, with pages edged in red. It was printed on thin paper that browned quickly. Of course, it was the King James, a red-letter version, with my name embossed on the front cover. I do not remember when it was given to me, but I think I had it before I went through confirmation in the fifth grade. I had no instruction or example of studying the Bible systematically, but I was fascinated with it. When I tried to read this Bible, I always started with Genesis 1, intending to read straight through. That did not work: I inevitably got bogged down. Usually the genealogies early in Genesis did me in.

That Bible sat on my shelf, black and squat, seeming to demand that I read it, and yet I couldn't.

Thus my earliest exposure to the Bible was actually through the stories and pictures printed in little four-page papers given to us in Sunday school, through the flannel-board depictions of Bible stories that were a major feature of Vacation Bible school, through the prints of popular religious paintings that hung in the church, through the stained-glass windows, and, of course, through the words of Sunday school teachers and sermons on Sunday morning. Through church and Sunday school, I was exposed to a body of stories embedded in the mind of our culture—Adam, Eve, and the Snake; Cain and Abel; Abraham, Isaac, and Jacob; Moses, Samson, David and Goliath, Jesus healing, Jesus teaching, Jesus working miracles, and that "wee little man," Zacchaeus, of whom so many children have sung.

I was exposed to two cultures: the culture of east central Kansas, where I grew up, and the culture of the Bible, mediated through story and picture. Seen through the lens of rural Kansas in the 1940s and 50s, the culture depicted in the Bible is both alien and familiar. The facets of its alienness are clear enough—biblical culture occurs in a much different time and place, with a very different climate and much simpler technology.

Biblical culture was familiar because the stories, characters, and images of the Bible pervade our souls. I am sure that my Sunday school teachers' conscious motivation was to make their students "good little boys and girls," to teach us the moral behavior and emotional responses that would allow us to fit into our society. Some of them may have also had more explicit notions of leading us to "salvation," of showing us how to please God. But by directing us to color Joseph in his coat of many colors, or showing us a flannelgraph depiction of Samson pulling down the Philistine temple, they were embedding and reinforcing imagery that shaped us at much deeper levels—of emotion, of our sense of personal identity, of what the world is and what people are.

There was a congruence for me between my life as a child on a farm and the lives depicted in the Bible. I could relate directly to Jesus' and David's metaphors about plants and weather. Our farm was on the edge of the Flint hills in Kansas, rolling grassy hills under a very large sky. The wind, clouds, heat, cold, rain, snow, dust—all were familiar accompaniments in my childhood.

When I was a child in the 1940s and early 1950s, rural Kansas was isolated and culturally simple. There were no freeways, no television, much less movies to rent on videotape. Radio, of course, was a major medium of entertainment and news, and even tiny (about five hundred people) Eskridge had a movie theater when I was young. But what came through the radio was usually consistent with the values and images around me, since my family listened mostly to a station that focused on issues of concern to farmers. Few people had any interests beyond the news, stock prices, and "Fibber McGee and Molly," or maybe "Amos and Andy."

The Thirst for Story

As a child I had a thirst for stories and myths that has not abated to this day. Gene Autry and Tarzan, as much as I enjoyed them, were not sufficient to quench it. I attended the first four grades in a one-room country school, where I was the youngest child, and the only child in my class. The library was very small, but it did have a volume of Greek and Roman myths, which I remember reading avidly. But there was very little reinforcement of my interest in story and myth, and I do not remember anyone who shared it.

Like Greek and Roman myth, but with greater actuality, the stories in the Bible present larger than life characters—huge, vivid figures that storm and weep, laugh, love, and go to war. The stories of Samson, Saul, and the others are primal stories—elemental narratives of the human condition. As such, the biblical stories I was exposed to in Sunday school and church thoroughly satisfied my need for story. In our ordinary lives, our passions overlap and blur each other, and our motives are mixed and uncertain. When biblical characters face moral dilemmas, their motives are clear and direct. Saul's disobedience has perfectly clear motives, for instance, even though the reader is saying, "Don't do it, Saul; God isn't fooling with you."

For contemporary readers, the Bible provides access to a world both like and unlike the one we live in; the biblical world is archaic and mythic in the sense of the largeness, simplicity, directness, and elemental nature of the characters and actions it depicts. The world of the Bible is larger than our lives, more intense and vivid; thus it enlarges and deepens our imaginations, giving us fundamental images to express our feelings.

The world in the Bible is rooted in the elemental rhythms of nature. The seasons in Palestine and Kansas are different, and yet life in both places depends on the flow and pattern of the seasons, on whether there will be adequate rainfall at the right time, whether insects will devour the crops or the livestock will die. In Kansas, massive dark clouds could blow a fierce storm out of the northwest. Job's whirlwind was entirely credible to me after my experience of the weather in Wabaunsee County, Kansas.

Bareback at the Crucifixion

An experience at a country church when I was around eight years old led directly to my poem "Bareback in Kansas," which deals with the crucifixion of Jesus.

I wrote "Bareback in Kansas"* one afternoon in 1965 when I felt at loose ends; my wife encouraged me to sit at the typewriter and write. Since I did not have anything specific in mind to write about, I just wrote whatever came to mind. Before long, I found myself writing into the rhythms and emotions of poetry.

The poem that resulted is rooted in my experience of nature and the Bible. Naturally, I had been exposed to the story of the Crucifixion since I was able to understand what was being said in church or Sunday school. Through Bible stories, Easter sermons, and my own reading of the Gospels, I was familiar with the events and images of the Passion story, and more important for poetry, the feelings it expresses.

In his essay "The Rabbinic Method and Biblical Criticism," Kalman P. Bland shows how the Bible involves the reader as an imaginative participant:

> The art of biblical narrative [and, one may add, poetry] consists of signals addressed to the sensitive reader. These signals function as agents which stimulate our intellect, our imagination, and our capacity for empathy in order to engage us in a mutual act of literary creation with Scripture itself. (21)

Like other readers of the Bible, I have been shaped at a deep level of imagination and feeling by the "signals" to which Bland refers. The reader who engages the Bible at this level finds that its imagery naturally expresses his or her own feelings.

Behind the country church was a small shed where coal was stored. Another boy and I went into the coal shed during a break. The rest of the children and the teachers were playing a game of some sort. In the coal shed, the other boy and I discovered a catfish that someone had left there. (A creek ran not more than a quarter of a mile from the church, and several ponds stocked with fish were nearby.)

We took a couple of the scraps of lumber that were lying around in the coal shed and fashioned them into a cross. Then we nailed the catfish to it, reciting words from the communion rite while we did so. We were consciously imitating the Crucifixion. While doing this, I felt that we were somehow honoring the crucified Christ, that we were imitating an important and mysterious event. I certainly did not intend any mockery of Christ. I know now that the fish was a symbolically appropriate creature for us to

*I published both "Bareback in Kansas" and "The Death of Saul" (mentioned later in this chapter) as Eugene Warren, not Gene Doty. Doty is my father's name; after my mother was divorced and remarried, I used my adoptive father's name, Warren, for a number of years. In 1988 I restored my original surname and have used it since. Whatever confusion the change has caused to others, it has meant a real reclaiming of identity for me.

crucify, but at the time, I only knew that it felt right. When I got home at noon that day, I told my mother what we had done. To my surprise and dismay, she was outraged. To her, what we had done was a terrible blasphemy, which had been far from my intention. In my confusion, I responded to her outrage with guilt and shame.

A second major source for "Bareback in Kansas" is the hours I spent on horseback when I was a child, either doing farm work or playing. Riding bareback, I often felt very close to God and to Jesus. I talked freely to Jesus and felt him as a very real presence.

The awe that I felt toward the Crucifixion and the guilt derived from my mother's response to the crucified catfish both came into the poem, as well as the rhythms of riding horseback. This poem expresses the childhood shame, guilt, and joy arising from those experiences and from my knowledge of the Gospels.

Formally, the poem uses parallelism, producing a rhythm that suggests riding a galloping horse across the prairies. My association of riding horses with feeling close to Jesus is at the heart of the rhythm of the poem, while the guilt and shame associated with my being a "crucifier" provides the emotional roots. The imagery comes from the Bible and from my experiences as a child and an adult. Here are two stanzas from the poem:

I am thinking of You
as her hooves bite the grass, spreading it;
I am thinking of Your face
bearded & serene, of Your eyes like the pond on a clear day,
a double depth cloudless;
I am thinking of the mouth in Your side
that spoke the fountain,
of the dark bloodcaked eyes in Your hands and feet weeping,
I am thinking that You loved me as I mounted the ladder
& shoved the thorns around Your skull,
I am thinking that the palms of Your outspread hands
watched me as I turned from the hill
& went laughing back to the city
to spill wine like blood down my throat
& tell whores of the Fool.
. . . .
And I know that this mare will rise with me,
that You will touch this body as well as spirit,
that the blossom will have its stem,
that Your city stands forever,
that the tree bears in season and out.

More than the rhythms of the Bible's poetry, more even than specific imagery drawn from the Bible (and in fact both rhythm and imagery have other sources as well), this poem is driven by a deep-rooted personal involvement with the Bible, with this ultimate story of human cruelty and selfishness, and divine mercy and power. When I wrote this poem, I was tapping deep emotional springs in myself, in my environment, and in the Bible itself, as it was mediated to me through Sunday school, Bible school, stained-glass windows, flannel boards, hymns, and sermons.

Imagery and Feeling

As a poet, my desire is to read the Bible with my eyes, mind, and heart open, to be aware of the feelings presented in its stories and poems. All through the Bible the authors and the characters explore their relation to God—not through intellectual endeavor, not through academic theology, but through story, image, rhythm, and speech.

The poets who wrote the Psalms had a common vocabulary of images and metaphors to draw on; they shared this vocabulary with their audience. This common vocabulary allows the psalmists to speak to and for their community in ways that express common feelings and values. Contemporary American poets do not have this advantage, since there is no common vocabulary of imagery in our culture, except for constantly shifting popular culture, which is limited in expressive capability.

A poet writing in the biblical tradition does have that set of images to draw on but cannot be sure that the reader will share those images. In discussing the Canadian poet Margaret Avison, Denise Levertov speaks of the advantage the Christian poet has in being able to synthesize "personal experience and the shared, or cultural, inheritance of emotive patterns . . ."; Levertov adds that such shared patterns "can most deeply penetrate the feeling-life of an empathic reader" (Levertov 83).

Any reader—and not just a poet—can participate imaginatively in the Bible's poetry. The reader must simply allow her or his imagination to be open to the intuitive ranges of meaning in the imagery. For instance, in reading Psalm 1, which has quite clear content, the reader can also imaginatively be like a tree planted by a stream of water, its roots searching through the soil for water, its leaves expanding upward and opening to the light. In the same psalm, the reader may also imaginatively experience being threshed into small bits and tossed into the wind or gathered into safety.

These imaginative experiences add a living dimension to the reader's intellectual understanding of the psalm's meaning.

King Saul's Fire

Almost twenty years after writing "Bareback in Kansas," I wrote a verse play, "The Death of Saul." I had been struck for some time with the tragic elements in the story of Saul. The imagery and pattern of action in that story express emotions to which I could relate, especially his bitterness and despair. Although I do not consider myself to be a playwright, I wrote a verse play with a chorus and several characters but not a lot of action. The following quotations from "The Death of Saul" illustrate how I used those emotions to express my own.

In this first quotation, Saul is speaking to Abner in their camp at Gilboa, opposite the Philistine army:

Silence, Abner. You are a warrior,
As you say. You have not known
The piercing oil of God that lights a fire
Deeper than your bones, blazing in your heart
Like constant lightning. No! you have not known
That shaking fire. And you have not known—
For which ignorance give thanks—
The hollowness left when that fire goes out,
Or leaps like a burning deer to another's heart.
Be blessed that you have not known
And cannot know the silence that follows
The final words God speaks to you,
Words that drain your heart of life and joy.

Oil, fire, bones, heart, deer, silence, words: all these crucial images come from the Bible, and yet they are universal enough to be expressive for contemporary readers.

In the next quotation, Saul tells Abner of his plan to consult the witch of Endor:

[God] gives me rancid butter, not sweet oil.
Let him object—let him do worse to me
Than he does, if he can think of worse.
I'll bear it or break.

In both of these quotations, images from the Bible express Saul's sense of loss combined with despondency and obstinance, an emotional climate with which the contemporary reader may identify.

As Saul is dying, the evil spirit from God speaks to him a last time:

When your story is written, I will be called
"An evil spirit from the Lord,"
And so I am. I am the image
Of your pride, of your refusal,
Of your jealousy, of your weakness.

This evil spirit is troublesome to many modern readers, who find it difficult to believe that God would send such a spirit to Saul. Seen imaginatively, however, the spirit may actually minister grace to Saul. The spirit calls Saul's attention to singing and dancing maidens, whom Saul hears faintly as he dies:

. . . I hear the maidens' dance whispering nearer;
They circle my misery, a bright whirl of grace.

In my play, Saul dies in his misery just as he does in the Bible. But the "bright whirl of grace" that surrounds Saul's death suggests a glimmer of light and beauty that appears to lie just out of his reach. Any reader of the Bible can identify with its characters and find in their stories imagery that expresses the reader's feelings and experiences. In writing this play I identified thoroughly with Saul and found that expressing his anguish worked powerfully as a way of expressing my own.

Reading the Bible Now

The Bible has influenced my poetry much more than supplying imagery and themes. The Bible gives us, through its characters, stories, and images, fundamental patterns with which to express our deepest feelings.

I hope to set aside my presuppositions, assumptions, prejudices, and doctrines when I read the Bible. I do not want to read the Bible to prove a point, nor do I want to read it defensively. Instead, I want to let it be what it is: a large, long, varied work made up of works written by a number of authors, some of whom are anonymous. It uses poetry, imagery, and symbolism extensively. Before reading the Psalms and the Gospels as theology and history, one should read them as poetry in order to discover their basic relevance to human experience.

I prefer to read the Jerusalem Bible because its literary quality seems high compared with other contemporary translations. It also transliterates the

Hebrew names of God, such as Yahweh and El Sabaoth, giving a greater sense of the linguistic power of the original. An example is this verse from the Song of Songs:

I sleep, but my heart is awake.
I hear my Beloved knocking.
"Open to me, my sister, my love,
my dove, my perfect one,
for my head is covered with dew,
my locks with the drops of night." (5:2)

The present tense gives the verse immediacy, and the music of vowel and consonant repetition adds to the richness of the imagery. The language flows, without any of the "biblical" diction that so many translations use, and without the flatness of many modern translations and paraphrases.

I like the Gelineau Psalter because it is an especially lyrical translation of the Psalms. Psalm 63 is one of my favorites (it is number 62 in the liturgical numbering used in this psalter). It begins:

O God, you are my God, for you I long,
for you my soul is thirsting,
my body pines for you
like a dry, weary land without water.
(*The Psalms: A New Translation* 62:2)

The rhythmic patterns in this translation are clear and regular because it is intended for singing. At the same time, the chant-tones written for it allow for flexibility that accommodates natural, spoken rhythms. The simplicity of the language allows the reader, or singer, to identify easily with the feelings expressed.

I prefer to avoid heavily annotated editions or overly literal translations, so that I may better apprehend the real mystery of the Bible itself via story, character, rhythm, and image. I believe this poetic response to the Bible is the necessary basis for further devotional, theological, literary, and historical readings of the Bible.

WORKS CITED

Bland, Kalman P. "The Rabbinic Method and Literary Criticism." *Literary Interpretations of Biblical Narratives.* Ed. Kenneth R. R. Gros Louis et al. Nashville: Abingdon, 1974. 1:16–23.

Jones, Alexander, gen. ed. *The Jerusalem Bible.* New York: Doubleday, 1966.

Levertov, Denise. *The Poet in the World.* New York: New Directions, 1973.

The Psalms: A New Translation From the Hebrew Arranged for Singing to the Psalmody of Joseph Gelineau. London and Glasgow: Fontana, 1966.

Warren, Eugene. "Bareback in Kansas." *Geometries of Light.* Wheaton, Ill.: Harold Shaw, 1981.

———. "The Death of Saul." Unpublished verse play. Performance directed by Priscilla Hayden and Susan Cheston. St. Louis: Grace and Peace Fellowship, 12 November 1983.

CHAPTER 38

The Value of a Literary Approach for Preaching

SIDNEY GREIDANUS
Calvin Theological Seminary

A literary understanding of the Bible has been prized by preachers from earliest times. The Bible, after all, is composed of *biblia,* books. The only way to preach the Bible's message is to read and interpret these Scriptures by making literary distinctions between, for example, plain speech and figures of speech and between historical narrative and apocalyptic narrative.

But recently preachers have been able to benefit from much more specialized literary studies of the Bible and its books. After decades of biblical scholars' preoccupation with the historical dimensions of Scripture, this sudden change to literary dimensions amounted to a "paradigm shift" (Robertson 548). Along with this shift in biblical studies came a shift in homiletics: as the main interest in biblical studies moved from history to literary genres, the cutting edge of homiletical research shifted from the content of the sermon to its form, particularly the narrative form. According to George Bass, "preaching began to turn 'the narrative corner' at the beginning of the 1970s" (83).

Since we are still in the middle of these literary developments in biblical studies and homiletics, it is difficult to get a bearing and compile definitive results. The task is further complicated by the great variety of literary approaches to the Bible (see Barton) as well as the variety of homiletical theories (see Eslinger, Robinson). There is no doubt, however, that the new literary emphases in biblical studies have been a breath of fresh air in the house of homiletics. We can sense these refreshing currents at work in several areas.

The Return to the Final Text

In his recent work *What Is Narrative Criticism?* Mark Powell states, "The objective of literary-critical analysis is not to discover the process through which a text has come into being but to study the text that now exists" (7). After decades of *pre*-textual studies, preachers can only welcome this return in biblical studies to the final text. For neither the hypothetical documents of source criticism nor the speculative life-settings of form criticism provide a solid foundation for preaching the word of God to his people today. For preaching purposes, only one foundation is firm and dependable and that is the canon the church received as its norm for faith and life. This does not mean that historical investigation, source criticism, form criticism, and tradition criticism cannot provide illuminating insights for preaching, but it does mean that the only reliable foundation for preaching today is the *final* text, the canon the church received as its inspired Scriptures. When Paul writes, "All scripture is inspired by God and profitable for teaching, for reproof, for correction, and for training in righteousness" (2 Tim. 3:16), he is referring not to hypothetical constructs behind the received text but to the final text of the Old Testament. Inasmuch as the new literary approach focuses on understanding the final text, it will benefit preachers more than any approach that focuses on pretextual levels.

Preaching the message of the final text also benefits the congregation, for it enables the hearers to test the sermon for biblical integrity. Already in his day, Paul recognized the maturity and responsibility of the congregation for testing a message before accepting it as the word of God. Wrote Paul to the church in Thessalonica, "Do not despise prophesying, but test everything; hold fast what is good" (1 Thess. 5:20–21; cf. 1 Cor. 14:29). Congregations have no way of testing sermons based on theoretical constructs behind the text, but the text itself gives them a handle for testing the sermon before accepting it as the word of God. In short, the literary approach works with the same text that is used by the congregation.

In contrast to source criticism and form criticism, the new literary criticism assumes the unity of the present text. The Old Testament scholar David Clines writes, "The holistic, total view, while always open to revision in the light of the merest detail, must have the last word in interpretation. In the quest for meaning, the essence, message, function, purpose . . . of the work as a whole is our ultimate ambition" ("Methods" 33). Literary critic Leland Ryken agrees: "Literary criticism, rightly so called, gives a reader the big picture—a clear pathway through a book or passage" (8). This emphasis on the big picture benefits preachers because it will help them to avoid preaching on isolated fragments of a text and instead to concentrate on a textual unit understood in the light of the whole book.

Both the return to the final text and the assumption of the unity of the text are of direct benefit to preachers. Studies such as *Narrative Art in Genesis* by J. P. Fokkelman and *Matthew as Story* by Jack Kingsbury are veritable gold mines for preachers.

The Textual Unit and Its Message

A second area where the new literary studies are benefiting preaching is that of detecting the textual unit and its message.

Common wisdom in homiletics advocates that a preaching-text should be a literary unit and not a fragment of a text, for fragments (phrases and isolated verses) can easily be misused to preach one's own likes and dislikes. Since the new literary approach concentrates on literary wholes, it is able to help preachers become aware of rhetorical structures and other literary devices that mark the boundaries of literary units. For example, in the story of David at Nob, Robert Alter points out that verse 10, "And David rose and fled that day from Saul, and went to Achish the king of Gath," concludes that unit: "The ancient Hebrew audience would have immediately recognized this last verse as the end of the episode because it invokes the formula of rising up and going off to a different place which is one of the prevalent biblical conventions for marking the end of a narrative segment" (65). Rhetorical criticism has uncovered other ancient rhetorical structures that mark the beginning and end of literary units—structures such as the key-word technique, inclusion, and chiasm. These and other literary devices are useful indicators for preachers for determining the proper boundaries of a preaching-text.

Since expository preachers seek to transmit the message of the textual unit to the church here and now, they are especially interested in the message (the *kerygma*) of the text. In this quest for the message of a passage, preachers can greatly benefit from the new literary studies. For despite major differences among contemporary literary theories, "all theories of literature . . . understand the text as a form of communication through which a message is passed from the author to the reader" (Powell 9). Literary studies help one discern the message of a passage by providing concrete details that enable one to enter into the story or poem and relive it. At a more theoretical level, a literary analysis aids understanding by a careful study of literary devices such as scenes, plot, characters, dialogue, point of view, symbol, metaphor, simile, irony, hyperbole, etc., and such rhetorical devices as the strategic location of key words, parallelism, contrast, chiasm, and inclusion.

More specifically, literary analysis aids preachers in detecting the particular theme of a passage. The repetition of a word, phrase, clause, or action is frequently a clue to the theme. A chiastic structure usually focuses on the pivotal thought around which the passage turns. Again, a character's speech or the narrator's point of view or comments may reveal the theme.

In contrast to some modern literary theories, expository preachers will seek to detect the original (historical) theme of a passage, for only this original theme provides assurance that one has understood the point of the text according to its original intentions and not according to one's subjective likes or dislikes. Moreover, this original theme, after possible adjustments in the light of the whole Bible, becomes the all-important sermon theme that guides the crafting of a unified, well-focused sermon.

Questions have been raised recently about the propriety of formulating a theme for a narrative text. For example, David Buttrick writes, "The preacher treats the passage as if it were a still-life picture in which some*thing* may be found, object-like, to preach on. What has been ignored? The composition of the 'picture,' the narrative structure, the movement of the story, the whole question of what in fact the *passage* may want to preach" (47).

Although Buttrick's warning against a rationalistic, scholastic approach is valid, one must not throw out the baby with the bath water. For every meaningful narrative has a theme. Dan Via has helpfully compared plot and theme and calls them the "two sides of the same formal principle with plot being theme in movement and theme being plot at a standstill" (96–97). The theme of a narrative is its plot at a standstill. This description makes clear that the theme of a narrative is not the narrative itself but only an abstraction, a summary statement that the preacher requires temporarily to craft a unified sermon that will make the same point today as that made originally by the biblical narrative. The narrative sermon itself, of course, should not simply state the theme but should help the congregation experience it holistically in the vivid retelling of the biblical narrative.

Historical Questions

As has already been intimated, for a good understanding of the message of a text, the literary approach must work hand in hand with a historical approach. Unfortunately, many contemporary literary critics not only ignore the historical approach but are intentionally nonhistorical. "These critics bracket out questions of history in order to concentrate on the nature of the text as literature" (Powell 8). They do not wish to deal with the uncertainties of historical authors and historical readers but seek to enter the self-contained story world with its implied authors and narrators and implied readers and narratees (see Greidanus, *Modern Preacher* 79, 192–93).

For proper interpretation of the Bible, however, the literary approach must necessarily break out of its self-contained story world. For, as Mark Powell perceptively observes:

> Narrative criticism demands that the modern reader have the historical information that the text assumes of its implied reader. . . . In a basic sense, this comprises practical information that is common knowledge in the world of the story: how much a denarius is worth, what a centurion does, and so forth. It may also include recognition of social and political realities that lie behind the story. It may involve understanding particular social customs and recognizing the meaning of culturally determined symbols and metaphors. (97)

With an ancient text like the Bible, genuine understanding necessarily requires a historical understanding of the culture, customs, figures of speech, and rhetorical structures that are not spelled out in the text but were taken for granted by the author and hearer.

In their attempt to concentrate on the text as literature, some literary critics also wish to bracket out the question of the historicity of the narrative, the historical referent. For example, James Barr explains that the issue of historicity makes no difference for the message of a parable, for "the message of the parable is something other than the story which it itself tells." But then he extends this principle to all biblical narratives by suggesting that "the story of Jesus' birth, or the story of his resurrection, or that of the exodus of the Israelites from Egypt" work on us like general literature. "Do they not exercise their power upon us quite apart from the question whether things happened as they are narrated in the external world? Is not their effect upon us essentially the same as that exercised by the myths, the patterns, the imagery and the symbols of all great literature?" (56–57).

Some homileticians follow this nonhistorical lead and are now advising preachers to ignore the question of historicity. For example, Mark Ellingsen writes, "The strength of the biblical narrative approach for preaching on the strange biblical accounts is precisely that formal historical claims are not made on their behalf" (68). "With regard to this matter, the preacher's job is simply to report the biblical accounts, not to insist that the strange stories happened" (92).

But surely preachers cannot simply neglect the question of historicity. Even from a literary point of view this neglect is objectionable. A respectable literary approach cannot simply interpret all biblical narratives as parables, for it recognizes that narratives come in different literary forms—forms such as parable, apocalyptic narrative, and historical narrative. It is true that the question of historicity makes no difference for understanding the message of a parable and hence can be bracketed out. It is also true that the question of historicity may not mean much for the message of a historical narrative when it teaches "something other than the story which it itself tells."

For example, when Luke 18:15–17 relates that parents brought their children to Jesus, we may assume the historicity of the event, but that issue does not directly effect the message (v. 17): "Truly, I say to you, whoever does not receive the kingdom of God like a child shall not enter it." Here the message clearly is "something other than the story which it itself tells." But when one preaches on Luke 24, the stories of Jesus' resurrection, the question of historicity cannot be bracketed out because here the message *is* "the story which it itself tells"; the message is precisely the historicity of Jesus' resurrection. To bracket out the historical referent here is to bracket out the *kerygma* itself. In the Old Testament, similarly, the story of God's redeeming his people from Egypt *is* the message. In these instances, as well as in many others, to bracket out the historical question is irresponsible because it brackets out the message itself (see further Greidanus, *Modern Preacher* 24–47, 80–101).

The Significance of the Form of the Text and Sermon

The new literary emphasis is making a positive impact on preaching also in the area of form, particularly with the perception that form and content are interrelated.

While there was always an intuitive awareness of the difference between, say, historical narrative and wisdom literature, this diversity in the forms of the texts formerly made little difference for developing the forms of the respective sermons. For centuries the sermon had its standard form, sometimes derisively called "three points and a poem." Actually it was a didactic form consisting of an introduction, a statement of the theme, development of the theme in three or four points in logical order, and a conclusion. Although this didactic form is much maligned today by the avant-garde, the problem is not with the didactic form as such but with the notion that one sermon form fits all texts.

Sermons are not like stretch socks, however, one size fitting all. The didactic sermon form, for example, does not properly fit all forms of texts. Thomas Long observes,

> An unfortunate result of overlooking the literary properties of biblical texts is the tendency to view those texts by default as inert containers for theological concepts. The preacher's task then becomes simply throwing the text into an exegetical winepress, squeezing out the ideational matter, and then figuring out homiletical ways to make those ideas attractive to contemporary listeners. (12)

Because of the new literary approach, there is greater awareness today that one cannot separate form and content, since form is integral to meaning. Clines observes,

> Rhetorical criticism, as has been amply attested in recent years, is not a mechanical matter of identifying stylistic devices, but, on the premise of the unity of form and content of a work of art, moves towards the work's meaning and quiddity from the standpoint of form rather than of content, of the "how said" rather than the "what said." (*I, He, We* 37)

Form is integral to meaning. To inquire about form is already to inquire about meaning, for the form of the text sets our expectations of the meaning of the text and guides us in the questions we ask (see Greidanus, *Modern Preacher* 16–18). The form also codetermines the meaning of the text, witness our different understandings of historical narrative and apocalyptic narrative.

The new interest in form in biblical studies soon spilled over into homiletics. If form is integral to meaning in the biblical text, there is no reason why this should not be the case for sermons: the form of the sermon also codetermines *its* meaning. The form of the sermon is not a secondary matter but is vital in communicating the desired message.

Moreover, the sermon form should do justice to the biblical form. Given the great variety of biblical forms, it will not do to have one sermon form fit all biblical texts. In his innovative work *As One Without Authority,* Fred Craddock asks,

> Why should the multitude of forms and moods within biblical literature . . . be brought together in one unvarying mold, and that copied from Greek rhetoricians of centuries ago? An unnecessary monotony results, but more profoundly, there is an inner conflict between the content of the sermon and its form. . . . The content calls for singing but the form is quite prosaic; the message has wings but the structure is pedestrian. (143–44)

The major "new" (but see Davis 157–62) form being investigated and promoted in homiletics today is the narrative form. This choice is not surprising, since much of the Bible is written in narrative form. Richard Jensen argues, "If the text 'makes its point' in story form then we ought to seriously consider constructing a sermon that is faithful to the content and the form of the biblical text. . . . Why should we de-story these stories in our sermons and simply pass on the point of the story to our listeners?" (128).

The popularity of the narrative form among homileticians does not, however, imply agreement on specifics. Some, like Jensen, would allow for story preaching as "imaginative recasting," that is, "we can . . . create and tell our own stories which elicit responses in the hearer similar to the responses to the original story" (125). Others, like Mark Ellingsen, validly argue that "the story model does not seem to take the biblical text and its particularity with sufficient seriousness" (58). Some, like Eugene Lowry, insist that *every* sermon be cast in a narrative, plot form: "A sermon is not a doctrinal lecture. It is an *event-in-time,* a narrative art form, a sacred story" (6). Still others, like Richard Eslinger, rightly hold that "it does not follow that a narrative model should always be imposed on non-narrative biblical material" (87).

In choosing a sermon form, one cannot always use the same form as that of the preaching text. If the text is a form of teaching, one can use the didactic form; if the text is narrative, one can use the narrative form. But what should one do when the text is a prayer or a hymn? This dilemma shows that preachers cannot simply copy biblical forms—nor should they want to. Thomas Long states, "The preacher's task . . . is not to replicate the text but to regenerate the impact of some portion of the text. While the literary form of the text may at times serve as a model for the form of the sermon, on other occasions the preacher, in order to be faithful to the text, will select for the sermon a markedly different pattern" (33–34).

Instead of slavishly trying to copy the form of the text, preachers should carefully examine the form of the text and allow its characteristics and mood to shape the form of the sermon. Thus, if the text is a narrative, one can use the narrative form by imaginatively retelling the biblical story. But if the text is a psalm, one would not try to copy its form but instead use the mood of praise or lament and the parallelism and/or metaphors to help shape the sermon. The preacher's goal is not simply to use the same form as the text but to expound the text relevantly so as to create the same effect and response today.

The Relevance of the Sermon

A final area in which a literary approach benefits preaching is that of relevance, specifically the relevance of narrative preaching. Mark Powell notes, "There is increasing appreciation among scholars today for the ability of stories to engage us and to change the way we perceive ourselves and our world. . . . The narrative form . . . corresponds in some profound way to reality and thus enables us to translate our experience of the story world into our own situation" (90).

In contrast to developing rational or intellectual understanding, the narrative form of preaching allows hearers to be involved more holistically. Research has shown that "we have linear, rational modes of perception and we have nonrational and intuitive modes of perception," the left brain hemisphere controlling "our rational, logical, sequential thought processes" and the right hemisphere controlling "our intuitive, holistic, imagistic thought processes" (Jensen 129). Narrative engages especially the right hemisphere and allows hearers to be involved not only rationally but also emotionally.

Another advantage of using the narrative form in preaching is that it allows the hearers to identify with a biblical character and relive the story through that character. Identification can range from empathy to sympathy to antipathy (Powell 56–58). However, the device of having the hearers identify with a biblical character must be used with extreme caution since it easily leads to shallow, moralistic preaching—the various characters functioning as positive models for the hearers to imitate or as negative examples of what the hearers ought not to do (see Greidanus, *Sola Scriptura* 65–83).

Moreover, since the meaning and significance of a narrative changes as readers identify with different characters, the device of character identification threatens to make interpretation arbitrary and subjectivistic. To avoid subjectivistic interpretation at this level, one needs to inquire about the relevance of the text for its first hearers. What was the original intention of this text? If the (implied) author intended his first hearers to identify with a certain character (e.g., Israel with Abraham, or the early church with the disciples), one can extend this identification from the Old Testament church or the early church to the contemporary church. But if the (implied) author did not intend his hearers to identify with a specific character, there seems to be little justification for contemporary preachers to do so—let alone using that character as an example of what to do or not to do (see Greidanus, *Modern Preacher* 161–86). The relevance of the Bible is found first and foremost not in what the biblical characters are doing but in what God in Christ is doing for his people.

The narrative form also enhances relevance because it captures and maintains interest in a natural way. Stories capture interest with their characters, scenes, and plot conflict and maintain that interest with suspense and the natural movement from conflict to resolution. Moreover, stories are not abstract and theoretical but concrete and visual.

To capture and maintain interest with a didactic sermon form, preachers need to work harder at making the teaching concrete and visual. Concrete illustrations are helpful. Most helpful is discovering in the text a metaphor that makes the teaching concrete and visual. Happily, biblical texts use many more metaphors than first meet the modern eye. Historical understanding will help unearth these ancient metaphors and their meaning. Terms like *redemption, adoption, peace, justification, expiation*—all are ancient metaphors frozen on the pages of Scripture. In fact, according to Terrence Tilley, "the key concepts of Christian faith—creation, fall, incarnation, atonement, church, eternal life, trinity—are all metaphors at rest, metaphors which have become Christian doctrines" (3). By recognizing these ancient metaphors for what they are, preachers can bring them to life again in order to carry their message today in a visual and relevant manner.

Finally, the literary approach enhances relevance with its emphasis on "the big picture," the *whole* story. The big picture of the Bible is the story of God's involvement with our world from the beginning of time to its end. Like a complex plot this story unfolds. The stage is set with God creating the world good. Conflict is generated by the human fall into sin and God's resolve to redeem his world through the seed of the woman (Gen. 1–3). Scene after scene shows God's involvement with the generations of Israel until a major climax is reached when God sent his Son Jesus to save the world. Still the story continues: scene after scene shows God's involvement with the early church until the resolution is reached with Jesus' second coming and the appearance of a new heaven and a new earth (Rev. 21–22). In essence, the whole story of the Bible is a universal *history* of God's involvement with his world from the first creation to the new creation. This universal history encompasses the story of every textual unit in the Bible as well as our own story today. Erich Auerbach remarks, "Far from seeking . . . merely to make us forget our own reality for a few hours, it [the world of the Scripture stories] seeks to overcome our reality: we are to fit our own life into its world, feel ourselves to be elements in its structure of universal history" (15). This universal history is the history of God's coming kingdom. Since every biblical text is part of this kingdom history, every biblical text is relevant for the church as it works and waits for the completion of the kingdom of God.

WORKS CITED

Alter, Robert, *The Art of Biblical Narrative.* New York: Basic Books, 1981.
Auerbach, Erich. *Mimesis.* Trans. Willard Trask. Princeton: Princeton UP, 1953.
Barr, James. *The Bible in the Modern World.* New York: Harper & Row, 1973.
Barton, John. *Reading the Old Testament: Method in Biblical Study.* Philadelphia: Westminster, 1984.
Bass, George M. *The Song and the Story.* Lima, Ohio: CSS, 1984.
Buttrick, David G. "Interpretation and Preaching" *Interpretation* 35, no. 1 (1981): 46–58.
Clines, David J. A. *I, He, We, and They: A Literary Approach to Isaiah 53.* Sheffield: JSOT Press, 1976.
———. "Methods of Old Testament Study." *Beginning Old Testament Study.* Ed. John Rogerson. London: SPCK, 1983. 26–43.
Craddock, Fred B. *As One Without Authority.* Nashville: Abingdon, 1981.
Davis, Henry Grady. *Design for Preaching.* Philadelphia: Fortress, 1958.
Ellingsen, Mark. *The Integrity of Biblical Narrative: Story in Theology and Proclamation.* Minneapolis: Fortress, 1990.
Eslinger, Richard L. *A New Hearing: Living Options in Homiletical Method.* Nashville: Abingdon, 1987.
Fokkelman, J. P. *Narrative Art in Genesis: Specimens of Stylistic and Structural Analysis.* Amsterdam: Van Gorcum, 1975.
Greidanus, Sidney. *The Modern Preacher and the Ancient Text: Interpreting and Preaching Biblical Literature.* Grand Rapids: Eerdmans, 1988.
———. *Sola Scriptura: Problems and Principles in Preaching Historical Texts.* Toronto: Wedge, 1970.
Jensen, Richard A. *Telling the Story: Variety and Imagination in Preaching.* Minneapolis: Augsburg, 1980.
Kingsbury, Jack Dean. *Matthew as Story.* Philadelphia: Fortress, 1986.
Long, Thomas G. *Preaching and the Literary Forms of the Bible.* Philadelphia: Fortress, 1989.
Lowry, Eugene L. *The Homiletical Plot: The Sermon as Narrative Art Form.* Atlanta: John Knox, 1980.
Powell, Mark Allan. *What Is Narrative Criticism?* Minneapolis: Fortress, 1990.
Robertson, David. "The Bible as Literature." *The Interpreter's Dictionary of the Bible Supplementary Volume.* Ed. Keith Crim. Nashville: Abingdon, 1976. 547–51.
Robinson, Wayne Bradley, ed. *Journeys Toward Narrative Preaching.* New York: Pilgrim, 1990.
Ryken, Leland. *The New Testament in Literary Criticism.* New York: Ungar, 1984.
Tilley, Terrence W. *Story Theology.* Wilmington: Michael Glazier, 1985.
Via, Dan. *The Parables: Their Literary and Existential Dimension.* Philadelphia: Fortress, 1967.

Author Index

Index of Biblical Passages

Index of Major Bible Stories and Characters

Index of Subjects